Routledge Revivals

Credit Marketing and Consumer Protection

The mid-20th century saw a significant expansion in the purchase of consumer goods and in the use of credit. At the same time, several changes in the nature of consumer credit took place. Credit cards made credit more readily available for goods and services and mass production, automated selling methods and the growth of consumer credit brought advantages. But they have also provided opportunities for predatory practices and deception. Originally published in 1979, and based on surveys and interviews, this book presents a review of some of these developments, together with an evaluation of some of the techniques of control over abuses in the marketing of consumer goods. The book discusses the financing of consumer goods, the variables that might have causative significance in leading to satisfactory or unsatisfactory transactions, and the legal positions of the time in relation to consumer problems.

Credit Marketing and Consumer Protection

Terence G. Ison

Routledge
Taylor & Francis Group

First published in 1979 by Croom Helm Ltd.

This edition first published in 2025 by Routledge
4 Park Square, Milton Park, Abingdon, Oxon, OX14 4RN
and by Routledge
605 Third Avenue, New York, NY 10158.

Routledge is an imprint of the Taylor & Francis Group, an informa business

ISBN 13: 978-1-041-07722-0 (hbk)
ISBN 13: 978-1-003-64194-0 (ebk)
ISBN 13: 978-1-041-07728-2 (pbk)
Book DOI 10.4324/9781003641940

CREDIT MARKETING AND CONSUMER PROTECTION

TERENCE G. ISON

CROOM HELM LONDON

Croom Helm Ltd, 2-10 St John's Road, London SW11

British Library Cataloguing in Publication Data

Ison, Terence George
Credit marketing and consumer protection.
1. Consumer credit – England
I. Title
332.7'43 HG3756.G7

ISBN 0-85664-728-4

Printed in Great Britain by
Biddles Ltd, Guildford, Surrey

CONTENTS

PREFACE

This book is about consumer protection in the marketing of durable goods and in the supply of consumer credit. Its purpose, as explained in Chapter 1, is to provide an argumentative background to the law, and a perspective on the significance of law; but not a comprehensive synthesis of legal doctrine. The primary interest of the book is expected to be among those concerned with the marketing of consumer durables, with consumer finance, with consumer protection and with law reform in these areas. For those who advise on consumer problems, the book may provide some ideas on strategy and some background understanding of current law. But, if used for advisory purposes, it needs to be read in conjunction with updated syntheses of legal doctrine.[1]

The opening chapters are largely descriptive, including the results of a consumer survey and other enquiries. The emphasis then shifts to argument, including ideas for reform. To the extent that consumer transactions involve injustice, the later chapters explain how this is, at least to some extent, institutional rather than aberrational. Hence it is argued that to eliminate the causes of injustice requires institutional changes of a fundamental nature rather than the amendment of particular rules.

During the final revision of the book, mainly in 1977, several provisions of the *Consumer Credit Act*, 1974,[2] were being brought into effect, and transitional provisions were part of contemporary literature. The focus of this book, however, is on issues of more perennial significance. Thus it is concerned with some of the background problems underlying the *Consumer Credit Act*, but not with transitional problems in the initial implementation of the Act and regulations.[3]

1. Unfortunately, there is no single work that covers the same subject area as this book. But relevant texts can be found in a law library under the subject headings of contract, consumer credit, consumer protection, consumer law, commercial law and trade descriptions.

2. Several excellent works relating to this Act are now available in loose-leaf form: *Consumer Credit Legislation*. R.M. Goode, 1977, Butterworths; *Encyclopedia of Consumer Credit Law*. A.G. Guest and M.G. Lloyd, 1975, Sweet and Maxwell; *Consumer Credit Law*, F.A.R. Bennion, 1976, Oyez Publishing.

3. By the time this book is published, most sections of the Act should be in effect. Anyone wishing to check whether a particular section has been brought into effect may find the answer in one of the reference works mentioned in footnote 2, or in the Commencement Orders published by the government from time to time in the Statutory Instruments. Alternatively (and particularly for those who do not have access to legal materials) the Office of Fair Trading is willing to respond to enquiries of this kind. The address is: Field House, Bream's Buildings, London EC4A 1PR.

In the research for this book, I have tried to add to existing knowledge, and particularly in the survey work, to use the methodology of the social sciences. In the data gathering phase of the survey, the methodology was in several respects more meticulous than is usual in survey work. No survey, however, can provide all the information relevant for rational judgments about reform. Thus the book also reflects a pragmatic recognition that the process of law reform inevitably includes argument and assumptions about the unknown and doing the best one can with limited data.

For information that has not been well known, or that differs from common understandings, I have tried to footnote references to the sources. Similarly I have footnoted the citations for propositions of law that may not be well known, or that may be controversial. But I have not referred to sources for statements of fact that are obviously part of the general knowledge of the community, or for propositions of law that are part of the ordinary textbook knowledge of the legal profession.

A great deal of information was obtained or confirmed in personal interviews. Sometimes an undertaking was given that the interviewee would not be identified, and in some other interviews that was implied. In some other instances, naming the source could be unfair to the person concerned.[1] Thus the convention I have generally followed is to refer to the source with sufficient particularity to identify the institutional derivation of the information, but not to name individuals.

For responding to my questions in interviews, or for supplying information in other ways, I am most grateful to officials of the Office of Fair Trading and other government departments, registrars and staff of the County Courts, Trading Standards Officers, Consumer Advice Centre personnel, Citizens' Advice Bureaux, newspapers, trade associations, manufacturers, financial institutions, department stores and other retailers, collection agencies and others. So far as the courts were concerned, these enquiries were much assisted by the Lord Chancellor's Office.

My special thanks are due to the former Consumer Council, the Consumers' Association, the National Association of Citizens' Advice Bureaux, the Hire Purchase Trade Association, Barclays Bank, and United Dominions Trust, for the substantial time that they were good enough to allocate in responding to my enquiries.

For similar assistance in the United States and Canada, I am grateful

1. For example, an official may have described to the writer a practice that he follows, and which is criticised in the text. But that practice may be unrepresentative of his work as a whole. To describe other aspects of his work may be irrelevant. But to name him only by reference to the criticised practice could give an unfair impression of the person.

to the various Better Business Bureaus, Credit Bureaus, Credit Counselling Services, Chambers of Commerce, financial institutions, government officials and others who were good enough to provide information, either in interviews or by correspondence.

To the Institute of Advanced Legal Studies (University of London) I am most grateful for research facilities.

For undertaking the survey contract, my thanks are due to Research Services Ltd.

For the discussion of ideas and the checking of material I am obliged to many colleagues. In particular, I would like to thank Professor Roy Goode of Queen Mary College (University of London), whose encyclopedic mind and the generosity with which he allowed me to delve into it was of immense help; Miss Susan Marsden-Smedley, formerly with the Consumer Council and now Director of the Legal Action Group, whose extensive knowledge and imaginative understanding of consumer problems was invaluable; and Mr C. McNeil Greig, Director of the Hire Purchase Trade Association, who generously allowed me to tap his long experience and intimate familiarity with matters of consumer finance.

To one person, I regret that my thanks can only be posthumous. The late Mr Registrar T.A. Riches, formerly of Grays Thurrock County Court, was kind enough to provide several unpublished memoranda containing interesting insights into the County Court system.

For encouragement at the beginning of the project, including comments on the research design, I am grateful to Professor Maurice Rosenberg of the School of Law, Columbia University. For detailed and most helpful comments on the typescript, and for an American perspective on particular points, I would like to thank Professors W.F. Young and P.G. Schrag of the School of Law, and Professor R.P. Shay of the School of Business, all of Columbia University, New York.

In Canada, my thanks are due to many colleagues, and particularly to Professor J.S. Ziegel of the Faculty of Law, University of Toronto. As well as being a leading contributor to the literature of commercial and consumer law, he has been most generous in supporting the work of myself and others. For reviewing the final script, I am grateful to Professor M.G. Baer of the Faculty of Law, Queen's University.

The views expressed in the text and any errors that remain, are, of course, my own responsibility.

For the necessary financial support, I am most grateful to the Social Science Research Council, whose grant covered in particular the cost of the survey work. For computer facilities and supplementary funding, I am grateful to Queen's University, Ontario. Finally, this book has been published with the help of a grant from the Social Science Federation of Canada, using funds provided by the Canada Council.

Kingston, T.G.I.
February, 1978.

1 INTRODUCTION

The expansion of consumer credit[1] and the diverse forms that it takes are two striking features of mass marketing in the twentieth century. Credit has become widely available for the general range of soft goods and services, as well as for hard goods. Revolving credit accounts (option accounts), operated by department stores, allow the purchase on instalment credit of items too small in value or too perishable to be the subject of a separate credit transaction. Multi-purpose credit cards issued by banks or other companies enable the user to buy a wide range of goods and services from a variety of outlets on a single account, and to pay by instalments. Personal loans and revolving loan accounts at the banks make credit available for an infinite variety of purposes. Thus credit marketing is no longer (if it ever was) a simple matter of bank loans and charge accounts for the well-to-do and hire-purchase for the workers. Competing sources and types of credit are now available to many sections of the population.

Diversification of the forms of credit has been facilitated further by the expansion and automation of credit reporting. These services make it more feasible to extend credit by reference to the payment record of the customer rather than by relying primarily on security in the goods. This process has also had an influence on collection methods, shifting emphasis from the threat of legal proceedings to the threat of an adverse credit report.

For the general public, intelligent choice in the use of credit is impaired by the tie-in of advertising with news and entertainment. Exposure to the exhortation to expand one's consumption and possessions has become an integral part of reading the paper, watching television, or going to the cinema. Lack of capital or income is not portrayed as cause for restraint. Moreover, there is no comparable level of exhortation to budget wisely or to shop with caution. Nor is there any comparable level of exhortation to seek happiness in the pursuit of other goals. Maximum consumption is still widely hailed as the paramount human aspiration, and any propensity of people to spend more than their income is nurtured by the inducements

1. Precise measurement is not possible because there is no system of statistical returns covering all types of credit grantors. In connection with the purchase of consumer durables, however, the total of instalment credit outstanding in Great Britain had reached over £1,000 million by the present decade. (See the *Report of the Committee on Consumer Credit*, 1971, Cmnd 4596, Vol. 1, pp.52-60.) Although the level fluctuates with monetary policy and economic conditions, the long-term trend has been one of expansion.

of their environment.

On the political scene, there has been an increase during the last two decades in the demand for consumer protection. Fraud, other misrepresentations, high-pressure salesmanship, price-fixing combinations, false advertising, hazardous products and the disclosure of the cost of credit, have all been the subject of legislative attention. In the field of credit marketing, the *Consumer Credit Act*[1] is now coming into effect, and more consumer protection legislation in the next few years is very possible.

The growth of credit marketing has brought obvious advantages. Apart from advancing the business of those in industry, commerce and finance, the growth of consumer credit may well have been a major factor in raising the standard of living of ordinary working people. But it has also provided the opportunities and incentives for predatory practices, deceit and other abuses. Complaints have been voluminous about, for example, misleading advertising, fraud, the concealment of credit terms, high-pressure tactics, defective goods, dubious accounting methods and oppressive collection tactics. These problems were not created by the expansion or new forms of consumer credit, but they may have been aggravated. For example, it is often thought to be easier for a high-pressure salesman to induce a signature on an instalment contract than to induce a signature on a cheque for the same amount. Again, the shift of emphasis from security in the goods to personal credit may sometimes make it less important to the seller that the customer be supplied with goods that will last, or that the customer will like.

Other problems derive from the failure of the legal system to adjust to the realities of mass production. It would not be in the best interests of consumers, or anyone else, if the manufacturing of consumer durables was aimed at achieving perfection in each unit. A point must be reached beyond which the marginal cost of preventing defects would exceed the marginal cost of suffering them (referring here to the total marginal cost to all parties). From a manufacturer's viewpoint, the downward pressure on prices that can derive from competition, as well as the desire to expand volume, militates against the use of the most durable materials, the most careful workmanship, supervision, and end-of-line inspection. Thus the prices of consumer durables have been relatively stable, and the possession of, for example, cars, refrigerators and washing machines has spread to wider sections of the population. Any over-insistence on durability and perfection might raise prices, and thereby restrict volume, to the detriment of consumers and workers as well as manufacturers. The sensible

1. 1974, Ch. 39

approach might well be to seek a level of performance that is acceptable and satisfactory on the whole, but which involves a regular proportion of defects. A crucial issue then is who should bear the loss when defects occur. Should the individual consumer take the loss as part of the luck of buying, or should the manufacturer assume the loss and allow for it in setting his price?

These are some of the questions and problems considered in the chapters that follow.

This book is not concerned with the protection of all consumer interests; only with integrity in marketing. Thus it is not concerned, for example, with price levels, product safety, or environmental control, unless a question of honesty in the marketing process is also involved. Nor is it concerned with monetary policy and the role of credit in the economy.

The focus on abuses by those engaged in selling and finance is, of course, not a denial of the theft and fraud perpetrated by consumers. But abuses on each side of the marketplace involve such different problems that it is surely excusable, if not desirable, for a book to concentrate on one or the other. Nor should the focus on abuses be construed as reflecting any negative overall judgment on credit marketing, or any morbid preoccupation with its incidental evils. It is simply the demand of a lawyer's discipline to be more concerned with transactions that result in dissatisfaction or conflict than with those that result to the benefit of all concerned.

To control abuses in credit marketing, various techniques have been debated and sometimes enacted. These include criminal sanctions, compulsory disclosure of the cost of credit, a cooling-off period during which a buyer may rescind the contract, the licensing of lenders and vendors, restrictions on legal claims for debt, making a buyer's defences available against a credit grantor as well as against the seller, and changes in the methods of execution available to creditors. It has also sometimes been argued that Control Orders, prescribing a minimum downpayment (deposit) and a maximum payment period, should be used for consumer protection purposes even when not required for monetary policy.

To make optimum choices among regulatory techniques obviously requires a background of ideas, information and argument. To contribute to that background is the purpose of this book.

With regard to information, the most intelligent choices among regulatory techniques could well be assisted by quantitive data about the nature and extent of marketing abuses. No comprehensive body of such data is, however, available. Possible sources of such data are the agencies dealing with consumer complaints. But the use of those sources involves three problems. First, these agencies do not have the resources to compile statistics with sufficient precision and detail to be usable for many purposes, or to keep files in a way that would permit such statistics to be compiled. Secondly, there is no predominant agency to which all consumer grievances are directed. For example, one person might complain to a trade association, another might go to a Citizens' Advice Bureau, a third might go to a Trading Standards Department, a fourth might write to a newspaper, and a fifth might write to the Consumers' Association.[1] Thirdly, a scrutiny of complaints can give a limited or distorted impression. It says nothing about the people who are not complaining and leaves no indication of the extent to which they are suffering from the same grievances compared with the extent to which their experiences have been satisfactory.

In the United States, several surveys have been made about the use of consumer credit. But they generally fall into one of two categories. First, there are those that examine the role of consumer credit in the economy. These studies are designed only to produce data required for monetary policy and are not relevant to the problems of integrity in marketing.[2] Secondly, surveys have been made of consumers who have become defendants in court proceedings or who have become insolvent.[3]

These studies of debt-troubled consumers are invaluable. But to examine marketing methods in a more complete perspective, the purchasing experience of that group needs to be compared with those whose transactions are satisfactory, and with those who have cause for complaint about their purchases but no debt or collection problems.

When this research was begun in 1967, therefore, it was decided to seek some data on consumer experiences by a survey of 1,540 households in England and Wales. The survey was carried out in 1969.

This survey work focused exclusively on the purchase of major con-

1. The Office of Fair Trading has begun to organise and collate some simple statistics of consumer complaints received by Trading Standards Departments, Consumer Advice Centres, and Citizens' Advice Bureaux. But more scrutiny is required on how the complaints are being classified before the comparability of the data can be assured.

2. Several such studies have been undertaken or sponsored by the Board of Governors of the Federal Reserve System.

3. See eg. *Debtors in Default*, D. Caplovitz, 1970, Bureau of Applied Social Research, Columbia University; *An Analysis of Economic and Personal Factors Leading to Consumer Bankruptcy*, R. Dolphin, 1965, Occ. Paper No. 15, Bureau of Business and Economic Research, Michigan State University; 'Families in Bankruptcy – A Survey of Recent Studies', R.O. Herrmann (1966) 28 *Journal of Marriage and the Family* 324.

sumer durables. Food is in many ways more important. There are, of course, marketing problems in relation to food, and it features more prominently in a consumer budget. But in some ways consumers may be more vulnerable in the purchase of durable goods. First, the infrequency of buying a major durable does not give a buyer much exposure to different sellers. Secondly, if a transaction is unsatisfactory, a consumer may have lost a substantial amount before learning from the experience. Thirdly, payment is out of future income which a consumer may be tempted or persuaded to commit more readily than present income. Fourthly, because the purchase of major durables is episodic, rather than regular, these transactions are more difficult to accommodate in a family budget. Unlike food, for which a family can budget by habit, the purchase of major durables requires planned budgeting if a family is to avoid the risk of insolvency or privation.

From a seller's standpoint, the price of major durables might be an incentive to aggressive or predatory sales tactics, and compared with the sale of perishables the risk of losing repeat business may be less cogent as a sanction.

Cash sales of consumer durables were, however, included in the study. Indeed, it is only by comparing cash sales with credit transactions that any assessment can be made of the significance of credit.

In addition to the household survey, a series of interviews and other enquiries was conducted with retailers, finance companies, manufacturers, court officials, government departments, trade associations, Citizens' Advice Bureaux, newspaper readers' advisory services and staff of the former Consumer Council and of the Consumers' Association. These interviews were conducted in 1968, 1969 and 1977.

In two respects, the book reflects a departure from patterns of thinking that have been traditional among lawyers. First, it has been traditional in consumer protection legislation, as in other areas, to legislate by reference to legal concepts rather than economic phenomena. The predictable result is that the effect of the legislation can be avoided by changing the formalities by which transactions are consummated. For example, if legislation protects consumers in hire-purchase and credit sale transactions, a seller who wishes to avoid the effect of the protection may switch to different methods of arranging credit. In the last ten years, however, there has been growing recognition of this problem. The Crowther Committee recommended: 'The adoption of a functional approach to regulation [which] involves identifying different forms of transaction possessing an essential unity of purpose and regulating these in the same way.'[1] That position was adopted in the *Consumer Credit Act*, 1974.

Secondly, it has been traditional in dealing with problems of integrity in marketing for lawyers to focus primarily on adjudication case by case. But the amounts involved in consumer transactions are usually small compared with the cost of litigation and it is very doubtful whether adjudication will ever occur with sufficient frequency to function as a regulatory device for the control of fraud and other predatory practices. Thus a major question in consumer protection is whether techniques can be devised to operate against fraud and other predatory practices across the board without at the same time being so restrictive or indiscriminate as to impair legitimate trade.

1. *Report of the Committee on Consumer Credit*, 1971, Cmnd 4596, p.184.

2 THE SURVEY

The purpose of the survey was to obtain information about the purchase and use of major consumer durables. It would have been ideal, therefore, to begin with a random sample drawn from the universe of all purchasers of these items. Unfortunately, however, there was no way in which this universe could be identified. Although it would have been possible to obtain lists of some purchasers of some items, it was not possible to obtain lists of all the purchasers of all items. It was decided, therefore, to begin with a random sample of households, and then to screen out those in which there had been no purchase within the preceding two years of any of the durables mentioned on a prepared list. The list was as follows:

Vacuum cleaner
Encyclopedia set or reference books (over £20)
Heating equipment (total over £20 bought at one time)
Cooking utensils (total over £20 bought at one time)
Sewing machine
Knitting machine
Typewriter
New motor vehicle
Secondhand motor vehicle
TV, radio, tape recorder, record player or combination
Dishwasher
Furniture (total over £20 bought at one time)
Rug or carpet (over £20)
Refrigerator
Deep freeze
Gas or electric stove
Washing machine, dryer or combination

Since the survey data were required primarily for a discussion of law reform, it was decided that Scotland, having to some extent different laws and institutions, should be treated as a separate jurisdiction. The survey was confined, therefore, to England and Wales.

Pretesting and a pilot survey were done in the summer of 1968. The main survey was carried out in the summer of 1969.

The sample was a random sample, mostly preselected. It was a two-stage probability sample clustered at 60 sampling points. What this means and how the sample was drawn are explained in Appendix A. The interviewers were instructed to make at least three calls, if necessary, to establish contact at a selected address. No substitution was allowed. The sample was composed as follows:

Households selected at random from the electoral register	1,460
Households selected at random from lists of new building areas	40
Non-elector households added[1]	23
Households added at multi-household addresses[1]	17
Total	1,540

It was anticipated that a sample of this size would produce useful data about the general run of consumer purchases of major durables, although it would be too small to yield much detail about rackets on the crooked fringe of retailing. Information about these marginal areas was gathered primarily from the other sources.

The distribution of the households in the sample by Registrar General's standard regions is shown in Table 2.1, below, together with an indication of how it compares with the distribution of population in those regions.

Table 2.1: Distribution of Households in Sample

Standard region	No. of households in sample	Percentage of households in sample	Percentage distribution of the population over 15 years of age in England and Wales[2]
North	103	6.7	6.8
North West	226	14.7	13.7
Yorkshire and Humberside	151	9.8	9.8
West Midlands	155	10.1	10.4
East Midlands	102	6.6	6.8
East Anglia	52	3.4	3.4
South West	125	8.1	7.7
South East	284	18.4	19.5
Greater London	267	17.3	16.3
Wales	75	4.9	5.6
Total	1,540	100.0	100.0

1. Why and how these households were added is explained in Appendix A.
2. Calculated from *The Registrar General's Statistical Review of England and Wales In the Year 1969*, Part II, Table A4 (Estimated Home Population by Sex and Age, as at 30th June, 1969), HMSO.

Upon making contact with a selected household, the interviewer would first identify herself and seek co-operation. Then she would produce the list of articles and ask if any of them had been purchased within the household during the preceding two years. Except for motor vehicles, items purchased secondhand were excluded. Items bought within the preceding two weeks were then excluded. Where one item on the list had been purchased, the interviewer was instructed to interview with regard to that item. Where two items had been purchased, the interviewer was instructed to seek two interviews, one with regard to each item. Where more than two items on the list had been purchased, the interviewer was instructed to seek interviews with regard to the first two items on the list and to ignore the remainder. In following this procedure, the interviewer used the contact report that appears as Appendix B.

The order in which the items appear on the list was deliberately calculated to result in those near the top being over-represented in proportion to their total sales compared with those lower down the list. The order was determined by the anticipated value of data relating to each item and also by the anticipated frequency of response for each item. For example, vacuum cleaners were placed at the top because they are a relatively standard item distributed through retail shops, by mail order, and by selling at the home. Hence data relating to vacuum cleaners would enable different channels of distribution to be compared more than data relating to say, cars. Again, sewing machines were placed ahead of motor vehicles to give them a greater chance of selection because it was anticipated that there would be enough motor vehicles in the sample in any event whereas the number of sewing machines might be small.

Once an item had been selected as the subject of an interview, the interviewer ascertained the buyer(s) of the item and the user (if a different person), and sought to interview them.

The questionnaire dealt with the following:

(1) What influenced the buyer:
  (a) to think of buying the particular type of goods,
  (b) to select the particular make and model, and
  (c) to select the particular seller?
(2) The type of retailing involved, and the manner in which the transaction was processed.
(3) Exactly how the purchase was financed.
(4) Any misrepresentations or other abuses involved in the sale.
(5) Any misrepresentations or other abuses involved in the financing.
(6) The subsequent experience of the buyer with the goods.
(7) Any complaints by the buyer, and the results of any complaints.

(8) The circumstances and results of any failure to pay instalments.
(9) The personal circumstances of the buyer.

The questionnaire is reproduced as Appendix C.

In addition to the sampling instructions, contact reports and questionnaires, the interviewers were required to study and to keep with them an instruction manual, part of which appears in Appendix D. The interviewers were also personally briefed by the writer.

The survey was undertaken by contract with Research Services Ltd. The survey documents and instructions were all prepared by the writer with assistance, particularly on layout, from Research Services. The sample was drawn by Research Services. The field-work, editing and coding were done by Research Services with supervision jointly by the writer and company officials. The analysis was done by the writer.

The results by household were as shown in Table 2.2, below. As may be seen, the survey resulted in acceptable interviews relating to 1,226 transactions.

Table 2.2: Results by Household

	Number of households	%
No contact	66	4.3
Interview refused	125	8.1
No items bought	468	30.4
Buyer or user not available	82	5.3
One item interview completed	360	23.4
Two item interviews completed	433	28.1
Item interview but not acceptable[1]	6	0.4
Total	1,540	100.0

1. These were households at which there were no acceptable item interviews. A further 8 item interviews were rejected in respect of households at which one or two other item interviews were accepted. The reasons for rejection of the 14 item interviews were:

item a gift and donee not interviewed	3
item bought overseas	1
item not new (and not sold as new)	1
item bought for business use	4
intra-family transaction	1
two item interviews already from same household	1
one buyer not interviewed	1
insufficient information obtained	2
Total	14

The distribution of the results by standard region is shown in Table 2.3, page 24, and the distribution by type of area is shown in Table 2.4, page 25.

Because of the method of selecting the total sample, the sub-samples of buyers of each type of item are not likely to be in quite the same proportion to each other as the total market sales of each type of item. This is not felt, however, to be critical, because the types of bias likely to be introduced by the sampling method are not the types of bias that are likely to distort the results. For example, goods which are sold evenly throughout the country would tend to be over-represented in proportion to their total sales compared with goods of a type which are sold more intensively in one area. Again, goods of a type which are bought one per household would tend to be over-represented in the total sample compared with goods of a type which are bought two or more per household. These factors might introduce some distortion if one considered only figures for the sample as a whole, but not when the results are checked item by item.

With regard to the reliability of the data, supervisory rechecks showed a high level of accuracy in the recording by interviewers of the answers given by the respondents. This is not, of course, a measure of the correctness of those answers, but there are other ways in which an impression of that could be gathered. First, it appeared from the briefing, from telephone communications with interviewers and from scrutinising the questionnaires (including the interviewers' observations) that generally the interviewers had a high level of understanding of the questions and possible answers, except that a few of the interviewers had difficulty in comprehending the different categories or types of credit. Secondly, it was possible to check some questions against others in the questionnaire for internal consistency. With regard to some other questions, it was also possible to compare answers received with information from other sources. The impression gathered was that, in so far as it could be checked, the data seemed generally reliable except that:

(1) the figures of purchasers who paid cash might include a few who bought on credit but were unwilling to say so;
(2) where respondents did not have documents available to refer to, they were sometimes confused about cash figures and other numbers;
(3) the term 'hire-purchase' was sometimes used and understood very loosely to refer to any type of instalment credit. The interviewers were warned about this at the briefing. But it is possible that some buyers who indicated that they bought on 'hire-purchase' may have been using some other credit arrangement.

Table 2.3: Household Returns Classified by Standard Regions*

	No contact		Refusal		No items bought		Buyer or user unavailable		Item interview(s)		Rejects		%	Total	
North	6	(6)	5	(5)	34	(33)	6	(6)	52	(50)	0	(0)	6.7	103	(100)
North West	9	(4)	22	(10)	59	(26)	8	(4)	128	(57)	0	(0)	14.7	226	(101)
Yorkshire and Humberside	14	(9)	6	(4)	51	(34)	9	(6)	71	(47)	0	(0)	9.8	151	(100)
West Midlands	4	(3)	10	(6)	57	(37)	8	(5)	74	(48)	2	(1)	10.1	155	(100)
East Midlands	8	(8)	11	(11)	30	(29)	9	(9)	44	(43)	0	(0)	6.6	102	(100)
East Anglia	0	(0)	3	(6)	19	(36)	2	(4)	28	(54)	0	(0)	3.4	52	(100)
South West	7	(6)	8	(6)	32	(26)	7	(6)	71	(57)	0	(0)	8.1	125	(101)
South East	10	(4)	32	(11)	78	(28)	13	(5)	149	(53)	2	(0)	18.4	284	(101)
Greater London	5	(2)	25	(9)	89	(33)	14	(5)	133	(50)	1	(0)	17.3	267	(99)
Wales	3	(4)	3	(4)	19	(26)	6	(8)	43	(57)	1	(0)	4.9	75	(99)
Total	66		125		468		82		793		6		100.0	1,540	

*Percentage figures shown in brackets.

Table 2.4: Household Returns Classified by Type of Area*

	No contact	Refusal	No items bought	Buyer or user unavailable	Item interview(s)	Rejects	Total
Conurbation	18 (3)	51 (9)	170 (31)	26 (5)	278 (51)	2 (0)	545 (99)
Urban: over 50,000 population	17 (4)	37 (10)	128 (33)	19 (5)	181 (47)	1 (0)	383 (99)
Urban: 10,000–50,000 population	16 (6)	19 (7)	78 (28)	13 (5)	155 (55)	1 (0)	282 (101)
Urban: 2,000–10,000 population	4 (8)	2 (4)	18 (36)	5 (10)	21 (42)	– (0)	50 (100)
Rural	11 (4)	16 (6)	74 (26)	19 (7)	158 (56)	2 (0)	280 (99)
Total	66 (4.3)	125 (8.1)	468 (30.4)	82 (5.3)	793 (51.5)	6 (0.4)	1,540 (100)

*Percentage figures shown in brackets.

On the pilot study, it had been noticed that there were sometimes gaps in the information, or answers that looked unreliable, in situations where only one of two buyers had been interviewed, or where the buyer had been interviewed but a different person was the user. These problems were avoided on the main survey by insisting that where there were two buyers, both must be interviewed, and that where the user was a different person from the buyer the user must also be interviewed.

In transactions financed by a credit arrangement or loan, the interviewers were instructed to look at the contract documents wherever possible. It was anticipated that buyers would not always recall accurately the contents of documents, and this proved to be so. Indeed, many people never read them. In several cases, the buyer did not recall having been informed that he could cancel the deal. Yet the interviewer found a notice of the right to cancel in the buyer's copy of the contract.

There was some concern about whether people who had not paid for an item would give honest answers to questions relating to payment. On the pilot study, 22 households were included that were known to have serious debt problems. Only 3 item interviews were completed within this group. These 3 appeared to contain accurate responses. However the proportion of addresses that resulted in 'no contact' and 'premises unoccupied' was much higher than normal. In two cases, the interviewers reported having seen occupants inside the house who refused to answer the door.

The main survey was a random sample of households. But credit reports were obtained by contract with a credit reference agency on most of the households in the sample. Unfortunately the information contained in these reports was not sufficient to identify with certainty any debt mentioned in the credit report with any item about which the buyer had been interviewed. But a comparison of these reports with the survey returns was helpful to form an impression. It appeared that, for the most part, questions relating to payment were probably answered correctly except that:

(a) There was a margin of cases in which the buyer probably answered incorrectly when responding to the question 'Have you ever been notified that payment for the [item] was overdue?'
(b) There may have been a margin of households that denied having bought an item for which they had not paid, and therefore were not interviewed with regard to that item.

It is interesting to note that the proportion of households with an adverse credit report (10 per cent) was the same for those at which item interviews were completed as for those at which no contact was made. It was also the same for households at which no item on the list had been bought. However, it is possible that if credit reports had been obtained from a different reference agency having different sources of information the results might not have been the same.

A difficult area is the reliability of the data relating to marketing abuses and consumer complaints. With regard to each transaction, the survey was designed to obtain information from the consumer. The research as a whole included interviews in the business community, and these provided some information with which to compare the survey data. But these interviews did not relate to the specific transactions involved in the consumer survey. One can imagine that in some instances, the retailer's story, if it could have been obtained, would not have been the same. But the risk of distortion that this might create is mitigated by three factors:

(1) A large proportion of transactions resulted in the complete satisfaction of the consumer, or in further handling of the matter by the retailer about which there was unlikely to have been any dispute. Thus it is only in a minority of transactions that there would be likely to be any significant dispute about the facts.
(2) The consumer grievances revealed by the survey were of the same type as those shown by other sources of information.[1]
(3) The primary purpose of the survey was to make comparisons between different channels of distribution, different categories of goods, different categories of sellers, different methods of financing, etc. If consumers have any propensity to exaggerate their woes, it seems unlikely that this would create a significant distortion for the purpose of these comparisons.

Apart from the risk of exaggeration, there is also a risk of underestimating predatory sales practices and defects in the goods. One possible cause is lapse of memory. It is the experience of the writer that people generally remember any serious grievances that they have about the goods better than they remember things said in the advertising or by the salesman. On the survey, therefore, the interviewers were instructed to probe with regard to representations by the salesman or in the advertising, and it was reassuring to find that on these matters the survey results generally did not vary much according to the lapse of time between the purchase and the interview.

1. Retailers, Citizens' Advice Bureau personnel, newspapers, *Which?*, trade journals, and the law reports.

Secondly, although retailers are aware of customers who are ready (almost anxious) to complain, many consumers are extremely reluctant. The enormous capacity of people to adjust to their environment seems to extend also to the acceptance of purchases that are less than satisfactory.

> We buy something and we may have some doubts about it, if we think about it at all, up to the time of delivery, but then it is ours. We grow used to it; we like it; it is part of our lives. Experimental psychologists tell us that this is the result of the operation of something called 'cognitive dissonance'; that is to say, once we reach a decision, a choice, we readapt our attitudes and opinions so as to forget about those attitudes and opinions that are inconsistent; that is to say, dissonant with that choice.[1]

A related factor is that, for psychological reasons, some people feel reluctant to admit that they have been fooled, or that they have made an imprudent purchase. Thus one respondent on the survey, in explaining why he had not complained to the seller about a defective item, said 'It's a matter of pride. One always likes to think that you can spot a pup when you see one.' In another case, the interviewer commented at the end of the questionnaire, 'Satisfied in every way with the car, but I get the feeling somehow that you would never hear it from them if they were taken.'

It was partly in response to these problems that the questionnaire was designed to probe each aspect of the transaction rather than simply to ask in general terms about any complaints. The other reason for the detailed questions was to achieve, as far as possible, comparability of results. The ideal would be a questionnaire designed to ensure that where two people have been treated in the same way, bought the same item and had the same experience with it, they would give answers indicating the same results. Unfortunately, it was not possible to rule out subjective criteria and language. But it was felt that a series of questions probing each aspect of the transaction would come closer to the ideal than a few more general questions.

Further comments on the reliability of various parts of the data will be made in the following chapters.

For analysis, each transaction was classified in one of four categories with regard to the selling methods, and again into the same four categories with regard to subsequent experience relating to the goods. The four

1. Letter from F.R. Sherwood of the Massachusetts Joint Banks and Banking Committee, reproduced in 'The Cooling-off Period in Door-to-Door Sales' Byron Sher, (1968) 15 *UCLA Law Review* 717, 730.

categories were:

(1) *Major Objections:* transactions involving fraud, other predatory practices, substantial non-performance, substantial failure of the item, or other problems sufficiently serious that the buyer would most likely not have entered into the transaction had he known the truth, or how it would turn out.

(2) *Substantial Objections:* matters thought to be less serious than in the first category, but involving some objection to the selling methods, performance of obligations, or condition or function of the item, of more than a trivial nature.

(3) *Minor Objections:* this category includes (a) objections of a trivial nature, and (b) problems that would have been serious if the seller had not put the matter right upon request or complaint from the buyer. Many cases in this category are very close to 'entirely satisfactory'.

(4) *Entirely Satisfactory:* transactions involving no objections at all.

The formulae by which the transactions were classified appear in Appendix E.

In setting the formulae for this classification system, as well as in designing the survey documents originally, an effort was made to avoid the temptation of assuming a general acceptance of one's own value judgements. The topics on which the questionnaire focused and the formulae for classification reflect value judgements derived from a mixture of:

(1) An observation of what courts and legislatures commonly regard as wrong. A prime example is deceit.
(2) A perusal of legal periodicals, trade journals, and newspapers to discover what marketing practices are regarded by substantial sections of the community as objectionable.
(3) Preliminary enquiries at agencies receiving consumer complaints, such as the Consumer Council (since abolished), newspaper readers' advisory services, and Citizens' Advice Bureaux, to discover the things about which people complain.

How the respondent to each questionnaire felt about the purchase emerged to some extent from the answers. But the questionnaire was already so long that it would not have been practicable, even if desirable, to include any type of gravity rating to discover how the consumer in the particular case would have rated the gravity of any abuse in the marketing, or of any defect in the item.

Most of the classifying was done by programming the computer. But to take account of other comments of the buyers, often recorded in marginal notes of the interviewers, and to ensure comparability as far as possible, every questionnaire was reviewed by the writer personally to check that like situations received the same codes.

One result of the survey is the overall impression that it gives of the extent of abuses in selling behaviour and of defects in the goods. It suggests that in the marketing of major consumer durables the majority of transactions were satisfactory with regard both to selling methods and to the condition of the goods. The proportion of transactions for which the buyers reported objectionable features was, however, a substantial minority and certainly more than a negligible fringe. Thus for the sample as a whole, selling methods were classified as open to major objections in 7.7 per cent, substantial objections in 10.5 per cent, and minor objections in 10.4 per cent, with 71.3 per cent entirely satisfactory. The condition of the goods was classified as open to major objections in 7.9 per cent, substantial objections in 10.5 per cent, and minor objections in 25.6 per cent, with 56.1 per cent entirely satisfactory.

Table 2.5, page 31, shows the extent to which the selling methods varied according to the type of item, and Table 2.6, page 32, shows the extent to which the condition of the goods varied according to the type of item.

With regard to both selling methods and condition of the goods, there was no significant variation according to how the households were selected (whether from the electoral register, from the lists of new building areas, additional addresses not on the electoral register and added by the interviewers, or additional households added by the interviewers at multi-household addresses).

There were no striking contrasts among the Registrar General's Standard Regions, except that buyers in Wales reported much better experiences than average, both with regard to selling methods and the condition of the goods.

The type of area was more significant. Thus, as Table 2.7, page 33, shows, buyers had the most satisfactory experiences with regard to selling methods in rural areas and small towns, and the least satisfactory experiences in the conurbations. Buyers in the larger towns fared in between. With regard to the condition of the goods, Table 2.8, page 33, shows that there was no clear pattern, but buyers in small towns and rural areas reported slightly better experiences than those in large urban areas and conurbations.

Table 2.5: Selling Methods Classified by Type of Item (All Cases)*

Type of item	Major Objections		Substantial Objections		Minor Objections		Entirely Satisfactory		Totals	
Vacuum cleaners	5	(3.5)	8	(5.7)	20	(14.2)	108	(76.6)	141	(100.0)
Encyclopedia set	3	(37.5)	1	(12.5)	0		4	(50.0)	8	(100.0)
Central heating	5	(11.6)	7	(16.3)	6	(14.0)	25	(58.1)	43	(100.0)
Electric fire	0		1	(5.3)	1	(5.3)	17	(89.5)	19	(100.1)
Gas fire	13	(24.5)	8	(15.1)	3	(5.7)	29	(54.7)	53	(100.0)
Other heating equipment	2	(7.7)	3	(11.5)	4	(15.4)	17	(65.4)	26	(100.0)
Cooking utensils	0		0		0		9	(100.0)	9	(100.0)
Sewing machine	3	(8.6)	2	(5.7)	6	(17.1)	24	(68.6)	35	(100.0)
Knitting machine	0		0		1	(25.0)	3	(75.0)	4	(100.0)
Typewriter	0		0		1	(7.1)	13	(92.9)	14	(100.0)
New motor vehicle	5	(6.7)	14	(18.7)	9	(12.0)	47	(62.7)	75	(100.1)
Secondhand motor vehicle	15	(7.2)	27	(12.6)	21	(10.1)	145	(70.0)	208	(99.9)
TV/Radio/Tape-recorder	1	(0.8)	11	(8.5)	14	(10.8)	104	(80.0)	130	(100.1)
Dishwasher	0		1	(25.0)	0		3	(75.0)	4	(100.0)
Furniture	23	(15.4)	19	(12.8)	15	(10.1)	92	(61.7)	149	(100.0)
Rug or carpet	12	(8.6)	12	(8.6)	10	(7.1)	106	(75.7)	140	(100.0)
Electric refrigerator or deep freeze	0		0		8	(15.7)	43	(84.3)	51	(100.0)
Gas refrigerator	1	(50.0)	1	(50.0)	0		0		2	(100.0)
Electric cooker	2	(8.3)	1	(4.2)	1	(4.2)	20	(83.3)	24	(100.0)
Gas cooker	2	(4.9)	6	(14.6)	3	(7.3)	30	(73.2)	41	(100.0)
Washing machine (or combination)	2	(6.9)	7	(24.1)	4	(13.8)	16	(55.1)	29	(99.9)
Dryer	1	(1.1)	0		1	(1.1)	19	(97.8)	21	(100.0)
Totals	95	(7.3)	129	(9.9)	128	(9.9)	874	(72.9)	1,226	(100.0)

*Percentage figures in brackets.

Table 2.6: Condition of the Goods Classified by Type of Item (All Cases Where Some Item Received)*

Type of item	Major objections		Substantial objections		Minor objections		Entirely satisfactory		Totals	
Vacuum cleaners	10	(7)	12	(8)	32	(22)	87	(61)	141	(98)
Encyclopedia set	1	(12)	1	(12)	1	(12)	8	(62)	8	(98)
Central heating	3	(7)	5	(12)	20	(47)	15	(35)	43	(101)
Electric fire	0		1	(5)	5	(26)	13	(68)	19	(99)
Gas fire	7	(13)	5	(9)	18	(34)	23	(43)	53	(99)
Other heating equipment	0		0		9	(34)	17	(65)	26	(99)
Cooking utensils	0		0		3	(33)	6	(66)	9	(99)
Sewing machine	1	(2)	2	(6)	8	(23)	24	(69)	35	(100)
Knitting machine	0		0		0		3	(100)	3	(100)
Typewriter	0		0		1	(7)	13	(93)	14	(100)
New motor vehicle	9	(12)	14	(19)	35	(47)	17	(23)	75	(101)
Secondhand motor vehicles	28	(14)	33	(16)	69	(33)	77	(37)	207	(100)
TV/Radio/Tape-recorder	8	(6)	13	(10)	31	(24)	78	(60)	130	(100)
Dishwasher	2	(50)	0		0		2	(50)	4	(100)
Furniture	11	(7)	19	(13)	33	(22)	85	(57)	148	(99)
Rug or carpet	4	(3)	9	(6)	12	(9)	112	(82)	137	(100)
Electric refrigerator or deep freeze	0		5	(10)	9	(18)	37	(73)	51	(101)
Gas refrigerator	0		0		0		2	(100)	2	(100)
Electric cooker	4	(16)	1	(4)	5	(20)	14	(58)	24	(98)
Gas cooker	2	(5)	3	(7)	11	(27)	25	(61)	41	(100)
Washing machine (or combination)	5	(17)	4	(14)	8	(28)	12	(41)	29	(100)
Dryer	1	(5)	1	(5)	2	(10)	17	(81)	21	(101)
Totals	96	(7.9)	128	(10.5)	312	(25.6)	684	(56.1)	1,220	(100.1)

*Percentage figures in brackets.

Table 2.7: Selling Methods Classified by Area Type (All Cases)*

Area type	Major objections		Substantial objections		Minor objections		Entirely satisfactory		Totals	
Conurbation	50	(12)	38	(9)	59	(14)	284	(66)	431	(101)
Urban area: over 50,000 population	18	(6)	33	(12)	26	(9)	200	(72)	277	(99)
Urban area: 10,000–50,000 population	10	(4)	33	(14)	28	(12)	172	(71)	243	(101)
Urban area: 2,000–10,000 population	1	(3)	1	(3)	1	(3)	28	(90)	31	(99)
Rural parish: over 2,000 population	2	(5)	5	(12)	2	(5)	32	(78)	41	(100)
Rural parish: under 2,000 population	14	(7)	19	(9)	12	(6)	158	(78)	203	(100)
Totals	95	(7.7)	129	(10.5)	128	(10.4)	874	(71.3)	1,226	(99.9)

*Percentage figures in brackets.

Table 2.8: Condition of Goods Classified by Area Type (All Cases Where Some Item Received)*

Area type	Major objections		Substantial objections		Minor objections		Entirely satisfactory		Totals	
Conurbation	33	(8)	47	(11)	110	(26)	239	(56)	429	(101)
Urban area: over 50,000 population	27	(10)	35	(13)	67	(24)	146	(53)	275	(100)
Urban area: 10,000–50,000 population	19	(8)	22	(9)	70	(29)	131	(54)	242	(100)
Urban area: 2,000–10,000 population	3	(10)	2	(7)	6	(20)	19	(63)	30	(100)
Rural parish: over 2,000 population	3	(7)	4	(10)	11	(27)	23	(56)	41	(100)
Rural parish: under 2,000 population	11	(5)	18	(9)	48	(24)	126	(62)	203	(100)
Totals	96	(7.9)	128	(10.5)	312	(25.6)	684	(56.1)	1,220	(100.1)

*Percentage figures in brackets.

There was no significant variation, either with regard to selling methods or condition of the goods, according to the number of calls required to make contact with the household. From this it might be projected that if contact could have been made at the households at which no contact was achieved, the addition of those households to the sample would probably not have made a significant difference.

An interesting variation appeared, however, according to the reaction of the household to the interviewer and to the survey. Those classified by the interviewer as reluctant (or terse, evasive, nervous or not much interested) fared better as regards selling methods and condition of the goods than those classified as willing (cordial or interested), and better also than households that were equivocal in their reaction (see Tables 2.9 and 2.10, page 35). A possible explanation is that those who were reluctant to be interviewed might be more discreet people who would tend to have more satisfactory buying experiences. Another possible explanation is that they might be the sort of people who are reluctant to complain. In any event, if it can be assumed that those who refused to be interviewed would be more likely to have characteristics in common with those who were reluctant than with those who were willing, it might be projected that if those who refused to co-operate had been interviewed, the results for those households would probably have appeared a little more satisfactory.

It was anticipated that certain categories of buyers might fare better than average. Thus cases were analysed separately where the buyer, or one of them, was in business, self-employed, or employed as a salesman, or where the buyer was an employee of the seller, or a personal relative or friend of the seller, or had a close business connection with the seller. It was found that in none of these categories did the buyers fare any better than the average for the sample as a whole, either with regard to the selling methods or condition of the goods, except for buyers who were employed by the seller. In cases where the buyer was an employee of the seller, his answers indicated that he fared better, both with regard to selling methods and condition of the goods.

The results were also analysed according to the number of items on the list that had been bought within the household. It was found that selling methods did not vary significantly according to the number of other items that had been bought within the household during the preceding two years. But the condition of the goods appeared slightly worse as the number of other items purchased within the household increased.

An interesting result is that although the buyers of motor vehicles reported worse experiences than the average for other types of goods, both with regard to selling methods and the condition of the goods, the contrast was not dramatic. The data do not support the view sometimes

Table 2.9: Selling Methods Classified by Reaction of Household*

Reaction	Major objections		Substantial objections		Minor objections		Entirely satisfactory		Total	
Willing (or cordial or interested)	85	(8)	111	(11)	114	(11)	734	(70)	1,044	(100)
Reluctant (or terse, evasive, or nervous)	0		7	(11)	6	(10)	48	(79)	61	(100)
One willing, one reluctant	2	(10)	1	(5)	2	(10)	16	(76)	21	(101)
Equivocal	8	(8)	10	(10)	6	(6)	75	(76)	99	(100)
Unascertained	0		0		0		1	(100)	1	(100)
Total	95	(7)	129	(11)	128	(10)	874	(71)	1,226	(99)

*Percentage figures in brackets.

Table 2.10: Condition of Goods Classified by Reaction of Household*

Reaction	Major objections		Substantial objections		Minor objections		Entirely satisfactory		Total	
Willing (or cordial or interested)	81	(8)	113	(11)	276	(27)	568	(55)	1,038	(101)
Reluctant (or terse, evasive, or nervous)	5	(8)	5	(8)	7	(11)	44	(72)	61	(99)
One willing, one reluctant	2	(10)	0		4	(19)	15	(71)	21	(100)
Equivocal	8	(8)	10	(10)	25	(25)	56	(57)	99	(100)
Unascertained	0		0		0		1	(100)	1	(100)
Total	96	(8)	128	(10)	312	(26)	684	(56)	1,220	(100)

*Percentage figures in brackets.

expressed or inferred that motor dealers (like horse traders before them) are the villians of retailing. If motor dealers have a bad reputation, it is probably less because they behave in ways significantly different from other retailers than because more money is involved. In other words, a customer who feels wronged by a motor dealer may make more fuss than one who suffers the same grievance at the hands of another retailer because the loss is greater. Moreover motor vehicles are one of the few consumer items involving enough money to make it worthwhile to resolve disputes by litigation. Thus, for example, a motor dealer who deceives a customer could find that he suffers the adverse publicity of a court action. But a sewing machine dealer who deceives the same customer is much less likely to be sued.

3 THE USE OF CREDIT

1. Introduction

The purposes of this chapter are to explain the use of consumer credit, to consider its significance with regard to integrity in marketing, and to provide background information for the chapters that follow.

2. Reasons for Using Credit

An obvious reason for using credit is to purchase now something for which the buyer does not immediately have the money to pay. But it is not the only reason, and may not be the most significant. For many families, the purchase of major items on instalment credit is a normal routine continued over many years. Over time, they have the money to pay cash for what they buy, and one might think that the same items could be purchased at less total cost if the family would save the money that it pays in instalments and make each purchase as enough is accumulated. For some families, the reason for not doing so is that the pressures of the moment are always stronger than the discipline or budgeting skill necessary for saving. Current demands may be enough to consume the whole pay packet, or if anything is left after paying for basic needs, the temptation is there to use it for transitory pleasures. Paying instalments to a seller or finance company may be perceived as a demand that must be met (like the rent and the food bill) whereas saving can be deferred. For families in this position, buying on credit is not only a way of purchasing major items; it is also a form of saving and a method of budgeting.

Even families that have savings in the bank may prefer not to use that money for the purchase of consumer durables. They may derive a sense of financial security and flexibility by keeping their savings intact for a rainy day. Moreover they may recognise that they will meet the obligation to pay instalments but lack the confidence that they would replace by instalments any savings that they withdrew.

Although the use of credit involves interest (finance charges) and other costs,[1] these are partly offset by inflation, and sometimes the interest cost can be more than offset. This can be so, for example, if the price of an item rises shortly after its purchase by more than the amount of the interest. If the use of the item enables other expenses to be avoided, this might also offset part of the cost of credit. For example, buying a washing

1. These are summarised in Chapter 8, p.199 (heading G).

machine may enable a family to avoid the expense of using a launderette.

Another reason some people use credit is a feeling that it puts them in a better position to reject unsatisfactory goods, or that it gives leverage with which to obtain repair or replacement if the goods prove defective. As one buyer of a television on the survey put it, 'I bought on HP so that I would have some sort of security against the seller if any faults appeared. When the set seemed OK, I paid it off in two instalments and avoided paying interest.'

Credit is also used for convenience. In particular, charge accounts or credit cards are used to avoid carrying cash or writing cheques for each item bought.

Advertising and the blandishments of salesmen can be another inducement to buy on credit. So much per week can sound easier than paying 20 times that amount now. Even when talk of easy payments is not needed to sell the item, the seller may still have reasons for preferring credit to cash sales. For example, in the motor trade the seller may receive a commission from a finance company on HP transactions. In the furniture trade, a seller may prefer credit because customers coming in to pay instalments increase the traffic flow to the shop. In these situations the use of credit may result from the seller's influence.

On the other hand, of course, sellers often have an incentive to prefer cash, particularly during periods of rising unemployment.

3. Types of Consumer Credit

Most consumer credit can be classified in one of the following five categories.

(1) Transaction Credit

This term is used throughout the book to refer to instalment credit arranged between buyer and seller for the purchase of a particular item. Thus transaction credit includes:

(a) Hire-Purchase. This is the most popular form of transaction credit used in England when the seller or finance company wants security in the goods (i.e., the right to repossess the goods if the instalments are not paid). In legal theory, hire-purchase is a hiring with an option to purchase, usually for a nominal sum, at the end of the hiring period. But in practice it is usually viewed by all concerned as simply a way of buying by instalments. Sometimes the credit is advanced by the seller. This is common, for example, with furniture, radios and sewing machines. Sometimes the credit is advanced by a finance company,[1] an arrangement common in motor

1. Sometimes called finance houses.

vehicle transactions. Theoretically the dealer sells the car to a finance company which then lets it out on hire-purchase to the customer.

(b) Conditional Sale. This is an alternative form of sale on credit with a right of repossession. It is a normal method in the United States and Canada but is used only for a minority of transactions in England.

(c) Credit Sale. This is the ordinary sale of goods on credit without security (i.e., if the instalments are not paid, the seller has a debt claim for the price but no right to repossess).

(2) Account with Seller

Instead of credit being arranged for the purchase of a particular item, the price may be debited to a continuing account that the buyer maintains with the seller. This may be an ordinary charge account, the buyer paying the balance in full at the end of the month. Or it may be a revolving credit account under which the buyer pays by instalments. Often the buyer has an option to pay either way, and this is sometimes called an option account. Or it may be a subscription account (budget account) in which the buyer pays continuing equal instalments of an agreed monthly amount, and can purchase up to, say, 24 times that amount. There are many variations. The seller may issue a credit card to be used when making purchases on the account.

(3) Loans

The buyer may pay cash to the seller by borrowing the money from a cash lender. Consumer loans can be divided into two major categories:

(a) Pure cash loans, i.e., the lender supplies money to the buyer independently of the seller. A common example is a customer borrowing money from his bank to buy a car. To estimate the risk involved, the bank may want to know how the money will be used, but it is not generally concerned where the car is bought.

(b) Transactions using the legal documentation of a cash loan but which are in substance a form of sales finance. The seller arranges with a finance company to advance the price of goods to be purchased, the customer undertaking on a loan form or promissory note to repay the finance company. In substance, these loans are a species of transaction credit.

(4) A Credit Card Company

The buyer may use a card of a multi-purpose credit card company, i.e., a company that operates a credit card system but does not itself supply the goods or services that the card may be used to purchase. The credit card company pays the seller, usually at a discount, and the buyer pays the credit card company. Usually the cardholder can pay the balance in full or by instalments.

These multi-purpose credit cards, for example the American Express Card, were first issued to people at upper-income levels and were used primarily for travel and dining. But the cards issued by the banks (the Barclaycard and the Access Card) are now the two major systems. The banks have extended the use of multi-purpose credit cards both with regard to the types of user and the types of goods and services that can be purchased through their use.

The banks began by aiming at upper-income users. But 'A few years ago we moved to aim at C1s. Now we have some C2s and Ds as card-holders.'[1]

Although only one case appeared in the sample (taken in 1969) of a multi-purpose credit card being used for the purchase of a consumer durable, their use has since become much more extensive. The bank credit cards are, for example, now used for the purchase of petrol, clothing, white goods, electronic equipment, furniture, photographic equipment, railway travel, hotel accommodation, meals, and a wide range of goods at department stores.[2]

The presence of the customer at a retail outlet and the signature of the customer on a charge slip are no longer necessary for the use of a credit card. For example, theatre tickets can be ordered by telephone quoting the card number, or camping equipment can be ordered by mail order.

The banks, however, impose a maximum limit on each customer's account. There is no limit on the amount of each individual purchase. But there is a limit on the total amount of credit that each customer is allowed to have outstanding. A limit of £300 to £500 would be typical. These limits make bank credit cards generally unusable for the purchase of motor vehicles and major items of furniture.

(5) Check Trading

This arrangement is similar to multi-purpose credit cards in that a separate

1. Interview in 1977 with the head office representative of a bank credit card. For an explanation of the social grades referred to in that quotation, see Appendix F.

2. Same interview in 1977. Also observations by the writer of window displays in 1977 showed that at appliance stores, radio stores and many furniture stores, there were signs indicating the acceptance of bank credit cards. Moreover they were displayed much more prominently than notices indicating 'HP terms available'. The acceptance of bank credit cards at these outlets had not been nearly so noticeable in 1969.

financing company is involved, i.e. the check trader. The customer is supplied with checks, for example in denominations of £20 or £30, which may be used to make purchases at shops named on a list with which the customer is supplied. The customer pays the check trader by instalments. A disadvantage is that if there is a significant time lag between receiving the check and making the purchase, the customer will be paying for credit that he is not using.

Check trading has been operating for many years. During the 1960s, however, a new type of check trading developed as a device for evading the Control Orders.[1] A department store, for example, would establish a corporate affiliate that would issue trading checks usable only at that store. Commonly, a trading check would be issued for a particular transaction, and in these situations, the arrangement is essentially a species of transaction credit.

A feature of the older style of check trading is that the instalments are collected by an agent so that the customer may receive more personal attention than with some other types of credit. For example, as one buyer of furniture on the survey put it, 'I like dealing with a check trader because if you get into arrears they allow you time to pay and don't worry you.' The Crowther Committee felt that check trading 'has given rise to fewer complaints and difficulties than many other forms of credit trading or lending'.[2]

Leasing is an alternative method of obtaining the use of an item by periodic payments. It is common with regard to television sets. But the focus of this study was on selling and buying, and lease transactions were not included.

4. Financing of Transactions in the Sample

Of the cases in the sample, the buyers indicated that they paid cash in 57 per cent, used transaction credit in 33 per cent, raised a loan in 5 per cent, bought on an account with the seller in 3 per cent, and used a trading check in 2 per cent.

Table 3.1, page 42, shows the method of financing classified by type of item. An interesting feature is that 62 per cent of cookers (stoves) were bought on transaction credit compared with only 37 per cent for cash. For most other types of goods, it was closer to the reverse. A possible explanation is that cookers are more of a necessity, and a larger proportion of

1. *The Hire-Purchase and Credit Sale Agreements (Control) Order 1964* (since repealed and subsequently replaced).

2. *Report of the Committee on Consumer Credit,* 1971, Cmnd 4596, Vol. 1, para. 8.2.13.

Table 3.1: Method of Financing Classified by Type of Item*

Item	Cash	Loan	Transaction credit	Account with seller	Credit card company	Check trader	Credit, but unascertained what type	Totals
Vacuum cleaner	88 (62)	1 (1)	39 (28)	9 (6)	–	4 (3)	–	141 (100)
Encyclopedia	2 (25)	–	5 (63)	1 (13)	–	–	–	8 (101)
Central heating	22 (51)	16 (37)	5 (12)	–	–	–	–	43 (100)
Electric fire	12 (63)	1 (5)	5 (26)	1 (5)	–	–	–	19 (99)
Gas fire	30 (57)	1 (2)	19 (36)	–	–	2 (4)	1 (2)	53 (101)
Other heating equipment	16 (62)	–	9 (35)	1 (4)	–	–	–	26 (101)
Cooking utensils	7 (78)	–	1 (11)	1 (11)	–	–	–	9 (100)
Sewing machine	19 (54)	–	13 (37)	1 (3)	–	2 (6)	–	35 (100)
Knitting machine	–	–	4 (100)	–	–	–	–	4 (100)
Typewriter	10 (71)	–	1 (7)	3 (21)	–	–	–	14 (99)
New motor vehicle	52 (69)	8 (11)	15 (20)	–	–	–	–	75 (100)
Secondhand motor vehicles	113 (54)	24 (12)	71 (34)	–	–	–	–	208 (100)
Radio/TV/Record player	77 (59)	1 (1)	44 (34)	7 (5)	–	1 (1)	–	130 (100)
Dishwasher	4 (100)	–	–	–	–	–	–	4 (100)
Furniture	85 (57)	1 (1)	55 (37)	3 (2)	–	5 (3)	–	149 (100)
Rug or carpet	91 (65)	1 (1)	37 (26)	6 (4)	1 (1)	4 (3)	–	140 (100)
Refrigerator	25 (49)	2 (4)	21 (41)	1 (2)	–	2 (4)	–	51 (100)
Deep freeze	1 (50)	–	1 (50)	–	–	–	–	2 (100)
Gas stove	13 (32)	1 (2)	27 (66)	–	–	–	–	41 (100)
Electric stove (and 2 stoves unspecified)	11 (46)	–	13 (54)	–	–	–	–	24 (100)
Washing machine or combination	13 (45)	–	14 (48)	1 (4)	–	1 (4)	–	29 (101)
Dryer	13 (62)	1 (5)	5 (24)	1 (5)	–	1 (5)	–	21 (101)
Total	704 (57)	58 (5)	404 (33)	36 (3)	1	22 (2)	1	1,226 (100)

*Percentage figures in brackets.

cookers in the survey were bought by families with low incomes who could less readily afford to purchase other items on the list. Another factor may be that, as the survey indicates, people who are just settling into new accommodation use transaction credit a little more than others, and this is also likely to be a time when cookers are purchased.

As the table shows, transaction credit was used more in the sale of secondhand motor vehicles than of new ones. This contrast is even more pronounced if private sales of secondhand motor vehicles are excluded. Approximately 44 per cent of secondhand motor vehicles purchased through a dealer were financed by transaction credit compared with 20 per cent of new motor vehicles.

The use of transaction credit dropped off for secondhand motor vehicles over five years old, no doubt because older cars are less valuable as security. For vehicles in the years up to that age, transaction credit was used in 35 to 48 per cent of cases, but in the years after that age it was 18 to 29 per cent. Conversely, the proportion of cash sales jumped at the five-year age line.

Transaction credit was used in a higher proportion of sales at the home than of sales made in other ways. Thus where the item was bought at a shop or garage, 61 per cent of buyers paid cash, 31 per cent used transaction credit, and 4 per cent raised a loan. In purchases from a heating engineer or builder, 60 per cent paid cash and 40 per cent raised a loan. In the mail order cases, 50 per cent used transaction credit, 28 per cent bought on accounts with the seller, and 17 per cent paid cash. In purchases at gas or electricity board showrooms, 47 per cent used transaction credit, 47 per cent paid cash and 2 per cent raised a loan. But in sales at the home, it was 55 per cent transaction credit, 35 per cent cash and 8 per cent on accounts with the seller.

The methods of financing indicated by the buyers did not vary significantly according to the lapse of time between the purchase and the interview.

There were some regional differences. In the use of cash, the South East and Wales were higher than average, and the North and North West were much lower than average. In the use of transaction credit, the North, North West and East Midlands were much greater than average, the South West and Greater London were slightly below average, and the South East and Wales were much below average. Check trading was heaviest in Greater London and the North, although there were only 22 check trader cases in the sample.

In the conurbations and urban areas with populations over 10,000, transaction credit was used in 35 per cent of cases. In the smaller towns and rural areas, transaction credit was used in 26 per cent of cases, and cash, loans and accounts with the seller were used proportionately more.

Cash was used proportionately more in social grades A and B, followed by C1 and housewife.[1] Transaction credit was used most heavily in social grades C2 and D, and in these grades, the proportion of items bought on transaction credit was about the same as the proportion bought for cash. Loans were used most heavily in social grades A, B and C1. Trading check were used most heavily in the social grades C2, D and housewife. There were 20 transactions involving trading checks in those grades, only 2 in grade C1 and none at all in grades A or B.

The use of cash was heaviest at the extremities of the income scale. Thus cash was used in 67 per cent of transactions by households with an income of up to £10 per week, and 78 per cent of transactions by households with an income of over £40 per week, dipping to a low of 48 per cent by households with an income in the range £21-£30 per week. Conversely transaction credit was used in the greatest proportion of transactions by households in the income range £11-£30 per week. Thus the proportion of cases involving transaction credit was 24 per cent for households with an income up to £10 per week, rising to a high of 40% for those in the income range £21-£30 per week, and dipping to 10 per cent for households with an income of over £40 per week.

The reason for the use of cash rather than transaction credit among households at the lower end of the income scale is most likely that these households often consist of retired people. They may be more likely to use savings rather than credit terms for the purchase of major durables Of the 62 transactions in households with an income of up to £10 per week, 41 per cent of buyers were 65 or over (compared with 4 per cent for the sample as a whole). Only 3 per cent of buyers in these households were under 40 (compared with 47 per cent for the sample as a whole).

Also in the sample as a whole, the use of cash showed an increase with age, ranging from 44-45 per cent of transactions by people in the age bracket 20-30 years up to 80 per cent of transactions by people in the age bracket 65-79 years.

The sample included 4 cases in each of which there were 2 buyers both under 21 (then the age of majority) and a further 20 cases in which 1 buyer was under 21. In these 24 cases, the distribution according to methods of financing was very close to that for the sample as a whole.

Buyers who could be expected to be better informed about business seemed to use cash proportionately more, and transaction credit proportionately less. Thus where the buyer was self-employed, cash was used

1. For a description of the social grades, see Appendix F.

much more than average for the sample and transaction credit much less. Where the buyer was a salesman, cash was used a little more than average, and transaction credit a little less.

There was also a correlation between the use of cash and the readership of *Which?*.[1] Of those who had never seen *Which?*, 45 per cent bought the item for cash, and 41 per cent used transaction credit. Of those who had seen *Which?* but did not check it when buying the particular item, 61 per cent paid cash, and 28 per cent used transaction credit. Of those who checked *Which?* before making the particular purchase, but did not buy a recommended item, 67 per cent paid cash and 23 per cent used transaction credit. Of those who checked *Which?* before making the purchase and bought a recommended item, 70 per cent paid cash and 12 per cent used transaction credit.

People living in a flat used transaction credit in a larger proportion of cases than people living in a house.

Not surprisingly, it was found that people in new accommodations tended to use more transaction credit. Thus in households that had been selected at random from the electoral register, 56 per cent of their purchases were for cash, and 32 per cent involved transaction credit. But for those selected from the lists of new building areas, it was 45 per cent cash and 45 per cent transaction credit.

There was a decreasing use of transaction credit with the length of time that the buyers had lived at the same address prior to the purchase. Transaction credit was used in 40 per cent of cases where the buyers had lived at the address less than one month, dropping to 30 per cent where they had lived there three or more years.

One of the points that the interviewers were instructed to note was 'How clean and tidy is the home (making allowances for children)?' In connection with this observation the interviewers were instructed: 'Ignore the quality of the building structure. We are only concerned with the orderliness of the household, i.e., how well they manage to keep whatever they have in a clean and tidy condition.' The answers were intended as a rough guide to the skill of the household in the management of domestic affairs. As table 3.2, page 46, shows, there was a direct correlation between the condition of the home and the use of cash.

As table 3.3, page 46, shows, there was an inverse correlation between the use of cash and the number of children in the household. The proportion of transactions paid for in cash was 68 per cent for households without children, falling to 42 per cent for households with over two children.

1. The monthly magazine of the Consumers' Association.

Table 3.2: Methods of Financing Compared with Interviewers' Observations on Condition of Home

Home Condition (as observed by interviewer)	Proportion of transactions paid for in cash	Proportion using transaction credit
	%	%
Immaculate	64	24
Good	54	25
Fair	42	42
Poor	25	56

Table 3.3: Methods of Financing Classified by Number of Children in Household

Number of children		Cash	Loan	Transaction credit	Account with seller	Check Trader
None	%	68	4	24	3	1
One child	%	55	5	36	2	2
Two children	%	44	7	45	2	2
Over two children	%	42	5	41	6	6

For households that had bought 1 to 3 items on the list within the preceding two years, the proportion paying cash ranged from 51 to 56 per cent, and the proportion using transaction credit ranged from 33 to 36 per cent. For households that had bought 4 or more of the items on the list within the preceding two years, the proportion using cash ranged from 63 to 65 per cent and the proportion using transaction credit ranged from 21 to 27 per cent.

In the 404 transaction credit cases, the instalments were usually payable monthly (56 per cent), but sometimes weekly (25 per cent) or quarterly (15 per cent).

5. Methods of Financing Compared with Outcome of Transactions

As Table 3.4, page 47, indicates, selling methods, as reported by the buyers, were more objectionable in credit transactions than in cash sales. Thus when cash was used, selling methods were classified as open to major objections in 6 per cent, substantial objections in 9 per cent, and minor objections in 9 per cent, with 76 per cent of the cases entirely satisfactory. In the transaction credit cases, the corresponding proportions were 10, 13,

Table 3.4: Selling Methods Classified by Method of Financing*

How item paid for	Major Objections	Substantial Objections	Minor Objections	Entirely Satisfactory	Total
Cash	45 (6)	61 (9)	63 (9)	535 (76)	704 (100)
Transaction credit	42 (10)	52 (13)	53 (13)	257 (64)	404 (100)
Loan	3 (5)	10 (17)	9 (16)	36 (62)	58 (100)
Account with seller	0	4 (11)	1 (3)	31 (86)	36 (100)
Check trader	5 (23)	2 (9)	2 (9)	13 (59)	22 (100)
Credit card company	0	0	0	1 (100)	1 (100)
Credit, but unascertained what type	0	0	0	1 (100)	1 (100)
Totals	95 (7.7)	129 (10.5)	128 (10.4)	874 (71.3)	1,226 (99.9)

*Percentage figures in brackets.

Table 3.5: Condition of Goods Classified by Method of Financing*

How item paid for	Major Objections	Substantial Objections	Minor Objections	Entirely Satisfactory	Total
Cash	44 (6)	68 (10)	155 (22)	434 (62)	701 (100)
Transaction credit	37 (9)	48 (12)	120 (30)	196 (49)	401 (100)
Loan	8 (14)	8 (14)	27 (47)	15 (26)	58 (101)
Account with seller	3 (8)	2 (6)	4 (11)	27 (75)	36 (100)
Check trader	4 (18)	2 (9)	6 (27)	10 (45)	22 (99)
Credit card company	0	0	0	1 (100)	1 (100)
Credit, but unascertained what type	0	0	0	1 (100)	1 (100)
Totals	96 (7.9)	128 (10.5)	312 (25.6)	684 (56.1)	1,220 (100.1)

*Percentage figures in brackets.

13 and 64 per cent. In the loan cases, the corresponding proportions were 5, 17, 16 and 62 per cent. In the check trader case, the corresponding proportions were 23, 9, 9 and 59 per cent. The category reporting the best experiences was the cases involving an account with the seller, where the corresponding proportions were 0, 11, 3 and 86 per cent.

With regard to subsequent experience with the condition of the goods, Table 3.5, page 45, shows that cash buyers again reported better experiences than those using transaction credit. Thus in the cash sales, the transaction was classified as open to major objections to the condition of the goods in 6 per cent, substantial objections in 10 per cent and minor objections in 22 per cent, with 62 per cent of the cases entirely satisfactory. In transaction credit cases, the corresponding proportions were 9, 12, 30 and 49 per cent. In the loan cases, it was 14, 14, 47 and 26 per cent. In the check trader cases, it was 18, 9, 27 and 45 per cent. Those using an account with the seller again reported the best experiences, and the corresponding proportions were 8, 6, 11 and 75 per cent.

These figures might be explained to some extent by the more frequent use of cash and accounts with the seller for some items that are simpler, less expensive, and that require little salesmanship. Conversely transaction credit may tend to be used more extensively for items that are more expensive, involve more salesmanship, and which have more complicated features that can go wrong. To test this possibility, the selling methods and condition of the goods were analysed separately for each item category that appeared in sufficient volume in the sample involving both cash and transaction credit cases. This analysis showed that the contrast between cash sales and transaction credit cases is partly explicable by different types of item being involved. In other words, when differences in the type of item were controlled, it was found that cash buyers still reported better experiences than those using transaction credit, but the differences were less than those which appear in Tables 3.4 and 3.5.

A check was also made to discover whether differences in the channels of distribution might have influenced the results. In particular it was throught possible that the adverse experiences of those using transaction credit, compared with cash buyers, might be partly explained by the greater use of transaction credit in sales at the home. It was found, however, that this was not so. Both with regard to selling methods and the condition of the goods, those who bought from a salesman who called at the home reported worse experiences than those who bought at trade premises. But in sales at the home, those using transaction credit reported worse experiences than those paying cash in roughly the same ratio as in sales at trade premises. Thus the combination of door-to-door selling and the use of transaction credit appears to be associated with adverse experiences (both with regard to selling methods and the condition of the goods) beyond those associated with either factor separately.

Overall, the data suggest that with regard to both selling methods and the condition of the goods, cash buyers fared a little better than those using transaction credit.

Three points should be added about this conclusion. First, the survey was not designed to measure value for money. Hence it does not show the extent to which, if at all, cash buyers may be in a better bargaining position over price. Secondly, the survey was not designed to measure any collateral consequences that might flow from the use of cash or of credit. Thirdly, although the use of credit does not seem to produce any broad deterioration in marketing standards generally, it could well be a crucial factor in the crooked fringe of business. For example, many of the frauds that have occurred in the sale of encyclopedias and of central heating would not have succeeded if the customers had been required to pay cash.

In 92 per cent of cash transactions, the buyer answered that the item was received in the condition in which it was expected to be. In loan cases, the proportion was 90 per cent; in cases involving an account with the seller it was 89 per cent; in transaction credit cases it was 87 per cent; and in check trader cases 77 per cent.

Subsequent defects in the goods were reported in 14 per cent of the cases involving an account with the seller, 21 per cent of the cash sales, 28 per cent of the transaction credit cases, 32 per cent of the check trader cases and 33 per cent of the loan cases.

With regard to money spent on repairs by the buyer, there were no significant contrasts between cash buyers and those using transaction credit.

The proportion of cases in which the buyer subsequently complained to the seller, or asked for something to be put right, or asked for some repairs to be done, was 44 per cent in the loan cases, 40 per cent in the check trader cases, 28 per cent in transaction credit cases, 21 per cent in the cash sales and 16 per cent where the item was bought on an account with the seller. 72 per cent of those who bought on an account with the seller felt that they had nothing to complain about, compared with 64 per cent for cash sales, 56 per cent in transaction credit cases, 40 per cent in check trader cases and 36 per cent in loan transactions. With regard to the loan cases, part of the explanation may be that loan finance was used mostly in connection with motor vehicles and central heating. Motor vehicles have more to go wrong with them than most of the items on the list, and central heating involves problems of installation, adjustment and suitability to the premises that are not involved in most of the other items on the list.

The proportion of cases in which the seller did nothing in response to the buyer's request or complaint was 8 per cent in loan cases, 12 per cent in the cash sales, 16 per cent in transaction credit cases, and 22 per cent in check trader cases. Of the cases in which the buyer complained, or asked for something to be put right or repaired, the proportion in which the buyer was satisfied with what the seller did in response to the request or complaint was 73 per cent in the loan cases, 72 per cent in the cash sales, 58 per cent in the transaction credit cases and 55 per cent where a trading check was used.

The contrast between cash and transaction credit with regard to complaints is not explicable by differences in the type of item. There was no overall striking contrast with transaction credit being used proportionately more for items that are more complaint-prone.

It is not possible to deduce from the survey results a clear reason why the transaction credit cases involved more requests or complaints than the cash sales, nor a clear reason why cash buyers who complained were more readily satisfied than credit buyers who complained. But several explanations are possible.

(1) People who buy on credit may feel more entitled to complain. There may be some inclination for a cash buyer to treat a transaction as final, and if an item is defective, a cash buyer may not feel a continuing sense of loss. A credit buyer may be inclined to feel that the seller owes him an obligation as long as he owes part of the price.

(2) Some people may be more prone to complain and it is possible that these people may be more likely to buy on credit to give themselves leverage for the complaints.

(3) People who buy on credit may have different expectations about the performance of the goods. In particular, they may expect that the item should retain its appearance, or at least continue to function, until it has been paid for. A cash buyer, on the other hand, may have no particular expectation about the length of time during which the item should retain its appearance, or should function.

(4) For three reasons, some people who buy on credit may tend to deal with merchants selling poorer quality goods:

(a) people using credit may be less cautious as shoppers, or may be more restricted in the extent to which they can shop around. The survey results show that the proportion of buyers who shopped around before buying was the same for cash buyers as for those using transaction credit (51 per cent in both categories). But it is still possible that cash buyers might be more mobile and better able to shop around in different districts;

(b) people buying on credit may be less able to afford the better quality items and therefore tend to buy items of a poorer quality that cause more trouble. This hypothesis, however, is not supported by the survey results. On the more standard items, a comparison of the average prices showed that for a majority of item categories those using transaction credit paid a higher cash price per item than did cash buyers. In many cases, however, the nominal cash price in credit transactions includes a concealed cost of credit. Where this occurs, credit buyers might be receiving poorer quality goods even though paying the same or a higher price;

(c) some credit buyers may go to poorer quality shops because they think (perhaps rightly) that they would risk a denial of credit at the better quality shops.

(5) The use of credit might be associated more frequently with selling methods that create a gap between a buyer's expectations and the performance of the goods.

A significant proportion of the loan cases were not pure cash lending, but were essentially a form of sales finance. The financing was arranged by the seller rather than by the customer. Only 1 out of the 18 bank loans was arranged by the seller, but 13 out of the 16 loans from a finance company were arranged by the seller. The loan was also arranged by the seller in 1 out of the 4 insurance company cases, in the 2 National Coal Board cases, and in the 2 transactions involving the AA Loan Scheme.

Using loan forms, rather than HP or credit sale forms, had the effect of denying the customer the benefit of the consumer protection sections of the *Hire-Purchase Act*, 1965, and no doubt in some situations that was the reason for their use. Another reason was to evade the Control Orders.

In their dealings with the seller, customers who borrowed from a bank reported better experiences than those borrowing from a finance company, both with regard to selling methods and the condition of the goods. Of those who borrowed from a bank, the selling methods were classified as open to major or substantial objections in 1 case out of 18, compared with 5 cases out of 16 for those who borrowed from a finance company. With regard to the condition of the goods, cases involving a bank loan were classified as open to major or substantial objections in 4 out of 18, compared with 6 out of 16 where the borrowing was from a finance company. In both categories, most of the loans were for the purchase of motor vehicles or central heating.

Other comments on the significance of credit appear in the chapters that follow.

4 SELLING METHODS

1. Advertising

In the sample, there were 127 cases in which the buyer contacted the seller in response to an advertisement for a particular item. There were a further 276 cases in which the buyer could recall that prior to buying the item, he had seen or heard some particular advertising for goods of the type that he bought.

Overall, those who could recall seeing or hearing some advertising (either for the particular item bought or for that type of goods) reported experiences slightly worse than those who did not recall having seen or heard any advertising at all. Thus with regard to selling methods, the cases in which the buyer reported having seen or heard some advertising were classified as open to major objections in 8 per cent, substantial objections in 13 per cent, and minor objections in 13 per cent, with 66 per cent entirely satisfactory. For cases in which the buyer did not recall having seen or heard any advertising at all, the corresponding proportions were 8, 9, 9 and 73 per cent. With regard to the condition of the goods, the cases in which the buyer remembered having seen or heard some advertising were classified as open to major objections in 10 per cent, substantial objections in 11 per cent, and minor objections in 27 per cent, with 51 per cent entirely satisfactory. For cases in which the buyer did not recall having seen or heard any advertising, the corresponding proportions were 7, 10, 24 and 58 per cent.

The contrast, however, was most pronounced in cases in which the buyer had responded to an advertisement for a particular item. Tables 4.1 and 4.2, pages 53 and 54, show, both with regard to selling methods and the condition of the goods, how those who contacted the seller in response to an advertisement for a particular item reported worse experiences than those who did not. Those who did so contact the seller, but then bought from him a different item from the one advertised, reported the worst experiences of all.

Where the buyer did not respond to an advertisement for a particular item, but had seen or heard advertising relating to the type of goods, the results reported, both with regard to selling methods and condition of the goods, were slightly worse than where the buyer did not recall having seen or heard any advertising at all, but only by a fine margin. A significant contrast appeared, however, between those who had seen or heard advertising that mentioned the name of a seller (mostly retail advertising) and

Table 4.1: Selling Methods Classified According to Whether Buyer Responded to an Advertisement for a Particular Item*

	Selling methods				
	Major Objections	Substantial Objections	Minor Objections	Entirely Satisfactory	Totals
Buyer did not respond to advertisement for particular item	80 (7)	110 (10)	104 (9)	802 (73)	1,096 (99)
Buyer responded and bought the item advertised	12 (10)	15 (13)	19 (17)	68 (60)	114 (100)
Buyer responded to advertisement of seller for particular item, but bought a different item	3 (25)	4 (33)	5 (41)	0 (0)	12 (99)
Unascertained	0 (0)	0 (0)	0 (0)	4 (100)	4 (100)
Totals	95 (8)	129 (11)	128 (10)	874 (71)	1,226 (100)

*Percentage figures in brackets.

Table 4.2: Condition of Goods According to Whether Buyer Responded to an Advertisement for a Particular Item*

	Condition of goods				
	Major Objections	Substantial Objections	Major Objections	Entirely Satisfactory	Totals
Buyer did not respond to advertisement for particular item	82 (8)	106 (10)	281 (26)	622 (57)	1,091 (101)
Buyer responded and bought the item advertised	12 (11)	16 (14)	30 (27)	55 (49)	113 (101)
Buyer responded to advertisement of seller for particular item, but bought a different item	2 (16)	3 (25)	2 (16)	5 (41)	12 (98)
Unascertained	0 (0)	1 (25)	1 (25)	2 (50)	4 (100)
Totals	96 (8)	126 (10)	314 (26)	684 (56)	1,220 (100)

*Percentage figures in brackets.

those who had seen or heard advertising that did not mention the name of a seller (which would generally be manufacturers' advertising). Both with regard to selling methods and the condition of the goods, those who had seen or heard sellers' advertising reported worse experiences. Those who had seen or heard only manufacturers' advertising reported slightly better experiences than those who did not recall having seen or heard any advertising at all.

Taking all cases in which any advertising had been seen or heard, buyers who recalled an advertisement mentioning the name of a seller reported worse experiences than those who saw only other advertising, generally that of a manufacturer. Thus where the buyer recalled advertising mentioning the name of a seller, the selling methods were classified as open to major objections in 11 per cent, substantial objections in 15 per cent, and minor objections in 15 per cent, with 59 per cent entirely satisfactory. Where the buyer saw or heard advertising not mentioning the name of a seller, the corresponding proportions were 3, 10, 12 and 74 per cent. With regard to the condition of the goods, where the buyer recalled advertising mentioning the name of a seller, the condition of the goods was classified as open to major objections in 13 per cent, substantial objections in 10 per cent, and minor objections in 30 per cent, with 46 per cent entirely satisfactory. Where the advertising did not mention the name of a seller, the corresponding proportions were 5, 11, 24 and 59 per cent.

It is also interesting to note that almost twice as many buyers saw or heard an advertisement mentioning the name of a seller as one that did not. Thus not only did those who recalled sellers' advertising report proportionately worse experiences than those who recalled only manufacturers' advertising, they also reported a greater total volume of adverse buying experiences.

Buyers were asked whether anything said in the advertising turned out to be wrong or untrue. Measured by the responses to this question, the advertising was reported to be false in 14 per cent of cases where the buyer responded to an advertisement for a particular item and 10 per cent of cases in which the buyer recalled other advertising. Taking all cases in which any advertising had been seen or heard, it was reported to be false in 12 per cent of cases where the advertising mentioned the name of a seller, and 9 per cent of the cases involving only manufacturers' advertising.

Misrepresentations by the salesman were also reported in a larger proportion of cases involving sellers' advertising than of cases involving manufacturers' advertising.

The differences that appeared between sellers' advertising and manufacturers' advertising are not explicable by any differences in the categories of goods involved.

It is not obvious why the buyers who recalled having seen or heard sellers' advertising should report worse experiences than those who recalled having seen or heard only manufacturers' advertising; but several explanations are possible.

(1) Manufacturers' advertising may be more vague or subtle, involving associations of ideas rather than statements of fact, so that if any deceit is involved it may be harder to recognise or harder to explain. Conversely, sellers' advertising might be more detailed or precise, giving rise to a greater or better articulated sense of grievance if expectations are unfulfilled.

(2) Where the buyer responded to an advertisement for a particular item (one category of sellers' advertising) the details would probably be remembered better than when other types of advertising were seen.

(3) There may be a greater range of honesty levels among retailers than among manufacturers. A manufacturer who continually told blatant and readily detectable lies in his advertising might expect the bulk of retailers to refuse his products. His distribution would then be limited to the less scrupulous fringe of retailers and to direct selling. Thus any unscrupulous person entering business to profit by deceit or predatory practices may find it easier to operate as a retailer than as a manufacturer.

(4) The advertising agencies, or the advertising media most used by manufacturers (television, national newspapers and magazines), may exert a controlling influence that is not present in the advertising channels mostly used for sellers' advertising (brochures, local newspapers, posters, the cinema and displays and notices on sellers' premises).

(5) The Advertising Standards Authority Ltd endeavours to promote and enforce ethical standards in advertising by promulgating and supervising the *British Code of Advertising Practice*. But its primary sanction is a 'recommendation of non-acceptance', i.e. a recommendation to the media that a specified advertisement should not be accepted. For that reason, it would be natural to expect the Advertising Standards Authority to have more influence on manufacturers' advertising through national media than on sellers' advertising through local channels.[1]

With regard to secondhand motor vehicles, the reported incidence of false advertising was higher in sales by a dealer than in private sales.

1. For further comment on this Code, see Chapter 12, p.340.

Of all the cases in which the buyer did not recall having seen or heard any advertising at all, there were 23 per cent in which he complained to the seller, or asked for something to be put right or for some repairs to be done, and in 16 per cent he was satisfied with what the seller did in response to the request or complaint, leaving a residue of 7 per cent. In cases in which the buyer responded to an advertisement for a particular item, the corresponding proportions were 29, 17 and 12 per cent. In cases where the buyer recalled having seen or heard other advertising, the corresponding proportions were 28, 17 and 11 per cent.

Of the cases in which the buyer responded to an advertisement for a particular item, and in which he bought the item advertised, the buyer complained to the seller, or asked for something to be put right or for some repairs to be done in 29 per cent. In 16 per cent the buyer was satisfied with what was done in response to the complaint, leaving a residue of 13 per cent. Where the buyer bought a different item from the one advertised, the corresponding proportions were 42, 16 and 24 per cent. Of the cases in which the buyer had seen or heard other types of advertising, and in which the advertising was by a seller, the buyer complained or asked for something to be put right or for some repairs to be done in 32 per cent. The buyer was satisfied with what was done in response to the request or complaint in 18 per cent, leaving a residue of 14 per cent. Where it was manufacturers' advertising, the corresponding proportions were 22, 12 and 10 per cent.

In none of these situations was there necessarily a connection between the request or complaint and the advertising. Nevertheless the data show a higher proportion of requests and complaints, and a lower proportion of satisfaction with the response to complaints, in situations in which the buyer recalled an exposure to sellers' advertising than those in which he recalled an exposure to manufacturers' advertising or to no advertising at all.

The data mentioned so far suggest some preliminary conclusions about legal techniques of control over abuses in advertising. First, any attempts to control false or misleading advertising would be inadequate if they aimed only at advertising on a national or regional scale, at manufacturers' advertising, at advertising through agencies, or at advertising through the media of television and national newspapers. If there is a need for further controls over abuses in advertising, the greatest need seems to relate to sellers' advertising through local channels. Secondly, it would be unwise to expect much further improvement to come through industry self-regulation. While self-regulation within the advertising industry might be valuable and may well be having a desirable effect, it is unlikely to provide extensive coverage of sellers' advertising at the local level. Thirdly, control through any type of censorship would be inappropriate to deal with what is now the greatest area of abuse. Various bodies established by government or industry exist for the censorship of certain categories of advertising, usually national or repeat advertising. But even if it were desirable, censorship would not be practicable to deal with what the data suggest is the major problem area, i.e. sellers' advertising through local channels.

In designing the questions relating to false advertising, it was thought possible only to identify the cases in which the buyer subsequently recognised the advertising to be wrong. Whether the advertising was wilfully untrue or was wrong by mistake would not be known to the buyer. No attempt was made, therefore, to make that distinction in the questions asked. Another consequence of having to rely on the buyer's recognition if the advertising was untrue is that the incidence of false advertising may be underestimated. Many types of false advertising infer rather than state facts, so that any falsity may pass unrecognised. Consider, for example, the case of a vacuum cleaner displayed in a shop window with the notice:

List price	£40
Our price	£36
Save	£4

A customer will only save £4 if, but for buying that vacuum cleaner at this shop for £36, he would have bought essentially the same model elsewhere for £40. This is commonly not so. While some manufacturers' list prices are genuine as an indicator of the prices at which the goods are normally sold at retail, many others state a fictitious price at which the goods are not sold to anyone.[1]

The reported role of advertising in the transaction did not vary markedly or in any significant way according to the length of time that the buyer had lived at the address before making the purchase, or according to the time that had elapsed between the purchase and the interview. There was, however, a variation according to the income of the household. The proportion of cases in which the buyer responded to an advertisement for a particular item rose from 2 per cent in households with an income of under £10 per week, to 12 per cent in households with an income of over £40 per week. Similarly, of the households that did not respond to an advertisement for a particular item, the proportion that recalled having seen or heard advertising for goods of the same type rose from 25 per cent

1. See e.g. *Review of the Trade Descriptions Act 1968*, 1976, Cmnd 6628, para. 210.

in households with an income of under £10 per week, to 34 per cent in households with an income of over £40 per week. Thus the data suggest that exposure to advertising increases with income (or possibly, that recollection of exposure to advertising increases with income).

Regulatory techniques in relation to advertising are discussed further in Chapter 12.

2. Bait and Switch

Joe Bloggs, thinking of buying a secondhand car, was reading the small ads column of a local paper. One car was described in very attractive terms, and at an attractive price. Compared with others, it was a bargain. Joe went to the dealer's premises and explained that he had come to see the car described in the advertisement. The dealer immediately showed Joe a different and more expensive model which he then pushed with a heavy sales pitch. Finally, Joe insisted on seeing the car described in the advertisement. Reluctantly, the dealer showed it to him. It was of the shabbiest appearance, rusty, had no windshield wipers, and one wheel was missing. Joe asked if it could be taken for a test drive, to which the dealer replied, 'No, the engine block is cracked. Anyway you wouldn't want *that* one would you?' The dealer then tried to resume pushing the more expensive model.

This case[1] is a classic example of the technique known as bait and switch. The advertisement serves the purposes of enticing the buyer to the premises, inducing the idea that he is going to buy something while he is there, and portraying the dealer as a dispenser of bargains. The potential customer having thus been placed in a mood to buy, the salesman then has to switch his focus to a different and usually more expensive model.

Apart from its use in the sale of a principal item, the bait and switch technique can be used with regard to the supply of a 'free' accessory. For example, in one case on the survey involving the purchase of a carpet, the buyer explained:

> They stated in the window 'free underfelt with carpet'. But when you get in the shop they tell you the free underfelt wouldn't last long or do a good job, then go on to recommend foam underlay. They don't knock anything off for not having the free one, but you feel you can't put a good carpet over a poor underfelt, so of course you buy the foam underlay.

1. This example was found by responding to advertisements in the small ads column of a local newspaper to discover what was being offered for sale and on what terms.

Another variation of the bait and switch technique is sometimes used for sales at the home. For example, a seller of sewing machines advertises a particular machine in glowing terms and with extra features that make it sound like a bargain at the price. When someone responds, a salesman goes round to the home. He produces the machine, which turns out to be a used one, shabby and dilapidated. The customer expresses disappointment, if not dismay. The salesman oozes grief, apologises for the advertisement and sympathises with the customer's attitude. In his contrition, he magnanimously offers to let the customer have a better model brand new at the same price. By coincidence, he just happens to have one in the car outside. With the salesman seeking forgiveness by offering such a favour, who could say no? The machine is then sold at a price probably a little higher than that for which a similar machine could be bought in the shops. One case of this type was found in the survey.

In the sample, there were 127 cases in which the buyer responded to an advertisement for a particular item. In 12 of these, the buyer bought a different item from the one advertised. As explained above, the buyers in these cases reported worse experiences than those who bought the item advertised, both with regard to selling methods and the condition of the goods.

Of these 12 cases, 3 clearly did not involve a bait and switch. On the statements of the buyer, 2 were clear bait and switch cases. Both involved sewing machines, and other types of deception, in addition to the bait and switch, were reported in both cases. The remaining 7 were possible bait and switch cases, but no conclusion on this could be reached on the information obtained from the buyer. Three of these involved motor vehicles, one central heating, one a sewing machine, one a dryer and one a refrigerator.

The bait and switch technique is open to several objections:

(1) The advertisement is a lie. It implies that the purpose is to supply the item advertised when that is not the advertiser's purpose. Indeed in many cases, the item advertised is not available or in a condition to be supplied.

(2) People responding to the advertisement are often induced to spend time and money attending the premises of the seller when they would probably not have gone there if they had known the truth.

(3) The sales resistance of the customer having been weakened by the expectation of a bargain, he may then be more vulnerable to high-pressure salesmanship and likely to make an imprudent purchase. He may be induced to buy a different item at a price higher than it could be obtained for elsewhere.

(4) The switch is to a transaction that the customer did not plan, one that is immediately consummated and that may involve a significant sum. The customer may therefore make an expenditure that would be an imprudent burden on the family budget. The practice of bait and switch can therefore contribute to privation and insolvency.

(5) The attraction of customers and their money to the deceitful advertiser is a diversion of funds that might have gone to more legitimate business. Like most forms of deceit in retailing, it operates to the detriment of legitimate merchants as well as customers.

(6) Bait and switch may facilitate or nurture less obvious forms of deceit. A dealer who does not see enough virtue in truth to stick to it in his advertising is surely unlikely to stick to it in the oral representations that he makes to customers. Moreover a dealer who makes a habit of deceit does not rely on repeat business for future income. This is the type of dealer who needs the bait and switch technique, or other types of false or gimmick advertising to maintain a flow of new customers to the premises. Thus prohibiting bait and switch may not only eliminate a deceitful form of advertising; it is also likely to have a downward influence on fraud in the sales pitch and on other predatory practices in selling.

In several of the United States, the practice of bait and switch has been made an offence,[1] but not in England. With regard to sales at home, bait and switch is prohibited by the *British Code of Advertising Practice.*[2] But the prohibition does not extend to sales at retail premises.[3] Moreover, the enforcement machinery of the Code (non-acceptance of advertisements by the media) is aimed primarily at national and repeat advertising whereas the practice of bait and switch is well suited to advertising through local channels.

1. E.g., in the *California Statutes, 1970 Regular Session,* Ch. 1550; S.1970 created the offence of 'Advertising goods or services with intent not to sell them as advertised'. A similar provision appeared in the *New York Statutes,* Art. 26, S.396.

2. 'Direct sale advertisements are not acceptable without adequate assurances from the advertiser and his advertising agency. . .that sales representatives when calling upon persons responding to the advertisement will demonstrate and make available for sale the products advertised. . . . . It will be taken as prima facie evidence of misleading and unacceptable bait advertising for the purpose of switch selling if an advertiser's salesmen seriously disparage or belittle the cheaper article advertised or indicate unreasonable delays in obtaining delivery or otherwise put difficulties in the way of its purchase.' *British Code of Advertising Practice,* 4th ed., 1974, Part IV, Article 1.

3. It is unclear why sales at retail premises should be excepted from the prohibition.

It is suggested that it should be an offence to advertise any item for the purpose of supplying to anyone responding to the advertisement a different item instead of the one advertised. The offence could be made part of the *Trade Descriptions Act* so that its enforcement would be in the hands of local trading standards officers.[1]

Bait and switch must be distinguished from loss leadering. The latter term is sometimes used where a merchant advertises something for sale at a low price, possibly an unprofitable price, for the purpose of attracting to the shop customers who may buy other items in addition to the one advertised. It is commonly alleged to be done in the grocery trade. The practice can be criticised as unfair competition if the dealer's selling price is below his buying price, but otherwise it is difficult to see anything wrong.

Bait and switch and loss leadering both involve the advertising of one item for the purpose of selling another. The difference is that with bait and switch there is no intention to sell the item advertised. With loss leadering the merchant intends those responding to the advertisement to buy the item advertised, but hopes that while they are in the shop they will buy other things as well.

There is another practice that falls somewhere between bait and switch and loss leadering. This is where a merchant advertises certain items for sale at a low price, but the extent of the advertising is so out of proportion to the number of items that he is willing to sell at that price that there will be a predictable excess of demand. The advertising campaign is planned so that only a small proportion of those responding to the advertisement will be able to buy one of the advertised items. The majority will be told that it is sold out, the hope being that they may then be persuaded to buy a more expensive model or a different item. The practice is open to the same objections as bait and switch.

In the *British Code of Advertising Practice*, this technique is prohibited when used with regard to sales made at the home, but not with regard to sales made at retail premises.[2] A common reason given for not making the practice an offence is that it is difficult to identify when it occurs. But it could surely be identified in at least the more extreme situations. A good start could be made by comparing the expenditure incurred on the advertising with the gross receipts expected on the stock of advertised

1. See Chapter 12.

2. Here again, it is difficult to see any reason for the distinction. The Code provides, in Part IV, Article 1: 'Direct sale advertisements are not acceptable without adequate assurances from the advertiser and his advertising agency that the products advertised will be supplied at the price stated in the advertisement within a reasonable time from stocks sufficient to meet the potential demand. . .'

items available for sale.

3. Misrepresentations

(a) Misrepresentations about the Goods

On the survey, the buyers were asked, 'When you were buying the [item] what did the salesman/seller/agent etc. tell you about it?' After listening to the response and probing for further answers, the interviewer continued, 'Did any of this turn out to be wrong or untrue?' Misrepresentations by the salesman were measured by the responses to this question. Where the statement of a salesman turned out to be wrong or untrue, the buyer would not generally know whether it was a lie or a mistake. No attempt was made, therefore, to make that distinction in the questions.

There was a total of 100 cases in which the buyer reported some misrepresentation by the salesman, this being approximately 8 per cent of the sample as a whole. The nature of the reported misrepresentations was as follows:

Item did not perform as well as salesman said it would	38
Item was not the quality that salesman said	34
Item did not wear as well as salesman said	14
Operating cost was more than salesman said	13
Delivery, installation or other service was promised but not carried out or not as promised	9
Parts or accessories were missing that salesman said would come with the item	6
Subsequent service or maintenance were not as promised	4
Parts or accessories were not new that were supposed to be new	4
Item was not new although sold as new	3
Parts or accessories were necessary that salesman said were not needed	2
Other misrepresentations	8
Unascertained	3
Total (100 cases: list includes multiple responses)	138

In some of these cases, the use of the word 'misrepresentation' might be inappropriate. Suppose, for example, the salesman assured the buyer that the car would do 40 miles per gallon, but it only does 30 miles per gallon. If other models of that car usually do less than 40 miles per gallon the salesman has made a misrepresentation. But if a case occurred in which other cars of that model do 40 miles per gallon and only this particular car does not, the salesman has said nothing deliberately untrue, and the situation could better be described as an unfulfilled prediction or promise.

In 2 per cent of the total cases in the sample, the buyer never spoke to a salesman, and in 29 per cent the salesman said nothing about the item. In 60 per cent, the salesman said something about the item but nothing which the buyer reported to be untrue.

In cases involving vacuum cleaners, heating equipment, sewing machines, typewriters, new motor vehicles, furniture, washing machines and dryers, the proportion reported to involve some misrepresentation by a salesman about the item was the same as in the sample as a whole (7-9 per cent). Cookers were slightly below average with 6 per cent, radio/TV/ record players, and rugs or carpets were below average with 4 per cent. Secondhand motor vehicles were double the average with 16 per cent, (17 per cent for secondhand motor vehicles sold by dealers and 15 per cent for the private sales). There were no misrepresentations at all about the item reported in the cases involving encyclopedias (8), cooking utensils (9), knitting machines (4), dishwashers (4), or refrigerators or freezers (53).

The proportion of cases reported to involve some misrepresentation about the item was a little higher in the conurbations and large urban areas than in the small towns and rural areas.

Comparing the cash transactions with the total of those using any type of credit arrangement, there was no difference. In both categories, misrepresentations about the item were reported in about 8 per cent of transactions. An interesting contrast appeared, however, with regard to the different types of credit. In the transaction credit cases (where any finance company that advanced the credit would be responsible for any misrepresentations of the seller) the proportion reported to involve some misrepresentation about the item was 7.6 per cent). But in the check trader cases and the loan cases (in which the financing company was not generally responsible for any misrepresentations of the seller) misrepresentations about the item were reported in 13.6 per cent and 13.8 per cent respectively.

Reports of misrepresentations by salesmen about the item were higher than reports of false advertising. Thus false advertising was reported in 3.5 per cent of cases in the whole sample, and 10.9 per cent of the cases in which any advertising was seen or heard. Misrepresentations by the salesman were reported in 8.1 per cent of the cases in the whole sample, 8.4 per cent of the cases in which the buyer spoke to a salesman, and 12.0 per cent of the cases in which the salesman said anything at all about the item.

These figures might indicate a higher rate of misrepresentations by salesmen than in the advertising. This would not be surprising. A great deal of advertising says nothing significant that can be either true or false, and appears to have no purpose except to promote recognition of the name of a product, a brand, or a seller. Another possible explanation is that buyers may be more conscious of any misrepresentation in a sales pitch than in advertising. Advertising is often in broad and vague terms so that any misrepresentation may not be apparent without the addition of inference or innuendo. A salesman may be more precise, and hence more obviously wrong. Moreover, a salesman may respond to questioning by the customer with precise and well remembered statements, and if they are wrong the falsity may be or become more apparent.

Of the cases in which the buyer did not recall having seen or heard any advertising at all for goods of the type purchased, misrepresentations by the salesman were reported in 6.6 per cent. This compares with 11.4 per cent of the cases in which any advertising was seen or heard. Of the cases in which the buyer responded to an advertisement for a particular item, misrepresentations by the salesman were reported in 15.0 per cent, and of the cases in which the buyer recalled having seen or heard other types of advertising, it was 9.6 per cent.

It may well be that the advertising of a particular item is associated with misrepresentations by salesmen more often than other advertising. But it is not easy to explain why the proportion of cases involving misrepresentations by the salesman should be higher for other types of advertising than where the buyer did not recall having seen or heard any advertising at all. It is unlikely that the explanation lies in any planned connection between advertising and misrepresentations, because misrepresentations were reported in a larger proportion of cases where the buyer bought a different model or type from the one portrayed in the advertising, or bought from a different seller. Moreover, a similar contrast appeared with regard to people who gathered information in other ways. Thus misrepresentations by the salesman were reported in a larger proportion of cases where the buyer had shopped around than in those where he had not, and in a larger proportion of cases where the buyer had checked in *Which?* than in those where he had not. There would seem to be at least three possible explanations:

(1) Exposure to advertising, or to other sources of information, may make people better informed and therefore better able to recognise any misrepresentations by a salesman.

(2) People who remember their exposure to advertising or other sources of information may in other ways be more attentive people, and therefore better able to recognise any misrepresentations by a salesman.

(3) People who have read advertising or who have otherwise sought information prior to buying may ask a salesman more questions, thereby

obtaining more answers and increasing the probability of the salesman saying something wrong.

There was a significant correlation between reported misrepresentation by the salesman, complaints to the seller and lack of response to complaints. Thus of the cases in which the buyer never spoke to a salesman, the buyer complained, or asked for something to be put right or repaired in 15 per cent, and was satisfied with what the seller did in response to the request or complaint in 7 per cent. Of the cases in which the salesman said nothing about the item, the buyer complained to the seller, or asked for something to be put right or repaired in 17 per cent and was satisfied with what the seller did in 12 per cent. Of the cases in which the salesman said something about the item, but nothing known to be wrong or untrue, the buyer complained to the seller, or asked for something to be repaired or put right in 24 per cent and was satisfied with what the seller did in response in 16 per cent. But of the cases in which the buyer reported some misrepresentation by the salesman about the item, the buyer complained (although not necessarily about the misrepresentation) or asked for something to be put right or repaired in 68 per cent, and was satisfied with what the seller did in response in 25 per cent.

Reports of misrepresentations by salesmen showed a peak for buyers in social grade C1. For grade A, the proportion reported to involve some misrepresentation by the salesman about the item was 3 per cent. For grade B it was 8 per cent, for grade C1 it was 10 per cent, for grade C2 it was 9 per cent, for grade D it was 7 per cent, for grade E 4 per cent, and for housewives 5 per cent.

On the income scale, the proportion of cases reported to involve some misrepresentation by the salesmen about the item peaked for households having an income of £31-40 per week. Thus for households with an income up to £10 per week, the proportion reported to involve some misrepresentation by the salesman about the item was 5 per cent. For households in the range £11-20 per week it was 6 per cent, in the range £21-39 per week it was 7 per cent, in the range £31-40 per week it was 15 per cent, and in the range of over £40 per week, it was 9 per cent.

The data mentioned above dealing with misrepresentations refer only to statements that the buyer recognised, either at the time or subsequently, as being wrong or untrue. But the marketing techniques for consumer durables sometimes include lies not generally recognised as such by buyers. One example is a practice used in the sale of furniture, sewing machines, and sometimes white goods. When the interest of the customer has focused on a particular model, the salesman adds assurance by stating that this is the model that he has at home.

Techniques of control over misrepresentations by salesmen are discussed in Chapter 12.

(b) Misrepresentations about the Price

In addition to being asked whether anything they were told about the item turned out to be wrong or untrue, buyers were asked 'Were you misled or misinformed in any way about how much you would have to pay for the [item]?' The buyers answered 'Yes' to this question in 28 cases (2.3 per cent of the sample). The ways in which these buyers were reported to be misled were as follows:

Charged for accessories that they had been told were included in the price, or charged more for accessories than they had been quoted	2
Charged for installation or delivery that they had been informed was included in the price, or charged more for installation or delivery than they had been quoted	4
Misinformed in some way about the instalments	4
Signed the contract in blank and seller inserted the wrong figures	2
Charged more than they were informed the item would cost	6
Not told about interest or other features of the financing	5
Charged for maintenance or other extras without having agreed to these	2
Miscellaneous	3
Total	28

The buyers were also asked 'At the time of the purchase, or before that, were you given to understand that the price you were paying for the [item] was less than the usual price?' Leaving aside 10 cases in which the information did not come from the seller, there were 306 cases in which the buyer replied 'Yes' to that question (25 per cent of the cases in the sample). No doubt in many of these cases, the price really was less than usual; but it would seem unlikely that this could be true of at least 25 per cent of the sales of consumer durables. The practice appeared to be prevalent in the sales of vacuum cleaners, encyclopedias, electric fires, food mixers, washing machines and dryers. In the sales of motor vehicles, reports of the practice were less than the average for the sample as a whole.

Since the survey was taken, misrepresentations about the price at which goods are ordinarily sold, or other misleading price comparisons, appear to have become even more widespread, in spite of the operation of the *Trade Descriptions Act*, 1968.

> Since the Act became law, the number and variety of price comparisons have proliferated, and the ordinary shopper now faces an almost constant bombardment of claims, not only about reductions from recommended prices, but also about the alleged previous selling price of the goods, about their alleged value or about other matters which suggest that the goods are worth more than the price being charged.[1]

One of the main provisions of the *Trade Descriptions Act* dealing with misleading price comparisons is as follows:

> S.11 (1) If any person offering to supply goods of any description gives, by whatever means, any false indication to the effect that the price at which the goods are offered is equal to or less than –
> (a) . . .or
> (b) the price at which the goods or goods of the same description were previously offered by him;
> or is less than such a price by a specified amount, he shall, subject to the provisions of this Act, be guilty of an offence.
> (2) . . .
> (3) For the purposes of this section –
> (a) An indication that goods were previously offered at a higher price or at a particular price –
> (i) shall be treated as an indication that they were so offered by the person giving the indication, unless it is expressly stated that they were so offered by others and it is not expressed or implied that they were, or might have been, so offered also by that person; and
> (ii) shall be treated, unless the contrary is expressed, as an indication that they were so offered within the preceding six months for a continuous period of not less than twenty-eight days;
> (b) . . .

But as a practical matter, that is obviously unenforceable. Given limited resources and the range of other statutes that they are expected to enforce, no one could reasonably expect Trading Standards Departments, on any

1. *Review of the Trade Descriptions Act 1968*, 1976, Cmnd 6628, para.199. The same impression was gathered by observations of the writer of shop window displays in mid-1977. See also *Bargain Offer Claims*, A Consultative Document, 1975, Office of Fair Trading.

broad scale, to maintain a continuing surveillance of the price at which a particular item is being offered at a particular outlet for six months *prior to* the date when an offence might be committed.

It has been suggested[1] that the Act be amended to put the burden of proof on the trader to show that the goods were offered by the trader at the higher price for a period of not less than 28 days in the preceding six months. Such an amendment would mitigate the difficulties of proof that face the prosecution at trial. But it would do little to ease the dilemma of a Trading Standards Officer in deciding which, among the array of advertised price reductions, should be selected for investigation or prosecution. If such an amendment should be followed by more prosecutions, there is an obvious risk that they would be prosecutions resulting from complaints rather than from systematic surveillance. The achievement of such an amendment may, therefore, be no more than a shift from non-enforcement to a process of enforcement that is intermittent, uneven and discriminatory.

Moreover, this suggested amendment, even together with other proposed amendments,[2] would still leave too many loopholes for any trader who wants to engage in misleading price comparisons, or who feels under competitive pressure to do so. Suppose, for example, a ladies' clothing shop wants to sell a particular dress at £32, having allowed for its usual mark-up. The dress could be placed in a remote corner with a price tag of say £40, but without any real expectation of its sale at that price. After 28 days, it could be placed in the window at £32 and marked as a genuine price reduction.

With regard to misleading price comparisons, there are probably four basic approaches that a government might take:

(1) *Impose no legal restraints, but maintain a public information programme.* Hope that the public will come to recognise that much of comparative pricing is useless and uninformative, and that the practice will then become counter-productive. It is difficult, however, to have any confidence in that approach. It is, in substance, the approach that the government has taken over the last ten years. Yet it has brought about no termination or even any apparent decline in price comparisons. Even if the publicity should result in fewer people being misled by the price comparisons, they are still likely to be confused. It is arguable too that this approach is a breach of faith with honest traders. Those who would prefer simply to quote the

1. In the *Review of the Trade Descriptions Act 1968*, 1976, Cmnd 6628, para.242.
2. Ibid.

price of their goods without misleading comparisons may find themselves under competitive pressure to participate in the gimmicks.

(2) *Adopt a selective programme of prohibitions aimed at the curtailment of misleading price comparisons while at the same time allowing the use of price comparisons that are truthful.* This is the policy that the Office of Fair Trading now seems to prefer.[1] The proposal mentioned above to reverse the onus of proof would be one step in such a programme. Another idea might be to require that any comparison of the price at which goods are being offered with any other price must be specific, stating when and where, and how or by whom the goods are or were being offered at the other price. Vague comparisons, such as '6p off' or 'Worth £95, our price £90' would be prohibited. But it is at least doubtful whether this approach can ever be effective. The variables of time, space, identity of the seller and identity of the goods that are involved in the price comparisons can make the detection and prosecution of offences of this type a high-cost matter. Some objectionable practices, such as '6p off' can be proscribed very simply. But it is at least doubtful whether a code could be drawn up sufficiently comprehensive and sufficiently enforceable that it would prohibit the objectionable practices while at the same time allowing the use of truthful price comparisons.

(3) *Adopt a general prohibition of misleading price comparisons, either instead of or in addition to these specific prohibitions.* For example, the *Combines Investigation Act* of Canada provides

> S. 36 (1) No person shall, for the purpose of promoting, directly or indirectly, the supply or use of a product or for the purpose of promoting, directly or indirectly, any business interest, by any means whatever, . . .
>
> (d) make a materially misleading representation to the public concerning the price at which a product or like products have been, are or will be ordinarily sold; and for the purposes of this paragraph a representation as to price is deemed to refer to the price at which the product has been sold by sellers generally in the relevant market unless it is clearly specified to be the price at which the product has been sold by the person by whom or on whose behalf the representation is made.

1. *Review of the Trade Descriptions Act 1968*, 1976, Cmnd 6628, Ch. VIII.

Prosecutions under that Section are few[1] and there is no systematic surveillance at the local level. Hence enforcement is intermittent and uneven. The section has not brought an end to misleading price comparisons in Canada, but it may well have had a dampening and beneficial influence.[2]

(4) *Prohibit all price comparisons.* The only price that a trader would be permitted to display in connection with the offer for sale of any item would be the price at which that item is being offered for sale. The display or quotation of any other price in connection with the offer of that item for sale would be prohibited. This might be augmented by requiring that when any item is being displayed for sale, the price at which the item is being offered should also be displayed.[3] The advantages of this approach are that the prohibition would be simple to understand and easy to enforce. Misleading price comparisons made orally by salesmen could still be difficult to detect. But at least the prohibition should be effective in preventing misleading price comparisons from being used as a way of attracting customers to the premises. The disadvantage of this approach is that a trader would not be able to use price comparisons as a way of drawing the attention of potential customers to any genuine price reductions. Truthful as well as untruthful indications of comparative prices would be prohibited. Customers would have to make their own price comparisons. It is at least arguable, however, that they could do this more easily if the prices displayed by each trader indicated nothing except the prices at which he is offering his goods for sale.

In the Office of Fair Trading, the fourth approach appears to have been ruled out so far, but not because of any judgment on its relative value compared with other approaches: '. . .clearly some further control is needed, provided that this can be done without preventing a trader making a truthful claim or the buyer obtaining a genuine bargain or paying a lower price.'[4] But why make such a proviso an absolute condition for regulatory action? That approach elevates the display of truthful price comparisons by traders to the status of a priceless benefit that has to be preserved

1. For example, there were only 17 cases tried under that Section in the year ended 31 March 1976. *Annual Report of the Director of Investigation and Research for the year ended 31 March 1976*, p.40.

2. Misleading price comparisons are still noticeable in Canada, particularly in the catalogues of discount operations.

3. With regard to some items, this is already required by orders made under Section 4 of the *Prices Act, 1974*. See e.g. *The Price Marking (Cheese) Order 1977.*

4. *Review of the Trade Descriptions Act 1968*, 1976, Cmnd 6628, para.201.

regardless of the cost.

The second and third approaches mentioned above, even if both are adopted, are not likely to be more than a limited success. The critical question then surely is: would the total harm done by the misleading price comparisons that would remain after adoption of the second and third approaches be greater or less than the total benefit derived from truthful price comparisons? It may well be that the question could not be answered except by a subjective appraisal of the inferences to be drawn from inadequate data. But that is normal in the political process, and the question posed is surely the relevant one that ought to be asked and answered.

4. Referral Selling

This term refers to the practice by which the seller of an item, in order to induce a sale, promises the buyer a commission in return for his help in making future sales. Usually the help required is the names and addresses of possible customers. The buyer is promised a commission on sales to the people whose names he supplies, or sometimes a commission is promised upon the buyer permitting the item to be demonstrated in his home to other potential customers.

The objections to the practice are as follows:

(1) As part of the sales pitch, the salesman sometimes makes unrealistic and fraudulent representations about the amount of commission likely to be earned.

(2) The practice occurs in the sale of expensive items on credit terms. Thus the customer is sometimes committed to the purchase of an item that he would not have purchased but for the representations of the salesman that he would not have to pay the full contract price. Sometimes the probability of earning the commissions is so emphasised in the sales pitch as to divert attention from the price that the customer is undertaking to pay. If the buyer defaults and is sued for payment, the complaint is that 'I understood from the salesman that if I supplied the names and addresses, I wouldn't have to pay anything.'

(3) Another complaint is that salesmen misrepresent the terms on which the commission is payable. For example, the contract provides that 'A commission of £10 will be paid on each sale made to a customer introduced to us by you.' But the salesman says that the commission is payable 'each time you allow us to bring a potential customer here and use your home as a showplace'.

(4) Sometimes the salesman has no intention of even following up the leads. If the price of the item is more than that for which it can be

bought elsewhere, the salesman may anticipate that the friends of the buyer will recognise this before he calls. For that reason he may not call at all. In other words, the purpose of the referral plan may simply be to make that particular sale rather than to obtain further customers. In these situations the presentation of the plan is a lie.

(5) The practice can create personal embarrassments particularly if the buyer, having given the salesman a list of the names and addresses of his friends, recognises thereafter that the purchase was imprudent.

(6) Complaints are common that the commissions, even when earned, are not received. In one case in the sample, the purchaser of a television mentioned that the salesman had been referred to him by a friend who had been promised £5 commission, but this commission had never been received.

The questionnaire was designed to seek some impression of the extent of these abuses and the extent of referral selling.

Questions about referral selling were asked in 362 cases in the sample, all cases involving transaction credit or loans. Referral selling was reported in 13 of these (3.6 per cent). In none of these 13 cases did the buyers say that they were relying on the commission in order to pay the instalments. In none did they actually earn any commission. None clearly involved any of the abuses mentioned above as being associated with referral selling. However in these 13 cases, the buyers reported worse experiences than in the sample as a whole both with regard to selling methods and the conditions of the goods.

In sales at the home, the buyers were asked, 'Did [the salesman] say that your name had been suggested to him by someone you knew?' Eight out of 88 replied 'Yes' to that question. The buyers in these 8 cases reported worse experiences than in the other sales at the home with regard to selling methods, but not significantly different experiences with regard to the condition of the goods.

Although the numbers involved are small, it would appear from the survey data that the abuses mentioned above as being the objections to referral selling are certainly not universal and probably occur only in a small minority of transactions in which the practice is used. In other words, the bulk of referral selling probably does not involve these abuses. On the other hand, cases involving referral selling seem to be less satisfactory with regard to other aspects of the selling methods.

In some jurisdictions, referral selling has been prohibited. For example, the *Consumer Protection Act* of Ontario provides:

> S.46a(1) . . .
> (2) No seller shall hold out to a buyer or prospective buyer any

advantage, benefit or gain to the buyer or prospective buyer for doing anything that purports to assist the seller in finding or selling to another prospective buyer.

(3) Notwithstanding the provision for or imposition of a penalty under this Act, any contract entered into following the holding out referred to in subsection 2 is not binding on the buyer.[1]

This section applies to any executory contract of sale or hire-purchase (this category coincides approximately with the transaction credit cases on the sample). A violation of the section is punishable by a fine of up to $2,000, or imprisonment of up to 1 year, or both.[2]

The prohibition of referral selling can be supported by the following four arguments.

(1) To prohibit only the objectionable features of the practice would be impracticable. It could not be done effectively without an unacceptably vast system of surveillance and detection. It should be easy to prove that a salesman has made the promise of a commission in order to induce a sale. But it could be much more difficult to prove, for example, that he misrepresented the amount of commission that buyers usually receive, or that he intended never to pay the commission.

(2) The evils of referral selling can be difficult to identify when they occur and their frequency may therefore be underestimated. For example, a buyer may respond 'No' to the question 'Did you rely on these commissions to meet the instalments?' Yet the promise and expectation of the commission may have been among the factors that softened him to make a purchase that he might not otherwise have made.

(3) The evils of the practice have to be balanced against the harm that would flow from the prohibition. Even if the evidence is that the serious evils only occur in a small minority of cases involving referral selling, there is no counterbalancing volume of cases in which the public derive any benefit from the practice. If the truth is that the practice is harmless in most cases, but is harmful more often than it is beneficial, there would seem more to be gained than lost by the prohibition.

(4) If the practice has any legitimate commercial utility, this must lie in bringing together salesmen with potential customers. That purpose can be accomplished without offering the first buyer a commission on

1. *Consumer Protection Amendment Act, 1972*, Ontario.
2. *Consumer Protection Act*, RSO, 1970, Ch. 82, S.48.

future sales as one of the inducements to buy. It can be accomplished just as well by sending customers an offer of the commission on some occasion after the goods have been bought. This would curtail most of the abuses but still permit commissions to be paid. Moreover, if the commission is offered on a subsequent occasion, after the buyer has had some experience with the goods, people are less likely to send in the names of their friends if they are not satisfied customers. The commissions are then more likely to promote the trade of sellers whose customers are satisfied than of those who leave a trail of dissatisfaction.

5. Documentation

Many grievances on the survey referred to the failure or refusal of the seller to document the transaction honestly and efficiently.

Of the 404 transaction credit cases, there were 36 in which the buyer reported that there never was any agreement in writing. In 20 of these the absence of a written agreement would be a failure to comply with Section 5 of the *Hire-Purchase Act 1965*, and in 10 it would also be an offence under *The Hire-Purchase and Credit Sale Agreements (Control) Order 1964.*

In a further 70 cases, the buyer reported not having received a copy of the agreement or contract document at the time of signing. In 58 of these cases, that would be a failure to comply with the *Hire-Purchase Act.* However, this figure may be high. Probably in some cases the buyer received a copy but forgot having done so.[1]

Buyers who received a copy of the agreement at the time of signing reported better experiences than those who did not, both with regard to selling methods and the condition of the goods.

Violations also appeared to be widespread of the requirement that the contract shall state 'the cash price of the goods'.[2] This meant 'the price at which the goods may be purchased by the hirer or buyer for cash'.[3] But the cash price stated in the contract sometimes appeared to be fictitious. One reason for a fictitious cash price was to evade the Control Orders. For example, suppose a deposit of 25 per cent was required by the Control Orders in respect of an item that normally sold for £60 cash. If a customer did not have the money for the deposit and the seller was

1. In an American study relating to conditional sales contracts, it was reported that 55 per cent of the buyers in the sample who responded to the question replied that they did not receive a copy of the contract at the time of sale, and 19 per cent replied that they never received one at all. *Debtors in Default*, D. Caplovitz, 1970, Bureau of Applied Social Research, Columbia University, pp.3-48.

2. *Hire-Purchase Act 1965*, S.7.

3. Ibid, S.6(2).

anxious for the business, he might document a hire-purchase transaction for a cash price of £80 (plus finance charges) with a deposit of £20, receipt of which was acknowledged but which was never actually received.

Another reason for using a fictitious cash price, and probably a more frequent one, was to conceal the cost of credit. To quote the hire-purchase price as the 'cash price' and to offer the goods on instalment credit terms with 'no finance charges' is not uncommon. If a cash customer then appears, he might be offered a 'cash discount'. Discounts may sound more acceptable than additional charges, and for this reason a retailer may find that if he quotes an inflated price that includes the cost of credit, and offers a discount for cash, his turnover is higher than if he quotes a legitimate cash price and adds finance charges for credit.

The frequency of fictitious cash prices and cash discounts cannot be measured with precision. But some indicators emerged in the survey results.

(1) In each transaction credit case, the buyer was asked 'How much was the cash price?' (where possible this was checked by the interviewer looking at the contract). Later the buyer was asked 'How much would the cash price have been if you had paid cash?' In 12 cases the answer to the second question was a lesser amount than the answer to the first question.

(2) In 298 of the transaction credit cases, the figures were available by which to calculate the interest. In 63 (21 per cent), the interest (hire-purchase charge) was reported as nil. It is highly probable that in these cases, the interest cost of the transaction was absorbed in an inflated 'cash price'.

(3) In the cash transactions, there were no questions specifically on the point. But even so, in 21 (out of 704) cases the buyers mentioned that they had received a discount for paying cash rather than buying on credit terms.[1] In most of these cases, it appeared that the cash discount was volunteered by the seller, but in some the buyer only received it after asking for it or bargaining.

The objection to the practice is, of course, that it hinders buyers from recognising the true cost of credit. This will be referred to later in the discussion of interest rate disclosure.[2]

Of the transaction credit cases to which Part II of the *Hire-Purchase*

1. Care must be taken to distinguish between a discount that is offered for cash rather than credit and a discount that is offered for paying the whole price rather than having a trade-in.

2. See Chapter 8.

Act applied (the part dealing with the provision of written agreements and copies to the buyer) the data indicated non-compliance in 31 per cent. Even this does not take into account violations of the requirements relating to the content of agreements. For example, in hire-purchase contracts seen by the writer, the goods were listed in terms such as 'one table' and 'four chairs'. Terms as general as that violate the requirement of the Act that the agreement must contain a list of the goods 'sufficient to identify them'.

It is clear from the survey data and other enquiries that non-compliance with the documentation requirements of the *Hire-Purchase Act* was widespread. However, this should not be surprising because there was no real sanction against non-compliance. Nor was there or is there any public official whose job it is to look for violations. The legal effect of non-compliance is only that the contract *might* not be enforceable in the courts by the seller or finance company. For several reasons, however this is unlikely to be a significant deterrent in many situations:

(1) In the vast majority of transactions, the buyer will complete the payments in any event.
(2) If a buyer does default, most sellers will normally use extra-legal methods of collection.[1] It is only in exceptional cases that they resort to the courts.
(3) Buyers are generally unaware of their rights. Only in an exceptional case will a buyer receive legal advice or other help necessary to recognise that a claim by the seller might be defended on the ground that the documentation requirements of the *Consumer Credit Act* (formerly contained in the *Hire-Purchase Act*) were not complied with. Even when a buyer recognises the availability of the defence, he may still feel threatened by the risks of litigation and an adverse credit report, and may therefore still pay.
(4) If the seller (or finance company) does sue and the claim is defended, the court is empowered to overlook non-compliance with the documentary requirements of the Act,[2] and to allow the claim. It would usually be difficult for a buyer to show that he was prejudiced by the non-compliance, and since a rejection of the seller's claim would amount to a loss of the goods without having received the price, sellers may be right in assuming that the courts would generally not allow what they perceive as a technical defence to defeat what they might perceive as a legitimate claim.

1. See Chapter 10, p.292.
2. *Consumer Credit Act*, 1974, SS.65 and 127. The corresponding earlier provision was the *Hire-Purchase Act*, 1965, S.10.

The *Consumer Credit Act*, 1974, has revised the substantive law relating to documentary requirements. But it has done nothing significant to improve the enforcement. Sections 61-64 prescribe the documentary requirements for a 'properly executed' agreement. Then Section 65 provides that:

> (1) An improperly-executed regulated agreement is enforceable against the debtor or hirer on an order of the court only.[1]
> (2) A retaking of goods or land to which a regulated agreement relates is an enforcement of the agreement.

At first glance, this may seem to place an obligation upon a creditor to seek a court order before proceeding with any enforcement. But it is obviously not going to work out that way. To begin with, unless someone else takes an initiative, there is nothing to require a creditor to make the distinction between properly and improperly executed agreements. If a seller wants to enforce an agreement by obtaining repossession, there is nothing to curtail the usual practice of seeking a voluntary surrender. If a creditor proceeds on a debt claim for the balance outstanding, he will obtain a default judgement in the ordinary course of things unless a defence is filed. Even if a buyer is advised on the terms of the Act, and the documentary defect is recognised, the buyer may still not want to risk the raising of a defence under a statute that makes the matter one for the discretion of the court, and therefore one in which the outcome is uncertain.

As a practical matter, compliance with the documentary requirements of the Act is almost voluntary. As with other attempts to regulate without sanctions, the result is to put legitimate traders who want to comply with the law at a competitive disadvantage, and to encourage those who are less careful or less scrupulous. Moreover, it is with regard to the less scrupulous retailers that the documentary requirements are most needed. If we seriously believe that such requirements are necessary for consumer protection, failure to comply should be an offence, and there should be someone in each locality whose job it is to look for violations and to prosecute when he finds them.

6. Add-on Contracts (Substituted Agreements)

Suppose a buyer who is currently purchasing something on HP wishes to purchase further items from the same seller. He can do so either by a totally new contract or by a 'Substituted Agreement' which varies the

1. The discretion and powers of the court are prescribed in S.127.

original HP contract to add on the new items and new terms.

During the period of the survey, one reason for using add-on contracts ('Substituted Agreements') was to permit additional items to be bought without the need for a deposit. Payments already made under the first contract could be treated as the deposit on the new items.

Another reason for using add-on contracts is to enhance the security of the seller. If the second transaction is dealt with by a totally new HP contract, the buyer obtains a clear title to the first items purchased as soon as he has paid the monies due under the first contract. But when an add-on contract is used, the buyer does not obtain a title to the goods covered by the first contract until he has paid the consolidated total of monies due under the second agreement.

The questionnaire did not include any questions to discover the frequency with which add-on contracts were used, but they were mentioned several times in the other comments of the buyers.

The way it worked for one buyer on the survey was explained as follows:

> We already had furniture on HP. We received a circular letter saying we could choose further goods without any increase in payments and without a deposit. When we went to the shop to make an instalment payment we saw our name on a board. We queried this and the assistant said that if we spoke to the manger we would hear something to our advantage. We spoke to him and then he told us about buying further goods without a deposit.

The manager of a major London department store explained in an interview that the practice of his store is to write to every customer six times during the currency of a hire-purchase contract seeking to persuade the customer to add on further items.[1]

The objections to the use of add-on contracts are:

(1) The security is too strong. If a buyer fails to pay the instalments, the seller can seize not only the most recently purchased item, but all other items purchased under the same chain of contracts even if enough has been paid to cover the price of the earlier items. Creditors' remedies that are this strong promote the over-extension of credit. This problem is, however, mitigated by the provisions of the *Consumer Credit Act*

1. Some letters of this type might, if they promise further credit upon production of the letter, now be an offence under S.51 of the *Consumer Credit Act*, 1974 (supplying a credit token without having been asked for it).

which restrict the seller's right of repossession where one third of the total price of the goods has been paid.

(2) The use of add-on contracts can induce customers to purchase further items on credit without making an intelligent choice about whether it would be preferable to use cash, or some other source of credit.

(3) The buyer may be induced to continue dealing with the same seller rather than considering other and possibly more advantageous sources of supply.

(4) Add-on contracts often involve accounting 'mistakes' that operate to the detriment of the customer. In the cases on the survey in which add-on contracts were mentioned, it was in the context of complaints about the accounting. An initial difficulty lies in settling a standard form of add-on contract that will permit all the relevant amounts to be shown in a manner that makes their significance clear. Some standard forms in use could not be followed by the writer without great difficulty, including one that was recommended by a reputable trade association. The essence of the buyers' complaints was that, somehow or other, they ended up paying more by the use of an add-on contract than they would if they had purchased the second item on a separate agreement. Some of the complaints related to the retention of the old payment card by the seller, and included an allegation by the buyer that more had been paid than the new payment card recorded. In one case the buyer paid a deposit at the time of signing the add-on contract, and although the amount of the deposit was shown in the agreement, the buyer was not given credit for it in the arithmetic.[1]

(5) Add-on contracts may encourage the marketing of shoddy goods. Suppose, for example, a customer is buying a dining-room suite on HP terms. He is happy with the furniture and is keeping up the instalments. The dealer then sells him a bedroom suite using an add-on contract. The bedroom suite turns out to be shoddy and defective, and the customer refuses to pay for it. The dealer may now seek to collect by repossessing the dining-room suite.

It is difficult to see any commercial need for add-on contracts, and it is suggested therefore that prohibiting their use would be the best way of meeting the objections. Similarly it should be prohibited for a seller (or lender where the loan is arranged by the seller) to take security on any-

1. Subsequently I examined this contract myself and found that this was so. The result was that the buyer paid £2.15*s*. (£2.75p) more by using the add-on contract than would have been paid if the second item had been purchased by the use of a separate contract form.

thing other than the item being sold.[1]

7. Ballooning

This term refers to the practice of writing an instalment credit contract so that the last instalment is much greater than the others (at least double the others). The practice occurs in the United States in the sale of major durables and was well known in nineteenth-century England in money-lending transactions.[2] Questions were included in the survey to discover whether it is a practice in England in the marketing of major durables.

The purpose of ballooning may be to create a financial predicament for the buyer at the end of the contract term out of which he can be 'helped' by the seller. The seller anticipates that the buyer will be able to meet the ordinary instalments as they fall due, but that he will have difficulty in meeting the exceptionally large instalment at the end of the contract period. The expectation is that the buyer will then welcome a proposal from the seller to overcome the problem by entering into a new transaction. This may involve the purchase of something else.

Four cases of ballooning occurred in the survey. Two of them, one involving a television and one a carpet, occurred in situations in which there appeared to be no explanation except that the arrangement was used by the seller as a device to promote further business.

In the other two cases it is possible, but paradoxical, that the ballooning may have occurred as a result of the Control Orders. In both of these two cases, the deposit was the minimum permitted, and the repayment period was the maximum permitted, so that it may be that the buyer had difficulty in meeting the terms of the Control Orders. It is possible that the seller's attention focused on obtaining the statutory deposit and limiting repayment to the period prescribed in the regulations (these being the best known features of the Control Orders) and that either deliberately or inadvertently the seller overlooked the requirement that instalments must be of approximately equal amounts.

Apart from the Control Orders, there is nothing in English law to prohibit ballooning.

The objections to the practice are:

(1) The buyer can be tricked into a financial predicament that makes him particularly vulnerable to a high-pressure sales pitch at the end of

1. Legislation on these lines has already been passed in some jurisdictions. See, e.g., *The Consumer Protection Act*, Ontario, RSO, 1970, Ch. 82, S.34.

2. *Report from the Select Committee on Money Lending*, Vol. 10 (House of Commons Sessional Papers for 1898), p.101, 104.

the contract period. The result may then be an imprudent purchase that the buyer might not otherwise make.
(2) The buyer is led into continued business with the same seller. If he needs something else at the end of the contract period, it might be prudent for him to look at alternative suppliers.
(3) The buyer is seduced into a continuing state of indebtedness rather than being encouraged to consider whether he would be better off to switch his buying habits to the use of cash.

On the other hand, there may be situations in which a balloon contract is what the customer really wants. The example often quoted is that of a travelling salesman who trades in his car every year or two and before the price has been fully paid. But other examples are hard to conceive. Apart from this possible justification of the practice in the sale of new motor vehicles, there appears to be no legitimate commercial reason for it. Thus the practice could well be prohibited except on the sale of new motor vehicles. There could also, of course, be a power to exempt by regulation any other situations in which a legitimate commercial reason is shown for balloon contracts.

The survey did not reveal any instances of ballooning in the loan cases.

8. Tie-ins

Buyers were asked 'In order to get the [item], did you agree to take some other thing, or some service, in addition to the [item]?' This was the first of a batch of questions designed to discover the extent and significance of one item being tied in with the sale of another. There were 25 cases in the sample (2 per cent) in which the question was answered 'Yes'.

Usually, but not always, there was some functional connection between the tying item and the one that was tied. Some examples of the tie-ins were: a maintenance contract with the sale of a television,[1] a table with the sale of a sewing machine, a clothes line with the sale of a spin dryer, and cutlery with the sale of a vacuum cleaner.

There are several objections to tie-ins:

(1) The buyer may be coerced into paying for an item that he does not want. To the extent to which this occurs, it is a form of economic waste as well as an unnecessary cost to the buyer.
(2) Even when the buyer does want the item, he is precluded from buying it in circumstances that permit an independent judgement with

1. Seven of the tie-ins involved maintenance contracts.

regard to that item and which permit him to obtain it at the best available price.

(3) In some situations, the practice may be a form of leverage permitting traders engaged in one line of business to project their monopoly power into another line of business. This objection may be significant with regard to maintenance contracts.

(4) The tied item is often of poor quality. One complaint about maintenance contracts is that while dealers may press customers to take out a maintenance contract when the item (often a television) is new, they may not be so anxious to keep the contract going as the item reaches a more troublesome age. 'As the set gets older, they tend to avoid servicing, and there is nothing you can do. If you threaten to cancel the contract that's just what they want.'[1]

On the other hand, in situations where the customer is not paying extra for the tied item, the practice is often supported on the ground that it is not significantly different from promotional advertising.

In the survey cases involving a tie-in, buyers reported experiences a little worse than in the other cases, both with regard to selling methods and the condition of the goods.

In response to the question 'Were you satisfied with the [other thing]?', buyers indicated that they were satisfied in 16 cases and dissatisfied in 9. Where the tying item was a sewing machine, the buyers were dissatisfied with the other thing in 3 out of 4 cases.

A tie-in is something that consumers would generally be well advised to view sceptically. But there are many situations in which a tie-in has advantages of convenience and economy for consumers. Consider, for example, the sale of cylinder-type vacuum cleaners with the attachments. If each cleaner is delivered through the distribution system together with attachments as one unit, the packing and distribution costs might well be minimised. Conversely, the administrative costs of dealing with an order for a cleaner only might be high. If the vast majority of buyers want the attachments, it is possible that the total marginal cost of supplying the attachments to those who do not want them is less than the total marginal cost of processing orders for cleaners only.

Thus a major problem with any attempt to regulate tie-ins would be the trouble and expense of seeking to distinguish between situations in which the tie-in is wasteful or a source of dissatisfaction and situations in which the practice is beneficial.

1. Complaint received from a householder during pretesting for the survey.

9. Delay in Delivery

Delivery of the item beyond the date by which delivery had been promised was reported in 12.2 per cent of the cases in the sample. The reported delay was 1-7 days in 4.6 per cent, 8-28 days in 3.8 per cent and over 28 days in 3.8 per cent. The delays were most common with regard to gas appliances, new cars, televisions, furniture and carpets. There was little or no delay reported in the delivery of encyclopedia sets, cooking utensils, sewing machines, knitting machines, typewriters or dishwashers.

There were 75 cases in the sample involving new motor vehicles, and this is too few to make a meaningful comparison between manufacturers. But of the 8 foreign vehicles, all were delivered when promised, and so were the 7 vehicles of the Rootes group. There were delays in delivery with regard to vehicles of the other British manufacturers.

Delay in delivery is sometimes viewed as a fortuitous circumstance, a petty misfortune, or at worst a broken promise. But it can reflect a lie at the time of sale. When a salesman assures a customer of delivery by a certain date or estimated delivery by a certain date, there is surely an implied representation that this is the date by which experience indicates that delivery can be expected. If the salesman knows that to be untrue, no euphemism can avoid the conclusion that he is lying.

In some cases, a salesman may feel the pressure of competition. For example, he may be apprehensive that if he tells the customer that the bedroom suites usually take three months to arrive, the customer will go to another dealer who might be less frank. In other cases, a salesman may be motivated by ordinary human optimism to expect delivery in less than the time that it has taken in the past. The lie becomes blatant when the salesman promises delivery in four weeks, and six weeks later he is explaining to the same customer that it usually takes two months.

Sometimes, of course, unrealistic optimism occurs in the customer rather than the salesman. Suppose, for example, delivery time for a type of item is known to fluctuate, and a salesman frankly tells the customer that it takes anywhere from two to ten weeks. If the customer is an eternal optimist, this may create an expectation of delivery in two weeks and disappointment if by that time the item has not arrived.

An unexpected result of the survey was that in the cases reporting a delay in delivery, the buyers also reported worse experiences subsequently with the condition of the goods. Thus of the 149 cases involving a delay in delivery, the condition of the goods was classified as open to major objections in 15 per cent, substantial objections in 15 per cent and minor objections in 29 per cent, with 40 per cent entirely satisfactory. In the cases not reporting any delay in delivery, the corresponding proportions were 7, 10, 25 and 57 per cent. This contrast is not explicable by differences in the type of item. When differences in the item categories were controlled, the same contrast appeared. These data would be consistent with the view that delays in delivery beyond the date promised or estimated are often due not to isolated or fortuitous circumstances but to weaknesses of integrity or of system.

Delay in delivery also creates problems with regard to payment. In several of the transaction credit cases on the survey, the buyers complained that they were expected to commence payment of the instalments before they had received delivery of the goods. Perhaps less noticeable, but more important, was that they were being charged interest for a period during which they did not have the use of the goods. In the transaction credit cases, 4 per cent reported a delay in delivery of over 28 days beyond the date by which delivery had been promised.

Those who pay cash at the time of ordering suffer a similar disadvantage. During the period of the delay they lose the use of their money without receiving the benefit of the goods. They also lose the leverage by which to threaten a cancellation of the order if the goods are not delivered by a particular date. Moreover the absence of this threat can help in enabling a seller to underestimate deliberately the time required for delivery. Thus if a seller requests cash at the time of ordering, it is probably wise for the buyer to treat that as a warning sign. As one buyer of furniture on the survey said, 'It's a mistake to pay cash before you receive the goods. I wouldn't do it again.'

Where a buyer requires an item for immediate use, another consequence of an unrealistically brief estimate of the delivery time is that the buyer may be deceived into ordering the particular item rather than another make, model or type of item that may be more readily available and serve the same purpose.

If the date of delivery is important, it may be wise for a customer to ask the salesman to write in on the contract or order 'Delivery by [date]'. The salesman might refuse to do so, but if he does, the explanation for the refusal may be enlightening to the customer about what the delivery situation really is. The customer will then at least be in a better position to decide whether he wants to go ahead with the order.

5 CHANNELS OF DISTRIBUTION

1. Channels of Distribution Compared

Most consumer durables are sold at retail premises, primarily shops, garages, and the showrooms of the electricity boards and the British Gas Corporation (formerly the area gas boards). Substantial proportions, however, are sold by door-to-door salesmen calling at homes, and by mail order. For the transactions in the survey, Table 5.1, page 87, shows the channels of distribution classified by type of item.

In the literature of consumer protection, it has commonly been assumed or asserted that those who buy from a door-to-door salesman suffer a larger proportion of unfortunate experiences than those who buy at retail premises. As can be seen from the tables, the survey data strongly support that view.

Tables 5.2 and 5.3, pages 88 and 89, show that taking the totals for the survey as a whole, those who bought from a salesman who called at the home reported worse experiences than those who bought in any other way, both with regard to selling methods and the condition of the goods. It may be more relevant, however, to compare the results for each category of goods. Table 5.4, page 90, shows that for most item categories in which sales at the home could be compared with either shop sales or mail order, the selling methods for sales at the home were reported to be worse. The totals for all item categories on that table show that the frequency rate and gravity of reported objections to the selling methods were roughly double for sales at the home than for either shop sales or mail order cases. Table 5.5, page 91, shows that the same contrasts appeared with regard to the condition of the goods.

It is no doubt correct, as the data suggest, that sales at the home involve a larger proportion of abuses in the selling methods and of trouble with the goods than sales at retail premises or by mail order. But even in the shop sales, the proportions reported to involve major or substantial objections are still high. Moreover, because the total volume of shop sales is so much greater, people buying at shops suffer a greater total volume of abuses in the selling methods, and a greater total volume of trouble with the goods, than those who buy from a door-to-door salesman. Any concentration of consumer protection legislation on sales at the home, therefore, cannot be justified on the ground that this is where the greatest volume of consumer grievances occurs. It might, however, reflect an assumption that this is where the greatest volume of preventable abuse

Table 5.1: Channels of Distribution Classified by Type of Item*

	Shop or garage[1]	Electricity or gas board	Whole-sale warehouse	Factory	Heating engineer or builder	Home of buyer[2]	Mail order[3]	Private seller	School	Unascer-tained	Totals
Vacuum cleaners	85 (60)	16 (11)	5 (4)	2 (1)	—	17 (12)	16 (11)	—	—	—	141 (99)
Encyclopedias	2 (25)	—	—	—	—	4 (50)	1 (12)	—	1 (12)	—	8 (99)
Heating equipment	21 (15)	69 (49)	9 (6)	2 (1)	29 (21)	8 (6)	3 (2)	—	—	—	141 (100)
Cooking utensils	7 (78)	—	1 (11)	—	—	—	1 (11)	—	—	—	9 (100)
Sewing machines	26 (74)	—	1 (3)	1 (3)	—	3 (9)	4 (11)	—	—	—	35 (100)
Knitting machines	1 (25)	—	—	—	—	—	3 (75)	—	—	—	4 (100)
Typewriters	7 (50)	—	—	—	—	2 (14)	5 (36)	—	—	—	14 (100)
New motor vehicles	73 (97)	—	—	1 (1)	—	—	—	—	—	1 (1)	75 (99)
Secondhand motor vehicles	140 (67)	—	—	—	—	—	—	67 (32)	—	1 (0)	208 (99)
Radio/TV etc.	100 (77)	—	10 (8)	1 (0)	—	7 (5)	12 (9)	—	—	—	130 (99)
Dishwashers	4 (100)	—	—	—	—	—	—	—	—	—	4 (100)
Furniture	139 (93)	—	2 (1)	3 (2)	—	1 (0)	4 (3)	—	—	—	149 (99)
Rugs/Carpets	109 (78)	—	9 (6)	1 (1)	—	11 (8)	9 (6)	—	—	1 (1)	140 (100)
Refrigerators or freezers	30 (57)	17 (32)	2 (4)	—	1 (2)	—	3 (6)	—	—	—	53 (101)
Cookers	3 (5)	50 (77)	1 (2)	—	—	11 (17)	—	—	—	—	65 (101)
Washing machines or dryers	34 (68)	10 (20)	1 (2)	—	—	2 (4)	3 (6)	—	—	—	50 (100)
Totals	781 (64)	162 (13)	41 (3)	11 (1)	30 (2)	66 (5)	64 (5)	67 (5)	1 (0)	3 (0)	1,226 (98)

*Percentage figures in brackets.

1. This column includes any retail premises at which goods are normally sold, except electricity or gas board premises. The column includes 18 cases where the purchase was consummated at a shop or garage, but was solicited by a call from a door-to-door salesman.
2. This column includes sales by a gas board where the transaction was consummated by a door-to-door salesman. One of the typewriters in this column was sold at the buyer's place of work.
3. This column includes 4 cases where the order to the mail order company was placed by a salesman who came to the home.

Table 5.2: Selling Methods Classified by Channels of Distribution*

	Selling methods									
	Major objections		Substantial objections		Minor objections		Entirely satisfactory		Totals	
Electricity or gas board	16	(10)	21	(13)	19	(12)	106	(65)	162	(100)
Other shop or garage	52	(7)	80	(10)	86	(11)	563	(72)	781	(100)
Wholesale warehouse	2	(5)	3	(7)	2	(5)	34	(83)	41	(100)
Heating engineer or builder	3	(10)	1	(3)	1	(3)	25	(83)	30	(99)
Factory	0		1	(9)	1	(9)	9	(82)	11	(100)
Seller called at home	14	(21)	8	(12)	11	(17)	33	(50)	66	(100)
Mail order	4	(6)	7	(11)	5	(8)	48	(75)	64	(100)
Private seller (secondhand cars only)	4	(6)	8	(12)	3	(5)	52	(78)	67	(101)
School	0		0		0	—	1	(100)	1	(100)
Unascertained	0		0		0		3	(100)	3	(100)
Totals	95	(8)	129	(11)	128	(10)	874	(71)	1,226	(100)

*Percentage figures in brackets.

Table 5.3: Condition of Goods Classified by Channels of Distribution*

	Conditions of goods									
	Major objections		Substantial objections		Minor objections		Entirely satisfactory		Totals	
Electricity or gas board	15	(9)	12	(7)	43	(27)	92	(57)	162	(100)
Other shop or garage	61	(8)	89	(11)	196	(25)	431	(56)	777	(100)
Wholesale warehouse	3	(7)	5	(12)	10	(24)	23	(56)	41	(99)
Heating engineer or builder	0		1	(3)	14	(47)	15	(50)	30	(100)
Factory	0		2	(18)	0		9	(82)	11	(100)
Seller called at home	9	(14)	10	(16)	13	(20)	32	(50)	64	(100)
Mail order	3	(5)	3	(5)	14	(22)	44	(69)	64	(101)
Private seller (secondhand cars only)	5	(8)	6	(9)	21	(31)	35	(52)	67	(100)
School	0		0		0		1	(100)	1	(100)
Unascertained	0		0		1	(33)	2	(67)	3	(100)
Totals	96	(8)	128	(10)	312	(26)	684	(56)	1,220	(100)

*Percentage figures in brackets.

Table 5.4: Channels of Distribution Classified by Selling Methods and Type of Item*

Item	Major objections		Substantial objections		Minor objections		Entirely satisfactory		Totals	
Shop sales (including sales at an electricity or gas board showroom)										
Vacuum cleaners	–		6	(6)	13	(13)	82	(81)	101	(100)
Encyclopedias	–		–		–		2	(100)	2	(100)
Central heating	1	(7)	3	(23)	3	(23)	6	(46)	13	(99)
Electric fires	–		–		–		9	(100)	9	(100)
Gas fires	12	(24)	7	(14)	3	(6)	28	(56)	50	(100)
Sewing machines	2	(8)	2	(8)	3	(12)	19	(73)	26	(101)
Typewriters	–		–		1	(14)	6	(86)	7	(100)
Secondhand motor vehicles	14	(7)	26	(13)	19	(9)	141	(70)	200	(99)
Radio/TV etc.	–		7	(7)	10	(10)	83	(83)	100	(100)
Washing machine, dryer and combinations	1	(2)	7	(16)	5	(11)	31	(70)	44	(99)
Carpets	8	(7)	7	(7)	9	(8)	85	(78)	109	(100)
Gas cookers	–		5	(17)	2	(7)	23	(77)	30	(101)
Totals	38	(5)	70	(10)	68	(10)	515	(75)	691	(100)
Sales at the home (including shop sales preceded by the visit of a door-to-door salesman)										
Vacuum cleaners	4	(22)	2	(11)	5	(28)	7	(39)	18	(100)
Encyclopedias	3	(75)	–		–		1	(25)	4	(100)
Central heating	3	(43)	1	(14)	2	(29)	1	(14)	7	(100)
Electric fires	–		–		–		–			
Gas fires	3	(50)	1	(17)	1	(17)	1	(17)	6	(101)
Sewing machines	1	(33)	–		1	(33)	1	(33)	3	(99)
Typewriters	–		–		–		2	(100)	2	(100)
Secondhand motor vehicles	1	(12)	1	(12)	2	(25)	4	(50)	8	(99)
Radio/TV etc.	–		2	(22)	2	(22)	5	(55)	9	(99)
Washing machine, dryer and combinations	1	(33)	–		–		2	(67)	3	(100)
Carpets	3	(23)	2	(15)	1	(8)	7	(54)	13	(100)
Gas cookers	2	(17)	2	(17)	1	(8)	7	(58)	12	(100)
Totals	21	(25)	11	(13)	15	(18)	38	(45)	85	(101)
Mail order										
Vacuum cleaners	1	(6)	–		1	(6)	14	(87)	16	(99)
Encyclopedias	–		1	(100)	–		–		1	(100)
Electric fires	–		1	(33)	1	(33)	1	(33)	3	(99)
Sewing machines	–		–		1	(25)	3	(75)	4	(100)
Typewriters	–		–		–		5	(100)	5	(100)
Radio/TV etc	1	(8)	2	(17)	2	(17)	7	(58)	12	(100)
Washing machine, dryer and combinations	1	(33)	–		–		2	(67)	3	(100)
Carpets	1	(11)	2	(22)	–		6	(67)	9	(100)
Totals	4	(8)	6	(11)	5	(9)	38	(72)	53	(100)

*Percentage figures in brackets.

Table 5.5: Channels of Distribution Classified by Condition of Goods and Type of Item*

Item	Major objections		Substantial objections		Minor objections		Entirely satisfactory		Totals	
Shop sales (including sales at an electricity or gas board showroom)										
Vacuum cleaners	7	(7)	6	(6)	24	(24)	64	(63)	101	(100)
Encyclopedias	—		—		—		2	(100)	2	(100)
Central heating	—		2	(15)	6	(46)	5	(38)	13	(99)
Electric fires	—		—		1	(11)	8	(88)	9	(99)
Gas fires	6	(12)	5	(10)	17	(34)	22	(44)	50	(100)
Sewing machines	—		1	(4)	8	(31)	17	(65)	26	(100)
Typewriters	—		—		1	(14)	6	(85)	7	(99)
Secondhand motor vehicles	28	(14)	32	(16)	65	(33)	74	(37)	199	(100)
Radio/TV etc.	5	(5)	12	(12)	22	(22)	61	(61)	100	(100)
Washing machines, dryers and combination	4	(9)	5	(12)	8	(19)	26	(60)	43	(100)
Carpets	3	(3)	6	(6)	10	(9)	89	(82)	108	(100)
Gas cookers	2	(7)	2	(7)	8	(26)	18	(60)	30	(100)
Totals	55	(8)	71	(10)	170	(25)	392	(57)	688	(100)
Sales at the home (including shop sales preceded by the visit of a door-to-door salesman)										
Vacuum cleaners	2	(11)	3	(17)	6	(33)	7	(39)	18	(100)
Encyclopedias	1	(25)	1	(25)	1	(25)	1	(25)	4	(100)
Central heating	2	(29)	1	(14)	2	(29)	2	(29)	7	(101)
Gas fires	1	(17)	1	(17)	3	(50)	1	(17)	6	(101)
Sewing machines	1	(33)	1	(33)	—		1	(33)	3	(99)
Typewriters	—		—		—		2	(100)	2	(100)
Secondhand motor vehicles	—		1	(12)	4	(50)	3	(37)	8	(99)
Radio/TV etc.	2	(22)	1	(11)	3	(33)	3	(33)	9	(99)
Washing machines, dryers and combinations	—		—		1	(33)	2	(66)	3	(99)
Carpets	1	(9)	2	(18)	1	(9)	7	(63)	11	(99)
Gas cookers	1	(8)	1	(8)	3	(25)	7	(58)	12	(99)
Totals	11	(13)	12	(14)	24	(29)	36	(43)	83	(99)
Mail order										
Vacuum cleaners	1	(6)	1	(6)	2	(12)	12	(75)	16	(99)
Encyclopedias	—		—		—		1	(100)	1	(100)
Electric fires	—		—		2	(66)	1	(33)	3	(99)
Sewing machines	—		—		—		4	(100)	4	(100)
Typewriters	—		—		—		5	(100)	5	(100)
Radio/TV etc	1	(8)	—		5	(41)	6	(50)	12	(99)
Washing machines, dryers and combinations	1	(33)	—		1	(33)	1	(33)	3	(99)
Carpets	—		1	(11)	1	(11)	7	(77)	9	(99)
Totals	3	(6)	2	(4)	11	(21)	37	(70)	53	(101)

*Percentage figures in brackets.

occurs. In other words, there may be some feeling that in any method of distribution, some unfortunate experiences are inevitable. But where the proportion of cases involving the unfortunate experiences is much higher in one channel of distribution than in the others, this may be an indication that abuses in that area are more amenable to remedial action.

With regard to the purchase of secondhand motor vehicles those who bought from a dealer reported worse experiences than those who bought from a private seller, both with regard to selling methods and the condition of the goods.[1]

Table 5.6, page 93, shows the channels of distribution classified by the method of financing. As the table shows, transaction credit was used proportionately more for sales at the home than for sales at retail premises.

In the cases involving secondhand motor vehicles bought from a dealer who also sold new motor vehicles, 45 per cent were for cash and 41 per cent transaction credit. Where the dealer did not also sell new motor vehicles it was 65 per cent cash and 23 per cent transaction credit.

In the use of finance companies, a contrast appeared between shop sales and sales at the home. When motor vehicle and central heating cases were excluded, it appeared that finance companies were involved in 8 per cent of transaction credit cases where the item was bought at a shop, but in 36 per cent of transaction credit cases where the item was bought from a salesman who called at the home.

Guarantors appeared more frequently in sales at the home. Where an item was bought at an electricity or gas board showroom, guarantors appeared in 6 per cent of the transaction credit cases. Where the item was bought at another type of shop or garage, they appeared in 13 per cent. Where the item was bought from a salesman who called at the home, they appeared in 16 per cent.

In the vacuum cleaner cases (the only category of goods for which this could be determined) it was found that the reported selling methods and the condition of the goods varied much more significantly according to the channel of distribution than according to the make of the cleaner.

There was a correlation between the condition of the home as described by the interviewer and buying from a door-to-door salesman. Thus, where the home was described as immaculate, 3 per cent of transactions involved

1. In the sales by a dealer, the selling methods were classified as open to major objections in 8 per cent, substantial objections in 14 per cent, and minor objections in 13 per cent, with 66 per cent entirely satisfactory. In the private sales the corresponding figures were 6, 12, 4 and 77 per cent. With regard to the condition of the goods, the sales by a dealer were classified as open to major objections in 17 per cent, substantial objections in 19 per cent, and minor objections in 35 per cent, with 29 per cent being entirely satisfactory. For the private sales the corresponding figures were 7, 9, 31 and 52 per cent.

Table 5.6: Channels of Distribution Classified by Method of Financing*

	Shop or garage	Electricity or gas board	Whole-sale warehouse	Factory	Heating engineer or builder	Seller called at the home	Mail order	Private sale (secondhand motor vehicles only)	School	Unascer-tained	Totals
Cash	474 (61)	77 (48)	38 (93)	10 (91)	18 (60)	24 (36)	12 (19)	49 (73)	0 (0)	2 (67)	704 (57)
Loan	32 (4)	3 (2)	1 (2)	0	12 (40)	1 (2)	1 (2)	8 (12)	0 (0)	0 (0)	58 (5)
Transaction credit	246 (31)	77 (48)	0	1 (9)	0	36 (55)	32 (50)	10 (15)	1 (100)	1 (33)	404 (33)
Account with the seller	11 (1)	1 (0)	1 (2)	0	0	5 (8)	18 (28)	0	0	0	36 (3)
Credit card company	0	0	1 (2)	0	0	0	0	0	0	0	1 (0)
Check trader	18 (2)	3 (2)	0	0	0	0	1 (2)	0	0	0	22 (2)
Credit but unascertained what type	0	1	0	0	0	0	0	0	0	0	1 (0)
Totals	781 (99)	162 (100)	41 (99)	11 (100)	30 (100)	66 (101)	64 (101)	67 (100)	1 (0)	3 (100)	1,226 (101)

*Percentage figures in brackets.

Note: The footnotes at the bottom of Table 5.1 apply also to this table.

an item bought from a salesman who called at the home. Where the home condition was described as good, the proportion was 4 per cent. Where it was described as fair, the proportion was 8 per cent. Where it was described as poor, the proportion was 22 per cent.

Table 5.7, page 95, shows the channels of distribution classified according to complaints by the buyer, and Table 5.8, page 96, shows the channels of distribution classified according to the results of the complaints. Looking overall at the complaint experience that these tables indicate, the differences among the principal channels of distribution were small.

2. Shop Transactions

Of the people who bought at a shop, those who bought at a department store[1] reported experiences a little better than those who bought at other types of shops, both with regard to selling methods and the condition of the goods.

Department stores had the highest proportion of customers who complained or asked for something to be put right or for some repairs to be done (19 per cent). This compared with 15 per cent for specialist shops. But the department stores also had the highest proportion of buyers who did not complain for reasons indicating that they had nothing to complain about (75 per cent). This compared with 71 per cent for specialist shops. The specialist shops had the highest proportion of buyers who did not complain for reasons indicating that they felt they had cause for complaint (6 per cent). This compared with 1 per cent for department stores.

Of the 16 department store cases in which the buyer complained, or asked for something to be put right, or asked for some repairs to be done, there were no cases in which nothing was done in response to the complaint, and there were no cases in which the buyer responded that he was 'not satisfied' with what was done. There were, however, 3 cases in which the buyer responded that he was only 'partly satisfied' with what was done. Of the 58 transactions at a specialist shop in which the buyer complained, or asked for something to be put right, or asked for some repairs to be done, there were 3 in which the buyer reported that nothing at all was done in response to the complaint, 7 in which the buyer was 'not satisfied' with what was done, and 5 in which the buyer was only 'partly satisfied' with what was done.

Because department stores sell a wider range of goods, a larger

1. 'Department store' was defined in the interviewers' introductions as meaning 'a shop appearing to have at least 25 sales staff and at least 3 departments'. 'Specialist shop' was defined as meaning 'any shop selling one category of goods, e.g. a furniture shop, a household appliances shop, etc.'.

Table 5.7: Channels of Distribution Classified by Complaints to Seller*

	Shop or garage	Electricity or gas board	Whole-sale warehouse	Factory	Heating engineer or builder	Seller called at the home	Mail order	Private sale	School	Unascer-tained	Totals
Buyer complained (or asked for something to be put right, or asked for some repairs to be done)	194 (25)	49 (30)	7 (17)	1 (9)	12 (40)	19 (30)	11 (17)	6 (9)	–	1 (33)	300 (25)
No complaint made, but for reasons indicating cause for complaint	41 (5)	3 (2)	5 (12)	1 (9)	1 (3)	2 (3)	2 (3)	7 (10)	–	–	62 (5)
No complaint made and no cause for complaint	496 (64)	101 (62)	26 (63)	9 (82)	17 (57)	41 (64)	48 (75)	53 (79)	1 (100)	2 (67)	794 (65)
No complaint, reason unascertained	46 (6)	9 (6)	3 (7)	–	–	2 (3)	3 (5)	1 (1)	–	–	64 (5)
Totals	777 (100)	162 (100)	41 (99)	11 (100)	30 (100)	64 (100)	64 (100)	67 (99)	1 (100)	3 (100)	1,220 (100)

*Percentage figures in brackets.

Note: The footnotes at the bottom of Table 5.1 apply also to this table.

Table 5.8: Channels of Distribution Classified by Results of Complaints (Cases where an Item had been Received, and where Buyer Complained to Seller or Asked for Something to be Put Right or Asked for Some Repairs to be Done)*

	Shop or garage	Electricity or gas boards	Whole-sale warehouse	Factory	Heating engineer or builder	Seller called at the home	Mail order	Private sale	Unascer-tained	Totals
Nothing done at all	21 (11)	8 (16)	1 (14)	–	–	4 (21)	–	1 (17)	–	35 (12)
Buyer not satisfied	26 (13)	6 (12)	1 (14)	–	–	3 (16)	1 (9)	–	–	37 (12)
Buyer partly satisfied	17 (9)	4 (8)	–	–	–	1 (5)	–	1 (17)	–	23 (8)
Buyer satisfied	121 (62)	31 (63)	5 (71)	1 (100)	12 (100)	10 (53)	10 (91)	4 (67)	1 (100)	195 (65)
Action pending	5 (3)	–	–	–	–	1 (5)	–	–	–	6 (2)
Unascertained whether buyer satisfied	4 (2)	–	–	–	–	–	–	–	–	4 (1)
Totals	194 (100)	49 (99)	7 (99)	1 (100)	12 (100)	19 (100)	11 (100)	6 (101)	1 (100)	300 (100)

*Percentage figures in brackets.

Note: the footnotes at the bottom of Table 5.1 apply also to this table.

proportion of their transactions are likely to be with regular customers, and this may result in complaints or requests for redress being made more readily. Department stores certainly have an incentive to maintain goodwill, and the making of complaints may be stimulated by a greater expectation on the part of customers that grievances will be remedied.

3. Sales at the Home

As mentioned above, and as shown in Tables 5.2, 5.3, 5.4 and 5.5, the survey data show that those who bought from a salesman who called at the home reported worse experiences than those who bought at retail premises or by mail order, both with regard to selling methods and the condition of the goods.

Different results appeared, however, with regard to different categories of door-to-door salesmen. In the literature of consumer protection, most of the discussion of abuses in sales at the home has focused on salesmen who sell one type of item and who have no retail premises. They sell consumer durables, such as heating equipment, vacuum cleaners, or double glazing, and they have no expectation of repeat business. Another category altogether are the people who call regularly selling a range of goods (sometimes called tallymen) and who maintain a continuing business relationship, often bordering on a friendship, with their clientele. A third category are the salesmen who call at homes but are selling for a retail outlet with established premises. This category includes the salesmen from the gas boards (British Gas Corporation). A fourth category are the agents who solicit orders for a mail order company.

For the cases in the sample where a salesman called at the home, Table 5.9, page 98, shows the transactions classified according to the categories of salesmen and the types of items sold by each.

Tables 5.10 and 5.11, pages 99 and 100, show how the reported selling methods and condition of the goods varied according to the type of door-to-door salesman. Unfortunately the numbers in most of the cells are small. However, the tables show that the worst proportion of unfortunate experiences was reported in transactions involving salesmen without retail premises who sell only one type of item. A little better were the transactions involving a salesman from an area gas board, and better still were the transactions involving salesmen from other retail premises. The best experiences of all were reported by those who bought from a salesman who called regularly selling different types of items. These buyers reported experiences among the best in the total

Table 5.9: Categories of Door-to-Door Salesmen Classified by Type of Item

Item	Called without appointment selling one type of item	Called with appointment selling one type of item	Called regularly selling different items	From the gas board, and called without an appointment	From the gas board, called with an appointment	From a shop, called without an appointment	From a shop, called with an appointment	Took orders for a mail order company	Totals
Vacuum cleaners	15	–	2	–	–	–	–	1	18
Encyclopedias	4	–	–	–	–	–	–	–	4
Central heating	1	4	–	–	–	–	2	–	7
Gas fires	–	–	–	3	3	–	–	–	6
Cooking utensils	–	–	–	–	–	–	–	1	1
Sewing machines	–	3	–	–	–	–	–	–	3
Typewriters	1	–	1	–	–	–	–	–	2
New motor vehicles	–	–	–	–	–	–	1	–	1
Secondhand motor vehicles	–	–	–	–	–	7	1	–	8
Televisions	2	2	1	–	–	–	1	–	6
Radio/Record player	1	–	2	–	–	–	–	–	3
Furniture	–	1	–	–	–	–	–	–	1
Carpet	6	1	4	–	–	–	1	1	13
Gas cookers	–	–	–	10	1	–	1	–	12
Washing machines	–	2	–	–	–	–	–	–	2
Dryers	–	–	–	–	–	–	–	1	1
Totals	30	13	10	13	4	7	7	4	88

Table 5.10: Selling Methods Classified by Type of Salesman (Sales at the Home, or at Retail Premises Preceded by a Call at the Home)*

Type of salesman	Selling methods: Major objections		Substantial objections		Minor objections		Entirely satisfactory		Totals	
Called selling one type of item	12	(28)	6	(14)	10	(23)	15	(35)	43	(100)
Called regularly selling different items	—		1	(10)	—		9	(90)	10	(100)
From the gas board	5	(29)	3	(18)	2	(12)	7	(41)	17	(100)
From a shop or garage	3	(21)	1	(7)	3	(21)	7	(50)	14	(99)
Took orders for a mail order company	2	(50)	—		—		2	(50)	4	(100)
Totals	22	(25)	11	(13)	15	(17)	40	(45)	88	(100)

*Percentage figures in brackets.

Table 5.11: Condition of Goods Classified by Type of Salesman (Sales at the Home, or at Retail Premises Preceded by a Call at the Home)*

Type of salesman	Condition of goods									
	Major objections		Substantial objections		Minor objections		Entirely satisfactory		Totals	
Called selling one type of item	8	(19)	9	(21)	9	(21)	17	(40)	43	(101)
Called regularly selling different items	1	(10)	—		1	(10)	8	(80)	10	(100)
From the gas board	2	(12)	2	(12)	5	(29)	8	(47)	17	(100)
From a shop or garage	—		2	(14)	7	(50)	5	(36)	14	(100)
Took orders for a mail order company	—		—		4	(100)	—		4	(100)
Totals	11	(13)	13	(15)	26	(30)	38	(43)	88	(101)

*Percentage figures in brackets.

sample.[1]

Sometimes door-to-door salesmen call at homes without prior selection, and without prior contact. Sometimes an item has been advertised in a magazine, or in a pamphlet pushed through letterboxes, and the potential customers have sent in names and addresses in response to the advertisement. Sometimes the households have been selected in some other way.[2]

It has sometimes been suggested that itinerant salesmen should be prohibited from calling at a home without having been requested or invited to do so by an occupier.[3] To discover whether an invitation to call makes any significant difference to the result, those who bought at the home were asked: 'Before the salesman came was an appointment made for him to come and see you?' It was found that where an appointment was made before the salesman called, the buyers actually reported worse experiences than where the salesman called without an appointment, both with regard to selling methods and the condition of the goods.[4]

The objections to door-to-door selling relate to every phase of the transaction. At the beginning, the salesmen may not introduce themselves in a straightforward way. They sometimes gain admission to the home and soften the household by representing themselves as something other than salesmen. The range of phoney introductions includes:

(1) Pretending to be conducting a survey and only to be seeking information.

1. Enquiries among advisory agencies did not indicate any substantial volume of complaints from customers about tallymen. But they are a source of complaints among social workers. In interviews in 1977, three social workers and one Citizen's Advice Bureau organiser mentioned that tallymen talk people into buying things that they cannot afford, charge high interest rates, and get families into debt beyond what they can reasonably cope with. See also *Debit and Credit*, 1977, Newham Rights Centre, London, p.40.

2. An example current in 1977 is for 'clipboard girls' to conduct a 'survey' by street interviews in London to identify potential customers for the salesmen.

3. Local ordinances to this effect can be found in some municipalities in the United States. In England, it can be an offence to canvass for the advance of a cash loan by calling at a home without having a previous written invitation to call. *Consumer Credit Act*, 1974, S.49.

4. After extracting sales by tallymen, it was found that where a salesman called at the home by appointment (32 cases), the selling methods were classified as open to major objections in 31 per cent, substantial objections in 13 per cent, and minor objections in 13 per cent, with 44 per cent entirely satisfactory. Where a salesman called at the home without an appointment (41 cases), the corresponding proportions were 24, 12, 27 and 37 per cent. Where the salesman called by appointment, the condition of the goods was classified as open to major objections in 17 per cent, substantial objections in 23 per cent and minor objections in 23 per cent, with 37 per cent entirely satisfactory. Where the salesman called without an appointment the corresponding proportions were 10, 12, 41 and 37 per cent.

(2) Pretending that the only purpose of the visit is to 'place' the item in the home for advertising purposes, or for viewing by potential buyers.
(3) Mentioning the names of children (previously ascertained) and creating the impression that the salesman is from the school, or from the local education authority.
(4) Pretending to have come for some type of technical inspection.

Phoney introductions were reported in 2 (out of 18) of the vacuum cleaner cases on the survey, 3 (out of 4) of the encyclopedia cases, 1 (out of 6) sales of gas fires, 2 (out of 8) sales of secondhand motor vehicles, 2 (out of 12) sales of gas cookers, and 1 (out of 13) sales of a rug or carpet.[1]

In another 3 cases on the sample, not involving sales at the home, the buyers mentioned that they had recently been visited at the home by encyclopedia salesmen posing with one of the phoney introductions mentioned above.[2]

A more difficult situation to assess is where the item was sold by someone who came to the home initially in response to a request for repair of an old item of the same type. This occurred in 6 cases in the sample. The situation is one in which there is obviously an opportunity for abuse. It is surely objectionable if a repair man is held out as being a workman who earns a standard wage for repair work (and whose advice about replacing an item by a new one might be treated as impartial) whereas actually he is being paid commissions on sales that are consummated by a salesman who follows his call. On the other hand, there are many small businesses in which repairs and selling are done by the same person, and there is surely no objection to that unless the blending of the repair and selling roles is concealed from the customer.

Once the salesman is inside the home, the more objectionable forms of door-to-door selling often include misrepresentations about the terms of the transaction and about the item, and high-pressure tactics, sometimes culminating in a closing line such as 'I know you want to get back to the television, so just sign here and I will fill in the details later.'

1. In a further 3 vacuum cleaner cases, it was reported that the salesman introduced himself by saying that he had come to demonstrate the item. That is surely acceptable unless something more is said to conceal that he is a salesman.

2. For a further discussion and examples of the phoney introductions, see 709 *House of Commons Debates*, 1964-5, cols. 964-1000; 718 *House of Commons Debates*, 1964-5, cols. 1225-6; and *How to Cope with Doorstep Salesmen*, 1976, pamphlet issued by the Office of Fair Trading.

Sometimes, however, a soft sell is used. One approach used with regard to encyclopedias is for the salesman to introduce himself with a cultivated public school accent. He follows this with a conversation that identifies his educational accomplishments with the use of the encyclopedia. Next, he spends half an hour developing a relaxing mood, a cordial rapport with the household, a warmth and friendliness. Then if the customer shows any reluctance to sign a contract, the salesman can react as if the customer is letting down an old and honourable friend.

Objections to door-to-door selling are not limited, however, to the high-pressure tactics and other predatory practices. In some areas of the United States where it is prohibited for salesmen to call without first being invited, one explanation for the prohibition is that the frequent calling of salesmen at the door is viewed as a species of nuisance.[1]

To illustrate some of the worst features of selling at the home, it might be helpful to mention an example. The following is a reconstruction of a typical encyclopedia case, based on interviews with people who have bought encyclopedias, on experience posing as a mooch listening to encyclopedia salesmen, and on the reading of a salesman's training manual. The transaction begins with a telephone call:

> *Salesman:* My name is William Brown. I represent the XYZ Publishing House. We have selected your name in view of your position in the community, and I would like to tell you about a programme in which I believe you will be interested.
>
> *Householder:* Are you selling encyclopedias?
>
> *Salesman:* No, certainly not. I am not selling anything. My company is bringing out a programme that I think will interest you, and I would like the opportunity of coming around and explaining it.
>
> *Householder:* Well, if you are not selling encyclopedias, you can come around.

The salesman comes to the home, ushers the husband and wife into the sitting room, sits them down, and launches into a pitch that takes about an hour to complete. Abbreviated, the essence of it is as follows:

'Of course you have heard of the XYZ Publishing House'.

A few minutes is then spent explaining the enormous size, respectability and virtue of the company, its worldwide connections and its contribution

1. E.g. in *Green v. Town of Gallup* (1941) 120 P2d 619, 622, Supreme Court of New Mexico, the reasons quoted by the court for the local ordinance prohibiting itinerant selling included both '. . .an early and very general tendency to defraud the unwary. . .' and '. . .the frequent ringing of doorbells of private residences by itinerant vendors and solicitors is in fact a nuisance to the occupants of those homes.'

to education, science and the arts. A map of the world is spread on the carpet and used to illustrate the extent of the company's operations.

'Have you seen the advertisements of our company on television?' The reply is negative.

'That's because we don't advertise. Do you know how much per year a company like ours could spend on advertising?'

The mooch confesses ignorance of advertising expenditures.

'It could run into millions. £10,000 for one spot on television alone. Our company is anxious to avoid all that expenditure on advertising. We decided that there are better ways of doing things. In a few months' time, the company will be introducing into Britain its . . *Encyclopedia*, but it won't be on sale for some time. In the meantime, the company has given a great deal of thought to promotion. We decided that instead of spending vast sums of money on advertising, we would instead spend the money on placing sets in certain selected homes, and in that way make the encyclopedia known. We have already placed the set with people, some of whose names are on this list.'

A glossy decorated list is then shown to the mooch. It includes two former prime ministers, several peers of the realm, filmstars, sportsmen and others with whom the mooch might like to be associated. It is then laid on the carpet.

'But to make the encyclopedia well known everywhere, we want to place it also with influential people in the local community.'

The salesman next produces a sample volume of the encyclopedia from his suitcase. He invites the mooch to turn the pages. The volume then joins the collection on the carpet.

'Now don't worry about the cost, there is no need for you to worry about that. All I am concerned with is would you like to have this magnificent set of reference works, and would you find it useful?'

The mooch is induced to say that he would. The salesman then pulls from his suitcase and spreads across the carpet a 6 ft x 3 ft glossy picture of the whole encyclopedia set installed in a cherry case. He comments on how magnificent this will look over there against that wall beside the fireplace.

'Now, in addition to this great set of reference works, you will be supplied with 75 enquiry forms on which you can write and ask a question on any matter of your choice, except legal and medical questions, and a report will come back to you from an expert on the subject that you have chosen. These enquiry forms can be sent in at any time during the next 10 years, and all this is free.'

The enquiry forms then are shown to the mooch with specimen reports that have been sent to other enquirers, and this material is then added to the collection on the carpet.

'In addition to all this, and to make sure that the information is never out of date, the company produces an annual supplement volume, and this too will be sent to you absolutely without charge.'

A specimen annual supplement volume is shown to the mooch and then squeezed into whatever space remains on the carpet.

'As you can see, it would be of no benefit to us to place these valuable sets with people who don't really want them. It is very important that we place them only with people who will appreciate them, and who will use them.'

The mooch assures the salesman that he will.

'To make sure, therefore, that we only place these sets in the right households where they will be appreciated, we do ask the household to assume a small portion of the cost by making a nominal token payment.'

The mooch asks how much.

'Now you will be receiving the supplementary volumes for 10 years, and the token payment that we ask amounts to only 10p a day. You will have to agree that that isn't really much. It's probably less than you spend on newspapers, and they offer you far less information.'

The salesman rambles on about what a trifling sum it is, particularly 'bearing in mind what the company is doing for you', the inference being that it would be petty and in bad taste to object to it.

'But of course you wouldn't want to be bothered by these trifling amounts over 10 years, so we compute them to have them paid off in the first three years.'

The salesman avoids mentioning how much per day that comes to, or how much in total. If the mooch insists on knowing how much in total, the salesman admits that it comes to £365.

'But that's nothing to what these sets will sell for when they are on the market. It will be at least £550. It's also nothing compared with the value that you are getting. And I haven't finished yet. In addition to these magnificent reference works, the company also supplies absolutely without charge the cherry bookcase, a world atlas, and an Oxford dictionary.'

As he reaches the climax of this crescendo, the salesman slips his pad of contract froms in front of the mooch for signature, together with a pen, at the same time keeping up the patter. The mooch says that he would like to think it over. The salesman is taken aback.

'The company is going to a lot of expense in placing these sets. They can't afford to have me calling back, and above all we only want to place the sets with people who are sure that they want them.'

The salesman refers back to the answers that the mooch gave about whether he wanted the set, would appreciate it and would use it, the inference being that if he denies that now he will prove himself a liar.

Sitting there entrapped in his own armchair, the contract pad on his knee, the glossy material littering the sitting room around him, the salesman perched on a footstool in front of him thrusting the pen towards him, and at the same time maintaining a patter to distract him from any rational thought, the mooch surrenders.

Theoretically of course contracts obtained in this way are voidable for fraud (deceit). But during periods of prosperity (when the encyclopedia racket and similar rackets have their greatest potential) most people will pay. If they do not pay willingly, they can be coerced by dunning letters and threats of an adverse credit report. If that is not enough, a court summons can be issued. The chances are that the householder will not have legal advice. Apart from the normal difficulties of obtaining legal services,[1] there is the reluctance to admit that one has been fooled. In most cases where a summons is issued, no proper defence will be filed, and judgment will be obtained by default. If a defence of fraud or some other defence is filed, the claim will probably be dropped. An operator of one of these rackets may well think it prudent to avoid any risk of the publicity that might follow from a trial on the merits,[2] particularly if a successful defence might thereby come to the attention of other buyers. Of course the 'contract' will be repudiated by some of the people who have signed. But that may not deter the seller as long as the proportion who pay is still high enough for the business to be profitable.

Predatory practices of the type described lead to some harsh feelings. In referring to door-to-door salesmen, the Maloney Committee reported that 'The activities of some of these men have provoked a greater wrath and indignation among our representors than any other single subject.'[3]

1. See Chapter 9.

2. It is difficult to know what happens in England if a case of this type does go to trial because County Court cases are not reported. In a Canadian case, involving the sale of a vacuum cleaner using a referral sale technique, the court had no difficulty in concluding that the transaction was voidable for fraud. '. . .[the seller] throughout misrepresented the transaction to the defendants. It was a clever, subtle and misleading scheme to sell a vacuum cleaner to persons who did not want one and could not afford it. From the time that Green appeared at the door until he left he stated he was not selling a vacuum cleaner but was giving the defendants an opportunity to earn money and receive a free vacuum cleaner as a bonus.' *Trans-Canada Credit Corp. Ltd. v. Zaluski et al.* [1969] 2 OR 496, 500. In another case involving high-pressure sales tactics at the home, the appellate court ruled simply that '. . .it would be unjust and inequitable to hold these ladies to a contract procured in the manner in which this one was.' *W.W. Distributors and Co. Ltd. v. Thorsteinsson et al.* (1960) 33 WWR 669, 672. But cf. *Thor Food Service Corp. v. Makofske* (1961) 218 NYS 2d 93.

3. *Final Report of the Committee on Consumer Protection*, 1962, Cmnd 1781, para.741.

The feelings of one buyer on the survey were apparent in the comment that high-pressure sales tactics should be met with capital punishment.

The effect of high-pressure selling shows through in some of the vacuum cleaner cases in the sample. For some salesmen, the discovery that the household already had a satisfactory vacuum cleaner was not reason to give up, but simply an indicator of the need for a change in the pitch. Thus in one case, the salesman persuaded the household to buy a vacuum cleaner in the expectation that it would be more efficient than the one that they already had. The household concluded afterwards that it was less efficient than their old one. (Indeed, one vacuum cleaner salesman told the writer that it was fairly common for him to sell a cleaner that was not as good as the one taken in part exchange.) In another case, the buyer was asked, 'Have you been using it during the last month?' The reply was 'No'. When asked 'Why not?', the answer was: 'I gave it away. I don't like anything electric.'

As the consumer movement gathered momentum in the 1960s, one of its demands in Britain and elsewhere was for action to curtail the predatory activities of door-to-door salesmen. The response of the government was the enactment of the cooling-off period.[1] Buyers who signed contracts at the home would be given a chance to reconsider the matter after being released from the compelling influence of the salesman. Thus the essence of the cooling-off period was that the buyer had four days during which the contract could be cancelled by sending a written notice of cancellation to the seller. The four-day period began when the buyer received the second copy of the contract document. This cooling-off period (or right to cancel) applied to any credit sale agreement where the total purchase price was between £30 and £2,000, and to any hire-purchase or conditional sale agreement where the total purchase price did not exceed £2,000, and where in any such case, the contract document was signed '. . .at a place other than appropriate trade premises'. To make the protection effective, the Act and regulations required that a notice informing the buyer of the right to cancel must appear in red on both copies of the agreement that the consumer received.[2]

Even before the enactment of the cooling-off period, there were grounds on which a contract to purchase could be avoided or rescinded; e.g., fraud, mistake, infancy, illegality, public policy, or non-delivery of the goods. The advantages of the cooling-off period were thought to be:

1. *Hire-Purchase Act*, 1965, SS. 11-15.

2. These provisions have been amended and replaced in the *Consumer Credit Act*, 1974, SS. 66-73.

(1) The buyer would be able to rescind the contract in all circumstances, whether or not there would otherwise be cause for doing so.
(2) Because the right to cancel would not be dependent on any showing of cause, the buyer would also be relieved of other problems; in particular the necessity for evidence of cause and the risks inherent in litigation, including the possibility that a judge might take a different view of the facts relating to the cause for cancellation.
(3) Although most buyers would be unaware of the circumstances in which they would otherwise be entitled to avoid or rescind a contract, the statutory right to cancel would be brought to their attention in the contract itself in simple and unmistakeable terms.
(4) If a buyer tried to cancel on one of the other grounds, the seller might still be able to coerce payment. He could challenge the buyer's right to cancel, and indeed his ignorance of the law may equal or exceed that of the buyer. The statutory cooling-off period, stated in clear terms in the contract, would confer a right of cancellation beyond doubt or dispute.

The value claimed for the cooling-off period is that a buyer is enabled to consider whether to be bound by the contract after being freed from any hypnotic influence of the sales pitch. A buyer can reflect on the transaction, consider whether he wants the goods, whether he wants them at the price required by the contract, and whether he wants to pay cash or buy on credit. Moreover, the period enables him to seek additional information and to engage in comparative shopping.

There were several reasons why it was thought that the problem should be tackled by a remedy that focused on sales at the home, rather than on retail transactions generally.

(1) In most types of retailing the buyer knows at least that he is dealing with a seller and can gauge his conduct accordingly. Many sales at the home, however, begin with a phoney introduction denying that the caller is a salesman. This may confuse the buyer and neutralise sales resistance.
(2) When buying a consumer durable at retail premises, a customer has at least taken the initiative of going there. The chances are, therefore, that he will have given some preliminary thought to whether the family needs the item and how much they can afford to pay for it. Conversely, when a salesman calles at the home, he may catch the family totally unprepared for any business transaction, let alone the purchase of the particular item that he is selling. Of those on the survey who bought the item from a shop or garage, 5 per cent replied that they did not

think of buying an item of that type before going to the seller's premises. Of those who bought from a salesman who called at the home, 16 per cent replied that they did not think of buying an item of that type before the salesman called. Of those who bought at a shop, 51 per cent reported looking at similar items for sale at other places before buying. Of those who bought from a salesman who called at the home, 26 per cent reported looking at items of that type in the shops prior to buying.

(3) The privacy of the home atmosphere makes the household more vulnerable to a high-pressure sales pitch. An efficient salesman can generally hold the attention of the household, and they cannot walk out as they can at a shop.

(4) Sometimes the presence of the salesman in the home and the length of time that he stays create an anxiety or weariness, and some buyers have even complained of acute physical fear.[1] There is sometimes an intense desire to be rid of the salesman, and signing what he wants the householders to sign may seem like the easiest way of inducing him to go. On the survey, most of the salesmen who called at the home seemed to have come at a reasonable hour and to have stayed a reasonable length of time. But in the case involving cooking utensils, the salesman was reported to be in the home for 4 hours terminating at 11 p.m., and in 2 of the vacuum cleaner cases, the salesman was reported to be in the home for 2 hours. In one vacuum cleaner case, the buyer complained to the interviewer that the salesman had stayed too long.

(5) Calling at homes is an expensive method of distribution. A car is generally necessary, and time must be spent arousing the interest of people who may have no initial desire for the product. The salesman's time and operating expenses may be covered by commission, and the desire to earn that commission can create an incentive to sell by whatever methods succeed. Moreover, there is commonly no countervailing interest. A merchant operating from retail premises often has goodwill to consider. He may want repeat business and a good reputation in the community. For these, he needs satisfied customers. A salesman who calls at homes selling only one type of item may have no such need.

(6) While some shops pressure customers to buy, most do not, and there is not the same necessity for pressure at retail premises. If a customer is browsing in contemplation of buying a major item, but does not seem inclined to purchase on this visit, there is still the chance that

1. *The Final Report of the Committee on Consumer Protection*, 1962, Cmnd 1781, para.742.

he may return. Salesmen who call at the home, however, feel compelled to take the view that it's now or never.

(7) Any allegations of fraud by a seller at retail premises are easier to investigate than allegations of fraud by a seller calling at the home. Salesmen, like the rest of us, tend to be creatures of habit. No doubt isolated instances of fraud occur. But in many of the more notorious rackets, the fraud is a planned scheme involving a constantly repeated performance. Thus if it is alleged that a misrepresentation is being made, it is an easy matter to send investigators to pose as customers at retail premises. It is much more difficult to locate door-to-door salesmen, to have investigators pose as potential customers, and thereby to obtain evidence of the sales pitch. This is relevant not only to the likely result of any inquiry, but also to the prospects of getting an inquiry started.

On the survey, questions were asked about cancellation and about notification of the right to cancel. Of the 39 transaction credit cases involving contracts signed at the home there were 2 in which notice of the right to cancel was not required. One was a credit sale for less than £30. The other was for a fitted carpet (which might be regarded as a contract for work and materials rather than for the sale of goods). Of the remaining 37 cases, the buyer claimed that there never was any written agreement in 2. In 19, the interviewer was not able to see a copy of the agreement. In 16, the buyer had one or both of his copies of the agreement available and permitted the interviewer to see them. The notice was there in 14 and not there in 2.

Earlier in the interview, the buyers had been asked 'Were you informed that you could return the [item], or cancel the deal, within a limited time?' For the 14 cases in which the interviewer saw the notice of cancellation in the contract, the answers to this earlier question are interesting. Six answered no, and only one answered that he recalled having been informed in the contract of a right to cancel. The remainder recalled that they had been informed of a right to cancel, but that they had been so informed by the salesman or in other ways than in the contract.

The survey results also showed that contracts including a notice of the right to cancel were used frequently in situations in which they were not required by law. There were 159 transaction credit cases in which the contract had been signed at a shop or other retail premises, and in which the interviewer was able to see the buyer's copy of the agreement. It was found that the notice of the right to cancel was present and in red in 46 of those cases. The notice was there but not in red in a further 21, and in 87 there was no notice of a right to cancel. Area gas boards and area electricity boards were prominent among those who included the right to cancel in contracts used for sales at trade premises.

It is not obvious why many retailers use contracts including the right to cancel for sales at trade premises, but in most cases it seems to be deliberate, not the result of inadvertence. A possible explanation is that it may help a large retailer to control any excessive zeal on the part of any salesman who may be inclined to talk a customer into ordering something that he obviously will not want. Another possible explanation is that it may foster goodwill and promote sales to provide that customers can change their minds. It may also serve to encourage cancellation by people with second thoughts about the purchase, so that those who are likely to default in payments are encouraged to cancel before delivery of the goods. A less healthy explanation is that once the cancellation period has passed, the notice can be used thereafter to convince the customer that he cannot cancel the contract, even though he may have good cause.

There were 2 transaction credit cases among the contracts signed at the home in which the buyer tried to cancel, in neither case within the cooling-off period. One was a vacuum cleaner case in which the buyer cancelled 14 days after receiving the second copy of the agreement. The seller agreed to cancellation and refunded the money that had been paid but did not return the cleaner taken in part exchange. The other case involved a television. The buyer tried to cancel 6 months after purchase and the seller refused.

As protection against the abuses sometimes involved in sales at the home, the cooling-off period had (and still has) severe limitations. First, the period during which the contract could be cancelled was four days commencing with the day on which the second copy of the agreement was received. The right to cancel, therefore, normally expired within a week or so from the date of the contract. This would commonly be before delivery of the goods. Thus while the cooling-off period may offer some protection against high-pressure salesmanship, it is no protection against the marketing of shoddy goods, or against misrepresentations as to quality. The cooling-off period could be modified so that the period would not begin until delivery of the goods; but no doubt sellers would object to the trouble and expense of delivering the goods while the contract is still subject to cancellation. As the mail order companies have shown, however, it is a possible way of doing business.

Secondly, only some buyers ever become aware of the right to cancel. Contracts involving transaction credit are sufficiently complicated in their form and jargon that the bulk of the population, and particularly those whose occupations do not involve the scrutiny of documents, can surely be forgiven for not reading them. A survey conducted by NOP Market Research Limited for the Crowther Committee[1] asked 'Did you know that with a doorstep salesman, you have the right to cancel any document that is signed, provided you do it fairly quickly?' Only 53 per cent answered yes,

1. Published by the Department of Trade and Industry (1971).

despite the leading form of the question and although it was only asked of those who had used any form of credit during the preceding year. Of the cases on the survey conducted by the writer in which the interviewer saw a notice of the right to cancel in the contract, only about 25 per cent of the respondents had answered earlier questions to the effect that they knew of the right to cancel because they had found it stated in the contract.

Thirdly, even if a buyer reads the contract in time and discovers the right to cancel, it still requires sending a 'notice of cancellation'. The survey data indicate that selling at the home is concentrated fairly heavily among people in the lower income ranges, in the social grades C2, D and E, and whose home conditions were described by the interviewer as fair or poor. For this section of the population, notices in writing are things that they receive, not things that they send. Like so many legal remedies, the cooling-off period protects the more sophisticated sections of the community, not those who need the protection most. This particular point might, however, be met to some extent by requiring a tear-off slip to be attached to the contract which the buyer can simply tear off and mail if he wishes to cancel.[1]

Fourthly, the people most vulnerable to selling at the home are not the most vigilant to defend themselves with documentary weapons. The crises of today preclude the development of habits that would enable them to plan their affairs to avoid the crises of tomorrow. A businessman may sit down and read a contract after the salesman has gone. But families scraping by on a marginal income are probably more likely to forget the matter until the goods arrive, or until the first instalment becomes due. It may be only the sight of the unwanted goods or of the unwanted bills that impresses upon them the necessity to do something.

Fifthly, there are many ways in which the cooling-off period can be avoided, or its significance evaded, by any unscrupulous seller. All of the following methods have been used.

(1) Selling items at a price slightly below £30 and using credit sale agreements so that the cooling-off period was not applicable. This practice has been widespread in the past although inflation may be making it obsolete.

(2) Using a credit sale agreement under which the price is payable by four instalments. The cooling-off period is then not applicable.[2]

1. This was recommended in the *Report of the Committee on Consumer Credit*, 1971, Cmnd 4596, para.6.7.3. The government indicated its intention to adopt the recommendation. *Reform of the Law on Consumer Credit*, 1973, Cmnd 5427, para.40.

2. This is still the position. See *The Consumer Credit (Exempt Agreements) Order 1977*, SI No. 326, Reg. 3.

It may well be that the instalments are too large for the buyer to pay, but, as an act of grace, the seller can subsequently allow each instalment to be paid in smaller amounts. A variation on this is to provide in the written agreement for a deposit payable immediately and the balance to be payable upon delivery or installation. But as a practical matter, the seller indicates a willingness to accept instalments.

(3) Shuffling the buyer's copy of the contract together with a collection of promotional literature. The whole collection can then be placed in a fancy envelope and stapled. The salesman impresses upon the buyer the importance of putting it away.[1] The second statutory copy may not be sent.

(4) At the climax of the sales pitch, the customer is taken out to the salesman's car and driven to some trade premises at which the contract is signed. In England, the cooling-off period is then not applicable. Some other jurisdictions cover this point by applying the cooling-off period to contracts solicited at the home, as well as those signed at the home.[2]

(5) The seller can ignore the cooling-off period and behave as if it had never been enacted. The statutory notification can be left out of the contract, or put in using some technique to keep it from the buyer's attention. Most people will pay, and if they refuse, they can usually be coerced by dunning letters, the threat of an adverse credit report, or the threat of court proceedings. If someone wants to cancel within the cooling-off period, he is told that it does not apply. If he sends a written notice of cancellation, the seller can ignore it and keep sending the bills. If the buyer still does not pay, a County Court summons can be issued. The chances are that the buyer will pay at that stage, or if not, that a default judgement can be obtained. If a particular buyer goes to a solicitor or otherwise pleads the notice of cancellation as a defence, that particular claim can be settled or abandoned. As long as the number of buyers in this category is small, the others may be enough to maintain a profitable business.

(6) The transaction can be dressed up to look like a sale of services which might be provided before or after payment, so that no credit is necessarily involved. For example, two contracts can be used, the first being a credit sale agreement for a 25-volume encyclopedia set

1. See 'How the Man With a Stapler Breaks the H.P. Law', *The Sunday Times*, 24 December 1967.

2. For example, the *Consumer Protection Act* of Ontario, S.33, makes the cooling-off period applicable 'Where a seller solicits, negotiates or arranges for the signing by a buyer of an executory contract at a place other than the seller's permanent place of business. . .'

at a price of £10, the other, which is signed at the same time, being a contract for an information service available over a period of years, costing £215, to be paid by instalments. If a case like this ever came to trial, the court might recognise the arrangement as a sham, and treat it as a contract to which the cooling-off period applies. This does not mean, however, that the ruse will not work. The device may be enough to convince the buyer that he is in trouble and had better pay.

(7) A similar device was to split the goods and use separate contracts, for example, one contract for the vacuum cleaner and another for the attachments. As long as each contract was a credit sale agreement under £30, each could be made to look like a contract to which the cooling-off period was not applicable. The legal consequences of this under the former *Hire-Purchase Act* do not appear to have been tested.[1] Under the *Consumer Credit Act*, 1974, it is now clear that these contracts will be treated as one regulated agreement to which the cooling-off period applies.[2]

(8) A loan form of finance could be used. The salesman acts as agent for the seller and also as agent for a finance company that advances loans. Each transaction is documented as a cash sale with the buyer obtaining the money by way of loan from the finance company. Here again, the legal position under the former *Hire-Purchase Act* was not fully tested in litigation.[3] However, one of the purposes of the *Consumer Credit Act*, 1974, was to provide that the consumer protection provisions that applied to sales finance could not be avoided by using the documentation of a loan. Thus the cooling-off period now applies to sales at the home whether documented by loan or sales finance.[4]

(9) If someone wants to cancel, his first move may be to telephone or call in person rather than send the statutory notice. If he does that, the seller can soothe him with evasive but encouraging responses. The buyer can be led to believe that his deposit will be returned, although without expressly promising that it will. Friendly and encouraging comments

1. 'As far as [Citizens' Advice Bureau] headquarters is aware, however, the point has not been tested in court and no enquirer at a C.A.B. has been willing (even on the advice of a solicitor) to stand the suspense of refusing to accept the commitment and waiting to see if the company concerned will bring the matter to court.' *Memorandum of the National Citizens' Advice Bureaux Council to The Committee on Consumer Credit*, 1969, p.4.

2. S.17 (3).

3. In a Canadian case not involving the cooling-off period in which the financing was arranged in this way, the court took the view that the loan company had so identified itself with the seller as to be subject to the same defences as if the seller and credit grantor were one. *Beneficial Finance Co. v. Kulig*, (1970) 13 DLR (3d) 134.

4. SS.67-73.

can be kept up until the cooling-off period has expired.

(10) The contract and any ancillary documents can be predated by seven days. The chances are that the buyer will not notice this at least until several weeks later. He is likely to remember receiving the second copy of the contract (or notice of the right to cancel) a few days after signing, but less likely to remember on which date either event occurred. If he sends a notice of cancellation, he can be told, after 3 or 4 weeks of delay, that it was too late. If his recollection of dates is not very accurate, he may actually believe it. Even if his recollection is accurate, he may not want to take the risk that a court would believe his recollection when it is inconsistent with the date on the contract.

(11) If a buyer gives notice of cancellation, the seller can keep the deposit or the item taken in part exchange. As long as the money involved is not large, the buyer may not sue. Also hints that the buyer would not recover his deposit, or the item taken in part exchange, might be enough to induce him to adhere to the contract rather than cancel.

Except for (7) and (8), the above methods of avoiding or evading the cooling-off period are still available.

The objections to the cooling-off period are not, however, limited to the ease of evasion. It is even arguable that the cooling-off period does more harm than good. The trouble with telling people that they have five days during which they may cancel a contract is that the converse is also implied, i.e., that the contract cannot be cancelled after that period. People may be induced to believe that once the period has expired they have no right of cancellation. This is not the law and never has been. Indeed, it is the experience of the writer that where a transaction credit contract has been signed with a door-to-door salesman, and where the buyer feels sufficiently aggrieved that he wants to cancel the contract, then in virtually every case he has legal grounds for doing so apart from the cooling-off period.

A usual ground is that the contract is voidable for misrepresentation. One reason why this defence is not recognised more often is that buyers are not usually cross-examined with a view to discovering its existence. In the typical case, the buyer does not go to a solicitor, a Citizens' Advice Bureau, or the office of a County Court, and say 'I want to cancel this contract because the salesman lied to me (or was wrong) when he said. . .' More commonly the buyer says simply that he cannot afford to pay, or that he was talked into it, or that he does not want the item, or that it does not work. It is only by thorough probing that a defence of misrepresentation can be discovered. For example 'How did the salesman first communicate with you? What did he say when you opened the door? What did he say next?' After the buyer has related the tale as best he can remember it in response to general questions, he can then be prodded with more specific questions, such as 'What did he tell you about how much you would have to pay? What did he tell you about the terms of payment? Did he tell you what the [item] normally sells for? Did he describe the [item]? What did he tell you about operating costs? What did he say the [item] would contain? What did he say it would do?', etc. After the representations have been ascertained in this way, their truth or accuracy can then be considered. Apart from the prospect of revealing a defence, cross-examination on these lines can reveal a counter-claim for damages for deceit or for breach of contract.

In many cases, other grounds for avoiding the contract are also available. Very often, objections can also be raised that the seller has failed to observe the legal requirements relating to documentation.

If a buyer wishing to cancel seeks advice from a Citizens' Advice Bureau, the normal practice is to determine first whether the cooling-off period is applicable. Once it has been determined, however, that the cooling-off period has expired, or is otherwise not applicable, the normal practice is then to conclude that 'there is no way out', or 'you are stuck with what you signed'. A common practice is then to attempt the negotiation of a compromise with the seller or lender.[1] But because there has been no probing to discover other defences, the chances are that in the negotiation of any compromise, the bargaining position of the buyer will have been under-estimated.

The results of the cooling-off period are not easily measurable. It may have had a depressing influence on door-to-door selling among the more articulate sections of the community likely to take advantage of the right to cancel. On the other hand, the survey showed that sales at the home still represented a substantial proportion of the sales of consumer durables, and that, notwithstanding the cooling-off period, they still involved the abuses with which door-to-door selling had long been associated.

Moreover, following the enactment of the cooling-off period, door-to-door selling expanded in some of its worse forms. The scandals in heating equipment sold by door-to-door salesmen emerged in the late 1960s. In some cases, deposits were taken with nothing further being done, and in others loan contracts were signed and enforced with no honest effort on

1. Interviews with CAB organisers in 1969 and in 1977. See also *I didn't realize it was a Contract, Fair Do's*, 1977, Office of Fair Trading, p.ii. This point is further discussed in Chapter 9, p.237.

the part of the sellers to perform the obligations that they had undertaken. The equipment supplied was often unsuitable or badly fitted, and buyers fared much worse than if they had gone to a local heating contractor. Another example during the same period was the expansion in the door-to-door selling of double glazing, again with the traditional abuses.[1] Then the freezer racket, known for years in North America, expanded into Britain.[2] This might well be thought the most insidious of all because it often seeks out for its victims families who are having difficulty in paying for food.[3]

Door-to-door selling still continues, along with the traditional complaints of phoney introductions, high-pressure tactics, misrepresentations, high prices and sometimes defective products or non-delivery. The type of item sold in this way, however, varies from time to time. For example, the door-to-door selling of encylcopedias and of vacuum cleaners appears to have been discontinued, at least for the time being. The sale of heating equipment and of double glazing in this way appears to have slackened. But the magazine racket continues, and the saucepan racket has been revived in recent years. The sale of home improvements, and of hearing aids[4] appears to have expanded, and a start has been made on the door-to-door selling of solar heating.[5]

There appears to be a widespread feeling that, except in relation to home improvements, there has been a reduction in recent years in the volume of complaints about door-to-door selling.[6] If this is correct, however, it could be due to factors other than the cooling-off period. Part of the explanation might lie, for example, in:

1. See e.g. *Report of the Committee on Consumer Credit*, 1971, Cmnd 4596, para.2.1.19.

2. *Which?*, July 1969.

3. The freezer racket takes various forms. Sometimes the household is offered a freezer at a bargain price, but the sale is tied in with the supply of frozen food, the price of which is concealed, but which turns out to be more than in the shops. Another variation is to sell the frozen food at a bargain price, the sale being tied in with the supply of a freezer, the cost of which is concealed, but which turns out to be much higher than the price of similar freezers in the shops. One way or another, the buyer pays more for the combination of food and freezer than he would pay if he bought the two separately in the shops. Complaints are also common that the quality, quantity, or availability of the food is not what the customer had been led to expect. See e.g. *Counsel for the Deceived*, P.G. Schrag, 1972, Pantheon Books, p.1.

4. See e.g. *The Provision of Health Aids by Commercial Organizations*, December 1975, evidence paper E75/2, National Association of Citizens' Advice Bureaux, London.

5. The information for these comments was mostly derived from interviews conducted in 1977 at Citizens' Advice Bureaux, Consumer Advice Centres, Trading Standards Departments, the Consumers' Association, the Office of Fair Trading, and a newspaper readers' advisory service.

6. Ibid.

(1) the extensive publicity surrounding and following the establishment of the Office of Fair Trading, which might have helped to make people more knowledgeable about predatory practices in marketing;
(2) the slackening of the economy, which may have made people more cautious about their spending, and about financial commitments, and which may also have made sellers more conscious of the risk of default;
(3) the operational improvements in the County Courts in relation to small claims, which may have made sellers more conscious of the possibility that a claim might be defended.

Many of the abuses have occurred in situations in which loan documentation has been used, and in which the contract might be considered one for work and materials, so that the cooling-off period was not applicable. But with the *Consumer Credit Act*, 1974, now coming into effect (in 1977) that gap is being closed. As explained above, however, other methods of avoidance or evasion still survive.

To deal with the abuses involved in door-to-door selling, another approach that has been tried is mediation. In 1969, and four years after the enactment of the cooling-off period, officials of the Board of Trade (as it was then called) were aware that the fraud and other abuses in door-to-door selling had not been eliminated. One way they tried to deal with the problem was by direct negotiations with encyclopedia companies and others engaged in selling at the home. But for several reasons, this approach was either a failure or a very limited success.

(1) People engaged in door-to-door selling, or likely to take it up, are too heterogeneous to be dealt with by solicitation through the old boy network.
(2) The approach has no deterrent effect.
(3) Some companies may recognise that they are not likely to market their products in substantial volume except by the tactics involved in door-to-door selling. Where that is so, it is unrealistic to expect them to be responsive to reasonable discussion.
(4) Mediation may be effective in some circumstances, for example, where responsible directors of a large company may not be fully conscious of what is happening at the grass roots. But it is not an approach that has any potential for dealing with small scale racketeers.

The approach currently being adopted is to require that those whose business involves selling on credit by canvassing off trade premises must have a special licence to do so.[1] For reasons discussed later,[2] that may be a marginal benefit, but it is not likely to stop the abuses.

In seeking to control abuses in door-to-door selling, it is extremely difficult to regulate the details of the selling behaviour. Any remedy would be inadequate if it depended upon an inquiry into the actual behaviour of the salesman in a particular case. Indeed, recognition of this is implicit in the enactment of the cooling-off period. Remedies must be aimed either at the market structure, or at having a general influence on behaviour.

It is suggested that the most promising approach would be to identify the category of door-to-door selling that gives rise to the abuses, and then impose a total prohibition on door-to-door selling of that type.

The more innocuous types of door-to-door selling that could be excepted from the prohibition might include:

(1) Those who sell for cash without requiring any payment in advance.
(2) Tradesmen making regular deliveries, for example, the milkman, the grocer, etc.
(3) The tallymen; those who call regularly within the same area on substantially the same customers selling a range of different goods.

Thus the prohibition would apply to itinerant salesmen selling one type of item on credit terms or who require part-payment in advance.

The argument for the prohibition is that it is the only effective way to eliminate the evils. The survey data show that, apart from the cases involving a salesman who calls regularly, 49 per cent of the sales at the home were reported to involve major or substantial objections either to the selling methods or to the condition of the goods. Many people are coerced into ordering what they do not want, and others do not receive goods of the quality that they have been led to expect. Moreover, the harm that flows from these transactions is not limited to the improvidence of the bargain. Added to that are the anxieties and domestic strains that result from wasted expenditure, and the diversion of funds from more necessary purposes. Moreover, the harm is not limited to that suffered by the buyers. Legitimate business suffers from the diversion of consumer expenditure, and from having to compete with the less scrupulous door-to-door operators in obtaining the payment of bills.

Further, there are the social costs incurred by society at large. The first of these is the economic waste of salesmen engaging their time on worthless activity. The second is the lack of integrity that is cultivated by the

1. *Consumer Credit Act*, 1974, S.23.
2. Chapter 12, p.385.

salesmen and then spread by teaching and example to the next generation. The third is a loss of confidence in a legal system that appears to condone and support the perpetration of fraud and other predatory practices.

By comparison, the harm that would flow from the prohibition does not seem great. First, some people who might otherwise buy an item from a salesman calling at the home would be put to the inconvenience of buying it from a retail outlet or by mail order.

Secondly, some people who have done nothing wrong would be denied the opportunity of carrying on the trade of their choice in the way in which they would like to do it, and which, so far as they are concerned, is not proven to be harmful. The survey shows that in the cases in which the item was sold at the home, otherwise than by a salesman who called regularly selling different types of goods, 23 per cent were reported to be entirely satisfactory both with regard to selling methods and the condition of the goods, and a further 28 per cent were reported to involve only minor objections. It appears, therefore, that a substantial proportion of selling at the home is legitimate business. This seems to be the most cogent objection to a prohibition of door-to-door selling. It is undesirable to restrict the freedom of one group to protect the public from harm done by another group. On the other hand, we frequently accept this as a necessary way to prevent harm that would otherwise result. Law cannot always be tailored for each individual. This principle is accepted, for example, in the way that cash loans are treated in the *Consumer Credit Act*. 'It is an offence to canvass debtor-creditor agreements off trade premises.'[1] It is suggested that, subject to some exceptions, door-to-door selling should be prohibited in the same way.

Thirdly, it might be argued that any foreclosure of a channel of distribution is an undesirable restraint upon competition. This argument, however, is a difficult one to press in the particular context. Door-to-door selling is a high-cost method of distribution compared with either shop sales or mail order. It is difficult to see what benefits of competition the public can possibly derive.

A more difficult area to tackle is the home improvement contracts: for example, contracts for central heating, roof repairs, or insulation. Anyone undertaking this type of contract would need to call at the home. The difficulty therefore lies in developing a workable formula and mechanism for distinguishing the legitimate heating contractor or builder from the itinerant rogue.

It is suggested that home improvement contracts should be dealt with in two ways:

1. S.49 (1).

(1) By making it an offence to engage in certain marketing techniques that are known to cause trouble; for example, obtaining a signed statement from the buyer that the work has been completed.
(2) By prohibiting the solicitation of home improvement contracts by anyone except an officer or employee of a company that itself undertakes work of the type being sold, or an individual who himself does the work, or his employee. In other words, no one should be allowed to solicit home improvement contracts unless he is in the business of doing home improvements. Recent changes have moved the law towards that position. Anyone taking orders for home improvements by canvassing off trade premises now requires a licence,[1] and it is apparently government policy that licences '. . .will not be available to independent salesmen who are not themselves, or who do not represent, either providers of the credit or sellers of the goods or services involved.[2]

The situation might also have been improved by the inclusion of home improvement contracts in the general provision that where a lender has advanced credit for the purchase of goods or services as a result of some prior connection or arrangement with the supplier, then no matter what documents are used or how the arrangement is described, all defences that the buyer would have on a claim by the supplier will also be available on a claim by the lender. Recent changes in the legal position on this are discussed in Chapter 11.

4. Electricity and Gas Board Sales

Since 1972, the area gas boards have become part of the British Gas Corporation. But the area names of the former gas boards are still used for the regions of the new corporation. These regional divisions of the British Gas Corporation are still popularly known as 'the gas board'.

As shown in Table 5.2, p.88, selling methods at electricity and gas board showrooms (grouped together and as reported by the buyers) were open to objection in proportionately more cases than at other retail premises.

A breakdown as between electricity boards and the gas boards, however, shows that it was in gas cases that more of the trouble was reported. Chart 5.1, page 122, shows the reported selling methods in the gas board cases compared with electricity boards, and with other sellers. Chart 5.2, page 123, shows the same comparisons with regard to the condition of the goods. Those who bought from a gas board reported unfortunate

1. *Consumer Credit Act*, 1974, S.23.
2. *Reform of the Law on Consumer Credit*, 1973, Cmnd 5427, para.33.

Chart 5.1: Electricity Boards, Gas Boards, and Other Sellers Compared (Except Mail Order Cases)

Item and seller	Selling Methods: Major objections	Substantial objections	Minor objections	Entirely satisfactory	Totals
Vacuum cleaners					
Electricity boards	–	–	5	11	16
Other sellers	4	8	14	83	109
Central heating					
Electricity boards	1	–	1	1	3
Gas boards	–	3	1	3	7
Other sellers	4	4	4	21	33
Electric fires					
Electricity boards	–	–	–	6	6
Other sellers	–	–	–	10	10
Gas fires					
Gas boards	12	8	3	22	45
Other sellers	1	–	–	7	8
Storage heaters					
Electricity boards	1	1	2	6	10
Other sellers	–	1	–	6	7
Refrigerators and freezers					
Electricity boards	–	–	2	13	15
Gas boards	1	1	–	–	2
Other sellers	–	–	6	27	33
Cookers					
Electricity boards	2	1	1	17	21
Gas boards	2	6	3	28	39
Other sellers	–	–	–	5	5
Washing machines, dryers, or combinations					
Electricity boards	–	4	1	5	10
Other sellers	2	3	4	28	37
Totals*					
Electricity boards	4 (5)	6 (7)	12 (15)	59 (73)	81 (100)
Gas boards	15 (16)	18 (19)	7 (8)	53 (57)	93 (100)
Other sellers	11 (5)	16 (7)	28 (12)	187 (77)	242 (101)

*Percentage figures in brackets.

Chart 5.2: Electricity Boards, Gas Boards and Other Sellers Compared (Except Mail Order Cases)

Item and seller	Condition of goods				
	Major objections	Substantial objections	Minor objections	Entirely satisfactory	Totals
Vacuum cleaners					
Electricity boards	2	1	6	7	16
Other sellers	7	10	24	68	109
Central heating					
Electricity boards	—	—	2	1	3
Gas boards	—	2	2	3	7
Other sellers	3	3	16	11	33
Electric fires					
Electricity boards	—	—	2	4	6
Other sellers	—	1	1	8	10
Gas fires					
Gas boards	7	5	13	20	45
Other sellers	—	—	5	3	8
Storage heaters					
Electricity boards	—	—	4	6	10
Other sellers	—	—	2	5	7
Refrigerators and freezers					
Electricity boards	—	1	—	14	15
Gas boards	—	—	—	2	2
Other sellers	—	4	8	21	33
Cookers					
Electricity boards	4	—	4	13	21
Gas boards	2	3	10	24	39
Other sellers	—	1	2	2	5
Washing machines, dryers, or combinations					
Electricity boards	1	1	3	5	10
Other sellers	4	4	6	23	37
Totals*					
Electricity boards	7 (9)	3 (4)	21 (26)	50 (62)	81 (101)
Gas boards	9 (9)	10 (11)	25 (26)	51 (54)	93 (100)
Other sellers	14 (6)	23 (10)	64 (27)	141 (58)	242 (101)

*Percentage figures in brackets.

experiences in proportionately more cases than those who bought items serving the same purpose from an electricity board or other seller. Those who bought from electricity boards and 'other sellers' were much closer together.

None of the electricity board cases involved salesmen calling at the home. Six gas fires and 12 gas cookers were sold by salesmen of an area gas board calling at the home (or were sold at the showroom following a call at the home). As Table 5.10, page 99, shows, salesmen from a gas board were among the categories of door-to-door salesmen having a high proportion of objections to their selling methods. During the year 1969/70, the area gas boards employed a total of about 4,300 outside or 'district' sales staff and their turnover was approximately £33 million. This compared with a turnover of appliance sales effected in the showrooms during the same year of approximately £38 million.[1]

It may be of interest to itemise the troubles reported in the gas board cases.

Central Heating

The sample included 7 cases of central heating sold by an area gas board. Two of these were classified as entirely satisfactory, both with regard to selling methods and the condition of the goods, and 1 was classified as having only minor objections. The problems reported in the remaining 4 cases were as follows:

(1) Delay in delivery 8-28 days beyond the date by which delivery had been promised. Within 2 months after installation, a switch broke. The buyer asked the gas board to repair the switch, but nothing was done in response to the request.

(2) The plumber finished all his part of the job, but the heating system was still not operative because the gas board failed to move the meter. Despite requests from the buyer, there was a long delay, and when the meter was eventually moved, it was still not connected to the furnace. In the meantime, the buyer wrote a letter of complaint to a newspaper. The buyer described the situation as 'terrible' and felt that the gas board should not be entitled to the full contract price. When the system was at last made usable, parts broke, but the gas board effected repairs.

(3) The central heating system was the gas board's own brand name. The buyer was induced by the advertising to expect it to be quiet in operation whereas it turned out to be noisy. The performance was not

1. *Memorandum Submitted by the Gas Council on Relations with the Public of the Gas Council and Area Gas Boards*, to the Select Committee on Nationalised Industries, 1971, p.5.

as good as the salesman said it would be, and the operating cost was more than the salesman said. Parts broke. They were repaired by the gas board to the buyer's satisfaction, but he was charged for the repair whereas he felt that it should have been done under the guarantee.

(4) The salesman erred in estimating the buyer's need. The salesman assured the buyer that he would not need a radiator in a particular room but the buyer found that he did. Parts broke, the unit overheated, and a timing device went wrong. However, repairs were done willingly by the gas board to the buyer's satisfaction and without charge.

Gas Fires

There were 44 cases in the sample in which a gas fire (or other type of gas room heater) was purchased from an area gas board. In 17 of these, the transaction was classified as entirely satisfactory both with regard to selling methods and the condition of the goods. In a further 4 cases, there were only minor objections. The remaining 23 cases were classified as involving major or substantial objections. In a sample 5 of these, the problems reported were as follows:

(1) When ordering, the customer was told by the salesman that the fire would have an automatic time switch, but it did not. The gas board mislaid the order and never gave the customer a copy although it was a HP transaction. The customer was not promised a specific delivery date, but it took 5 months from the date of the order and the customer missed the entire heating season. When she got fed up with the fire not coming, the customer tried to cancel the order but was told that she could not because the fire had already been delivered. Half an hour later the supervisor phoned to apologise for the mistake. The buyer was annoyed when the gas board started demanding payment for the fire before delivery. The gas board then agreed to payments being suspended until installation.

(2) The salesman stated that the outer case of the fire that the customer was ordering would not get hot, but it does. Delivery was delayed in excess of 28 days beyond the date by which delivery had been promised. On arrival of the fire, the back plates were missing and a tube was broken by the installer. The fire kept jamming and did not operate properly. The automatic ignition was defective. Repairs were effected by the gas board without charge, but the customer had to wait a considerable time for the repairs to be done. The customer complained that the gas board made a claim for overdue payments when no payments were overdue, but subsequently they apologised.

(3) The customer bought a gas space heater. When the customer was buying the unit, the salesman assured him that the casing would not get hot, but it reached 210°F. Following the customer's complaint, the salesman stated that his office had never fitted this type of equipment before. The customer felt that he should have been told this in the first place so that he would know he was taking a chance on an item about which the gas board personnel had no knowledge. The unit was not properly installed, but operated correctly after modification. The gas board tried to solve the problem of excessive heat on the casing, but unsuccessfully.

(4) The customers discovered that the gas pipe was not adequate for the full capacity of the fire. They felt that they should have been warned of this possibility at the time of ordering. They tried to cancel the contract, but the gas board would not agree to cancellation. The gas tubes were smashed in transit and the automatic ignition did not work properly. The gas board refitted the fire without charge and it then worked satisfactorily, but the customers still had some regrets about ugly pipes being visible where they did not want them. Also the response of the gas board to their complaints was very reluctant. The customers had to insist a great deal and had to wait three months during the winter for things to be fixed.

(5) There was a delay in delivery of 8-28 days beyond the date by which delivery had been promised. After delivery of the unit, a further delay of 2 months occurred before installation. The salesman who had called at the home originally to solicit the order told them that the equipment would fit their fireplace, and continued to maintain that view, but the fitter insisted that it would not. The salesman and the fitter called several times alternately, the one saying that it would fit and the other that it would not. The customers described the mixup as 'disgusting'. The gas board personnel kept losing records. The customers added that they want to get central heating, but they dread going to the gas board.

Gas Cookers

There were 39 cases in the sample involving the sale of a gas cooker by an area gas board. In 19, the transaction was classified as entirely satisfactory both with regard to selling methods and the condition of the goods, and in one of these cases, the buyer described the gas board as 'a good solid firm'. In these cases, there were no objections as far as the customer was concerned, but one case seemed to involve an evasion of the deposit requirement of the Control Orders and the quotation in the contract of a fictitious cash price. Also the period prescribed for paying the instalments exceeded the maximum permitted by the Control Orders. In a further 10 cases, there were only minor objections. The remaining 10 cases were classified as involving major or substantial objections. In a sample 5 of these, the problems reported were as follows:

(1) There was a delay in delivery of 8-28 days beyond the date by which delivery had been promised. The automatic lighter would only operate one ring. Some parts broke and others became loose. The customer complained to the gas board but nothing was done in response.
(2) When the cooker arrived it did not work properly. The customer complained about the timer being defective. It was finally repaired, but only after substantial confusion, four house calls and the failure of the gas board personnel to keep appointments. On the contract, the customer found the cash figures were confusing, and the interviewer found that they had been written in the wrong places.
(3) The cooker did not perform as well as the salesman said it would. It arrived chipped, and the automatic grill did not light. The customer complained to the gas board, but she had to insist a little before they would do anything. Then they attempted a repair, but unsuccessfully.
(4) A salesman from the gas board called at the home uninvited and secured the attention of the household by misrepresenting the purpose of his visit. The cooker arrived marked, and after delivery, parts became loose. The customer complained to the gas board and parts were replaced to the customer's satisfaction.
(5) There was a delay in delivery, and after delivery, the gas board failed to install. The customer threatened to take legal action to obtain installation, and only then, and after a further delay of 3 weeks, did the gas board install the cooker.

Refrigerators

The sample included 2 sales of gas refrigerators by area gas boards. Both involved a significant delay in delivery.

Another indicator of relations between some of the area gas boards and their customers might be seen in the proportion of cases in which they were notified that payment was overdue. Of the 44 cases involving the sale of a gas fire by an area gas board, the customers were notified that payment was overdue in 7. Of the 18 sales of electric fires by area electricity boards and other sellers, the customers were notified that payment was overdue in 1. Of the 17 sales of storage heaters by area electricity boards and other sellers, there were none at all in which the customer was notified that payment was overdue.

Of the 39 sales of gas cookers by area gas boards, the customer was notified that payment was overdue in 4. Of the 21 sales of electric cookers by area electricity boards, the customer was notified that payment was overdue in 1.

The publications of the gas industry do not portray a different picture. On the contrary, they may explain how the situation described above came about.

A paper delivered in 1970 by two representatives of the Gas Council included the following:

> . . .natural gas presents a unique challenge and. . .the key to its exploitation is the application of marketing. . .
>
> The record of sales performance in the gas industry over the past decade is of a high order and has enabled gas as a fuel to rise from a position of near despair to one that has a growth pattern almost unique in commercial life at the present time. Obviously the change in feeding stocks – from coal to oil derivatives and subsequently natural gas – has been basically responsible for this revolution. However, an essential part has been the sales promotion efforts of the 12 Area Boards, which took advantage of the market situation. . .
>
> Perhaps we should consider looking on these centres [the showrooms] more as shops where profit is the dominant theme[1] associated with trading.
>
> If this is so, then showroom staff of a different type may be required, which would affect our selection and recruitment techniques and our training and personnel development programmes.
>
> It would also encourage showroom managers to be discerning in the presentation of appliances to enable them to meet their profit objectives. . .
>
> This does not mean, however, that there is not a need for spreading retail coverage to take advantage of impulse buying.[2]

The annual reports of some area gas boards and of some consultative

1. In view of this, one cannot help wondering what the authors regard as the purposes of nationalisation.

2. *Exploiting the Riches of Britain's Gas*, A.I.D. Frith and E.A. Haynes, 1970, The Institution of Gas Engineers, Communication 819.

councils indicate the same enthusiasm for an expansion of business. For example,

> 85. The Board recognize the importance of achieving their sales targets and thus contributing significantly to the expansion not only of their own business but also that of the industry as a whole.
>
> 86. To this end a reorganization of the sales force was undertaken and in particular recruitment began of Special Salesmen, who after training will work in teams concentrating on achievement of substantial sales of load building appliances, particularly central heating.[1]

Emphasis was placed on the payment of staff by commission, and on the recruitment of door-to-door salesmen.[2]

The next step, and one which at least some people may feel went beyond the bounds of commercial honesty, was to extend the payment of commissions to non-sales staff; for example, repairmen, meter readers and collectors.[3] A small commission became payable to a repairman (or meter reader or collector as the case may be) if he gave a lead to a salesman that resulted in a sale. In the North Eastern area for the year ended 31 March 1972, it was stated that: 'The value of appliances sold on Prospect Cards during the year was £162,915. This came from the sale of 3,132 appliances, . . .'[4]

There seemed to be no recognition in the reports that this method of payment created a conflict of interest and duty, or a form of deception. In some types of small business, for example a radio shop, it may be normal for someone making service calls to be also a salesman, and this would surely be recognised by the public. But the gas boards are not organised in that way. Repairmen, meter readers, and salesmen are different people. A repairman is someone held out to the public as paid to do repairs, and similarly a meter reader is someone held out as paid to read meters. Thus if a householder whose cooker has broken down asks the repairman whether the unit is worth repairing, she might well expect

1. *Annual Report of the North Thames Gas Board* for the year ended 31 March 1970, p.13.

2. See e.g. the *Annual Reports of the South Western Gas Board* for the year ended 31 March 1966, p.11; and for the year ended 31 March 1971, p.11.

3. *Pay of Staff Workers in the Gas Industry*, Report No. 86 of the National Board for Prices and Incomes, 1968, Cmnd 3795, para.22; and letter from the Gas Council to the writer, 1972.

4. *Annual Report of the North Eastern Gas Board* for the year ended 31 March 1972, p.19.

impartial advice from someone whose own income does not vary according to the answer. Instead, she may receive the advice of someone who is paid a commission on the sale of a new appliance, but not on the repair of an old one. Similarly, if a householder is having a discussion with a meter reader about the efficiency of older appliances compared with newer ones, she may never suspect that she is speaking to someone who is paid a commission if he induces her to buy a new appliance, but not if he leaves her content with her old one. It seems incredible that the payment of commissions to non-sales personnel was not viewed as a device calculated to divert those employees from the impartial performance of their duties, and to mislead the public about the measure of performance by reference to which those employees are paid. With regard to a repairman in particular, the practice creates a disincentive to fulfil the very purpose for which he is summoned and for which he is ostensibly sent. Moreover, the practice, as well as creating an incentive to dishonesty, puts a premium on incompetence. A repairman who successfully repairs an old appliance is paid only his normal wage. One who is unable to effect the repair, and thereby induces the householder to buy a new unit, receives the additional benefit of a commission.

The results of the new selling methods, measured by the figures for sales of appliances, were impressive. But the impact on the integrity of selling methods did not pass unnoticed. Complaints about deceitful and high-pressure sales tactics were received by some of the area boards and consultative councils.[1]

Some of the problems arose out of the conversion to natural gas. Where an area was switching to natural gas, householders were entitled to a free conversion, or to a replacement appliance free of charge if their existing unit could not be converted. It is hardly surprising that this was sometimes a source of complaint if the medium of personal communication between an area gas board and a household was a salesman who was paid a commission on the sale of a new appliance, but not on the conversion or free replacement of an old one.

A step which may have been intended to restrain abuses in selling methods was the use of contracts containing the cooling-off period clause even in showroom sales. The usual practice of the area gas boards was to include the notice of the right to cancel for sales made at showrooms as well as sales made at the home. But as mentioned above, the cooling-off

1. *Annual Reports of the East Midlands Gas Consultative Council* for the year ended 31 March 1966, p.60; of the *Eastern Gas Consultative Council* for the year ended 31 March 1968, p.55; and for the year ended 31 March 1970, p.61; and of the *North Eastern Gas Consultative Council* for the year ended 31 March 1969, p.58.

period is not always a benefit. It confers upon the buyer the right to cancel within a few days without showing cause. But it can also be used to convince a buyer that he has no right to cancel thereafter, no matter what the circumstances may be. Two gas boards sales were found in the sample in which the buyers tried to cancel the order several weeks after it had been placed, but were told that they could not do so. In at least one of those cases there would, if the facts stated by the buyer were correct, be good legal grounds for cancellation.

The annual reports are barren of evidence that either area gas boards or consultative councils seriously came to grips with the problems of integrity in marketing. Codes of conduct for door-to-door salesmen were promulgated, and there is mention of threats of disciplinary action or dismissal for high-pressure selling. But there is no mention of how many, if any, salesmen actually were dismissed. Nor is there mention of any prosecutions. Above all, there appears to have been no recognition that the predatory practices were not the fleeting aberration of particular salesmen, but the usual concomitant of the combination of door-to-door selling by people who were not relying on repeat business, and the payment of commission. Unless there was the most incredible ignorance of the usual consequences of this type of door-to-door selling, sections of the nationalised gas industry seem to have decided that a drop in the integrity of selling was a price worth paying for the expansion of sales. Following the discovery of natural gas below the North Sea, the desire to expand markets for gas and appliances appeared to become so convulsive that other values fell victim in its path.

A perturbing feature is that deceit, conflicts of interest, and gimmick salesmanship should have become an established part of a nationalised industry. If these were the standards that government set for itself, how could anything better be expected in the performance of its role of protecting the public against predatory practices by private industry? One might have expected that government would set an example by establishing the nationalised industries as models of integrity. Surely they have sufficient monopoly power to make that feasible. Yet without great competitive pressure to do so, sections of the gas industry seem to have adopted marketing standards lower than those prevailing in the private sector of the economy. A sad example was thus set, not only to other entrepreneurs, but to young people entering the gas industry itself.

As mentioned earlier, the transactions in the sample involving electricity boards were reported to be better. It seems, however, that some of the electricity boards, possibly inspired by the competition from gas, were proposing or adopting questionable selling techniques. For example, in 1968, the South Eastern Electricity Board began the payment of commission for sales leads submitted by non-selling staff.[1]

Against this background, the survey results come as less of a surprise. As indicated in the gas cases listed above, some of the problems related to misrepresentations about the appliance. It seems likely that in some of these cases, the salesman was purporting to have knowledge of something of which he was ignorant rather than saying things which he knew to be wrong. In some cases, problems occurred with regard to fitting and installation.

Unfortunately, the approach in the programme for recruiting the new type of salesman (the payment of commission and the use of promotional gimmicks) does not seem to have been matched by any technical training. In the annual reports, the emphasis is on salesmanship rather than meeting the needs of the customer. A letter by the writer to the Gas Council included the following questions relating to the period 1967-69 during which the items were purchased that were covered by the survey:

> Was there any formal training course for gas appliance salesmen? If so, how long was the course, and were they all required to take it? How much time on the course was spent on:
>
> (a) How to calculate the capacity of heating appliances that a customer would need?
>
> (b) Problems of installation?

The reply was to the effect that:

> . . .All gas fires are capable of providing a high standard of heating in something like 95% of all domestic living-rooms. There is a limited number of models capable of heating very large rooms and, for the largest rooms, it is usually found that the house is already centrally heated and all that a gas fire is required for, is to provide radiant heat to sit around during winter evenings, and also for occasional use during the summer months should the weather turn wet or cold. In this latter situation, customers use the gas fire rather than switch on the central heating plant. Sales training courses, therefore, only spend a short time on the subject of the heating capacity of gas fires. All the salesman needs to know is how to identify those large rooms without central heating (only 1% or 2% of all living rooms) where it is necessary for the heating requirements of the room to be specially checked before an appliance is sold.

1. *Annual Report of the South Eastern Electricity Board* for the year ended 31 March 1969, p.4.

Complaints from customers regarding inadequate heating capacity of gas fires are very rare indeed.

Similarly, a salesman only needs a limited training regarding the installation of gas fires. Almost all gas fires are fitted to a traditional fireplace with a 9" x 9" brick flue. In these circumstances, flueing problems are almost unknown, the flue being oversized already. The only other element of the installation is the provision of a gas supply. Most older houses have wooden floors, and the usual method if there is not a gas point by the fireplace, is to run a supply either under the floor or around the skirting board (or baseboard). Post-war houses mainly have solid floors but in these dwellings, if there is a gas supply installed, then there will almost always be a gas point fitted adjacent to the fireplace.

You ask if there have been any major changes in marketing methods concerning the relationship between the salesman and the customer. The answer is that there have been no major changes although, today, rather more sales training is being done to improve the salesman's presentation of the product to the customer and to improve his general knowledge about gas, gas prices, and the competitive points that he needs to know relating to gas and electric appliances.

There was no other mention of improving the salesman's knowledge of the appliances themselves, or of installation.

One conclusion from the survey results and the literature of the gas industry is that the nationalisation of an industry is not of itself any assurance of integrity in marketing.

Since 1974, the world energy crisis has reduced the pressure to find expanding markets for North Sea gas. But most of the problems relating to appliances appear to be continuing. Examples of problems reported by consumers to Citizens' Advice Bureaux during 1975 were remarkably similar to the examples, listed above, that were found on the survey in 1969.[1] Enquiries at advisory agencies during 1977 indicated the same problems of delays in delivery, appliances arriving with parts missing or broken, installation difficulties, poor servicing, failure to effect repairs, poor accounting procedures, and lack of effective response to complaints. Observation of the window displays of British Gas Corporation showrooms indicated that gimmicks are still being used, such as misleading price comparisons. Schemes for the payment of commissions to repairmen

1. *Statutory Complaints Procedures*, Evidence Paper E75/1, June 1975, National Association of Citizens' Advice Bureaux.

and meter readers still continue[1] although the volume of sales made in this way may be small.

The situation with regard to door-to-door selling appears, however, to have improved. Specially selected outdoor salesmen are still used to cover housing areas on a cold canvass basis. But a significant portion of their remuneration is by salary, and the numbers of gas appliance salesmen engaged in this way is small compared with what it was in the late 1960s.[2] Enquiries among advisory agencies during 1977 (unlike 1969) did not indicate any significant volume of complaints about deceptive introductions or high-pressure tactics being used by outdoor salesmen of gas appliances.

The survey data also shed some light on the functioning of the gas consultative (now consumer) councils.[3] These were established (one for each area board) to deal with relations between the board and the public, including consumer grievances. But there are several weaknesses in their operation. First, action by a council depends upon an aggrieved consumer knowning of the council's existence and writing a letter of complaint. Of the cases in the sample, none of the buyers who felt aggrieved by an area gas board wrote to a consultative council. In a survey undertaken by Social Surveys (Gallup Poll) Ltd for the former Consumer Council, it appeared that of gas customers who had some complaint, only about 1 per cent communicated with a consultative council, and of electricity customers who had some complaint, less than 1 per cent did so. Of those who did complain to the consultative councils, however, 22 out of 26 gas complainants were satisfied with the outcome, and 12 out of 18 electricity complainants were satisfied with the outcome.[4] Thus the consultative councils seem to have obtained redress for an aggrieved consumer in a majority of the complaints that they tackled, but they were only seeing a small tip of the iceberg.

Secondly, it did not appear from the annual reports of the consultative councils that the redress of individual complaints was followed by any

1. Interview in 1977 with a regional manager of domestic sales, British Gas Corporation.

2. The same regional manager of domestic sales indicated that in his region, the number of outdoor salesmen was now about a quarter of what it had been a few years ago.

3. Formerly, there was a Consultative Council connected with each area gas board. Since the *Gas Act*, 1972, there is a National Gas Consumers Council, and also a Regional Gas Consumers Council for each region of the British Gas Corporation.

4. *Consumer Consultative Machinery in the Nationalized Industries*, Consumer Council, 1968, pp.4-9.

systematic inquiry to determine whether a change of structure or of system might be needed to prevent further problems arising from the same cause. A similar limitation appeared with regard to the complaints received by the consultative councils about high-pressure salesmanship. They seem to have perceived a behavioural problem, and they discussed with the area boards ways of amending a salesman's approach. The problem does not appear to have been tackled as one of structure, and the reports show no record of the consultative councils taking or even considering the position that door-to-door selling on commission was so inherently conducive to high-pressure salesmanship and other predatory practices that the most appropriate response would be to terminate that method of selling.

For the redress of consumer grievances, what seems to be needed is a much more powerful body and one that is self-initiating. It is suggested that this function ought to be transferred to a corps of full-time inspectors, independent of the industry, and operating much more like weights and measures inspectors than like the consumer councils. They could be locally based and centrally organised. Their functions could be:

(1) To receive and investigate complaints. This should be done not merely with a view to seeking redress for the individual complainant, but also, where the complaint is well founded, with a view to analysing the cause of the problem and considering what steps are necessary to prevent the recurrence of similar grievances.

(2) To make spot checks, for example, by obtaining lists of people who have recently bought appliances, and communicating with them to ascertain the selling methods used and the subsequent satisfaction with the unit.[1]

The powers of these inspectors could include:

(a) To order an area board (gas region) to remedy a particular grievance, for example, by paying compensation in cash, or by rescinding a purchase and taking back an appliance.

(b) To make recommendations individually to an area electricity board or regional office of the British Gas Corporation relating to matters of structure, system, or personnel.

(c) To make recommendations collectively in an annual report to the minister. This should be published.

The inspectors here proposed would not be judges or arbitrators in a formal

1. This is apparently not done by the British Gas Corporation at the moment (interview in 1977 with a regional manager of domestic sales).

sense. They would be essentially part of the quality control mechanism of the government-operated fuel industries. An aggrieved consumer who preferred the judgement of a court would still be free to seek it.

5. Mail Order

As Table 5.1, p.87, shows, a surprising range of consumer durables are sold by mail order. Tables 5.2, 5.3, 5.4 and 5.5, p.88-91, show that those who bought from a mail order company reported experiences which were at least as good as those who bought from a shop, and perhaps even better. Thus mail order seems to be among the most legitimate channels of distribution for major durables with high levels of customer satisfaction.

Part of the explanation no doubt lies in the practice of mail order companies of promising that a customer can return the goods if he is not satisfied and his money will be refunded whether or not he has cause for complaint. Another factor is the ways in which mail order companies solicit business. One method is advertising in national newspapers. Here the newspapers themselves have an interest in seeing that the advertisements are legitimate, and that the advertisers are reputable. Another way is through the operation of local agents. This type of marketing involves repeat business and that requires satisfied customers.

Enquiries at advisory agencies indicate a substantial volume of complaints arising out of mail order transactions, but of course that does not show what proportion those represent of the total volume of mail order business. Usually the complaints relate to fumbling in the processing of orders or accounts, or in delivery, rather than to the condition of the goods. If there are any real shysters left in the mail order business, they were not selling major consumer durables in sufficient volume to be apparent on the survey.

There are complaints about mail order record clubs and book clubs, perhaps the most common complaint being the delivery of an item different from that ordered. There have also been complaints of rackets in which orders and advance payment are received, and nothing is supplied in return. But these seem to have avoided transitory operators and relatively small amounts.[1] This research did not reveal any evidence of any rackets involving the sale of major durables by mail order, or involving the department store type of mail order companies.

1. *The Mail Order Transactions (Information) Order*, 1976, now requires some types of advertisements to contain better identification of people who are advertising goods to be ordered by mail with payment in advance.

6 COMPLAINTS, REPAIRS AND GUARANTEES

1. Complaints and Requests for Repair

Complaints by consumers to the various advisory agencies show the range of things about which people complain. The statistics of complaints to these agencies are, however, only usable as a rough indicator of a floor level of consumer grievances.

There are three major problems in any attempt to make any greater use of aggregated data from these sources. First, there are the obvious difficulties of record keeping, classification, and how to inspire a uniform and continuing enthusiasm among the staff concerned for the recording of statistical data, particularly when, as in the Citizens' Advice Bureaux, many of the advisers are volunteers.

Secondly, there is the problem of how to assure comparability of data from various agencies that are under different control.

Thirdly, the data input is subject to the influence of so many independent variables that the aggregated data collated from the advisory agencies are virtually useless as an indicator of the nature and extent of consumer grievances.

The third point is illustrated by the following:

(1) About six years ago, we had 6,000 complaints a year. Now we have 20,000 complaints a year. We do not advertise the service because we would not have the staff to cope.[1]

(2) If an inspector spots a type of violation he may mention it in the office, and then we may be more on the lookout for that type of thing.[2]

(3) Q. How do you manage to keep the number of staff specialising in each subject area in line with the number of enquiries in that area? A. . . .and of course the incoming mail is not entirely beyond our control. As well as advising readers, we sometimes write up a problem and a solution for publication in the paper. But we would not pick a topic on which we already have as much mail as we can handle.[3]

(4) It is expected that bureaux will continue to undertake the same volume of consumer work as at present – approximately 17 per cent

1. Interview with a Chief Trading Standards Officer, 1977.
2. Interview with a Supervisory Trading Standards Officer, 1977.
3. Interview at a newspaper readers' advisory service, 1968.

of their total workload – but they will not seek further promotion of this area.[1]

One of the purposes of the survey, therefore, was to obtain some impression of the nature and extent of consumer grievances in proportion to transactions, and the nature and extent of consumer grievances in proportion to complaints.

The buyers on the survey were asked 'Did you ever at any time complain to the shop/dealer/seller about this purchase, or ask for something to be put right, or ask for any repairs to be done?' Those who answered 'No' were then asked 'Why not?'. The answers to these questions were as follows:

	Number	% of sample
Buyer complained to the seller, or asked for something to be put right, or for some repairs to be done	300	25
Buyer didn't complain because:		
Nothing to complain about	734	60
Too trivial to complain	42	3
Defects not more than expected	18	1
Plan to complain soon	12	1
Would not expect him/them to do anything	16	1
Would take too much time and trouble	4	0
Never knew where to find him/them	3	0
Guarantee had expired	6	0
Moved from the area where item was bought	2	0
Other reasons	10	1
No particular reason	9	1
Reason unascertained	64	5
Total (all cases where any item received)	1,220	98

As the list shows, there were 300 cases (25 per cent) in which the buyer complained or asked for something to be put right or for some repairs to be done, and a further 53 cases (4 per cent) in which the buyer did not complain for reasons indicating that he felt he had cause for complaint or that repairs were needed.

1. *Annual Report for 1976-77 of the National Association of Citizens' Advice Bureaux*, p.13.

For the cases in which the buyer complained (or asked for something to be put right or for some repairs to be done) Table 6.1, page 140, shows what the buyer requested the seller to do, classified according to what the seller is reported to have done in response to the complaint.

This table shows that, to a large extent, sellers and buyers were agreed about what should be done, but there was a substantial margin of cases in which they differed.

Table 6.2, page 141, shows the reported experience of the buyers classified by type of item, and Table 6.3, page 142, shows the reported experience classified by channels of distribution.

In the 300 cases in which the buyer complained to the seller (or asked for something to be put right, or for some repairs to be done), the buyer's satisfaction with the results of these complaints was as follows:

	Number	% of sample
Buyer satisfied with what the seller did	195	65
Still waiting (repairs pending, etc.)	8	3
Partly satisfied	23	8
Not satisfied	37	12
Seller did nothing in response to complaint	35	12
Unascertained	2	–
Total	300	100

With regard to defects in the goods when received, the data show no significant distinction between the results of complaints according to whether the item was received with a static defect (e.g., chipped, stained, or rusty) or in a malfunctioning condition. There was, however, a perceptible distinction between cases in which the item was not working properly, and those in which the buyer could point to a more readily identifiable defect, such as broken parts, or the item not working at all. The buyer was satisfied with the action taken by the seller in a larger proportion of the cases where parts were broken or the item was not working at all. Similarly, with regard to subsequent defects, there was a perceptible contrast between cases in which parts broke and those in which parts came loose or noisy. The buyer was satisfied with the action taken by the seller in a larger proportion of cases where the parts broke.

One explanation may be that defects that are obvious are remedied more easily or more effectively than those which require a diagnosis. Another factor may be that complaints about broken parts or the item not working at all are more often indisputable, whereas complaints that the item does not work properly allow more scope for differences of

Table 6.1: Complaints and Requests of Buyer, classified by the Response of the Seller

What buyer asked seller to do	What the seller did												
	Repaired the item or replaced parts	Replaced the whole item	Reinstalled or refitted	Supplied additional parts or accessories	Cancelled the deal and refunded the price	Refunded part of the price	Cancelled the deal refunded the price and paid compensation in addition	Other	Inspected but did not remedy the problem	Said there was no cause for complaint	Nothing	Unascer-tained	Total
Repair the item or replace parts	188	2	–	–	–	–	–	10	3	1	22	–	226
Replace the whole item	7	12	–	–	–	–	–	1	–	1	–	–	21
Reinstall or refit	–	–	2	–	–	–	–	–	–	–	–	–	2
Supply additional parts or accessories	–	1	1	8	–	–	–	–	–	–	1	–	11
Cancel the deal and refund the price	1	–	–	–	–	–	–	–	–	–	1	–	2
Refund part of the price	–	–	–	–	–	1	–	–	–	–	1	–	2
Cancel the deal, refund the price and pay compensation in addition	–	–	–	–	–	–	–	–	–	–	1	–	1
Nothing	–	–	–	–	–	–	–	–	–	–	5	–	5
Other	–	–	–	1	–	–	–	18	–	1	2	–	22
Don't know, wasn't sure, wanted him to investigate	1	–	–	–	–	–	–	–	1	3	2	–	7
Unascertained	–	–	–	–	–	–	–	–	–	–	–	1	1
Total	197	15	3	9	–	1	–	29	4	6	35	1	300

Table 6.2: Complaint[1] Experience Classified by Type of Item*

Item	Did not complain because nothing to complain about[2]	Complained and satisfied with what seller did	Did not complain, reason unascertained or no particular reason	Complained and action pending	Complained and partly satisfied with what seller did	Did not complain for reasons indicating cause for complaint	Complained and seller did nothing	Complained and not satisfied with what seller did	Complained, result unascertained	Totals	Grievances unresolved by seller[3]
Vacuum cleaners	102 (72)	15 (11)	12 (9)	–	–	6 (4)	4 (3)	2 (1)	–	141 (100)	12 (9)
Encyclopedia sets	7 (87)	–	–	1 (12)	–	–	–	–	–	8 (99)	–
Central heating	20 (47)	17 (40)	1 (2)	–	2 (5)	–	2 (5)	1 (2)	–	43 (101)	3 (7)
Electric fires and storage heaters	27 (75)	5 (14)	2 (6)	–	–	1 (3)	–	1 (3)	–	36 (101)	2 (6)
Gas fires	24 (45)	16 (30)	5 (9)	–	3 (5)	1 (2)	2 (4)	2 (4)	–	53 (99)	5 (9)
Other heating equipment	8 (89)	1 (11)	–	–	–	–	–	–	–	9 (100)	–
Cooking utensils	7 (78)	1 (11)	1 (11)	–	–	–	–	–	–	9 (100)	–
Sewing machines	26 (74)	3 (9)	4 (11)	–	–	–	1 (3)	1 (3)	–	35 (100)	2 (6)
Knitting machines	1 (33)	–	2 (67)	–	–	–	–	–	–	3 (100)	–
Typewriters	14 (100)	–	–	–	–	–	–	–	–	14 (100)	–
New motor vehicles	26 (35)	33 (44)	1 (1)	2 (3)	3 (4)	–	3 (4)	7 (9)	–	75 (100)	10 (13)
Secondhand motor vehicles	120 (58)	36 (17)	5 (2)	1 (0)	6 (3)	17 (8)	11 (5)	11 (5)	–	207 (98)	39 (19)
Radio/TV, etc.	88 (68)	23 (18)	5 (4)	–	4 (3)	5 (4)	2 (2)	2 (2)	1 (0)	130 (101)	9 (7)
Dishwashers	2 (50)	2 (50)	–	–	–	–	–	–	–	4 (100)	–
Furniture	97 (66)	16 (11)	10 (7)	2 (1)	5 (3)	10 (7)	3 (2)	4 (3)	1 (0)	148 (100)	17 (11)
Rugs or carpets	112 (82)	2 (1)	15 (11)	1 (0)	–	3 (2)	3 (2)	1 (0)	–	137 (98)	7 (5)
Refrigerators or deep freezers	40 (75)	4 (8)	7 (13)	1 (2)	–	1 (2)	–	–	–	53 (100)	1 (2)
Electric cookers	16 (67)	3 (12)	1 (4)	–	–	1 (4)	1 (4)	2 (8)	–	24 (99)	4 (17)
Gas cookers	27 (66)	10 (24)	1 (2)	–	–	1 (2)	1 (2)	1 (2)	–	41 (98)	3 (7)
Washing machines and combinations	14 (48)	5 (17)	–	–	–	6 (21)	2 (7)	2 (7)	–	29 (100)	10 (34)
Dryers	16 (76)	3 (14)	1 (5)	–	–	1 (5)	–	–	–	21 (100)	1 (5)
Totals	794 (65)	195 (16)	73 (6)	8 (0)	23 (2)	53 (4)	35 (3)	37 (3)	2 (0)	1,220 (99)	125 –

*Percentage figures in brackets.

1. Complaint means that the buyer complained, or asked for something to be put right, or asked for some repairs to be done.
2. This column includes cases where the buyer did not complain because (a) nothing to complain about, (b) too trivial to complain, or (c) defects not more than expected.
3. This column includes cases where (a) buyer did not complain for reasons indicating cause for complaint, (b) buyer complained and seller did nothing, (c) buyer complained and not satisfied with what the seller did.

Table 6.3: Complaint Experience Classified by Channel of Distribution*

Where or how bought	Did not complain because nothing to complain about	Compalined and satisfied with what seller did	Did not complain, reason unascertained or no particular reason	Complained and action pending	Complained and partly satisfied with what seller did	Did not complain for reasons indicating cause for complaint	Complained and seller did nothing	Complained and not satisfied with what seller did	Complained, result unascertained	Totals	Grievances unresolved by seller
Garage	93 (43)	65 (30)	5 (2)	3 (1)	8 (4)	10 (5)	13 (6)	18 (8)	–	215 (99)	41 (19)
Shop	403 (72)	56 (10)	48 (9)	2 (0)	9 (2)	24 (4)	8 (1)	8 (1)	4 (0)	562 (99)	40 (7)
Electricity board	56 (69)	11 (14)	6 (7)	–	–	1 (1)	4 (5)	3 (4)	–	81 (100)	8 (10)
Gas board showroom	44 (54)	22 (27)	3 (4)	–	3 (4)	2 (2)	4 (5)	3 (4)	–	81 (100)	9 (11)
Heating engineer or builder	17 (57)	12 (40)	1 (3)	–	–	–	–	–	–	30 (100)	–
At the home	41 (64)	10 (16)	3 (5)	1 (2)	1 (2)	1 (2)	4 (6)	3 (5)	–	64 (102)	8 (13)
Mail order	48 (75)	10 (16)	3 (5)	–	–	2 (3)	–	1 (2)	–	64 (101)	3 (5)
Private sale	53 (79)	4 (6)	1 (1)	–	1 (1)	7 (10)	1 (1)	–	–	67 (98)	8 (12)
Other unascertained	38 (68)	7 (13)	3 (5)	–	–	6 (11)	1 (2)	1 (2)	–	56 (101)	8 (14)
Totals	793 (65)	197 (16)	73 (6)	6 (0)	22 (2)	53 (4)	35 (3)	37 (3)	4 (0)	1,220 (99)	125 (10)

*Percentage figures in brackets.

Note: the footnotes to Table 6.2 apply here also.

opinion between buyer and seller about the way in which the item should be expected to function.

Those who complained were asked 'What did you complain of?' The replies to that question were classified as follows:

Failure of the seller to document the transaction properly	2
The odometer having been turned back	1
Overcharging (or other grievance about price, financing, or charges for repairs)	8
Non-delivery of the item	8
Item not new	1
Failure of item to function at all, failure to install, or total collapse of item	11
Faulty installation	2
Missing parts or accessories, or parts or accessories not new	18
Bumps, dents, marks, scratches, stains, rust, chipped, dirt, discolouring or other aesthetic defects	29
Parts or accessories loose, undone, noisy, blocked-up, broken or otherwise defective	166
Failure of item to function properly	44
Leakage in mechanical parts	13
Item required adjustment or setting	14
High operating cost	4
Three or more different complaints about condition of item	13
Other	3
Total (300 cases; multiple responses permitted)	337

As the list shows, complaints to the seller were much more numerous about the condition of the goods than about the selling methods. Yet the proportion of cases in the sample involving major or substantial objections to the selling methods is the same as the proportion involving major or substantial objections to the condition of the goods (20 per cent in both cases). Thus the data suggest that defects in the condition of the goods are more likely to result in complaints to the seller than abuses in the selling methods.

Interviews at advisory agencies also showed that the bulk of consumer complaints made to them relate to the condition of the goods, including subsequent breakage and servicing. Relatively few relate to selling methods. Similarly, in so far as court actions are now brought by consumers, the complaint is almost always about the condition of the goods rather than the selling methods.[1]

These results are not surprising. Complaints about defects in an item may be motivated by the expectation of a remedy. There is less likely to be any expectation of a remedy for complaints about abuses in selling. Also a predatory practice at the time of sale may have only a transitory impact, if any, on the mind of a buyer, whereas a failure of the item to function may produce a more enduring sense of grievance. Documentary evidence of the advertising or other promotional gimmicks may not be retained. Moreover any complaints about selling methods may involve conflicting recollections or perceptions of what occurred, and differing judgements about what is acceptable selling behaviour. Present defects, on the other hand, are often demonstrable, and buyers may be more confident about what they are entitled to in the performance or condition of the item. Another factor is that the legal materials available to the advisory agencies equip them to advise on the initiation of claims for defective goods, rather than claims relating to false advertising or predatory selling methods.[2]

Other data indicated that most of the complaints on the survey related to problems that appeared after delivery. Thus of the 166 cases in which the complaint to the seller was about 'Parts or accessories loose, undone, noisy, blocked up, broken or otherwise defective', the condition of the item when received was as the buyer expected it to be in 125.

Buyers who had complained to the seller, or who had not complained for reasons indicating cause for complaint, were asked: 'Did you ever complain to anyone about this purchase, or discuss any complaints with anyone apart from the seller?'. The responses to this question indicated that in 48 cases the buyer complained to friends, generally to no avail, although in 3 cases the friend was able to repair the item or otherwise solve the problem. In 8 cases, the buyer complained to the manufacturer. In 5 of these, the manufacturer remedied the complaint, in 1 the manufacturer induced the seller to remedy the complaint, and in 2 nothing was done. In 4 cases the buyer complained to the finance company, and in 2 this resulted in the seller solving the problem. In 3 cases, the buyer complained to another dealer and in 2 the other dealer repaired the item or

1. Interviews with County Court Registrars and office personnel, 1977.
2. This is explained in Chapter 9, p.254.

otherwise solved the problem. In 1 case, the buyer consulted a solicitor and was told there was nothing that could be done. In 1 case, the buyer wrote to a newspaper and the problem was subsequently resolved by the seller. In 1 case the buyer wrote to a motoring organisation and the problem was subsequently resolved by the seller. There were no cases in the sample in which the buyer went to a Citizens' Advice Bureau.

Although the numbers involved are too small for detailed conclusions, they do indicate that for aggrieved consumers to complain in search of a remedy is not an exercise doomed to failure. If a buyer has a grievance that the seller refuses or fails to remedy, the data show that complaining to the manufacturer or finance company, or to a neutral agency such as a newspaper readers' service or a motoring organisation, succeeds in obtaining a satisfactory solution of the problem in at least some cases.

An interesting result in the survey is the very slight use that buyers made of the advisory agencies. Of the cases in which the buyer complained to the seller, or asked for something to be put right, or for some repairs to be done, there were 30 in which the buyer expected the seller to do something in response to the complaint, and in which the seller is reported to have done nothing. There were 37 in which the buyer was not satisfied with what the seller did, and a further 23 in which the buyer was only partly satisfied. Thus there was a total of 90 cases in which, having failed to obtain satisfaction from the seller, the buyer might have turned to an advisory agency. Yet in only 2 cases in the sample did the buyer actually do so. If the data were representative, they would suggest that the complaints received by advisory agencies were only a tiny tip of the iceberg in the total volume of consumer grievances arising out of the purchase of major durables.

Even so, enquiries in 1968-9 at the advisory agencies showed that complaints to these agencies about repairs, servicing, and guarantees (warranties) were widespread and persistent. Files were bulging with correspondence about defective items, failure to obtain replacement parts, failure of retailers or manufacturers to respond to the complaints, failure to make service calls, and deliberate failure or refusal to honour warranty obligations. Moreover, a perusal of trade literature did not reveal any conflict of evidence. For example, in a feature article dealing with the electrical trade, it was written in 1970:

> Everyone loses with things as they stand at the moment. The consumer has a product which does not work and is irritated, often infuriated; the dealer considers the service call is going to be unproductive and unprofitable and the manufacturer would much rather plan more production than cope with repairs and complaints

on existing or old products.[1]

Commenting on the article, a retailer wrote: 'It took us from May until October to get any answer to our letters to one major manufacturers service organization, and then only by threatening to write to the Sunday press.'[2]

There were 161 cases in the sample in which the buyer reported asking for repairs under a guarantee, and in which the results of the request for repair were known at the time of the interview. According to the answers of the buyer, the guarantee was willingly honoured in 121 cases (75 per cent). In 13 cases the guarantee was reluctantly honoured (8 per cent), and in 27 cases the guarantee was not honoured (17 per cent). The following list shows the breakdown.

All Cases in which Buyer Asked for Repairs to Which He Thought He was Entitled under a Guarantee, and in which Result of Request was Known at Time of Interview

		Total
All repairs done which buyer requested	121	121
Repairs done, but buyer had to insist a little	5	
Repairs done, but buyer had to insist a great deal	8	13
Repairs done but buyer was charged when he thought he should not have been	5	
Repairs done but buyer had to insist a little and was charged when he thought he should not have been	5	
Repairs done but buyer had to insist a great deal and was charged when he thought he should not have been	2	
Only some repairs done	6	
Only some repairs done, and even for those buyer had to insist a great deal	3	
Only some repairs done and buyer was charged when he thought he should not have been	1	
Only some repairs done, and even then buyer had to insist a great deal and was charged when he thought he should not have been	1	
Repairs not done at all	4	27
Total		161

Although the survey data support the view that the failure to honour

1. *Electrical Marketing*, January 1970, p.12.
2. *Electrical Marketing*, February 1970, p.3.

guarantee obligations was widespread, they show nevertheless that in the majority of cases where repairs were sought pursuant to a guarantee, the guarantee was honoured.

The data do not support the assumption sometimes made that the dishonouring of guarantees is a greater problem with regard to new motor vehicles than with regard to other categories of goods. There were 35 cases in the sample in which the buyer of a new motor vehicle reported asking for repairs under a guarantee and in which the result was known at the time of the interview. According to the buyers, the repairs were done willingly in 30. In 1 case the repairs were not done at all, in 2 only some were done, in 1 the buyer was charged when he thought he should not have been, and in 1 the buyer had to insist a great deal before the repairs were done.[3]

With regard to secondhand motor vehicles, however, the data confirm the impression gathered from other sources that guarantees are a subject of great dissatisfaction. There were 29 cases in the sample in which the buyer of a secondhand motor vehicle reported asking for repairs to which he thought himself entitled under a guarantee, and in which the result was known at the time of the interview. According to the buyers, the guarantee was willingly honoured in only 15 cases. The results of the remaining 14 cases were as follows:

Repairs done after buyer insisted a little	1
Repairs done after buyer insisted a great deal	2
Repairs done, but only after the buyer insisted a little and was charged when he thought he should not have been	3
Repairs done, but only after the buyer insisted a great deal and was charged when he thought he should not have been	1
Repairs done, but the buyer was charged when he thought he should not have been	2
Only some of the repairs were done and then only after the buyer insisted a great deal	2
Only some of the repairs were done and the buyer was charged when he thought he should not have been	1
Only some of the repairs were done and then only after the buyer insisted a great deal and was charged when he thought he should not have been	1
Repairs not done at all	1
Total	14

3. Worse results than this appeared, however, in a survey relating to new car warranties conducted by Social Surveys (Gallup Poll) Ltd for the Consumer Council in 1967. See 'When a New Car Runs Into Trouble', *Focus*, September 1967, p.2.

The reasons for the widespread dishonouring of guarantees by used car dealers may not be hard to find. The performance of guarantee obligations is not really governed by law,[1] and the used car business is one in which many dealers may not feel the pressures that come from a need to maintain goodwill or repeat business. Moreover, there is no manufacturer involved with an interest at stake and who might be anxious to maintain at least a minimum standard. Perhaps most important of all, there is no reimbursement. A new car dealer can generally charge most of the cost of warranty work to the manufacturer, but a used car dealer who issues a guarantee must generally bear himself the cost of any repairs.

Many manufacturers and retailers undertake repairs without charge beyond the extent required by any guarantees that they have issued, but it would have been impracticable to seek any measure of the extent of this on the survey.

With regard to express guarantees, two conclusions emerge. First, guarantee obligations are honoured in a substantial majority of cases in which repairs are sought pursuant to the terms of an express guarantee. Secondly, the minority of cases in which guarantees are dishonoured is still high, and the non-fulfilment of guarantee obligations is a significant problem in the integrity of marketing.

Interviews at advisory agencies in 1977 indicated a general impression among those dealing with consumer complaints that there has been some improvement in recent years both with regard to the honouring of guarantees, and with regard to servicing and repairs generally. There does not appear to be any single explanation, but several developments may have been influential:

(1) The *Supply of Goods (Implied Terms) Act*, 1973, was followed by extensive publicity emphasising retailers' obligations to supply goods of merchantable quality and that are fit for their purpose, and retailers' obligations to deal with complaints. This may have contributed not only to some improvement in service by retailers, but also to some retailer pressure on manufactures.

(2) In several industries improvements have been made in the mechanisation and automation of record keeping for the stocking of spare parts.

(3) Wage controls may have made consumers more cautious in their expenditures, and hence made retailers more conscious of a need to please.

(4) Codes of practice that have been promulgated by several trade associations in conjunction with the Office of Fair Trading might

1. See *infra* Chapter 9(1).

have had some influence. Alternatively, the publicity associated with the introduction of the codes might have had some effect.

(5) Improvements in the County Court system might have made traders aware that consumers can sue in respect of defective goods. Although the number of such claims is still small, it has risen in recent years from being almost zero to being a small trickle.

In spite of the improvements, however, complaints to the advisory agencies about defective goods, poor servicing and failure to honour guarantees still constitute a substantial volume.

2. The Problems with Express Guarantees

Many complaints about guarantees relate to the document itself. Some guarantees put the buyer to considerable trouble and expense to obtain the repair. For example, some require the buyer to send the item back to the manufacturer. While the cost may not be overwhelming, it is often significant compared with the price of the item.

A common problem is that although the document purports initially to be a 'guarantee', the subsequent wording makes the performance of the obligation a matter for the discretion of the manufacturer or seller. For example, 'In the event of any breakage or malfunction due to defects in material or workmanship, of which the manufacturer shall be the sole judge, . . .' In much the same category are the guarantees sometimes issued by used car dealers promising that in the event of breakdown within a specified period, the dealer and the buyer will each bear a stipulated percentage of the cost of repair. The difficulty, of course, lies in ascertaining the percentage of what.

Some guarantees provide that only the parts are free, leaving the buyer to pay for the labour. If the labour cost exceeds the cost of the parts, which is often the case, it is surely bordering on fraudulent to describe a document worded in these terms as a 'guarantee'.

As the Chief Inspector of one Trading Standards Department put it:

> Guarantees or warranties seem to provide a constant source of confusion to the purchasers of consumer durables, such as electrical and household goods or cars. The average purchaser of a new appliance tends to assume without even glancing at a manufacturer's guarantee that its terms will embrace a remedy free of charge for any fault arising within the stated period. Unfortunately, certain guarantees give only limited protection and, indeed, some are almost

worthless in financial terms.[1]

Other problems arise out of the assumption that guarantees confer rights additional to the rights that a buyer would otherwise have. That is now the legal position. But it may not work out that way in practice. Guarantees often confer real benefits. But they can also divert attention from a buyer's alternative remedies. In particular, an express guarantee can divert attention from the implied conditions of fitness for purpose and merchantable quality. In cases where the complaint indicates a defect in the goods at the time of sale, some retailers still try to avoid their liabilities under those implied conditions by directing the customer to claim service under a manufacturer's guarantee.[2]

Some guarantees provide that the buyer must have the item serviced at regular intervals at a franchised dealer of the manufactuer. This creates a tie-in of servicing with sales and precludes the buyer from seeking the service of his choice. The use of such terms in a guarantee is sometimes followed by complaints about over-servicing, or complaints that when the customer takes the item in for servicing, he is treated as a captive audience for a sales pitch on other items.

Some guarantees fail to make it clear how or where repairs can be obtained, and some do not even make it clear whether the guarantee is being issued by the seller, the manufacturer, or by whom. Usually the guarantee identifies the issuer by description, e.g. 'the manufacturer', but often the full name and address is not included.

Special problems arise with regard to durability. Consider, for example, a guarantee that reads 'Your watch is guaranteed against original defects in material or workmanship for a period of one year from the date of purchase'. Suppose that six months from the date of purchase the item ceases to function not because of any production error, or because of breakage, but simply because it has worn out. It ought surely to be implied in any guarantee of this type that the materials are of sufficient durability to last for at least the guarantee period.

Some guarantees deal expressly with durability by phasing out the obligations of the guarantor. For example, in the sale of tyres and batteries, it is common to offer a guarantee for, say, 24 months, the terms being that if the item wears out before that time, the buyer will be credited with a portion of the price on the purchase of a replacement, the amount of the credit being inversely proportionate to the use that has been obtained. At first impression, this may seem reasonable. If someone buys a battery

1. *Annual Report of the Trading Standards Department of the County Borough of Grimsby, 1971-72*, p.23.

2. Interviews at advisory agencies in 1977.

on the promise that it will last 24 months, and it wears out after 23 months, it would seem an excessive remedy that the buyer should be entitled to a new battery free of charge.

Guarantees of this type are, however, a source of complaint. One objection is to the use of the word 'guarantee' or 'warranty' to describe this type of promise. The word 'guarantee' is commonly understood by the public, and also in trade, to mean a promise of restoration of the item to a condition of functioning efficiency without charge. It is not generally understood to mean that in the event of a breakdown, the buyer will receive a credit for some portion of the price. This problem could be met by another choice of description for the document promising the credit, for example, 'durability period'.

Another objection to 'guarantees' of this type is that they tie the buyer to a further purchase from the same manufacturer. This is in restraint of trade. It precludes the buyer from switching to a manufacturer whom he may feel offers a better product, or from a manufacturer by whom he may feel he has been duped. While it would seem reasonable to have a sliding scale of refunds according to the use that has been made of the item, it is suggested that anyone promising an allowance of this type should be required to pay the refund in cash, and it should be an offence to make it payable by way of a credit on a further purchase.

Apart from complaints about the terms stated in a guarantee, many complaints relate to the failure of a retailer or manufacturer to carry out the repair or replacement. Often parts are not available, repairmen lack the skill or equipment necessary for diagnosis of the fault, or sometimes a repairman is just difficult to get hold of at all. Even if the repairs are eventually carried out, the customer suffers periods of waiting and frustration while an item for which he has paid or is paying, and which he expected to be using, is out of operation. In many cases the failure to honour the guarantee results from administrative inefficiencies. But if these become so persistent and widespread that non-performance is a normal routine, it is difficult in those situations to escape the conclusion that the gap between promise and performance is deliberate. If a manufacturer finds it impossible to provide the repairs that he has promised, he could at least stop issuing the guarantees.

Complaints have also been voluminous about the failure of manufacturers to provide an adequate stock of spare parts for servicing and repairs after the expiration of the guarantee period. In several trades, measures have been taken in recent years to establish conventional periods during which spare parts will continue to be available. For example, the *Principles for Domestic Electrical Appliance Servicing by Electricity*

Boards[1] provide (through arrangements made with the Association of Manufacturers of Domestic Electrical Appliances) that functional parts should be available for refrigerators for at least eight years, and cookers for at least ten years. Concern has been expressed, however, that legislated or conventional minimum periods of this kind can tend to become in practice maximum periods. If it works out that way, the prescription of a minimum period for the availability of spare parts could have the effect of shortening rather than lengthening the life cycle of domestic appliances.

It is sometimes suggested that the willingness with which a guarantee will be honoured is directly proportionate to the ease with which the repair can be carried out, and there is no doubt that some of the most serious problems and conflicts arise when the defect is one that defies a ready diagnosis or treatment. This is a relevant factor in understanding the survey data. Although, according to the buyers, guarantees were not honoured in 17 per cent of cases in which repairs were requested to which the buyer thought himself entitled under a guarantee, the percentage could well be higher if the measurement had been by reference to the gravity of the defects, or the cost of repairs, rather than numbers of cases.

The problem of the persistent defect (sometimes known as the lemon problem)[2] is handled in several ways. If a manufacturer or retailer is unable to repair an item in circumstances in which a free repair has been promised, he ought to replace the whole item; and with regard to many types of goods, manufacturers or retailers often do so. Some manufacturers and retailers are reluctant, however, to supply a replacement item. One approach, and perhaps the most disreputable, is to keep attempting patchwork treatments until the guarantee period has passed. If the buyer subsequently returns to complain that the attempted remedy is ineffective, he can then be told that the guarantee has expired. No questions were included specifically on this in the survey, but one buyer complained that this is what had occurred to her.

Another less reputable response is resort to the theory, maintained by motor vehicle manufacturers in particular, of the inter-changeability of parts, i.e. that any defect can be remedied by the identification and replacement of the defective part.[3] If a defect is persistent despite

1. This document is a Code of Practice prepared by the Electricity Council jointly with the Electricity Boards and the Electricity Consultative Council, in consultation with the Director General of Fair Trading.

2. See e.g. *What to do with your Bad Car: An Action Manual for Lemon Owners*, R. Nader *et al.*, 1971, Grossman, New York.

3. The theory of the inter-changeability of parts can be found in motor vehicle warranties. For example, the 'Owner Service Statement' issued by Leyland Cars in its 'Supercover' publicity begins: 'Should any part of the vehicle require repair or replacement as a result of a manufacturing or material defect within twelve months. . .'.

successive attempts at repair, the theory can be used as justification for refusing a total replacement of the item. The theory is no comfort, however, to a buyer who has returned the item several times only to find that the defect has not been remedied.

Many of the particular problems are aggravated by the lawlessness of the warranty system. While customers are encouraged to believe at the time of sale that the guarantee confers upon them clearly recognisable rights of repair or replacement, the rights are not so readily recognisable or enforceable when a breakdown occurs. Retailers and manufacturers commonly do not perceive the matter as a question of: (a) what obligations have been undertaken by the terms of the guarantee? (b) what must now be done to fulfil those obligations? Complaints are perceived and discussed as a question of company policy, availability of parts, budgets and appropriations, goodwill and the importance of the customer.

Complaints to the manufacturer sometimes result in a solution of the problem. But sometimes the only response is speculation that the problem might have been caused by some fault of the buyer, coupled with a refusal to look at the facts to discover whether that is so.

These responses are possible because the legal machinery for the enforcement of warranty obligations is hard to move. Cases can be found of a buyer suing for the enforcement of a motor vehicle warranty, and there are now some cases of buyers suing for the enforcement of other warranties. But it is still generally true at the retail level that the amounts involved make it uneconomical for buyers to sue as a general practice for the enforcement of warranty obligations.

One consequence of the lack of efficient legal machinery for the enforcement of warranty obligations is that performance is likely to vary according to the bargaining position as between consumer and retailer, and as between retailer and manufacturer. A regular customer or one likely to bring repeat business may find the retailer more responsive to his plight, and similarly a retailer with a high turnover may be able to extract a higher level of performance from a manufacturer than one who deals in the product only occasionally.

Apart from the problems of consumers, guarantees also involve disputes between manufacturers and retailers. Where manufacturers' guarantees include the cost of labour performed by retailers, the retailers often complain that the reimbursement received from manufacturers is inadequate. In other cases, manufacturers complain that retailers seek to obtain free parts for repairs not covered by guarantees.[1]

1. In one case on the survey, the buyer reported having discovered that the garage had used his guarantee to obtain from the manufacturer parts that were fitted to another customer's car.

3. Guarantees and Law Reform

In discussing legislative policy with regard to guarantees, a vital consideration is that defects occurring after delivery are not simply the result of mistake or accident; they reflect a planned risk. To a large extent, they are the predictable consequences of earlier decisions relating to design, the durability of materials, the quality of workmanship and the amount of money, if any, spent on end-of-line inspection. More care taken within the plant can reduce the incidence of subsequent defects. Conversely, a greater reliance on repairs after delivery can reduce the need for expenditure on care within the plant. As the Maloney Committee pointed out, however:

> It must be recognised that quality control and inspection cost money; the more thorough they are, the more they cost. Each successive advance can only eradicate a lesser proportion of defective goods than its predecessor and there must come a point at which it is cheaper to replace or repair a defective article when its fault comes to light in the buyer's hands than to develop the quality control system so as to pick it up at an earlier stage. Since any increase in manufacturing costs will be passed on to the consumer by way of higher prices, it is in the interests of both consumers as a whole and of manufacturers to strike a proper balance over the intensiveness of the control of product quality.[1]

The crux of the matter, however, is that the point of balance which would be optimum for the manufacturer is not the same as the optimum point for consumers. In the interests of the consumers of a product, and in the public interest, the optimum point of balance is the position that results in the lowest total cost of the product. For manufacturers, however, the optimum point is the one that results in maximum profit. These two points will tend to diverge to whatever extent a manufacturer is able to shift part of the cost of the product on to consumers (in addition to the price). To take a hypothetical example, suppose a new motor vehicle is fitted with a battery that does not carry enough charge to assure starting of the vehicle in adverse weather conditions. The average cost of fitting a more powerful battery in the plant may be £2 per car. The average cost to the motorist of having the less powerful battery might be £10 per car. This will represent the costs of getting the car started from wherever it is, getting the battery recharged, and possibly replaced. These costs may

1. *Final Report of the Committee on Consumer Protection*, 1962, Cmnd 1781, para.202.

be borne by the motorist and not shifted back to the retailer or manufacturer. Where this is so, there may be nothing to induce the manufacturer to take these costs into account in arriving at the point of balance, notwithstanding that it would be in the best interests of consumers to have the better battery fitted as part of the original equipment.

To a large extent, the cost of defects can be thrust on to consumers. Even if the actual repair cost is borne by the manufacturer, the peripheral costs of repair are often absorbed by the consumer, for example, the cost of food wastage through a malfunctioning refrigerator. Moreover, the cost of using alternative facilities or equipment while the particular item is broken down is usually absorbed by the consumer. Sometimes even the basic costs of repair are borne by the consumer, particularly when they are not covered by the fulfilment of an express guarantee. Thus, in arriving at a point of balance between care in the course of production and reliance upon repairs after delivery, a manufacturer can ignore breakdown costs until the point is reached at which their infliction upon the consumers creates a sense of grievance or dissatisfaction that has an adverse effect on sales.

If a point of balance is to be reached intelligently between care taken before delivery and reliance upon after-sales service to remedy defects, the balancing must be done by the manufacturer. No-one else has the power or the accounting resources. But if the optimum point of balance is to be reached in the public interest, the manufacturer must be compelled to take all costs into account. In other words, as far as possible, it is desirable that all costs should be borne by the manufacturer of defects that occur sufficiently soon after delivery that they could have been prevented by greater care in the plant. This is required not simply to compel performance of contractual obligations or expectations, but for good cost accounting and economic efficiency. This could be achieved by requiring that:

(1) The manufacturer or retailer must repair the item, or pay the cost of repairs, and the incidental costs of the breakdown, for a specified period after delivery.

or

(2) The retailer must make it abundantly clear to the buyer before sale that neither the retailer nor the manufacturer will accept any responsibility for repairs required by breakdowns after delivery. If this is made crystal clear to buyers prior to sale, one would expect it to have a downward influence on price and the cost of repair would be passed back to the manufacturer in that way.

If these arguments are accepted, they are not reflected in the present legal position.

There is a range of legal techniques by which the cost of defects can now be turned back to the manufacturer, but none of them is suitable for general use. For example, the consumer may sue the retailer under the implied conditions in the *Sale of Goods Act.*[1] Or he might sue the manufacturer for breach of an implied warranty consisting of a statement made in the manufacturer's advertising, or by notice attached to the goods.[2] Alternatively, a manufacturer might be sued for negligence. Other possibilities are an action against the seller for rescission or damages, alleging deceit or a 'fundamental breach' of the contract. Except in extreme situations, however, all of these remedies involve an element of vagueness about the circumstances in which a buyer will succeed, and about the extent of the success. Considering also the cost of litigation, it

1. The implied conditions most relevant here are as follows:

S.13.(1). Where there is a contract for the sale of goods by description, there is an implied condition that the goods shall correspond with the description; and if the sale be by sample, as well as by description, it is not sufficient that the bulk of the goods corresponds with the sample if the goods do not also correspond with the description.

(2) . . . . . .

S.14.(1) . . . . . .

(2) Where the seller sells goods in the course of a business, there is an implied condition that the goods supplied under the contract are of merchantable quality, except that there is no such condition –

(a) as regards defects specifically drawn to the buyer's attention before the contract is made; or

(b) if the buyer examines the goods before the contract is made as regards defects which that examination ought to reveal.

(3) Where the seller sells goods in the course of a business and the buyer, expressly or by implication, makes known –

(a) to the seller, or

(b) where the purchase price or part of it is payable by instalments and the goods were previously sold by a credit-broker to the seller, to that credit-broker,

any particular purpose for which the goods are being bought, there is an implied condition that the goods supplied under the contract are reasonably fit for that purpose, whether or not that is a purpose for which such goods are commonly supplied, except where the circumstances show that the buyer does not rely, or that it is unreasonable for him to rely, on the skill or judgement of the seller or credit-broker.

. . . . . .

(4) . . . . . .

(5) . . . . . .

(6) . . . . . .

Sale of Goods Act, 1893, as amended.

2. *Carlill v. Carbolic Smoke Ball Co.* [1893] 1 QB 256. Some American courts have shown a greater readiness to allow claims of this type. See e.g., *Randy Knitwear v. American Cyanamid* (1962) 226 NYS 2d 363, and *Ford v. Lonon* (1966) 398 SW 2d 240.

is generally not worthwhile using any of these techniques to obtain redress for defective items unless the defect is of a serious nature in an expensive item, or there is personal injury or other consequential damage.

Another possibility is for the consumer to claim performance of the obligations created by an express guarantee. The problems arising out of express guarantees have been outlined above, and as a practical matter, people do not usually seek their enforcement through the courts. Thus for the general run of complaints about defective goods, there is no practical legal remedy.

A strict enforcement of express guarantees would, of course, do nothing directly to thrust on to manufacturers the costs of defects occurring after the expiration of the guarantee period. A manufacturer of shoddy goods might try to avoid the cost of repairs by, for example, issuing a guarantee for only one month. But if he does that, he will surely not command the same price for his product as a manufacturer who offers a twelve month guarantee. The likely result would be that although he is not compelled to absorb the cost of the defects by paying for the repairs, he is compelled to absorb the cost through a lower price. A manufacturer of a more sturdily built item would then have an incentive to issue a longer guarantee period than the manufacturer of one less sturdy, and there would be a disincentive to issue a guarantee for a longer period than the manufacturer would expect the item to last without breakdowns. In other words, if express guarantees can be made more readily enforceable and more universally honoured, they will become more valid as an indicator of the durability of the product. If, as might well be expected, price levels follow guarantee periods, the net result would be that manufacturers of more durable items are able to obtain higher prices than those who produce less durable alternatives. Consumers could make more reliable assessments of what the product is worth when comparing prices; and here again, the net result would be improved efficiency in the operation of the price mechanism in the market.

There is no easy way to control the abuses connected with express guarantees, and no simple way of assuring that the expectations that they create will be honoured. The amounts involved in complaints relating to guarantees are generally too small to deal with the problem efficiently by adjudication on each claim. The aim must be, therefore, to devise a system that creates pressures for the fulfilment of guarantee obligations, but avoiding as far as possible any need for adjudication case by case.

The objective should be to secure for consumers the performance of what they were led to expect at the time of sale, and to assure that the cost of achieving that performance is borne by those who created the expectations. As suggested above, the objectives include not only honesty but also efficient operation of the market economy and good cost accounting. To make the achievement of these objectives worthwhile, the techniques used must not in themselves involve a significant counter-balancing cost.

The achievement of these goals requires measures to deal both with express guarantees, and with situations in which no guarantee is issued.

Most important is the need for some drastic improvement in the techniques of enforcement of warranty obligations.

One of the limitations of litigation for the solution of warranty disputes is the traditional view that if a warranty is not honoured, the consumer cannot return the item and reclaim the price. He can only sue for damages. Under sale of goods law, the right to reject the goods usually terminates, at the latest, when delivery has been accepted by the buyer. This made sense in trade sales of bulk goods because there were generally no continuing obligations of the seller outstanding. This branch of the law was, however, never really designed to deal with situations in which the seller undertakes a continuing obligation by issuing an express warranty relating to after-sales service. Where the warranty is dishonoured, rescission of the contract would surely be the most effective remedy.

Even as the law stands, rescission of the contract and recovery of the price can sometimes be obtained. For example, in some of the lemon cases, a consumer has been able to rescind the transaction and recover the price by alleging a 'fundamental breach' of the contract.[1] But the dilemma that this remedy creates is obvious. Just how bad does the situation have to be before a consumer can be confident that a judge will classify the breach as 'fundamental'? Another possibility might be an action for deceit. Suppose, for example, a retailer issues a repair warranty knowing full well that the spare parts that would be necessary to effect repairs are not available, and that in the ordinary course of events they are unlikely to be available. It is surely implicit in a repair guarantee that spare parts are available, or at least that there is an expectation that they will be available, and in these circumstances, one would expect the contract to be voidable for deceit. But the courts are naturally reluctant to arrive at a conclusion of fraud, and the cost of collecting and presenting the evidence would often be substantial. Neither of these grounds for rescission is, therefore, suitable for general use. The need is for a remedy that would be more clearly available in circumstances that can be precisely defined so that the rights and obligations of all parties can be readily understood by manufacturer, retailer and consumer alike.

It is suggested that where a defect has been notified to a seller or manu-

1. See e.g. *Farnworth Finance v. Attryde* [1970] 2 All ER 774.

facturer (being a party liable under a guarantee), and the consumer has become entitled to repair or replacement under the guarantee, he should be entitled to rescind the contract where either:

(1) The party liable on the guarantee has stated that he is unwilling or unable to effect the repair or replacement; or
(2) The item has been accepted for repair but has been redelivered to the customer without the defect having been remedied; or
(3) At any time after the request for repair or replacement, the consumer has given 14 days' notice that if the repair or replacement is not effected by the expiration of that period, the contract will be rescinded.

Upon such a rescission, the consumer should become entitled to a full refund of all money paid, and the seller should be entitled to recover the item. In other words, the essence of the proposal is that those liable on the guarantee should be allowed an opportunity to repair the item, after which the consumer should be entitled to rescission and recovery of money paid without further delay, and without waiting for further or successive attempts at repair.

This remedy is suggested not in the expectation that it would be exercised frequently, but rather to give consumers enough leverage to ensure the performance of warranty obligations, and hence to elevate the overall level of performance.

The proposal might, at first impression, seem like a penal remedy. For example, in the case of a 12 month guarantee on a motor vehicle, it might seem odd that a consumer who has had the use of a vehicle for 10 months should become entitled to a refund of the price in full. But there are several reasons why he should. First, in cases of this type, the consumer will generally have suffered collateral losses through the defect. For example, he may have had the expense of renting another vehicle or the inconvenience of going without, plus the trouble and expense of seeking to have the defect remedied. Indeed, in many of the serious warranty problems, the buyer has not had satisfactory use at all. The greatest advantage, however, of the simple right to recover the full price is that the solution does not involve any problems of measurement. All parties would generally know what the buyer is entitled to, and no one would have an incentive to litigate on the measure of damages. To try to measure the actual loss of the buyer in each case would involve a decision-making process the cost of which would generally be out of proportion to the amount in dispute. Thus it is suggested that the value of the remedy, together with the greater certainty and simplicity of the right, plus the economy of proceeding with an action for debt rather than a claim for damages, would create for the first time a legal pressure on those who issue repair guarantees to ensure that the obligations thereby created are fulfilled.[1]

Procedural measures that should also help to remedy the problems involved in guarantees are discussed in Chapter 9.

Other improvements could be made in the substantive law relating to warranty obligations. First, the use in a guarantee form of terms that have been a bane for consumers could be prohibited. Some examples are:

(1) The use of the word 'guarantee', or the word 'warranty', to describe any document issued in connection with a consumer sale[2] other than a document that, for a specified period promises to repair or replace free of charge to the consumer any item that proves defective otherwise than by reason of misuse or accident after delivery.

(2) Any clause that purports to make the person liable under a guarantee, or any person nominated by him, the judge of the buyer's rights under a guarantee, or whether the guarantee obligations have been fulfilled.[3]

(3) Any clause that requires a buyer to pay a portion of the cost.

(4) Any clause that requires the buyer, in order to obtain the repairs, to return the item at his own expense to any place more distant than the place at which he received delivery.

To prevent evasion, there would have to be a statutory power to add to the list by regulation.

Merely to declare such terms void would not be enough to make them ineffective, and it is suggested that wherever the objectionable terms can be defined with sufficient precision, their use in a guarantee form should be made an offence.

For many years, guarantees often took away some of a consumer's rights. In the motor industry and in some other trades, it was normal to include in a guarantee or a contract of sale a clause excluding the conditions that would otherwise be implied under the *Sale of Goods Act.*[4] Because of their vagueness and the cost of litigation, these implied con-

1. Actions for damages, or for rescission on other grounds, could still be available, but they would be significant only in a small minority of claims.

2. For a discussion of suggested definitions of 'consumer sale' see the *First Report on Exemption Clauses in Contracts*, the Law Commission and Scottish Law Commission, (Law Com. No.24), 1969.

3 Clauses of this type are now prohibited in some other jurisdictions. See e.g., *The Consumer Products Warranties Act*, 1977, Statute of Saskatchewan, 1976-7, Ch.15, S.17(3).

4. See footnote 1, p.156, *supra*.

ditions are of limited value in consumer transactions. But they are sometimes useful, and it was considered important for consumer protection that the rights that they confer should be preserved.

The Law Commission recommended that: 'the statutory conditions and warranties implied by sections 13-15 of the Sale of Goods Act should apply to a sale to private consumers notwithstanding any term of the contract express or implied to the contrary'.[1] That proposal would have the advantage that if there is a term in a contract or guarantee inconsistent with the implied conditions, but advantageous to the buyer, he could elect between the rights conferred by the contract or those conferred by the *Sale of Goods Act*. That proposal would also avoid the need to define the objectionable exclusion clauses. A limitation of that proposal, however, is that unless combined with a criminal prohibition, sellers could still insert exclusion clauses in contracts or guarantees and use them for their bluff value.

Unfortunately, that recommendation of the Law Commission was not adopted. Instead, it was enacted that:

> In the case of a contract of sale of goods, any term of that or any other contract exempting from all or any of the provisions of section 13, 14, or 15 of this Act shall be void in the case of a consumer sale. . .[2]

This may well create problems of definition in the process of deciding which are terms 'exempting from' and which are not. Moreover, once it is concluded that a term comes within the void category, there may then be problems on whether severance will be permitted in a clause that purports to exempt the implied conditions, but also to confer some alternative advantage on the buyer. If a court declines to sever the advantages from the exempting part of the clause, the whole clause will be void, and the buyer could lose an advantage that he might have retained if the recommendation of the Law Commission had been adopted.

The other difficulty with the Act of 1973 was that it contained no criminal prohibition. It was predictable that sellers who had been using exemption clauses in their contract and guarantee forms would continue to do so for the bluff value of having the clauses in their forms. That problem however, has recently been remedied by making the use of the exemption clauses in contract forms and other documents relating to consumer transactions an offence.[3]

1. *Law Commission Report No. 24*, 1969, para.80.
2. The *Supply of Goods (Implied Terms) Act*, 1973, S.4, amending the *Sale of Goods Act*, 1893, S.55(4).
3. *The Consumer Transactions (Restrictions on Statements) Order 1976*, SI No. 1813, Reg.3.

It is still open to a seller or manufacturer, however, to defeat the implied conditions in other ways. An express guarantee or other document can be produced that does not contain any terms expressly 'exempting from' the implied conditions, but which simply portrays buyers' rights that are more limited. The effect may be to focus the attention of the buyer on the terms contained in the express guarantee and to create the impression that they are the only rights that the buyer has.

In an attempt to deal with this problem, it is now required that an express guarantee must contain a statement to the effect that it '. . .does not or will not affect the statutory rights of a consumer'.[1] But it is difficult to see how this can be of much help. If the buyer has legal or para-legal advice, the statement is superfluous. Conversely, if the buyer is acting without such advice it is hard to see how he could be much assisted by a sentence referring to some unidentified statutory rights.

Regulation 4 does not prescribe any particular form of words to be used, nor does it even require the statement to explain that the statutory rights are rights against the retailer.

It is suggested that where printed contract forms are being used, or printed guarantees, it should be required that they include the full text of the statutory rights, or possibly a colloquial summary that could be prescribed by regulation.

Further legislation relating to exemption clauses is now being considered in Parliament.[2]

Even apart from exemption clauses, express guarantees can be used by retailers as an excuse for disclaiming responsibility in respect of defects that existed at the time of delivery. The aggrieved consumer sometimes receives a run-around between the retailer and the manufacturer. A related question is who, as between consumer and manufacturer, should bear the loss when the retailer has become insolvent, gone out of business, or is otherwise unlikely to honour the guarantee. A similar problem arises with regard to the possibility of a manufactuer becoming insolvent, failing to produce spare parts, or otherwise failing to fulfil his guarantee obligations.

It is suggested that the manufacturer and retailer should both be liable to the consumer for the performance of all obligations under any guarantee that has been issued by either of them with the knowledge of the other, and the consumer should be able to claim performance under the guarantee from either. As between the manufacturer and retailer, the ultimate responsibility could rest with the originator of the guarantee, unless otherwise determined by contract. Apart from resolving the problems mentioned above, this proposal is also supported by the view

1. Ibid, Reg.4.
2. *Unfair Contract Terms Bill*, 1977.

that the manufacturer and retailer can generally apply more pressure to each other than the consumer can apply to either, and it is not satisfactory that they should evade responsibility by involving the consumer in the internal wrangles of the trade.[1]

It may appear, at first impression, that a retailer or a manufacturer could become saddled with responsibilities that he has never undertaken. But with careful legislation, this should not be so. A retailer would be liable on any guarantee that he delivered to his customer, or which he knew, at the time of sale, would be delivered by the manufacturer to buyers of the particular type of goods. Similarly, a manufacturer would be liable only on any guarantee that had emanated from him, or which he knew would be supplied to buyers of the particular type of goods.

In some situations, this proposal may seem harsh. For example, it might seem unfair that if a manufacturer fails to produce the spare parts necessary to honour a guarantee, the retailer should be liable to the consumer. But as between retailer and consumer, it is generally the retailer who is in a better position to bear the loss, to remedy the problem, or to guard against the occurrence of the event. Moreover, it would be consistent with the provisions of the *Sale of Goods Act* which can make a retailer liable for manufacturing defects that exist at the time of sale. The proposal would create an incentive both for manufacturers and for retailers, when establishing a course of trade, to beware of those who do not meet their guarantee obligations.

It is also important in relation to express warranties, as in other areas, that the law on the subject should be published and available for anyone to read. In this connection, it is surely necessary to take a broader perception of the nature of law than has been taken so far. The service that a consumer receives under, for example, a motor vehicle warranty, does not necessarily depend upon the terms of the warranty, or upon any branch of published law. The manufacturers of motor vehicles have a commanding position. They exercise considerable power, and part of the exercise of that power is the distribution to dealers of warranty policy manuals specifying how the warranty system is to operate. If law is perceived as consisting of the whole body of rules by reference to which decisions are made that govern the lives and fortunes of individuals, the warranty policy manuals are as much a part of law as anything emanating from the more formal branches of government. It is surely indefensible that the industry should be allowed to treat operating rules of that kind as

1. Some steps in this direction are contained in *The Consumer Products Warranties Act*, Statutes of Saskatchewan, 1976-7, Ch.15, SS.10 and 13.

secret documents.[1] There should be statutory provisions requiring publication.

Where there is no express guarantee, a buyer might theoretically claim the cost of any necessary repairs under the implied conditions of fitness for purpose and merchantable quality.[2] These implied conditions are often useful in commercial cases but, as mentioned earlier, they are too vague for broad scale use in consumer transactions. Consider, for example, the sale of a couch that wears out after six months. Could the buyer be entirely confident that a court would come to the conclusion that, as at the time of sale, the couch was unfit for its purpose or not of merchantable quality?[3] A related problem is that these implied conditions are not known to many retailers or recognised by them as giving buyers any rights. If a buyer seeks a repair or claims the cost of a repair in a situation where there is no express guarantee, and if the retailer does not wish to carry out the repair, the customer may be told simply that 'there is no guarantee'. As a practical matter, he may be unlikely to obtain any redress without going to the trouble and expense of litigation, and for the amount involved it is not usually worthwhile.

To deal with this problem, it is suggested that in addition to the present implied conditions under the *Sale of Goods Act*, there should be an implied condition, applicable to a defined category of consumer durables,[4] that the item will remain functional in accordance with the reasonable expectations of the buyer for at least twelve months from the date of purchase. To meet this obligation, the retailer should have the option of repairing the defects, replacing the item by another of the same model, or paying the cost of repairs. This implied promise could be excluded by issuing an express guarantee, or by giving notice that there is 'no guarantee period'.

It is suggested that to avoid liability under this implied guarantee, it

1. Following the introduction of the new 'Supercover' by British Leyland, the writer requested in 1977 a copy of the Policy Manual issued to dealers for the administration of the new coverage. The company did not deny the existence of such a manual, but it declined to provide a copy.

2. See footnote 1, p.156, *supra*.

3. The Court of Appeal decided in one case that where a car will not go for a reasonable time after sale, that may be evidence that it was unfit for its purpose at the time of sale. *Crowther v. Shannon Motor Co.* [1975] 1 All ER 139. However, there is still considerable uncertainty about how far the implied conditions of fitness for purpose and merchantable quality can be used to incorporate a notion of durability. This is discussed in *Law of Contract: Implied Terms in Contracts for the Supply of Goods*, Working Paper No. 71 of the Law Commission, 1977, pp.43-6.

4. The category might include such items as motor vehicles, heating equipment, electrical appliances, furniture, household fixtures and clocks.

should be necessary for a retailer to state boldly 'No guarantee period', or to specify a shorter guarantee period: (a) in any advertising of the item or type of item; and (b) by notice on the item itself if displayed, or on any display model of that type of item; and (c) by clear notice on the front page of any contract or order form.

At first impression it may seem inconsistent that retailers should be entitled to contract out of obligations to remedy subsequent defects but should otherwise be bound by the implied conditions of the *Sale of Goods Act*. There are, however, reasons for making this distinction. The obligation to remedy subsequent defects is easily comprehensible by buyers, and if the exclusion of this liability is dependent upon giving notice in the ways proposed, then the exclusion of the obligation should be sufficiently comprehensible to buyers that one would expect it to result in a downward influence on price. Indeed, goods offered under these conditions might be difficult to sell. The present implied conditions under the *Sale of Goods Act*, on the other hand, are less known or understood so that their exclusion would normally leave buyers in ignorance of what they were losing. Moreover, these implied conditions are not generally used to compel repairs but to reject the goods or to claim for personal injury or other consequential damage resulting from defects, and it is not suggested that there should be any right to contract out of those liabilities.

When a manufacturer is outside the country, it is suggested that the importer should be liable for performance of the manufacturer's obligations.

7 PAYMENT

1. Payment Overdue

On the survey, all buyers were asked whether they had been notified that any payment for the item (or any instalment on the relevant account) was overdue.[1] Out of 1,222 cases in which the question was answered, there were 62 in which the reply was 'yes'. In 11 of these, the buyer stated that payment never was overdue and the notice was a mistake.[2] This left 51 in which the buyer agreed that a payment had not been made (including cases in which the buyer felt that there was good reason for non-payment). Classified by method of financing, they were as shown in Table 7.1, below.

Looking at the transaction credit cases, Table 7.2, page 167, shows payments overdue classified according to the number of months between the date of purchase and the interview. Not surprisingly, the proportion of buyers who were notified that a payment was overdue increased with the length of time between the purchase and the interview. No doubt some of the cases in which the interview was conducted early in the payment

Table 7.1: Buyers Notified of Overdue Payments

Method of financing	Total cases in sample	Notified payment overdue	Agreed that payment was overdue
Cash	704	4	4[3] (0.6%)
Loan	58	4	3 (5.2%)
Transaction credit	404	53	43 (10.6%)
Account with seller	36	0	0
Credit card company	1	0	0
Check trader	22	1	1
Credit (unascertained)	1	0	0
Totals	1,226	62	51

1. This was thought to be a more acceptable question than asking whether they had missed a payment.
2. Some of these were no doubt cases in which the payment had been posted, but a 'reminder' had been sent before the payment had been received or recorded.
3. These would be cash transactions in that no credit arrangement was made, but for some reason the cash was not paid as planned.

Table 7.2: Overdue Accounts Classified according to Months between Date of Purchase and Interview

Months between date of purchase and date of interview	Total transaction credit cases	Number in which buyer notified that payment overdue	Per cent
1–6	129	6	5
7–12	130	13	10
13–18	97	22	23
19–24	48	12	25
TOTALS	404	53	

period would involve a non-payment at some later stage. This would tend to make the cases with the longest gap between the date of purchase and the date of interview more representative. On the other hand, when the transaction credit cases involving interviews within 12 months from the date of purchase were analysed separately, it was found that the proportion involving an overdue payment at that stage was roughly double for those having a payment period of over 12 months than for those having a payment period of less than 12 months. Again, this is not surprising. Longer payment periods tend to be coincident with greater financial commitments and one might expect these cases to involve more difficulty with payments.

Other data indicated a tendency for the proportion of cases in which the buyer was notified that payment was overdue to increase according to the number of calls required to make the contact at the household, and for the proportion also to be greater in cases in which the buyers were reluctant to be interviewed than in those in which they were willing. It seems probable therefore that if interviews had been accomplished at households at which no contact could be made, and at those where an interview was refused, the proportion involving payments being overdue would have been greater. Considering the data as a whole, it is the impression of the writer that in transaction credit cases, the buyer would be notified that payment was overdue at some stage of the payment period in somewhere between 12 per cent and 40 per cent of transactions.

Most of these cases are not, of course, serious default situations. Thus in the 51 cases in which the buyer agreed that payment was overdue, the results reported were as follows:

Paid off in full	47
Settled for part of the amount claimed	1
Nothing more was paid	2
Repossession, but no further cash payments	1
Total	51

2. Reasons for Non-payment

The reasons given by the buyer for a payment being overdue were as follows:

Stopped paying because of dissatisfaction with the seller or with the item	8
Interruption of earnings through sickness or injury	2
Out of work for other reasons	1
Money all spent paying other bills	4
For other reasons, did not have the money to pay	4
Just forgot/too busy	24
Other reasons	7
Unascertained	1
Total	51

There is, however, a perceptible obscurity about reasons for non-payment. No doubt dishonesty among buyers sometimes produces a distortion, but even apart from that, people often have difficulty in recognising their own motivations.[1]

One phenomenon that appeared[2] early in this research was that even when buyers refuse or suspend payment because of some grievance against the seller, they commonly do not give that as the reason. Several checks were made of the data to seek a measure of the extent to which this occurred on the survey. Table 7.3, page 169, shows the cases in which the buyer agreed that a payment had not been made, classified according to the reported selling methods and condition of the goods. Thus, of the cases in which payment was overdue ostensibly for reasons other than dissatisfaction with the seller or the item (43 cases), there were major or substantial objections to the selling methods or to the condition of the goods in 56 per cent. This compares with 27 per cent for the sample as a whole and 33 per cent for the transaction credit cases.

Another indicator was found in the situations in which two items were bought on transaction credit within the same household. There were 5

1. In survey work generally, it is notoriously more difficult to determine the motivation of the respondents than to discover events.

2. From the advisory agencies and from observing court proceedings.

Table 7.3: Overdue Accounts Classified according to Reported Selling Methods and Condition of Goods

Reason given for non-payment	Cases involving major or substantial objections to selling methods or to condition of goods	No serious objections to selling methods or condition of goods
Stopped payment because of dissatisfaction with seller or item	8	0
Interruption of earnings through sickness or injury	2	0
Out of work for other reasons	1	0
Money all spent paying other bills	1	3
For other reasons, did not have money to pay	2	2
Forgot/too busy	13	11
Other reasons	5	2
Unascertained	0	1
Totals	32	19

such households in the sample in which a payment was overdue on one item but not the other, in which there were major or substantial objections to the selling methods or the condition of the goods in respect of the one item, but not the other, and in which, nevertheless, those objections had not been given as a reason for non-payment.

Thus the data show a correlation between non-payment and reported facts which could be legal grounds for non-payment, even in some of the cases where those grounds were not given as a reason for not paying. This does not mean, of course, that in those cases the factors mentioned by the buyer as the reason for non-payment (e.g. sickness or too busy) were not present. But it suggests that they were probably not the decisive factor. All in all, the data suggest that there were probably about nine cases in which payment was withheld because of dissatisfaction with the selling methods or the condition of the goods, and yet in which some other reason was given to the interviewer. The same phenomenon was noticeable in the observation of court cases and in observing the work of legal advice centres.

It is not entirely clear why buyers who have stopped payment because of dissatisfaction sometimes give another reason, but several explanations are possible. First, if someone does not recognise that fraud, non-delivery, or defects in the goods, etc. are possible defences to a claim for payment, it may be natural to put forward some other explanation. In response to questioning by an inverviewer, a buyer may give whatever reason seems the most innocuous (e.g. forgot or too busy). Or in response to a summons, a buyer may state as the reason for non-payment whatever recent event seems likely to arouse the most sympathy (e.g. sickness or unemployment). Secondly, when someone is unsure of his position, there may be an ordinary human propensity to seek security in the explanation that the course adopted was inadvertent or forced by circumstance, and not a deliberate choice. By pretending (and perhaps even convincing himself) that no choice has been made, the buyer avoids the risk of condemnation for having made the wrong choice. Thirdly, expressing dissatisfaction with the seller or the item could involve the buyer in controversy, whereas being sick or forgetting to pay does not involve the animosity of a dispute. Moreover, a dispute about the goods or the selling methods can involve the buyer in a discussion of problems that he may feel unable to understand, or about which his understanding or ability to explain would be less than the seller's. He may be apprehensive about being made to look silly. Fourthly, if the real motivation for non-payment is dissatisfaction resulting from defective goods or fraud, there may be some feeling of guilt for not having been more prudent in the first place, and a reluctance to confess to having been duped. For example, the buyer of a shabby carpet that has worn out after nine months may be reluctant to say that he was told by the salesman that it would 'last a lifetime'. To have believed that could seem idiotic; though it may have sounded so convincing the way the salesman said it at the time.

Whatever the causes of the phenomenon, one of its consequences in court proceedings is that when a buyer gives as the reason for non-payment some excuse that is not a defence in law, this does not mean that he has no lawful ground for suspending or reducing payment.

3. Seller's Right to Payment

One of the questions on the survey was 'Do you feel that the seller is/was *entitled* to be *paid* in full for the [item]?' This question was asked in cases in which the buyer had complained, or asked for something to be put right, or asked for some repairs to be done, and in cases in which the buyer had not complained for reasons indicating some cause for complaint. Out of the 362 cases to which the question applied, the answers were:

Yes	263
No	54
Don't know	6
Unascertained	39
Total	362

Of the cases in which there were major or substantial objections to the selling methods, there were 88 in which the buyer thought that the seller was entitled to be paid in full, and 39 in which the buyer thought that he was not. Of the cases in which there were major or substantial objections to the condition of the goods, there were 124 in which the buyer thought that the seller was entitled to be paid in full, and 51 in which the buyer thought that he was not. There were no significant contrasts according to methods of financing.

Of the cases in which the buyer was not satisfied with what the seller did in response to his complaint, or request for repair, the buyer still thought that the seller was entitled to be paid in full in 19, though not in 14. Of the cases in which nothing at all was done in response to the complaint, or request for repair, the buyer thought that the seller was entitled to be paid in full in 20, though not in 10.

The data suggest that probably the majority of consumers with grievances against a seller did not perceive those grievances as grounds for withholding or reducing payment. A possible explanation is the tendency for people's perception of their rights to be influenced over time by the availability of enforcement machinery. Sellers' rights are commonly enforced by the courts; the rights of buyers at the consumer level are not.[1] It should be no surprise if rights that are not enforced become unrecognisable. A related problem is that a buyer's claim against a seller is usually more difficult to express in a cash figure, and even people who recognise that they have a claim are often unclear about whether there is a right of set-off. The *Sale of Goods Act*,[2] entitles a buyer to reduce the price in respect of a breach of contract by the seller, but this is not widely known.

4. Stopping Payment

There were 13 cases in the sample in which the buyer reported stopping payment because of dissatisfaction with the seller or the item. There were another 48 cases in which the buyer did not think that the seller was entitled to be paid in full, and yet in which he did not stop payment. The reasons for not stopping payment in these 48 cases were as follows:

Paid before discovering (the cause for not paying)	25
Felt responsible for paying	9
Complaints are against the seller and not the finance company	3
Afraid they would take court proceedings	2
Afraid of repossession	2
Afraid of trouble (no particular trouble specified)	3

1. See Chapter 9(1).
2. S.53(1).

Grievances were not serious	2
The seller rectified the complaint	2
Other reasons	3
Unascertained	2
Total (48 cases; multiple responses permitted)	53

Thus there were about 20 cases in which the buyer thought that the seller was not entitled to be paid in full, in which he had an opportunity to suspend or reduce payment, and yet in which he did not do so. The high proportion in which the buyer 'felt responsible for paying' is perhaps indicative of the reluctance of many buyers to reduce or suspend payment, even in situations in which they think they have a right to do so.

Where an item is being bought on some instalment credit arrangement and the buyer has a grievance that the seller refuses or fails to remedy, stopping payment might well be an appropriate way of securing attention. Indeed, although the survey data show that many buyers with complaints are very hesitant to stop payment, others do so as a way of coercing a remedy.

Stopping payment is, of course, not without risks. It is only appropriate when a seller has failed or refused to provide something to which the buyer is entitled. If a buyer withholds payment in circumstances in which the seller has fully performed his obligations, the seller may sue for payment and obtain a judgment which will add some of the costs of the action to the original claim.

What is often perceived as a greater risk is that the seller or finance company may seek repossession of the item. In that event, a buyer may lose the benefit of the instalments that he has already paid, and there may even be a risk of having to pay a further sum after repossession. It is primarily because of the risk of repossession that some advisory agencies[1] have a policy of never advising a buyer to stop or suspend payment. A difficulty with recommending a buyer to suspend payment is that it may involve a risk to the advisory agency itself. If the buyer stops payment after receiving advice to do so, the seller repossesses and the buyer loses the benefit of payments previously made, and possibly even is sued for more, he is likely to be annoyed with the advising agency. On the other hand, if he is advised to see a solicitor (however unlikely it is that he actually will) the advising agency avoids any risk of subsequent complaints. It is the impression of the writer that the risk of repossession is sometimes given undue prominence, and that buyers are not advised to stop or reduce payment as often as that advice would be sound. If the

1. See Chapter 9, pp.238, 246.

amount involved is not enough for good legal advice to be worthwhile, it is probably better for a buyer to decide this question by using his own judgment.

In many situations, repossession is not a serious risk. First, a seller or finance company has a right of repossession only if security in the goods has been preserved. This is usually done by the use of a hire-purchase contract or a conditional sale agreement. If the transaction is by a credit sale agreement, there is no right of repossession.

Secondly, repossession involves trouble and expense for a seller as well as a possible loss of goodwill. If the grievance of a buyer is, for example, failure to replace a defective part pursuant to the terms of a guarantee, suspending payment of the instalments may well be effective to coerce a remedy.

Thirdly, in some situations, repossession is what the buyer wants. This might be so, for example, where furniture has been bought which is not of sufficient durability to last even for the period of the instalments.

Fourthly, fraud and predatory practices often occur in situations involving little or no downpayment (deposit). Where this is so, it is an optimum situation for stopping payment. The buyer has paid very little on account, so that repossession would involve no significant loss of equity. Moreover, it is often good tactics in these situations for the buyer to refuse redelivery of the item until the seller tenders repayment of all monies already paid. Where the sales pitch was fraudulent or the goods significantly defective, it is unlikely that court proceedings will be commenced against a determined buyer, but if they are, a defence and counterclaim can be presented.

Fifthly, even where a hire-purchase or conditional sale agreement has been used, the seller (or finance company) is not entitled to repossession without court proceedings after one third of the hire-purchase price (or total purchase price) has been paid.[1] Thus where more than one third has been paid, the seller may well hesitate to sue if the buyer is alleging good cause for non-payment. The buyer can stop payment and see what happens. He will at least receive attention, and probably a remedy of his grievance. On the other hand, if the seller issues a summons for repossession, the buyer can decide at that stage whether to (a) consult a solicitor, (b) file a defence and counterclaim on his own, (c) pay, or (d) allow the seller to repossess.

Finally, for most categories of goods, their resale value compared with the cost of repossession makes it an uneconomic remedy for the seller. Repossession is a common remedy when the item is a motor vehicle.

1. *Consumer Credit Act*, 1974, S.90.

But for other items, such as household furniture, the cost of collecting the goods, the cost of resale, and the low prices that secondhand goods command, are often enough to make sellers reluctant to repossess, and in many cases it is just not worthwhile.

For these reasons, it is thought that the risks involved are often overestimated, and that stopping payment could be used much more extensively than it is to achieve a remedy for consumer complaints.

Where a buyer does stop payment because of dissatisfaction with the seller or the goods, it is important to state in writing to the seller (or finance company) the reason for non-payment, and to keep a copy of the letter. A buyer obviously runs the risk of his credibility being questioned if he stops payment for no apparent reason, and then, at some subsequent stage, explains that it was because of dissatisfaction.

8 INTEREST

1. Interest Rates

A. Rates Being Paid

Out of the 404 transaction credit cases in the sample, there were 298 in which enough data were available for the interest rate to be calculated. The distribution was as follows:

Number of cases	Interest rate (%)
63	Nil
9	0.1 – 5.9
14	6 – 8.9
24	9 – 11.9
41	12 – 14.9
19	15 – 17.9
29	18 – 20.9
31	21 – 23.9
21	24 – 26.9
17	27 – 29.9
14	30 – 32.9
5	33 – 39.9
3	40 – 49.9
4	50 – 74.9
2	75 – 99.9
2	100 –150.0
Total 298	

For the cases in which some interest was charged and in which the rate was calculated, the median was about 20 per cent. The average was 21 per cent.

Among the loan cases, there were 8 bank loans in which enough data were available for the interest rate to be calculated and the median was 11.5 per cent. There were 9 finance company loans with enough data available and the median for those was 14 per cent.

A national survey of 300 retail outlets was conducted by the Consumers' Association in 1969,[1] and based on the information obtained,

1. *Evidence to the Committee on Consumer Credit*, 1969, Consumers' Association, p.3.

the rates of interest being charged were calculated as given in Table 8.1, below.

Table 8.1: Comparison of Rates of Interest Being Charged in 1969

	No. of rates	Mean rate (%)	Lowest rate (%)	¾ in percentage range	Highest rate (%)
Electrical showrooms	19	11.1	6.3	7.8 – 13.3	17.0
Gas showrooms	13	14.0	9.3	12.4 – 16.7	17.9
Department stores	42	17.6	5.5	9.4 – 26.3	40.3
Co-operative stores	16	18.1	8.5	13.8 – 26.1	27.0
Carpet shops	23	25.5	7.0	13.2 – 38.5	48.5
Furniture shops	58	29.0	3.3	18.1 – 38.8	110.9
Radio and electrical shops	55	27.6	8.1	17.2 – 40.2	63.2
Car showrooms	53	23.2	6.3	12.5 – 34.6	40.8

Source: Consumers' Association.

With regard to loans from moneylenders, the Crowther Committee reported that interest rates 'are often 40 per cent to 50 per cent, and may be as high as 70 per cent to 80 per cent'.[1] Contract forms seen at a newspaper readers' advisory service in 1969 indicated that rates were often in the range of 65 per cent to 95 per cent, although rates in the range of 40 per cent to 50 per cent may have been more usual.

In 1977 typical interest rates were roughly as follows:

Personal bank loans	16 – 17 per cent
Multi-purpose credit cards	24 per cent
Transaction credit by retailers	25 – 30 per cent
Personal loans from finance companies	24 – 30 per cent
New motor vehicles	30 – 43 per cent
Used motor vehicles	39 – 50 per cent

B. Public Awareness of Interest Rates

The survey data indicate that most people have no idea what interest rates they are paying on consumer credit transactions. In the transaction credit cases, buyers were asked (before looking at any documents) 'What rate of interest was payable on this agreement?' The responses were as listed on page 177. Of those who responded with a percentage rate (92), the rates quoted ranged from 2 to 45 per cent with clusterings at 5 per cent

1. *Report of the Committee on Consumer Credit*, 1971, Cmnd 4596, para.2.4.19.

Buyers' Impressions of Rate of Interest Charged

	Number of cases	%
Nil	61	15
Percentage rate quoted	92	23
Don't know	242	60
Don't understand question	5	1
Unascertained (no comprehensible answer recorded)	4	1
Total	404	100

(16 cases), 10 per cent (12 cases), and 12 per cent (14 cases).

In 71 transaction credit cases, enough data were available to compare the percentage rates that the buyers thought they were paying with the rates that they were actually paying, as calculated from figures they gave or that were found in their documents. In only 2 cases was the rate the same, and only in another 14 cases was it within 4 per cent. In 10 cases the buyers were actually paying lower rates than they thought, and in 59 they were paying higher rates. Of the rates that the buyers thought they were paying the median was 10 per cent, and of the rates that they were actually paying in the same cases the median was 20 per cent.

The loan cases also indicated that actual interest rates were generally higher than the buyers thought they were paying. Of the 23 cases in which the buyers indicated a rate that they thought they were paying, 17 stated 5, 6, or 7 per cent. Unfortunately, there were only 12 cases in which the buyers indicated a rate that they thought they were paying and in which enough data were also available to calculate the actual rate. In these 12 cases, the average rate of interest on the loans was 4.3 per cent higher than the buyers thought they were paying.

In the 55 transactions involving a charge account, credit card, or trading check, most buyers again had no idea what rate of interest they were paying. Two answered that they did not understand the question, and 28 replied 'don't know'. Sixteen answered nil, and in only 3 of these was the answer likely to have been correct. Only 6 responded by quoting a percentage rate, and 5 of these were obviously lower than the prevailing rates.

Similar results have appeared on other surveys. For example, in a survey conducted in the United States prior to the compulsory disclosure of interest rates, it was found that the average of the rates being charged in the sample was 23.2 per cent. The average of the rates that the consumers thought they were paying was 8.3 per cent.[1]

Although people are uninformed about interest rates, it does not follow that they are unconcerned about the rate or amount of interest that they are paying. Indeed, concern about interest was expressed in several 'other comments' in the sample. In one case, the interviewer reported:

> During the interview the collector from . . . called, so the informant asked him the interest on the voucher. He was not able to tell them without looking it up. When he told them it was 3/6d in the pound, the housewife was rather shocked.

The public ignorance of interest rates is something that the practices of many credit grantors do nothing to dispel. 'Easy terms' and 'low payments' are commonly offered with no mention of the interest rate being charged. Where a percentage rate is quoted at all, it is often the flat rate (add-on rate). In other words, the credit grantor quotes the interest as a per cent per annum based on the cash price, or the initial advance, rather than as a per cent per annum based on the balance outstanding from time to time. When this is done, the true rate of interest is almost double the rate quoted.

The *Advertisements (Hire-Purchase) Act,* 1967, required that where goods are advertised as being available on hire-purchase and an interest rate is quoted in the advertisement, it must be the true rate. But the Act contained no provision for its enforcement and has been widely ignored.[2]

By going to the shop and making enquiries, a consumer is not likely to be more accurately informed. The salesperson may either respond with the flat rate, or simply guess at a rate. Often the sales staff are themselves uninformed. Based on a national sample of 300 retail outlets in 1969, the Consumers' Association reported that:

> . . .the true rate is almost always understated. Of the rates intelligibly quoted, 65 (33 per cent) were so misleading as to be under even the 'flat' rate (i.e. well below half the true rate). Next, 57 (29 per cent) were around the 'flat' rate (i.e. quoted at about half the true rate). As for the rest, 52 (26 per cent) were not so much seriously deceptive as just randomly inconsistent – falling uncertainly, as they did,

1. *Consumer Sensitivity to Finance Rates: An Empirical and Analytical Investigation*, F.T. Juster and R.P. Shay, 1964, National Bureau of Economic Research, p.51.

2. 'Misleading Credit Advertisements', M. Zander, (1968) 118 *New Law Journal* 1034; *Evidence to the Committee on Consumer Credit*, 1969, Consumers' Association, p.3.

> between the 'flat' and 'true' rates. The percentage actually near the rate was extremely low (about 10 per cent). Six (3 per cent) were actually above the true rate.[1]

The problem for consumers is not, however, limited to obtaining an accurate quotation of the percentage rate. Often they also have difficulty in obtaining the cash cost of credit.

> In only 8 out of 33 cases were shoppers given completely accurate figures. Although in a further 4 cases the figures given were only marginally inaccurate. In 17 out of 33 cases shops could not give the Total Credit Price, or got it wrong.[2]

During the 1960s, it was common for shops displaying major consumer durables to have a price notice on each item that would show at least the cash price, deposit, amount of each instalment, and total HP price. During the 1970s, however, that practice disappeared.[3] By 1977, it was only at very few shops that price tags were still displaying this information.

2. Compulsory Rate Disclosure

A. The Rationale

Except with regard to loans made pursuant to the *Moneylenders Acts*, there has been no legal obligation on credit grantors to disclose their rates of interest.

> In the result one finds that either a rate per cent is not quoted at all or, if it is, the rate quoted is a flat rate calculated on the original amount of the advance regardless of the repayments that are made over the period of the loan. The borrower (whether he be a borrower in the conventional sense or a hirer or buyer) is thus placed

1. *Evidence to the Committee on Consumer Credit*, 1969, Consumers' Association, p.24. The same situation was found in subsequent reports. See: *Survey of Credit Charges on a Three-piece Suite and a Double Bed Carried Out in London*, 1972, Consumers' Association, p.3; 'Higher Purchase', *Manchester Guardian Weekly*, 27 May 1972, p.18; *An Investigation into Cash and Credit Charges for a Hoovermatic Deluxe Twin Tub Washing Machine*, 1972, Consumers' Association, pp.2 and 5.

The same situation was found by the writer making enquiries in shops in 1977.

2. *Survey of Credit Charges on a Three-piece Suite and a Double Bed Carried Out in London*, 1972, Consumers' Association, p.3.

3. It is not entirely clear why the practice disappeared. Perhaps the most credible explanation is that the higher interest rates currently prevailing made it no longer attractive to display the difference between the cash price and the credit price.

> at a serious disadvantage. He cannot readily calculate the effective cost of the loan and it is difficult, if not impossible, for him to compare the rate charged by one type of financing institution with that charged by another, or even to compare rates of two financing institutions of the same type. In consequence he has no means of shopping around for the best buy and may be quite unaware of the wide disparity between the interest charges of one concern and those of another. Hence the forces of competition which might otherwise operate in a free market are substantially diminished.[1]

Following the recommendations of the Crowther Committee[2] the *Consumer Credit Act,* 1974, provides for compulsory disclosure of the true rate of interest in consumer credit transactions.

The main argument for interest rate disclosure is that it would provide buyers and borrowers with the information to shop around for the cheapest credit in the same way as shopping for the best prices of goods. It is unrealistic to expect the bulk of the public to figure out the percentage rate for themselves. Moreover, disclosure only of cash figures is not adequate to provide a basis for comparison. In particular, the repayment period may be different at one credit source from another, and the only effective way for a consumer to control for this is to know the percentage rate.

Another advantage is that the consumer credit market would be more truly competitive. The shopping around that could be expected to result from interest rate disclosure would have a limiting effect on the control of credit grantors over interest rates, would make them more truly responsive to the influences of supply and demand, and would tend to promote the other advantages of competition, particularly the optimum allocation of resources. Moreover, by facilitating competition between sales finance and direct cash lending, rate disclosure creates a pressure for the reduction or elimination of the commissions paid by finance companies to dealers.

To facilitate comparison shopping is not, however, the only purpose of interest rate disclosure. Another purpose is to facilitate more intelligent decisions about the use of credit compared with buying for cash. Informing consumers of the cost of credit in terms of the percentage rate gives part of the basic information necessary to avoid the over-use of credit by those who might be better off to save and pay cash, and to

1. 'The Legal Regulation of Lending' – R.M. Goode, *Instalment Credit*, ed. A.L. Diamond, 1970, Stevens, p.77.

2. *Report of the Committee on Consumer Credit*, 1971, Cmnd 4596, para. 6.5.16.

prevent the under-use of credit by those who are saving to pay cash in circumstances in which the use of credit might be more advantageous.

Moreover, interest rate disclosure enables a consumer to make comparisons between consumer credit and other sections of the consumer money-market. Probably the most relevant is savings accounts. A significant proportion of people who buy on instalment credit have a savings account at the Post Office or some other savings institution. For several reasons,[1] they may prefer to use instalment credit for a major purchase rather than to draw on savings. But the choice can be made intelligently only by comparing the advantages of using credit with the cost. To calculate this, an essential starting point is the difference between the two interest rates.

The other relevant section of the consumer money-market is house mortgages. Comparative shopping between consumer credit and the mortgage market may be useful for two purposes. First, it can sometimes be worthwhile for someone planning the purchase or construction of a house to consider an unsecured demand loan from a bank rather than an ordinary first mortgage from a mortgage lender. It is just possible that in some situations, the interest rate might be lower. This could occur, for example, where the credit standing of the individual is good, he is known to the local bank, the amount required is modest compared with his income, but the property has features that put it in a high risk category. Secondly, when a consumer is building a house, there may be alternative sources of credit for fixtures and fittings. For example, credit terms might be offered by the seller of heating equipment, or by the seller of cupboards or furniture. The rates offered by these sellers, compared with the mortgage rate, can be relevant information to assist the consumer in deciding whether to try and have the cost of central heating included in the house for the purposes of the mortgage, and how far to use built-in cupboards rather than furniture.

The quotation of percentage rates would also be an indicator to consumers of changes in the cost of credit. It has been argued that consumers should be made aware of these changes not only because they may be interested individually but because their response to the information contributes to optimum efficiency in the operation of the economy.

> If consumers understand the price of credit as they understand the price of other articles and services, their choices can help to combat inflation or a recession. When finance charges go up in a

1. See Chapter 3, p.37.

> period when inflation threatens, the consumers – if they know the cost of credit is going up – will be encouraged to postpone credit purchases; or when recession threatens, the knowledge that finance charges are lower can encourage consumers to buy.[1]

Finally, there is the argument that truth is a virtue *per se* regardless of its economic significance. It can hardly inspire public confidence in financial institutions if they are found to be quoting, for example, a true rate of interest on deposit accounts but a flat rate on consumer loans.

Fears have sometimes been expressed that compulsory interest rate disclosure might be the thin end of a wedge leading to rate regulation, and there is no doubt that prescribing a common formula for the calculation of interest provides a tool that could be used for that purpose. But the advocacy of interest rate disclosure springs from a desire to make the market mechanism effective, not to bring about its abandonment in favour of rate regulation. 'The essence of [interest rate disclosure] is to restore full information to the consumer credit field – to insure full disclosure of the cost of credit – and thus to permit the market system to function more effectively.[2]

Several arguments have been raised against interest rate disclosure, but most of them will not stand serious reflection.[3]

With regard to small amounts and to short-term credit, it is often argued that the cash amount of interest is more significant than the percentage rate. No doubt this is so: but this is an argument for quoting the cash amount in addition, not for withholding the percentage rate both in those and other consumer transactions. In any event, one would think that most instances of credit for small amounts or short terms occur as items on a continuing account rather than as isolated transactions. Where this is so, it is not suggested that the credit grantor need do more than quote the rate applicable to the account.

Another argument is that the public are not greatly interested in percentage rates. But there are three answers to that. First, it is difficult to see why the exact proportion of people who are interested should be critical. Those who are interested have not been able to obtain the information: '. . .when shops are not obliged to work out their rates of interest by any standard method, it is completely useless asking them

1. Per Senator Proxmire, 113 *Congressional Record* 90th Congress, 31 January 1967, p.2043.

2. Ibid.

3. Most of them are succinctly stated and answered in the *Report of the Royal Commission on the Cost of Borrowing Money, Cost of Credit, and Related Matters*, Nova Scotia, 1965, pp.366-80.

what it is'.[1] Secondly, that the public do not generally enquire about interest rates when seeking credit does not mean that they would not welcome the information. What they enquire about is largely determined by their expectations (created by advertising or prior experience) of what the credit grantor is willing or able to discuss. Thirdly, a survey conducted for the Crowther Committee concluded that 'Compulsory disclosure of a "real" rate of interest was wholeheartedly supported, although it is unlikely that all understood the concept. . .'[2]

Perhaps some of the reluctance in the credit industry to welcome interest rate disclosure rests on a more general objection to anything perceived as government interference. It may seem that the country can prosper best if businessmen, like the rest of us, are free to make their own choices. The difficulty with applying that general proposition to the disclosure of the true interest rate is that on this matter businessmen are never free to make their own choices. Whether we like it or not, there are some matters on which society has to make a collective choice because individual decisions are not possible. Interest rate disclosure is in that category. If the individual credit grantor is not under a legal obligation to disclose the true rate of interest, he is usually compelled by competitive pressures not to disclose. For example, no department store can advertise appliances on hire-purchase at an interest rate of 26 per cent, or quote that rate to enquiring customers, if its competitors are enticing the public with quotations of 13 per cent (being a flat rate roughly equivalent to a true rate of 26 per cent), or with 'easy terms', or 'low monthly payments'. Thus the absence of compulsory disclosure legislation does not leave credit grantors a free choice. The effect is compulsory non-disclosure.

B. Calculating the Rate

To make interest rate disclosure effective, the first requirement is a statutory formula. This is now prescribed in *The Consumer Credit (Total Charge for Credit) Regulations 1977*.[3]

The principal sum on which interest should be calculated is not usually difficult to determine. In cash lending it will begin with the amount of the

1. *An Investigation into Cash and Credit Charges for a Hoovermatic Deluxe Twin Tub Washing Machine*, 1972, Consumers' Association, p.5.

2. *Surveys carried out by NOP Market Research Ltd for the Committee on Consumer Credit*, 1971, Department of Trade and Industry, Part One, Section One, p.18.

3. SI No.337. For discussion of the mathematical aspects of interest rate disclosure, see, e.g.: *Introduction to the Consumer Credit Act 1974*, R.M. Goode, 1974, Butterworths, Appendix A; *Report of the Committee on Consumer Credit*, 1971, Cmnd 4596, Appendix IV; 'The Calculation of Interest at a Rate "Per cent Per Annum"', C.L. Pannam, (1967) 40 *Australian Law Journal* 376.

advance, in sales transactions it will begin with the cash price of the goods (less any part-exchange allowance), and in both cases it will be the balance outstanding from time to time. A more controversial issue is what should be included as interest in the formula. Credit grantors have sometimes argued that although part of the finance charge paid by a consumer represents a return on their investment, another part represents costs incurred in the granting of credit. Thus only part of the 'finance charge' is 'pure interest'. This argument might be relevant if disclosure were required for some purpose relating to the business of the credit grantor, but it is not. To assist a consumer in comparative shopping for credit, the vital thing is the cost *to him* of obtaining the credit from one source rather than another. All charges, therefore, payable by a credit buyer and not payable by a cash buyer should be counted as interest in calculating the percentage rate.

To secure the inclusion of the whole cost of borrowing in the percentage rate has been a political difficulty in other jurisdictions. In Canada, for example, government commissions and committees, one after another, recommended legislation for interest rate disclosure. When it became clear that outright opposition would be unsuccessful, some sections of the credit industry switched to lobbying for the exclusion from the percentage rate of some items of cost. This lobbying was partly successful, with the result that the percentage rate now disclosed does not in all cases reflect the true cost of borrowing. For example, in Ontario sums charged for insurance or official fees are treated as principal in the calculation rather than being treated as part of the cost of borrowing.[1]

Loopholes of the same kind appear in the British regulations, for example, with regard to maintenance contracts and damage insurance. Credit grantors will be able to obtain extra charges through contracts of this type. As a practical matter, these collateral contracts can be signed as part of a sale on HP, while being given the appearance of separate contracts freely entered into by choice of the buyer with someone independent of the credit grantor.

It would be much easier to foreclose loopholes of this kind by tighter wording of the disclosure regulations than by market surveillance to prevent such abuses occurring. The result may then be that the amount and percentage rate quoted as the total charge for credit would include some items such as maintenance and damage insurance. But credit grantors would be free to state this so that consumers can recognise what the credit charge covers when comparing rates.

1. *Consumer Protection Act*, Ontario, RSO, 1970, Ch.82. The 'official fees' are the filing fees for the security documents and therefore a direct cost of credit, and the word 'insurance' in the Act is not defined to exclude credit life insurance.

A problem arises when there is a significant delay between the date of contract and delivery of the goods. There is usually no difficulty with cash lending because interest generally runs from the date when the principal sum is advanced. But in retail transactions, it is normal to calculate interest from the date of contract, and to provide for instalments to commence by reference to that date, commonly one payment period thereafter. This is fine if the goods are delivered immediately or within a few days. But it creates a problem when there is a delay (often unexpected) of several weeks or months. Suppose, for example, a consumer orders furniture on hire-purchase with instalments payable over 24 months. If the furniture does not arrive for three months, but he has been paying instalments in the meantime, he is being charged interest on balances outstanding for a total of 24 months when he has received the benefit of the credit only for a period of 21 months. Because he is being charged unearned interest, the effective rate would be higher than the rate quoted.

When there are significant delays in delivery, sellers often agree to delay the commencement of instalments, and that mitigates the problem. But cases arose on the survey involving substantial and unexpected delays in delivery and in which the buyers had difficulty in getting the sellers to agree to corresponding delays in the instalments. It is suggested that when credit is granted by or arranged through a retailer, it should be required that the contract provide for the instalments to commence on delivery, or a specified period thereafter.

Another problem arises with regard to cash lenders who also operate current, deposit or savings accounts, particularly the banks. It might be argued that when a customer has two accounts, one with a credit and the other with a debit balance, they should be consolidated, and interest should be quoted and charged on the net amount owing by the consumer. It is suggested, however, that this argument should be rejected. The fair way to deal with the banks is surely to put them, as closely as possible, in the same position as any other cash lender. The banks should not be allowed to use current accounts as a vehicle for imposing upon consumer-borrowers additional costs of borrowing beyond those disclosed in the interest rate. But conversely, there is no justification for subjecting banks to obligations with regard to loan accounts greater than those imposed upon other cash lenders. To compel consolidation would mean that a consumer with a loan account at a bank would be charged interest calculated on a different basis from one with a loan account at a finance company. This would militate against comparability in the quotation of interest rates.

To the extent that the banks are willing to allow overdrafts, however, a consumer can obtain the advantage of consolidation. Unless the loan interest rate is significantly less than the rate charged on overdrafts, it will usually be cheaper for a consumer to seek an overdraft authorisation rather than a loan.

Compulsory interest rate disclosure can be legislated most readily for transaction credit and loan cases. With continuing accounts, it is more difficult to disclose the rate of interest actually being charged, but it is also less vital. It is more difficult in that the actual rate of interest paid will vary according to the time of the month that purchases are debited, and the time of the month that payments are made. On the other hand, if the consumer knows the rate being applied to any balance carried over, that may be more significant to him than the rate applicable to each transaction. With regard to revolving credit accounts, the Crowther Committee thought

> . . .that the matter can best be dealt with by requiring the credit grantor to state the basis of calculation of the credit charge before the first transaction takes place – e.g., that the charge is one per cent a month on the balance carried forward from the end of the billing cycle – and to show the effective annual equivalent of the quoted rate, on the basis of annual compounding.[1]

This is probably the best that can be done without making the matter unduly complicated. Two provisions, however, need to be added. First, there should be standardisation of the terms used to identify the principal sum to which the interest charge is applied. For example, one credit grantor might refer to an interest charge of 2 per cent per month (roughly 24 per cent per annum) charged on the balance carried forward from the end of the monthly billing cycle. Another might refer to it as charged on the previous month's closing balance. Another might refer to it as applicable to the amount outstanding at the end of the month, and a fourth might refer to it as applicable to the amount brought forward.[2] It may not be obvious whether these terms mean the same thing or something different. To avoid confusion, it is desirable to establish standard descriptive phrases so that the same basis for calculation is described in the same terms.

1. *Report of the Committee on Consumer Credit*, 1971, Cmnd 4596, para. 6.5.21. For the formula to be used, see *The Consumer Credit (Total Charge for Credit) Regulations 1977*, SI No.327.

2. See e.g., 'The Big Hole in Truth-in-Lending', (1967) 32 *Consumer Reports* 470.

Secondly, it would be well to prescribe that the consumer be supplied with a statement of account at the end of each billing cycle. This should contain the information necessary to check, if the consumer wishes, to ensure that interest is being charged according to the rate and formula quoted. It is normal practice to provide this type of statement.

Check trading is a problem in that there is usually some interval between the time that the consumer receives the check and the time it is used. Probably the best that can be done is to require each issuance of trading checks to include a statement indicating the effective rate by reference to a sample of possibilities. For example:

> These trading checks enable you to buy goods or services for a total price of £ ____ .
>
> The total cost to you of these trading checks is £____, payable by instalments of £____ per______ commencing on ______.
>
> The effective annual rate of interest that you are paying for these checks varies according to when they are used. For example:
>
> (a) If you use them immediately you are paying interest at ____% per annum.
> (b) If you use them after two weeks you are paying interest at ____% per annum.
> (c) If you use them after four weeks you are paying interest at ____% per annum.

The rates disclosed will be less than the effective rate being received by the check trader because of two other benefits that he receives. One is the discount from the retailer, and the other is the advantage of the delay between the use of the check and the reimbursement of the retailer. But here again, it is the cost to the consumer that must be quoted in the rate, not the gross profit margin to the credit grantor.

On some types of accounts, pre-computation is not used and the interest is not payable at a fixed rate throughout the duration of the credit. It is calculated from time to time at a rate that varies according to the bank rate, or according to some other indicator of prevailing rates. In these cases, the credit grantor should be required to calculate interest according to the statutory formula, and to disclose it in terms of: (a) the rate prevailing at the commencement of the credit; and (b) the manner in which it is subject to change, e.g. 2 per cent above bank rate.

C. Where and How to Disclose

The *Consumer Credit Act*, 1974, contains the statutory authority to require interest rate disclosure by regulation. The formula for calculation has been prescribed. But at the time of writing, the disclosure requirements are still pending.

There are basically three phases at which disclosure might be required:

(1) In any advertising.

(2) In any pre-contract discussion or negotiation, or in response to any consumer enquiry.

(3) In the contract itself, or some other document issued at the consummation of the transaction.

What to do about the advertising of credit terms is a major dilemma in the preparation of disclosure requirements. The failure to advertise interest rates and the other terms of credit is obviously an impediment to comparative shopping. On the other hand, a credit grantor must be entitled to vary his interest rate according to the estimated risk involved in each transaction. For this reason, compulsory disclosure of interest rates in advertising is inappropriate. Moreover, it would be misleading to permit the quotation of any interest rate in advertising unless it is the rate at which transactions are consummated.

One suggestion sometimes made is that where a credit grantor varies the rate of interest according to the estimated risk, he should be entitled to advertise the range of rates. But this obviously has potential for abuse. Consumers could be lured by the quotation of attractively low rates at the bottom end of the scale that are seldom used and then subjected to a sales pitch to consummate a transaction at the upper end of the scale.

Probably the best that can be done is to require credit grantors to elect between two positions:

(1) If a credit grantor has only one rate, he should be allowed to advertise that rate. The quotation should comply with the statutory formula, and all transactions should be consummated at that rate. He may quote different rates according to the amount of the advance, and that too should be permitted, provided that the same rate is applicable to all customers receiving an advance of the same amount.

(2) If a credit grantor does not wish to advertise a percentage rate, or if he does not use a standard rate for all his transactions, he should be prohibited from making any mention at all in advertising of interest rates, or of any other terms of credit. The prohibition should extend to the mention of any particular rate, the mention of any range, the mention of the amount of each instalment or any other terms, and the use of any vague language

> implying a level of interest rates, such as 'low finance charges', 'modest terms' or 'easy credit'.

Thus any credit grantor would be free to advertise simply that credit is available. But if he wishes to say anything about credit beyond that, he must quote the rate calculated according to the statutory formula and make that rate applicable on all his transactions.

Another possibility might be to require credit grantors to state the rate and amount of interest orally prior to consummation of each transaction. But this would be difficult to enforce. Forgetfulness, inadvertence, a reluctance to disclose information that might discourage a customer, and a reaction against being told what to say, could all operate against this requirement being effective. A scrupulously law-abiding credit grantor who honestly made the disclosure in every case could soon be at a competitive disadvantage. Moreover the courts would surely be reluctant to impose any significant sanctions against conduct that may be no worse than ordinary forgetfulness. Without the prospect of either willing compliance or effective enforcement it is better that this form of disclosure should not be required.

On the other hand, to make no legislative provision with regard to oral representations would almost certainly result in the continuation of credit grantors quoting the flat rate, and other false rates, in pre-contract negotiations. Indeed, this is what has happened to some extent in Canada. There should, therefore, be a prohibition of the oral quotation of any percentage rate of interest (or cost of borrowing) except the true rate calculated according to the statutory formula. Enforcement would still be difficult, but forgetfulness and inadvertence would be less readily available as excuses. It is, in any event, probably easier to enforce a prohibition than a positive obligation.

To require the rate and amount of interest to be disclosed in writing to a consumer prior to a transaction would be useless. It would just add one more to the documents that are not read.

The only practical form of disclosure that can be required universally is in the contract document itself, or in some other document issued at the consummation of a transaction, such as a payment card.

That contract documents are not generally read in consumer transactions before signature is a limitation of this form of disclosure, but for three reasons, it does not render the disclosure useless.

First, interest rates on consumer transactions vary from time to time according to the money-market. For this reason, the percentage rate is likely to be written in by hand rather than becoming a printed part of a contract form. Although few consumers read the fine print before signing a contract, some read the figures inserted by hand.

Secondly, even more people who do not read anything before signing might still look at a contract when they get home. If, as suggested below, an account can be pre-paid without loss to the consumer, someone who reads a contract when he gets home would still be able to consider whether he can obtain a loan elsewhere at a cheaper rate and pay off the account.

Thirdly, the achievement of interest rate disclosure legislation cannot be measured simply by reference to the people who become aware of the rate prior to each transaction. Interest rate disclosure is advocated not merely because the information might be useful for the particular transaction, but as a vehicle for increasing public awareness of the interest rates charged by different sources of credit. Indeed, the most significant benefit of disclosure may be the delayed impact. Successive transactions can inform people of the credit sources at which interest is higher or lower.

In Canada there were indicators that interest rate disclosure resulted in a greater rationalisation and perfection of the market for consumer credit. Following compulsory disclosure, a larger proportion of borrowers seemed to obtain credit from the most advantageous sources available to them. One example was in the purchase of new motor vehicles, where there was a trend away from sales finance companies (then charging interest at 14-16 per cent) to the banks (then charging interest at 11.8 per cent).

D. Enforcement

To ensure compliance is probably the greatest difficulty with disclosure legislation. As appears from earlier chapters, experience with consumer protection legislation so far is no cause for optimism. For example, the formal requirements of the *Hire-Purchase Act*, 1965, have been widely ignored.[1] If profit margins are at stake, the incentive to non-compliance can be strong. Unless honest merchants who willingly comply are to be penalised by less scrupulous competitors, the sanctions for violation of the legislation must be sufficiently tough and sufficiently certain of application that compliance is very close to 100 per cent. If a government is not willing to enact tough sanctions and to provide the resources for their consistent application, it would be better not to have enacted compulsory disclosure legislation at all.

Violations of the legislation could be made an offence, but this in itself would not assure compliance. One indicator is the experience with the *Advertisements (Hire-Purchase) Act*, 1967. As mentioned earlier in

1. See Chapter 4(5).

this Chapter, the requirements of that Act are widely ignored. Although possibly to a lesser extent, it seems that interest rate disclosure legislation in the United States suffered a similar fate. The Federal Trade Commission made a survey of five classes of retailers: (1) new and used automobile dealers; (2) TV and appliance dealers; (3) home improvement companies; (4) jewellery stores; and (5) furniture stores. Combining the responses, it was found that 69 per cent of those extending credit were using contract forms which were in total compliance with the *Truth-In-Lending Act*, 17 per cent were using contract forms that were in substantial compliance, and 14 per cent were using contract forms in serious violation of the legislation.[1] Moreover, this survey was by a questionnaire mailed to credit grantors and returned by them. The survey was designed to measure only the extent of defects in the contract forms and took no account of the manner in which they were completed. Thus one would expect lower levels of compliance to be disclosed if the survey had been carried out by investigators visiting retail premises or obtaining completed contract forms from consumers. In any event, enforcement machinery that results in compliance levels as low as this illustrates the risk that compulsory interest rate disclosure can be an illusion.

Although making violations of the disclosure requirements an offence would not be enough to assure compliance, it is surely an essential starting point. In the *Consumer Credit Act*, however, even that starting point has not been reached. Anyone who violates regulations made under Section 44, relating to the form and content of advertisements, commits an offence under Section 167. But it is apparently no offence to violate regulations made under Section 60, relating to the disclosure of interest information in the agreement.

Even to the extent that the Act creates offences, the effectiveness of these provisions is limited by Section 168, which provides that

> . . .it is a defence for the person charged to prove –
> (a) that his act or omission was due to a mistake, or to reliance on information supplied to him, or to an act or omission of another person, or to an accident or some other cause beyond his control, and
> (b) that he took all reasonable precautions and exercised all due diligence to avoid such an act or omission by himself or any person under his control.

If interest rate disclosure is not to be rendered futile by evasion and non-compliance, violations must be made an offence with strict liability, and

1. *Report on Surveys of Creditor Compliance with the Truth-In-Lending Act*, 1971, Federal Trade Commission, Washington, DC, p.7.

there must be someone in each locality whose job it is to look for violations and to prosecute when he finds them. Some functions, such as the checking of contract forms, might be done best at the national level. But the effectiveness and fairness of interest rate disclosure depend primarily on a system of detection and prosecution at the local level. Even with such a system, there would still be problems with the use of criminal sanctions. These are discussed below.[1]

Another difficulty with the *Consumer Credit Act* is that it does not deal in any adequate way with the significance of non-compliance to the contractual relationship between credit grantor and consumer. The effect of Sections 60, 65 and 127 is that if the credit grantor fails to state the amount and rate of the total charge for credit in the agreement as required, there is no automatic penalty. The result lies in the discretion of a court. A court might decide that, notwithstanding the failure to disclose as required, the full sum prescribed in the contract as payable to the credit grantor must still be paid. Or the court might '. . .reduce or discharge any sum payable by the debtor or hirer,. . .so as to compensate him for prejudice suffered as a result of the contravention in question'.[2] This is surely the worst of all possible positions. Adjudications of this type in consumer transactions involve a decision-making process the cost of which would generally be in excess of the amount at issue. Even when a consumer is prejudiced, no issue will usually be raised. The civil consequences to the contractual relationship, therefore, will be no deterrent against non-compliance.

An alternative possibility would be that where there has been non-compliance, the whole of a creditor's claim would be uncollectable. This sanction has been used, for example, with regard to the claims of unlicensed moneylenders. But this would be too severe a penalty for conduct that may be no more blameworthy than a clerical error.

Another possibility would be to allow a consumer to rescind the contract, repaying the principal of the loan or returning the goods, and recovering any instalments already paid. But this too would have its problems. An item traded-in might already have been resold by the vendor. Items purchased on a revolving credit account may have been consumed. A new motor vehicle may have been used extensively before the non-compliance with the disclosure legislation is discovered.

Probably the best solution would be to provide that where a credit grantor has failed to comply with the disclosure requirements, he should

1. Chapter 12(4).
2. S.127(2).

be entitled to recovery of the principal amount of the loan, or the cash price of the goods, but not to any interest. Instalments would be payable on the terms of the contract until the principal or the cash price has been paid. This may seem like rough justice, but it has the advantages of certainty, of avoiding litigation on the amount, and of creating an incentive to compliance. As a practical matter, consumers are likely to exercise the right of withholding interest only in a minority of situations in which they would be entitled to do so, and the sanction would not be any too severe.

A third vehicle for enforcement is the licensing provisions of the *Consumer Credit Act*, 1974. The potential of licensing is discussed in Chapter 12(5).

E. Avoidance and Evasion

Apart from simple violations of the disclosure legislation, several techniques of avoidance or evasion are likely to be used unless they are precluded.

(1) A retailer can quote an inflated 'cash price' to credit buyers together with a low rate of interest and allow a discount to cash buyer.

> In all cases shops were asked their cash prices, and the shoppers enquired whether the shops would reduce this price at all. Many shops had already made a reduction on the manufacturer's recommended retail price in their marked prices. But 9 shops gave a further reduction of these marked prices for cash. Sometimes this was actually advertised, sometimes the shop gave a discount only when asked. Only 1 out of the 9 shops however used this new low price when working out its credit charges.[1]

A similar problem arises in the use of trading checks. In 11 out of the 15 shops that accepted them, it was found that the price charged for the goods was higher than that charged to cash customers.[2]

Where a cash discount is freely offered, it would be an obvious evasion of disclosure legislation and a prohibition should be easy to enforce. A more difficult problem is where a retailer does not volunteer a cash discount but will allow one to a customer who bargains.[3] It is suggested that as long as the retailer offers the goods to cash customers at the quoted 'cash price', and does not suggest that they should bargain or otherwise seek a discount, the quoted 'cash price' should be accepted as a legitimate cash price to use in calculating the interest rate.

1. *Survey of Credit Charges on a Three-piece Suite and a Double Bed Carried Out in London*, 1972, Consumers' Association, p.4.

2. *An Investigation into Cash and Credit Charges for a Hoovermatic Deluxe Twin Tub Washing Machine*, Consumers' Association, 1972, p.7.

3 See Chapter 4, p.76.

(2) Where a customer is trading-in another item, the part-exchange allowance can be made payable at the end of the credit period rather than being deducted from the price at the beginning. The effect is to inflate the balance outstanding and so make the interest rate look artificially low. Two cases occurred on the survey of this being done, although presumably for other purposes. In both cases, the buyers were complaining of never having received the part-exchange allowance.

(3) The amount and rate of interest can be quoted, but included with other information and arranged to ensure that it will not be read, or that it will not be understood. This should be precluded by regulations providing in particular that the interest rate must be disclosed on the front page of any contract document and in a paragraph that deals with nothing else.

(4) If a disclosure requirement applies only to instalment credit, it can be evaded by making demand loans, the understanding being that in practice the loan will be repaid by instalments. This is done in Canada. The customer signs a promissory note on which the interest rate and other terms of the loan are set out, but does not receive a copy.

(5) The credit grantor might seek to gain additional benefits from the credit arrangement, and impose additional costs on the consumer, by requiring or inducing the consumer to enter into collateral transactions. Some obvious possibilities are credit life insurance, maintenance contracts, and the opening of a savings account on which a minimum balance will be maintained.

The *Consumer Credit Act*, 1974, and the regulations made so far recognise this last problem, but as mentioned above, they are not drawn tightly enough to close the loophole.

There is, however, one technique for the avoidance of disclosure that cannot be precluded by legislation. Some retailers might react to compulsory disclosure by including the cost of credit in the price of goods, thereby having no separate cash price and credit price. This already happens to some extent. Of the 404 transaction credit cases in the sample, there were 63 in which the interest was shown as nil. Moreover, these were generally cases in which one would expect the interest to be significant. For example, 32 involved amounts of over £30, 59 involved payment periods exceeding three months, and 44 involved payment periods exceeding 6 months.

Classified by channels of distribution, these cases were as given in Table 8.2, page 195. Classified by type of item, they were as given in Table 8.3, page 195.

It is thought, however, that whether a retailer discloses a credit charge or includes the cost of credit in the quoted price is determined by market

Table 8.2: Interest Shown in 404 Transaction Credit Cases

	Total transactions credit cases	Number in which interest reported as nil	%
Shop or garage	246	18	7
Electricity or gas board	77	4	5
Factory	1	1	
Seller called at home	36	5	14
Mail order	32	30	94
Private sale	10	5	
School	1	0	
Unascertained	1	0	
Totals	404	63	

Table 8.3: Transactions Shown in Table 8.2 Classified According to Item

	Total transaction credit cases	Number in which interest reported as nil	%
Vacuum cleaner	39	8	21
Encyclopedia set	5	3	60
Heating equipment	38	4	11
Cooking utensils	1	0	–
Sewing machine	13	4	31
Knitting machine	4	3	75
Typewriter	1	1	
New motor vehicle	15	0	–
Secondhand motor vehicle	71	6	8
Radio/TV etc.	44	12	27
Furniture	55	4	7
Rug or carpet	37	10	27
Refrigerator or deep freeze	22	5	23
Stove (cooker)	40	1	2
Washing machine, dryer, or combination	19	2	10
Totals	404	63	

considerations that would not be altered significantly by the compulsory disclosure of interest. For example, in areas where there are competing firms selling the same type of goods and a significant volume of cash customers, it is difficult for a retailer to raise prices to include the cost of credit without risking a loss of cash business. Where a retailer includes the whole or a substantial portion of the cost of credit in his quoted price, it must surely be because his marketing is aimed essentially at credit customers. Either he has made an initial decision to accept a loss of cash business, or there was no expectation of a significant volume of cash customers in any event.

Any attempt to prohibit the cost of credit being included in the quoted price is bound to fail. The merchants concerned could respond by quoting a low cost for credit, and who would say that it was fictitious? The allocation of cost is often at best an arbitrary process, and no court or other government agency could be expected to determine the level of credit charge which would reflect a fair allocation of each retailer's total costs.

The prospect of some merchants continuing to include the cost of credit in the price is, therefore, a weakness of disclosure legislation that has to be accepted. The lesson for consumers, of course, is to compare prices as well as credit terms and to be chary about buying for cash at any outlet that does not make a charge for credit at about the level of prevailing rates.

A variation of the problem occurs when a retailer quotes an amount for interest, but lower than a realistic charge for the cost of the credit. Part but not all of the cost of credit is concealed in the cash price. Here again, the possibility has to be recognised as one of the weaknesses of disclosure that cannot be prevented by legislative proscriptions. However, to the extent that retailers are in competition for cash customers, and to the extent that credit customers compare prices as well as interest rates, these are limiting influences on the feasibility of the practice.

One thing that might be done is to prohibit a merchant who includes the cost of credit in the quoted price from obtaining an unfair advantage through misleading advertising. The Crowther Committee felt that it was misleading to advertise goods as being available on credit 'with no credit charge', and that this practice should be prohibited.[1] Presumably the prohibition would extend to the use of any language indicating that credit is free.

A similar problem arises with regard to banks. The opportunity is there

1. *Report of the Committee on Consumer Credit*, 1971, Cmnd 4596, para. 6.4.15. This practice was still observed by the writer in major department stores in 1977 with regard to credit up to 6 months for items over £50.

to include part of the cost of a loan or overdraft in the charges made for the operation of a current account. Apart from the interest that is overtly charged on a loan, there used to be a practice of imposing a charge for the opening of a loan account, and of charging for the transfer of payments from the current account to the loan account.

The cost of setting up a loan should clearly be borne out of the interest, and no separate charge should be allowed. But an argument can be made for permitting a charge for the transfer of payments. If the customer had obtained the credit elsewhere, he may well have made the payments by cheque or standing order, and in that event, he would have paid a charge to the bank for effecting the transfer of payments. Thus for a bank to make a separate charge for transferring payments from a current account to a loan account makes the interest charged on the loan cover the same items of cost as it does with other credit grantors. Thereby the practice contributes to comparability. For this reason, it is suggested that a charge for the transfer of payments ought to be acceptable as long as it is at the same level as the charges for other in-house transfers.

Apart from legitimate transfer charges, the inclusion of part of the cost of loans in the charges made for operating current accounts might be prevented by requiring each bank to establish and publish a formula for its current account charges. Even apart from interest rate disclosure, this is desirable to enable consumers to make intelligent choices about the use of banking services. Publication of the formulae used for banking charges was recommended by the Prices and Incomes Board,[1] and it appears to be the current practice.

F. The Extent of Disclosure

Disclosure of the amount and rate of interest has generally been discussed in England so far only in relation to the granting of consumer credit. For example, the *Consumer Credit Act*, 1974, excludes from regulation the typical mortgage loan from a building society for the purchase of a house.

But it is difficult to see any rational ground for this limitation, and it is suggested that the disclosure requirements should extend throughout the consumer money-market, including savings accounts, bonds and house mortgages. This is desirable for two reasons. First, it would enable comparative judgments to be made in situations involving choices between consumer credit, savings and mortgages. As explained above, consumers often have a choice between buying on credit or drawing on savings, and sometimes also a choice between buying an item on credit

1. *Bank Charges*, National Board for Prices and Incomes, Report No.34, 1967, Cmnd 3292, p.46.

or including it in a mortgage loan.

Secondly, even when there is no transaction connection, the establishment of a uniform method of calculating and quoting interest throughout the consumer money-market is desirable. An analogy can be drawn here with weights and measures. We do not require uniform weights and measures to be used only with regard to goods in competition with each other. The use of varying or non-standard weights or measures has long been recognised by merchants, government and consumers alike as a source of fraud, discord and inefficiency. Thus for five centuries it has been established that one pound weight and one yard measure should mean the same thing any time, anywhere, and for any commodity.[1] Standard weights and measures are not simply indices of weight, length or volume necessary to establish quantity in a particular transaction. They establish reference points which people absorb by experience, and to which they refer, often subconsciously, to assess the significance of any new input of quantitive data, reacting to it as being light or heavy, long or short, high or low. For the same reasons, we need a standard method of calculating interest throughout the consumer money-market. The public should know, for example, that when paying or receiving 10 per cent interest in dealing with one businessman, it means the same thing as 10 per cent interest in dealing with another. Anything less is at best confusing and inefficient, and at worst an encouragement of deceit.

The connection between consumer credit and savings is particularly important where a cash lender is also the recipient of savings deposits. Lenders of this type may feel an incentive to minimise public recognition of the difference between their lending rates and their savings rates. So far, it has been possible to do this by quoting a flat rate of interest on loans and a true rate on savings. If they are compelled to quote a true rate on loans, however, without any regulation of the quotation of rates on savings, an incentive is created to devise techniques for showing an artifically high rate on savings accounts. It should be no surprise that in the United States, the enactment of truth in lending was closely followed by a demand for truth in savings legislation.[2] In Canada, the banks, following statutory disclosure requirements with regard to loans, now quote a true rate of interest on their personal loans, but still quote a misleading rate on their savings accounts. For example, the rate on a savings account may be quoted as 5 per cent, but it is calculated on the minimum monthly or quarterly balance while the loan rate is applied to

1. See e.g., the *Weights and Measures Act*, 1494, II Hen. VII, Ch.4.
2. 'Maybe We Need "Truth in Savings" too', 25 *Changing Times*, February, 1971, p.7.

the balance outstanding from day to day.

It may well be that so far in England the general practice has been to use a true rate on savings and deposit accounts. But it would surely be reckless to rely on that to continue following the enactment of a statute that creates an incentive to do otherwise.

G. The Limitations of Interest Rate Disclosure

For the reasons mentioned above, it is suggested that compulsory disclosure is worthwhile. It is however, no panacea. It does not give a consumer all the information needed for deciding whether to use credit, nor for selecting among alternative sources of credit.

Probably the greatest limitation of disclosure legislation is that it relates only to the cash cost of borrowing. Just as the use of credit can have monetary and non-monetary advantages[1] so it also has monetary and non-monetary costs. The most significant monetary cost of using credit is usually the interest, including all charges payable in respect of the credit. However, some additional monetary costs are often incurred. For example, if the instalments are payable by cheque through the post, there is an additional cost to the consumer in banking charges, stationery and postage.

Another cost is the risk of becoming unable to meet the instalments. It is common to think of default as a risk of the credit grantor; but it is a risk of the consumer too.[2] Default in making payments can involve repossession with consequential loss of the benefit of payments already made. It can also involve other monetary costs for a consumer, particularly if court proceedings are commenced, and non-monetary costs in terms of embarrassment, anxiety and tension.

Possibly the most significant non-monetary cost is the loss of flexibility. Most people are bound to apply a significant proportion of income to food and housing. Additional credit obligations add to the proportion of income required for expenditure that *must* be met, thus reducing the amount of discretionary income available for other purposes. Hence a consequence of using credit is to reduce the flexibility with which each pay packet can be used, and to reduce the capacity of a houshold to make sudden changes in its expenditure pattern to meet any unexpected change of circumstance.

For people at lower income levels, the use of credit may also restrict the extent to which they can shop for the most advantageous prices. A

1. See Chapter 3, p.37.

2. For the credit grantor, the aggregate risk of default is covered by the aggregate interest charged. But the risk to the consumer of default is not covered in any similar way.

low-income consumer may be able to obtain credit at a neighbourhood shop, where prices are high, but unable to obtain credit (or afraid to ask for it) in the town centre, or in a nearby larger town, where prices are lower.[1]

Thus to make an intelligent choice about whether to use credit, and if so from what source, a consumer cannot simply consider whether the benefits are worth the interest. The critical question is whether the total package of monetary and non-monetary benefits is worth the total package of monetary and non-monetary costs. Interest rate disclosure, however, is a considerable help in providing a standard measurement of a major item in the cost package.

Another limitation of disclosure is that the benefit is likely to be derived primarily by people in middle and upper income groups who can shop for credit and who recognise the significance of doing so. For people in lower income ranges, or who for other reasons are regarded as poor risks, the opportunities to shop for credit are less, and hence knowledge of the interest rate is less useful.

After the introduction of interest rate disclosure in Canada, enquiries by the writer among banks and new car dealers indicated a substantial increase in customer awareness of interest rates and a substantial increase in shopping around for the most advantageous terms. On the other hand, enquiries among small loan companies and used car dealers indicated no significant change, with the customers still enquiring primarily about the cash amount per month that they would have to pay.

No doubt one reason why people in lower income ranges do not enquire about the percentage rate is that they sometimes do not recognise its significance. But another and perhaps more common reason is a lack of expectation that could do better by shopping around. Commonly they are not aggressive shoppers for credit and do not perceive themselves as people with a bargaining position.

H. Conclusions on Interest Rate Disclosure

It has been suggested above that disclosure is worthwhile. But the legislation must be designed to achieve the objective. To enact disclosure requirements without the sophisticated and thorough enforcement machinery necessary to make disclosure effective is a breach of faith with consumers and honest businessmen alike. With regard to the substantive rules for disclosure, much depends on the content of regulations yet to be promulgated. As explained above, however, the *Consumer Credit Act*,

1. See e.g., *Report of the Committee on Consumer Credit*, 1971, Cmnd 4596, para. 3.6.5.

1974, does not contain any adequate collection of sanctions for the enforcement of disclosure requirements, and that deficiency cannot be remedied by regulations.

The administrative structure prescribed in the Act is sound. The Director General of Fair Trading is to provide the national leadership, and local weights and measures authorities are to initiate enforcement at the local level. But many of these authorities have barely enough staff to carry out their existing duties and there does not appear to be any nationally organised programme of budget increases to cope with the new function. Bearing in mind the inverse correlation between the strength of sanctions and the need for enforcement staff, it seems unlikely that the public will actually receive the benefit of interest rate disclosure.

If disclosure requirements are to be effective, the enforcement machinery must be strong. For those who do not feel that the achievement is worth the systematic application of strong sanctions, the rational alternative is not to pass interest rate disclosure legislation at all.

3. Pre-computation and Rebates

There are various ways in which interest can be charged. For example, a traditional method with demand loans at banks has been to calculate interest at fixed intervals and add it to the principal or charge it to the customer's current account. Another method, common in mortgage transactions, is to apply each instalment first to the payment of interest then due, and secondly to the reduction of principal. For consumer credit transactions, however, the usual method is pre-computation. The credit grantor calculates the total amount of interest that will be payable if the consumer pays according to the contract, and that amount is added to the principal at the beginning. The total is then divided by the number of instalments to arrive at the amount of each instalment.

There are several reasons why credit grantors prefer pre-computation. No doubt the most important is that a large proportion of consumers pre-pay, either by paying instalments ahead of time or by paying the whole outstanding balance. For example, one finance company informed the writer that on its motor vehicle accounts, mostly payable over two years, about 50 per cent are paid off within the first 18 months.

Credit grantors may allow the consumer a rebate in respect of the unearned interest, but they have not been required to do so. When a rebate is allowed in practice, it is usually for less than the unearned interest, and some companies only allow the rebate when it is requested. Thus the effect of pre-computation is that credit grantors keep interest charged in repsect of periods during which, in the event, no credit is outstanding.

Another reason why credit grantors might prefer pre-computation is that it may be thought to create a better impression with a consumer. She is able to see the balance outstanding in her payment book reduced by the full amount of each payment. The consumer has to be told at the beginning of a significant sum payable as interest, but does not have to be reminded of the interest when each instalment is paid.

The explanation generally given to justify pre-computation is that it saves time in calculating the interest when each instalment is received. But this is hardly a credible argument for banks and finance companies. Even if the interest is not calculated by computer, tables are available by which interest can be determined readily on the balance outstanding. Retailers are in a slightly different position. But even for them, anyone who is capable of pre-computation should be able to calculate interest on the balance outstanding from time to time.

One objection to pre-computation is the over-charging of interest in cases of pre-payment. The credit grantor receives more than the interest that has been earned. Looking at it another way, a credit grantor can receive interest from two consumers at the same time in respect of the same principal sum. Calculating interest on the balance outstanding from time to time would have the advantage that the consumer pays and the credit grantor receives exactly the interest that has been earned, no more and no less.

The main concern, however, is that pre-computation is a barrier to the effectiveness of interest rate disclosure. Consider the following example. Joe Bloggs is contemplating a new car. He starts browsing by going to a dealer, perhaps two or three dealers. He has no intention of buying on that day and consequently has not thought about financing. At one dealership, he is persuaded by an attractive car and a convincing salesman to make a purchase there and then. Like everyone else, he signs a collection of forms without reading them. One of them is a hire-purchase contract with a finance company. An interest rate of 35 per cent is stated but not read by Joe at the time. When he arrives home in the evening, however, he begins to meditate on what he has done. He fumbles with the documents, and for the first time glances at the contract. He notices the 35 per cent. He also remembers the personal loan scheme that he saw advertised at the local bank. He calls at the bank the following day and is told that he is eligible for a personal loan at 17 per cent. He arranges this and promptly goes back to the car dealer to explain that 'I have come to pay cash'. If interest rate disclosure is to be effective, he must be allowed to do so without any credit charge or penalty.

Enquiries by the writer at banks, motor vehicle dealers and sales finance companies in Canada revealed that this example is typical of what happened there after the introduction of interest rate disclosure.

Sophisticated consumers may shop for credit prior to or simultaneously with making a purchase. But it is understandable for a large proportion of the public to shop for a major item first, and then, if at all, to shop for the credit. To the extent that this is so, interest rate disclosure will be effective only if people are free to shop for credit *after* they have been informed of the interest rate. For this purpose, people cannot be regarded as informed of the interest rate until at least a day *after* receiving a copy of the contract in which it is disclosed.

Moreover, it is surely in the public interest that dealers should have no incentive to divert consumers from their cheapest source of credit. When a consumer enters retail premises, it may well be thought that he is fair game for a sales pitch and should be bound by any contract that he signs for the goods on sale. But with financing it is different. To treat a signature on a form as binding a consumer to pay interest that has not been earned creates an incentive for a dealer to hook a consumer on credit terms which the dealer knows are less satisfactory than the consumer could obtain, and in circumstances in which the consumer has commonly not thought about the credit aspects of the transaction.

It may seem at first impression that to allow a consumer to pay off a credit arrangement the following day without some loss would be a hardship on the dealer or finance company. They have incurred the trouble of documenting the credit arrangement, and perhaps of obtaining a credit report. But no significant volume of hardship would be incurred in this way. Prohibiting pre-computation or compelling a full rebate of unearned interest upon a pre-payment would create a disincentive for a dealer to hook a consumer on a hire-purchase contract when he knows the consumer can obtain cheaper credit elsewhere. The likely result would be that hire-purchase contracts would be signed by people who would not be eligible for a bank loan, or who would not think themselves eligible. These people are not likely to pay the finance company off immediately or quickly, so that, as a practical matter, it is difficult to see that dealers or finance companies would suffer any significant loss in administrative overhead. If they suffer a loss, it is more likely to be through the transfer of business to low-cost sources of credit, particularly banks. It would be counter-productive to enact disclosure legislation and at the same time permit the imposition of charges that impede that result from occurring.

Unfortunately, the *Consumer Credit Act*, 1974, condones rather than prohibits pre-computation. The Act provides for a rebate of unearned interest to be allowed on early settlement,[1] and regulations are expected to provide the formula for calculating the rebate. But it is apparently

1. SS.94-7.

the intention of the government to allow a creditor to charge for pre-payment an amount equal to interest for three months beyond the date of settlement.[1]

If interest rate disclosure is to result in a more perfect market for consumer credit, either pre-computation should be prohibited, or a consumer must be entitled to pay off the balance and be credited for the *full amount of unearned interest.*

A prohibition of pre-computation is clearly preferable. A statutory right to pre-pay and obtain a rebate of the unearned interest has obvious difficulties. One is that a statutory right to the rebate would not be enough to result in rebates actually being allowed. There could be a requirement that a consumer be informed of the right by a notice in the contract. But the probabilities are that few consumers would read the contract document at the time of pre-payment, even if they still have it available. Scrupulously honest creditors may allow the rebate to anyone who pre-pays an outstanding balance. But for others, the practical result is likely to be that full rebates according to the statutory formula are paid to well informed and attentive consumers who ask for them, but not to those who are ill-informed or for other reasons less demanding. To seek the enforcement of rebates through criminal sanctions and the exercise of licensing powers would add to the burdens of surveillance over the credit market, and the cost and inconvenience of the whole process of enforcement would surely exceed any benefit that can be derived from the use of pre-computation.

If it is right that pre-computation is not a substantial cost-saving device, that it will frustrate the effectiveness of interest rate disclosure, and that it enables credit grantors to obtain unearned interest, it is suggested that by far the simplest and most effective solution would be to prohibit pre-computation. Using tables that are readily available for the purpose, interest could then be calculated on the balance outstanding from time to time, as it is now for savings accounts, demand loans and some other types of accounts.

Accounts for consumer credit could still be paid by instalments of equal amount. As in mortgage transactions, each instalment could be applied first to the payment of interest then due, and secondly to the reduction of principal.

4. Rate Ceilings

The rate at which it should be permissible to charge interest has for centuries been a topic of discussion in the literature of philosophy, theology,

1. *Reform of the Law on Consumer Credit*, 1973, Cmnd 5427, App. III, para.18.

law and economics.[1] In more recent years, it has also featured in the literature of marketing and of social work. Usury laws at various times and places have specified maximum interest rates, commonly 6 per cent or 10 per cent per annum. In the twentieth century, in England and the Commonwealth countries, there appears to have been a tendency to move away from statutory ceilings on interest rates. No ceiling is prescribed in the *Consumer Credit Act*, 1974.

The arguments on the desirability of a statutory ceiling vary according to the level being considered.

During the 1960s, it was enacted or advocated in some of the United States that there be a maximum of 12 per cent on credit granted by retailers. The purpose was clearly regulatory. Since this rate was below prevailing levels, the objective was to effect a reduction in interest charges.

Following the introduction of a 12 per cent ceiling on interest rates, the first reaction one might expect is that, as far as possible, merchants would transfer part of the cost of credit to the prices of goods, either by raising price levels generally or by increasing the prices of items most commonly sold on credit. But the extent of this would be limited by competition for cash customers. Merchants anxious to retain cash business could be expected to hold their price levels and restrict their credit business to the better risks to whom it was profitable to advance credit at 12 per cent. Other merchants could be expected to specialise in sales on credit to those in poorer risk categories. These merchants would include the bulk of their credit costs in inflated prices, accepting as a consequence that they would not expect cash customers.

People in low income groups would become more dependent upon a limited range of merchants, and the increase in monopoly power that this stratification of retailing would give to those merchants would reduce any pressure on them to sell good quality merchandise at reasonable prices. Not only would low income consumers pay at least the same amount for credit as without a rate ceiling, but they would be more restricted in the shops at which they could deal, and thus be more the victims of predatory practices and shabby goods.

If it is a goal of consumer protection to foster the establishment of business relations between reputable merchants selling good quality products and low income consumers, a ceiling on interest rates as low as 12 per cent would be counter-productive.

1. For a brief summary of the history of this, see 'Interest and Usury', R.W. Johnson, *The Realities of Maximum Ceilings on Interest and Finance Charges*, 1970, Conference on Personal Finance Law (New York), p.5.

If a rate ceiling as low as 12-18 per cent was applied to cash lending, the consequences could be even worse. Those not eligible for a bank loan (perhaps a majority of consumers) would be disqualified from borrowing on the legitimate lending market. The result would be a tremendous unfulfilled demand, thereby creating an opportunity for loan shark operations on a large scale. Moreover, because their methods of collection would be extra-legal, there is a risk that these loan shark operations would be affiliated with other sections of organised crime.

For these reasons, it is highly undesirable to establish a rate ceiling at the lower end or near the middle of the range of prevailing rates.

Establishing a ceiling at the upper end of prevailing rates would make these objections less applicable. But it may appear to give a statutory blessing to the upper end of the scale. A rate of, say, 30 per cent is not far above the median of current rates. Hence making that rate a statutory ceiling might encourage credit grantors to move up to it, and it might encourage consumers to feel that this is a rate that Parliament has found reasonable.

Different considerations would apply to a ceiling well above the range of prevailing rates, for example, a ceiling of 55 per cent. This is too high for prevailing rates to move up to it. It is also too high to have any regulatory effect; indeed, it would have no influence on the bulk of credit transactions. But it may still be advantageous. Primarily the argument rests on unabashed paternalism. People who cannot qualify for credit at a rate of 55 per cent must be in dire circumstances. Their incomes must be so low or uncertain in relation to their needs that paying interest at rates higher than 55 per cent can only aggravate their plight.

> . . .there is a level of cost above which it becomes socially harmful to make loans available at all, even if the cost is not disproportionate to the risk and expense incurred by the lender. There may be cases where, in view of the poor financial standing of the borrower, interest of 100 per cent would not yield an excessive profit to the lender; but if the borrower falls into a risk category as low as this, then we feel he ought not to be eligible for loans from the private sector. We recognise that such a borrower has to live; he has to have money from somewhere. But we feel that this is a problem which, assuming it to be capable of solution at all, must be solved through social welfare services rather than by the granting of loans at enormous interest rates.[1]

1. *Report of the Committee on Consumer Credit*, 1971, Cmnd 4596, para.6.6.6.

The argument also rests on a feeling that we should not deviate from or undermine social measures for the relief of poverty, nor should we encourage financial despair through the incurring of debt obligations that people cannot repay without inflicting privation upon themselves and their families, or raising the money by resort to criminal activity.

> The modern state can ill afford to permit its citizens to exchange for present relief promises for the future which imply the risk of economic peonage and add to the public burden through poverty and crime.[1]

Moreover, people who borrow at such high rates often have prior debt obligations outstanding. It is unfair to creditors who have made advances at reasonable rates that they should be subjected to increased risks and to competition in their collection endeavours by lenders who are charging high rates commensurate with high-risk lending.

Another argument is that a ceiling in this range would prevent a credit grantor from taking advantage of those consumers who place a blind confidence in the reasonableness of the businessmen with whom they deal. Consider, for example, a merchant who charges competitive rates of about 24-28 per cent to sophisticated customers, but charges up to 65 per cent to those who appear to lack the intelligence or attentiveness to recognise the significance of the rate, or to shop elsewhere, notwithstanding that they are good risks. A statutory ceiling of 55 per cent would be some protection to people in this category.

A ceiling, even as high as 55 per cent, would be too low for credit transactions involving small amounts or short time periods. This, however, is no reason for not applying such a ceiling to ordinary long-term consumer transactions. Exceptions could be prescribed for small amounts and for short periods.

For the above reasons, it is suggested that a ceiling on interest rates for consumer transactions is desirable provided that it is substantially above the range of prevailing rates. For a ceiling to be workable, it is essential that

(1) The level be high enough to embrace all reasonable credit transactions so that there would be no unfulfilled demand large enough to create a pressure for the development of loan shark operations.
(2) The system of social security (Supplementary Benefits or whatever it is called for the time being) must be sufficiently available,

1. 'Three Experiemnts with Small-Loan Interest Rates', R. Nugent, (1933) 12 *Harvard Business Review* 35, 39.

prompt and responsive to meet the needs of those in dire straits.

(3) There must be somebody whose job is to detect and prosecute illegal lending operations.

Probably the greatest difficulty with this proposal is one of image on the political scene. Any politician who advocates a statutory ceiling substantially above the range of prevailing interest rates is vulnerable to the criticism (however undeserved) that he is pandering to the credit industry rather than making a rational judgement in the public interest.

5. Unconscionability (Extortionate Credit Bargains)

Apart from a ceiling on interest rates, another possibility is to provide by statute that the courts may vary the rate of interest stipulated in a contract whenever it is thought to be harsh or unconscionable (or nowadays 'extortionate'). A provision on these lines was contained in the *Moneylenders Act*, 1900, and a similar principle is now being extended to the general run of consumer credit transactions.[1]

An unconscionability provision can occasionally be useful, and if perceived in that way, as a long-stop measure, it can be helpful. The danger is, however, that an unconscionability provision can be perceived as an alternative to a rate ceiling. This was the context in which the proposal appeared in the report of the Crowther Committee, and unfortunately, this is what appears to have happened in the *Consumer Credit Act*, 1974.

An unconscionability provision has the advantage of flexibility, enabling a court to take into account the risks and circumstances of the transaction. This can be a valuable feature in commercial cases. But for consumer transactions, there are two important respects in which an unconscionability provision is very different from and inferior to a rate ceiling.

First, it is of paramount importance in consumer transactions that the legal result should be, as far as possible, clear, predictable and certain, so that creditors and consumers alike will know where they stand without incurring the cost of litigation over small amounts. A rate ceiling provides that certainty. Conversely, unconscionability provisions require an adjudication at the behest of someone who is usually ill equipped to undertake litigation. In Canada, similar provisions[2] have not been used extensively, and when they are invoked, it is often by commercial borrowers rather than consumers. Because unconscionability prescribes no clear rule of illegality, these sections of the Act give little guidance for out of

1. *Consumer Credit Act*, 1974, SS.137-40.
2. E.g. the *Unconscionable Transactions Relief Act*, RSO 1970, Ch.472.

court settlements.

Secondly, the value of a rate ceiling is that, together with the law relating to creditors' remedies,[1] it can be used to define the perimeters of consumer credit. It is a tool that enables societal judgements to be made about the extent to which consumer credit should be allowed to expand before the point is reached at which the dangers to society or the individual exceed the benefits. An unconscionability provision can never be used for this purpose, partly because of the rarity of its invocation, and partly because the criteria that the courts are required to use by these provisions relate to the fairness of the interest rate having regard to the risk involved, rather than to the propriety of the interest rate having regard to social policy or other objectives.

For these reasons, an unconscionability provision, though it can be helpful, is not an alternative to a rate ceiling.

1. See Chapter 10.

9 THE RESOLUTION OF CONSUMER DISPUTES

1. The Courts

A. The Traditional County Court System

When discussion and negotiation fail, the official way of resolving disputes is through litigation in the courts. But this can be expensive and the bulk of consumer disputes involve relatively small amounts.

England has no special courts for small claims. Those not settled must either be brought in a County Court or abandoned. By the beginning of the present decade, however, there was increasing concern about the processing of small claims in the adversary system.[1]

A common misconception about courts was that they were engaged primarily in the task of adjudication. Of claims brought in the County Courts, however, the largest category was debt claims arising out of retail transactions. With regard to these claims, it was nearer the truth to describe the County Courts as like collection agencies, enforcing the claims of sellers and finance companies regardless of their legitimacy. So universal was the absence of any scrutiny of the legitimacy of claims that even those made void by statute were enforced. 'There is a charming, but not harmless, innocence about those who believe that a gaming debt cannot be recovered by court action. The County Courts entertain thousands each year, even to the point of enforcing them by commitment.'[2] Only by way of exception was there any enquiry into the merits of a claim. Moreover there was an almost total absence of claims by buyers.

Unfortunately, civil judicial statistics are not broken down into very useful categories. But a rough impression was gained by enquiries among County Court registrars and office staff. While debt claims by credit grantors could be counted in hundreds or thousands a year, claims by buyers in the same courts could be counted in ones or twos.[3] The contrast

1. The contribution of the writer to that discussion is contained in 'Small Claims', (1972) 35 *Modern Law Review* 18. An excellent paper, and the one which probably had the greatest political effect, was *Justice Out of Reach*, The Consumer Council, 1970, HMSO.

2. Per a County Court registrar in a memorandum, 1966. It is, however, professional misconduct for a solicitor to threaten or to issue proceedings for the recovery of a gaming debt. See *The Guide to Professional Conduct and Etiquette*, T. Lund, p.86.

3. The enquiries of the writer in 1968 and 1969 were confirmed by the Consumer Council study, *supra*, pp.13-14. A study of 1,238 actions in County Courts did not reveal a single case of an individual suing a firm in a consumer matter, except for one possible case.

was even more striking when it is recalled that claims by sellers are generally limited to credit transactions, whereas theoretically claims by buyers are not. Meanwhile, the remoteness from reality of the official perception of the courts was illustrated by the assertion that the County Courts '. . .are adapted to the needs of the great masses of the population. . .'.[1]

If an adjudication occurred at all in a consumer case, it was likely to result from a defence being filed to a claim initiated by a seller. Defences to the claims of sellers were more common than claims initiated by buyers. But even here, there was cause for concern and reason to believe that defences were only filed in a small proportion of cases in which a defence would be available.

Among consumers aggrieved by unsatisfactory transactions, there was a feeling of helplessness,[2] and the courts were not perceived as a place to go for redress.

In connection with the work of the Payne Committee,[3] several interesting memoranda were written by County Court registrars, and they saw a different picture. From their vantage point, the scene was an array of 'delinquent' buyers ('debtors'). Some were seen as inadequate people who never seem to predict the consequences of what they do; some overcommit themselves through not budgeting; some meet hardship through a loss of income; some dispute a claim but never file a defence; some are swindlers. Many are evasive. Proposals for reform were made that centred on how to get money from 'delinquent' buyers more swiftly, more cheaply, or more humanely.

This depressing perception of a segment of the buying public is, of course, not difficult to explain. Delinquent buyers were commonly hauled into court. Delinquent sellers were not.

B. The Reforms of the 1970s

Rather than establishing any new kind of small claims court, the Lord Chancellor's Office sought to ameliorate the situation by improvements in the County Courts.

One step was to provide for the adjudication of small claims by 'arbitration', rather than trial. This differs, however, from conventional arbitration

1. *The County Court Practice 1970*, p.3.
2. The same phenomenon was observed in the United States:
'Some consumers feel unhappy about the marketplace because it provides nobody to complain to. The marketplace is impersonal. The blame for any fault is shifted to the company – no person may be identified and the place is inaccessible.' *Consumer Protection in the States*, 1970, Council of State Governments, p.7.
3. Committee on the Enforcement of Judgment Debts. The Committee reported in 1969, Cmnd 3909.

in that it does not usually depend upon the consent of both parties, and the adjudicator is usually the registrar, not an arbitrator chosen by the parties. In those respects, the adjudication is still like a trial, rather than like a commercial arbitration. It is labelled 'arbitration', probably to convey the intention that it should be simpler and less formal than a trial. The strict rules of evidence need not be observed, the registrar is unrobed, the oath can be dispensed with, and most arbitrations nowadays take place in the registrar's office rather than in a courtroom.

Some registrars interviewed by the writer seem willing to use their knowledge and experience more in arbitrations, and more willing to dispense with expert evidence. In other ways, too, some registrars take a more active role in arbitrations and try to help the parties to a greater extent than they would think appropriate in a trial.

> In arbitrations, I do not interrupt a litigant in person. We cannot expect litigants in person to cross-examine. I ask each party to say his piece in turn. Then I ask any questions that I think need to be asked.[1]

It is often said that arbitrations follow inquisitorial rather than adversarial procedures. But this is true only to a limited extent. The procedure is inquisitorial to the extent that registrars ask questions to bring out the case that each party is presenting. But it is still adversarial in that each party is expected to decide for himself what case it is that he wants to present. Each litigant is still expected to decide what he should be asking for, and on what grounds he should be claiming or defending.

To some extent, the informality of arbitration may be more apparent than real. For example, when asked in what ways arbitration is less formal, one registrar replied:

> In a trial by registrar, I have to tell a litigant to present his evidence now and his argument later. This is when he tries to present his evidence and argument in one presentation. But on an arbitration I can say 'Let's just have the facts now. The commercials come later'.[2]

The need for reform in the adjudication of small claims cannot be met by observing the rigid procedures of the adversary system with a more colloquial vocabulary.

The main limitation of arbitration is that it is only a simplified form of

1. Interview with a County Court registrar, 1977.
2. Interview with a County Court registrar, 1977.

trial; while most of the difficulties that consumers experience in dealing with courts relate to pre-trial proceedings. For this reason, the new 'arbitration' procedure is probably less significant than the other reforms mentioned below.

Far more cases have been affected by the introduction of pre-trial review. Where a general summons is issued, or a defence has been filed to a default summons, a date is fixed for a hearing. But this hearing is now a pre-trial review, not a trial.

The official purpose of pre-trial review is to clarify the issues, and to make interlocutory decisions in preparation for the trial or arbitration. Cases are listed for pre-trial review at about 5 or 10 minute intervals, and the process can function like the traditional summons for directions in the High Court.[1]

In the minority of cases that involve substantial sums and that are going for trial by a judge, pre-trial review can have obvious advantages in preparing the case. But it is surely counter-productive in relation to small claims. Any aggrieved consumer must already overcome so many hurdles in the quest for adjudication that to add another interlocutory stage seems pointless and discouraging. It is hardly surprising that many people attend a pre-trial review expecting it to result in a decision on the claim, only to feel dejected upon being told that that is not the purpose of the event.

An achievement claimed for pre-trial review is that it facilitates settlement. Indeed, 76 per cent of cases going to pre-trial review go no further.[2] In pre-trial reviews in 1976, it appears that only 27.63 per cent resulted in directions being given for trial or arbitration. In 35.94 per cent, judgment was entered or damages assessed (perhaps by default or admission), leaving 36.42 per cent in which the claim would have been settled, abandoned or otherwise disposed of without the disposition becoming part of a judgment or order.[3]

No doubt pre-trial review does play a positive role in achieving a genuine settlement in some cases. The meeting of the parties on neutral ground and clarification of the issues may enable them to see possibilities of settlement that had not been apparent before. The real problem, however, is how to distinguish genuine settlements from capitulations resulting from frustration at the failure of the court to provide any opportunity for prompt adjudication.

It is often alleged that pre-trial review is used to coerce settlements and

1. In one court visited by the writer, a standard form was used for the order on a pre-trial review, and it was very similar to the traditional summons for directions.

2. *Small Claims*, W.H. Elliott, 1977, International Congress on the Law of Civil Procedure at Ghent, p.6.

3. Calculated from the *Judicial Statistics for 1976*, Cmnd 6875, p.71.

this was confirmed by the enquiries and observations of the writer. For example, in one case observed by the writer, the parties were sent out of the room to see if they could settle the matter notwithstanding that one of them objected that there was no hope of settlement and that he wanted a court decision. Another registrar explained that his practice was to send the parties to another room to settle the case. If they did not settle, he told them they would have to come back at the end of the list for that day. Thus if they did not settle, their pre-trial review would not be completed until the end of the list that day, and they would have to come back again on a subsequent occasion for the arbitration or trial. One need hardly say that this puts pressure to concede on whichever party can least afford to spend so much time at the courthouse. A third register explained that he perceived the main purpose of pre-trial review as achieving a settlement.

Among these registrars, it did not appear to be recognised that pressures were being created to settle on terms that may have nothing to do with the merits of the case. A fourth registrar interviewed was, however, very conscious of the problem, and maintained the traditional view that it would be improper for him to suggest that a case be settled.

The prevailing view in the County Court system appears to be that the settlement of a case is a success, and that therefore pre-trial review is successful because it brings about settlements. But it is surely perverse to regard settlements as a success when a proportion of them (perhaps a majority) result from a structure and procedures that, in substance, amount to a denial of adjudication.

Apart from settlements outside the registrar's office, both pre-trial review and arbitration can be used as occasions for conciliation, with the registrar acting as conciliator. There is no measurement of the extent of the practice. But it certainly happens some of the time, and possibly to a greater extent than is recognised.

Conciliation has obvious advantages in situations involving a continuing relationship between the parties, such as in labour relations. But it is pernicious in small claims.

Conciliation means attempting to locate a point somewhere between the positions taken by the parties at which they can be persuaded to agree. It penalises people with more agreeable attitudes, or who are more easily intimidated, and it gives an advantage to the party with the most aggressive temperament, the most experience of litigation, or who feels the most comfortable with the procedures of the court. The party with the most urgent need for disposition of the case may feel at a disadvantage. Again, a litigant may feel that if he declined conciliation, or declined to accede to the registrar's suggestions for settlement, the registrar might be influenced by his stubbornness in the subsequent adjudication. If the conciliation fails, there is still a need for adjudication, and hence there may be a wasteful duplication of effort. Moreover, conciliation tends to legitimise procedures that avoid rather than provide prompt adjudication.

However well intended, conciliation can amount to a denial of justice. Far from allowing conciliation, it would be well to prohibit registrars from ever suggesting possible terms of settlement, or even from suggesting that a case be settled.

In relation to consumer problems, the need is not for a courthouse that promises adjudication and then pressures people into accepting the institution as a forum for settlement. It is particularly inappropriate for people who went there in the first place because they had not received what they were led to expect. Nor is there a need for another conciliation service, particularly when those services are already offered elsewhere. The desperate need is for quick and cheap adjudication.

For these reasons, it is suggested that pre-trial review is counter-productive in relation to small claims, and that it ought to be abolished. The result could well be that some cases will reach trial or arbitration without adequate preparation. But it would surely be better to meet that problem by adjournment in those cases rather than by telling those who are ready for adjudication that they must settle or come back another day.

Pre-trial review could have greater potential if it was used in actions commenced by a default summons and where no defence has been filed. But it is not used in those cases. Thus pre-trial review is not a mechanism for checking on the validity of undefended claims.[1]

Perhaps the most important reform has been in public relations. Previously, the County Courts seemed to be perceived as passive institutions, operating on the assumption that people in need of adjudication will somehow find their way there. But recently the Lord Chancellor's Office has been actively informing the public of the services offered. Booklets[2] and pamphlets on how to make use of the County Courts receive a wide circulation, and a liaison has been established between the County Courts and the advisory agencies. County Court personnel also talk about their courts at meetings of local groups.

1. Special procedures apply, however, to an action for the recovery of goods under a hire-purchase or conditional sale agreement, and in the course of those proceedings, the court might discover and consider a defence, even though no defence has been filed. (The writer saw this happen in 3 cases.)

2. A 73 page booklet on *Small Claims in the County Court*, Michael Birks, 1975, Lord Chancellor's Office, is available free to the public at offices of the County Courts, at Citizens' Advice Bureaux, and at other agencies.

Other helpful reforms of recent years are:

(i) Court forms have been revised to make them more readable and court staff are encouraged to help people complete the forms.
(ii) The postal service can now be used more in dealing with the court so that fewer attendances at court offices are now needed.
(iii) There is less insistence that corporations be represented by a solicitor, and in routine matters, many corporations are now represented by a member of their office staff.
(iv) With regard to costs, a litigant in person used to be at a serious disadvantage compared with one who retained a solicitor. Two reforms now put them on a more equal footing. First, in claims not exceeding £100, no lawyer's fees can be recovered by a successful party, except the fee for issuing the summons. Secondly, in more serious cases, a successful litigant in person will not nowadays be denied the costs of preparing and presenting his case simply because no solicitor was retained.[1]

These reforms have been an improvement. But they have not changed the basic role and image of the County Courts. In relation to most claims filed, the County Courts still function like collection agencies for credit grantors processing claims in bulk. Some of these companies have standing arrangements with some of the courts that any offer of any payment in settlement of a claim should be accepted without reference back to the plaintiff. Some also have standing arrangements with regard to the action to be taken in the event of a defence being filed.

The reforms have benefited some sections of the population, particularly small business. Many small businessmen now bring claims themselves, whereas previously they might have gone to a solicitor or not sued at all.[2] It also appears that more actions are now brought with regard to individual matters, for example, a householder suing his neighbour for the repair of a fence, intra-family disputes relating to property, and small damage claims resulting from motor vehicle collisions. But with regard to claims by consumers, the reforms have been a predictable disappointment. Claims by consumers have risen from almost zero to a small trickle, but that is all.

As the assistant chief clerk of one County Court saw the situation in 1977 'People still haven't cottoned on that they can sue'.

The difficulty, however, is not simply lack of information. 'When recourse to the County Court is recommended, there is often reluctance

1. *Litigants in Person (Costs and Expenses) Act*, 1975.
2. Interviews with court staff, 1977.

to become involved with "the Courts", though the case amply justified this.'[1] Enquiries at advisory agencies in 1977 indicated that although there is now a trickle of consumer claims, there is still a widespread fear among consumers of going to court to sue a business enterprise. Typical comments were:

(i) People don't have faith in courts. They fear the courts. They are afraid of ritual and formality.
(ii) Consumers get concerned whenever we mention courts.
(iii) In most people's minds, courts equals police equals crime.
(iv) People are afraid of courts.

There are no recorded statistics that identify claims brought by consumers in the County Courts. An impression was gathered, however, from information obtained during interviews with the staff of four County Courts in 1977. If those courts are representative, it would appear that somewhere about 70 per cent of actions commenced in County Courts are claims by businesses against consumers, while somewhere about 1 per cent are claims by consumers against businesses.

C. The Potential for Further Improvement

The Lord Chancellor's Office seems to perceive the reform process as continuing, and no doubt other reforms could be made within the structure of the County Court system. For example, further improvements are pending to simplify court forms and to use more colloquial language.[2] Also, if pre-trial reviews are to be continued, a notice may be needed explaining to the parties the purpose of the event.

Similarly, signs outside the courts could be improved. For example, outside the offices of one County Court visited by the writer in 1977, there was a sign indicating 'Plaint Office'. That is fine for someone who already knows that he wants to be a 'plaintiff'. But for those who are less certain how their aspirations in relation to the legal system should be designated, there was no notice of an entrance for 'Enquiries'.

More could also be done to adapt the courts to the ordinary habits of human discourse, rather than expecting litigants in person to adjust themselves to the formalities of legal process. For example, the informality of 'arbitration' could become more universal through a rule change providing that 'A litigant in person shall not be required to separate evidence from

1. *Annual Report of the Consumer Services Department to the Greater Manchester Council for the year ending 31st March 1975*, p.26.
2. Interview at the Lord Chancellor's Office, 1977.

argument'.

Similarly, there could be a rule change recognising the role of a companion to a litigant in person. The fear of courts that many people have is sometimes overcome by the company of a friend, a member of the family, or perhaps someone from a Consumers' Advice Centre or Citizens' Advice Bureau. Some registrars relax the formal rules and allow the companion to participate in proceedings. But others will not allow anyone to say anything unless he is first classified in one of the categories of people eligible to speak. Traditionally, these categories are a litigant in person, a barrister, a solicitor, an ordinary witness, an expert witness, or an interpreter. This can be frustrating for a companion who does not understand these categories, but who 'just wants to say something'. It would surely be an improvement to have a simple rule that a companion to a litigant in person should be allowed to speak, reserving a discretionary power to terminate any presentation that becomes irrelevant.

The furniture of the courts could be changed to a layout more suitable for small claims. Most 'arbitrations' are conducted in a registrar's office with a T layout. The registrar sits behind his desk. In front of the desk, and perpendicular to it, is a table, with the litigants sitting each side. With the table only 3-4 ft wide, this may be too much of a confrontation for people who are sometimes angry. In any event, they have not come there to speak to each other. On the other hand, holding an arbitration in a courtroom puts the parties in line abreast, and is in other ways too formal. The ideal furnishing for this type of event would surely be a triangular arrangement.

Fortunately, the architectural tone of austere grandeur in courthouse design is disappearing. Newer courthouses visited by the writer are more functional and attractive. But the value of this reform can be undermined by the decisions on dress and decoration. For example, at one fairly new courthouse visited by the writer, the registrar was dressed in a congenial lounge suit. In dealing with pre-trial reviews, he was very courteous to people, trying hard to put them at ease, and explaining things in language they would understand. But a courtroom was being used as the waiting room for those who were waiting their turn, and people were shown into the registrar's office by an usher in a black robe. In the superior courts, dark clothing may have some value in emphasising the gravity of the event. But in relation to small claims, features like this can, in their cumulative effect, explain why ordinary people are afraid of courts. They are inconsistent with the image of justice as a service industry. If some kind of uniform is desirable to identify court staff to the public, surely a neat-looking blazer would lend a more congenial atmosphere. Respect and dignity can be preserved without making a place look gloomy.

Another reform would be to abolish the concurrent jurisdiction of the High Court in relation to claims against consumers. The benefit of reforms in County Court proceedings, which could make it easier for consumers to defend a claim, are undermined if a small claim can still be pursued by the intimidating procedure of a High Court writ.

Section 141 of the *Consumer Credit Act*, 1974, may have been intended to solve this problem. It provides that in England and Wales, the County Court shall have jurisdiction to determine any action by the creditor to enforce a regulated agreement, and 'such action shall not be brought in any other court'. That would be a promising start if the Act contained further provisions to make the prohibition effective. But it does not. It goes on to provide that where such an action is brought in the High Court, '. . .it shall not be treated as improperly brought, but shall be transferred to the county court'.

Even if the staff of the High Court were specifically trained for the function it would still be impossible in many cases to distinguish a writ for the enforcement of a regulated agreement from writs in other matters. If, as appears to be the case, the burden is placed upon the consumer to become aware of his rights and to make application for the transfer, the problem has been retained of confronting ordinary people with technical proceedings that may involve communication with a distant court, instead of providing them with a simple opportunity of defending a claim in their local County Court.

If it is intended to terminate the unfair advantage that a business plaintiff can derive through the concurrent jurisdiction of the High Court, the prohibition of the issuance of High Court process should be enforced by some kind of penalty, perhaps some amount or percentage that would be automatically deductable from the claim.

D. Counter-productive Changes

Not all changes in the County Courts in recent years have been improvements for consumers. In particular, the public need for an adjudication service on a local basis has run counter to government economy moves. These have included holding down the opening of new court offices, or the appointment of additional registrars, and even the closing of some court offices.

How many court offices there should be in any given area is not a question that can be answered simply by reference to the distances that people travel. It is also important to consider the significance of size. Of the four County Court offices visited by the writer in 1977, there was a perceptible difference between the largest and the smallest. In the largest court, communication between the staff and the public was through a glass barrier. The number of staff working in one room was too many for the most cordial forms of inter-personal communication, and a division of labour appeared to result in a great deal of repetition work. The staff did not, as they did in the smallest court, have the sense of achievement that comes from seeing matters through from the beginning to the end.

Staff in each of the courts were asked how they felt about litigants in person, and consumer cases in particular. It may not be a coincidence that the reply indicating the most warmhearted enthusiasm came from a clerk in the smallest court. In this court, the same clerk dealt with claims coming in bulk through the mail and with the counter enquiries.

> I like dealing with people at the counter. Those cases are more interesting and you can follow it through more. Otherwise we would just be doing paperwork. . .Spending time with people at the counter is very important. They come in extremely nervous, like they were criminals. It is worth spending time with them at the beginning.

A similar contrast appeared in the replies to questions about how the staff respond to enquiries from people who need advice on whether to sue. Again, it was the clerk in the smallest court who seemed to be offering the most help.

> We are not allowed to advise people whether they should sue. But I try to help a bit. If I think someone has a good case and they just seem frightened, I say something encouraging, like 'Why not have a go and see what happens'. . .If the person they want to sue has several judgments against him already, and the other people are not getting their money, I would say something to put them off. I am not allowed to say anything about the other judgments. But I would mention the difficulties of enforcing a judgment, and put the emphasis on that. I don't like to see people waste their money.

Helpful hints of this kind did not appear from interviews with staff at the larger courts.

Of course isolated experiences do not prove that small courts are better than large ones. But they do leave one wondering whether the advantages of smallness are fully considered when the decisions are made on the merger or division of court areas.

There has also been some backtracking in the publicity. In 1975, posters were telling people that: 'County Courts are There to Help. It's simpler and cheaper than you think.' In 1977, however, posters were telling the public that they can sue in the County Court 'As a last resort'.

The earlier poster tended to create the impression that County Courts provide a quick and cheap system of adjudication, readily available to the public. The subsequent poster appears to reflect official recognition that this is not the case, and not likely to be.

The lack of any structure for quick and cheap adjudication may have been aggravated further by the *Consumer Credit Act,* 1974. This seems to expand the range of issues determinable by judicial discretion.

Finally, the addition of divorce jurisdiction to the County Courts has been no help to the administration of small claims. Not only does it add to the workload of registrars, but it will tend to preclude them from becoming specialists in small claims adjudication.

E. The Endemic Problems

Whatever changes are made in County Court practice, there are some problems that are unlikely to disappear in a court that is oriented primarily to the adversary system.

To appreciate the significance of these problems, it is important to consider the background from which the consumer cases arrive at the courthouse.

Consumer disputes do not arise among people of equal bargaining power, with equal capability of presenting claims, and with equal capacity for approaching the court. For a seller or finance company, a dispute with a customer can be handled as a business routine. For the consumer, it is more likely to be a disturbing experience. The use of forms (e.g. invoices and bills) can give a seller another psychological advantage. By having a figure in his books and showing that figure in documents that he sends, his claim is given an aura of righteousness. A buyer has no such formal trappings in which to dress a claim against a seller. Similarly court forms may seem strange and awesome to a buyer, but routine to a seller.

Moreover, the socio-economic milieu of a judge or registrar is closer to that of a businessman than to that of a low-income consumer. While a seller may feel at ease at the prospect of talking to the judge or registrar, a working-class buyer may feel that he would have to communicate with one of 'them', not one of 'us'. The buyer may anticipate that the bewilderment and discomfort of dealing with 'them' will make him inarticulate, and this in turn can add to anxiety. It may well be that in any adjudication, the registrar would be patient and sympathetic in listening to him. But that is irrelevant for someone who is never going to get that far.

Another psychological difference relates to the risk of losing a case and having to pay costs to the opposing party. Where a claim exceeds £100, these costs can include a solicitor's fees. For a buyer, this can threaten an intolerable burden on what is already a tight budget.[1] For a seller or finance company, it is simply the risk of another business expense.

Economies of scale can be another advantage for a seller. There are various ways in which a seller can process economically very small claims. If he has a large number, he can handle them himself in bulk. If he has fewer, he can use a collection agency. One way or another, sellers find it economical to process claims even as low as £10. Indeed, the majority of money claims in the County Courts are for less than £50.[2] For a buyer, on the other hand, a claim against a seller, or the defence of a claim, may be his only experience of litigation. He cannot go to a collection agency, and if he went to a solicitor charging an economic rate, the cost of bringing or defending a claim to trial would not usually justify handling cases involving less than £250.

Where the assistance of a solicitor is required, the system is again organised to facilitate the processing of sellers' claims in bulk. In most areas, there is at least one solicitor (often known as a 'local advocate') who gathers the claims of retailers, finance companies, and sometimes collection agencies, and will deal with them economically by appearing in several cases at one sitting of the court. Other solicitors who prefer to avoid litigation, or who do not have enough volume in the particular court, often brief him to act as their agent.

There is no push-button legal service of this type available to buyers. The greater variety of grievances that buyers can suffer reduces the opportunities for processing buyers' claims in bulk. In low-income areas, solicitors are sometimes hard to find. Moreover the fees that can be charged, compared with the work involved, make consumer grievances unattractive to them, and because consumer problems do not generally receive legal advice, most solicitors do not develop expertise in handling them. Legal aid does not seem to have made much difference, except with regard to large ticket items in middle-class communities where solicitors are more readily available.

Citizens' Advice Bureaux are often helpful, but they are limited in several respects. First, in low-income areas, they are bound to feel restrained in the number of cases that they can refer to the few solicitors who are available and willing to act. Secondly, if a consumer does not characterise his problem as a disputed claim, it is unlikely that any defence will be uncovered. If he regards the matter simply as a debt problem, the chances

1. In Saskatchewan, there is now provision that party and party costs will not be awarded against an unsuccessful consumer '. . .unless, in the opinion of the court, the action, defence or counter claim was frivolous or vexatious'. *The Consumer Products Warranties Act*, Statutes of Saskatchewan, 1976-7, Ch.15, S.29.

2. *Judicial Statistics for the Year 1976*, Cmnd 6875, p.67.

are that a Citizens' Advice Bureau will do the same.

Another discouragement to buyers is that the courts operate at hours convenient to the legal profession and the business community rather than to the public at large. The ordinary working person who wants to pursue or defend a claim may have to take into account loss of wages in the process as well as court fees and any other costs. Moreover he may feel some embarrassment in asking for time off work to go to court.

Buyers can, of course, sue in the County Court without a solicitor, and nowadays some of them do. But most buyers are likely to feel some uncertainty about the extent of their rights, and the remedies available. Many (perhaps most) buyers never realise that they have rights against a seller. For example, even where a buyer is alleging fraud or seriously defective goods, he may be so conditioned to accept a state of helplessness in the legal system that he still believes he has an obligation to pay the contract price.[1] In this respect, legal aid made little difference; but the publicity programme of the government following the *Supply of Goods (Implied Terms) Act*, 1973, and the publicity of the Office of Fair Trading seem to have resulted in greater awareness of legal rights among consumers. For the reasons mentioned below, however, going to an advisory agency does not always result in sufficient advice being received.

Even when buyers know their substantive rights, they often overestimate the problems of evidence. In particular, buyers often assume that they cannot prove anything unless they have an independent witness. Some advisers in Citizens' Advice Bureaux make the same assumption.

When a buyer recognises a legal ground for not paying a seller's claim, he may still feel no motivation to allocate the time and expense necessary to defend. In particular, a large proportion of defendants are insolvent or close to insolvency, living on incomes that provide for no more than necessities. If a defendant is oppressed by financial worries and is not able to pay the claims being made against him, he may see little point in seeking to defend any that are invalid.

One phenomenon that appeared in this research[2] was that even when buyers do refuse or suspend payment because of some grievance against the seller, they commonly do not give that as the reason. Often they will say simply that they forgot, or that because of sickness, unemployment, or some other reason, they did not have the money to pay. Thus a proportion of cases in which a buyer raises a legally irrelevant defence (such as sickness or unemployment) are cases in which a legally valid defence would be available. Some explanations of this phenomenon are outlined

1. See Chapter 7.
2. From the survey data, from observing courts, and from the advisory agencies.

above.[1] Whatever the explanation, however, the net effect is that judgment is commonly given for the seller in situations in which, if there had been a real adjudication on the merits of the case according to law, judgment would have been given for the buyer.

Another handicap is that buyers are often people who think and plan for relatively short time periods, and who do not keep records. When a summons is issued against a buyer, supervening events may have so preoccupied his mind that without legal advice and probing, he has long ceased to regard the original transaction as relevant. The case of a student who spoke to the writer shows that the problem in not limited to low-income groups. About a year previously, he had foolishly signed a three-year magazine subscription with a doorstep salesman. The student refused to pay and was now being threatened with suit. From questioning him, it appeared that the high-pressure sales pitch had included several fraudulent misrepresentations. But the student had almost forgotten the sales pitch until questioned about it. The collection agency had been impervious to any explanation of his refusal to pay, and he had become convinced that 'No one listens if you try to explain why you don't owe the money'. He was preparing to defend the claim by explaining to the court the oppressive collection methods tried against him during the month preceding the summons. The chances are that judgment would have gone against him without the real defence ever coming to light.

Not surprisingly, most people do not understand the adversary system. While there is fear of the courts, there is also an element of uninformed pride among the public about the administration of justice in England, and sometimes an assumption that there must be someone whose job it is to seek out the truth and to adjudicate according to law. Hence people do not react to the service of a summons in a way that is intelligently responsive to the demands of the adversary system. One defendant explained his reaction following the service of a summons as follows: 'So, as I did not owe them money, and not knowing what to do, I put it on the mantelpiece trusting in British justice and then a man came to take away the furniture.'[2] Although this degree of naivety may be unusual, even people who recognise the system as an adversary one often have little comprehension of how it works. To participate in it, they must overcome any fear of the unknown. To many people, litigation means engaging in some kind of public combat with unknown weapons and unknown rules against a professional adversary, often not even being clear what the significance will be of winning or losing. 'The psychological pressures may be considerable,

1. See Chapter 7.
2. Letter to a newspaper readers' advisory service, 1968.

weighing heavily on the [alleged] debtor and his family. He encounters, perhaps for the first time in his life, the subtle terrors which legal processes can inspire in those who do not understand them'.[1]

Although people do now bring and defend claims without a solicitor, they must still take the risk that the other side will be represented by a solicitor whose relationship to the court they do not understand. A 'local advocate' has been described by one observer as follows:

> One such solicitor may appear in very nearly all the actions of his local county court. He will develop an acute sensitivity to the idiosyncrasies of 'his' Registrar and judges, and inter-action will often be non-verbal. He will know what orders are acceptable, will understand esoteric cues, and will acquire the ability to make his behaviour completely complementary to that of the judge.[2]

As long as small claims are determined in a tribunal primarily oriented in the adversary system, there will be a perpetual risk that the specialised vocabulary and communications rapport operating between members of the legal profession will militate against the ready participation in the system of ordinary people. Registrars observed by the writer have striven to overcome this problem. But it requires a continuous effort to operate contrary to the natural propensity of the structure. A change in the structure would surely be more effective.

Perhaps the greatest impediment to justice in consumer cases is that a consumer cannot simply ask for the adjudication of a matter without first taking a definite position, which he is then called upon to justify. In so far as the reforms of recent years have resulted in some shift from adversarial to inquisitorial procedures, this has occurred at the hearing stage. The full demands of the adversary system are still imposed upon each litigant at the stage of initial pleading.

The rules of civil procedure require a distinction between disputed and undisputed claims. That may make sense in the High Court, but it is unrealistic in the context of small claims. It assumes that at some stage someone will decide into which category each case should fall. But for the reasons explained, buyers are not only discouraged, inhibited and impeded from defending; they are also often disabled from making any intelligent decision about whether they want to defend.

1. *Report of the Royal Commission on the Cost of Borrowing Money, Cost of Credit and Related Matters*, 1965, Nova Scotia, p.335.
2. 'Observations on Debt Collections', P.E. Rock, (1968) 19 *British Journal of Sociology* 176, 182.

Of the 971,862 judgments entered in the County Courts in 1976, the breakdown according to how the judgment was reached was as follows:

	%
Judgments in default of defence	55.40
Judgments on admission	28.46
Judgments by consent	1.09
On hearing by registrar with one party present	8.37
On hearing by judge with one party present	1.78
By judge after trial	2.03
By registrar after trial	2.02
After arbitration	0.85
Total	100.00

Thus of judgments entered in the County Courts in 1976, 83.86 per cent were by default or admission.[1]

The staff of the court will assist a litigant to complete the appropriate form, once the litigant has decided for himself what he wants to say. They will also help in some other ways, such as advising a potential claimant in which court the action should be brought, and perhaps whether some notice is required before suit. But they are not allowed to advise on what is a good cause of action or a good ground of defence. If a defendant comes to the counter in one of the larger courts not knowing what to do, the clerk will probably run through the questions on the standard admission/defence form and ask:

(1) Do you admit the claim?
(2) Do you admit part of the claim?
(3) Do you dispute the claim?

For any timorous or bewildered individual, an affirmative answer to either of the first two questions at least has the advantage that the discussion ends and he can go home. But an affirmative answer to the third question results in the defendant being asked 'What are your reasons for disputing the plaintiff's claim?' Suppose, for example, the claim is for payment for a washing machine. If the defendant says that she is not paying because the machine does not work, the clerk will show her the defence part of the form where she should write the reason for non-payment. But if the

1. *Judicial Statistics for the Year 1975*, Cmnd 6875, p.69. It is impossible to say in what proportion of cases where judgment goes by default or admission a good defence would be available. Court files are treated as confidential in England. There is no right of access that would permit a random sample of court files to be used for research with field interviews of the parties.

claimant says simply 'I don't know what to do', the clerk will not run through a list of questions, including 'Does the machine work?'

Of all court claims, it is surely among those admitted or undefended by an unassisted litigant that there is the greatest incidence of injustice. Yet the Lord Chancellor's Office seems committed to the idea that the obligation should lie upon each defendant, unassisted by the court, to determine whether a claim should be defended. It has even been argued that this is an advantage of the County Court system, and a reason for not establishing small claims courts.

> One prime advantage was the methods of dealing with undefended cases by means of a default summons and judgment. The majority of small claims would remain undefended and the Lord Chancellor's officials responsible for the administration of the civil courts felt that this default procedure must be retained.[1]

If a litigant says something by way of claim or defence, and the matter reaches the registrar, the situation then changes. There may then be some relaxation of the principle that the onus lies upon each party to decide what the case is that he wants to present. In interviews with four registrars in 1977, the following example was put. Suppose someone sues on an express warranty. Suppose it should appear from the evidence that the warranty is inapplicable, perhaps because it was not issued by the defendant, but that the plaintiff has a good claim against the defendant for breach of the implied conditions under the *Sale of Goods Act*. What would you do in that situation? Two replied that they would try to give judgment in accord with the merits of the case, and would try not to be hampered by the pleadings. The other two replied that they would adjourn and advise the plaintiff to see a solicitor, a Consumer Advice Centre, or a Citizens' Advice Bureau, to obtain help in revising his pleadings.

When a buyer does file a defence, the claim is likely to be abandoned if the amount is fairly small. But if payment for a motor vehicle is being claimed, a finance company is more likely to proceed. In these cases, even after a defence is filed, a buyer without a solicitor may still need courage and perseverence if he is not to be talked out of his day in court.

> Where a defence is raised without a solicitor, I write and suggest that they make an offer of deferred payments and withdraw the defence. This often works. We don't have any difficulty in dealing with

1. *Small Claims,* W.H. Elliott, 1977, International Congress on the Law of Civil Procedure at Ghent, p.8.

buyers themselves, but solicitors sometimes give us trouble.[1]

It should be no surprise that many defences are raised for the first time in the course of execution processes after a default judgment. This is usually the first stage in the proceeding at which the defendant meets a court official. If a defence is raised in discussion with a bailiff, the 'judgment debtor' will probably be advised to make application to the court to set aside the judgment. If the defence is raised in an execution proceeding before a registrar, the practice varies. Some registrars will adjourn the execution proceeding for long enough to enable an application to be made to set aside judgment. Others may be willing to consider on the spot whether the judgment should be set aside. Sometimes the defence is accommodated in a less formal way. For example, in two 'disposal' proceedings observed by the writer, the British Gas Corporation was seeking orders for the repossession of cookers. The corporation was willing to have each repossession order suspended conditionally upon the defendant meeting instalment payments which the court would determine. No defence had been filed in either case, but the defendants objected orally that the cookers did not work. In both cases, the registrar adjourned the applications, indicating that he would not order the commencement of instalments until the cookers were working.

The criteria by which registrars will set aside a judgment also vary. Some registrars follow the orthodox rules of the adversary system, requiring that for a default judgment to be set aside, the 'judgment debtor' must show a *prima facie* defence, and a good reason for not having defended in the first place. Other registrars show greater recognition of the plight of an unassisted litigant, and will set aside a default judgment as long as a *prima facie* defence appears. Another registrar will stay proceedings for 14 days and order a default judgment to be set aside only if the amount of the judgment is paid into court within that period.

Another feature of the County Court system incompatible with justice in small claims is the 'list'. It seems to be a paramount goal of government policy not to 'waste judicial time'. To assure judicial productivity, judges and registrars must be kept preoccupied with a 'list'. One day for example, a registrar may be dealing with pre-trial reviews. The list of cases ready for pre-trial review is his agenda for that day. Another time he may be dealing with an arbitration list, and another time with a divorce list. The rigidity of the list system requires litigants to adapt themselves to a range of semi-automated court procedures. Little flexibility is left for the court to adapt

1. Interview with the head of the collections department of a finance company, 1969.

its procedures to the needs and expectations of litigants. Suppose, for example, two people go to the office of a County Court with a dispute that they would like to have resolved on the spot. The court cannot cope. If a dispute arises on a building site and the parties would like to have the matter adjudicated on the spot before conditions change, again the court cannot cope. If the parties attending on a pre-trial review both indicate that they are ready for adjudication, they will most likely be told to come back another day for arbitration, because today the registrar is fully occupied with his 'list'.[1]

All four registrars interviewed by the writer in 1977 indicated that they do not usually take views of the scene of events, because the pressure of the list would make it very difficult to fit in the travelling. However, one of them knew of another registrar who does take views.

Another consequence of the semi-automated processes associated with the list may be an undue preference for documents rather than oral testimony. This is critical in consumer transactions involving standard form documents prepared by one party and almost never read by the other. The substance of what the parties agreed to is often more likely to be obtained from the oral testimony than from the printed form. But with 'the list' is a pile of files, and getting through 'the list' means working through the pile. Of course oral testimony is received and considered, particularly when the event is a 'trial' or an 'arbitration'. But instances are still found of a reluctance to adjudicate on oral testimony and an undue preference for documents. An example put by the writer to one registrar was a deficiency claim brought by a finance company for monies alleged to be due following a repossession by 'voluntary surrender'. 'Suppose the defendant testifies that "The agent told me I would not have to pay any more if I let him take the car".' The Registrar replied 'That is not a valid defence unless the agent admits saying it.'

Of course fixed time appointments are necessary to some extent. But if we are to develop an efficient system for the adjudication of small claims, it must include a judicial capacity to deal with events as they arise.

Moreover, the system is one with built-in delays. Adjudication usually takes place, if at all, several weeks after service of the summons. This may be satisfactory for debt claims by tradesmen, but it can be a serious impediment to a consumer. Suppose, for example, someone has bought a secondhand motor car from a dealer, together with a written guarantee.

1. Of the cases in which directions are given on pre-trial review for trial or arbitration, it appears that only 2.4 per cent are set down for hearing on the same day, leaving 97.6 per cent set down for hearing on another day. *Judicial Statistics for the Year 1976*, Cmnd 6875, p.71.

The car is seriously defective. The buyer claims repairs under the guarantee, but the seller refuses to carry them out. The need for transportation, possibly for work, may mean that the consumer has to make a quick decision. He may want the car repaired by another dealer. But there may be different ways of repairing the defects, some better and more expensive than others. Without a quick determination of his rights, how can he decide which to order? Worse still, if the repair cost is high compared with his income, then without knowing what the decision of the court will be, he may find it difficult to decide whether to have the repairs done at all or to sell the car as it is. The delays of litigation can require a buyer to make choices before trial which he cannot make most advantageously until after judgment.

The period between summons and judgment is not, however, a period during which the litigants are free to apply themselves entirely to other matters. It is a period during which they must communicate with the court at irregular intervals as the action proceeds through its various stages.

To an aggrieved consumer, the discovery that this is how the court works can be a frustrating disappointment. The buyer may already have been back to the seller several times with regard to the complaint. There may also have been correspondence with the manufacturer. The buyer may have been to a Citizens' Advice Bureau (CAB) or other agency that attempted to settle the matter. Attendances by the buyer at the shop and at the CAB have turned out to be fruitless. Rather than give up, he has now come to the court to bring the matter to an end. Now he discovers that instead of being, as he thought, an end of the matter, going to court is only the beginning of another series of attendances. 'People are disappointed when they find that the case will not be decided quickly. A litigant says "I don't want to come here again, I have been here four times already".'[1]

Examples can be found of County Court personnel using their initiative to alleviate the problem. Perhaps the most common is the steps taken by court staff to assist people in dealing with some stages of an action by post to save them a journey to the court offices. In one court, the registrar helps by doing pre-trial reviews from the file without requiring the attendance of the parties if the claim does not exceed £100. In another court, the registrar has a volunteer arbitrator standing by when he is dealing with the pre-trial review list so that if both parties are ready for adjudication, they can be offered the services of the volunteer arbitrator. No doubt other steps could be taken to reduce the attendances. But an efficient system of justice in small claims is never going to be achieved through

1. Interview with a County Court registrar, 1977.

institutions and procedures that are an adaptation of the High Court system.

Moreover, no adjustments in the adversary system can remedy the basic problem that the adversary procedures of the County Court are far too expensive for the general run of small claims. For example, in one case, the claim was for £10.50, and judgment was eventually entered for £7. Yet it was estimated by an impartial observer that the total cost of the action would be about £100.[1]

F. Conclusions

In relation to small claims, the basic problems with the County Courts are not behavioural aberrations. They are the natural consequences of the structure. An adequate system for the adjudication of small claims will never come about simply through adaptations within a structure that is primarily oriented to the adversary system.

If reform can only come through the adaptation of existing systems, justice in small claims is more likely to be achieved by adapting Trading Standards Departments to the role of adjudication than by attempting any further adjustments to the County Courts.

2. Solicitors

As explained above, the courts and the legal profession do not offer consumers the same automated service available to those claiming to be creditors. The study by the Consumer Council concluded that '. . .solicitors do not welcome clients with potential consumer claims; that some solicitors will not accept such clients at all; and that, as a result, people with consumer claims may be shuffled from one solicitor to another'.[2]

A major problem is, of course, that solicitors are highly trained people with an overhead to meet, and no solicitor could make a living by advising and litigating for consumers on the general run of transactions. To charge a reasonable fee on a time basis would be equivalent to turning people away. On the other hand, to keep the fee reasonable having regard to the amount in dispute would create pressures for superficial and inadequate work. 'Universally, solicitors told us that consumer cases are a dead loss, financially – whether court proceedings are involved or not. Many added some such phrase as "if we never saw another, we'd be happy".'[3]

An aggravating factor is that those who most need a solicitor (i.e. those

1. *Small Claims Tribunals : A Challenge to the County Court : A Preliminary Report*, J. Neville Turner, 1973, University of Birmingham, pp.49-53.
2. *Justice Out of Reach*, The Consumer Council, 1970, HMSO, p.5.
3. Ibid., p.10.

least able to function as litigants in person) often get into trouble in the first place through their gullibility, forgetfulness, or lack of capacity for the orderly management of their affairs. They cannot state the problem clearly and briefly. Hence no proper advice can be given without spending time trying to extract the relevant facts from an incomprehensible story. This adds to the difficulty of giving legal assistance at a cost that makes it worthwhile. In other ways too, individual clients can be more troublesome than business clients. 'One solicitor, who said that he acted almost entirely for firms, explained frankly that he found individual clients in contentious matters "a bloody nuisance". He added "they pester the solicitor and make it difficult to settle a case".'[1] It is obviously easier for a solicitor to help an articulate client who can crisply state his problem and understand the advice that he receives.

A solicitor's help is obviously more valuable if a consumer has suffered a substantial loss. For example, if someone has paid £4,000 for a new car that is useless, or if he has suffered a serious injury through its defects, he may have no difficulty finding a solicitor to pursue the claim. Conversely, if someone has bought furniture for £40 that breaks immediately upon use, and the seller has refused a remedy, it is not worthwhile to have a solicitor provide the attention required to go to trial. Indeed, the consumer could be out of pocket even if he wins.

> Our solicitors [a sample of 43] almost to a man told us that they invariably advised clients against taking a disputed case to court. The main reason, of course, was economic: they said that the costs awarded to the successful party in a county court action were not sufficient to meet the legal fees and other expenses of bringing an action.[2]

The cost of legal services is, however, not the only restriction on their use. Even apart from the fear of fees, several factors may deter a consumer from communicating with a solicitor. People in low-income groups in particular often do not perceive 'the law' as something that can be used to their advantage. Also, consulting a solicitor may involve communication across a class barrier. Another major problem is a lack of recognition by the general public of the circumstances in which legal services can be helpful. In the survey conducted by the writer, there were many cases in which the buyer might have had legal grounds for claiming against the seller, or defending a claim for payment, several cases in which he probably would

1. Ibid., p.10.
2. Ibid., p.11.

have liked to do so, and some in which he might have been well advised to do so.[1] Yet in only one case did a buyer actually consult a solicitor.[2] In another survey conducted for the Crowther Committee, it was reported that 'There was a general ignorance of the value of professional legal advice, and a disinclination to be involved with the legal profession'.[3]

When consumers do consult a solicitor, his communication with the seller is sometimes all that is needed to solve the problem. On the other hand, it is sometimes alleged that, because of the low fees that can be charged in consumer cases, solicitors are inclined to seek the quickest termination of a matter rather than the solution most favourable to the consumer. For example, some organisers of Citizens' Advice Bureaux complain that solicitors are not much help in dealing with dubious contracts, and that they too readily come to the conclusion that a consumer is stuck with what he has signed. Even when a consumer is complaining of misrepresentations, a solicitor may dwell on the possibility that the client will not be believed rather than the possibility that the seller will recognise the merit of the defence. Another allegation is that solicitors sometimes persist in futile negotiations when the prompt issuance of a summons would be more appropriate.[4]

Part of the problem is that most solicitors do not receive consumer grievances in sufficient volume to develop the experience for recognising the best strategy. For example, many solicitors are not conversant with the sales pitches commonly used by racketeers. Consequently, they may not ask the questions that would reveal a defence of deceit, nor do they always recognise that on filing that defence, the claim would most likely be discontinued. In the Consumer Council study, it is reported that: 'In one case, where a couple were being sued for arrears on a carpet that had worn badly after six months, we were told that the solicitor advised them on

1. The questioning was not sufficiently intensive to arrive at precise figures for this purpose. Also the interviewers were not lawyers. In so far as inferences can be drawn from the data, however, it is the writer's impression that out of the total of 1,226 transactions there were somewhere about 330 in which the buyer might have had legal grounds on which to claim against the seller, about 60 in which he would probably like to have done so, and about 26 in which he might have been well advised to do so.

2. In that case, the buyer reported having been advised that there was nothing that could be done.

3. *Surveys carried out by NOP Market Research Ltd for the Committee on Consumer Credit*, 1971, Department of Trade and Industry, Part I, section 1, p.25.

4. 'My experience is that consumers rarely, if ever, start proceedings against the seller or anybody else. They consult a solicitor, and matters drag on through interminable negotiations until the consumer is exhausted or his available funds are exhausted.' Per an adviser at a newspaper readers' advisory service, 1969.

grounds of cost, to pay rather than defend.'[1] Yet when a sample of County Court records was analysed in the same study, it was shown that:

> The defendant filed a defence or counterclaim in 50 of our sample of trader cases – which amounts to seven per cent of the summonses actually served by traders on consumers. We examined the case papers for each of these. The most striking thing that emerged was that in 32 cases (64 per cent) the action was withdrawn after the defence was filed. We could rarely tell why from the papers. The reason may have been that the firm thought the defence sound, or that it preferred simply not to fight. But there must surely be a lesson here for solicitors consulted by consumers who are being sued for arrears of hire-purchase or other forms of debt: it may well be worth defending.[2]

Another factor relevant to the development of expertise is that the education of solicitors tends to avoid consumer problems. A course on consumer protection is still not a part of the normal law curriculum in most British universities. Nor do solicitors have much informational backup for dealing with consumer cases. A solicitor dealing with tax cases, for example, can subscribe to several publications that will keep him up to date in his field. But there is not the same intensity of periodical literature or textbooks for solicitors handling consumer cases.[3]

It would be wrong, of course, to leave any impression that in consumer cases, solicitors are never helpful. As the Consumer Council study shows, 'Not all solicitors disliked consumer cases, however – apart from the fact that they were unremunerative. Some enjoyed the fight and others gained satisfaction from the help that they were able to give people whom they thought needed it.'[4] Moreover, '. . .some solicitors pursue claims painstakingly and resourcefully. . . Several had taken pains over visiting to inspect the goods and obtaining reports from experts.'[5] Many solicitors of course specialise in other types of work, and a consumer who wants to consult a solicitor would be well advised to select one accustomed to court work, and if possible, one known to take an interest in consumer cases.

For people who cannot afford a solicitor's fees, many areas have legal clinics, sometimes associated with a Citizens' Advice Bureau. Two of these

1. *Justice Out of Reach*, Consumer Council, 1970, HMSO, p.11.
2. Ibid., p.15.
3. Probably the most useful legal periodical that includes consumer problems is the *Legal Action Group Bulletin*.
4. *Justice Out of Reach*, Consumer Council, 1970, HMSO, p.10.
5. Ibid., p.11.

clinics were visited by the writer. Several of the cases were consumer problems, and the quality of the advice was impressive. To what extent this produces a satisfactory result is hard to know because most of the clients do not return. Feedback on the results is therefore limited. These clinics do not, however, handle litigation, and a consumer in need of an advocate to pursue or defend a claim will be advised to go to a practising solicitor at his normal office.

The development of Neighbourhood Law Centres in recent years has provided another source of legal advice. But they are available only in some areas. Moreover, giving their attention to other subjects may seem more urgent, and with their limited resources, it is not surprising that assistance with consumer problems is not one of their highest priorities.

The changes of recent years in County Court practice have, of course, had some spill-over effect on solicitors. Complaints are still heard that some registers discourage litigants in person, and suggest that people should go to a solicitor. But the official policy (indicated in the procedural changes, the publicity from the Lord Chancellor's Office and the instructions to court staff) is to encourage and assist litigants to conduct small claims without solicitors. One consequence is that solicitors can now more readily contribute to the conduct of a claim without undertaking the case entirely. In particular, solicitors often assist in the pleading stage of a case while leaving the litigant to act in person at any hearings. Here again, however, business clients may derive the benefit more often than consumers.

3. Advice and Negotiation

There are several agencies to which an aggrieved consumer might go for advice, or for someone to negotiate with the seller, manufacturer, or finance company. The main ones (referred to in this book as the advisory agencies) are the following.

A. Citizens' Advice Bureaux (CABs)

These offices are supported out of public funds but are not under any direct form of government control. They advise on a wide range of problems, including consumer matters. Many enquirers simply need information. With regard to consumer disputes, a bureau will advise the enquirer what course seems best calculated to solve the problem. If the enquirer has already attempted to negotiate a solution, the bureau will often communicate with the retailer. Writing a letter explaining the problem, perhaps more articulately than the consumer could explain it, often results in a solution.

The local bureaux are supported by a national office to provide for the constant inflow and arrangement of new information.

As of March 1977, there were 710 Citizens' Advice Bureaux in the United Kingdom. During the year 1976/7, there were about 481,000 enquiries classified as 'Consumer, Trade and Business', this being about 16.6 per cent of total enquiries.[1]

The bureaux are generally well informed about other sources of help. For example, if a consumer needs technical assistance for a claim, a bureau will probably know where the technical help can be obtained. If the testing of an article is needed, a bureau will most likely know what testing facilities are available. If a trade association might help, a bureau will know which trade association is appropriate. If the consumer needs legal advice, a bureau can probably say which solicitors in the area deal with litigation, and if he cannot afford a solicitor, a bureau can help to obtain legal advice without charge. A large proportion of the advisers are part-time volunteers.

A disadvantage of the CABs is that the advisers are not specialists. For example, the same people advise on consumer problems, employment, housing, social security, marital problems, etc. On the other hand, because they are generalists, they may be able to recognise related problems and assist in their solution. For example, if a client comes in with debt problems arising out of consumer transactions, it might appear to a CAB adviser that budgeting anxiety is resulting from a failure to collect supplementary benefits.

Sometimes the lack of specialisation is overcome by referring the client to a more specialised agency. For example, the organiser of one bureau informed the writer that: 'All complaints relating to secondhand cars we send to the Consumer Advice Centre. They know the rogues in the business and are more successful at dealing with them.'

Perhaps the most serious limitation on CAB effectiveness is that the advisers do not have available to them any adequate digest of legal materials.[2] It may be because of this that there is still a widespread belief among bureau advisers that 'you are stuck with what you signed'. Unfortunately, that belief has even found its way into the literature emanating

1. *Annual Report for 1976-77 of the National Association of Citizens' Advice Bureaux*, pp.6 and 7.
2. See this chapter, p.254.

from head office.[1]

Another difficulty with the CABs in the past has been that usually the advisers have been unfamiliar with the County Courts. Consequently, when negotiations failed, they were in no position to advise a consumer whether court proceedings might be appropriate, or what would be involved. This problem, however, has been recognised, and in the last few years a collaborative programme has evolved between the National Association of CABs and the Lord Chancellor's Office, and between local bureaux and County Courts. Training sessions have been organised that include County Court procedure, and liaison arrangements have been established under which bureau advisers observe court proceedings.

When negotiation is unsuccessful, the practice varies. Some bureaux still maintain the older view that they have a duty of impartiality, and that hence, in the negotiation of disputes, they should simply explain the position of each side to the other. If negotiations fail, that is an end of their function.

The trend, however, is to take a more active role, and probably most bureaux now perceive themselves as there to assist the ordinary citizen in dealing with bureaucratic institutions, whether they be government agencies or business enterprises. Most bureaux nowadays will advise a client on the possibilities of County Court proceedings. Some carry a stock of court forms and will assist clients in completing them. Some advisers will go further and accompany the client to court proceedings, but that is not a general practice.

One complaint about the bureaux is that they tend to be over-cautious when the client would be better advised to take a chance. For example some bureaux never advise a client to stop payment of the instalments relating to a credit transaction no matter how appropriate that course may be in the particular case.[2] Again some bureaux, as a normal routine, continue to advise clients to obtain expert evidence prior to the commencement of proceedings. The evidence will probably not be needed, and in any event the registrar can be asked for his comments on that at the pre-trial review.

It is difficult to measure the success of Citizens' Advice Bureaux in the

1. *The Provision of Health Aids by Commercial Organisations.* Evidence Paper E75/2, December 1975. On p.12, there is a list of predatory practices, including some in which it is reported that the signature of the client was obtained on the contract form by deceit. Yet the resulting documents are still described on the same page as 'legally binding documents'. In one case, it is reported that a solicitor wrote to the firm stating that 'the contract was not a valid document' (p.14). Yet the evidence paper goes on to repeat the position that contracts obtained in this way are 'a legally binding document' (p.15).

2. See Chapter 7, p.172.

resolution of consumer disputes because there is commonly no feedback of the outcome. There is no doubt, however, that these offices play a useful role in the supply of information, and in the resolution of those problems that are susceptible of a solution by negotiation.

B. Consumer Advice Centres (CACs)

During the twentieth century, the Weights and Measures Departments of local authorities became responsible for the enforcement of a range of consumer protection and trade regulation statutes in addition to the weights and measures legislation. These departments also undertook an advisory role in relation to trade and consumer problems. During the 1960s, some local authorities began to develop the advisory role in a more organised way by opening Consumer Advice Centres to negotiate disputed claims, and to deal with consumer enquiries, including pre-shopping advice.

The passing of the *Trade Descriptions Act,* 1968, gave this development a new impetus. Criminal sanctions were enacted against false trade descriptions, and the enforcement function was assigned to the weights and measures authorities. Thus the tasks performed by the Weights and Measures Departments of local authorities came to include such a range of trade regulation responsibilities that they were generally renamed. 'Trading Standards Department' or 'Consumer Protection Department' are names now in common use.

A common limitation of Trading Standards Departments is that they are not readily accessible to the shopping public. There may be only one office of a Trading Standards Department in a major conurbation, or in a county, and even that office may not be in a major shopping area. To overcome this problem, the development of Consumer Advice Centres continued. As of December 1976, there were about 108 Consumer Advice Centres, plus some mobile units.[1] These centres are usually located in a shopping area. They are separate offices from the Trading Standards Departments, but usually under the same management.

The advisers at these centres are full time, and many have a relevant professional or academic background. At one centre visited by the writer, all 7 advisers were university graduates, including 3 in law and 2 in home economics.

The following extract from an interview with a senior trading standards officer responsible for the supervision of a CAC gives some impression of

1. Estimated from a list of Consumer Advice Centres produced by the Department of Prices and Consumer Protection. For a critical commentary on Consumer Advice Centres, see 'Down With Consumer Organisations?', P. Toynbee, *Manchester Guardian Weekly*, 18 December 1977, p.5.

how they deal with consumer disputes.

> If a consumer comes here, we first determine that he lives in our area, or has bought something in our area. Then we determine that he has tried to obtain satisfaction himself, and that he has a prima facie complaint. Then we take the matter up with the retailer, sometimes by phone, sometimes by a visit. Sometimes we look at the goods first. Sometimes we bring the customer and retailer together, particularly if the matter involves building repairs, paving work etc. Sometimes the matter is settled on the spot.

An advantage of CACs is that they are the offspring of departments oriented primarily in field work, rather than office work. Perhaps because of this, CAC advisers go to people's homes or elsewhere to look at equipment, or for other purposes. If negotiations are unsuccessful, many advisers will accompany a consumer to court if that seems appropriate. In some areas, they often help in adjudication by telling the County Court registrar what they found on their inspection of the goods.

Where there is no CAC, advice and negotiation services are usually provided by the Trading Standards Department. The issues involved in having the negotiation of disputes conducted in the same office as the prosecution of offences are discussed in Chapter 12.

C. Newspapers

There are two situations in which an aggrieved consumer might obtain redress by writing to a newspaper. The first is where an item was bought in response to a newspaper advertisement and has turned out to be not as advertised. The newspaper may be willing to pursue the matter with the advertiser, particularly where the consumer has relied exclusively on the advertisement, as is usual for items bought by mail order.

Secondly, some newspapers operate a readers' advisory service.[1] These services advise on a range of problems, most of which do not involve any prior connection with the newspaper. They have staff specialising in consumer problems, and other staff specialising in other areas – housing, immigration, etc. They are similar to the CABs with regard to the range of matters on which they advise, but similar to CACs in that the advice is given by someone specialising in the subject area. Like the other advisory agencies, they provide advice to consumers, and they also communicate where appropriate with the business concerned to negotiate a solution.

1. Probably the largest is now the *Daily Mirror* Readers' Advisory Service, PO Box 644, 66-73 Shoe Lane, London EC4P 4RB.

These services are independent of the news columns of the paper. Occasionally, letters from readers provide a lead for a newspaper story, and a journalist might be assigned to it. But for the most part, these offices operate as a service to readers rather than a source of news material. In any event, enquiries are treated as confidential, and there is no publicity identifying an enquirer, except by agreement with the enquirer.

An obvious limitation of these services is that they cannot usually cross-examine the enquirier, or otherwise deal with the matter by personal discussion. This creates a danger of undue significance being attached to the documents, and a risk of oral exchanges between contracting parties being overlooked. These services often try to overcome that problem by writing back for further information before advising, or by arranging a telephone discussion with the enquirer. Another obvious limitation is the time lag involved in mail communication. For someone in a state of serious distress, the CABs and CACs offer the opportunity of dropping in for an instant discussion.

On the other hand, a newspaper readers' advisory service may have some advantages compared with a CAB. These are:

(1) A mail service may be more convenient to people living in remote areas.

(2) Some people may prefer to communicate personal problems to strangers in a distant city. It is the policy of other advisory agencies to require their advisers to observe the confidentiality of clients' affairs. But some people, particularly in rural areas, may still be apprehensive about communicating personal problems to people who live in the same community.

(3) The specialisation and centralisation may be an advantage with regard to some types of problems, particularly when the business concerned is small scale but operating on a national basis.

(4) It may be easier to select advisory staff who will empathise with enquirers, because the clientele may be more concentrated in the same socio-economic grouping.

(5) The risk of adverse publicity may sometimes act as a stimulant to remedial action. These services do not threaten adverse publicity. But simply receiving a letter from a newspaper may create an apprehension of the risk.

The BBC includes consumer problems in it current affairs' programmes, both on television and radio, including national and local programming. Listeners and viewers are invited to write or telephone with their complaints or queries. Sometimes the programmes include investigative reporting.

Unlike newspaper readers' advisory services, however, the main purpose of these programmes is consumer information and education, rather than to provide a vehicle for the resolution of individual problems. Although the BBC does sometimes help consumers to obtain redress or otherwise solve their problems, it does not set out to offer such a service, and will normally direct consumers with particular problems to one of the advisory agencies.

D. Better Business Bureaux (BBBs)

These offices are organised by retailers in major cities of North America to deal with enquiries and complaints by consumers. Suggestions have sometimes been made that they could be introduced into Britain, and it may be of interest to mention them.

Like the other agencies mentioned above, Better Business Bureaux are useful in the solution of negotiable problems. But there are several limitations on their success.

Better Business Bureaux are creations of the retailing community financed by the subscriptions of retailers. Hence they do not have the structure for a position of impartiality between buyer and seller: still less can they act as advocate or champion of the consumer interest. Moreover

> The Bureaus' programs for aiding consumers are motivated, in the main, by a desire to forestall governmental intervention in the marketplace and to cool the anger of aggrieved consumers against the business community.[1]

Many bureaux do not have enough staff to deal with incoming phone calls, and their telephone lines are constantly engaged. When a caller gets through to make a complaint, he is told that he must do so in writing. The normal practice is to take his name and address and send a form. This rules out the prospect of assistance to those who are inarticulate or otherwise unable to complete a written report. Yet in many situations, it is because he is inarticulate that the consumer has been unable to negotiate a solution himself. Estimates of the proportion of forms that are completed and returned vary among different bureaux from 30 to 80 per cent.[2]

Once a complaint in writing has been received, the practice is to forward a copy to the retailer and to invite his response. Many problems are solved this way. But a sense of grievance is often felt when they are not,

1. 'Report on the Better Business Bureaus' B.S. Rosenthal, (1971) 117 *Congressional Record* No.199, Part II, p.E13764.
2. Estimates obtained by enquiries of the writer to bureau personnel.

and people are inclined to feel that they have been misled. What they want (and what they often assume a Better Business Bureau to be) is an organisation that can make the retailer remedy the grievance, not one that will simply explain his refusal. 'Stated another way, the consumer is urged by the BBB to bring his problems to them, to expend his energy in their system, and is often left with no resolution to his problem.'[1]

For the hard core situations in which no solution is possible without adjudication, Better Business Bureaux are no use. They can waste people's time and sap their energies.

One consequence of insisting that a complaint should be in writing is that there is generally no cross-examination. Moreover advice about the validity of contracts is often given without seeing the document, let alone questioning the buyer about the circumstances in which the transaction came about, and there is a readiness to assume that a consumer is 'stuck with what he signed'.

Statements by the Vice-President of one bureau illustrate the level of the advice given in some of the more common situations.

> One of the most common complaints we get is from someone who says that he bought an item, has taken it home, changed his mind about it and wants his money back. Our girls answering the phone are instructed to tell him to forget it. They are liable to pay.[2]

From follow-up questions on this point, it appeared that the girls do not ask the enquirer why he changed his mind, nor pursue any other questions to determine whether he might have grounds for rescinding the contract.

With regard to complaints about price, the same Vice-President stated: 'If a customer complaint is about over-charging, we say that there is nothing he can do about that, he must pay.' In response to follow-up questions on this point, the position taken was that the customer's obligation is to pay what the tradesman asks. There was no recognition that where a price has been agreed at the time of ordering, that is the price that the customer is liable to pay, or that where no price has been agreed, the customer's obligation is to pay a reasonable price. At least as far as that bureau is concerned, one could not help wondering whether consumers might not find a better quality of advice at the local pub.

Membership of a Better Business Bureau tends to be concentrated among the more established retailers of a city. This means that the less

1. 'Report on the Better Business Bureaus', B.S. Rosenthal, (1971) 117 *Congressional Record* No.199, Part II, at p.E13774.

2. Interview with the Vice-President of a Better Business Bureau in Canada.

stable fringe of the business community lies beyond the reach of any admonitory influence that a bureau may have. But it also makes it easier for a bureau to take a more aggressive approach to those operations. For example, some bureaux issue press releases about fraudulent operations, or take steps to foreclose the use of advertising media to those engaged in the more extreme types of consumer fraud. On the other hand, it is often alleged (but denied by the bureaux) that they do not take effective or aggressive action when dealing with complaints against their members. For example, it is alleged that if a complaint is against a member, they do not refer an enquirer to the courts, to a lawyer, or to the police, in situations in which that would be appropriate.

Another complaint is that the bureaux focus excessive attention on predatory practices that operate to the detriment of local businessmen rather than those that operate to the detriment of consumers. For example, some bureaux have taken aggressive and effective action with regard to solicitations among retailers for trade listings or advertisements in dubious publications. Another example relates to itinerant salesmen engaged in fraudulent or predatory practices. The allegation is that the bureaux swing into action more readily and effectively if the goods being sold are in competition with those available at local retail outlets.

Perhaps the most serious complaint is that Better Business Bureaux consistently lobby against consumer protection legislation, at least until it is clear that the legislation is going through anyway. Indeed, a feature of the sales pitch used by the bureaux when soliciting memberships is that they can help to 'save' the business community from more government regulation.

Better Business Bureaux also advise consumers prior to buying. Someone who contemplates a major purchase from a particular retailer can phone a bureau and ask what the complaint experience is with regard to that retailer. The response varies. Some bureaux seem reluctant to say much more than whether the retailer is a member. Others will give some detail about the volume of complaints and whether the retailer is responsive in dealing with them. But the value of the reports is doubtful.

> The quality of BBB telephone reports to consumers on the integrity and reliability of business firms, is extremely poor. With a few modest exceptions, these reports are misleading, inaccurate, incomplete and couched in vague generalities:
>
> Telephone calls to BBB's in four cities (Washington, D.C.; Chicago; Philadelphia; New York City) requesting reports on 25 firms against which disciplinary action has recently been taken by a Federal, State

> and local law enforcement authorites disclosed that: in only *one* instance did Bureau operators make any reference to such legal action; and, in only *three* other instances (16 per cent) did Bureaus report adversely on any of these 25 firms;[1]

Even apart from the quality of the information transmitted, enquiries are often dealt with very briefly and one complaint is that the response is too curt.[2]

The Better Business Bureaux have a national organisation but are not subject to central control. Hence the bureaux vary a great deal in different cities. No doubt Better Business Bureaux are useful in communities that have no other office mediating in consumer disputes. As far as England is concerned, however, it is suggested that the introduction of Better Business Bureaux would be a wasteful duplication of services already available. Moreover, involving as they do a clear conflict of interest, Better Business Bureaux may provide a poorer quality consumer service as well as a new lobby group against legislative reform in the consumer interest.

E. Conclusions on Advice and Negotiation

The agencies mentioned above perform a range of useful functions apart from those stated. Hence it would be beyond the scope of this work to present a full and fair description of their activities. With regard to consumer complaints, however, the crucial point is that these agencies are best suited to deal with the negotiable problems. They cannot coerce a solution when the parties are unable to agree. Thus, although these agencies achieve a resolution of a large proportion of the complaints that they receive, and perhaps a majority, there is still a substantial proportion that cannot be resolved by discussion. These agencies are therefore not a substitute for adjudication.

As explained above,[3] a readily available adjudication service is not offered to consumers by the courts. If the demands of a consumer have evoked no response from the trader concerned, and attempts at negotiation by an advisory agency have failed, a consumer must either give up or plod through the successive stages of a County Court action.

The absence of a readily available adjudication service is not simply a cause of frustration in the cases that have not been settled. It is also a negative influence in the cases in which a settlement is negotiated.

1. 'Report on Better Business Bureaus', *op.cit.*, p.E13764.
2. Referring to telephone enquiries about a merchant, the manager of one bureau told the writer 'They only have about 30 seconds'.
3. See this chapter, p.211.

In consumer cases, a settlement is not usually brought about, as it is in some other areas of law, by a common prediction of the likely result of court proceedings. If the parties do not willingly agree, a settlement is more likely to result from a recognition of the pressures and incentives operating in the situation. Because the negotiating agency lacks coercive power and no quick and cheap system of adjudication is available, the consumer is commonly under pressure to settle for less than his legal rights. Thus the absence of readily available adjudication is a cause of injustice even with regard to claims that are settled.

The lack of any adequate digest of legal materials is another factor weakening the advisory agencies in the negotiating process.[1]

A related matter is a tendency sometimes to give non-controversial advice when more aggressive action could be more appropriate and successful. For example, some agencies never advise people to stop payment. Yet in many situations, this can be the most prudent course.[2] Similarly, there is often a reluctance to suggest the commencement of a County Court action when success is uncertain. If the client sues and fails, the agency runs the risk of subsequent resentment. There is no similar risk if the client is discouraged from suing. Yet it may be in the best interests of the client to take the risk.

Again, where proceedings are being suggested, some agencies are over-cautious in preparations before suit. For example, in one case[3] a client complaining about defective shoes was advised to send them for expert examination prior to commencing an action against the retailer. If the client wished to pursue the claim, it would surely have been better simply to commence the action. If it was defended, the registrar could decide on pre-trial review whether an expert's report was needed. The risk of wasting money on court costs would surely be less than the risk of wasting money on an expert's report.

When communicating with a business organisation, the advisory agencies often receive the attention of a different management official, or a different department, from the one that deals with consumers. This may obtain the satisfaction of a particular claim. But it has the disadvantage of taking the heat off by obtaining special treatment for those aggrieved consumers who complain through one of the advisory agencies while leaving untouched the practices of the firm in its treatment of those who only complain direct to the firm.

The advisory agencies are, of course, aware of this limitation on their

1. This is explained under the next heading below.
2. See Chapter 7, p.171.
3. Found by the writer at a CAB in 1977.

effectiveness. For example:

> Consumer problems continue to occupy much of our time and although we are pleased by the success of our efforts, the number of traders who agree to reductions or settlement of alleged debts on receipt of a letter from us asking for their comments when the enquirer's personal representations have met with failure, causes us some concern. One wonders what happens to the alleged debtor who does not seek our advice in dealings with firms where the complexity of administrative machinery often causes payments made by the customer to go unrecorded or to be overlooked.[1]

Again,

> It is a constant source of amazement to me that firms can brush off letters and phone calls from customers who have spent a great deal of money with them, who presumably might be in a position to spend more, and influence others to do the same. Yet the same firms will charge into action to put things right the instant they get a call from the BBC.
>
> . . . . . .
>
> The midnight knock from the media sometimes helps to clear that particular blockage: whether the system itself is reviewed and improved is another matter.[2]

In other situations too, the advisory agencies often perceive their role as remedial rather than preventive. One example noticed by the writer in 1969 involved a firm engaged in the same fraudulent marketing scheme year after year. There was a continuing flow of complaints to the advisory agencies from customers of the firm. In response to each complaint, an advisory agency wrote to the firm and a refund was promptly received. Yet refunds had not been obtained when the same customers complained to the firm. Nor was anything being done to solve the problem by measures that would prevent future customers from being deceived.

This problem might, however, be solved as the Office of Fair Trading becomes more firmly established. One of its roles, which it is now developing, is to monitor the complaints received by the advisory agencies to see

1. 'Annual Report of the Citizens' Advice Bureau of Islington', *Citizens' Advice Bureaux in Central London 1966-67*, Family Welfare Association, p.24.

2. Per John Turtle in 'Marketing and the Consumer', supplement to *Marketing*, October 1975, p.vii.

what can be learned from them about the need for preventive action at the national level.

In summary, the advisory agencies play a useful role in advice and negotiation. But they cannot meet the public need for adjudication, nor can they be considered an alternative to government action against abuses in marketing.

4. Arbitration

For many years, some trade associations have operated arbitration schemes for the resolution of disputes between consumers and members of the trade. This practice was given a new impetus by the *Fair Trading Act,* 1973. Pursuant to the Act, trade associations are encouraged to devise Codes of Practice in co-operation with the Office of Fair Trading. These codes include provision for conciliation and for arbitration.

An independent and more general scheme for the arbitration of consumer disputes has been operating in Manchester since 1972, and another operates in Westminster.

Arbitration is usually supported on the ground that it should be quicker, cheaper, more casual and less hostile than court proceedings.

Arbitration need not require repeated attendances, and it is often more efficient than the courts in other ways. For example, when a complaint to the Manchester Arbitration Scheme relates to a building dispute, the arbitration is held on site.

The consumer arbitration schemes usually deal only with complaints by consumers. This has the advantage that a scheme can focus on disputes without the distraction of an overwhelming volume of debt claims by traders. But it is also a limitation on their effectiveness. The arbitration schemes deal with one defect in the County Court system, i.e. the lack of a readily accessible adjudication of consumer complaints. But the arbitration schemes do not mitigate the other main defect of the County Courts, i.e. debt claims passing from summons to judgment without intermediate investigation, and being enforced by the courts regardless of their validity.

Arbitration has the advantage that disputes which cannot be resolved by discussion are brought to a resolution instead of being negotiated to a deadlock. But it has several limitations.

A normal benefit claimed for arbitration is that the parties can select the arbitrators. No doubt this can be an advantage in commercial arbitration, or in labour relations. But selecting arbitrators in each case would be too clumsy and time consuming for the amounts usually involved in consumer disputes. A possible alternative is a fixed arbitration panel for all disputes relating to a particular trade, or to a particular shopping area. But a fixed panel deprives arbitration of one of its advantages.

Arbitration can be simpler than court proceedings. For example, in disputes over dry cleaning (if they are worth an adjudication at all) it may well be simpler to have an expert in cleaning processes as an arbitrator rather than to bring experts as witnesses to a court trial. But the assumed simplicity of arbitration can sometimes be illusory. For example, an amendment of the claim might be more difficult on an arbitration because the statement of claim may have determined the issue on which the jurisdiction of the tribunal was agreed.

Another advantage of arbitration is that it may provide an alternative forum for people who may be intimidated by the thought of court proceedings. Even the word 'court' is frightening to some people. The privacy of arbitration can be an advantage. But this too has an attendant risk. The law developed in arbitration cases is not usually digested in any readable form, and hence is not amenable to the ordinary processes of law reform. Moreover, when there is no reporting of decisions and no simple appeal structure, there may be a risk of arbitrators arriving at conclusions not according to law at all, but by reference to their own intuition. The result could be an abandonment of the rule of law and impairment of one of the essentials of justice, i.e., that like cases be treated alike.

The merchants most likely to agree to arbitration are surely those operating in a legitimate and reasonable way, and who rely on repeat business. Retailers selling shabby goods by predatory tactics may find no incentive to agree. 'When retailers won't settle, they generally dig their heels in and won't agree to arbitration either.'[1] But some of the more dubious merchants do agree to arbitration. 'Merchants selling shoddy merchandise can look respectable by co-operating. They can respond to the tip of the iceberg. The majority of people do not pursue their complaints.'[2]

Perhaps most important, arbitration does not meet the primary objection to the County Courts. The main problem is the burden that the adversary system puts on the individual to present his own case, or find his own champion. Even in the Manchester Arbitration Scheme, which is in many ways well designed to help ordinary people, the publicity document describing the scheme still speaks of the claimant proving his case. What people need for the resolution of consumer disputes is someone who takes the initiative, and who performs the task of investigation as a prelude to adjudication. This is not normally the case with arbitration. Something may be gained by moving from the intimidating milieu of the courthouse. But a satisfactory system for the adjudication of consumer disputes cannot

1. Interview at an advisory agency, 1977.
2. Interview with the organiser of an arbitration scheme, 1977.

be established simply by moving the adversary system from one forum to another.

Another problem is that arbitration is sometimes confused with conciliation, and perhaps for this reason, the decision is not always perceived as binding. In some cases, a merchant perceives an award of an arbitrator as signalling a need for negotiations, rather than a decision to be honoured. Where a consumer succeeds and the award of an arbitrator is not paid, an action must still be commenced in the County Court for enforcement of the award.

On enquiries at the advisory agencies about their reasons for not referring cases to arbitration, the two most commonly mentioned were: (a) the difficulty in getting merchants to agree; and (b) the risk of having to take court proceedings subsequently to enforce the award.

There are further difficulties with arbitration schemes organised by trade associations. One is an obvious risk that the process will be, or appear to be, dominated by the trade. A panel can be composed of representatives from the trade and from consumers. But the business representatives may be more knowledgeable about the normal practices of the trade, and their views may still tend to dominate. Moreover, there is a tendency for arbitrators to adjudicate by reference to normal trade practice rather than by reference to the more impartial doctrines of the law of contract.[1] Thus a practical consequence of arbitration may be for each trade or retailing community to make its own law. To the extent that this happens, it would deprive justice of impartiality, would be inconsistent with the democratic process, and would leave arbitration dangerously close to industry self-regulation.

The determination of consumer disputes in the courts at least has the advantage of adjudication by people trained in the rules developed in commercial cases. Of course those rules should not be applied automatically in consumer cases. But an awareness of the rules developed in commercial cases should result in a more impartial justice than the application of rules developed by a trade for its own dealings with its customers.

The arbitration schemes organised by trade associations can also be expensive, the total cost sometimes being more than the amount involved. Some of them also involve the problems of communication with people at distant places.

In the advisory agencies, the proliferation of arbitration schemes can add to the workload. With each scheme having its own jurisdiction, its own rules and its own practice, the resulting total can add significantly to the

1. For an example of this happening, see 'Arbitration in Action', *The Motor Trade Executive*, March 1972, p. 24.

volume and complexity of material that must be handled in training advisers.

One of the objectives of the Manchester Arbitration Scheme was to provide a model for the possible development of small claims courts. Hence it is a challenge to the official position of the Lord Chancellor's Office that the County Courts can cope with small claims, and that there is no need for the separate development of small claims courts. Possibly for this reason, the scheme has not usually received the enthusiastic support of the central government, although it has been supported by some of the authorities in Manchester.

The Trading Standards Departments do not provide any official arbitration service, but many of them come close to it. When a complaint is presented to a merchant by a consumer, or by a Trading Standards Department, it is common for the merchant to ask a Trading Standards Officer what he thinks would be the fair thing to do. If the Trading Standards Officer gives a definite answer, it does not have the official status of an arbitration award. But as a practical matter, it might have the same significance.

Arbitration plays a useful role in the resolution of consumer disputes, and it is helpful to fill a gap in adjudication services. But arbitration can never meet the need for adjudication in small claims by a tribunal having compulsory jurisdiction, i.e., a court.

5. The Significance of Law

One consequence of the absence of a readily accessible forum for the investigation and adjudication of consumer disputes is a divergence between law as it appears in appellate judgments (and consequently in legal textbooks) and law as it operates in the consumer marketplace.

Retailers commonly do not perceive consumers as having rights accorded by law. A retailer's decisions relating to customers are more often determined by habit, his own sense of fairness, profitability, and sometimes a desire for repeat business. Interviews with top management of large retail operations showed a working knowledge of the law relating to retailing; but interviews with local managers and others dealing with the public indicated generally not the slightest understanding of sale of goods law. Habit, company policy, trade practice, and profit, seem to be the dominant influences. When pressed to state what they felt the law to be on a particular problem, the normal answer was simply a reflection of their own practice. For example, when questioned about the circumstances in which a buyer would have a legal right to return an item, one retailer replied that a buyer is always entitled to return anything as long as it has not been used. Another answered that a buyer is never entitled to return anything once he has taken it away, or it has been delivered. A third answered that a buyer is entitled to return it if it does not work. Another answered that a buyer is entitled to return it as long as it is in a condition to be resold as new, but otherwise he is not entitled to return it no matter what complaints he may have.

The publicity[1] following the *Supply of Goods (Implied Terms) Act*, 1973, was helpful, and there seems to be a consensus in the advisory agencies that there has been an improvement in retailers' understandings of their obligations. But 18 months after the circulation of that publicity, the Director General of Fair Trading was still reporting that: '. . .I have been dismayed in my discussions with trade organisations at the lack of knowledge shown by many traders concerning their legal obligations towards their customers.'[2]

Again, following a review of answers received from 350 Citizens' Advice Bureaux relating to footwear complaints, the National Association of CABs concluded that:

> It seemed that the overall difficulty in getting the problem satisfactorily concluded was the unwillingness of the shop to accept responsibility. This often overlapped with a referral to the manufacturer, and both imply a refusal (not necessarily deliberate) on the shop's part to recognize its obligations under the Sale of Goods Act (as amended by the Supply of Goods (Implied Terms) Act).[3]

Even when retailers know the law, they may also know that there is no programme of systematic enforcement, so that compliance is to a large extent optional.

> If we quote law to traders, they sometimes say 'We don't do that in our firm'.[4]
>
> Some shops offer a replacement at half price. If he is not smart, the customer can end up paying 1½ times the price for one useable item.[5]

In particular, the concept of damages is not widely understood. When an

1. E.g. *A Retailers' Guide: Changes in the Law relating to the Sale of Goods*, 1974, pamphlet by the Department of Prices and Consumer Protection.
2. *Annual Report of the Director General of Fair Trading for 1975*, p.9.
3. *Footwear*, Evidence Paper E74/5, November 1974, National Association of Citizens' Advice Bureaux, p.3.
4. Interview at an advisory agency, 1977.
5. Interview at another advisory agency, 1977.

item is defective, and a consumer is aggrieved by a lack of remedial action, the typical demand is that 'I want my money back'. Similarly, the complaint may be considered by the retailer in terms of whether the customer is or is not entitled to his money back. That he may be entitled to a partial rebate of the price is less likely to be recognised.

The same phenomenon appears at the advisory agencies. Claims are often settled for a partial rebate of the price. But this is usually perceived as a compromise of a buyer's claim for rescission rather than as satisfaction of a buyer's right to damages.

The same phenomenon appears in arbitrations.

> When damages are awarded, the shops want the goods back. . .Retailers never understand damages beyond the price. Claimants feel short-changed if they recover damages as a settlement when they think they are entitled to full recovery of the price.[1]

Similarly in court offices, the possibility of a consumer claiming damages is not as well recognised as the possibility of claiming rescission. For example, the particulars of claim forms provided in the County Courts include specific forms for:

(1) return of money paid for defective goods;
(2) return of money paid for work not carried out or goods not delivered;
(3) cost of making good faulty workmanship/completing unfinished work.

But they do not seem to include a specific form for a partial rebate of the price of defective goods, or damages for the cost of repairs.

In interviews with registrars and court staff, the possibility of a consumer claiming damages was generally recognised, but not always. In one court, the clerk dealing with counter enquiries was asked what she would do if someone complained about defective goods, and wanted to claim back the whole price that was paid. She replied that 'We can issue a default summons'. She was then asked what she would do if the enquirer wanted to claim back part of the price. She replied that 'That has to be argued out with the manager of the shop'. When the registrar of the same court was asked similar questions, he replied that 'If someone wants to claim recovery of part of the price, it would be better to suggest that they go to the Trading Standards Department'. Yet he had no doubt that the County

1. Interview with the organiser of an arbitration scheme, 1977.

Court was the right place for anyone claiming recovery of the whole price.

A major problem in the role of law in consumer transactions is that the advisory agencies do not have a comprehensive digest of legal material. In spite of the expenditures, changes in institutional structure, and the pamphlets that have been issued, the advisory agencies still do not have any comprehensive manual of consumer law. The pamphlets issued by the Office of Fair Trading and the Department of Prices and Consumer Protection relate primarily to legislative changes. Similarly, the digests of law supplied to Citizens' Advice Bureaux from the national office are digests of statute law and regulations. The advisory agencies do not have any comprehensive manual that is a blending of common law and statute.

The result is predictable. Advisers interviewed by the writer all understood that when goods are defective, a buyer might claim 'under the Sale of Goods Act'. But the possibility of a buyer claiming rescission or damages for deceit was not generally recognised. Again, examples were mentioned by agency advisers of cases in which no defence to a claim was perceived, and yet in which *non est factum* would be a probable defence. Similarly, the writer was told several times in interviews at advisory agencies that in relation to a particular situation (e.g. private sales) there are no rules, because 'no Act covers it'.

The focus of the advisory agencies on statute rather than common law may partly explain why, when consumers bring or defend a claim, the case invariably alleges defective goods rather than misrepresentations in the sales pitch or in the advertising.[1]

There is a desperate need for a comprehensive manual of common law, statute and regulations relating to consumer protection, and classified under topic headings that are relevant to the everyday work of the advisory agencies. As well as being a consolidation of legal doctrine, there are two other areas that such a manual would need to cover:

(1) Alternative strategies for dealing with various situations, illustrating the significance of negotiating techniques and legal options.

(2) Checklists: for example, there is a desperate need for checklists of possible defences to various types of claims, and checklists of alternative strategies that should be considered in various problem situations.

Of course the production of a comprehensive manual that would blend common law, statute law, and alternative strategies would require first-class legal talent. It would be a difficult thing for any agency or department

1. Other explanations for this are suggested above in Chapter 6, p.144.

of the central government to produce. But without such a manual, it is infinitely more difficult for advisers at the local level to achieve this blending themselves.

Of course the advisory agencies refer some cases to solicitors. But this does not counteract the blinkering effect of reference material limited to statute law, and it is not an alternative to a comprehensive manual.

6. A New Procedure for Small Claims

A. Introduction

As explained above, there is no readily accessible system now available throughout the country for the adjudication of small claims. On the other hand, it is difficult to conceive of any system of adjudication that could handle the enormous potential volume of consumer disputes, most of which involve amounts of under £25. One approach obviously is to consider possible ways of reducing the need for adjudication. Three possibilities are:

(1) Maintaining and improving the services available for advice, and the negotiation of those claims that are susceptible of a solution by discussion. Some comments on that are made above.
(2) Changes in the substantive law to reduce the total volume of claims. A proposal on this is made in Chapter 10 (4).
(3) Changing the system of costs to create pressures for the settlement of claims without adjudication. A suggestion on this is included in the proposal that follows.

Whatever reforms are adopted to reduce the volume of disputed or unpaid claims, however, there will always be a residual category of small claims for which adjudication must be readily available or justice denied.

An expansion of legal aid is obviously not the answer. The main problem with small claims is not a lack of funds for professional advocacy. It is that the amounts involved make professional advocacy too extravagant even when funds are available by which the fees could be paid. A judge and two advocates (total 3 lawyers) is just too many lawyers for the disposition of small claims at reasonable cost.

A possible reform in England would be the introduction of small claims courts of the type functioning in Canada and the United States. But they would not be more than a marginal improvement. They are open to the same basic objections as the County Courts and suffer from the same defects. They are used extensively for the collection of trade debts and alleged debts, and there is the same picture of defences not being raised when they are available, and of relatively little use of the courts by consumers as plaintiffs. As one distinguished American judge has put it, '. . .there is little correspondence between the professed aims of these courts and the ends they serve.'[1]

A study by the Consumers' Union included several examples of small claims courts being used by consumers as plaintiffs. Nevertheless, the study concluded:

> Small claims courts have been in large part a disappointment to those who thought they would serve the poor by creating a forum where costs were low, lawyers were unnecessary, procedures were simple and justice was nevertheless dispensed. The poor man who is a debtor is likely to stop paying when he discovers the merchandise is defective, the transaction is fraudulent, or the price is excessive. He then becomes a defendant in a case brought by the retailer or the finance company. Then the small claims courts, like other civil courts, become a weapon against poor people. All the trappings intended to serve them, will victimize them instead. The speediness of the procedure takes on the character of railroading.[2]

There are, however, substantial variations in the achievement of small claims courts in different communities, and the proposal that follows is partly the result of reflection on these variations.

The trouble with small claims courts is that although they use a more simple procedure than the higher courts, they still operate on basically the same principles. The small claims judge tends to imitate his superiors in the adversary system. If justice is ever to be done in small claims, the approach must be far more iconoclastic. Indeed, almost every principle that a common lawyer has cherished must be abandoned. The adversary system, the separation of adjudication from court administration, the concept of the trial; all must go: and we must brace ourselves for such innovations as a judge speaking on the telephone to one of the parties in the absence of the other. Above all, the judge's function must be recognised as first and foremost the task of investigation, with adjudication being an ancillary role.

1. Per Skelly Wright, J., a justice of the US Court of Appeals for the District of Columbia circuit, in an article 'The Courts Have Failed the Poor', *New York Times Magazine*, 9 March 1969, p.26, 102. The impressions of another observer are apparent in the title of her work, viz. 'The Persecution and Intimidation of the Low-Income Litigant as Performed by the Small Claims Court in California', B.A. Moulton, (1969) 21 *Stanford Law Review* 1657.

2. 'Buyer vs. Seller in Small Claims Court', 36 *Consumer Reports*, October 1971, p.624, 627.

The break with the adversary system must be total. To achieve this, small claims should be handled by totally different personnel operating separately and at different premises from the County Court. Reform through adjustments to the County Court system will never meet the need for readily accessible adjudication in small claims.

The following is the outline suggested for a new type of small claims court.

B. Procedure

The system must be run by judges without the help of professional advocates. The primary guide rule should be that responsibility for reaching the just conclusion of a case rests on the court, not on the litigants. From non-business parties, the court should expect co-operation, but it should not expect initiative.

Contact with a defendant need not necessarily begin with a summons. Suppose, for example, a buyer comes to the court office with a complaint against a retailer. It might be helpful for the judge to phone the retailer while the claimant is still in the office to see how far the matter can be dealt with over the phone. Putting the retailer's story to the customer may reveal that even on his own evidence the customer has no case. The claim could then be dismissed. Or the retailer's story may show that even on his evidence, the claim is obviously valid, and judgment could then be given. Or it may appear that inspection of the goods is necessary and this could be arranged. Or it may appear that there are issues that need to be determined by a hearing, and the judge could then arrange a time, advise both parties of the types of documents to bring, and discuss with them witnesses or other evidence. There should be no 'onus of proof' on anyone except the judge.

The essence of the proposal is that the judge should proceed as he thinks appropriate in the particular case until he feels that the investigation has been sufficiently thorough for a conclusion to be safely reached. At that point he should give judgment whether or not there has been anything that would be recognised as a trial in the traditional sense. Described by comparison with existing institutions, the *modus operandi* of a small claims judge should approximate more closely to that of a police detective or Trading Standards Officer than to that of a High Court judge. Perhaps some rules of procedure could usefully be formulated after some experience with the system, but few should be prescribed initially.

There should be no default judgments, and the system should not depend upon a defendant taking the initiative to raise a defence. Summonses should be used sparingly, if at all. The claim should normally be put into writing by the claimant, the judge, or a court clerk, and this would be enough to open the file. Where a statement of the claim is sent to a non-business defendant, it should be accompanied by a pamphlet listing and briefly explaining the defences that might be available to the particular type of claim. If communication by mail or telephone is unsuccessful, a process server could deliver the statement of claim and the pamphlet describing possible defences, and then explain that 'I have come to arrange an appointment for you to meet the judge and talk to him about it'. If a defendant is sick, shy or frightened about going to the court, the judge should willingly go to the defendant. Once the two come together, the judge can discuss any possible defence with the defendant (or his representative), or if there is clearly no defence, can discuss how the judgment will be satisfied.

Implicit in the proposal is a recognition that different categories of litigants have different capacities to function within the legal system. Regular business litigants in particular have a natural advantage, and rules designed to treat everyone alike discriminate in practice against the working class.

No judgment should be entered against a non-business litigant until both:

(1) He has been given a list of possible defences to the particular type of claim, and except where there is some urgency given seven days to consider; and

(2) The judge has made a sufficient enquiry into the facts, including a personal discussion with the defendant, to satisfy himself that there is no defence.

A judge should never begin by asking a defendant 'Do you owe the money?' Most people have no idea. Far from soliciting admissions of this type, which necessarily involve an opinion on law, the judge should cross-examine on any confession of liability by a litigant in person, not to ensure that the defendant understands the significance of the confession, but to discover any defence that might be available. It should be assumed that a non-business litigant is ignorant of possible defences and it should be the judge's responsibility to raise any available defence unless it is expressly disclaimed by the defendant.

The court office should be organised to ensure that anyone wishing to bring or defend a claim is given a cordial reception and prompt attention, and it should be the judge's responsibility to arrange this. Much depends on the temperament of the court clerk who meets the public when they enter the office.[1]

Except in remote areas, judges should be assigned three or more per court so that each day there would be at least one judge not preoccupied with fixed time appointments.

Where a hearing is needed, and one of the parties is a worker, the hearing should be scheduled for the evening unless he requests a day-time hearing. This should be done as a routine, not treated as a privilege.

The assumption that some interval must elapse between presentation and determination of a claim should be abandoned. There are many situations in which justice must be instant or be denied. Consider, for example, a situation where a tenant is just moving out of a flat. The landlord demands £100 for structural damage. The tenant says there is nothing beyond fair wear and tear. Would anyone seriously suggest that the parties should testify later about the condition of the premises, or worse still, call expert witnesses to testify later? Why should they not be able to phone for a judge to come, inspect the premises, and decide on the spot? Or where two people walk into a court office with a dispute that they want the judge to decide, why should he not do so if he can? Again, what happens when a visitor to a town has a dispute with a local tradesman? The present system is virtually a denial of justice. Why should the visitor not be able to obtain a judgment the same day, followed if necessary by instant execution? In the thirteenth century, some courts provided instant justice in such cases;[2] why not today?

If there are not enough judges to serve the public at this level of convenience, an obvious answer is more judges. It may be hard to imagine a judge moving round the community, resolving disputes on the spot, and keeping in touch with his office by two-way radio; but why not? Meeting the public need for justice must surely take precedence over any sentimental attachment to the perception of a dignified and sedentary judge presiding over structured proceedings. Apart from meeting the need for instant justice, a small claims judge must also be mobile, like any detective, to view the scenes of events, talk to possible witnesses, inspect documents, etc.

A collateral advantage of viewing the scene and talking more freely to parties and witnesses is that small claims judges should develop some expert knowledge with regard to the larger categories of cases, and thus

1. In one Canadian city, I discovered the unusual phenomenon of claims being brought in the small claims court in substantial numbers by buyers against sellers. This occurred in spite of a cantankerous judge. Much of the explanation lay in the warmth, charm, personality and efficiency of the court clerk.

2. *Select Cases Concerning the Law Merchant, 1270-1638*, Vol 1; *Local Courts*, London, 1908 Selden Society, Introduction, p.xxiii.

help to minimise costs by reducing the need for expert evidence.

Another conceivable arrangement would be to have a more conventional and sedentary judge assisted by a field investigator. But for the following three reasons, this would be unworkable:

(1) The processes of communication between judge and investigator would involve tremendous time and expense. They would also involve errors and omissions, with the risk of consequential injustice. Moreover, there is a limit to how much can be conveyed in a briefing or in a report. An investigator would not have the same awareness of what he was looking for, or the same recognition of the significance of what he found. Nor could an investigator take advantage of opportunities that occur to resolve disputes in the field.

(2) It is unlikely that people of sufficient calibre would be attracted to act as investigators unless they were also entrusted with the task of adjudication.

(3) Having an investigator would make it difficult to enforce the requirement that the judge must speak to every non-business defendant. There would be too much risk of the procedure becoming like a system of default judgments.

C. Selection of Judges

If they are to function as suggested, small claims judges must be people of high intelligence, they must be in some ways more versatile than High Court judges, and yet they must be willing to forgo the prestige that comes from 'sitting on the bench' and listening to advocacy. They must above all be willing to meet the convenience of working-class litigants.

How would people of sufficient calibre be attracted to the position? Probably the only way is to pay them well and appoint them young. By the time they have reached their early thirties, people of the calibre required will generally have found other positions with higher incomes, or that they find more satisfying, more enjoyable, more challenging, more prestigious or having greater prospects of advancement. Small claims courts would fail miserably if they became, as they have in some jurisdictions, repositories for lawyers who, because of senility, incompetence, or ill health, had become an embarrassment in some other position.

The suggested minimum qualifications for appointment are:

(1) The candidate should be a university graduate with honours, a barrister (honours), a solicitor (honours), a qualified social worker, or a Trading Standards Officer. If the candidate is a barrister or solicitor, he should not have been in practice for more than six months, including

articles or pupilage, during the preceding five years. (This is to disqualify those who have become accustomed to the adversary system.)

If the candidate is not a law graduate, a barrister or solicitor, the appointment could be conditional upon reaching a satisfactory level in a training programme of, say, twelve months.

(2) At least where the candidate is a lawyer, he should be under 33 years (with compulsory retirement at 45 years).

(3) The candidate should not be a former official or employee of any court or tribunal using an adversary system.

(4) The candidate must be enthusiastic about fieldwork, and not be someone who sees the position as sedentary.

The reason for early retirement is the expectation that people of sufficient calibre would not want the position for more than a few years before moving on to something else. Thus without compulsory retirement at an early age, the court would become overweighted with those least able to find other positions, and who may therefore be the least able. Some small claims judges might go to higher courts, or find positions in academic life, or transfer to the central office (described below). Others might move to professional practice, government, social agencies or business.

To recognise the importance of small claims and to attract people of the required calibre, salaries should be close to those of County Court judges.

D. Jurisdiction

The proposed court might cover claims involving less than, say, £500. The important thing, however, is that the jurisdiction should be exclusive. This is not just because forum shopping is wrong in principle. In places where a small claims court has concurrent jurisdiction with higher courts, some tradesmen admit that they bring their claims in the higher courts because it makes it more difficult for customers to defend.[1] Claims above the prescribed limit would be left to the County Courts.

E. Representation

Whether lawyers should be allowed as advocates is a sensitive question. It is suggested that legal representation should not be allowed. Some of the objections to lawyers are fairly obvious – increasing the cost, increasing formality, giving an advantage to business litigants and discouraging those

1. This appeared from interviews in Western Canada questioning tradesmen and their solicitors about their reasons for preferring to sue in the higher courts for amounts within small claims court jurisdiction.

without a lawyer from litigating. But another reason is even more compelling.

The procedure would be in many respects more demanding on judges than the adversary system. Hence there would be a constant temptation to slip into the adversary system unless the avoidance of that temptation is built into the institutional framework. Because lawyers are accustomed to the adversary system in other courts and because of the prestige of their presence in a small claims court, they would be a powerful influence promoting the adoption of adversary procedures. Once this occurred, the benefit of the reform would be lost.

Two objections to the exclusion of lawyers have sometimes been discussed, but neither seems very substantial. The first is that corporate litigants would have to appear by a representative, and if an employee of a company appears regularly on its behalf, he will develop a familiarity with the court and many of the same characteristics as a lawyer. But a corporate representative would not have the most objectionable characteristics of lawyers, i.e. he would not through his experience in other courts have become accustomed to the adversary system, nor would he have the prestige with which to coerce the small claims court into adopting adversary procedures.

Secondly, it has been said that the proposal would be a denial of legal services, unfair both to the legal profession and to the public. But small claims are not generally receiving legal services at the moment. Paradoxically, it may only be by denying lawyers the right to act that a readily accessible legal system for the adjudication of small claims can be established successfully.

F. Costs

If the system depended on government revenues, it would be an obvious target for economy drives by officials who might not be sympathetic to the importance of small claims. Yet the success of the proposal depends on a sufficient number of judges being appointed at a substantial salary. To relieve pressure for holding down the number of judges, the system should be self-supporting. On the other hand, it would be unjust to follow the High Court practice that costs are nearly always ordered to be paid by the losing party.

The suggestion is that a scale of court charges be drawn up that would be a maximum scale so calculated that, if always applied, it would yield about three times the revenue required for operating the system. The judge should have a discretion to order payment of court costs of anywhere up to the scale figures. In exercising this discretion, he should consider: (1) the conduct of the parties, and in particular whether the claim was one that the judge feels should not have been brought, or should have been paid; and (2) the ability of the parties, or generally the losing party, to pay. The same criteria could be used with regard to party and party costs, and these could be awarded up to the amount actually incurred.

Thus, apart from providing the revenue to sustain the court, the system of costs would be used blatantly as a regulatory device to encourage legitimate claims and defences, and to discourage those that are patently bad.

An initial fee deposit for commencement of an action should be required, but kept low so that it would not be a discouragement. It is also hoped that the regulatory and penal impact of the system of costs would help to stimulate the payment of legitimate claims and keep the number of cases for adjudication down to a manageable level.

G. A Central Office

The system would require a central office for co-ordinating the administration of the courts, selecting judges, keeping statistics, drawing forms, publishing advice pamphlets to litigants, etc. The office should also maintain a continuing programme of research on the efficiency of the system.

H. Appeals

A liberal right of appeal would make the system uneconomic. A right to a trial *de novo* in the County Court, such as exists in some parts of Canada, would be open to the same objections as forum shopping.

On the other hand, to allow no appeals would insulate the higher courts from exposure to the impact of the legal system on small transactions. The law applicable to small claims would be that prescribed by the higher courts in dealing with larger sums. If small claims are to be determined according to rules developed in the higher courts, it is essential to the intelligent development of the jurisprudence that appellate judges should be exposed to the impact of those rules in the context of small claims.

There could be an appeal by case stated wherever the judge who decided the case, or another small claims judge, or the Director General of Fair Trading, certifies that a significant point of law is involved. On points of substantive law, the appeal could lie to the Court of Appeal. On a point of procedure, there should be one final appeal to a specially appointed Senior Judge of Small Claims. He should have the status of a High Court judge with exclusive power to determine his own jurisdiction. He should also be responsible in any appeal for deciding whether it lies to himself or to the Court of Appeal. Although appeals to the Court of Appeal on procedural points could be satisfactory, it would be unwise to take the risk. There is at least a danger that the Court of Appeal judges may, albeit subconsciously, measure the virtue of the procedure by the extent to which it coincides with the system to which they are accustomed. No risks should be taken that might allow contamination from the adversary system.

The system must be designed to recognise that in small claims, appeals are not being allowed primarily to review the justice of the decision in the individual case. The primary purpose here in allowing appeals is to use the cases as examples through which the appellate courts will review and develop the applicable law.

A problem with appeals is that a non-business litigant may have no interest in the result compared with the costs involved. A business litigant might be concerned about the impact of a decision on future cases, but a non-business litigant usually will not. If decisions of small claims judges are appealed when the result favours a consumer, but not when the result favours a businessman, there is an obvious risk of distortion in the development of new law.

To facilitate consumer appeals, the Office of Fair Trading should have standing to take over a consumer case, by consent of the consumer, and initiate an appeal.

For all appeals in small claims, there should be a central fund available to retain counsel to argue the cause, but not necessarily the case, of a non-business party. The small claims central office or the Office of Fair Trading might select, wherever possible, some organisation having interests in common with the non-business litigant, for example, the Consumer's Association or a tenants' rights group. That organisation could then be invited to brief counsel to appear in the Court of Appeal at the expense of the central fund. Thus it would be the responsibility of the central office to ensure that, one way or another on every appeal, the case for a non-business party is presented. Similarly the case for a business litigant might be presented by a trade association, but that would not require any special provision.

The small claims judge could also be allowed to appear *amicus curiae* in the Court of Appeal. Much might be gained by exposing appellate and small claims judges to each other's thinking, and for the small claims judge, the break from his normal routine, and discussion with the appellate judges, might be a stimulating experience. This would also help to restrain any despotic tendency that might otherwise result from a small claims judge not being exposed to the arguments of lawyers in his daily routine.

I. The Government Position

The official position of the Lord Chancellor's Office has been that there is no need for a separate system of small claims courts.

Initially, there was no apparent recognition of anything significantly wrong with the County Courts. That subsequently changed to a belief that problems could be corrected by reforms within the County Court structure. Apprehension about the cost of any new system of small claims courts has also been an influential factor. 'In economic terms the Government was looking for a reduction in public expenditure and, therefore, new court buildings and new judicial appointments could not be looked upon favourably.'[1] The Government does not appear, however, to have produced any appraisal of the cost of *not* adopting a new system of small claims courts. These costs would include at least:

(1) the costs incurred by the advisory agencies, and by people dealing with the advisory agencies, in negotiating processes that are probably slower and less productive than they would be if prompt and efficient adjudication were a readily available alternative;
(2) the economic waste and other costs associated with standards of integrity in marketing lower than they would probably be if litigation was a readily available response to the breach of obligations;
(3) the wastage now involved in processing small claims through the cumbersome procedures of the adversary system.

The absence of perceived need is partly explained by the absence of any systematic process for the assessment of need. The Lord Chancellor's Office has not included a research wing with a capability for periodic assessments of public needs in the administration of justice. Nor has it included staff and other provisions for systematic and empirical enquiry into other aspects of court efficiency.

It is also unfortunate that the Lord Chancellor's Office has not received as much help as it might have done from the research of others. Partly this results from the secrecy attending the operation of the courts. Trials and some other proceedings are exposed to public view. But the bulk of court claims never reach such a proceeding. They start and finish in files that are treated in England as confidential, and not freely available for academic research. It is an old adage that justice must not only be done, it must manifestly be seen to be done. But in practice, the application of that adage is limited to a tiny minority of court actions.

Here too, however, there has been some improvement in recent years. The Lord Chancellor's Office has been helpful in assisting several research projects, including this work; and there is a healthy willingness to facilitate,

1. *Small Claims,* W.H. Elliott, 1977, International Congress on the Law of Civil Procedure at Ghent, p.8.

at least to some extent, the work of those who may not share the departmental view.

J. Conclusions

One cannot make a proposal such as the above without being conscious of the difficulties, the risks and the weaknesses. But the risk of error should not be the excuse for inertia. Nor should the test, when considering a new system, be one of perfection. Surely the relevant questions are: would the proposal be a significant improvement on what we now have, and can we think of anything better? If the objective is to minimise the frequency and severity of injustices, it is suggested that a court system functioning on the model proposed offers the best hope.

10 DEBT CLAIMS

1. Introduction

It is traditional in legal thinking for the regulation of marketing to be seen as separate from the law relating to the collection processes that follow a default in payment. But there is a close business connection. Rational behaviour by a credit grantor at the time of a sale or loan is likely to be conditioned, directly or indirectly, by predictions of how and when the credit will be repaid, and with what cost of collection. Changes in the law relating to collections can, therefore, have an impact on marketing behaviour, and possibly a greater impact than attempts to influence that behaviour by more direct forms of regulation. For this reason, a discussion of debt claims and collections is essential to the study of credit marketing and consumer protection.

2. The Collection Dilemma

It has been argued above[1] that, in spite of the improvements of recent years, the County Court system still operates to a large extent like a machine for enforcing the claims of credit grantors regardless of their legitimacy. This does not mean, however, that claimants always recover the money swiftly, easily, or at all. Although default judgments can be obtained with relative ease, recovery of the money is often another matter.

Where a claim has not been paid because of some grievance or resentment, or in the hope that the claim will not be pursued, the commencement of proceedings or the entry of judgment may be enough to induce payment in the majority of cases. The problems for credit grantors usually lie with those who are determined not to pay, those who have not sufficient income, and those who are so over-extended in debt that although they could pay some claims, there is no hope of paying all.

Judgment creditors often allege, understandably, that courts are too sympathetic to judgment debtors. One problem is, of course, that in the application of his income, a judgment debtor must be allowed priority for the necessities of life for himself and his family, and once this provision has been made, there is commonly nothing left. Thus criticism of the system sometimes exceeds the justification. No system can be efficient in extracting money from people who neither have it, nor have the earning

1. Chapter 9 (1).

power to obtain it.

The first problem for a judgment creditor is that the court is not self-motivating. If he wants to maximise the prospects of collection, a creditor must keep track of the judgment debtor, both with regard to his location and his affairs. The judgment creditor must decide which among the possible methods of execution to use, and must apply for the orders. Sometimes a judgment debtor is summoned for an examination as to means. But successive orders for his appearance may be needed before a satisfactory examination can be completed. Each of these phases involves time and expense for the judgment creditor and sometimes the services of a solicitor. Even if the costs of execution are ultimately recovered in addition to the judgment debt, the costs allowed by the court will not be a total indemnity for the time and expense. Often, a judgment creditor cannot deal with the judgment debtor on a one-to-one relationship because of competition from the unco-ordinated moves of other creditors. Repeated applications to the court are often necessary for the enforcement of one judgment, and there is no assurance of success.

It is not surprising that credit grantors sometimes complain that collection through the courts is slow, cumbersome, time-consuming, expensive and uncertain. Instances appeared during this research of credit grantors running what seemed to be legitimate businesses expressing desperation at the failure of the legal system to recover the money on judgments obtained in respect of instalment credit transactions. The system can seem particularly harsh to a small trader, perhaps one whose expertise lies in technical matters rather than business and who is not sophisticated in making credit decisions.

Thus the system can fail the innocent and law-abiding on both sides of the marketplace. An unscrupulous seller can use the courts to enforce invalid claims against ordinary people while an unscrupulous buyer can learn from experience how to manipulate the machinery of execution to wear down his creditors.

One cause of uncertainty is the occasional feed-through into the execution process of feelings about the validity of a claim. The theory, of course, is that once a default judgment has been entered, the validity of a claim is no longer in issue and cannot be questioned except on proceedings to set aside the judgment. This is not, however, the way things always work. The failure of the system to screen out invalid claims prior to judgment is not something to which judges, registrars and bailiffs are universally insensitive. For example, where it appears in the course of execution proceedings that a judgment debtor had a good defence to the claim, a judge or registrar may, rather than suggesting a motion to set aside the judgment, be tempted to compromise by ordering small or even derisory instalments.[1] Similarly, bailiffs as a practical matter exercise some discretion in executions, and it is not unknown for the exercise of this discretion to be influenced by a bailiff's perception of the merits of a claim or class of claims. It may seem that rough justice is better than none, but practices of this type can generate confusion and undermine confidence in the integrity of the system and the rule of law.

Where a claim is unpaid, however, the causes of a creditor's dilemma do not always begin at the time of judgment. Often there was no reasonable ground at the time of advancing the credit for any expectation that the money would be paid or collectable.

> Many persistent Debtors have no regular employment, and some have not worked for many years. In many cases sickness explains the unemployment: – Bronchitis the dust (Pneumoconeosis), Nerves and headaches (Neurasthenia), etc. But if a man has a wife and 4 children, and no special skill, he is not likely to get a job in which his take home wages will equal, still less exceed, the £12 or more which the state gives him in National Assistance.[2]

Yet these 'debtors' are, *ex hypothesi,* people who have been receiving credit.

Although some credit grantors ask a range of questions and obtain credit reports at the time of advancing credit, others do not. After a study of judgment debtors who had been to prison under commital orders, a County Court judge concluded that, with two exceptions, 'all the creditors were large commercial concerns trading on the basis that they give credit to customers and are repaid by periodic instalments'. Referring to four lists of judgment summonses heard in different courts, he continued:

> It is clear that an overwhelming majority of the creditors who use the judgment summons procedure are of this kind. It seems likely they constitute 95% of all judgment creditors, at least, in industrial areas. For them the judgment summons procedure is part of their normal business routine and the County Court. . .a debt collecting agency.

1. In one proceeding observed by the writer in 1968, the judgment debtor stated facts which were not disputed by the judgment creditor and which were not recognised by either party as being a defence to the claim. Yet those facts would clearly constitute a defence. The result was that on a judgment for £80, the judgment debtor was ordered to pay 1/- (now 5p) a month. That this amount was too small to be worth collecting was a consequence the registrar was willing to accept.
2. Per a County Court judge in a memorandum, 1966.

> Credit traders of this kind :
> a. Habitually give credit without making any enquiries about the creditworthiness of the debtor so that sometimes the same creditor is issuing judgment summonses against the debtor while through their agents they are persuading that debtor to accept further credit.[1]

The failure of many credit grantors, however, to obtain credit reports, or otherwise to make a reasonable assessment of the prudence of a transaction, is not an aberration susceptible of remedy by exhortation. It is a form of market behaviour encouraged by the legal system. In creating a system of debt collection by coercion, the law encourages optimism on the part of credit grantors and promotes an expectation that money can be recovered in situations in which a debtor is unwilling or unable to pay.

A major problem in the discussion of creditors' remedies is that the area is sometimes perceived as a matter relating to the administration of justice. A consequence of classifying any matter as relating to 'The Administration of Justice' is that it then becomes almost exclusively a preserve of the legal profession, and the Lord Chancellor's Office, or the Home Office. A functional classification of creditors' remedies (including methods of execution) would surely require that the area be treated as a matter of monetary policy, of trade, of social policy, and of integrity in marketing.

First, it is a matter of monetary policy in that the law relating to creditors' remedies is a primary factor determining the perimeter of consumer credit. Any strengthening of creditors' remedies that increases recovery rates creates an incentive to expand the granting of credit into more marginal categories of risk. Conversely, any retraction of creditors' remedies will tend to increase bad debt ratios and thereby create an incentive to retract the perimeter of consumer credit in the marginal categories of risk. It is surely undesirable for any revision of creditors' remedies to be made independently of some assessment of how much consumer credit is good for the economy.

Secondly, credit has, from ancient times, been recognised as having a potential for evil. Insolvency through the over-extension of credit can create anxieties, deterioration in morale, loss of pride, family tension and sometimes privation. In extreme cases, the consequences can be worse, including the break-up of marriages and suicide.

> Financial strain is seen as one of the main agents operating against families and keeping family and personal problems ahead of any

1. Per another County Court judge in a memorandum, 1966.

> other category. Many bureaux report that marriage difficulties are stemming directly from money troubles in general and debt in particular.[1]

On the other hand, the under-use of credit can mean relegation to a standard of living lower than can reasonably be achieved. Also it could result in some diversion of income to transitory pleasures rather than buying major durables of more lasting benefit. It is, therefore, a matter of moral value judgments and social policy to arrive at a point in the expansion of consumer credit that is thought to achieve the optimum good. Individual choices and market mechanisms can do this only to a limited degree. Whether we like it or not, the state influences the perimeter of consumer credit when it settles the law relating to creditors' remedies. Thus decisions relating to the strength of creditors' remedies can be made intelligently only if those making the decisions are conscious of this significance.

Thirdly, the law relating to creditors' remedies can have a significant influence, for better or worse, on the integrity of sellers and of buyers.

Creditors' remedies were revised in 1970,[2] but unfortunately, as explained below, these aspects of the matter were almost entirely ignored.

3. The Garnishment of Wages (Attachment of Earnings)

For a century before 1970, the inviolability of the wage packet was one of the traditions of English labour law. In 1870, Parliament consolidated this position with *The Wages Attachment Abolition Act,* subsequently described as:

> . . .the culmination of a movement to protect the wages of the working man and it was passed through both Houses of Parliament in 1870 without a dissentient voice and without a Division. It was part of a movement in which we are still living, through the nineteenth and twentieth centuries, to protect the position of the wage earner.[3]

Various deductions from wages came to be accepted, particularly for income tax and social insurance contributions. The most significant retreat from the Act of 1870 came in 1957 when the Government introduced the Maintenance Orders Bill, providing for wage garnishment for the enforcement

1. *Annual Report for 1976-77 of the National Association of Citizens' Advice Bureaux*, p.6.
2. *Administration of Justice Act.*
3. Per R. Bell, in (1957) 565 *Parliamentary Debates (Commons)* col. 1550.

of maintenance orders.[1] At that time concern was expressed, both inside and outside the House, that this might be the thin edge of the wedge leading to wage garnishment for the enforcement of consumer debts. The Home Secretary set minds at rest in the following terms:

> People may ask whether, when we are introducing this Bill for the attachment of wages, we are to extend the principle of attachment to such matters as civil debt, hire-purchase agreements, fines or any other purposes. I have been approached by some Hon. members who are trade unionists, and I have given an answer to them officially, and I now give it in my speech. It is not the intention of this Government to extend attachment to any of these things or any other purposes. I hope that will be an undertaking which will give satisfaction to trade union members.[2]

On the second day of August 1971, the garnishment of wages in England for ordinary consumer debts began.[3]

Against the strength of this tradition and background, one might think that wage garnishment would not be introduced as a method of execution without first being studied by a commission or committee established specifically for that purpose. This is not, however, what happened. Concerned about over-crowding in the prisons and a variety of anomalies arising out of execution proceedings, the Government appointed in 1965 the *Committee on the Enforcement of Judgment Debts* (Payne Committee). Given that the topics referred to the committee included all methods of execution, the harassment of debtors, and orders for possession in mortgage actions, it is hardly surprising that the committee was appointed under the auspices of the Lord Chancellor's Department. The committee consisted almost entirely of lawyers, the only concession to the social sciences being the inclusion of one sociologist.

The paramount concern of the Government, and of the committee, seemed to be the abolition of imprisonment for debt. It is in this context that the garnishment of wages came to be considered. Thus it was perceived as an alternative to imprisonment rather than as a new development

1. Usually orders for the support of wives or children. A definition of the 'maintenance' orders to which wage garnishment may apply is now contained in the *Attachment of Earnings Act*, 1971, Sch.1.

2. Per R.A. Butler, Home Secretary, in (1957) 579 *Parliamentary Debates (Commons)* col. 1545.

3. Wage garnishment was first introduced in the *Administration of Justice Act*, 1970. The current legislative provision appears in the *Attachment of Earnings Act*, 1971. The Act applies to salaries and private pensions as well as wages. But it may only be with regard to wage-earners that the Act has significant effect.

in monetary and social policy. Hence the composition of the committee did not include, as a committee on the garnishment of wages might well have done, a psychologist, a social worker, a personnel officer, a union official and an economist specialising in monetary policy. The briefs submitted to the committee included a substantial number from the institutions of the legal system and from credit grantors. There were also briefs from some social agencies; but no submission was received or apparently invited from the Treasury or from the Bank of England.

Many of the briefs submitted to the committee supported the garnishment of wages, but again, they were submitted in the context of seeking an alternative to imprisonment. Even the Trades Union Congress filed a brief[1] supporting wage garnishment, and the committee regarded this as highly persuasive.[2] In understanding that brief, however, four points are significant.

(1) The TUC is a federated body. It did not undertake an independent study of wage garnishment but compiled a brief that was primarily a consolidation of the replies of member unions to a questionnaire prepared by the Payne Committee.
(2) As the brief itself explains, the head offices of member unions are in a creditor position when dealing with local officials and have occasion to make debt claims for the recovery of union funds.
(3) The brief makes no real appraisal of the effects of garnishment on the lives of workers. It suggests that garnishment would be helpful to creditors in 'that it would save the creditor much of the trouble and expense incurred by the present cumbersome procedure for securing the repayment of debt'.[3] But it gives no indication of how wage garnishment is likely to benefit union members, except 'that it is preferable to imprisonment'.
(4) There is no indication that the enquiries to member unions went beyond national officials.

In these circumstances, there was surely too much conflict of interest as well as detachment from the rank and file to accept the TUC position on wage garnishment as reflecting the views and interests of wage-earners.

Another feature of the committee's work was the absence of any evaluation of wage garnishment in the United States and Canada. In these countries, wage garnishment for consumer debts had been in effect for

1. *Memorandum to the Committee on Enforcement of Judgments*, 6 September 1965, Trades Union Congress.
2. *Report of the Committee on the Enforcement of Judgment Debts*, 1969, Cmnd 3909, para.590.
3. *Supra*, note 1, para.7.

many years and had been heavily criticised.

Entrenched in the view that '. . .the law must provide adequate machinery for debt collection',[1] the committee moved from the proposition that imprisonment should be abolished to the conclusion that it should be replaced by wage garnishment. To abolish imprisonment without replacing it by anything was not seriously considered.[2]

In Parliament, the matter was handled in much the same way. Wage garnishment was introduced in an omnibus Bill[3] containing a disparate assortment of topics, including the reorganisation of the superior courts, the abolition of imprisonment for debt, discovery procedures, and actions by mortgagees for possession, as well as the miscellaneous provisions.

Under the heading 'Advantages of Extending Attachment of Earnings to Civil Debts', the Payne Committee gave its reasons for recommending the garnishment of wages.[4] Most of them are however, difficult to take seriously. For example:

> (e) The debtors who wish to fulfil their obligations but are in financial difficulties (and these we think are the majority) will welcome a regular system of deduction which will enable them to pay off their debts in an orderly fashion.

(If the factual assumptions are correct, this is an argument for a system of voluntary attachment of wage (assignment), not for compulsory attachment (garnishment).)

> (f) The reluctant payer might not welcome the deductions, but even he may come to prefer the regular and relatively painless method of deduction to the continuance of a haphazard system of recurrent crises.

(But the only recurrent crises were those created by the system, particularly the threat of imprisonment.)

Probably the most plausible reason given by the committee was that:

1. *Report of the Committee on the Enforcement of Judgment Debts*, 1969, Cmnd 3909, para. 593.

2. For an excellent critique on the report and the subsequent Bill, see 'Administration of Justice Act 1970: Enforcement of Debt Provisions', C. Glasser, (1971) 34 *Modern Law Review* 61.

3. *The Administration of Justice Bill*, 1970.

4. *Report of the Committee on the Enforcement of Judgment Debts*, 1969, Cmnd 3909, para.592.

(c) Most judgments that have to be enforced arise because the debtor has undertaken to purchase goods or services out of periodical income. Attachment of wages applies this principle and would enable the debtor to pay in accordance with his original intentions.

Leaving aside the euphemistic use of 'enable', compulsion to carry out original intentions can have an appearance of justice. But it calls for reflection on the social and economic significance of moving from the intention to the compulsion and whether the consequences of that step are desirable.

There is a traditional feeling that the use of credit for the purchase of capital goods is more prudent than the commitment of future income to meet current or transitory needs. Indeed the report of the Crowther Committee,[1] although recognising the use of credit for other purposes, places significant emphasis on the use of credit to enable people to build up a stock of capital goods. Without garnishment (or some other legal proceeding such as bankruptcy) a debtor is free to pay creditors in his own choice of order. This creates a tendency for secured creditors to be paid before those who are unsecured. But garnishment is available to all judgment creditors regardless of the purpose for which the credit was advanced. While the secured creditor retains the advantage of his security, he may lose the advantage of priority in the receipt of instalments. It is the unsecured creditor who has the greatest need for wage garnishment and who is probably the most likely to invoke it. This result promotes the extension of credit, not where it is a form of saving and therefore probably the most prudent use, but for transitory or current needs. To promote the expansion of credit to meet current needs or transitory pleasures, and to compel repayment for that type of credit out of future income, promotes consumer insolvency. It is also uncomfortably close to ancient concepts of bondage.

This ground for concern is reinforced by a study of the use of wage garnishment in the US.

> Finance companies [meaning cash lenders in this context], by every account, are the most systematic users of wage garnishment. They make many marginal loans; indeed, they are often the last commercial source of credit for the debtor in financial trouble. They are willing to make relatively risky loans because they are carefully

1. *Report of the Committee on Consumer Credit*, 1971, Cmnd 4596, e.g. at para.3.7.1.

> organised to maximise collections. Their loan applications explicitly seek the information necessary to initiate a successful garnishment action. They begin collection efforts almost as soon as a debt becomes delinquent. The creditor questionnaire revealed that while retail stores often waited 30-60 days before considering an unpaid account delinquent, finance companies often waited less than a week.[1]
>
> . . . . . .
>
> Businessmen and professionals who cannot alienate their customers or do not wish to also hesitate to use wage garnishment because they are aware of the bitterness it engenders.[2]

Another argument of the Payne Committee (perhaps the next most credible) was that:

> (j) If it became widely known that default in payment for goods acquired on credit might result in regular deductions from wages, an over-optimistic purchaser might reflect more seriously before embarking on new credit ventures. Most citizens would not be affected but the credit extended to extravagant spenders might be reduced.[3]

But how were people becoming 'extravagant spenders'? One explanation could be seen in letters to a newspaper editor in 1972. 'The Access credit card which has arrived uninvited in a vast number of homes is to be condemned. . .it encourages people to spend beyond their means. . .'[4] Obviously, 'One of the consequences of allowing creditors to seize wages for the payment of debts is that creditors shape their lending policies to take account of that eventuality.'[5] Credit grantors have control over the

1. *Debtors in Court: The Consumption of Government Services,* H. Jacob, 1969, Rand McNally and Co., Chicago, p.81.
2. Ibid, p.85.
3. *Report of the Committee on the Enforcement of Judgment Debts*, 1969, Cmnd 3909, para 592.
4. This and three other letters on the same subject appear in the *Manchester Guardian Weekly*, 4 November 1972, p.2.

Under the *Consumer Credit Act*, 1974, S.51, it is an offence to give a person a credit token if he has not asked for it. It seems to have been intended that this should prohibit the sending of unsolicited credit cards. But it is doubtful whether the bank credit cards come within the definition of 'credit token' in S.14. In any event, termination of the particular practice described in the text would not invalidate the point that credit grantors are not simply docile respondents to the demands of consumers.

5. *Debtors in Court: The Consumption of Government Services,* H. Jacob, 1969, Rand McNally & Co., Chicago, p.73.

process, and if the policy is to discourage extravagant spending it will not be promoted by creating a new incentive to extravagant lending.

Another problem with wage garnishment is the projection of the personal affairs of an individual into his working environment. First, a loss of privacy is suffered through the problems of the worker being made known to his employer, or at least to fellow employees in the pay office.[1]

Secondly, the system is troublesome to employers with no compensating benefit. An employer is allowed to deduct 13p 'towards his clerical and administrative costs'.[2] Even on a marginal cost basis, that must fall well short of reimbursement.[3] Moreover, the costs borne by employers are not limited to administration. Employers also take the risk of liabilities arising from any failure to comply with a court order, perhaps through some mistake. Employers also suffer from any damage to working morale. The net result is that employers are compelled to subsidise credit marketing.

It is hardly surprising if employers sometimes extricate themselves by the discharge of workers affected by wage garnishment. The extent of this practice has not been assessed in England, but from interviews at the advisory agencies, County Courts and credit grantors in 1977, it emerged that wage garnishment is commonly followed by a change of employment. County Court statistics give the same impression.[4] But it is unclear to what extent this is because:

(1) the worker was discharged by the employer as a result of the wage garnishment;
(2) the worker was discharged by the employer for reasons independent of the wage garnishment, for example, because the worker handles cash and is classified as untrustworthy by reason of the debt problems, or because insolvency has produced anxieties that impede work efficiency;
(3) the worker left the employment to avoid the garnishment;
(4) the worker left the employment for other reasons; or

1. During enquiries at the advisory agencies and County Courts in 1977, the most commonly mentioned complaint of workers about wage garnishment was that they were upset about their employers being told of their personal problems.

2. The *Attachment of Earnings (Employer's Deduction) Order,* 1975, SI No. 1868.

3. In 1970, when the permissible deduction was 5p, an estimate of the actual cost was 37½p for the first payment and 19p for each subsequent payment. 'Administration of Justice Act 1970 – II', S. Cretney, (1970) 114 *Solicitors Journal* 596, 597.

4. During 1976, there were 59,927 attachment of earnings orders made. 16,142 orders were 'redirected to other employers', and 21,362 lapsed. (Under S.9, an attachment of earnings order lapses when 'the person to whom it is directed ceases to have the debtor in his employment'.) Only 18,119 were discharged during that year by being 'fully paid'. *Judicial Statistics for the Year 1976,* Cmnd 6875, p.79.

(5) judgment debtors against whom attachment of earnings proceedings are taken tend to be people who change employment frequently.

The difficulty of distinguishing between categories (1) and (2) is the reason why the problem of discharge is not one that can readily be solved by making it an offence to discharge an employee because an attachment of earnings order has been made.

A study conducted for the Payne Committee of garnishment orders in maintenance cases showed that 'Of the 600 cases in which the order had been discharged, and in which the reason for discharge had been ascertained, 85 per cent (507) of the orders had been discharged because the respondent to the order had left his employment'. The committee found comfort in the reflection that:

> The type of person who becomes liable for payment under a maintenance order is probably, in general, more 'foot loose' than the average judgment debtor possibly by temperament and also by virtue of the fact that in most cases he has left his wife and has no family to move around with him;[1]

Another view was, however, that '. . .an extension of the existing procedure [of wage garnishment for the enforcement of maintenance orders] to County Court judgments would meet similar difficulties especially as the type of defendant most likely to be the subject of such an order changes his employment frequently'.[2]

Even if the percentage of judgment debtors who are discharged or who leave their employment to escape the impact of an order is lower than in matrimonial cases, it is still difficult to justify a system that creates such an incentive to disrupt employment. Honest regular work is made less remunerative, and an incentive is created to secure an income by engaging in casual or transitory work, by seeking to qualify for sickness or unemployment benefits, or worse still, by criminal activity.

Even when a judgment debtor is not discharged from employment, his advancement might still be prejudiced. Where this occurs, a judgment debtor who already has a budgeting problem may be further entrenched in poverty and insolvency by the wage garnishment rather than being extricated. Moreover, employers have an incentive to avoid the hiring of people with overdue debts likely to result in wage garnishment. This can operate

1. *Report of the Committee on the Enforcement of Judgment Debts*, 1969, Cmnd 3909, para.602.

2. Per a County Court registrar in a memorandum, 1966.

to the detriment of debtor and creditors alike.

Another problem is that worker morale and enthusiasm for work can be damaged by wage garnishment. Wages are subject to income tax and other deductions, but most of these are shared in common with other workers. An individual is surely more likely to feel aggrieved about a deduction that is levied specifically against him. The Payne Committee recognised that with regard to garnishment for the enforcement of maintenance orders, 'Many husbands (and no doubt wives) part from their spouses suffering from a grievance and feel resentful of the liability imposed on them by a court order.'[1] The committee was, however, '. . .convinced that bitterness of this kind is nothing like so prevalent among ordinary debtors'.[2] But the bitterness of estranged husbands surely results not just from the residual pains of matrimony but from the continuing wage deductions. This cause of bitterness has been introduced into the employment relationship in respect of ordinary consumer debts.

If wage garnishment does result in bitterness, a judgement debtor might fail to comply with the procedural requirements of the *Attachment of Earnings Act.* For example, he might refuse to inform the court of his place of employment. The remedies are a fine, which aggravates the debt problem, or imprisonment, which, to the extent that it is used, detracts from the reason for introducing wage garnishment in the first place.

In 1976, 190 people were imprisoned under the *Attachment of Earnings Act,* 1971. This may be roughly 10 per cent of the number who would have been imprisoned in that year if the old system of judgment summons and committal had continued.[3] But the system has not been wholly successful even in ending the imprisonment of judgment debtors.

Another objection to wage garnishment is that it creates an excuse for those claiming to be creditors to communicate with employers of alleged debtors. Sometimes there is a legitimate need to communicate with an employer to obtain information required for garnishment. But there is nothing to limit such communications to occasions when they are really needed for garnishment purposes. Nor is there anything to require that such communications will only occur after judgment, or after the commencement of proceedings. Thus wage garnishment gives an aura of legitimacy to an extra-legal method of collection that may impel an employee to pay a claim regardless of its validity. Even solicitors are now free to engage in the practice. Prior to 1971, it was a rule of professional conduct

1. *Report of the Committee on the Enforcement of Judgment Debts*, 1969, Cmnd 3909, para.602.

2. Ibid.

3. Roughly estimated from figures contained in the Civil Judicial Statistics for 1969 and the Judicial Statistics for 1976.

for solicitors 'that it is not in accordance with proper professional practice for a solicitor to communicate or threaten to communicate with a debtor's employer or commanding officer'.[1] But the Law Society subsequently ruled

> . . .that there is nothing professionally improper in a solicitor communicating with a debtor's employer or Commanding Officer in order to obtain information as to his status or means, although to threaten to do so is improper and might be a criminal offence.[2]

Thus communications are permitted for the purpose of seeking information. But once any communication with an employer is permitted, it is impossible to limit its purpose or effect. Moreover the Law Society ruling does not limit a solicitor to communicating with an employer only after judgment. Thus the practice can create a pressure to pay a claim regardless of any opportunity to defend.

A further objection is that wage garnishment may discriminate among creditors in favour of the most aggressive and unreasonable. Consider the example of an ambitious young man in steady employment who wants to buy a car. He goes to his bank and borrows £900 for the purpose at an interest rate of 16 per cent. Before he has repaid very much, he becomes engaged. Inspired by upward mobility aspirations and anxious for a honeymoon in the Mediterranean, he returns to the bank. The manager, after careful arithmetic, tactfully suggests that he should settle for a week in Torquay. The young man then notices the seductive advertising of another credit grantor, possibly a moneylender or a travel organisation. He incurs a further £400 of liability at an interest rate of 40 per cent. After the honeymoon, his wife becomes pregnant and fails to obtain a job that she had expected. Instalments on the bank loan by itself could have been maintained, but the total is too much and both accounts fall into arrear. In this situation, it may well be the second credit grantor who is first in applying for a garnishment order. Yet it is the second credit grantor who is charging an interest rate commensurate with the greater risk, and it is the second credit grantor who could have avoided the predicament. Thus wage garnishment can be a stimulant to high-risk credit grantors, placing at an unfair disadvantage the healthier and most reasonable sections of the credit industry.

Where wage garnishment fails to effect collection of the debt, possibly because of the discharge of the employee, the harm in loss of privacy,

1. *Guide to Professional Conduct and Etiquette,* T. Lund, p.86.
2. *The Law Society Gazette,* June 1971, p.246.

anxiety, humiliation or loss of employment has been inflicted with no counterbalancing achievement. Even to the extent, however, that wage garnishment or the threat of garnishment succeed in coercing the payment of claims, this still cannot be counted an unmitigated success. Indeed, the achievement would be incompatible with other national policies. The enforcement of debt claims by wage garnishment can enable future income to be used as current money. It is an inflationary pressure,[1] and an incredible remedy for any government to introduce when it was the stated policy of that same government to curb inflation.

Moreover the effects of the expansion of consumer credit that wage garnishment could be expected to produce are not limited to inflation. The social consequences must also be considered. Whether consumer credit has expanded beyond healthy bounds is a matter on which judgments may differ. On the one hand, the majority of consumers have not been burdened by insolvency. In the NOP survey, 63 per cent of respondents felt that their total credit commitments were about right, and 30 per cent felt that they could take on more.[2] Another indicator has been the high proportion of consumers who pre-pay on instalment credit transactions.

On the other hand, among the less fortunate minority there is a significant proportion of consumers overburdened by debt obligations that they cannot meet. One indicator is that on the NOP survey, 5 per cent of the respondents felt that their total credit commitments were too high.[3] Another is the estimate that in Britain one car in 40 taken on hire-purchase is repossessed.[4] Interviews with County Court judges and registrars indicated that with regard to a substantial proportion of consumers who default on payment, it is not simply because of recalcitrance or grievances against the seller. After paying for necessities, many do not have any discretionary income left to pay instalments arising out of credit transactions. Indeed, in some cases it is the pressure of expenses above income that motivates the use of credit in the first place.

For present purposes, however, it is not necessary to demonstrate a particular level of consumer insolvency, or to make moral judgments about that level. The crucial point is that the enforcement of payment by wage garnishment is not calculated to expand consumer credit among

1. Cf. *The Report of the Committee on Consumer Credit*, 1971, Cmnd 4596, pp.124-8.

2. *Survey by NOP Market Research Ltd* for the Crowther Committee, Department of Trade and Industry, 1971, Table 254.

3. Ibid.

4. *Report of the Committee on Consumer Credit*, 1971, Cmnd 4596, para. 6.6.47.

those who can pay with ease. The expansion is most likely among those who can be induced to pay by the threat or implementation of wage garnishment, and these are surely likely to be families for whom the incursion of further debt is no blessing.

The procedure by which attachment of earnings orders are made is also a cause for concern. The Payne Committee recommended that the sum to be deducted should be determined '. . .after full consideration of all the circumstances'. Also 'In the great majority of cases the process would be simple, straightforward and inexpensive'.[1] There seemed to be no recognition that these are inconsistent goals. In the result, it is the 'full consideration of all the circumstances' that has been sacrificed. To the extent that imprisonment for debt has been abolished, so too has the judgment summons. There is, therefore, usually no examination of a judgment debtor before wage garnishment. If an issue is raised or a hearing is requested, an application for an attachment of earnings order will be listed for hearing. But in the majority of cases, enquiry forms are sent to the judgment debtor and his employer, and where an attachment of earnings order is issued, it is following a perusal of the replies on those forms.

A final objection is that wage garnishment, as it operates at the moment, is a system of deductions from wages on behalf of those claiming to be creditors without any effective system of enquiry and adjudication on the validity of their claims.[2]

The significance of wage garnishment has, however, been limited by two factors. First, the court is required to establish an amount of 'protected earnings', having regard to the resources and needs of the judgment debtor. This amount is exempt from garnishment. But the state of the economy in recent years, including wage controls, has been such that a large proportion of wage earners have nothing beyond protected earnings to which wage garnishment could apply. Those at higher levels of earnings may own goods that could be seized under a warrant of execution. Thus the category of cases in which an attachment of earnings order may succeed when an execution on goods has failed may not be a very large one.

Secondly, it is still the normal practice to use execution on goods as the

1. *Report of the Committee on the Enforcement of Judgment Debts*, 1969, Cmnd 3909, para.592.
2. See Ch. 9(1).

first method of enforcing a judgment.[1] During 1976, there were over a million warrants of execution against goods issued by the County Courts. But the number of attachment of earnings orders made was a little under 60,000.[2]

For the reasons explained above, it is suggested that wage garnishment for consumer debt ought not to have been introduced, and that it ought to be abolished.

Garnishment for maintenance orders is, however, another matter. There are several factors that distinguish wage garnishment for the enforcement of maintenance orders from wage garnishment for consumer debt.

(1) Failure to pay on a maintenance order cuts off the income of one or more other person. A trade creditor, on the other hand, is not usually dependent on one consumer account. Moreover, he has control over his bad debt ratio through his credit granting policy.

(2) Failure to pay on a maintenance order can create burdens for the state. People may feel, therefore, that there is a greater community interest in the claims of dependants.

(3) The dimension of the problem is different. More people have consumer debts than maintenance orders outstanding, and those who do have maintenance orders outstanding do not usually have more than one. Thus an employer receiving a garnishment order for maintenance does not see it as indicating a probability of other claims.

1. Possible reasons why execution on goods is usually tried first are:
(1) Under the pre-1971 practice, imprisonment was treated as a last resort. Thus it was established practice to attempt execution on goods first, and that may have continued partly because it was the habit.
(2) Execution on goods can be issued immediately. It does not require preliminary information as an attachment of earnings order does.
(3) Executions on goods can be issued in bulk without having to distinguish between people who are employed, and those self-employed, or unemployed.
(4) A warrant of execution brings a baliff into communication with the judgment debtor. The visible presence of the arm of the law entering the home might have a psychological impact that induces payment regardless of what the bailiff actually does when he is there.
(5) In response to an application for an attachment of earnings order, a judgment debtor only has to deal with a document. In response to a warrant of execution, he has to deal with a person, i.e. the bailiff. This gives the bailiff an opportunity to use his persuasive influence to promote payment.
(6) Some credit grantors, or their solicitors, may be apprehensive that an attachment of earnings order could result in a loss of employment, thereby reducing the prospects of payment.
(7) Where a judgment creditor is unfamiliar with the choices available, execution on goods is the method most likely to be suggested by court staff.
2. *Judicial Statistics for the Year 1976*, Cmnd 6875, pp.78-9.

(4) Most important of all, several of the arguments against wage garnishment relate to the feedback effect on marketing behaviour. Wage garnishment creates an incentive to extend credit in marginal situations, thereby inducing imprudent transactions. It would take a cynical mind to suggest that garnishment to enforce maintenance orders has any comparable effect.

For these reasons, it is suggested that wage garnishment to enforce maintenance orders is a separate problem about which it is not necessary to come to the same conclusion.

4. Should Debt Claims be Enforced?

The suggestion that wage garnishment ought to be abolished invites a further question. Should debt claims arising out of consumer transactions be enforced at all? Discussions of creditors' remedies usually focus on court procedure, methods of execution, or priorities among creditors. The initial assumption that courts ought to enforce the payment of debts is not usually questioned. Thus it is difficult to find in legal literature a rational argument why they should. The case is usually expressed in terms of principles rather than policies. For example.

> We start from the assumption that citizens ought to repay legally binding debts and that the community recognises a social and moral obligation to honour obligations freely contracted. *Pacta sunt servanda* is not only legal doctrine; it is moral precept too. The function of law is to compel observance of the rule in those marginal cases where moral and social sanctions fail.[1]

As applied to consumer transactions, almost every word of the dogma rests on unwarranted assumptions. Indeed, 'It has long been recognised that freedom of contract has little meaning in consumer transactions'.[2]

Our law does not jump from the proposition that obligations ought to be honoured to the conclusion that fulfilment should be compelled. Indeed, there are many categories of contractual obligations, such as social engagements and wagering contracts, which are not (or not supposed to be) enforceable at law. Policy judgments have been made and are commonly made about which categories of contracts ought to be enforced. Even a conclusion that the fulfilment of obligations ought to be compelled

1. *Report of the Committee on the Enforcement of Judgment Debts*, 1969, Cmnd 3909, para.46.
2. *Report of the Committee on Consumer Credit*, 1971, Cmnd 4596, para.6.1.12.

still leaves a choice among possible methods of enforcement. Not only is there a choice among methods of execution on a money judgment, but there is also a choice between court proceedings and other methods of enforcement, such as social or business sanctions, an adverse credit report, or repossession.

There are other difficulties too with the simple proposition that contracts should be enforced. First, the enforcement is not reciprocal. For the reasons explained in Chapter 9(1), the obligations of a consumer are enforced by courts much more readily than the obligations of a retailer or manufacturer.

Secondly, the simple doctrine that contracts should be enforced is remote from the current realities of mass distribution. The concept of the bargain reached by free people negotiating on equal terms is unrealistic for the bulk of retail transactions. The blandishments of advertising (much of it seductive and some of it false or misleading) carefully prepared with the expertise of modern psychology and widely disseminated, and the subtle pressures of experienced salesmen, are all brought to bear on the ordinary consumer. Only by a small fringe of buyers is a seller subjected to any comparable level of skilled persuasion. The documents used in retail transactions are prepared by sellers and finance companies (or their legal advisers) and routinely signed by consumers in circumstances in which they are not read. In what meaningful sense do they reflect 'obligations freely contracted'? Moreover, credit reports are available to assist a seller in estimating the probability that a buyer will pay. There is no comparable system through which a consumer can determine whether a seller's obligations are likely to be fulfilled.

To decide, in these circumstances, what legal significance should be attached to retail transactions requires an appraisal of policy objectives that is not supplied by the bald iteration of *pacta sunt servanda*.

For the reasons that follow, it is suggested that debt claims arising out of retail transactions ought to be abolished.

(1) If it is too difficult or too expensive to develop a system that would give full effect to buyers' rights, the courts ought not to be enforcing sellers' claims regardless of their legitimacy. In other words, if the government is unwilling or unable to develop an effective system of adjudication for consumer cases, the courts ought not to be giving judgment at all. It may seem that this argument could be met by introducing the new type of small claims court suggested above.[1] But as a practical matter, the probability of successfully introducing that system may be inversely proportionate to the anticipated volume of claims. Debt claims arising out of

1. See Chapter 9(6).

retail sales are the largest single category of small claims. Unless litigation is to reach a volume that creates an intolerable burden on the legal system, on merchants and on consumers alike, the need for adjudication must be limited to exceptional situations. The general run of consumer transactions and disputes must be resolved by the normal routines, incentives and pressures of the market. If it is uneconomical or unduly burdensome to devise a system of adjudication case by case for the broad range of consumer transactions, the alternative is to aim at what might be called a just balance of power over-all between sellers and buyers. In other words the aim should be a system in which creditors' remedies are strong enough to make credit marketing feasible, but not strong enough to make it profitable to embark on fraudulent schemes, high-pressure techniques, or the deliberate sale of defective goods. It is suggested that this balance of power could be achieved if retailers' claims for debt are abolished, leaving repossession and an adverse credit report as the sanctions against non-payment. Moreover, making a seller more dependent on the security in the goods would reduce the incentive to sell shoddy or defective goods. As an influence on selling behaviour, the abolition of debt claims has the advantage that the law would be carried into effect with a minimum of trouble and expense. Indeed, it would result in a saving of costs. Compared with that, any attempt to influence selling behaviour by direct prohibitions and controls would require a substantial cost in policing.

(2) A seller can default on a contract in various ways and it is difficult for a buyer to protect himself in advance. Conversely, there is generally only one major grievance suffered by sellers, i.e. not being paid. This is a risk against which a seller can protect himself in several ways without relying on court proceedings. He can, for example, obtain a credit report, or he can insist on a significant deposit (down-payment) coupled with a right of repossession. Moreover, the well-being of a retailer does not depend on the enforcement of all his claims. It is enough that he can achieve a satisfactory outcome in the vast majority of his transactions; and in the long run, the default rate of his customers is under his control. A seller does not have it exclusively within his power to determine the result of each transaction; but through adjustments in his credit policy, he does have it within his power to determine over time what his bad debt ratio is going to be.

(3) The granting of credit would be done with greater care. In respect of each credit transaction, someone should be making an intelligent judgment about whether the use of credit is prudent. Yet all too often, the buyer lacks the capacity and the seller lacks the incentive.

Experience shows that when judgment has been obtained and

> instructions are given to enforce it judgment creditors have little or no knowledge whether the judgment debtor has any and if so what assets. Further enquiries show that in many cases credit was given without the judgment creditors ascertaining whether they were likely to be paid. It is usually these creditors who bitterly complain that the law does not recover their money for them but tends to favour the judgment debtors.[1]

To place the burden primarily on the buyer is unrealistic.

> Most wage earners have been brought up on a tradition of budgeting for 7 days ahead and only too often they are incapable of appreciating the financial implications involved in an agreement which commits them to payments for several years. Thus many people will enter into hire purchase agreements on the strength of a few weeks overtime and it only require[s] a short spell of sickness or unemployment to produce utter disaster. Moreover the majority of debtors have no business experience; they are not accustomed to writing letters and once in financial difficulties they have little idea of how to extricate themselves. Add to this a background of continual sales pressure and it is hardly surprising that so many people fall into debt although they earn enough to live quite comfortable lives.[2]

A significant factor is that credit sellers are usually accustomed to working with documents. Buyers very often are not. As long as a consumer gives honest answers to questions, it is usually the credit grantor who has the experience and arithmetical skill to avoid the granting of credit where the consumer is likely to have difficulty in meeting the payments. It would surely make sense, therefore, to place the incentive to caution on the seller rather than the consumer. Under the proposal, credit by retailers would be limited to families that can repay with ease, and there would be no incentive to push credit on those who can only be made to repay by the threat of court proceedings. Sellers would be more cautious about checking credit reports, and about security in the goods. Hence the anxieties, family tensions, and other social problems of consumer insolvency, as well as loss to other creditors, would be mitigated.

(4) For marginal credit risks, there would be a reduction in sales financing and some diversion to loan financing. The plan would be to permit debt claims to continue for cash loans, so long as the loan is not arranged

1. *Memorandum of the Institute of Legal Executives to the Payne Committee,* 1965.

2. Per a County Court registrar in a memorandum, 1966.

by the seller. This diversion to loan financing would have two advantages. First, the cost of credit would be more readily identifiable. Secondly, going to another place to arrange the loan would create a brief period for contemplation during which the consumer would be released from any hypnotic influence of the sales pitch. To allow consumers a chance to think before they buy, and to think in the absence of the salesman, would be a valuable step in the encouragement of prudence by consumers, and the prevention of high-pressure tactics.

(5) The abuses connected with deficiency claims would be ended. A large proportion and probably the majority of repossessions are not carried out pursuant to the *Hire-Purchase Act* (now being replaced by the *Consumer Credit Act*), but are carried out by a 'voluntary surrender'. It is often alleged by the consumer that he was induced to agree to the surrender by being told or led to believe that this would terminate any liability for payment. Moreover, the sale following the repossession, which determines the amount to be credited to the account, is a trade sale, which may make it doubtful whether the best price was obtained. For both of these reasons, people can feel swindled when they find, after surrendering the item, that they are still being pursued for further payment.

There is, of course, scope for refinement in defining the category of claims for which the action of debt would be abolished. The essence of the proposal is that debt as a cause of action should be abolished for the price of goods sold at retail. The abolition would extend to cash loans when made for a specific purchase, or by arrangement with the retailer, or at the premises of the retailer, or in the presence of any agent of the retailer; and to claims by credit card companies in so far as they arise out of sales transactions. But claims for the repayment of ordinary cash loans would still be enforceable as debts; so too would claims for services, and for work and materials.

There are several reasons why debt claims in respect of ordinary cash loans should be retained.

(1) There are fewer categories of abuse in cash lending. The consumer normally receives from the lender what he bargained for, and if he does not, at least the shortage is usually identifiable.
(2) The homogeneity of the product makes the policing of cash lending easier than the policing of retailing as a method of preventing abuses.
(3) The need and the purpose of the loan are normally independent of the lender. Thus the interval between the decision to buy (or other reason for the loan) and the arrangement of the loan provides an obstacle to high-pressure or impulsive transactions.

(4) The cost of the credit is more obvious. At least it cannot be concealed in an artificially high cash price.
(5) The operation of a cash lending industry within the legal system is important to restrain the development of loan shark operations that may operate outside the scope of legal purview, and that may resort to abusive and oppressive methods of collection. There is no comparable risk of retailers operating in that way.

Thirty years ago, the suggestion might have seemed untenable. No doubt it would have been said that to abolish the action for debt in respect of retail sales would stifle consumer credit. But much has changed. The broad scale of credit reporting gave a new sanction to credit grantors, and the risk of an adverse credit report may now be as valuable for collection purposes as the threat of a judgment. If so, to abolish debt claims on retail sales might simply be restoring the strength of creditors' remedies, and their influence on the perimeters of consumer credit, to the same position as they were some years ago. Moreover, many credit grantors function very well at the moment without using legal or other coercive techniques of collection. Examples of this can be found among grocers, solicitors, and even some cash lenders. Also the development of teenage credit (even before the age of majority was lowered to 18) suggests that the retraction of consumer credit that would result would not be more than marginal. The hope is that the margin would be wide enough to include deceptive sales and defective goods cases.

In considering where the retraction would come, it might be helpful to reflect on the significance of the proposal to different categories of buyers.

(1) *Ordinary solvent and satisfied customers.* Most people pay their bills and could be expected to go on doing so. If they are not impelled by feelings of obligation, they are surely likely to be motivated by the risks of an adverse credit report and of repossession. Where a reasonable merchant is selling reasonable goods to customers who can afford them, these sanctions are surely enough.

(2) *The rogues* – those who obtain credit by false statements with no intention of paying. The proposal would not make a significant difference in this category. For protection against rogues of this type, sellers must rely in any event on diligence at the time of sale, and on criminal sanctions against obtaining credit by fraud. Debt claims are of no general use. For the odd case where a rogue is available and worth suing, the action for deceit in respect of the false statements would still be available.

(3) *Bad payers* – people who do not plan to avoid payment, but who somehow lack the organising capacity to maintain the regular flow of instalments. Here again, the risks of an adverse credit report and of repossession should generally provide enough sanctions. Where they fail, people

in this category would soon find they are denied credit.

(4) *Over-extended buyers* – those who, perhaps because of economic pressures, undue optimism about future income, difficulty in budgeting, or the allurements of advertising, have taken on greater obligations than they can meet. This is a social problem that can best be alleviated by minimising the incentive to advance credit in these situations, not by rallying the coercive power of the state in aid of credit grantors.

(5) *Unfortunate buyers* – those who made a prudent purchase at the time, but subsequently became unemployed, disabled, or for some other reason have suffered a reduction of income. Here again, there is a social problem for which coercion to pay is not the answer. One approach is the development of social insurance to a point where an interruption of earnings through circumstances beyond the control of the individual does not result in a major reduction of income. In any event, it is a value judgment how much pressure people should be under to pay in these circumstances, and it is suggested that loss of one's possessions is too much.

(6) *Irate and dissatisfied buyers* – those who are determined not to pay because of fraud or other misconduct of the seller, or because of defects in the goods. If the proposal results in sellers being paid less often in these situations, that is surely an improvement. There is, of course, the risk of buyers making unfounded allegations of this type as an excuse for non-payment. But a buyer could not do that very often before producing an adverse credit record and finding that he can no longer shop as a credit customer.[1]

Three red herrings need to be mentioned. The first is that:

> Every restriction on a creditor's remedy has to be paid for. To the extent to which the creditor is not himself willing or able to absorb the loss or expense in which he is involved by the restrictions imposed on him, this must be passed on to his customers. Hence the good customer is made to subsidise the bad.[2]

This can be true only to a very limited extent. It would be true if credit grantors were few in number and a closely knit oligopoly. But that is not the case. Consumer credit is supplied by large numbers of separate operating units, and is fairly competitive. While interest rates tend to become standardised to some extent, there is also significant variation according to the category of risk in which a credit grantor places his customers in

1. For a discussion of credit reporting, see Chapter 13.
2. *Report of the Committee on Consumer Credit*, 1971, Cmnd 4596, para.6.1.16.

general, or according to the category in which he places individual customers. Thus any credit grantor who seeks to deal with an increase in his bad debt ratio by raising his interest rates may find that he loses his better customers.

Secondly, it is argued that:

> . . .the burden of bad debts bears particularly harshly on the small trader, who may be ill-able to afford to write them off and may be in no position – because of competition – to pass them on to his customers in the form of increased prices.[1]

This might be so if the level of bad debts was something over which the trader had no control. But here again, that is not the case. Every credit grantor has an optimum bad debt ratio at each level of interest. If his actual bad debt ratio exceeds his optimum, he is losing more in bad debts than he is gaining by the profit made on the business of the marginal risks. If his actual bad debt ratio falls below the optimum, he is losing more in lost profit from marginal risk business being declined than he is saving by the avoidance of bad debts. Indeed, some credit grantors calculate their optimum and then aim at a constant bad debt ratio. If a credit grantor finds his bad debt ratio increasing more than he wishes, his obvious response is either to retract the granting of credit among the marginal risks, or if it is possible to use different interest rates, to increase the rate in the maginal categories of risk. Thus if the adoption of the proposal resulted in any loss of profit, it would not be because of any increase in bad debt ratios but because of a reduction in the total volume of credit business. What is at stake here is not bad debt ratios; it is the perimeter of consumer credit.

Thirdly it is said that:

> There is a limit to the extent to which a creditor can be deprived of legal remedies without being induced to have recourse to extra-judicial (and perhaps illegal) measures of self help.[2]

Retail credit grantors by and large do not use the more obnoxious extra-legal methods of collection. The ill-will that they generate is bad for business, and that is not going to change. At the moment they can, and often do, go to collection agenices using such tactics. But this would be terminated if, as suggested below, collection agencies are abolished.

1. Ibid.
2. Ibid.

A major problem is the use of extra-legal and abusive methods of collection by unlicensed moneylenders. It is suggested that this problem should be dealt with by:

(1) Keeping the action for debt in respect of cash loans. This is for the reasons explained above, one of which is to facilitate the operation of a legitimate consumer lending industry.
(2) Establishing a more effective system of licensing for moneylenders.[1]
(3) Making it somebody's job to detect and prosecute unlicensed moneylending.

For these reasons, it is suggested that the abolition of the action for debt in respect of retail transactions would provide optimum conditions for consumers and for reasonable credit grantors. If those engaged in high-pressure tactics, those who sell defective goods, and those who advance credit to people who (predictably) cannot meet the payments, find that it is no longer profitable to operate in those ways, this surely ought to be an acceptable result.

5. Extra-legal Methods of Collection

> What I would like to know Sir is are they allowed to pester you in such a way as to persecute you and maybe make a nervous wreck out of you.[2]

A. Introduction

Court proceedings are not the only method of pursuing debt claims, and probably not the most common.

When a payment is missed, most credit grantors send one or two friendly reminders. Usually that is all that is necessary. When requests for payment fail, however, there is no standard collection procedure in general use among credit grantors. There are several options, and the following six are in common use.

(1) Write off the debt.
(2) Pursue the alleged debtor by a programme of persuasion.
(3) Seize any security.
(4) Contact a solicitor or County Court office to commence a court action.

1. This was recommended by the Crowther Committee and is now provided for in the *Consumer Credit Act*, 1974.
2. Letter to a newspaper readers' advisory service. The tactics reported to have been used against the enquirer in this case included the threat to 'send the van'.

(5) Pursue a programme of threatening or aggressive communications.
(6) Send the account to a collection agency.

Some credit grantors habitually follow the same course, others make a judgment in respect of each account.

Where an account is sent to a collection agency, the process begins anew with one or two ordinary demand letters. If they fail, the collection agency usually selects among the first five options mentioned above.

The advantages that a credit grantor might see in a collection agency are:

(1) A new element of bluff is added to the pursuit of the claim. Many people assume that a collection agency can or will do something, though they are not sure exactly what. Thus fear of the unknown may result in payment.
(2) The credit grantor may be able to dissociate his business name from the collection process sufficiently to permit the use of collection methods that would generate ill-will and a consequential loss of business if used by the credit grantor directly.
(3) A small credit grantor may not have staff experienced in the pursuit of claims.
(4) Collection agencies can operate with economies of scale that could not be matched by smaller creditors.
(5) Collection agencies offer ancillary services. In particular, they may have the equipment and staff necessary for skip-tracing.
(6) Collection agencies are generally willing to act for a percentage of the recovery on the successful claims.

Sometimes debt claims are assigned to a collection agency. Otherwise the agency acts as agent for the creditor. Collection agencies have no special status in the legal system and no legal powers beyond those of the creditor.

The exact methods used by collection agencies are not well documented, partly because the agencies themselves have no interest in contributing to a description of their work. All they need for their own purposes is a sufficient description to attract the business of credit grantors. To the extent that they rely for their success in collections on bluff, anxiety and fear of the unknown, it would be counter-productive for them to contribute to a clear public understanding of exactly what they do and do not do.

> If debt collection is kept as undramatic as possible, and if it is handled as a private system of control which merits no press commentary, public understandings of the process should be marked by

> some confusion and lack of interest. It is these understandings which provide the contexts for enforcement activity and the definitions which debtors apply to their own default. The uncertainty and anxiety which surround enforcement are important materials for exploitation by collectors. Public ignorance provides opportunities for the manipulation of threats to the person and social standing of the defaulter.[1]

Related to this, collection agencies are one of the few categories of business in which there might be some commercial value in a bad reputation. For example, if it is rumoured in a particular community that the local collection agency engages in coarse and aggressive behaviour, the agency may see no advantage in denying the rumour, regardless of the truth.

Apart from court proceedings, the main collection techniques that might be used are summarised in sections B-J following.

B. Dunning Letters

Large volume credit grantors usually have a series of standard form letters that are sent automatically to customers who have missed a payment. If no payment results from the initial friendly reminders, the series may continue, changing the tone to firmer demands. Most of these letters in the early stages are innocuous. People who have simply missed a payment, or possibly two payments, include good customers whom it would be unwise to alienate by treating as financially irresponsible.

If the initial series of letters fails, a technique sometimes used at that stage is to 'transfer' the account from one person or department to another. For example, the account may be 'transferred' from the 'Accounting Department' to the 'Collections Department'. All this may mean is that the next batch of letters is signed by the person at the next desk. The purpose is to create a psychological impact – to impress upon the recipient that he is no longer regarded as a routine customer and has been singled out for some extraordinary but still undefined treatment.

The creditors' series of letters sometimes culminates in a threat of court proceedings, sometimes in a transfer of the file to a collection agency, sometimes both. Often the letter notifying the transfer to a collection agency is itself designed to have a psychological effect. The hope is that reclassification of the consumer from 'customer' to 'delinquent account' will induce a fear of some impending doom. In case the alleged debtor may not attach a sinister significance to the transfer of the account to a

1. *Making People Pay*, P. Rock, 1973, Routledge and Kegan Paul, p.11.

collection agency, a creditor may add an explanation. An extreme and imaginative example is as follows:

> We are sorry to have to inform you that since we are not receiving regular payments we find it necessary to hand over your account to our local collection Agents.
>
> Before doing so, in all fairness to you, we think it right to brief you on a few of the methods of collecting payments. For instance, a bailiff may be appointed to call on you each week on a given day who will not leave your premises until he has received payment. There are times, we admit, due to domestic circumstances, when it is virtually impossible to make the payments and in cases like this the situation can be very embarrassing. However, this perhaps may not apply to you, nevertheless, it must be pointed out that all bailiffs have a legal right of entrance through skylights and open windows or back doors, of course, without the use of force and this method is only applicable in the event of you not answering the door. Here again you will notice the embarrassment. To cut a long story short, you can term the situation as a 'Harassing one'.
>
> You have now five days to decide your preference. On the seventh day your account will be handed over if a substantial payment of £1.15s.0d., has not been received.
>
> . . .
>
> In conclusion, may we add that it is with the greatest reluctance that we are resorting to this action as it is the only alternative. Of course, it may be understood that any letters not accompanied by payments will be turned down.
>
> We are sorry to have to do this, but in the circumstances we must.[1]

The problem for the legal system is what credit grantors or collection agencies should be allowed to do once reminders, requests for payment, or offers to discuss the matter have produced no result. Obviously a creditor may threaten a court action for payment. The problem is what, if anything should be allowed apart from that.

One tactic commonly used by creditors, by collection agencies, and sometimes even by solicitors, is to threaten an adverse credit report. 'Although few people know much about how credit records are established, where they are maintained, or who has access to them, most people

1. *Memorandum of the National Citizens' Advice Bureaux Council to the Committee on the Enforcement of Judgment Debts*, 1966, Appendix, p.5.

vaguely feel that it is nice to have a good one.'[1] It will be argued later[2] that credit reporting, including the filing of adverse reports by credit grantors, is socially desirable. But *threatening* an adverse credit report is another matter. Like other extra-legal methods of collection, it by-passes the courts and seeks to coerce the payment of claims while denying the opportunity to defend. The threat of an adverse credit report is, of course, all the more compelling if the collection agency is also the operator of a credit reporting service.

Sometimes the threat is overt, sometimes more oblique, such as a passing mention of the need to maintain a good credit record.

Sometimes there is a threat of embarrassing publicity going beyond the simple threat of an adverse credit report. For example:

> 'Dear Sir/Madam,
>
> Re: the sum of £. . .owed to. . .
>
> The Creditor named above has authorised us to collect this debt from you and henceforth all correspondence, monies, etc. must be sent direct to us.
>
> We have your Creditor's assurance that all appeals to your sense of decency have met with no response and therefore we do not intend to waste any time on such measures.
>
> It is our experience that PUBLICITY of the debt is most distasteful to many people and it is our intention to give the FULLEST POSSIBLE PUBLICITY TO THE MATTER in all possible ways. This we know from long experience, you will find most unpleasant.
>
> We would PREFER that you agree to come to some amicable arrangement with us in this matter and to this end we will allow you a further seven days from the above date in which you may commence payments or if you are ill or unemployed, for WRITTEN PROOF of same to us.
>
> However, if you want it the hard way we assure you the ultimate result will be the same.
>
> Yours faithfully'

(This letter came in an envelope on which the words 'APPLICATION FOR PAYMENT' were distinctively printed on both sides.)[3]

1. *Credit and Collection*, E.H. Barnes, 1961, Prentice-Hall, Englewood Cliffs, NJ.
2. Chapter 13.
3. *Memorandum of the National Citizens' Advice Bureaux Council to the Committee on the Enforcement of Judgment Debts*, 1966, Appendix, p.3.

Another common threat is to communicate with the employer of an alleged debtor causing embarrassment at his place of employment.

Another tactic is threats of dire consequences deliberately vague or ambiguous so that the recipient of the letter is left to imagine the worst. An example is the threat to 'send the van'. The letter containing the threat has a picture, included in the letter heading, of a van with bars at the windows and 'BAD DEBT COLLECTIONS' prominently displayed across the side.[1] (As far as is known to the writer, the van does not exist.) The alleged debtor is left to imagine what will happen when the van arrives; for example, whether he will be taken away to some kind of institution, whether the furniture will be taken, or whether the van will simply park outside to cause embarrassment. Another example is the use of a two-page collection letter, the first page of which is never received (or written). The second page reads 'and you wouldn't want *that* to happen would you? Yours truly.'

Many of the vague and ambiguous threats are open to the interpretation that violence is one of the possible consequences of not paying the claim. But they are usually sufficiently vague or ambiguous that this could be denied if it ever became an issue in court proceedings or in a government inquiry. Some collection letters contain a denial of any intention to use violence. Yet it is difficult to see any reason for the denial except to create the impression that there is some risk of violence being used.

Sometimes, however, crude threats of violence have been made with no subtlety at all. For example, a letter from the 'Commando Bad Debt Collections Service' is reported to have ended with the following passages:

> We give notice that no threat of personal violence against yourself or your family is contained or implied in this letter. Our operators are expressly forbidden to resort to such means. Any such action is unauthorised by the company and is not the liability of the company.
>
> But we must remind you that our operators are not selected by us on account of their patience and self-control.[2]

A series of letters used by a collection agency (ostensibly a reputable one) in Canada illustrates the art of arousing anxieties by the threat of dire but

1. For using this threat, at least one collection agency has been convicted under S.40 of the *Administration of Justice Act*, 1970. See 'Woman is Fined £20 for Debt Collection Threat', *The Times*, 18 June 1971, p.3. But reports of the practice were still found in 1977.

2. 'Pay-up demands terrified man who owed only 45s', *The Sun*, 26 June 1965.

unspecified consequences. The series includes letters of this type and some containing specific threats. The first letter informs the recipient that: 'It is my job to collect this account, this I can do with or without your co-operation, I would prefer to collect from you in a friendly manner.' The second letter threatens an adverse credit report. The third is as follows:

> Why bother? Why not forget your responsibilities, wouldn't it be wonderful, or would it, would it be wonderful if our leaders, our businessmen, our police our citizens said let's forget our responsibilities. No, it would not be wonderful it would be disastrous, it would mean looting, robbery, murder, a complete loss of our whole way of life. Are you forgetting your responsibilities? It is our job to first remind you of them by letter and then if this fails by action. You may be much better off to consider settling this account now rather than face future action.
>
> I trust I have managed to convey my meaning.
>
> Send full payment immediately by money order or certified cheque directly to this office.

The fourth is:

> Your disregard of my last three letters leaves me to believe that you are acting in an irresponsible manner. Irresponsible people have to be governed by firm methods which may be considered harsh. If you wish to be treated as a responsible person, act now, and take time to settle this account.
>
> Remit your payment at once.

The fifth letter threatens court proceedings, and the sixth communication is a simulated court form headed 'INTENTION to issue SUMMONS'.[1]

Sometimes costs of collection are demanded (even though there is no legal right to such costs) in addition to the alleged debt.[2]

1. If no payment is received by this stage, the usual practice of this agency is to write off the account, but court proceedings are commenced in some cases. (Interview at the collection agency, 1970.)

2. The Office of Fair Trading is trying to stop this practice through the exercise of its licensing powers under the *Consumer Credit Act,* 1974. Some collection agencies who engage in this practice have been issued 'minded to refuse' notices in response to their applications for licences. (Interview at the Office of Fair Trading, 1977.)

Most of these letters are bluff, although, as indicated below, some are not. Their purpose is to build anxiety and nervous tension, thereby to induce payment. Even when they culminate in a threat of court proceedings, it is still common and perhaps usual for the proceedings not to be commenced.

If, instead of sending a payment or ignoring the letters, a consumer sends an explanation for not paying, the reaction varies. A sympathetic reaction can be expected from credit grantors handling their own collections, particularly when dealing with a customer who has fallen on hard times, and who previously had a good payment record. Moreover, many retail credit grantors want to know why a customer is not paying. In a large department store, for example, customer feedback in the collections department can provide management with a source of intelligence about the purchasing department, the complaints department, and the credit office. Also if the matter can be resolved amicably the store may retain the goodwill of the customer.

Collection agencies are in a different position. They usually have no interest in the goodwill of the alleged debtor. Their income depends entirely upon the receipt of payments. They make nothing on excuses, however valid, legitimate, or inevitable.

A common complaint about collection agencies is that they ignore letters explaining why the money is not due and keep sending the standard form letters.[1] If the claim is admitted and the debtor is sending regular instalments, collection agencies often acquiesce though the instalments may be at less than the level demanded. The complaints usually relate to situations where the alleged debtor is trying to explain why the money claimed is not due.

Sometimes collection agency letters invite an alleged debtor to call at the office, or telephone, to discuss the matter. These invitations may be wholly or partly genuine. An alternative purpose, however, may be to discover weak points of the alleged debtor to which pressure might be applied, or to secure an opportunity for 'shouting down'. A literal though extreme example of this practice is a collector (interviewed by the writer) who, when he receives a telephone call from an alleged debtor, sometimes stands on his desk so that he can deliver his admonition with a resounding echo, punctuated by percussion effects from stamping his feet on the desk.

There has been no systematic scrutiny in the past of standard form letters used by collection agencies. But the Office of Fair Trading is now requiring copies of standard collection letters to be submitted as part of

1. Interviews at the advisory agencies, 1969 and 1977.

the licensing requirements.[1]

C. Telephone Calls

The telephone is not used as much in England as in North America for collection work. A large proportion of alleged debtors do not have a telephone, and those who do are commonly out during normal office hours. But the telephone is used to some extent.

Credit grantors handling their own collections sometimes use the telephone for friendly reminders, or to reaffirm the whereabouts of an alleged debtor, to discuss any reasons for non-payment, and to induce payment by persuasion.

Some collection agencies use the telephone in a sophisticated way, persuading an alleged debtor to recognise first the obligation to pay, secondly the possibility of payment, and thirdly the wisdom of payment.

Unfortunately, however, these are not the only purposes for which the telephone is used. Making abusive telephone calls, calling with harassing frequency, including telephone calls in the night, are part of the arsenal of some less scrupulous collection agencies.

The telephone has the potential advantage of being a vehicle for two-way communication. Unfortunately, however, it is not always used in that way. Some collection agencies feel that it is profitable to use the telephone as a normal routine only to convey standard messages in much the same way as they use form letters. Sometimes the telephone calls are made by staff who are not of the type to discuss disputed claims, or to deal with serious financial problems.

D. Telegrams

Telegrams do not appear to be used on a broad scale in collection work. But there are reports of telegrams being used, perhaps to induce a fright or a sense of urgency. Sometimes the alleged debtor is induced to make a long-distance telephone call. For example: 'Absolutely imperative that you contact Mr. Preston at [a London telephone number]'.[2]

E. Personal Calls at the Home

A great deal of collection work is done by having collectors call at the home. It is a normal method of collection for tallymen, check traders, and mail order companies. Also one of the major national collection agencies[3] has a network of collectors who call at the home, and this is offered as one

1. Interview at the Office of Fair Trading, 1977.
2. 'Credit Card Frightener', *Sunday People,* 28 December 1975.
3. Credit Data Ltd.

of its services. The bulk of collection work done in this way does not appear to result in any significant volume of complaints. It is an expensive method of collection, but it has two advantages. The first is convenience to the debtor. Some people who might not take the initiative to send a payment by post may willingly pay a collector who calls. The second is that the physical presence of a collector may be more compelling than a collection letter. It is easier to ignore letters than to ignore someone at the front door.

Where a claim is being pursued by a collection agency or an unlicensed moneylender, however, there are some reports of calls at the home being used for coercion. For example

> The collector calls at our home every Monday afternoon. He hammers strongly on the front door, then goes to the windows and raps and raps, peering closely to get a look inside, his scowling face frightens my wife. Shouting abuse, making insulting remarks, while people walk the pathway. . .She tried to reason with him, wanting to explain that I was working, and would renew the payments. So angry was he that he refused to listen to her.[1]

The practice of bawling (shouting collection demands from the roadway outside the house) does not appear to be in general use in England. But collection agencies sometimes make their demands on the doorstep in a loud voice so that neighbours can hear.[2]

F. Communicating With the Employer of an Alleged Debtor

If no reply is received to communications addressed to the home of an alleged debtor, a common practice of collection agencies, moneylenders, and finance companies, is to communicate with his employer. The ostensible purpose is often to establish contact with the alleged debtor because no response has been obtained from his home address. Sometimes the employer is asked for the new address of the alleged debtor, sometimes he is asked to forward a communication, and sometimes he is asked more explicitly to use his influence to induce payment.

Even solicitors are now allowed to communicate with the employer of an alleged debtor as long as it is 'in order to obtain information as to his status or means'.[3] Such communication is not limited to situations where a judgment has been obtained.

1. Letter to a newspaper readers' advisory service, 1968.
2. Interviews at the advisory agencies, 1968 and 1977.
3. 'Council Opinion', (1971) 68 *The Law Society's Gazette* 246.

Among the larger industrial employers, the personnel office will probably just forward the communication to the employee. But smaller employers often discuss the matter with the alleged debtor, and this can be a form of coercion to pay. Occasionally, however, the tactic can rebound, particularly if the employer sympathises with the employee and arranges for him to receive legal advice.

In addition or as an alternative to writing, telephone calls are often made to the place of employment and sometimes also personal visits. Some callers ask to speak to the employer and some to the employee. Often they leave without speaking to either, but if the alleged debtor hears that they have called, that's the important thing.

No doubt there are occasions on which a collection agency, money-lender, or finance company is unsure whether communications addressed to the home of an alleged debtor have been received, and is therefore resorting to the place of employment to establish communications. There are, however, two difficulties with allowing this type of communication. The first is that as long as communication with the employer, or with an alleged debtor at his place of employment, is permitted, there is no practical way of limiting its purpose or effect.[1] Secondly, as long as the alleged debtor hears of the communication, he will probably assume that the employer has been informed of the claim. The vital thing is not the exact content of the communication to the employer, but what the employee can be induced to think has been communicated, for this is the measure of the coercion that has been applied. Moreover, there is no doubt that many letters, telephone calls, and personal visits to the place of employment of an alleged debtor are designed to coerce payment by causing embarrassment, and indeed some are blatantly for that purpose. For example, 'We should advise you of this matter so that your employee will not find it necessary to absent himself from work to attend court.' (Enclosed with this letter was a payment notice which the employer was asked to include in the employee's wage packet.)[2]

G. Publicity

Apart from communicating with the employer of an alleged debtor, other types of adverse publicity are sometimes used. One is to communicate with an alleged debtor by an open postcard, including in bold letters words

1. For a discussion of this problem in America, see 'Creditor's Pre-Judgment Communication to Debtor's Employer: An Evaluation', K.M. Block, (1969) 36 *Brooklyn Law Review* 95.

2. Included in correspondence received by a newspaper readers' advisory service, 1968.

such as 'BAD DEBT' or 'FINAL NOTICE'.[1] Much the same effect is achieved by a letter sent in an envelope on which 'OVERDUE ACCOUNT' is boldly printed. Even having the name of a collection agency on the envelope might be regarded as a species of adverse publicity. Another example is a notice reported to have been found by an alleged debtor on his front door and reading: 'S. . .LOAN CO. BAD DEBT I WILL CALL FOR PAYMENT AGAIN SAT.'[2] Even the scattering of lists of 'defaulters' on the streets of London is reported to have happened.[3]

A more common practice is to make telephone calls or personal visits to neighbours of an alleged debtor, and to local shops. This is often done ostensibly to ascertain the whereabouts of the alleged debtor, but the reason for the enquiry is made sufficiently obvious to cause embarrassment.

H. Personation

Collection agencies sometimes feel that it helps if their communications can appear to emanate from an organisation having some kind of official status. One way of achieving this is to locate the office at some official-sounding address, such as 'Town Hall Chambers'. Another way is to use language which, although not actually saying so, conveys the impression that the agency has some connection with the police.

Another example is the use of the simulated County Court summons. The collection agency sends a form which has in large print the language of a summons. Only in the small print does the language make it clear that it is not a summons but a demand from a collection agency. To those who gather an impression from the total image without reading all the language, it looks like either a summons, or a court document preceding a summons. In any event, if the purpose is to cause an initial fright rather than to convey a specific message, it can have that effect even on those who read and understand the small print.

I. Violence

So far as is known to the writer, actual violence is not used as a routine in the collection of consumer debts.[4]

Reports were discovered of a collector visiting the home with an Alsatian dog, but no report of the dog making a bite. Similarly reports were received of collectors having an aggressive appearance, being

1. See e.g., 'Insulting cards to HP debtor', *Daily Mirror*, 1 December 1971.
2. Letter to a newspaper readers' advisory service, 1968.
3. 'Confidential Files in a London Street', *The Times*, 14 December, 1970, p.3.
4. Possibly violence is used for the collection of large gaming debts. However, this research was not directed to that area and the only information received about gaming debts was third-hand rumours.

tall, broad-shouldered men, sometimes attending two at a time. But judging from the reports of their behaviour[1] it would seem that their instructions were simply to look ferocious, not to touch anyone.

No doubt most credit grantors would regard violence as abhorrent and beyond their own standards of integrity. But even for those who have no scruples, violence is not likely to be good business. The risk of imprisonment means that the agent engaged for the purpose would require a substantial fee, and this would make the use of violence uneconomical for the collection of small claims. Moreover, there may not be a very wide range of people who can be intimidated into payment by the use of violence but who could not be induced to pay by the threat of violence. Hence if the threat does not work, it may not be very often that carrying it out will result in payment. Violence could be used against one alleged debtor to induce others to pay. But it can only have that effect if the violence becomes widely known, and that, of course, creates two other risks. First, it increases the risk of detection and imprisonment. Secondly, it may frighten people to the point of discouraging new business. Again, if the violence causes serious injury, that may prevent the alleged debtor from working and thereby deny him the income with which to pay. Finally, there is the risk of counter-violence. While the ordinary debtor does not wait with the proverbial shotgun, a collector who made a habit of violence may sooner or later find one who does.

For these reasons, it is thought that the use of violence is not a serious risk in ordinary debt collections, at least not unless the standards of policing fall significantly.

J. Repossession

Where a seller uses a hire-purchase or conditional sale form, a right is reserved to repossess the item upon default in payment. If a repossession is carried out according to law, this might be regarded as a method of collection through the legal system rather than an extra-legal method. However, many, and possibly a majority of repossessions are not carried out in that way. Often the buyer defaults in payment after one-third of the hire-purchase price (or total purchase price) has been paid. The seller is then not entitled to repossession without a court order, but he can still call at the home to solicit a 'voluntary surrender'. Sometimes the item is repossessed in circumstances which, according to the collector's version of the facts, amounted to a voluntary surrender, but which according to the consumer's version of the facts, amounted to an unlawful repossession.

Even when a credit sale contract has been used and the seller has no

1. From interviews and the perusal of documents at the advisory agencies.

right to repossession, a repossession often takes place. Here again, it is done by soliciting an agreement with the consumer. But as in the hire-purchase cases, there is sometimes a conflict of evidence or recollection about what actually occurred. The consumer's recollection of the event is that he was persuaded to part with the item upon the promise or understanding that this would be a discharge of any monies owing on the account. But according to the subsequent statements of the collector, and according to the agreement that the consumer signed without reading, it was agreed that the item would be repossessed and resold, that if the sale price (less the cost of sale) exceeded the amount outstanding on the account, the consumer would receive a credit for the surplus, but if it was less than the amount outstanding on the account, the consumer would be liable for the deficiency. Of course it is usually less. The consumer is then distressed to find that he has parted with the item and yet is still being pursued for part of the price.

K. Legal Remedies for Extra-legal Methods of Collection

The Payne Committee concluded that'. . .there should be some provision making it unlawful to employ unreasonable extra-judicial methods for the collection of debts'.[1] This recommendation was implemented in Section 40 of the *Administration of Justice Act,* 1970, as follows:

> 40. (1) A person commits an offence if, with the object of coercing another person to pay money claimed from the other as a debt due under a contract, he –
>
> (a) harrasses the other with demands for payment which, in respect of their frequency or the manner or occasion of making any such demand, or of any threat or publicity by which any demand is accompanied, are calculated to subject him or members of his family or household to alarm, distress or humiliation;
>
> (b) falsely represents, in relation to the money claimed, that criminal proceedings lie for failure to pay it;
>
> (c) falsely represents himself to be authorised in some official capacity to claim or enforce payment; or
>
> (d) utters a document falsely represented by him to have some official character or purporting to have some official character which he knows it has not.
>
> (2) A person may be guilty of an offence by virtue of subsection (1) (a) above if he concerts with others in the taking of such action as is

1. *Report of the Committee on the Enforcement of Judgment Debts*, 1969, Cmnd 3909, para.1238.

described in that paragraph, notwithstanding that his own course of conduct does not by itself amount to harassment.

(3) Subsection (1)(a) above does not apply to anything done by a person which is reasonable (and otherwise permissible in law) for the purpose –

(a) of securing the discharge of an obligation due, or believed by him to be due, to himself or to persons for whom he acts, or protecting himself or them from future loss; or

(b) of the enforcement of any liability by legal process.

(4) A person guilty of an offence under this section shall be liable on summary conviction to a fine of not more than £100, and on a second or subsequent conviction to a fine of not more than £400.

A major difficulty, however, is that neither the committee report nor the statute contain any special provision for enforcement. The effectiveness of this enactment could be predicted from experience with similar legislation in the past. The first extra-legal method of collection listed by the Payne Committee[1] was the use of a simulated County Court summons, as described above. The document has the appearance (except to lawyers) of having been issued under the authority of a County Court. In 1970, this practice was made an offence under Section 40(1)(d). Yet the same practice had been for many years an offence under the *County Courts Act.*[2] If a prohibition is ineffective because of no provision for its enforcement, it is surely absurd to see a solution in re-enacting the prohibition in another statute that also contains no provision for its enforcement. Predictably, the practice still continues.[3]

The police may investigate and prosecute in response to a complaint. But it was predictable that they would not undertake any systematic programme of surveillance and detection. In the result, few prosecutions under Section 40 are actually brought. In 1971, for example, there were five convictions under this section in England and Wales.[4]

Nevertheless, Section 40 has offered some hope of improvement, and among the criminal sanctions for extra-legal methods of collection, it may be the only one actually used. Another criminal provision that might be invoked is Section 78 of the *Post Office Act*, 1969, which, *inter alia,* makes it an offence to use a telephone persistently for the purpose of causing annoyance, inconvenience or needless anxiety to another. In extreme situations, there might also be an offence under Section 21 of the *Theft*

1. Ibid., para.1232.
2. S.189 of the *County Courts Act*, 1959.
3. Interview with a County Court registrar, 1977.
4. Per the Home Office in response to an enquiry.

Act, 1968.[1]

It is sometimes assumed that no civil action is available against extra-legal methods of collection. But that is not the law. For the reasons explained in Chapter 9(1), a victim of these practices does not usually seek redress by civil action. In the odd case, however, where an alleged debtor has enough determination and finds a good solicitor, an action for damages might succeed, at least where the collection tactics have caused significant harm.

An argument can be made that Section 40 of the *Administration of Justice Act*, 1970, gives rise to an action for damages for breach of statutory duty. It is an open question. Even if the courts do not take that view, the statute can still be relevant in a civil action. For example, if the case is pleaded as a conspiracy to injure, the statute might be used in reply to any defence that the conduct was only the legitimate pursuit of the defendants' self-interest.

Probably the most promising causes of action, however, are libel and slander. Libel was the cause of action on which an alleged debtor succeeded in a Canadian case[2] in which a collection agency had written to his employer. The judge stated:

> . . .I have no doubt whatever that the publication complained of. . . is defamatory.
>
> Taking the letter by itself and without anything else, it's a clear indication that the plaintiff is being branded as one who does not pay his bills. It's one of these sneak-up type of matters. As I say it's just the choice of language that is somehow or other insulting: 'The above person' – 'person' even used in this connotation has got an element of insult to it –
>
> 'The above person, whom we understand is in your employ, is indebted to our client.

1. The Section reads as follows:

'(1) A person is guilty of blackmail if, with a view to gain for himself or another or with intent to cause loss to another, he makes any unwarranted demand with menaces; and for this purpose a demand with menaces is unwarranted unless the person making it does so in the belief –

(a) that he has reasonable grounds for making the demand; and

(b) that the use of the menaces is a proper means of reinforcing the demand.

(2) The nature of the act or omission demanded is immaterial, and it is also immaterial whether the menaces relate to action to be taken by the person making the demand.

(3) A person guilty of blackmail shall on conviction on indictment be liable to imprisonment for a term not exceeding fourteen years.'

2. *Sawatzky v. Credit Bureau of Edmonton*, Unreported, Supreme Court of Alberta, 1970, file no. 62766.

> It is our wish to endeavour to have this account settled with the least possible cost or embarrassment to the debtor. However, despite numerous requests by letter and/or telephone, the debtor has as yet shown no inclination to make satisfactory arrangements for payment.
>
> We feel that possibly a word from you could impress on him the advantage of avoiding legal proceedings and while we dislike bringing the matter to your attention, your assistance could bring about amicable results.'
>
> Now this type of correspondence put in the hands of an employer cannot help but be defamatory.

It does not appear from the judgment that the plaintiff established any significant harm beyond embarrassment. Even so, the court considered exemplary damages appropriate and awarded a total of $1,000. There were, however, three aggravating circumstances:

(1) The defendant (the collection agency) had made a mistake. The debt being claimed from the plaintiff was due, if at all, from someone else.
(2) The plaintiff had denied the debt to the defendant prior to its communication with his employer.
(3) After discovering the mistake, the defendant made no correction or apology.

An action for libel does not depend, however, on the debt claim being invalid. Once a court has concluded that the meaning of the communication is that the plaintiff is 'one who does not pay his bills', a defence of justification could not then succeed upon proof only that one debt is unpaid, particularly if there is a bona fide dispute about the validity of that claim.

Other grounds upon which a tort claim might be founded, in appropriate circumstances, include assault, trespass to land, and the intentional causing of nervous shock.

In Texas, causing harm by unreasonable collection methods has been recognised as itself a tort at common law.[1] It is possible that English courts might take the same view. There are passages in English judgments

1. For a good synthesis of the Texas law on this, see 'Effectively Regulating Extra-Judicial Collection of Debts', Julavits and Stuntebeck, (1968) 20 *Maine Law Review* 261, 271-82.

that could be cited in support, or used by analogy, at least where the collection tactics have involved an interference with an employment relationship. For example,

> . . .if a person who, by virtue of his position or influence, has power to carry out his design, sets himself to the task of preventing, and succeeds in preventing, a man from obtaining or holding employment in his calling, to his injury, by reason of threats to or special influence upon the man's employers, or would-be employers, and the design was to carry out some spite against the man, or had for its object the compelling him to pay a debt,. . .then that person is liable to the man for the damage consequently suffered.[1]

Again,

> If he failed to pay a just debt, the law provides ample means for enforcing payment of it. . .If the existence of the default or debt were admitted as a valid excuse for depriving a defaulter or debtor of his employment, a punishment might be inflicted upon him far greater than that which is allowed by law.[2]

The choice of arguments and cause of action must obviously vary with the circumstances. But where extra-legal methods of collection have caused significant harm, such as a loss of employment or emotional distress, there is enough legal ammunition for a lawyer advising a victim to consider seriously an action for damages.

The validity of a debt claim is not, theoretically, affected by the use of unreasonable or harassing collection methods. But as a practical matter, if an alleged debtor is well advised, the use of unreasonable or harassing tactics by a seller, lender, finance company, or collection agency might have the effect of extinguishing a claim. An alleged debtor may think it not worthwhile commencing an action in respect of any harassment. But if he plans in any event to defend a debt claim on the merits, it may well be worthwhile to add a counter-claim for damages in respect of the collection tactics. If a solicitor is acting for an alleged debtor and counter-claims for damages for harassment, that may well result in the abandonment of the claim.

A relevant consideration here is that debt collecting, particularly in

1. Per Romer L.J. in *Giblan v. National Amalgamated Labourers'* Union [1903] 2 K.B. 600, 620.
2. Per Stirling L.J., ibid., p.624.

small claims, is an automated process. If consumers are afraid of litigation, so too are collection agencies when the matter cannot be disposed of without a trial. To proceed with a disputed claim means that it can no longer be processed by lower paid clerical personnel. It must now receive management attention as well as executive time from the client. The addition of a counter-claim in respect of the collection tactics looks like even more trouble. Moreover, the fear of the unknown and the risk of condemnation that afflict consumers in their apprehension of courts sometimes also afflict collection agencies. Many collection agency personnel are self-conscious, unsure of their legal position, and understandably uncertain about the extent to which their practices would be condoned or condemned in any court proceedings. There may also be a risk of attracting adverse publicity and further attention from government. A collection agency may well consider, therefore, that it is good business to operate with a low profile. For these reasons, as well as the expense of litigation, it is highly probable that when a consumer threatens to defend a claim in court, the claim will be abandoned; the more so if he has a solicitor and particularly if a counter-claim is added.

L. The Effect of Extra-legal Methods of Collection

A reason sometimes given by collection agencies and credit grantors for the use of extra-legal methods of collection is to save an alleged debtor from the trouble, embarrassment and expense of court proceedings. But it is hardly credible that extra-legal methods of collection are motivated by concern for the well-being of the alleged debtor. If they are saving him from anything, it is from a system that involves a risk, however slight, that he might perceive an alternative to paying the claim, i.e., filing a defence.

Extra-legal methods of collection received a brief mention in the report of the Payne Committee. The committee accepted '. . .that creditors ought to be permitted a proper latitude in their attempts to obtain payment of overdue debts;'.[1] But there seemed to be no recognition that use of the words 'creditors' and 'debts' in this context was begging the question. The use of extra-legal methods to pursue claims cannot be justified by the assumption that the claims are 'debts' when the very methods of pursuit deny the opportunity of using even the inadequate machinery that we have for distinguishing debts from invalid claims.

It is not possible to arrive at any precise estimate of the proportion of claims that are legally invalid, but some indicators are available.

(1) In the survey conducted by the writer relating to consumer durables,

1. *Report of the Committee on the Enforcement of Judgment Debts*, 1969, Cmnd 3909, para.1235.

there were 51 cases in which the buyers acknowledged having been notified that a payment was overdue, and in which they agreed that a payment was overdue. Yet in 32 (63 per cent) of these, there would probably have been a total or partial defence to the claim. This proportion may be high because those with serious financial problems were probably undersampled. But the proportion could be much lower and still be cause for concern.

(2) Enquiries at the advisory agencies indicated large numbers of debt claims being pursued by sellers, lenders, finance companies and collection agencies in situations in which a defence could probably be raised successfully to the whole or part of the claim. These situations included:

Deceit in the advertising or in the sales tactics
Defective goods
Account already paid in full
No right to the interest being claimed
An additional amount, e.g., for services, being added to the account in excess of the amounts agreed, or for items that were never ordered
Non-delivery
Wrong goods.

Although it is not possible to estimate exactly what proportion of claims pursued are legally invalid, it is also not crucial. The point is that a significant proportion of claims are invalid, and that they are pursued by extra-legal methods of collection that deny even the limited opportunities that we have for adjudication.

The pursuit of invalid claims is not, however, the only objection to extra-legal methods of collection. In establishing courts and execution processes, society has made its judgments not only with regard to adjudication procedures, but also with regard to acceptable techniques of coercion. Moreover, the law has traditionally leaned against self-help and insisted that execution proceedings should be in the hands of government employees (sheriffs and bailiffs). When societal judgments have been made through the democratic process about acceptable types of coercion, which then become enacted as methods of execution, it is surely absurd if claimants are still left free to use any other coercive techniques that the wit of man can conceive. There is no doubt that some of the extra-legal methods of collection can be very frightening.

The iniquity is compounded when the other methods of coercion, possibly more severe than those used by the courts, can be applied without adjudication either on the merits of the claim or on the reasonableness of the instalments being demanded.

If an alleged debtor goes to a solicitor, extra-legal methods of collection can still be used, even at that stage, to prevent the legal advice from being effective. A collection agency can ignore the solicitor, keep up the pressure on the alleged debtor, and sometimes still coerce a payment. To counteract this, it may be prudent for a solicitor to (a) warn the client that this may occur and advise the client to let him know if it does, (b) request the collection agency to direct all further communications to himself, and (c) warn the collection agency that if any further demand is made to the alleged debtor, a claim may be presented against the agency as well as the creditor for damages for harassment.

Even when a claim has gone to court and judgment has been given, that does not necessarily mean that extra-legal methods of collection will be ended, or even that they will be brought into accord with the court decision. When a court has ordered payment by instalments, it still sometimes happens that a collection agency continues to demand the full amount, or instalments of higher amounts.[1]

M. Proposals

Proposals have been made above[2] relating both to the categories of claims that should be enforceable at law, and to the procedures of adjudication and execution that should be available for the pursuit of those claims. If we are to have a system of justice in small claims, however, forum shopping must be prevented not only as between one court and another, but also as between courts and other institutions. Perhaps the point can be illustrated by the following extracts from an interview conducted in Canada with a furniture dealer in a community in which the Small Claims Court was exceptionally efficient.

. . .

Q. 'How often do you receive customer complaints?'

A. 'Our customers don't have any complaints'.

Q. 'Surely it must sometimes happen that a customer complains about goods being damaged, or not being what he ordered, or something like that?'

A. 'When the furniture is delivered we require the customer to sign a form saying that it has been received in good order and condition and that any complaint must be notified to us within twenty-four hours. If the customer comes back with some grievance I show him the form and I say "You don't have any complaint".'

. . .

1. Interviews at advisory agencies, 1977.
2. Chapters 9 and 10.

Q. 'How do you handle your collections?'
A. 'We try to collect ourselves by sending out a series of three letters. If that fails, we use a collection agency.'
. . .
Q. 'Do you use the Small Claims Court?'
A. 'We used to, but they kept deciding cases against us so we don't think it pays to use courts any more. Now we use the collection agency.'. . .

To achieve a system of justice in the courts would be to a large extent futile if we were still to tolerate the existence of agencies whose function is to apply coercion without adjudication.

The approach taken in Section 40 of the *Administration of Justice Act*, 1970, is an attempt to apply behavioural controls to collection procedures. But this is unsatisfactory. Even if it were somebody's job to enforce the legislation it would still be a Herculean task. Where abusive collection tactics are used, a large proportion of victims come from sections of society least articulate in expressing complaints. Spot checks could be made on the content of written communications, but there is no practical way in which the content of telephone conversations or of personal calls at the home can be monitored and offences detected.

Under the *Consumer Credit Act*, 1974, collection agencies are now required to be licensed. That would make sense if the business being licensed was providing a public benefit and the problem being tackled consisted of behavioural aberrations the nature and extent of which could be monitored. But that is not the case. Like the *Administration of Justice Act*, the *Consumer Credit Act* seems to assume that a distinction can be and should be made between reasonable and unreasonable techniques of extra-legal coercion. It is difficult to see how such a distinction can either be made in practice or justified in principle. All such techniques apply pressure to pay regardless of the legitimacy of a claim. It is surely preferable, therefore, that these practices be eliminated as far as possible by structural change to prevent their use, not curtailed by behavioural controls to prevent excess.

The *raison d'être* of collection agencies is to apply coercion to pay by techniques that deny an opportunity for adjudication. They are surely an affront to the rule of law and ought to be abolished.

One of the ancillary services now performed by collection agencies is skip-tracing, and it is not of course suggested that this function should be abolished. No doubt it would continue to be carried on by credit reporting services and others. Most skip-tracing in any event is done by the use of directories and in-file information, and this could be continued without communicating with the alleged debtor, his employer, or others.

To make the abolition of collection agencies effective, assignments would have to be prohibited of debt claims against consumers, and it would need to be an offence to seek the recovery of a consumer debt otherwise than in the name of the seller or lender. Thus a credit grantor would know that his collection methods become part of his business reputation.

The elimination of collection agencies would still leave the question of what to do about extra-legal methods of collection by credit grantors themselves. Because they usually have business goodwill at stake, this is less of a problem. In any event, structural change is not possible here, and behavioural controls are the only approach possible.

It is suggested that the aim should be a framework that will discourage and impede harassment but still allow credit grantors to present their demands for payment, threaten court proceedings, collect instalments and negotiate settlements. For these purposes, credit grantors may legitimately need to use the telephone, and to make personal calls at the home of an alleged debtor, as well as using the post.

Probably the best approach would be to itemise what is permissible, and then legislate a prohibition on any other method of attempting collections. In addition, all known techniques of coercion could be specifically prohibited, including:

(1) Threatening or indicating any action except court proceedings or the discontinuance of business by the credit grantor with the alleged debtor.
(2) Threatening action without specifying exactly what.
(3) Sending more than three communications to the alleged debtor without receiving a reply.
(4) Making telephone calls to an alleged debtor between 10 p.m. and 8 a.m.
(5) Making more than three telephone calls to an alleged debtor except at his request.
(6) Communicating with the employer of an alleged debtor in connection with a claim, or with an alleged debtor at his place of employment.
(7) Communicating with neighbours or acquaintances of an alleged debtor in connection with a claim.
(8) Giving any publicity to a claim otherwise than by reporting it to a credit reporting service.
(9) Bawling outside the home of an alleged debtor.
(10) Calling at the home of an alleged debtor after being requested not

to do so, or remaining on the premises after being requested to leave.
(11) Communicating with an alleged debtor after being requested to address any further communications to a solicitor or other agent.

Rules on these lines would clarify what is permissible collection behaviour. Primary responsibility for surveillance and prosecution could be assigned to the Trading Standards Departments, and the licensing system under the *Consumer Credit Act* could also be used as a vehicle for enforcement.

Any retraction in credit marketing that might result from adopting these proposals would not be likely to occur evenly across the board. At the time of granting credit, the collection methods likely to be used in respect of that transaction are generally predictable. To the extent that this is true, the elimination of harassment by extra-legal methods of collection is only likely to result in a retraction of the types of business that rely on those methods. Moreover, other types of creditors who view such tactics with disdain may find it easier to obtain the payment of their bills if, when demanding payment, they are not subject to competition from those less scrupulous. Thus it is suggested that the elimination of harassment by extra-legal methods of collection would help to promote a healthier credit market as well as relieving oppression.

Perhaps the most important point in this chapter is the view that changes in the law relating to collections can be a much more sensitive and efficient mechanism for influencing marketing behaviour, particularly with regard to high-pressure salesmanship, than any attempt at control by the more direct regulation of marketing.

11 FINANCE COMPANIES AND THE CONSUMER

This chapter deals with three-party transactions. An item is purchased by a consumer from a dealer, the price being advanced by a finance company to the dealer, and being repaid in instalments by the consumer to the finance company.

A major issue in consumer protection during the 1960s was whether a finance company should be allowed to enforce the payment of instalments when a consumer has been the victim of a fraud by the dealer, or when the dealer has otherwise failed to meet his obligations. This issue has received considerable legislative attention, but has not yet been entirely resolved.

To understand the matter, it is important to recall the various ways in which an instalment credit transaction might be financed. The most important are summarised in Chapter 3, p.38. For present purposes they can be classified roughly into the three categories below.

(1) The credit may be supplied by the retailer. The transaction might take the legal form of hire-purchase, credit sale or conditional sale; or the item might be charged to a continuing account between consumer and retailer. Any failure of the retailer to fulfil his legal obligations to the consumer can be raised as a total or partial defence, or as a counter-claim, in any action by the retailer for payment.

(2) Independently of the retailer, a consumer may arrange a loan and deal with the retailer as a cash buyer. For example, a consumer may arrange a loan from his bank. In this case, the loan is an independent transaction from the purchase, and the consumer's obligation to repay does not vary according to whether the dealer has fulfilled his obligations to the consumer.

(3) The credit may be supplied by a finance company but arranged through the retailer. The legal form this usually takes in England is for the retailer to 'sell' the goods to a finance company, which then supplies the goods to the consumer on a hire-purchase or credit sale contract. The finance company becomes legally the 'owner' or 'seller'. Alternatively, loan documentation might be used. In North America, the legal form is often a conditional sale contract between retailer and consumer, the retailer's right to payment under this contract being assigned to the finance company (acceptance company). But whatever the documentary formalities, the substance is that the finance company

> is advancing the capital for the retailer to supply the item to the consumer on instalment credit terms. The issue has been whether, under this type of arrangement, the right of a finance company to payment should depend on the performance by the dealer of his obligations to the consumer; or whether, like an independent cash lender, the finance company should be entitled to payment regardless of any default by the dealer.

When the financing is arranged through the retailer (whatever the documentary formalities), the arrangement is described in the report of the Crowther Committee as 'connected lending'. When the financing is arranged by the consumer independently of the retailer, it is described as 'unconnected lending'.

In the transaction credit cases in the sample, buyers were asked 'Who have you been paying the instalments to, or who were you expected to pay them to?' This question was intended to provide a rough guide for distinguishing cases where the credit was advanced by a finance company as a contracting party with the consumer from those in which it was advanced by the retailer. The results showed that co-ops and gas and electricity boards generally carried their own financing. In department stores and chain stores, finance companies advanced the credit to the consumer only in about 5 per cent of transaction credit cases. In specialty shops it was about 12 per cent.

Excluding motor vehicle sales, financing was by the retailer in 91 per cent of transaction credit cases where the sale occurred at a shop or other trade premises, and 61 per cent where the sale was made at the home. In the sale of motor vehicles on transaction credit, however, finance companies were predominant. Thus in the transaction credit cases involving new motor vehicles, only 13 per cent were financed by the dealer, and in cases involving secondhand motor vehicles, only 15 per cent.

The larger finance companies, the members of the Finance Houses Association, finance mostly motor vehicles and home improvements on the consumer side of their business. They do not, for example, generally finance the purchase of kitchen appliances, radios, televisions, or furniture. There were 21 cases in the sample in which financing for goods of this type was arranged with a finance company through the retailer. In all except one of these cases, the finance company was either known to the writer as a corporate affiliate of the retailer, or not recognisable at all. Apart from central heating and motor vehicle cases, it seemed that when financing was arranged by a retailer it was usually supplied either by the retailer or by a corporate affiliate.

Of the loan cases in the sample, 19 involved loans arranged through the dealer and 27 were unconnected lending.

In the transaction credit cases, it was not possible to compare buyer experiences between those where the financing was by the seller and those where it was by a finance company because of differences in the type of item. In the loan cases, this comparison was more feasible because they generally involved a motor vehicle or central heating, but the numbers were small. Where a bank loan was used, the selling methods were classified as open to major or substantial objections in 1 out of 18, compared with 5 out of 16 where the loan was from a finance company. With regard to the condition of the goods, the cases in which a bank loan was used were classified as involving major or substantial objections in 4 out of 18, compared with 6 out of 16 where the loan was from a finance company.

The legal position most accommodating to finance companies would be to compel the consumer to pay the instalments regardless of any grievances that he may have about the dealer or the goods. Indeed the traditional argument raised by finance companies was that they were simply in the position of cash lenders, and that they should be entitled to recover their advances in the same way as unconnected lenders regardless of any dispute between consumer and dealer.

On the extent to which finance companies can achieve that position, English law has been muddled. The doctrine of freedom of contract (in this context, the freedom of a finance company to settle the terms upon which it deals) had been subjected to legislative intervention on behalf of consumers. But until 1977 (when the relevant provisions of the *Consumer Credit Act*, 1974, came into effect) this had not been done in any coherent way.

Prior to that year, if a finance company used a hire-purchase, conditional sale or credit sale form, it was bound by the implied conditions of fitness for purpose and merchantable quality,[1] and was bound by any representation made by the dealer with respect to the goods during antecedent negotiations.[2] Paradoxically, the finance company was probably not bound by any misrepresentation of the dealer relating to the financing. Whether a finance company was bound by a manufacturer's repair warranty probably depended upon whether a court could conclude that the dealer gave an undertaking that the warranty would be honoured.

If a loan form was used, a finance company had none of the ordinary obligations of a seller, nor was it automatically bound by representations of the dealer. It was still, however, not in quite the same position as an unconnected lender. For example, if a salesman of the goods also acted as

1. *Supply of Goods (Implied Terms) Act*, 1973, SS.3 and 10.
2. *Hire-Purchase Act*, 1965, S.16.

agent of the finance company in arranging the loan, a court might conclude that he was acting in that capacity when making any misrepresentations. Similarly, a court might have concluded on the facts of a particular case that a finance company and dealer had acted in concert towards the consumer and behaved as business partners to such an extent that they should be so treated and held jointly liable to the consumer. In a Canadian case, for example, the court ruled that a finance company, even when using loan forms, 'may so identify itself with the dealer as to deprive itself of all defence against the equities of the transaction'.[1]

From a consumer point of view, there were two main problems with this state of the law. First, a finance company could avoid responsibility for the goods, and for the representations of the dealer, by documenting the transaction on loan forms.

Secondly, in so far as the law imposed obligations on finance companies, it did so in a confusing way through a conceptual framework that required key words to be understood differently from their colloquial meaning. In particular, a finance company became privy to the obligations of a dealer by becoming 'the seller' under a credit sale agreement, or 'the owner' under a hire-purchase agreement. But it was difficult for people to perceive a finance company as 'the seller' when in colloquial speech that phrase would normally refer to the dealer.

The *Consumer Credit Act,* 1974, deals with the first of these problems. Thus, the obligations of a finance company are now more uniform whether the documentation is on a hire-purchase, credit sale, loan, or other form. The language identifying parties is usually descriptive of their commercial functions. But there are still conflicts between colloquial and technical meanings.

For tripartite situations, where a dealer supplies the goods, and financing is provided through arrangements with a finance company, the Act now provides that:

> If the debtor under a debtor-creditor-supplier agreement falling within section 12(b) or (c) has, in relation to a transaction financed by the agreement, any claim against the supplier in respect of a misrepresentation or breach of contract, he shall have a like claim against the creditor, who, with the supplier, shall accordingly be jointly and severally liable to the debtor.[2]

There is some ambiguity about whether 'the supplier' refers to the dealer

1. *Beneficial Finance v. Kulig,* (1970) 13 DLR (3d) 134, 150.
2. S.75 (1).

only when loan documentation is used, or in all cases, but this may be unimportant. Where hire-purchase or credit sale documentation is used, the obligations of 'owner' or 'seller' are imposed upon the finance company directly by the pre-existing law, particularly the *Supply of Goods (Implied Terms) Act*, 1973. Where loan documentation is used, the above section imposes the same obligations on a finance company jointly and severally with the dealer. The Act also makes the dealer the agent of the finance company in respect of antecedant negotiations.[1]

To understand these obligations, it may be helpful to consider why finance companies should be liable at all in respect of defects in the goods or the conduct of dealers.

First, finance companies are the only major grantors of consumer credit having no goodwill at stake among consumers. Most retailers and cash lenders expect repeat business with the same customers or others in the same community, and this surely must be a limiting influence on abuses in business behaviour. But that is not the position of finance companies. Their flow of new business depends on goodwill among dealers, not among consumers. While this does not of itself indicate that finance companies should be under any particular liability with regard to a dealer's conduct or the goods, it is ground for a sceptical reaction to any suggestion that they ought to be immune.

The strongest argument for some measure of liability is that sales finance arrangements can play a catalytic role in the perpetration of fraud.

As two observers in the United States have written:

> Consumer-fraud criminals frequently operate freely in the marketplace. The responsible business and legal communities are often too willing to accept the machinations of fast-buck operators without first questioning their propriety. Banks and finance companies too frequently close their eyes to specious transactions, which depend upon the negotiability of commercial paper, in the interest of promoting business.[2]

In England, the central heating rackets illustrate the point. Consider the case of a seller with no established place of business, no technical competence and no integrity, who makes a prior arrangement with a finance company to advance the credit for his transactions. He then moves

1. S.56. For an excellent pamphlet explaining these reforms, see *Equal Liability*, 1977, Office of Fair Trading.

2. 'Criminal Consumer Fraud : A Victim-Oriented Analysis', D.P. Rothschild and B.C. Throne, (1976) 74 *Michigan Law Review* 661, 676.

through one community after another with high-pressure salesmen calling at houses that appear to have no central heating, working on householders with a skilfully prepared sales pitch. This builds up to a climax at which a householder is induced to sign an array of documents, one being an order form, another being a loan form or promissory note, and a third being an acknowledgement that the installation has been completed to the customer's satisfaction. The householder, while subjected to the skilful manoeuvering and constant patter of the salesman, signs the documents without reading them. The seller then obtains payment from the finance company. Some kind of heating may be delivered or installed, but nothing like the central heating that the consumer was led to expect. The consumer complains, but nothing significant is done even if the seller can be located. The consumer refuses to pay, but the finance company demands payment, insisting that it is in no way responsible for the default of the seller. If the consumer still refuses to pay, the finance company may sue and obtain a default judgment for the full amount of the 'loan'.

But for the participation of the finance company, frauds of this type could not be perpetrated. Cash buyers cannot usually be deceived and pressured in this way, nor can those who make their financing arrangements with unconnected lenders. The clincher is the facility that enables a salesman to consummate a transaction simply by obtaining signatures on forms and thereby to obtain payment without supplying what the consumer was led to expect. Thus, although connected lending is often a legitimate method of extending credit, it is also sometimes a weapon for the perpetration of fraud, and the argument is that those who supply such a weapon should not be allowed to thrust upon others the losses resulting from its abuse.

With unconnected lending it is different. There is generally an interval between the decision to buy and the arrangement of the loan. Hence the consumer has a chance for second thoughts about the transaction, a release from the pressure of the salesman, a chance to enquire about the reputation of the seller, a chance to compare prices and quality, a chance to consider alternative models and terms, and an opportunity for discussion with friends. All these aids to rational decision-making are denied when a salesman, supported by a prior arrangement with a connected lender, pressures or deceives a consumer into signing on the spot.

It is not suggested that fraud by dealers is usual in sales finance transactions. Although some finance companies have been behind some scandalous frauds, they have also been behind an infinitely greater number of satisfactory transactions. The argument for liability, however, does not rest on establishing that any particular proportion of sales finance transactions involve fraud or other abuses in the selling process. Even assuming abuses to be unusual, that would be no reason why finance companies should not be liable when they occur. Moreover, instalment credit purchases are not simply divisible into satisfactory transactions and frauds. There are many other grievances that consumers suffer, not necessarily involving dishonesty or catastrophic losses, but which have a higher frequency rate. These include the supply of shoddy goods, delivery of the wrong item, late delivery, and failure to honour repair warranties. An advantage of buying on credit is that a consumer retains the opportunity to stop or suspend payment, and this can be used to induce a remedy for a seller's defaults. Making finance companies liable for the obligations of dealers preserves that leverage and creates an incentive for a finance company to put pressure on a dealer to resolve complaints and to fulfil his obligations.

Again, finance companies are intimately involved in the business operations of their dealers. It is a continuing relationship. Often a finance company will provide the capital for a dealer's stock as well as financing his retail sales. The transactions with consumers are consummated on forms supplied by the finance company. Usually the finance company will do the credit checking, will determine the interest rates, and will allow the dealer a commission for the business. For all practical purposes, the dealer is a salesman of the finance company and acting as its agent. 'To a considerable extent the finance house and the dealer are engaged in a joint venture'.[1]

When a finance company is involved in the sale of goods other than motor vehicles or home improvements, it is commonly not an independent company but a corporate affiliate of the retailer. It would be iniquitous if a retailer, in relations with consumers, could obtain a legal position stronger than the law would otherwise allow simply by binary fission, conducting his business through a selling company and a captive finance company.

Further, it is surely acceptable policy to promote legitimate, fair and honest business, and to discourage fraud, predatory practices, and the habitual failure to honour obligations that have been undertaken. But who is in the best position to make the distinction between different types of retailers and to exert an influence? With regard to a major durable it is not the consumer, because he does not buy one often enough to learn from comparative experience in dealing with different retailers. Yet businessmen, like the rest of us, tend to be creatures of habit, operating at levels of honesty and efficiency that are fairly constant. Thus a finance company that deals with a retailer consistently over time has an infinitely better opportunity to assess his business methods and the results of his trans-

1. *Report of the Committee on Consumer Credit*, 1971, Cmnd 4596, para. 6.6.22.

actions than a consumer who is approaching him for the first time.

There are several sources of information available to finance companies. The most obvious is the complaints that they receive from consumers who object to paying the instalments. Also the Finance Houses Association maintains a register of all dealers who have been reported by members as unsatisfactory either because of fraudulent practices, or because they otherwise do not honour their obligations. Names added to this list are circulated periodically to the member companies. It is more difficult with regard to new dealers, but even here it may be possible to obtain information from a credit reporting service or by discreet enquiries among agencies dealing with consumer complaints.

The greater experience and information available to a finance company, compared with that available to a consumer, may be seen as relevant in two ways. One is to regard the situation as appropriate for the rule in *Lickbarrow v. Mason*[1] to be invoked 'wherever one or two innocent persons must suffer for the acts of a third, he who has enabled such third person to occasion the loss must sustain it.' Secondly, finance companies have the capacity to discriminate between legitimate dealers and those less reputable, and the power to restrain the business operations of disreputable dealers by drying up their sources of credit. It is at least arguable that because they have the power they should have the responsiblity. It is extremely difficult and expensive to control fraudulent or predatory business operations by direct policing, and it is surely cheaper and more efficient to minimise their survival by withdrawing legal support for a type of credit structure that enables them to receive payment without fulfilling the obligations that they have undertaken.

In Canada, when a claim for payment is brought by a finance company, it is now subject to most of the defences that would have been available if the claim had been brought by the dealer. When questioned by the writer about the effect of this legislation, the manager of a local finance company replied 'We now have to be more careful about weeding out bad dealers'.

It is sometimes suggested that if a consumer is a victim of fraud, or otherwise does not receive the item for which he is paying, he has adequate recourse in a legal action against the dealer. But this is no answer.

> There are many reasons why in practice a legal right which the buyer may have against his seller is not sufficient protection. Where the seller is reputable he will usually be prepared to deal with justified complaints and rectify the matters complained of. The majority of

1. (1787) 2 TR 64, 70. Per Ashhurst, J.

> the cases in which the buyer is likely to suffer are those where a seller is of doubtful repute and is able to continue in business only because of the financial support he receives from the lender. The buyer supplied with defective goods may find that to secure redress from such a seller he has to incur the worry and expense of litigation, in which the burden of taking the initiative lies on him; and that in some cases the seller's financial position is so poor that it is doubtful whether he will be able to meet the judgment even if the buyer is successful. The buyer's difficulties of pursuing the claim against the seller are enhanced if, whilst wrestling with the financial problems of litigation, he has to go on paying the lender under the loan agreement.[1]

For the reasons explained in Chapter 9(1), the majority of consumers are unlikely to begin legal proceedings against a retailer. The most that can generally be expected of consumers by way of forensic initiative is that, given a sporting chance, they might defend themselves when sued. It is essential therefore that the opportunity for adjudication on a consumer's grievance should be available by way of defence to the claim for payment, and not simply by way of a separate claim against the retailer.

Moreover, to allow a finance company immunity from responsibility for a dealer's actions created a sense of bewilderment among consumers as well as feelings of frustration and injustice.

> We have a lot of problems arising out of the purchase of cars and particularly the use of exclusion clauses. The typical case is a young man who buys a car. He signs a contract that includes exclusion clauses that he never read or understood. The car turns out to be unroadworthy. Repairs are very expensive. He fails to pay, the finance company serves a termination notice of the hiring. The buyer doesn't understand the notice, and does not reply. Hence it is difficult for the court to protect him. The buyer is faced with an endless passing of the buck. If he declines to pay, the finance company insists on payment telling him to take his complaint to the dealer. The dealer will refer him to the manufacturer who will refer him back to the dealer. He gets the eternal run-around.[2]

To allow a consumer's grievances to be raised by way of defence or counter-

1. *Report of the Committee on Consumer Credit*, 1971, Cmnd 4596, para. 6.6.25.
2. Per an adviser at a Citizens' Advice Bureau, 1969.

claim in the action for payment is surely just. If a consumer has been defrauded or is not receiving what he is paying for it is natural that he should see his remedy in stopping or reducing the payments. There is also a feeling of outrage against the idea of someone being compelled to pay for something when he is not receiving the thing for which the payment was agreed. To regard the claim of a finance company as an independent claim has a ring of chicanery when it is presented by someone who is obviously a business collaborator of the dealer. Not least important, it could also bring the legal system into disrepute.

Moreover the right of a consumer to seek redress from the dealer is sometimes rendered useless by the dealer's mobility, obscurity, or insolvency. Here again it is finance companies that are in the best position to check on the solvency and availability for suit of their dealers. Indeed, since finance companies are often creditors of the dealer as well as creditors of his customers, a dealer's solvency and availability are matters in which they have a primary interest. If a finance company sustains the business operation of a dealer who does not have sufficient capital for the conduct of an independent business, and who could not operate without the advances of the finance company, it is surely reasonable to expect that company to ensure that the dealer is sufficiently solvent and available to meet his obligations.

Making finance companies liable for the obligations of their dealers might result in a loss of some marginal business, but they should not otherwise suffer. They can either advance the credit with full recourse against the dealer in the event of non-payment by the consumer, or they can stipulate for a right of recovery against the dealer in situations where the consumer has not paid because of grounds for non-payment. Where there is no contractual term covering the point, a finance company now has the right to be indemnified by a dealer for any loss suffered by the finance company in satisfying a liability of the dealer.[1]

With regard to the level of the liability of finance companies, there are several possibilities. One would be to make a consumer's grievances available by way of defence and set-off in any claim for payment by a finance company, but not to make the finance company liable for damages beyond the amount of its claim. This approach has a superficial attractiveness in that it might seem to place a consumer in the same position as if no finance company had been involved. In that situation, a consumer would have a right of action against the dealer for damages, together with a right of set-off on any claim by the dealer for payment. This level of liability would meet some of the policy arguments for making finance companies

1. *Consumer Credit Act*, 1974, S.75 (2).

liable, but it would not meet others. For example, it would provide no deterrent against the provision of finance company backing to dealers who sell shabby goods that fall apart at the end of the payment period, or who fail to honour long-term repair warranties. Further, it would not meet the argument that finance companies should be responsible for the solvency and availability for suit of the dealers that they support.

A second possibility might be to limit the liability of finance companies to the total price of the goods. But it is difficult to find any rational argument for stopping at that point.

A third possibility is simply to make finance companies liable for the obligations of dealers, including any liability for damages in excess of the total price of the goods. This is the level of liability that was applied by the *Hire-Purchase Act,* 1965, and also the level recommended by the Crowther Committee.[1] This is the level that is continued in the *Consumer Credit Act,* 1974. This meets all the policy reasons for imposing the liability.

In defining the situations in which a finance company will be liable for the obligations of a dealer, the *Consumer Credit Act,* 1974, tries to avoid the mistakes of the past. In particular, the distinction between connected and unconnected lending does not now depend as much as it did previously on the formalities or documents used.

There are, however, still problems of potential evasion.

If connected lenders are made the guarantors of a dealer's obligations while unconnected lenders are not, there is obviously an incentive for finance companies to seek ways of producing the legal result of unconnected lending while at the same time retaining the economic substance of connected lending.

This is what happened to some extent in the United States and Canada when legislation gave increased consumer protection in sales finance transactions (connected lending). One method was for a dealer to make prior arrangements with a cash lender, and to seek to avoid the result of connected lending by introducing each customer to the cash lender. This was done, for example, by a motor dealer driving the consumer to the office of the lender. The practice had all the disadvantages of connected lending; the consummation of the transaction by obtaining a signature on a form while the consumer is under the continuing pressure of the sales pitch, no opportunity to shop for credit after the decision to purchase, and no opportunity for second thoughts or for discussion with family or friends.

The provisions of the *Consumer Credit Act*, 1974, that make a finance

1. *Report of the Committee on Consumer Credit*, 1971, Cmnd 4596, para.6.6.28.

company liable for the obligations of a dealer[1] relate to '. . .a debtor-creditor-supplier agreement within section 12(b) or (c). . .'.

Section 12(b) relates to a regulated consumer credit agreement to finance a transaction between the debtor and a person (the 'supplier') other than a creditor and made by the creditor under pre-existing arrangements, or in contemplation of future arrangements, between himself and the supplier.

Section 12(c) relates to a regulated consumer credit agreement being an unrestricted-use agreement which is made by the creditor under pre-existing arrangements between himself and a person (the 'supplier') other than the debtor in the knowledge that the credit is to be used to finance a transaction between the debtor and the supplier.

Section 187 provides that:

> (1) A consumer credit agreement shall be treated as entered into under pre-existing arrangements between a creditor and a supplier if it is entered into in accordance with, or in furtherance of, arrangements previously made between persons mentioned in subsection (4)*(a)*, *(b)* or *(c)*.
>
> (2) A consumer credit agreement shall be treated as entered into in contemplation of future arrangements between a creditor and a supplier if it is entered into in the expectation that arrangements will subsequently be made between persons mentioned in subsection (4)*(a)*, *(b)* or *(c)* for the supply of cash, goods and services (or any of them) to be financed by the consumer credit agreement.
>
> (3) Arrangements shall be disregarded for the purposes of sub-section (1) or (2) if –
>
> *(a)* they are arrangements for the making, in specified circumstances, of payments to the supplier by the creditor, and
>
> *(b)* the creditor holds himself out as willing to make, in such circumstances, payments of the kind to suppliers generally.
>
> (4) The persons referred to in subsections (1) and (2) are –
>
> *(a)* the creditor and the supplier;
>
> *(b)* one of them and an associate of the other's;
>
> *(c)* an associate of one and an associate of the other's.
>
> (5) Where the creditor is an associate of the supplier's, the consumer credit agreement shall be treated, unless the contrary is proved, as entered into under pre-existing arrangements between the creditor and the supplier.

1. SS.56 and 75.

Section 184 defines 'associate' by reference to family relationships, partnership arrangements, and corporate affiliations.

It is doubtful, however, whether these definitions will be effective to prevent evasion. For the odd case that goes to trial and is fully argued there or on appeal, the definitions provide a sufficient mixture of clarity and flexibility to enable a good judge to make the distinction between connected and unconnected lending according to the economic realities. The difficulty is that the definitions do not identify features that are readily recognisable to ordinary businessmen and to advisers at the agencies to which consumers go for advice.

The law would surely be clearer to ordinary people (and therefore more likely to be applied) if it were prescribed that a finance company will be liable for all obligations of a dealer when any of the conditions listed below exist.

(1) Any prior arrangement or understanding between seller and lender with regard to the financing of consumer transactions.
(2) Any corporate affiliation between seller and lender.
(3) Supply of contract documents, forms, brochures, advertising, or other materials by lender to seller, or vice versa.
(4) Presence of the lender or any agent of his on the premises of the seller either usually or in connection with the particular transaction.
(5) Escorting of the consumer to the premises of the lender by any employee or agent of the seller.
(6) Unless by coincidence, the presence of any agent or employee of the seller at the premises of the lender when the credit arrangement is made.
(7) Any agent of the seller acting also as agent of the lender.
(8) Any other participation of the seller in arrangement of the financing.
(9) Direct transmission of the advance by lender to seller.
(10) Any specification by the lender that the advance should be used for purchasing from a particular seller.
(11) Payment of any commission by lender to seller in respect of the particular transaction, or in respect of other transactions.
(12) Location of the lender, or any office or department of the lender, in the same building as the seller.

No doubt there would be scope for discussion with regard to exactly what features should be included in such a list. The immediate purpose, however, is not to justify each item on the list but rather to illustrate the kind of list that is needed if the distinction between connected and unconnected lending is going to be applied effectively in the advisory agencies and elsewhere. If the distinction remains dependent upon broad definitions that involve uncertainty, and that also require a high level of legal talent to understand and apply, there is an obvious risk that consumers may tend to concede the issue rather than face the prospect of legal involvement and litigation. Much of the expected benefit of the reform will then be lost.

A development that might follow the curtailment of immunity for connected lending, together with the introduction of interest rate disclosure, is the establishment of branch offices by finance companies for the conduct of ordinary cash lending. This could be in the public interest. But it could also raise the prospect of several techniques of evasion being developed, the making of demand loans being one. A finance company is still immune from liability for the obligations of a dealer if loan documentation is used and the number of payments to be made by the consumer does not exceed four.[1] Thus if it is willing to forgo the pre-computation of interest, a finance company can still evade the obligations of a dealer by making demand loans, or loans repayable by four or less instalments, with a tacit understanding that payment by a longer series of instalments would be acceptable. Another technique would be to consummate a connected lending transaction, and then subsequently seek to blend that account with others into a consolidation loan. This may not change the legal position in theory. But in practice, it may well result in people losing sight of the liability of the finance company for the obligations of the dealer. Both of these practices have been used in Canada.

The use of a promissory note endorsed over to a finance company has in the past enabled the company to claim the status of a holder in due course. The Crowther Committee recommended that no negotiable instrument other than a cheque should be taken in connection with consumer transactions,[2] and this recommendation was adopted in the *Consumer Credit Act,* 1974.[3] Unfortunately, however, the Act does not make it an offence to take a promissory note in a consumer transaction. This may not have any broad significance because the licensing provisions of the Act would surely deter any established finance company from accepting promissory notes as an endorsee. But it may still be significant in some situations, and the prohibition would surely be more emphatic if the taking of promissory notes in consumer transactions was made an offence.

Another technique of evasion may be to use loan documentation, and to include clauses purporting to limit or exclude the rights and defences of

1. *The Consumer Credit (Exempt Agreements) Order 1977,* SI No. 326.

2. *Report of the Committee on Consumer Credit,* 1971, Cmnd 4596, para. 6.6.39.

3. SS.123-5.

the consumer in relation to the finance company, and to divert consumer grievances to the dealer. Such exclusion clauses are now void.[1] But that is not enough to prevent them from being effective in the negotiation of disputed claims. The elimination of such clauses may need to be achieved through the regulation-making and licensing powers of the Director General of Fair Trading.

In some jurisdictions, such as Canada, legislation making a finance company responsible for the obligations of a dealer has not covered credit card companies. The result is an obvious loophole. Fortunately, this was recognised by the Crowther Committee in reporting that:

> . . .there is in fact a close business relationship between an issuer and the suppliers who have agreed to accept that issuer's credit cards. The issuer, through provision of the card, swells the turnover of the supplier, and for conferring this benefit usually receives by way of discount an agreed percentage of the invoice price of the goods or services supplied. Moreover, a cardholder dealing with a reputable issuer has every reason to assume that the issuer will list only reputable suppliers.
>
> There is a close analogy between the credit card business and that of check trading. We have already indicated our view that where the lender is not independent but has a business relationship with the supplier of goods or services. . .the lender should be answerable for failure in performance by the supplier (having a right of indemnity against the supplier) and that the debtor should in addition be entitled to set off his claim for such failure against any sum payable under the loan agreement. We feel that the same considerations should in principle apply to transactions financed by credit cards. This should not impose an undue burden on the issuer, who is much better placed than the cardholder to secure redress from the offending supplier, and who because of the further delay in payment. . . would almost invariably be in a position to exercise its right of indemnity against monies payable to the supplier. Moreover agreements between issuers and suppliers usually impose an express obligation on the supplier to deal promptly with legitimate complaints by cardholders.[2]

Credit card usage has expanded considerably. Although multi-purpose credit cards are not in general use for the purchase of motor vehicles or

1. *Consumer Credit Act*, 1974, S.173.
2. *Report of the Committee on Consumer Credit*, 1971, Cmnd 4596, p.316.

home improvements, they are in general use for the purchase of, for example, furniture, white goods, electrical appliances and radios. It is vitally important, therefore, that credit card companies should be subject to the same obligations as finance companies.

Following the recommendations of the Crowther Committee, the protective sections of the *Consumer Credit Act*, 1974, apply to all transaction credit cases (hire-purchase, credit sale, and conditional sale), to connected loans, credit cards, check trading, and any other form of tripartite arrangement involving a consumer, seller and creditor.

There is, however, one respect in which multi-purpose credit card companies are in a different position from finance companies. Access Card and Barclaycard have between them very close to a monopoly in multi-purpose credit cards for the bulk of the consumer market. Hence in their hands, any threat to terminate business relations could be a powerful weapon.

At the time of writing, there was not sufficient experience on which to discuss the consequences of the introduction in 1977 of the legislative changes mentioned above. The mutli-purpose credit card companies might well accept their new obligations with good grace. Better still, they might react by terminating arrangements with any trader whose methods are clearly unsatisfactory. But the range of theoretical possibilities includes some other options. For example, if an item on a credit card account relates to defective goods for which the consumer refuses to pay, the credit card company could react by cancelling the card, perhaps perceiving the consumer as 'a nuisance'. At the other extreme, arrangements with a trader might be cancelled in response to isolated incidents, and the trader might complain of arbitrariness or over-reaction.

In view of their monopoly position, the government may have to consider at some stage whether multi-purpose credit card companies should have such powers over credit card usage, or whether there should be some regulation of the cancellation of credit cards, or arrangements with traders.

In summary, the loopholes have not yet all been closed. But the *Consumer Credit Act*, 1974, has gone a long way towards making finance companies liable for the obligations of the dealers with whom they participate in credit transactions.

If new regulations and orders are issued as required, and if the provisions of the *Consumer Credit Act* relating to this subject are administered with vigilance, and any amendments passed as required, a major system of institutional support for fraudulent and predatory sales practices may at last be laid to rest.

12 TECHNIQUES OF CONTROL OVER ABUSES IN MARKETING BEHAVIOUR

1. Introduction

Strength and sophistication in sanctions have not always been features of consumer protection legislation. One explanation is, of course, the incidence of political power. Following the industrial revolution, the rising pre-eminence on the political scene of those controlling industry and commerce brought not only the wholesome notion of free trade, but also the more dubious ancillary doctrines of *laissez-faire* and *caveat emptor.*

> The excesses to which unmitigated freedom of economic action gave rise need not be recounted in any detail; the legislative history of Nineteenth Century Britain is replete with efforts to alleviate its harsher consequences. Such was the influence of the prevailing political and economic doctrines, however, that an oddly apologetic note attended most reforms. It was believed that free market forces, governed solely by economic motives, could alone promote the prosperity of the whole community. Laws were to be judged by their 'utility' and as any law which impinged on freedom of economic activity must by definition be inutile, no acceptable intellectual argument could be deployed in its support. Hardship was accepted as necessary for some, so that others might prosper – even if the latter were disproportionately few in relation to the former. It became incontestible doctrine that interference by government with business, except for fiscal reasons, was pernicious and unsound. The authority of the doctrine was assured not merely by its eager acceptance by the magnates whose predominance in Parliament was on the increase, but by the memory of the struggles with the Stuart kings and by the previous history of the dissenting and non-conformist sects, in whom had been bred an almost instinctive mistrust of anything more than the indispensable minimum of government, and who now constituted an important voice in industry and commerce.[1]

Against the lobbying power of corporations and business organisations, there is no sustained and powerful lobbying in the consumer interest.

1. *Report of the Royal Commission on the Cost of Borrowing Money, Cost of Credit, and Related Matters,* 1965, Nova Scotia, p.219.

Consumer organisations have expanded considerably, and at the national level England has the Consumers' Association and the National Consumer Council. These organisations have an influence. But they have to work hard to make the most of limited resources. Whether measured by size of staff, numbers of publications, volume of advertising, number of MPs on the payroll, political contributions, numbers of people engaged in lobbying, common club memberships and other affiliations with the civil service, career interchanges, or in almost any other way, consumer organisations are small creatures on the political scene compared with the total organisations of industry, commerce and finance. The voting power of the consuming public often creates a pressure for parliamentary action which politicians heed. But it does not provide a well financed organisation for continuous monitoring to sustain a clearly articulated demand for detailed and specific action over the broad spectrum of consumer interests and throughout the administrative departments of government.

The political power of business is not, however, the only explanation for the weakness of sanctions in consumer protection. Another restraining influence may be the reflection that it is upon the functioning of industry and commerce that the prosperity of us all depends. Allied to this is the influence of advertising in moulding community values, placing maximum consumption at the forefront of contemporary aspiration, thereby militating against any reform that may seem calculated to impede the maximum flow of goods and services.

Moreover the opposition to consumer protection does not rest simply on economic self-interest. For example, a reputable business may oppose a reform aimed at curbing its less scrupulous competitors. Any government action may be feared as the thin end of a wedge, perhaps leading to a more comprehensive system of government control.

> ...[the Office of Fair Trading] goes to great lengths to consult business interests before deciding whether or not to take a new initiative. But the responses of business are almost always negative, rarely positive, though there are occasional heartening exceptions.[1]

Restrictions, regulations and government supervision can be perceived in the business community as a threat to the operation of a free market and to the independence of businessmen. Hence a business may react intuitively against any government proposal for consumer protection regardless of the merits and whether or not the particular enterprise would be affected by

1. 'Management and the Consumer Movement', J. Mitchell, (1976) 3 *Journal of General Management* 46.53.

the legislation. Thus an industrial spokesman was not referring to the merits of any particular legislation when commenting that: 'The current trend appears to be towards legislation and it will be difficult to find a manufacturer who will welcome this.'[1]

When a businessman does feel personally threatened by government proposals, it may even then be psychic security at stake rather than economic well-being. Most people are in occupations in which they take orders from above. But the aspiration of businessmen is often to avoid that condition. The ordinary shopkeeper, along with the corporate director of a manufacturing firm, may conceive of himself as having to get along with others and as being subject to the limitations of the market; but not as one who takes orders in matters relating to his trade. From his independence he may derive comfort, pride, and a sense of freedom; and any regulations may seem an intrusion of this regime, regardless of their content or value. Thus opposition to the regulation of business can spring from deep-rooted causes that may have little to do with the merits of any particular legislation.

Businessmen are, of course, also consumers. But when acting in that capacity they are surely better able than most people to look after themselves and to assess the credibility of what they are told. This may militate against a sensitive understanding of the predicament of those who lack the same acumen. It may also partly explain the occasional use of the argument that the resources of the state should not be used to save fools from their folly.

Although this view does not always prevail, there is an ambivalence in political debate about the extent to which it is feasible or desirable to legislate in matters of honesty. If salesmen are allowed to speak (as presumably they must), it is difficult to preclude the creation of false impressions. Moreover sanctions against fraud, for example, can involve drawing lines between puffery and misrepresentation, exaggeration and lie. Hence salesmanship can be seen not as a process that should be expected to involve honesty, but as a psychological game, akin to a sport, in which cunning, avarice, lying and bluff all have an acceptable role. On this view, buying is analogous to gambling. It is a battle of wits between buyer and seller, and anyone who complains that he never received what he ordered can be dismissed as a bad loser. It could be these feelings, as well as others, that supported the doctrine of *caveat emptor*. But they are cruel arguments if used to abandon the ordinary consumer, seeking to make his marginal income most effective, to the wiles of any unscrupulous seller or lender.

It would not be surprising if the pressures of the political scene should

1. Per G. Batchelor of Lever Bros, 'More Law Means Higher Prices', *Marketing and the Consumer*, supplement to *Marketing*, June 1976, p.vii.

result in some untenable compromises, and this may be what has sometimes happened. If consumer groups are demanding prohibitory or regulatory legislation, and a government is under pressure from sections of the business community to do nothing significant, there is an obvious temptation to enact prohibitions without the enforcement machinery or sanctions to make them effective.

Even apart from the influences that operate specifically in consumer protection, ineptitude in the selection of sanctions has been a general characteristic of legislation. It was otherwise in the early development of the common law. Procedure, remedies and sanctions were paramount. Indeed, the essence of the forms of action at common law was the prescription of a remedy for a wrong. But in the legislative process, there is a tendency, both at the preparatory stages and in parliamentary debate, to focus on the substantive rules, with the choice of sanctions receiving only parenthetical treatment. Exactly what legal consequences will follow from a violation of the rules is sometimes omitted, or is stated vaguely or incompletely, so that it has to be decided subsequently by the courts or other tribunals.

Another handicap in consumer protection has been the tendency to legislate by reference to formalities rather than the substance of a transaction. For example, the consumer protection provisions of the *Hire-Purchase Act*, 1965, were limited to hire-purchase agreements, credit sale agreements, and conditional sale agreements. Thus the requirements of the Act could be and were evaded by using a loan form. This problem was well recognised in the report of the Crowther Committee and is now largely resolved by the *Consumer Credit Act,* 1974.

Problems of the same type occur in the courts with regard to the common law doctrine of public policy. Sometimes it has been recognised that in decisions on public policy, it is essential for the courts to apply their own system of classification. In other cases, however, the courts have been content to adopt uncritically the classification that the dominant party to the transaction used in selecting the contractual documents, or in selecting the cause of action on which to sue.

The problem is illustrated in the law relating to penalties. Suppose a tradesman is persuaded to sign a contract for 3 years of advertising in a magazine at a total price of £1,200, payable by instalments of £200 every 6 months in advance. The day after signing, he notifies his intention to cancel. If the contract form provides that in the event of any default or repudiation, the magazine company can recover £500 as liquidated damages, and if the company sues for that sum, the court will probably conclude that this provision is void as a penalty. The company is only entitled to damages to the extent of its proven loss. Suppose, however, that instead of the liquidated damages clause, the contract form contains an acceleration clause making the whole price due in the event of default or repudiation. If the company ignores the cancellation, proceeds with the unwanted advertising, and sues for the total price of £1,200, the court will most likely conclude that since the action is for a debt rather than damages, the law relating to penalties is not applicable and the magazine company can recover the whole £1,200.[1]

If consumer protection provisions (whether statutory or common law) and other doctrines of public policy are to achieve their purpose, the courts must make their own classification of the subject matter. To allow the application of these doctrines to depend upon procedural or documentary choices made by the dominant party to a transaction can create flagrant opportunities for evasion.

To enact consumer protection legislation without adequate sanctions or enforcement machinery is unsatisfactory in three respects. First, it is surely reasonable to assume that the least scrupulous sections of the business community are also the least likely to comply. Yet it is probably against those sections that the legislation was most needed. Secondly, legislative reform with regard to marketing must aim at fairness among businessmen *inter se* as well as consumer protection. For both of these reasons, regulatory or prohibitory legislation in the consumer interest should include enforcement machinery and sanctions sufficiently severe and certain of application to assure a high rate of compliance. The absence of adequate enforcement machinery or sanctions is not only calculated to result in a failure of the legislation to achieve any significant consumer protection; it also places honest and law-abiding businessmen at a disadvantage compared with any less scrupulous competitors. Thirdly, without adequate sanctions and a thorough enforcement programme, the money spent on half-hearted enforcement can be a waste of public resources.

Particular sanctions and other techniques of control are discussed below.

2. Industry Self-regulation

Throughout industry, commerce and finance, there exists a range of trade associations, some being organisations of manufacturers, some organisations of distributors or retailers in a particular trade, and others organisations of retailers in a particular area. In addition there are organisations, such as the Automobile Association and the Royal Automobile Club, that include in their membership consumers and suppliers. Many of these organisations include integrity in marketing among their objectives. Thus

1. *White and Carter v. McGregor* [1962] AC 413; and *Granor Finance v. Eastore* [1974] SLT 296.

when regulation is demanded for abuses in marketing, an issue often raised is whether the problems should be met by government action or by industry self-regulation.

An advantage of self-regulation is that if remedial measures can be achieved by industry agreement, this may avoid any resentment or resistance that could accompany government action. Another advantage is that the familiarity which a trade association may have with the affairs and technology of an industry can be valuable, particularly when the problems involve technical issues.

On the other hand, there are several objections to any significant reliance on trade associations for consumer protection. First, the democratic process is by-passed if the acceptable level of integrity in any trade should be determined by those on one side of the marketplace.

Secondly, there are often conflicts of interest between consumers and a trade association. One such conflict may be with regard to the optimum level of competition. Anti-competitive restraints and practices may be advantageous to the suppliers in an industry but undesirable for its consumers. That trade associations do sometimes organise restraints upon competition appears from the reports of cases decided in the Restrictive Practices Court. Again, a trade association, or its director, may perceive a paramount need to maximise the membership, and hence be reluctant to expel members for misconduct, or to apply other significant sanctions. Another conflict could be seen in the discussions on the grading of garages. A main issue was whether garages should be graded by equipment and facilities, or whether they should also be graded by the service rendered.[1] If the grading and publication of the grades are being administered or determined by an association that is wholly or substantially dependent upon trade membership, there is an obvious risk that it may prefer the grading system that is easiest to administer or least offensive to the trade rather than one that is more informative to consumers.

Thirdly, trade associations carry out a mixture of functions. These may include the exchange of technical or marketing information, the dissemination of news relating to the industry (including the movement of personnel and patterns of business behaviour), and the monitoring of political events relating to the industry. Many associations publish periodicals for these purposes. Often the association will represent an industry in dealing with government inquiries, and in lobbying with regard to legislative change or administrative action. If members have joined an association primarily for these purposes, the communications of the association

1. See e.g. 'We Cannot Sweep "Which?" Findings Under the Carpet', M. Bradstock, *Motor Trade Executive*, February 1971, p.5.

will tend to be mainly within the trade, i.e. with people who recognise the difficulties and costs of remedial action to prevent consumer grievances, rather than with those who are suffering the grievances. Hence the role of an association in seeking to maintain or improve standards of integrity within the trade may be assigned a relatively low priority.

Fourthly, when trade associations do become actively involved in consumer protection, it is often from motives that do not augur well for the success of the endeavour. Abuses in marketing often stimulate a public demand for government action, and it is to head off such a response that action by a trade association is commonly advocated. Within the trade it is explained as an attempt to forestall 'government interference' and outside the trade is commonly explained as a demand 'for a chance to put our own house in order'. For example, after portraying a sad state of affairs with regard to repairs and service, a writer in the electrical appliance industry continued:

> The weight of consumer opinion is growing, their dissatisfaction mounting.
>
> The people who speak for them know full well that in the not too distant future things will have reached a stage where they can demand government action.
>
> That is the last thing which industry wants.[1]

If remedial action by a trade association comes about only in response to public pressure, there is an obvious risk that the effort will lose vitality once the heat is off.

Fifthly, few trade associations have any real machinery for the discovery and investigation of marketing abuses. Moreover few have any effective sanctions. An exception is in the professions, where the organising bodies can impose sanctions ranging up to termination of the professional practice of the offender. Outside these areas, however, sanctions are generally limited, non-existent, or not used.

Sixthly, when members of a trade association are concerned about abuses in marketing, they are often concerned about the image of the industry as well as the prospect of government regulation. Usually, however, it is legitimate businessmen who are concerned about image and who join trade associations. Yet a large proportion of fraud and other predatory practices occur, not as an aberrant by-product of legitimate business, but as the exclusive occupation of racketeers who show no desire to run a

1. *Electrical Marketing*, January 1970.

legitimate business at all, still less to join a trade association or chamber of commerce. This point was mentioned repeatedly during enquiries made in the course of this research. For example:

> Trade associations are usually helpful if we have a complaint against one of their members. Most will co-operate in taking some action to pressure their members, but most of our complaints are about firms that are not members of trade associations. For example, the garages that we have trouble with do not belong to the British Motor Trade Association, or to the AA or RAC.[1]

To the extent that this situation obtains, abuses in marketing will not be ended by the exhortation and persuasion of trade associations.

The advertising industry claims a significant level of success in self-regulation. There are, however, several features that distinguish this industry and that may combine to make self-regulation more effective.

(1) The enormous power of advertising to shape societal goals, individual life styles, political views, and consumption patterns, makes the industry vulnerable to criticism. Hence the fear of increased government regulation provides an incentive to self-control.
(2) The Advertising Association has promulgated a code of advertising behaviour[2] and issues supplementary directives from time to time. This code is not merely a recital of platitudes. It is fairly specific in its proscriptions.
(3) The Advertising Standards Authority (which works in conjunction with the Advertising Association) meets regularly and has a staff devoted exclusively to supervising compliance with the code.
(4) There is an effective sanction in that through the co-operation of the media, the Advertising Standards Authority can foreclose the use of the media to advertisers who fail to comply with the code.
(5) This sanction is available against non-members as well as members of the Association.

Even with these advantages, however, self-regulation in the advertising industry has not been an unmitigated success. The system has been criticised over the years as lacking initiative, vitality and effective preventive

1. Per an adviser at a Citizens' Advice Bureau, 1969.
2. This is obtainable from the Advertising Standards Authority, 15 Ridgmount Street, London, WC1E 7AW.

and remedial action. Criticism came to a climax at the conference of the Advertising Association in 1974.[1] Following that conference, the Code of Advertising Practice was revised, the budget of the Advertising Standards Authority was greatly increased, and new staff were hired in a renewed effort to make self-regulation effective. Also a new publicity campaign was introduced by the Advertising Standards Authority to let the public know of its existence.

In spite of these efforts, subsequent pressures were needed for further revamping of the Advertising Standards Authority,[2] and it was still felt necessary at the 1976 conference to discuss whether the system of self-regulation is working. In reporting that conference, the marketing editor of the *Financial Times* commented that: '. . .There is obviously a danger that the industry will slip back into the complacency which marked the years up to 1974.'[3]

Trade associations often assist in the resolution of consumer complaints, and many of their activities may promote integrity in marketing. But for the reasons listed above, trade associations can never be a satisfactory or universal substitute for government action against fraud and other predatory practices.

In an attempt to bolster the role of industry self-regulation, the *Fair Trading Act*, 1973,[4] imposed a duty on the Director General of Fair Trading to encourage trade associations to prepare codes of practice for guidance in safeguarding and promoting the interests of consumers. By the end of 1976, eleven such codes had been issued.[5]

The response of industry to the legislative and administrative initiatives of government has not, however, been as enthusiastic, spontaneous, or broad-scale as might have been hoped. Thus the *Annual Report of the Director General of Fair Trading for 1975* contained a mixture of hope and despair.

> My aim is that, encouraged and persuaded by my Office, trade and industry should create for themselves the high standards which people in this country have a right to expect. . .My Office has, all too often, had to look outside this country for examples of a positive

1. See e.g. 'Attack on "inadequate" advertising reforms', *The Times* 4 May 1974.
2. See e.g. 'The Reformed A.S.A. : Calm policeman of advertising', *Financial Times*, 5 February 1976.
3. 'Rhetoric hides the realities', *Financial Times*, 22 July 1976.
4. S.124(3).
5. *Annual Report of the Director General of Fair Trading for 1976*, p.11.

> approach to consumers. Now, gradually, the balance is being redressed as more British firms are adopting marketing practices which benefit their companies and their customers.[1]

Another official of the Office wrote: 'The general reluctance of business in the UK to analyse the implications of the consumer movement and to take the initiative in starting a constructive dialogue is baffling and disappointing.'[2]

The codes of practice typically cover about 10-15 pages and are produced in bulk in pamphlet form. They are distributed to manufacturers and traders by the trade associations, and are available to the public through the advisory agencies.

An advantage claimed for codes of practice is that since they were drawn up by the industry, they should be more acceptable to the industry than government regulations. This is not seen simply for its convenience in saving public officials from embarrassing confrontations. The argument is that since members of the industry have been responsible for the promulgation of the code, they will also feel responsible for making it effective.

Unfortunately, the codes of practice are open to the same objections as other forms of industry self-regulation. They are codes drawn up by trade associations whose membership is all on one side of the marketplace. There is a process of consultation with the Office of Fair Trading, but there is some ambivalence about what the role of the Office in this process is intended to be.

If a code of practice is to be taken seriously as reflecting consumer as well as supplier interests, one would think that it ought to come into existence as a result of:

(1) a negotiating process between an organisation representing the trade and an organisation representing consumers; or
(2) a government decision by a department or tribunal responsible for making an impartial judgement; or
(3) a decision by a body that is, directly or indirectly, elected by the public.

The role of the Office of Fair Trading does not fit into any of those categories. The function that it undertakes is one of consultation and

1. Ibid., p.10.
2. 'Management and the Consumer Movement', J. Mitchell, (1976) 3 *Journal of General Management* 46,52.

negotiation. But the posture that it maintains is one of impartiality.[1]

Theoretically, the codes of practice could be of some significance in legal proceedings.[2] But in practice, they are rarely mentioned.[3]

Among the advisory agencies, there are different impressions of the value of the codes. Some advisers feel they are useless while others find them helpful in some cases. Among the latter, one view expressed was that:

> Where a trader subscribes to a code of practice, it gives us or the consumer, something to refer to which he recognises as applying to that situation. If we quote law to traders, they sometimes say 'We don't do that in our firm'.[4]

One objection to the codes is that in conferring rights upon consumers, they are sometimes weak and offer no more protection than the common law. Indeed, from a consumer point of view, they can be counter-productive in two ways.

(1) While a common law court might elect between strict liability or a duty of care, a code might limit the range of possible consumer arguments and maximise the evidentiary problems of the consumer by prescribing only a duty of care.[5]

(2) Although called 'codes', these documents are not exhaustive statements of traders' obligations. By specifying only some obligations, they may divert attention from others.

Another disadvantage of the codes is that in their combined effect, they create a multiplicity of remedial procedures that makes the job of the

1. 'I do not regard the Office as being exclusively either a champion of consumers or a defender of trade and industry. It is not, and should not be seen to be, the partisan voice of consumer interest. . .' *Annual Report of the Director General of Fair Trading for 1973-74,* p.13.

2. 'Fair Trading Codes of Practice : the Legal Implications', R.G. Lawson, (1977) 121 *Solicitors' Journal* 4.

3. County Court registrars interviewed in 1977 were asked whether the codes of practice are ever mentioned in consumer cases. The four replies were 'Never', 'Never', 'Rarely', 'Only in one case that I can remember'.

4. Interview at an advisory agency, 1977.

5. For example, Clause 4 of the *Code of Practice for Domestic Laundry and Cleaning Services,* in dealing with the loss or destruction of an article, or damage to an article, seems designed to exclude any possible cause of action alleging strict liability. Similarly, in dealing with the 'Overbooking of Hotels', the *Code of Conduct Between ABTA Tour Operators and Members of the Public* (drawn up by the Association of British Travel Agents), imposes only a duty of care. If the objective is to protect the public from overbooking, strict liability would surely be more effective.

advisory agencies more complicated.

While a code of practice is often seen as an alternative to government regulation, a code may be sometimes a prelude to regulation. A code of practice might serve to establish norms that are acceptable to most members of an industry. If the code is then ineffective because some members of the industry refuse to comply, it may be more difficult to forestall government regulation by the argument that industry should first have a chance to put its own house in order. The regulation of price signs outside petrol stations may be an example of this. An agreement between the Office of Fair Trading and the petroleum industry was announced in 1976.[1] But this was ineffective and was followed by government regulation in 1977.[2]

While codes of practice may be useful in some situations, it is doubtful whether they can ever be a major vehicle for consumer protection, and their overall impact might even be counter-productive.[3] In any event, they are not a broad-scale alternative to the other techniques of regulation mentioned below.

3. Civil Actions

Viewed individually, civil claims by consumers are a medium through which an aggrieved individual may seek redress. But in aggregate, they could be an influence on marketing behaviour. For the reasons explained in Chapter 9(1), however, civil actions by consumers are so few that their total influence on marketing behaviour must be negligible. Moreover very few consumers withhold payment for goods when they have a right to do so.[4] The same phenomena appear in other countries. For example, in Canada it has been observed that:

> Even for the rare consumer who may be aware of some element in his contract entitling him to legal redress, there are many difficulties in the way of its attainment. He must first muster the resolve to beard his creditor and this has not been characteristic of consumer-borrowers, whose dependence on credit and lending sources has increased so immensely in the last few decades. He may have to miss work getting advice (although in Halifax the Legal Aid Committee

1. *Annual Report of the Director General of Fair Trading for 1976*, p.14.
2. *The Petrol Prices (Display) Order 1977*, SI No. 1057.
3. For some interesting commentaries on codes of practice, see 'Voluntary Codes of Practice', S.E. Marsh (1977) *New Law Journal* 419; and 'CODES OF PRACTICE: Not Worth the Paper they are Written On', A.P. Allen (1977) 85 *Monthly Review* (of the Institute of Trading Standards Administration) 55.
4. See Chapter 7, p.171.

> holds consultations in the evening); he must certainly do so when his case goes to court.
>
> The reluctance of individuals to take such cases to court is notorious, and there are excellent reasons for it. The loss of time, the expense (which may be high in proportion to the amount involved, unless legal aid is available, and only those who cannot pay for legal services are eligible for it), the prospect of future difficulties in obtaining credit, the fear of notoriety and the uncertain prospects of success – for the forms of transaction are weighted in the creditor's favour – these circumstances weigh heavily on the private consumer. Consequently, in all the circumstances, it is not surprising that the courts are resorted to so seldom in these cases and, therefore, that the law has in some ways remained static for fifty years. For judges, when they have the opportunity will always seek to do justice, as some of the cases which have been mentioned clearly indicate, but the opportunities have been rare.[1]

Similarly in the United States it has been said that:

> . . .we erect a huge structure of protective laws around consumers who are not in an economic position to pay cash for their goods and services and are not sophisticated, but, to an extent, these laws give consumers rights that only people with economic resources and a good bit of sophistication can enforce.[2]

One problem with civil actions in consumer cases is that the law relating to the marketing of consumer goods evolved as part of the private law of contract. As standard form contracts came to be used by sellers and lenders, the courts treated these, like negotiated contracts, as almost conclusive evidence of the terms on which the parties were dealing. This approach is breaking down. To the extent that it still prevails, however, it ignores the realities of mass distribution. The terms on which a consumer buys (i.e. the terms on which he is induced to believe and commonly believes he is buying) are contained in the advertising, the catalogues, and the statements of salesmen; rarely if ever in the terms of a standard form contract. These forms are seldom read by consumers and sometimes not even read by the merchants using them. The courts and Parliament have

1. *Report of the Royal Commission on the Cost of Borrowing Money, Cost of Credit, and Related Matters*, 1965, Nova Scotia, p.357.

2. 'Translating Sympathy for Deceived Consumers into Effective Programs for Protection', (1966) 114 *University of Pennsylvania Law Review* 395, 409.

moved towards a recognition of these realities, but there is surely a need to go much further.

Apart from contractual or statutory rights, a ground on which a consumer might seek to recover damages from a seller, or on which he might seek rescission of a contract, is deceit. Both the survey data and enquiries at other sources indicate, however, that deceit is raised as an issue in only a tiny proportion of the cases in which it occurs. There are several explanations.

First, consumers do not always recognise false representations when they occur. If a consumer consults a solicitor, the advice is sometimes based on the face of the documents, and the consumer may not be cross-examined in depth to discover any false representations. Unless a consumer complains specifically of deceit, this cause of action or defence may not be unearthed. Even when a representation is recognised as false, this may still not be perceived as ground for any remedy. For example, in the classical encyclopedia case described in Chapter 5, page 103, it is the experience of the writer that people who want to avoid the contract seldom make a clear complaint that they have been deceived, although it emerges if they are questioned. If a consumer goes to one of the advisory agencies and mentions the false representations, a claim or a defence may still not be filed on that ground. There is sometimes a tendency to dwell on the possibility that the consumer might not be believed in his testimony about the representations rather than the possibility that they will not be denied, or that the denial will not be believed. Coupled with this, consumers are sometimes advised that a claim or defence could not be sustained, or would not be wise, unless there is an independent witness to the representations.

Secondly, to found an action or defence on deceit, the representation must relate to past or present facts. It must not be simply a promise, or a prediction of future events. With regard to representations by sellers, deceit is a false statement made knowing it to be untrue, or recklessly not caring whether it be false or true, for the purpose usually of inducing a sale. If the representation consists of a promise that is subsequently unfulfilled, or the prediction of an event that subsequently does not occur, the matter may be treated as a breach of contract if it is any wrong at all, but it is not a ground for rescission of a contract, or for exemplary damages, or for a criminal prosecution.

It is sometimes recognised that a promise or prediction may have implicit within it representations relating to existing facts. What is not generally recognised, however, is that this is commonly and perhaps usually the case. Consider the example of an ordinary repair warranty. A manufacturer or retailer warrants that he will repair an item free of charge if it breaks down within 12 months. If he has been issuing the same warranty for some time, it is surely implicit in that promise that he has some facility, arrangement or system for the repairs to be carried out, and that warranties of this type are being honoured. If the truth is that he has no such facilities, or that he is otherwise systematically dishonouring the warranties that he has issued, there is surely a false statement of existing fact. Again, suppose a salesman assures a potential customer that an item can be delivered within 3 weeks. Implicit in this is a subsidiary statement that the salesman has some knowledge or experience upon which to base such an assurance. If the truth is that, to the knowledge of the salesman, delivery takes about 3 months, and that it cannot be speeded up, he has made a false representation about existing conditions.

This distinction has, however, featured prominently in the failure of the legal system to deal effectively with fraud in marketing. The courts recognise that promises or predictions may have implicit within them representations of existing fact. But for the most part in practice, it seems to be only misrepresentations that are on the face of them statements of fact that are treated as deceit.

Another difficulty with deceit is that it may not avail a consumer who discovers the truth prior to consummation of the transaction. To succeed on an allegation of deceit, a consumer must show that he acted on the misrepresentation (usually by entering into the contract). A court may conclude against the consumer if it appears that although false representations were deliberately made, the truth became apparent prior to signing the contract form. This result may be satisfactory when the discovery of the truth and the signing of the form occur on separate occasions. But in the normal case, they occur on the same occasion. Should it be relevant that a consumer discovers the truth if there is no opportunity for reflection on the significance of that discovery? The classical encyclopedia case illustrates the point. The salesman misrepresents the purpose of calling at the home, misrepresents the reason for selecting the household, and misrepresents the nature and terms of the proposed transaction. Yet the falsity of all these statements may be apparent prior to the signing of the contract form. Surely it would be absurd to conclude that this discovery of the truth by a consumer should be enough to deny his remedy for deceit. The truth is only discovered while the consumer is still subject to the continuing patter of the sales pitch, and thereby denied an opportunity to reflect on the significance of what he has discovered.

The matter might be tested by asking why a salesman uses false representations if their falsity will be discovered prior to consummation of the transaction. They are used to soften the mooch, stage by stage, to induce a state of mind in which he will sign. If salesmen systematically make false representations notwithstanding that the truth will be discovered prior to consummation of a transaction, this surely is evidence in itself that the discovery of the truth will not cancel the effect upon the mind of the misrepresentations.

As a matter of law, the point does not seem to be concluded by decided cases. But it is suggested that discovery of the truth prior to consummation of a transaction ought not to defeat an allegation of deceit unless the truth was discovered in sufficient time prior to the transaction to permit reflection upon the significance of the discovery.[1]

Another discouragement of actions for deceit is the restrictions on the circumstances in which exemplary damages can be awarded.[2]

Where deceit consists of misrepresentations by a salesman, a further handicap is the difficulty of proving exactly what was said, particularly when the discussion was lengthy and the consumer's recollection is vague. In some cases, such as those involving motor vehicles, salesmen may not follow a set patter. But in other cases, particularly in doorstep selling, salesmen commonly follow a set routine with each household. In these cases, it may be possible to use the testimony of other customers to confirm the content of the sales pitch.[3] There is a risk, however, of a court treating the testimony of other customers as irrelevant, and therefore inadmissible as evidence of what was said to a particular customer. In an appropriate case, such as the classical encyclopedia case, this risk might be avoided by pleading a conspiracy to defraud, as well as deceit. This should make evidence clearly admissible of what the salesman said to other customers, and probably also evidence of what other salesmen of the same company said to other customers. A further advantage of pleading a conspiracy to defraud is that it should broaden the enquiry sufficiently to permit the training manuals of the salesmen and other instruction circulars from the company to its salesmen to be inspected on discovery, and if necessary to be adduced in evidence. If the company and the particular salesman are insolvent, the allegation of conspiracy might also be useful in establishing a cause of action against people of more substantial means.

Even when an action for deceit is clearly available, it is often not used to its fullest potential. One example is the practice of taking action only against the selling company, and not against individual officers or salesmen.

1. In prosecutions under the *Trade Descriptions Act*, a trader can be convicted of a false representation even if customers discover the truth prior to the consummation of any transaction. *North Western Gas Board v. Aspden, The Times*, 20th February 1970, p.17.

2. See in particular *Cassell v. Broome* [1972] 1 All ER 801.

3. For an example of a case in which evidence of this type was allowed, see *Beneficial Finance v. Kulig* (1970) 13 DLR (3d) 134.

A tragic case of this type came to the attention of the writer. The company was in the business of selling central heating, but apparently not in the business of supplying central heating. Two officers of the company (who were also the salesmen) obtained the signatures of householders on contract forms and took substantial deposits. But they did not in retrospect appear to have any facilities or arrangements for fulfilling the contractual obligations. Some consumers who had paid deposits sued the company and obtained judgments. These remained unsatisfied notwithstanding that the officers of the company still appeared to have substantial assets. It did not seem to have occurred to those advising the plaintiffs that the officers of the company should have been joined as defendants.

Enquiries at consumer advisory agencies, and even among some solicitors, revealed a tendency to assume that as long as a seller is incorporated those carrying on the business are immune from personal liability. This is generally so with regard to claims for breach of contract. But where an action is for deceit, every individual who has deliberately brought about the perpetration of the fraud, whether through a company or otherwise, is personally liable. Any vicarious liability of the company is additional. It does not displace the personal liability of each tortfeasor. In the case mentioned above, if the officers of the company had been sued and the truth of the facts alleged had been established, they would surely have been held liable for deceit in respect of their implicit representations that the company had some capacity or arrangement for the performance of the obligations being undertaken, and an intention to perform.

With regard to advertising, there is no civil cause of action simply for false advertising. The courts have long recognised the possibility of an action for damages by a consumer against an advertiser where messages in an advertisement are untrue, or where they create expectations that are not fulfilled. But success on such a claim is limited to situations that fit within a traditional cause of action.

With regard to sellers' advertising, the traditional legal approach is to treat the advertising as superseded by any written contract. The *Misrepresentation Act*, 1967, now permits an action for damages (as well as rescission) if such advertising contains a misrepresentation negligently made. But the requirement of negligence makes the decision-making process too complicated and expensive for this cause of action to be of general use for consumer grievances, and it is rarely invoked. Some jurisdictions are now facing the realities of mass distribution by providing that statements relating to the goods in a seller's advertising are express warranties.[1]

1. E.g. *Consumer Protection Act*, Revised Statutes of Manitoba, 1970, Cap. C.200, S.58(8).

The courts do not generally regard manufacturers' advertising as creating any rights for a consumer unless the advertising contains a clear promise that is broken[1] (when an action may lie for breach of contract), or contains untrue statements deliberately or recklessly made (when an action may lie for deceit). The *Misrepresentation Act* does not allow a consumer to recover damages against a manufacturer for negligent mis-statements unless the manufacturer sells direct to consumers. Except in direct selling cases, to succeed on a claim for damages in respect of false advertising by a manufacturer, a consumer must establish deceit, or a collateral warranty, or try to invoke (and perhaps expand) the nebulous cause of action at common law for negligent misrepresentation.

The statute with the broadest application and now dealing with misrepresentations in advertising or by salesmen is the *Trade Descriptions Act*, 1968. But it is a criminal statute. Violation of the Act is an offence, but it does not make any resulting contract void,[2] nor does it give rise to an action for damages.

The *Review of the Trade Descriptions Act 1968*, published in 1976, reported that: 'we see no grounds. . .for recommending that breach of the duty to comply with the provisions of the Trade Descriptions Act should automatically give rise to a civil action.'[3] The only reasons given for that conclusion were:

(a) violations of the Act would usually result in pecuniary loss rather than personal injury; and
(b) offences under the Act often do not give rise to any damage.

While these comments are no doubt true, it is difficult to see their relevance to the conclusion.

Although it does not *per se* create a civil cause of action, the *Trade Descriptions Act*, 1968, is relevant to civil claims in several ways. First, the enforcement of the Act has expanded the role of the Trading Standards Departments of local authorities, and this role has come to include the negotiation of consumer disputes with tradesmen, particularly in areas with no Consumer Advice Centre.

Secondly, evidence gathered in an investigation with a view to criminal proceedings might, in the event, be useful in a civil claim by the consumer. Section 28 provides:

1. As in *Carlill v. Carbolic Smoke Ball Co.* [1893] 1 QB 256.
2. S.35.
3. Cmnd 6628, para.251.

(5) If any person discloses to any person –
(a) . . . or
(b) any information obtained by him in pursuance of this Act; he shall be guilty of an offence unless the disclosure was made in or for the purpose of the performance by him or any other person of functions under this Act.

This has been construed to mean that it would be an offence for a Trading Standards Officer to disclose evidence obtained through investigations under the Act to an aggrieved party, or in civil proceedings.[1] But that interpretation of the section is not uniformly accepted, and in some Trading Standards Departments, the officers do sometimes appear as witnesses in civil proceedings to testify with regard to facts discovered in the course of an investigation.[2]

Thirdly, a consumer may invoke the combined effect of the *Trade Descriptions Act*, 1968, and the *Powers of Criminal Courts Act*, 1973, to seek a compensation order in a criminal court. Not only do these provisions offer an alternative forum, but they also provide an alternative body of substantive law. Where a trader is convicted of an offence under the *Trade Descriptions Act*, and an application is made for an order requiring the trader to compensate an aggrieved consumer, the issue is not whether the consumer would have a civil cause of action for damages. It is whether the consumer has suffered any personal injury, loss or damage resulting from the offence.

Compensation orders are not the usual result of convictions under the *Trade Descriptions Act*, but they are made in some cases. Sometimes, however, the magistrates refuse to consider a request for compensation, leaving that to a separate County Court action, even though the amount involved may be trivial compared with the trouble and expense of a separate proceeding.[3]

In respect of the period 30 November 1968 to 31 March 1975, the Office of Fair Trading was aware of 8,489 prosecutions under the *Trade Descriptions Act*, resulting in 7,477 convictions on one or more counts, with total fines being imposed of £567,036. In respect of the same period, the Office was aware of 517 cases in which compensation orders had been made, and the total compensation payable amounted to £39,901.[4]

1. *Review of the Trade Descriptions Act, 1968*, 1976, Cmnd 6628, paras.257-64.
2. Interviews at Trading Standards Departments, 1977.
3. See e.g. 'Holiday company fined over "sitting together" clause', *The Times*, 11 March 1975.
4. *Review of the Trade Descriptions Act, 1968*, A Consultative Document, 1975, Office of Fair Trading, App. II.

Although there is not yet a general cause of action for damages for losses sustained through false or misleading advertising, the law seems to be moving slowly in that direction. The evolution of doctrine through the judicial process is, however, impeded in the ways explained in Chapter 9(1). As a practical matter, it is rare for any consumer to sue for false advertising.[1]

In the United States, some courts have treated a manufacturer's advertising as a warranty of the matters stated and implied in the advertisement; and without seeking to overcome the lack of privity by any fictions, they have allowed a consumer to sue the manufacturer on a tort claim for damages for breach of warranty notwithstanding the absence of any contractual relationship.[2]

Canadian courts too are beginning to recognise the realities of mass distribution and to suggest that a manufacturer is liable to fulfil undertakings made to consumers in his advertising.

> It seems to me the time has arrived for an examination of our law upon the obligation of manufacturers and vendors of products to implement their undertakings given in the news media by nationwide advertising. By such means they stimulate reliance upon the safety and the quality of their products; and in order to stimulate sales offer a host of prizes. To allow a producer to evade the fair implication of his advertising is to permit him to reap a rich harvest of profit without obligation to the purchaser. . .By newspaper, radio and television every home has become the display window of the manufacturer, and the stand of every pitchman. By extraordinary skill the printed and spoken word together with the accompanying art form and drama have become an alluring and attractive means of representation of quality and confidence.[3]

It is suggested that all advertisers should be strictly liable for the truth of statements made or implied in their advertising, as well as for the performance of promises. Perhaps this could best be achieved by providing that every advertisement for goods or services is a warranty of the matters stated, to every purchaser and user of the product or service in respect of all sales occurring within a specified period (say six months) after the last publication of the advertisement. The remedy would be a claim for damages, but it would be defined as a tort claim so that the contractual

1. Interviews with County Court Registrars and office staffs, 1977.
2. See e.g. *Manheim v. Ford Motor Co.* (1967) 201 So. 2d. 440.
3. *Ranger v. Watts* [1970] 2 OR 225, 234, affirmed on appeal [1971] 3 OR 450.

doctrines of privity and consideration would not apply.

This general liability for truth in advertising would be more comprehensible than the present array of diverse causes of action, and more consonant with honesty in business. It is surely iniquitous that any manufacturer, or other advertiser, should be allowed to reap the benefit of false advertising and thrust onto others the costs. Moreover, if civil claims by consumers are ever to reach a sufficient volume to influence marketing behaviour, it is surely essential that an advertiser should be liable simply for being wrong or misleading. There is no good reason why liability should depend upon arguments about collateral contract, enquiries into fault, or proof of deceit. One distinction that would seem to make sense, however, is that where deceit is proved, exemplary damages should be recoverable.

With regard to false statements by salesmen, it is again difficult to see why success on a claim for damages should depend on establishing that the representation was a term of a contract, that it was fraudulent or that it was negligent. If a consumer relies on the *Misrepresentation Act,* 1967, in a claim against a seller, the burden is on the seller of proving 'that he had reasonable grounds to believe and did believe up to the time the contract was made that the facts represented were true'. But at the time when he must decide whether to sue, a consumer is unlikely to know the extent of the evidence that the seller has on this point. Hence the uncertainty of litigation may be as much a deterrent to a consumer as if the burden of proof on this issue lay upon himself. Wherever the burden of proof lies, it is unrealistic to expect a consumer to undertake the risks of litigation if a defence of reasonable care is available, and if the evidence on that issue is almost exclusively in the hands of the seller. Thus the failure of the legal system to give consumers a clear right of action simply upon proof of being induced to buy an item by false representations of a salesman adds to the probability that they are unlikely to sue even in situations in which a claim would succeed. The obvious need is for a clearly defined right based on facts that are obvious to both parties, not a right that arises only in circumstances about which the seller has the critical evidence.

Finally, if the law of marketing is to become realistic, it should no longer be regarded as part of the law of negotiated contracts. It is commonly through the allurements of advertising and the blandishments of salesmen that consumers are induced to buy, and it is out of accord with the realities (as well as sometimes an inducement to duplicity) if courts attach crucial significance to a standard form contract, seldom if ever read by the consumer buyer, and not always read by the seller. As one Canadian study found: '. . .all the purchasers seem to have accepted the word of the salesman, even when it was flatly contradicted by the words of the document they signed.'[1]

Where the terms offered by a seller in advertising or in the statements of salesmen, and the terms of his standard forms are inconsistent, one would expect ordinarily that in the selling process the emphasis would be upon the terms most advantageous to buyers. It would be fair, therefore, that these should be the terms by which a seller should be bound. It is suggested that where there is any inconsistency between the terms of a seller's advertising or the statements of his salesmen, and the terms of a standard form contract, the buyer should be entitled to elect which to treat as the terms of the transaction.

To make this effective, it should also be an offence to include in any form used in consumer transactions any clause purporting to exclude liability for any statements made in advertising or by salesmen.

Another possible development would be to allow a class action to be brought on behalf of all consumers who have substantially the same type of grievance against the same manufacturer or distributor. This subject has been discussed extensively in North America and an example of that discussion is reproduced below in Appendix G.

Another possibility, adopted in other jurisdictions, is to enact that a government agency may sue on behalf of an aggrieved consumer.[2] While this may occasionally be useful, it can have the disadvantage of diverting the resources of government from preventive to remedial action.

In summary, civil actions are not sufficiently frequent or sufficiently available to make them a significant influence in the integrity of marketing behaviour. Suggestions have been made, however, through which they could become more significant.

4. Criminal Sanctions

A. The Difficulties with Criminal Proceedings

Prosecutions for offences committed in the course of retail trade are usually brought, if at all, by the Trading Standards Departments of local authorities. Before discussing their role, it may be helpful to comment on the operation of criminal law generally in relation to trade offences, including the role of the police. This is of interest for the following reasons:

1. *Report of the Minister's Committee on Franchising,* 1971, Ontario, p.12.
2. See e.g., *Trade Practices Act,* 1974, Statutes of British Columbia, Ch.96, S.24.

(1) It provides an historical and comparative perspective from which to see the role of Trading Standards Departments.

(2) The authority of Trading Standards Departments is defined by reference to statutory titles rather than business functions. They are responsible for enforcing particular statutes rather than being responsible for law enforcement in respect of defined categories of behaviour. Thus if an offence is not under a statutory provision that has been assigned to the Trading Standards Departments for enforcement, any prosecution may still be a matter for the police, even when the offence is committed in the course of trade. Examples are:

- (a) obtaining money by deception (S.15 of the *Theft Act*, 1968);
- (b) using harassing methods of collection (S.40 of the *Administration of Justice Act*, 1970);
- (c) selling a motor vehicle in an unroadworthy condition (S.60 of the *Road Traffic Act*, 1972).[1]

(3) People may go to the police with complaints about false trade descriptions or other offences in the course of trade, particularly in towns where there is no office of a Trading Standards Department. How the police characterise the problem may, therefore, influence the direction that a complaint then takes.

(4) The position of criminal law generally and the role of the police may be crucial in other jurisdictions where there may be no equivalent of the Trading Standards Departments.

Law enforcement is obviously easier when aimed at conduct recognised throughout the community as criminal. For example, complaints to the police of violence are treated seriously, and the police often receive public support in the apprehension and prosecution of offenders. But there is a different attitude to crime committed in the course of business. Indeed there is a reluctance to recognise and prosecute white-collar crime at all.

During 1971, for example, there were 104,424 cases reported to the police of consumers taking out of shops goods for which they had not paid (i.e. shoplifting).[2] There were no comparable statistics of consumer complaints to the police about goods and services that people had paid for but never received. Any failure of a business to supply goods that have been paid for, or any other default of a trader, is generally classified by the police as a civil matter. For example, in one case on the survey, the buyer

1. Some Trading Standards Departments prosecute under this section, but others, and probably the majority, do not. They do, however, prosecute under the provisions of the *Road Traffic Act* relating to overloading.

2. *Report of H.M. Chief Inspector of Constabulary for 1971*, p.36. The figure appears to relate to England and Wales except for the Metropolitan Police.

of a used car paid the dealer, but apparently the car was never delivered. The buyer told the interviewer that he complained to the police, but they refused to act, saying that it was a civil matter. There was apparently no enquiry to determine whether the dealer ever had a title to the car, or whether he was in the habit of taking money for cars that he never delivered. Indeed, the general practice seems to be that such complaints are not even recorded.

Enquiries among the advisory agencies about fraudulent practices also revealed several instances of complaints made to the police, but none in which they had taken any action. For example, in one case, the buyer alleged that he bought a television as new, subsequently discovering that it was a reconditioned set in a new cabinet. Again, the police were reported to have said that it was a civil matter. There was apparently no enquiry to discover whether the facts might amount to an offence under Section 15 of the *Theft Act*, 1968.

With regard to official reports, *The Report of the Commissioner of Police for the Metropolis for the year 1969*, for example, includes a description of police action in respect of frauds perpetrated by consumers against retailers.[1] But the report contains no similar description of police action in respect of frauds perpetrated by retailers against consumers.

The Office of Fair Trading recognises that some deceptive business practices, such as false bargain offers, can be an offence under Section 15 of the *Theft Act*, 1968. But that recognition does not lead the Office to expect prosecutions under that section.[2]

When the *Trade Descriptions Act* was passed in 1968 and the weights and measures inspectorate began prosecuting for false representations by retailers, they were breaking new ground and expanding on what used to be the prosecutions under the *Merchandise Marks Acts*. But they were not taking over from the police any case-load of prosecutions for obtaining (or attempting to obtain) money by false pretences.

In the course of this research, isolated instances were found of the police prosecuting in some cases where a business was systematically receiving payment for goods or services that were never supplied,[3] but other instances were found of no action being taken even in response to this type of complaint. Moreover, it is rare for the police to treat a

1. Cmnd 4355, p. 48.
2. *Bargain Offer Claims*, A Consultative Document, 1975, Office of Fair Trading, p.3.
3. For example, according to a news report, a firm of financial consultants acting as mortgage brokers received fees from the public over a period of 6 months, but never arranged a single mortgage. The prosecution was for conspiracy to defraud. 'Court told of £21,000 swindle', *Liverpool Daily Post*, 27 January 1976.

consumer complaint as possibly involving a crime if the seller supplies something, albeit not what was ordered. Thus although occasional examples can be found of the police taking action in respect of frauds against consumers,[1] it is not part of their normal routine.

Prosecuting a merchant is, of course, generally more difficult than prosecuting a consumer and may involve more sensitive judgments. For example, distinctions may be required between exaggeration and puff on the one hand, and lies on the other. Distinctions may also be required between a failure to fulfil promises, and obtaining money by representations known to be untrue, or without any intention of fulfilling the obligations undertaken. Moreover, an unfounded allegation of crime against a businessman might cause more harm than a similar allegation against some other types of people, and businessmen commonly have the status within the community and the self-confidence to make complaints against the police.

The potential volume of consumer complaints against business may be another fear. The police might be apprehensive that if they were to treat every such complaint that could involve a crime as ground for an investigation to determine whether a crime was committed, they would be overwhelmed by the workload. Except for the limited and specialised role of fraud squads, a policeman's usual rule of thumb for distinguishing between crime and a civil matter seems to be that it's not crime if it's business.

Another influence may be that much of criminal law is directed to the protection of property, and this may encourage a perception of businessmen as victims of crime rather than perpetrators. It also establishes retailers as a section of the community with whom the police co-operate, and from whom they obtain co-operation. Thus a prosecution for business crime could arouse resentment among sections of the community with whom the police are accustomed to co-operation and popularity. Compared with these costs, and compared with other demands on their time, they may not see any achievement that would make the endeavour worthwhile.

There may also be a feeling that honesty is never 100 per cent and that to some extent 'everybody is on the fiddle'. Corporate executives and civil servants might be perceived as padding their expense accounts, grocers as putting a margin of rotten apples in with the good ones, office employees as using company stamps on their personal letters, and dustmen (garbage collectors) as taking their perks out of the collections. On this view of the

1. One such case is *Levene v. Pearcey* [1976] *Criminal Law Review* 63. That case involved a London taxi driver deceiving a patron. The Metropolitan Police have, however, traditionally exercised a supervisory role in relation to London taxis, and that may help to explain why the complaint in that case resulted in a prosecution.

world, it may seem an over-reaction to prosecute someone whose conduct was no worse than a marginal error of judgment about the acceptable level of dishonesty, the more so if he was acting under competitive pressure.

To some extent, however, the differences in police behaviour towards traders and consumers may be part of a broader phenomenon involving a different police response to institutional compared with individual behaviour. There is a tendency to assume that established institutions, including business enterprises, are law-abiding while crimes are committed either by individuals, or by organisations that have no other apparent purpose.

Related to this is the view that criminal proceedings involve a symbolic rejection of an individual by society, and some people are easier to reject than others. Thus police response to behaviour may be influenced by the socio-economic status of the actor. To some extent this is apparent. For example, if a person of no regular employment or place of abode obtains goods from a trader by drawing a cheque on a bank at which he has no account, the police will almost certainly recognise the complaint as relating to crime, and the offender may go to gaol. But an established merchant who obtains money from a consumer by falsely promising to supply goods that he does not have, and which he knows are unobtainable, runs only a negligible risk of a police response.

Another perception of the problem is that when people (including policemen) are in situations of conflict, there is a tendency to act at the equilibrium established by countervailing pressures. The pressures may be of two kinds.

(1) Pressure on the individual to behave in the manner of the group. Only someone with a strong personality and self-confidence is likely to deviate openly and deliberately from what is regarded as normal conduct for people in his position. With regard to the prosecution of business crime, this influence may be reinforced by the need for equity in enforcement. It would be unfair if one trader is prosecuted for conduct that is permitted to a rival. To the extent that enforcement officials are conscious of this, it could create a tendency for enforcement action to settle at the lowest common level.

(2) Pressures operating on the group as a whole. These might consist, for example, of:

(a) pressure from the general community to detect and prosecute crimes of violence;

(b) pressure from people with property to detect and prosecute offences relating to property;

(c) influences, often subconscious, from the more powerful sections of the community against prosecuting white-collar crime.

A problem with consumer protection, whether through regulatory legislation or the use of ordinary criminal law, is that the influences of organised groups are commonly against enforcement.

Moreover, in consumer protection, there is no consistent countervailing pressure from public alarm. In news reporting, alarm about trade offences is stimulated only episodically. Newspapers can, for example, easily report crimes of violence with a sense of urgency and excitement. Reports of trade offences, by contrast, require special journalism if they are not to be dull reading. Moreover, local newspapers may hesitate to report, or to report prominently, what is embarrassing to advertisers. Even when a particular firm is not an advertiser in the paper, peer group sensitivities may still discourage any emphasis of dishonesty in a business enterprise. Crimes of violence often make the front pages of newspapers. But adulterated food, short weight, or false representations on the sale of used cars, are more likely to rank a mention in the middle pages, if reported at all.

The risk of a libel action can be another restraining influence on the reporting of business crime. If a consumer is complaining of adulterated food or fraudulent advertising by a local shop, a report of the event would be of no interest to readers unless the shop is named. Yet it would be folly for a newspaper to do that until at least a summons has been issued. By contrast, a malicious wounding or a murder may be newsworthy in a local newspaper even if the assailant is unknown. Thus to the extent that news reports stimulate an expectation of action by the police or other law enforcement officials, crimes of violence are more provocative than business crimes.

Another factor sometimes thought to influence the level of enforcement with regard to trade offences is that the prosecuting responsibility generally lies with men, while the bulk of consumer buying is done by women. In the discussion of sex discrimination, it is sometimes alleged that the police or other law enforcement officials treat complaints by women less seriously than complaints by men. There is no systematic research known to the writer, and relevant in the context of consumer protection, either supporting or disproving that hypothesis.

B. The Trade Descriptions Act

An attempt to deal with some of these problems was made in the *Trade Descriptions Act*, 1968. The Act contains offences relating to false representations in the course of trade, and the local weights and measures authorities are responsible for enforcement. Even prior to 1968, the responsibilities of the Weights and Measures Departments (Trading Standards Departments) of local authorities had expanded well beyond the enforcement of the *Weights and Measures Act*, 1963. Thus they (or at least some of them) were responsible for the enforcement of, for example, the *Petroleum (Consolidation) Act*, 1928, the *Food and Drugs Act*, 1955, the *Consumer Protection Act*, 1961, and the *Pharmacy and Poisons Act*, 1933. With the enactment of the *Trade Descriptions Act*, these authorities came close to having a general responsibility for the prosecution of offences committed in the course of trade. But as explained above, they have not taken over from the police a total responsibility for the prosecution of business offences.

In respect of the period 30 November 1968, when the *Trade Descriptions Act* came into force, to 31 March 1975, the Office of Fair Trading has recorded 8,489 prosecutions resulting in the conviction of 7,477 defendants on one or more counts.[1] Total convictions under the Act are, however, still only about 1,350 a year.[2]

The prosecuting activity of the Trading Standards Departments is, however, uneven. Some areas have a vigorous programme of prosecutions. Many, and perhaps most, Trading Standards Officers are dedicated people concerned to make the legislation effective.[3] But in some other areas, the number of prosecutions per year can be counted on the fingers of one hand, and as one observer has commented: 'some of their departmental colleagues seem to prefer the security to be found in an unquestioning commitment to the proven and familiar, being content to parry all but the truly inescapable call to act with a practised evasiveness.'[4]

Although the low level of prosecutions for trade offences is a recognised phenomenon, there is no unanimity about the appropriate government response. One view is that prohibiting an objectionable practice may be useful even if the criminal sanctions prescribed are not seriously enforced. The objectionable practices will not be eliminated, but any extension of them might be discouraged.

Another view is that prohibitions in consumer protection legislation with no thorough machinery for their enforcement are highly objectionable. It can be seen as a fraud on the public to enact a level of protection

1. *Review of the Trade Descriptions Act 1968*, A Consultative Document, 1975, Office of Fair Trading, App. II.

2. Figures obtained from the Office of Fair Trading in respect of the years 1975 and 1976.

3. Of the six Trading Standards Officers interviewed by the writer in 1977, four appeared to be of this type.

4. 'CONSUMER ADVICE CENTRES – More on Liaison with Trading Standards Officers', G.H. Bishop, (1977) 85 *Monthly Review* (of the Institute of Trading Standards Administration) 57.

with no realistic machinery for its achievement. It can also create inequities among businesses. If compliance involves effort or expense, or a restraint upon business opportunities, a law-abiding businessman who complies may be at a competitive disadvantage. A pressure may thus be created for non-compliance to become widespread. Not only may consumers and honest traders suffer, but there is also a cost in terms of respect for law.

> If a law is to be effective then it must be properly enforced. The correct way to deal with unjust or archaic laws is to amend or repeal them. To adopt a passive administrative policy of non-enforcement not only weakens the moral force of legislation but is unfair to those who observe the law and suffer the prescribed restrictions on their business activities.[1]

The corollary is that prohibitions should never be enacted simply in response to a judgment that certain practices are undesirable. The critical question is whether the harm suffered by tolerating the practices exceeds the total cost of enforcing the prohibitions. This involves an appraisal of the nature and extent of the harm, of the possible techniques of prohibition and enforcement, of the methods likely to be adopted to evade the prohibitions, and of the techniques necessary to prevent the evasion.

If the *Trade Descriptions Act* is to be effective, the Trading Standards Departments must have the budget and other resources necessary to enforce that Act, and to carry out their other responsibilities in a systematic way. They also need moral leadership at the political levels of government, and the support of adjudicative and reform processes aimed at the Act being interpreted and revised to achieve its policy objectives. Unless they receive this supporting structure, there is an obvious risk that they will become discouraged and lose their sense of purpose to a point where their effectiveness will be undermined.

The consumer movement of the 1960s was, of course, seeking a structure for remedial as well as preventive action. Thus it was necessary to consider how far Trading Standards Departments should be responsible for advice and the negotiation of disputed claims, as well as the prosecution of offences. To deal with that question, many local authorities opened the Consumer Advice Centres (CACs) mentioned above.[2] In those areas, the CACs were intended to deal primarily with advice and the negotiation of disputed claims, while the Trading Standards Officers would deal primarily

1. 'The Legal Regulation of Lending' R.M. Goode, in *Instalment Credit*, ed. A.L. Diamond, 1970, Stevens, London, p.57.
2. Chapter 9, p.239.

with inspections, the investigation of possible offences, and prosecutions. Some overlap and interaction among these functions was, however, inevitable, and became more so when the criminal courts were authorised to award compensation to anyone who had suffered harm as the result of an offence.[1]

Whether Trading Standards Departments should undertake both prosecuting and negotiating roles is a debatable issue, particularly in areas where there is no CAC. On the one hand, it has been argued that having prosecutions and the negotiation of claims handled by the same personnel, or at least within the same department, facilitates a cross-flow of information.

> . . .there is no doubt that when law enforcement and advisory services are administered (not necessarily operated) conjointly that one service compliments *(sic)* the other in providing knowledge of trade practices and customer habits. Requests for consumer advice do from time to time reveal infringements of the law, sometimes trivial, occasionally serious, which enables the Department to improve the degree of protection offered to the public. It is, of course, not always deemed appropriate to supply the ultimate legal sanction in such cases. A warning to a trader, coupled with suitable advice, may often achieve the desired result, and traders are frequently grateful that such guidance is available.[2]

Other arguments in support of this view are that:

> . . .the efficient internal transfer of complaints permitted by the combination assists complainants. Neither the complainant nor referring agencies, e.g. Citizens' Advice Bureaux, police, are sufficiently informed to differentiate accurately. If the services were completely separate complainants who happen to approach the inappropriate service first, would have to go to another office and repeat their story.[3]

And that:

> Weights and Measures Offices are dealing with an evergrowing

1. A broad provision for this was enacted in the *Criminal Justice Act*, 1972, and is now contained in the *Powers of Criminal Courts Act*, 1973.
2. *Annual Report of the Trading Standards Department, County Borough of Grimsby*, 1972, p.17.
3. 'The Problems Involved in Combining a Consumer Advisory Service with that of a Law Enforcement Service,' G.W. Bishop, (1972) 80 *Monthly Review* (of the Institute of Trading Standards Administration), p.311, 315.

> number of complaints arising from the Trade Descriptions Act and it is natural that the consumer should turn to them whenever there is cause for complaint. The members of the public do not differentiate between civil and criminal matters and, from their point of view, it is most unsatisfactory to be denied help on the ground that no offence is disclosed. Civil breaches of contract can involve considerable sums of money and be very frustrating. The ordinary consumer does not understand the difference between criminal and civil matters and, if he is denied help, the standing of the Weights and Measures Service is accordingly lowered in his estimation.[1]

Another argument for blending the services is that the designation of a case as one for law enforcement or as requiring the negotiation of a claim may not be obvious until enquiries have been made.

> For instance, some actions by traders which are [Consumer Advisory Service] matters can become [Law Enforcement Service] matters if they have been, or are, persisted in. Suppose that a trader carefully makes a statement as to a service that is later shown to be false. For example, he may advertise in a paper "all makes of shavers repaired". A complaint is received that he has carried out an unsatisfactory repair to a shaver apparently because the spares for that particular make are no longer obtainable. Enquiries by a LEO establish that the false statement was not made either knowingly or recklessly. There would seem to be no offence under the Trade Descriptions Act, 1968. Should the trader, however, repeat the advertisement without amendment he would appear to be acting knowingly and may commit a Trade Descriptions Act offence.[2]

On the other hand, there are several objections to prosecuting and negotiating roles being played by the same officials. The first is the traditional fear of any structure that might result in the threat of criminal proceedings being used to coerce the payment of a civil claim. Any threat of a prosecution in the negotiating process could be a form of coercion to pay by a technique that denies the opportunity for adjudication on the validity of the claim. Of course a trader could defend any criminal

1. 'Considerations Regarding the Setting up of a Consumer Advisory Service', E. Childs, 1972, unpublished working paper, Institute of Trading Standards Administration.

2. 'The Problems Involved in Combining a Consumer Advisory Service with that of a Law Enforcement Service', G.W. Bishop, (1972) 80 *Monthly Review* (of the Institute of Trading Standards Administration), p.311, 315.

proceedings, and possibly be acquitted; but the threat of a trial in a criminal court can be a form of pressure to pay regardless of the risk of conviction.

The Departments are, however, sensitive to this issue. The traditions of the service derive from years of prosecutions under weights and measures legislation, and all six Trading Standards Officers interviewed by the writer in 1977 were well aware of the proprieties connected with prosecutions. The potential problem is recognised and the prevailing view within the service seems to be that it can be met by appropriate behaviour without requiring a complete structural separation of functions. As the controller of one Trading Standards Department put it in an interview: 'It's a question of how you handle people as to whether they think they are being blackmailed.'

It is not difficult, however, to think of situations where a problem could arise. Suppose, for example, a trader refuses to settle a claim that has been presented to him through a Trading Standards Officer. Shortly thereafter, the officer, or another officer from the same Department, discovers an offence committed by that trader. It may be the duty of the officer to prosecute. But if he does, there might surely be a risk that he will be accused of retaliating.

Possibly the real risk is not that Trading Standards Officers will use the power of prosecution to coerce the payment of civil claims, but rather that they may bend over too far backwards to avoid any such suspicion.

Blending the roles of prosecution and the negotiation of claims could also have a downward influence on the vigour with which claims are pursued. The law enforcement function requires a Trading Standards Department to be impartial between consumer and trader. But what an aggrieved consumer needs is someone to negotiate on his behalf, and where that fails, to pursue the claim on his behalf. Impartiality is not the stance that is most helpful to a consumer in the pursuit of a claim unless it is taken by someone with a power of adjudication.

Another downward influence that a blended system might have on consumer claims is that the training and experience of Trading Standards Officers lie primarily in the enforcement of criminal statutes. Hence they may be less familiar with the law relating to civil obligations, and the lower standard of proof required in civil courts. This might, perhaps, explain the complaint that: 'We find the Trading Standards Department very unwilling to take on any sort of case which is controversial in nature, or about which they are doubtful of success.'[1]

Apart from any risk of the prosecuting function having an adverse

1. Letter to the writer from a Neighbourhood Law Centre, 1977.

influence on the negotiation of claims, there is also a risk that the negotiation of settlements may have a perverse influence on prosecutions.

> The making of restitution by the trader does sometimes occur during the course of inquiries by a [Law Enforcement Officer] into an alleged offence. LEO's are used to this and most will endeavour to to exclude it from their minds when deciding what action is called for. It has been known, however, for such an offer to be made through the enquiring LEO with the explicit condition attached that it would be dependent on the LEO not taking proceedings. It may be difficult for the [Consumer Advisory Service]-minded LEO to treat such an offer with the contempt many officers would feel it deserves. One of his objectives as a CAO is to minimise the loss to the complainant. He may be tempted to accede to just such a calculated proposal on the basis that at least the outcome will then be one he is used to viewing as satisfactory.[1]

Related to this,

> . . .the CAO frequently relies on traders for information of trade practices and for informed opinions in [Consumer Advisory Service] matters. In many instances he will find it helpful in assessing the merit of complaints to have the benefit of the specialist knowledge and the experience of local traders. Obviously he will obtain this assistance in a discreet way. Normally the traders are pleased to be able to help and seem to expect nothing in return. Should the LEO, however, subsequently encounter apparent offences committed by the helpful traders he may well find it difficult to dismiss from his mind their kind co-operation.[2]

Perhaps the most serious objection to blending the prosecuting and negotiating roles is that it may have an eroding effect on prosecuting activity. Prosecutions can involve meticulous preparation, conflicts of evidence, arguments in court, unpleasantness, and sometimes hostility. The action of the enforcement officer is exposed to public scrutiny and possible criticism. The sympathy of the court for the prosecution's position is not assured, and following a conviction, the penalty is sometimes so slight

1. 'The Problems Involved in Combining a Consumer Advisory Service with that of a Law Enforcement Service', G.W. Bishop, (1972) 80 *Monthly Review* (of the Institute of Trading Standards Administration) p.311, 313.

2. Ibid., p.315.

that the effort may hardly seem worthwhile. In these circumstances, and bearing in mind the general influences against prosecutions for business offences, any official confronted with a choice between prosecution or negotiation may be tempted to see the negotiation of individual claims as the easier route, particularly if he has a heavy case-load. If that happens, predatory practices may be met by settlement of the claims of those who complain rather than by steps to deter the practices.

Again, a prosecution in one case might engender hostility that could endanger the settlement of other claims. Because negotiations are more numerous than prosecutions, and because they involve a present clientele waiting for claims to be settled, a recognition of this danger may have a downward influence on prosecutions rather than on settlements.

A blended system can also result in undue significance being attached by traders to the decisions of a Department on whether to prosecute. 'If we decide not to prosecute, a merchant sometimes uses that as ground for rejecting a civil claim. After a conviction, they usually settle a civil claim.'[1]

A sceptic might also see a blended system as putting a Trading Standards Department in a situation involving a conflict of interest and duty. It is surely in the public interest to minimise the occurrence of trade offences by the deterrent of prosecutions. But offences that have been prevented by deterrence are not a visible achievement. Successful deterrence cannot usually be demonstated by statistics, or even by examples of grateful clients. There are no accolades for frauds prevented.

Conversely, recovering money for a consumer who complains is an obvious achievement, and the officer has the satisfaction of helping a known person. Moreover, negotiation and conciliation can maximise the popularity of a Trading Standards Department. Retailers may be happier because they can settle individual claims without exposure to the adverse publicity of a prosecution. Even a retailer of no integrity or respect for law may be content if he can respond to complaints by settling the claims of hardy individuals who persist to the Trading Standards Department, but is not required to change his general practice. Consumers who complain may be happy when their complaints are satisfied. Parkinson's Law[2] may also be relevant in this situation. The chief of a Trading Standards Department who reduces predatory practices within his area by a vigorous programme of prosecutions may not see the same expansion in the work and staff of his department as one who takes little preventive action and who puts the emphasis on negotiating settlements and recovering payments.

1. Interview with a Senior Trading Standards Officer, 1977.
2. 'Parkinson's Law or the Rising Pyramid', Chapter 1 of *Parkinson's Law*, C.N. Parkinson, 1957.

There are, however, some countervailing influences that tend to keep up the number of prosecutions. The Trading Standards Departments hail from a long tradition of enforcing weights and measures legislation. The officers are trained specialists with a proud tradition of competence and integrity, operating a service that has its own literature, association, and examinations. The goal has been to protect the public from dishonesty in trade by a programme of prevention and deterrence that includes notifying traders of legal requirements, checking for compliance, and prosecuting offences. 'Detect and prosecute' has often featured as an operational motto, though it has never been the only role of the service. Negotiating settlements for aggrieved consumers is more recent, and to some officers a more compromising role.

In North America, the annual reports of consumer protection bureaux often show the amount of compensation recovered for aggrieved consumers as an indicator of their success.[1] Moreover, publicity relating to the amount of compensation recovered is sometimes used for political credit. For example, the first sentence of the news release accompanying the Annual Report of the Department of Justice (Consumer Protection Division) of Iowa for 1976 begins: 'Final figures released by Attorney General Richard Turner show that the Consumer Protection Division of his Office saved more than One Million Dollars for Iowans in 1976.' This phenomenon does not, however, seem to have affected Britain, at least not so far. The annual reports of the Trading Standards Departments include a mention of the compensation recovered for aggrieved consumers, but the emphasis is still on the protection of the public through inspection and deterrence. Any increase in the amount of compensation recovered might be seen not as cause to applaud the success of negotiation, but rather as cause to lament the failure of prevention. Again, Trading Standards Departments, as prosecuting agencies, try to maintain an image of impartiality, and any advertising of the amounts recovered for aggrieved consumers as a benchmark of success might seem incompatible with that image.

With regard to crimes committed in the course of business, if prosecutions are to be sustained in the long run at a credible level for deterrence, it is the view of the writer that this can be done only by appointing officials whose job it is to detect offences, to prosecute when they find them, and who are not allowed to do anything except prosecute. In cases where it is more appropriate to negotiate claims or seek injunctive relief, this should be left to others. There must be a department, or section of a

1. See e.g. the *Annual Report of the Bureau of Consumer Frauds and Protection*, State of New York, 1976.

department, whose job it is to prosecute and nothing else.

Possibly the optimum structure is the one that has been adopted by many local authorities. Consumer Advice Centres are established separately from the Trading Standards Departments and at separate locations, but under the same top management. The division of personnel between the two offices can clarify whose role it is to negotiate disputed claims, and whose role it is to detect and prosecute. Having the same top management can make the information flow between the two offices more effective than if they were entirely separate.

The negotiation of claims and the limitations on staff resources could also create a tendency to prosecute only in hardcore cases where an offence is obvious, being content with the recovery of compensation in more marginal situations. If this happens, the result is to create a deterrent against hardcore and obvious offences but no deterrent against those less serious or more marginal. Indeed, in a study of tax offences in the United States:

> Some respondents reported that they began to cheat on their tax returns only *after* convictions for tax evasion had been obtained against others in their jurisdiction. They explained this surprising behaviour by noting that the prosecutions had always been conducted against blatant violators and not against the kind of moderate offenders which they then became.[1]

In the enforcement of the *Trade Descriptions Act*, however, at least some Trading Standards Officers have been testing the perimeters of the legislation.[2]

Another factor limiting the effectiveness of the *Trade Descriptions Act* is the extensive reliance on complaints. Some Trading Standards Departments will screen the small ad columns of local newspapers and follow up those that look suspicious. Some Trading Standards Officers will browse at advertisements in shop windows, make other types of inspections on premises and, in suspicious circumstances, have shoppers make spot purchases. Some officers make regular calls to exchange information at Citizens' Advice Bureaux and police stations, in addition to Consumer Advice Centres. Many and probably most Departments, however, do not function in that way. This is not because of any failure to

1. 'Two Studies of Legal Stigma', R.D. Schwatz and J.H. Skolnick, (1962) 10 *Social Problems* 133.

2. See e.g. *Wickens Motors v. Hall* [1972] 3 All ER 759, and *Beckett v. Cohen* [1972] 1 WLR 1593.

recognise the importance of these methods of surveillance, but because of the budgeting constraints and consequential limitations on resources that have occurred in recent years. As one Department put it, in explaining its role under the *Trade Descriptions Act:*

> The activities of the enforcement staff have been almost entirely concerned with the increasing number of complaints and the small number of original visits of inspections is shown in the Summary totals. When these figures are considered against an approximate number of 45,000 trading premises likely to be concerned with trade descriptions, it can be quickly appreciated how limited is the effect of the amount of departmental resources devoted to preventing offences occurring.[1]

Again,

> The number of inspection visits to trading premises are at a very low level and the net result of this is that in many areas the only consumers who are receiving adequate protection are those who complain to the department. The significant increase in prosecutions. . . despite this low level of activity, again shows the decline in standards of trading practices when effective enforcement is not carried out.
>
> . . . . . .
>
> . . .The variations which petrol retailers come up with seem endless and many of them are considered to be on the very borders of legality and some undoubtedly would be held to be contravening the Act if a prosecution were taken, but because of workloads in other areas only those which are the subject of a complaint are investigated.[2]

Some Departments have their officers check for violations of the *Trade Descriptions Act* at the same time as making inspections primarily for the purposes of the *Weights and Measures Act.* But in those circumstances, they may only have time to look for obvious violations. Some Departments proceed more systematically, for example by checking the odometer readings on motor vehicles displayed on dealers' forecourts, and then tracing the registrations. Some Departments rely almost exclusively on

1. *Annual Report of the Consumer Services Department of the Greater Manchester Council for the Year ended 31st March 1975,* p.8.

2. *Annual Report of the Consumer Services Department of the Greater Manchester Council for the Year ended 31st March 1976,* pp.10 and 11.

complaints for the initiation of investigations, though where no complaint has been made, an enquiry may be initiated if suspicious circumstances are brought to their attention.

Extensive reliance upon complaints is disquieting in several ways. One is the tendency for people to complain about the unexpected, or deviations from the normal. To the extent that this is an influence, it can result in the probability of a complaint about a predatory practice being inversely proportionate to its frequency. If a practice becomes well established, the result could be that people do not complain because they have grown accustomed to it, or because they assume from its regularity that it must be legal. If the authorities do not prosecute because there are no complaints, there is an obvious risk that some predatory practices will become legitimated by repeated use. Conversely, if people perceive as illegal the types of conduct for which prosecutions are brought, the prosecutions will influence the categories of complaints received. The result will be a tendency to more prosecutions for the same types of abuses, rather than a systematic programme spreading prosecutions over the full range of offences that are occurring.

For similar reasons, the level of complaints does not indicate a level of well-being. Preventive programmes and other influences on integrity in business will obviously influence the level of complaints. But this level can also go up or down according to public information programmes, changing patterns of consumer vigilance, changing expectations of remedial action, and any other changes in community expectations relating to trading standards.

There are also many types of false trade descriptions from which people are likely to suffer, but about which they are not likely to complain. One example is in the sale of men's clothing. If a consumer specifies a size, but that size is out of stock, some clothing shops will select the nearest size in stock, hope that the customer will not check the label himself, and tell him that it is the size requested. If he notices that it is not, an apology can be made for the 'mistake'. This is surely an objectionable practice that could probably be stopped fairly easily by spot checking and a few prosecutions. But it could go on for years without a complaint being made.

Another consequence of extensive reliance upon complaints is that enforcement action is more likely in respect of abuses perpetrated against those most prone to complain, i.e., people in middle and upper socio-economic groups.

People in lower socio-economic groups may complain by walking into a Consumer Advice Centre if one is immediately available in their shopping area. But they are surely less likely to communicate by letter or telephone to an office of a Trading Standards Department in a different town.

The response of the courts to prosecutions under the *Trade Descriptions Act* has been more vigorous than some might have feared, but on the whole is still not very enterprising. Average fines are about £202 for offences relating to the misdescription of motor vehicles, about £101 for the misdescription of other goods, about £85 for false price indications, and about £115 for false statements about services.[1] Fines of this order are not much for business enterprises. For any reputable business, however, the embarrassment of prosecution and conviction is probably more significant than the amount of the fine.

One weakness of the system is in dealing with business rogues for whom a criminal conviction will involve no loss of reputation, and probably no loss of business. An example is secondhand motor dealers who turn back the odometer readings, or who fail to check that the odometer readings are genuine. This practice appears to be widespread and out of control.[2] With regard to this problem, the Court of Appeal has used firm language.

> The Trade Descriptions Act 1968 was intended by Parliament to provide protection for the public against unscrupulous and irresponsible traders. Section 1(1)(a) deals with those who are proved to have been actively unscrupulous, as for example, by turning back mileometers; and section 1(1)(b) with those who do not take the trouble to check as best they can that mileometer readings are genuine. In this case the prosecution did not allege that the defendants had been actively unscrupulous; but they for their part did not seek to prove that they had taken all reasonable precautions and exercised all due diligence. In plain English they took a chance that the mileometer readings were genuine. Traders in secondhand motor cars should not take such chances; and if they do and are prosecuted to conviction the courts should discourage them by taking all the profit out of the transaction and a good deal more.[3]

But the complaint is still heard that the fines imposed by the courts are not high enough even to take the profit out of the transactions that are prosecuted.

> The fines are often inadequate. We have been prosecuting a case involving odometer readings on 40 cars. They can make an *extra*

1. Calculated from figures obtained from the Office of Fair Trading relating to 1976.
2. As one senior Trading Standards Officer put it in an interview in 1977, 'We could employ 5 officers full-time on odometer checks'.
3. *R. v. Hammertons Cars Ltd.* [1976] 1 WLR 1243.

> profit of £50 or £100 per car by turning the clock back [taking a middle figure of £75, that would amount to a total of £3,000]. But they were only fined a total of £1,500.[1]

Even if fines were imposed at the level prescribed in the Hammertons case, the courts would still be setting their sights far too low. Where a false trade description is applied not as an isolated event, but systematically as part of a business routine, the resulting fine, if it is to have any deterrent effect, should be enough to take all the profit out of that course of business, not simply the profit out of the particular transaction that led to the prosecution.

Another limiting factor is that upon summary conviction, the maximum fine under the *Trade Descriptions Act* is only £400. That maximum is imposed only in a minority of cases. But such a low maximum could well be a downward influence on the general level of fines.

Some Trading Standards Departments try to overcome this by proceeding on indictment in the Crown Court[2] where there is no maximum to the fine that can be imposed. But that is not a general practice.

Bearing in mind the traditional reluctance to impose significant sanctions for business crime, and the availability of appeals on sentence, the risk that fines will be too low is surely much greater than the risk that they will be too high. The maximum fine on summary conviction could well be raised to £10,000.

Another important weakness is the failure to use imprisonment. This sanction is often used for offences committed by consumers against retailers, but rarely for offences committed by retailers against consumers. For example, it appears that 71,935 defendants were convicted of shoplifting in England and Wales in 1976, and 2,685 were sent to gaol (3.733 per cent).[3] During the same year, it appears that about 1,328 defendants were convicted in Great Britain of offences under the *Trade Descriptions Act*,[4] and of these, only about 1 was sent to gaol (0.075 per

1. Interview with a Senior Trading Standards Officer, 1977.
2. E.g. the *Report of the Controller of the Trading Standards Department to the Fire Brigade and Public Control Committee*, Cheshire County Council, March 1977, para.7.3; and *Annual Report of the Consumer Services Department of the Greater Manchester Council for the Year ended 31st March 1975*, p.9.
3. *Criminal Statistics : England and Wales*, 1976, Cmnd 6909, pp.102 and 228.
4. Figures obtained from the Office of Fair Trading.

cent).[1]

A possible explanation for the minimal use of imprisonment is that offences committed in the course of trade are not seriously regarded as 'crime'. Yet surely one reason they are not regarded as 'crime' is because people committing those offences are not sent to prison.

It is not suggested that imprisonment should be the normal sanction for offences under the *Trade Descriptions Act.* But there are many cases in which, although the offence may be one of strict liability, there is ample evidence of actual intent to deceive. For example, there have been convictions for turning back the odometer readings on motor vehicles for the purpose of misrepresenting the mileages to potential buyers, and yet only fines or suspended sentences have been imposed. In other ways too, many convictions under the Act have involved outrageous frauds.

Another limiting factor is that Magistrates' Courts have no power to impose imprisonment for offences under the *Trade Descriptions Act.* The only provision for imprisonment is that where the prosecution proceeds in the Crown Court, there is power to impose up to two years.[2] Here again, offences committed by traders are treated differently from offences committed against traders. Magistrates' Courts can impose a sentence of imprisonment on summary conviction with regard to offences committed by consumers against traders (such as shoplifting). But Magistrates' Courts have no power to impose imprisonment under the *Trade Descriptions Act* no matter how appropriate that may be in a particular case. It is suggested that on summary conviction under the Act, Magistrates' Courts should be empowered to impose imprisonment up to six months.

With regard to the evolution of substantive law, the Act received a mixed reaction from the courts, as might be expected for any new consumer protection statute. From an enforcement point of view, some of the decisions have been unfortunate. As one Chief Trading Standards Officer put it '. . .a number of High Court cases have resulted in parts of the Act being virtually unenforceable'.[3] But in other cases, the language of the Divisional Court treats the Act seriously and shows a conscientious regard for enforcement. For example, in one case the odometer of a motor

1. So few defendants are sent to prison for offences under the *Trade Descriptions Act* that there are no annual statistics on the point. For the first few years of the Act, none at all were sent to prison, but it now appears that sentences of actual imprisonment are being imposed at the rate of about 1 per year. (*Review of the Trade Descriptions Act 1968*, A Consultative Document, 1975, Office of Fair Trading, App. II; 'Used-car Dealers gaoled for altering mileages', *The Times*, 3 August 1975; and interviews at the Office of Fair Trading and at Trading Standards Departments, 1977.)

2. S.18.

3. *Annual Report of the Chief Trading Standards Officer for the Year 1975-76*, Hertfordshire County Council p.4.

vehicle had been turned back by a person other than the seller. The defence raised was that this had occurred despite the taking of all reasonable precautions and the exercise of all due diligence by the seller. In delivering judgment Widgery C.J. stated:

> I would, however, in view of the prevalence of this particular kind of fraud, invite justices when examining the defence of the seller to such a charge as this to be meticulous in their consideration of all the courses which the seller might have adopted. This is a matter in which justices, if they are to fulfil their duty to the public, should be very quick and alert to consider whether there are further proper precautions which might have been taken and to consider whether those precautions in the circumstances of their case are reasonable. It is an alert consciousness of their duty in this respect which, in my judgment, is the best safeguard for the future against the continued repetition of these offences.[1]

The career of the Act in the House of Lords has, however, been less fortunate. In the leading case of *Tesco Supermarkets v. Nattrass,*[2] a supermarket was alleged to be charging more for an item than the price at which that item was being advertised, contrary to Section 11(2) of the *Trade Descriptions Act*, 1968. The defence was that the contravention was due to the act or default of the local manager, and that the company had used all due diligence to secure compliance with the Act. In the Magistrates' Court, the company was convicted and fined £25. On appeal to the Divisional Court, the conviction was sustained. The House of Lords, however, allowed the appeal, deciding in effect that the company was not responsible for the acts of its local manager.

It is interesting to compare that case with another decided by the House of Lords only the following year. In *Heatons Transport v. Transport and General Workers' Union,*[3] employers sought and obtained an injunction against a union for 'blacking' their lorries. Local shop stewards did not comply with the injunction, and in the National Industrial Relations Court the union was fined sums of £5,000 and £50,000. The Court of Appeal allowed an appeal by the union, but the House of Lords restored the original decision, saying in effect that the union was responsible for acts of its shop stewards.

The *Tesco* decision created a predictable handicap in the enforcement

1. *Naish v. Gore* [1971] 3 All ER 737, 742.
2. [1971] 2 All ER 127.
3. [1972] 3 All ER 101.

of the Act. Where an offending retail outlet is operated by a small merchant, a Trading Standards Department can proceed by detection and prosecution. But where an offending retail outlet is part of a chain, or otherwise part of a large corporate enterprise, a Trading Standards Department must either investigate the corporate structure to decide who to prosecute, or prosecute the company first to discover who the real defendant ought to be. The result was bound to be a curtailment of prosecutions against chain stores and other large companies.

> . . .the present situation is clearly unsatisfactory with enforcement authorities unwilling to prosecute employees because they feel that offences stem from the system these employees are asked to operate, and unwilling to prosecute the employer because they feel that in the light of the *Tesco* Judgment the trader might successfully plead the statutory defence. It is also unfair to individual traders if the effect of the law is to allow *mens rea* to apply to corporate traders in an area where the law creates absolute offences.[1]

In the review of the Act conducted in 1975-76 by the Office of Fair Trading, the possibility of imposing strict liability upon corporations for the acts of their employees was considered, but not recommended. The authors of the report were persuaded by a passage of the late Lord Reid in *Tesco*:

> It is sometimes argued – it was argued in the present case – that making an employer criminally responsible, even when he has done all that he could to prevent an offence, affords some additional protection to the public because this will induce him to do more. But if he has done all he can how can he do more?[2]

But the argument, with respect, overlooks the practical dynamics of regulatory techniques and enforcement processes. If the objective is a very high degree of care, that may be achieved by prescribing strict liability, but not by prescribing a duty of care.

The difficulty with the argument quoted is that it presupposes a capacity in the courts to adjudicate, systematically, regularly, and accurately, on whether a corporate employer has done all that it could to prevent the

1. *Review of the Trade Descriptions Act 1968*, Cmnd 6628, 1976, para.60.
2. [1971] 2 All ER 127, 135. For an example of the same argument being rejected in another context, see *Decision No. 167* (1975) 2 *Workers' Compensation Reporter* (BC) 234, 258.

offence. If that question were put to a management consulting firm, it might well take 3 months or longer before it could complete the enquiries necessary to produce a thorough report. Moreover the methodology for such an enquiry could include several attendances at the premises of the company to examine plant, equipment and systems, as well as to question staff in their working environment. These attendances would probably be required at the company head office as well as a local branch and possibly other premises. It is surely unrealistic to expect that, in relation to any large corporate enterprise, an enquiry into managerial structures and techniques of managerial control can be completed by a Magistrates' Court in the course of an ordinary trial in which other issues may also be involved.

On any such prosecution, the structure and operation of the company are within the knowledge of the defence, and they can adduce evidence of the precautions taken. The prosecution will not have the resources or opportunities to have the inside organisation of the company examined before trial by experts in managerial techniques. Moreover, a defendant might feel that co-operation in such an investigation would be analogous to self-incrimination. In any event, the cost would be enormously out of proportion to any likely fine. Yet without such an investigation, the prosecution cannot be prepared adequately to cross-examine on the issue of due diligence.

The prohibition of deceit and other predatory practices will never be achieved effectively without strict liability, including the responsibility of a company for the acts of its employees.

C. The Improvement of Criminal Sanctions

Some of the concepts and structural features of criminal law and procedure are an impediment in the enforcement of the *Trade Descriptions Act*. The purpose of the Act is surely to require that traders maintain honest procedures and accurate communications so that consumers will not be misled. But the criminal process tends to focus on an isolated transaction constituting a particular offence. It also requires a conclusion in terms of 'guilty' or 'not guilty'. Traders and business behaviour do not fall naturally into those two categories, and achieving the objectives of the Act surely requires a recognition of the gradations between those extremes. Certainly there are rogues in business who sell by techniques that involve planned deceit, and at the other extreme, there are businesses that go to great lengths to ensure honesty and accuracy in their dealings. But between those extremes is a great body of business enterprises operating at varying degrees of honesty and efficiency. In this connection, the objective of the Act is to require a high degree of care to avoid untrue statements, not simply to punish any deceitful intent. For this reason, as well as the evidentiary difficulties of proving intent, enforcement requires strict liability.

A complicating factor here is that honesty and efficiency are not neatly separate. For example, false statements in advertising or packaging might result from inefficiency in a manufacturing plant, perhaps involving poor communications between the production department and the publicity department. But the impact on consumers could be the same as if the misrepresentations had come about by decision of the board of directors. In any event, running a business without taking care to avoid false statements can be seen as a species of dishonesty.

There will, however, always be some situations in which a misrepresentation will occur in spite of the highest achievable degree of care, and recognition of this may well explain the reluctance to impose strict liability.

Thus the problem is how to promote a high standard of care to prevent false statements while not attaching a criminal stigma to a trader who is using that degree of care, but who has made an isolated mistake. The *Trade Descriptions Act* seeks to resolve this by the defence of mistake and due diligence.[1]

The difficulty with that defence, as explained above, is that where the defendant is a large corporate enterprise, it casts an almost impossible burden on the courts to adjudicate on the structure and efficiency of the business. This difficulty is compounded when the prosecution does not

1. 24. (1) In any proceedings for an offence under this Act it shall, subject to subsection (2) of this section, be a defence for the person charged to prove –

(a) that the commission of the offence was due to a mistake or to reliance on information supplied to him or to the act or default of another person, an accident or some other cause beyond his control; and

(b) that he took all reasonable precautions and exercised all due diligence to avoid the commission of such an offence by himself or any person under his control.

(2) If in any case the defence provided by the last foregoing subsection involves the allegation that the commission of the offence was due to the act or default of another person or to reliance on information supplied by another person, the person charged shall not, without leave of the court, be entitled to rely on that defence unless, within a period ending seven clear days before the hearing, he has served on the prosecutor a notice in writing giving such information identifying or assisting in the identification of that other person as was then in his possession.

(3) In any proceedings for an offence under this Act of supplying or offering to supply goods to which a false trade description is applied it shall be a defence for the person charged to prove that he did not know, and could not with reasonable diligence have ascertained, that the goods did not conform to the description or that the description had been applied to the goods.

have sufficient material or prior opportunities for enquiry to cross-examine effectively, or to adduce evidence in rebuttal.

Even apart from the statutory defence, a court may be reluctant to impose a severe penalty for what might seem like liability without fault. Related to this is the propensity of Trading Standards Departments to prosecute primarily for offences that are deliberate or repetitious. Commonly the trader will have been warned on prior occasions, though the evidence in the current prosecution may inform the court only of one offence. In this situation, the most likely risk is not the condemnation of the innocent but rather that sanctions for particular offences will be too light to serve as a significant deterrent, and lighter than a court might impose if it could see more of the defendant's compliance record.

It is suggested that rather than attempt to deal with issues of care and business efficiency by evidence on a prosecution relating to a particular transaction, a better approach might be to see whether some procedure can be devised to provide the court with a better record of previous violations by the defendant.

Trading Standards Departments often issue warnings, but except as an indicator of the future intentions of the Department, they are not of much legal significance. Occasionally, a prior warning may be mentioned in evidence on sentence to rebut any testimony of the accused that he had never been warned, or did not know that the conduct was an offence. But prior warnings are not normally admissible in evidence on a trial for a subsequent offence, and they are not usually adduced in evidence even with regard to sentence after a conviction. When a person is accused or convicted of a crime, there is a traditional reluctance to allow evidence of past misconduct in respect of which the defendant was never convicted or even charged. Such evidence could be unfair, because the defendant may not have kept records that might refresh his memory or rebut the allegations which he would have had if charged at the time, and other types of evidence may no longer be available.

To produce a more complete and admissible record of violations, it is suggested that on a prosecution under the *Trade Descriptions Act,* a court should not be limited in its options to 'guilty' or 'not guilty', nor should a defendant be limited in his plea to those alternatives. There could be a third plea available, and a third verdict possible, of 'inadvertent violation'. This could replace the present defences under Section 24. A verdict of 'inadvertent violation' would mean recognition by the court that the violation could have been an isolated mistake, and that the record of the defendant is consistent with a programme of compliance with legislative requirements.

At first impression, it may seem troublesome to commence criminal proceedings likely to result only in a record of a violation having occurred. But the process could be streamlined if written pleas are permitted. A business deciding to respond in this way could simply file a written plea of 'inadvertent violation' following the receipt of a summons. The prosecution will already have considered the merits of that plea before deciding to prosecute. In most cases, one would expect the prosecution to respond by filing a note accepting the plea, and that would be an end of that prosecution. Alternatively, the prosecution could proceed to trial, aiming at a guilty verdict. Where the plea of 'inadvertent violation' is accepted, however, the record would be established simply by the filing of two documents without anyone spending time in court. The suggestion is that the increase in the warning value of this procedure (compared with unrecorded warnings) and its subsequent evidentiary value would be worth the marginal increase in cost.

A verdict or plea of 'inadvertent violation' would not result in any sanction. Its value, compared with 'not guilty', is to record that the violation occurred. It could then be provided that previous convictions, and previous verdicts or pleas of 'inadvertent violation' would be admissible in any future prosecution to rebut a further plea of 'inadvertent violation', as well as being evidence on sentence in the event of a conviction. As well as having educative or warning value, this procedure should provide the court with a better measure of culpability.

Evidence of culpability or of due diligence would not be declared inadmissible, but it would become less critical, and less important compared with the record of prior offences for deciding whether the verdict in the particular case should be 'guilty' or 'inadvertent violation', and if guilty, for deciding on sentence.

The success of the idea would largely depend on acceptance by the courts of its rationale, i.e., that a record established in this way would usually be a more reliable indicator of culpability than any evidence of culpability adduced in the particular case.

One problem, relevant to this proposal, is the difficulty of maintaining comparable records in respect of convictions or other decisions relating to corporations. Consider the example of two chain stores, each consisting of 100 shops. In chain A, all the shops are owned and operated by the same company. In chain B, each shop is owned and operated by a subsidiary of a parent company that organises the chain. Suppose that there has been one conviction under the *Trade Descriptions Act* in respect of each of the 200 shops in the two chains. If further offences are now committed by one shop in each chain, the records will be quite different. For a shop in chain A, the record will show 100 previous convictions. But for a shop in chain B, the record will show only one previous conviction.

There is no easy answer to that problem. In the recording and use of previous convictions, it has not been customary to pierce the corporate veil or to refer to the convictions of affiliated companies. So far, the administrative difficulties of maintaining such records may have precluded consideration of that possibility. But such records are now being created in the licensing system under the *Consumer Credit Act*, and it may soon be necessary in any event to reconsider the structure to be maintained for the recording and use of previous convictions.

More emphasis on the prosecution of individuals, rather than companies, may be another way of alleviating the problem. Trading Standards Departments have been reluctant to prosecute individuals where the offence is committed by a large corporate enterprise. The feeling seems to be that while complicity can be proved most readily against lower echelon personnel, the pressures resulting in the offence are generated by people at higher levels of management against whom the offence cannot be proved, at least not by the enquiries that local authorities are equipped to undertake. This problem might be alleviated if the Office of Fair Trading, or possibly some other agency of the central government, undertakes a role of investigation and prosecution in relation to offences committed by companies trading on a national or regional scale, and where the offence does not appear to be a local deviation.

The substantiation of advertising claims is another area in which a traditional doctrine of criminal law has been invoked to frustrate the effectiveness of the Act. The *Review of the Trade Descriptions Act 1968* explained that:

> Much criticism of advertising arises from suspicion that claims put forward as to, for example, the product's performance are untrue though direct evidence of this is not readily available owing to the high cost of making tests or for some other reason. The obvious remedy in such cases is to impose an obligation on the advertiser to make good his claims; and we considered whether the Act could and should be amended in order to reverse the burden of proof in this way.[1]

The report then recommended rejection of that suggestion for no reason except that: 'It is a generally accepted principle of our criminal law that it is incumbent upon the prosecution to show that an offence has been committed.'[2]

1. 1976, Cmnd 6628, para.184.
2. Ibid, para.186.

That reasoning has a certain logic as long as the objective of the Act is perceived as the prevention of false representations. But the matter would take on another light if one objective was perceived as truth in advertising, and if a purpose of the Act was to require advertisers to limit statements of fact to those known to be true.

Where an advertiser makes a statement of fact, there is implicit a subsidiary assertion that he has knowledge of the matter. If he has no knowledge whether the statement be true or false, that is a species of deceit.

While not recommending a general provision for the substantiation of advertising claims, the Review recommended instead that the substantiation of an advertising claim could be required where it appears to be false. The recommendation was:

> . . .that where the enforcement officer has reasonable cause to suspect that an offence under the Act has been committed in relation to a particular statement he may, for the purpose of ascertaining whether it has been committed, require the production of books, documents or any information however recorded relating to the statement; and may require recorded information which is susceptible to being recorded in a legible form to be reproduced in a legible form; and may be able to take copies of any information he requires.[1]

But if that power is still associated only with offences that relate to false statements, it still misses the point. The discovery procedure proposed in that recommendation could, at best, only assist the prosecution where an advertising claim can be shown to be false.

Many propositions of natural science, for example, are not susceptible of proof or disproof. There may simply be no knowledge of the matter. Thus even if the proposals in the Review were adopted, an advertiser would still be free to claim anything as long as it is either: (a) true; or (b) a claim which cannot be demonstrated to be true or false.

The originator of an advertisement would still be allowed to deceive the public by proclaiming knowledge that he does not have. For example, a manufacturer might proclaim in his advertising that 'Breakfast cereal X is good for slimming'. If the truth is that no one has any knowledge of the effect of cereal X on weight, the statement will not be proved false by allowing enforcement officers discovery of the information available to the manufacturer. Yet it would surely be absurd if, in that situation, no offence could be proved unless the enforcement agency itself undertakes tests of the significance of the cereal on body weight.

1. Ibid, para.193.

It is difficult to see any ground on which advertisers should be allowed to mislead the public by advertising claims that cannot be substantiated.[1] This could be prohibited by amending the Act to provide, in effect, that:

(1) No person shall originate an advertisement for goods, credit or other services without first having information to substantiate every claim made in the advertisement;
and
(2) Any such person must supply that information upon request to any Trading Standards Officer, or the Director General of Fair Trading.

Failure to comply with either of those requirements could be made an offence.

Some subsidiary rules would obviously be required, relating in particular to the time during which substantiating information must be available. But at least the facts constituting the second offence would be within the knowledge of the prosecution (i.e. the advertisement, the request and the failure to comply).

In spite of the problems discussed above, the *Trade Descriptions Act* seems to be at least a partial success. The specificity of the offences and the provision of a specialised enforcement agency militate in favour of successful enforcement. It may help to discuss these points in turn.

Much of the conduct that is now an offence under the *Trade Descriptions Act* could have been prosecuted in earlier days as a common law or statutory crime, such as conspiracy to defraud or obtaining money (or attempting to obtain money) by false pretences. The perimeters of those offences in relation to trade activity were, however, never tested. For the reasons explained above, the police rarely perceived business behaviour towards consumers as being subject to the general proscriptions of criminal law. Prosecutions are surely more likely if the legislation applies specifically to trade, and if the conduct constituting the offence is more precisely defined.

Under the *Trade Descriptions Act*, the definition sections make the offence of applying a false trade description fairly specific. But in this respect, the Act could go further. Consider, for example, a retailer who displays in his advertising or in his window a refrigerator with 10 cu.ft. capacity along with a notice saying: 'From £80'. The 'from' is in very

1. At least some retailers agree with consumer organisations in believing that such advertisements ought not to be displayed. For example, the *Code of Practice of the Croydon Chamber of Commerce* provides an obligation on retailers: 'To ensure that advertising which cannot be substantiated shall not be displayed.' Para.3.2.

small print, and the '£80' in very large print. Only by going into the shop and submitting himself to the sales pitch does a customer discover that £80 is the price of a model with 5 cu. ft. capacity. The one displayed in the advertisement or in the window is sold for £180. This is a common practice. Probably it is an offence under Section 11(2) of the *Trade Descriptions Act.*[1] But surely the probabilities of a prosecution being brought, and of retailers recognising the practice as criminal, would be increased if it was made specifically an offence to publish any picture or display of any model or type of item in association with a price unless the price is that at which the advertiser is willing to sell the model or type of item in the picture or display. Similarly, where an advertisement or display portrays or describes several models or types of an item, it could well be made an offence to quote the price of one of those models or types without also quoting the prices of the others.

Another approach that can sometimes be used to make offences more specific and enforcement more effective is to proscribe distribution of the tools of deception rather than the end result. An example may be manufacturers' resale price lists. These limits are commonly used for one of two purposes (1) as an aid to resale price maintenance; or (2) as an aid to retailers in deceiving consumers into believing that the price at which the goods are being offered is less than the usual retail selling price. Since the first of these purposes violates a policy expressed by Parliament,[2] and the second involves deceit, it is difficult to see why the distribution of these lists should be allowed. The Monopolies Commission considered this matter, but concluded that the use of recommended resale price lists might be defensible in some situations. A total ban was, therefore, not recommended.[3]

The *Trade Descriptions Act* is more specific than much other consumer protection legislation. For example, in the *Consumer Credit Act,* 1974, Section 46 creates an offence of false or misleading advertising. But the requirements relating to the form and content of advertisements are left to be prescribed by regulation.[4]

To some extent, this may be inevitable. It may also have potential advantages of flexibility, enabling specific abuses to be proscribed as they become known. A problem can arise, however, that those responsible for

1. S.11(2): 'If any person offering to supply any goods gives, by whatever means, any indication likely to be taken as an indication that the goods are being offered at a price less than that at which they are in fact being offered he shall, subject to the provisions of this Act, be guilty of an offence.'

2. In the *Resale Prices Act,* 1976.

3. *Recommended Resale Prices,* 1969, Report of the Monopolies Commission.

4. S.44.

making the regulations may be subjected to lobbying primarily in one direction. Industry, commerce, and finance are organised for continuous lobbying in political and administrative processes, and the techniques of influence available to them are wide ranging. Lobbying in the consumer interest tends to be more episodic, and the techniques of influence available to consumer groups are less extensive. For consumer organisations, therefore, it may be better to press for specific proscriptions in the legislation, rather than to rely on assurances that the details can be supplied later by regulation.

With regard to the conduct of prosecutions, in so far as the *Trade Descriptions Act* has been a success, this is surely attributable in part to the assignment of prosecuting responsibility to officials already specialising in the prosecution of trade offences. Not only did this assure knowledge, technique and focus, but it also provided access to support services. Perhaps most important, some Trading Standards Departments operate their own laboratories, and others have arrangements for access to laboratory facilities.[1]

The specialised structure could, however, be carried further. In areas that do not have Consumer Advice Centres, the function of detection and prosecution is bound to be undermined unless some other section of the Department can undertake the negotiating and advisory roles.

Other anomalies can result from authorising Trading Standards Officers to prosecute only under a specified list of statutes. Suppose, for example, the sale of a used motor vehicle involves false representations as well as defects in the vehicle. A Trading Standards Officer can prosecute under the *Trade Descriptions Act* (for applying a false trade description), but in most areas he cannot prosecute under the *Road Traffic Act* (for selling a motor vehicle in an unroadworthy condition).[2] He may even be precluded by Section 28(5) of the *Trade Descriptions Act* from assisting the police in a prosecution under the *Road Traffic Act* by making available to them the evidence that he has obtained.

In some areas, a good liaison exists between Trading Standards Departments and the police. But it is suggested that the most efficient structure would be one in which the Trading Standards Departments can prosecute in respect of any offence committed against consumers in the course of

1. For interesting examples of laboratory work in connection with consumer protection, see the Annual Reports of the Consumer Services Department of Greater Manchester Council.

2. A few local authorities authorise their Trading Standards Departments to prosecute for this offence (see e.g. the *Annual Report of the Consumer Services Department of the Greater Manchester Council for the Year ending 31st March 1975*, p.10). But most do not.

industry, trade or finance, rather than only those offences contained in a prescribed list of statutes. Apart from prosecutions under statutes focusing on trade, this would enable Trading Standards Departments to prosecute under the general proscriptions of the criminal law in any situation in which that seemed appropriate. This would not, of course, exclude the right of the police or others to prosecute.

5. Licensing

The licensing of trades and professions is an ancient technique of legal control. The essence of licensing is usually that the conduct of a trade or profession is prohibited except by those to whom a licence is granted.

Licensing systems have been used at various times for different purposes. Among the objectives have been the raising of revenue by licence fees, the restriction of new entry into a trade or profession as a privilege for those already engaged upon it, or regulation to maintain standards of health, competence, or honesty, or the promotion of some other public interest.

In England, moneylenders and pawnbrokers have required licences. But there has not until recently been a general licensing system applicable to all consumer credit. Such a system was, however, recommended for Britain by the Crowther Committee,[1] and is now (1977) being phased in.[2]

Where the objective is integrity in trade, licensing can be used:

(1) To foreclose entry into the trade to those thought likely to engage in prohibited practices.
(2) As a system of sanctions, providing for the suspension, revocation, or non-renewal of a licence in prescribed circumstances.

Licensing systems are often advocated to control abuses in marketing that may not be prevented effectively by civil actions or criminal sanctions.

With regard to civil actions, the reasons why buyers do not generally pursue claims against sellers have been explained in Chapter 9. Even with an efficient system for the adjudication of small claims, there would still be several reasons why, in many situations, buyers would not pursue claims. For example, a predatory practice may be of a subtle kind not recognisable by the majority of buyers. Or the loss sustained by each individual may be too small to seek remedial action, but the losses

1. *Report of the Committee on Consumer Credit*, 1971, Cmnd 4596, Ch.7.2.
2. *Consumer Credit Act,* 1974, and regulations thereunder. For an earlier example of the licensing of credit grantors elsewhere, see the *Consumer Protection Act,* Rev. Stat. of Nova Scotia, 1967, Ch.53.

sustained by the public as a whole may be enormous. The operation of some mortgage brokers may illustrate the problem:

> Conduct which may give cause for concern when considering fitness for a licence is the persistent flouting of provisions of the Consumer Credit Act designed for the protection of consumers. Section 155 is a typical example. This valuable provision applies to brokers in the field of house purchase and certain other credit. It states that a broker can charge only a nominal fee of £1 unless the client gets his mortgage within 6 months; if he charges more than this the client can demand the return of the excess. However, my Office, as well as local consumer advice services are receiving a considerable number of complaints about the activities of a small minority of brokers.
>
> These people advertise their services, often in local newspapers. They offer to obtain mortgages and obviously attract a lot of attention from would-be first-time home buyers. The basis of the complaints is that various fees are paid to the broker over a period, sometimes in excess of £100 in total, without any mortgage facilities forthcoming but that the client finds it difficult or impossible to get his money returned, despite the existence of Section 155.[1]

The difficulties with the enforcement of criminal sanctions have been outlined above. While some of those difficulties apply also to a licensing system, others do not. In particular, a licensing authority is in a better position to assess the behaviour of a business over time. Also a fine, or even imprisonment, may not be enough where someone has manifested no intention of ever conducting an honest business.

The Crowther Committee explained its support of licensing in these terms:

> The protective methods listed. . .above are all concerned with individual transactions. Hence, though they are important, their efficacy is in practice limited by the fact that, for reasons we have already given, a single individual may be unaware of his rights or unable or unwilling to exercise them; and the more unscrupulous type of credit grantor may well take the view that the occasional check on his malpractices by a determined consumer in an isolated transaction is not a serious deterrent, and is outweighed by the financial advantages that he may derive from evading the law. There

1. *Speech of the Director General of Fair Trading* to the 25th Newspaper Advertising Conference, 19 April 1977, p.6.

> is thus a need for an agency entrusted with the continuing supervision of consumer credit grantors, with power to investigate trading practices, require production of accounts and records and, in the case of serious malpractice suspend or revoke the offender's licence.[1]

The potential advantage of licensing is that, to the extent that the system works, it can terminate the business of a trader engaging in fraudulent or predatory practices, or who persistently fails to comply with statutory requirements, instead of imposing sanctions that may only be of transitory significance.

Apart from screening or regulatory functions, licensing can also be used for psychological effect. The requirement of a licence to engage in a type of business may foster a perception of the role as one involving responsibilities, and this may help to make regulations relating to that type of business more acceptable. This can be reinforced if a licensing authority issues, along with the licence, a pamphlet outlining the responsibilities of licensees.[2] Licensing also establishes a mailing list that could be used to notify changes in statute law or regulations to those required to comply, or for the mailing of other literature that may promote standards of integrity in trade.

Under the *Consumer Credit Act*, 1974, a licence is required for carrying on any consumer credit business. This includes hire-purchase transactions, instalment sales, cash loans, overdrafts, budget or subscription accounts, mortgage agreements, credit cards, trading checks, and any other form of credit. A licence is also required by those engaged in consumer hire, credit brokerage, debt adjusting or debt counselling, and by collection agencies. A licence is not required, however, if the amount involved in each transaction exceeds £5,000. There are also some other qualifications and exemptions.[3] A licence is also required to operate a credit reference agency.

As of 1 July 1977, a total of 37,315 applications for licences had been received at the Office of Fair Trading, and 22,662 applications had been

1. *Report of the Committee on Consumer Credit*,1971, Cmnd 4596, para.6.3.3.
2. The pamphlet *Responsibilities of a Licensee*, 1976, Office of Fair Trading, does not fulfil this purpose. It focuses on the formal obligations of a licensee. It does not itemise, even in summary form, the standards of integrity to be observed in carrying on business. For example, it does not refer to the requirements of the *Trade Descriptions Act*, 1968.
3. The legal definitions and other provisions relating to licensing requirements are contained in various sections of the *Consumer Credit Act*, 1974, and statutory instruments made thereunder. They are explained in a more colloquial way in *Do You Need a Licence?*, 1977, a pamphlet of the Office of Fair Trading.

granted.[1]

In any system of licensing for regulatory purposes, it can be a major problem to identify licensees in a way that is relevant for achieving the objectives of the legislation. Under the *Consumer Credit Act,* 1974, a licence is required by the person who carries on the business. Often that will be a company. Thus the Office of Fair Trading cannot determine whether an applicant is a fit person (having regard to any previous convictions, etc.) unless the people controlling the company are identified. They will be identified if an applicant answers accurately and honestly the questions in the 'Application for a Standard Licence' form. So far, however, neither the Office of Fair Trading nor the Trading Standards Departments have been able to establish the resources to check on the honesty and accuracy of the answers provided, even on a sample basis.[2]

If a purpose of licensing is to distinguish honest from dishonest credit grantors, that objective will not be achieved to the extent that the system depends initially upon the honesty of all. For example, an unscrupulous individual could, perhaps by retaining title to several trade premises and other assets, operate through several companies, each having a nominal 'controller' whose name would be provided to the Office of Fair Trading. If the licence of one of the companies is eventually revoked, another may be incorporated to take its place, and meanwhile, any racketeer operations could be continued by the other companies.

> The corporate vehicle is an immensely flexible instrument of business organisation and the types of changes of control, direct and indirect, which may result from manipulation of the corporate vehicle are complex. This is so even in the case of corporations or groups of corporations held by a relatively small number of people, with no shares traded publicly, and is even more so in the case of corporations with publicly traded shares.[3]

The problem might be mitigated if, on any proceedings for the suspension, revocation, or non-renewal of a licence, the Office of Fair Trading initiates field enquiries to identify the individuals controlling or managing the business. Upon proper notice, any adverse decision relating to the business

1. Figures provided by the Office of Fair Trading.
2. When licensing was being introduced, every applicant was required to notify a Trading Standards Department of the application. But that procedure was adjudged to be too timeconsuming and expensive, and was abandoned. (Interview at the Office of Fair Trading, 1977.)
3. 'Transport Regulation in Canada', I.R. Feltham, (1974) 6 *Transportation Law Journal* 43, 61.

might then be treated and recorded as a decision also relating to those individuals. This could then be a ground for denial of a licence, or for revocation proceedings, with regard to any other company with which those individuals are associated in any significant way.

With regard to any type of business in which salesmanship is a critical factor, for example in the sale of motor vehicles, it may be desirable to require that each salesman should be licensed as well as the operator of the business. There is no provision for this in the *Consumer Credit Act.* But it has been done in some parts of Canada, and it may be useful to prevent a shady salesman moving from one company to another.

For some types of rackets, however, it may be impossible to prevent the licensing system from being undermined by the camouflage of identities. Thus one consequence of the identification problem is that licensing may have its greatest potential as a device for improving the ethical standards of those engaged in basically legitimate business. For dealing with rogues, the need is for a range of sanctions among which enforcement agencies can select. Licensing cannot be relied upon exclusively, though it can, along with imprisonment and other sanctions, sometimes play a useful role.

The Crowther Committee recommended that the issuance of a licence should be almost automatic:

> A licence should be granted to every applicant, on the first occasion, unless the Commissioner has some reason, arising out of the applicant's record or known character (or in the case of companies those of its directors or principal shareholders), to believe that he would not be a proper person.[1]

That is the way the system is working. Only a few licence applications have met with a 'minded to refuse' notice.

The licensing system is organised by the Office of Fair Trading on a national basis, though local Trading Standards Departments may assist in the conduct of any investigations under the Act.

A national system would seem most appropriate when the purpose is to regulate trading practices, rather than (as under some other licensing systems) to asses the suitability of local premises.

A problem with licensing is that the clerical workload can tend to generate a perception of the licensing function that falls short of the aspirations of those responsible for recommending or initiating the system. The burden of the clerical routine, and continuing problems of classification and recording, can tend to demand and attract people whose role

1. *Report of the Committee on Consumer Credit*, 1971, Cmnd 4596, para.7.2.9.

perception may lie in the smooth operation of administrative routines. Countervailing pressures might be insufficient to maintain a continuing sense of purpose.

The Crowther Committee felt that the licensing authority would exercise a supervisory role over the credit industry which would include watching and inspecting, but not snooping.[1] The distinction is not obvious. If it is implied that an inspector should not pose as an ordinary consumer to see how customers are being treated by a business, that would surely be absurd. Posing as ordinary consumers is just what inspectors ought to be doing for thorough law enforcement. In any event, to supervise effectively, inspectors must call periodically at the premises of credit grantors to:

(1) Obtain and check samples of standard forms in use, and send them to the national office;
(2) Make spot checks to see how transactions are consummated;
(3) Monitor advertising for compliance with the regulations and follow up advertisements to see whether the expectations that they create are fulfilled.

It does not appear, however, that sufficient local budgets have been provided for these purposes.

Another problem that must be tackled in the design of a licensing system is how and to what extent licensing decisions should be reversible on appeal. A major problem (and one which bedevils licensing systems in Canada) is how to design an appellate structure that will not create such a distortion in favour of leniency that the licensing system is ineffective. This problem appears in the *Consumer Credit Act,* 1974. A licensee or applicant has both the legal right and the incentive to appeal against an adverse decision. There is enough flexibility in the Act that someone with an incentive or duty to oppose such an appeal could be allowed to do so.[2] But there is no right of appeal against favourable decisions, and no-one whose job it is to review initial decisions that are favourable to licensees or applicants to determine whether, in the public interest, any of those should be appealed.

Where an appeal structure operates only one way, this may not only bias the results of appeals; it can also have a weakening influence on the decisions made at first instance. In ordinary civil litigation, a judge is subject to overruling if he decides either way. He is not under constant pressure in one direction. But such a pressure is surely created under the

1. Ibid, paras.7.4.2. and 7.4.4.
2. S.41(2).

Consumer Credit Act, 1974. A licensing official at the Office of Fair Trading knows that his judgment is open to question and possible overruling if he takes a firm position in the public interest, but not as long as he meets the wishes of licensees and applicants. Moreover to have a decision overruled can be more embarrassing for a licensing official than for a judge because of the continuity of contact with the people who have successfully challenged his decision.

This problem is aggravated in the *Consumer Credit Act* because roles of administration, adjudication, and advocacy are combined in the Office of Fair Trading. The Office deals with the routine administration of the licensing system, it adjudicates on any issues involved in the rejection of a licence application, or in the revocation, suspension or non-renewal of a licence, and the Director General of Fair Trading is also the potential opponent in any appeal by an applicant or licensor from a licensing decision.[1] This problem might be mitigated by either:

(1) Assigning the role of initial adjudication on contentious issues to a simple administrative tribunal associated with the Office of Fair Trading, but independent and not subject to the instructions of the Director General; or

(2) Assigning the role of investigation and advocacy on appeals to an official who would not be part of the Office of Fair Trading.

It is surely undesirable that appeals from licensing decisions should be available only one way, and that even in those situations, they should be treated by procedures analogous to a *lis inter partes.* To facilitate better protection of the public interest, as well as legitimate trade interests, it would surely be desirable to provide that an appeal may be brought from any licensing decision by any consumer organisation, Trading Standards Department, or trade association, and that these organisations should also have a right to be heard on a licensing appeal.

Past experience with licensing has not been encouraging. The licensing provisions of the *Moneylenders Acts* in particular have not been a marked success. '. . .in practice, the nature of the licensing system and the absence of any effective enforcement agency have limited the value of this protection. . .renewals are rarely refused. Indeed it is extremely rare for a certificate to be suspended or revoked.'[2]

1. *The Consumer Credit Licensing (Appeals) Regulations 1976,* SI No. 837.
2. *Report of the Committee on Consumer Credit,* 1971, Cmnd 4596, paras. 6.3.2. and 6.6.4.

Experience in North America has been similar.[1] While examples can be found of a licensing authority suspending or revoking licenses, these seem to be exceptions rather than general practice. One problem is that a licensing authority usually has more continuity of contact, and often more direct forms of contact, with people in the industry than it has with aggrieved consumers, and it may be part of human nature for a cordial rapport to develop among those continually in association. The incidence of political power may also be relevant here. In at least some jurisdictions, the job security of a licensor may be determined more by his acceptability to associations representing licensees than by his effectiveness in the public interest.

Of course the value of a licensing system cannot be assessed simply by reference to the numbers of licences suspended or revoked. Supervision coupled with a risk of revocation can have a significant effect. But the frequency of revocations and of suspensions can be indicators of the willingness of the licensing authority to invoke those sanctions, and thereby some indicator of the virility, if not the effectiveness, of the system.

There are other indicators too of industry dominance in licensing processes. For example, when a licensing system is established, draft bills and regulations may be discussed and circulated among the industries to be regulated, but not always among consumer organisations and others concerned with consumer protection. Sometimes trade association representatives have even written the legislation under which the industry is ostensibly to be regulated.[2] Thus licensing can sometimes amount to little more than the use by an industry of the authority of government to augment what is in substance a system of industry self-regulation.

Under the *Consumer Credit Act*, the risk of industry domination may be minimised by having one licensing system for all consumer credit, rather than, as is usual in North America, separate licensing systems for different sections of the credit industry.

An argument for licensing is that it can facilitate a more flexible response to abuses than is possible with other sanctions. How far this is so may depend on the criteria by which a licence may be refused, suspended or revoked. In this connection, the *Consumer Credit Act*, 1974, provides that a licence may be refused, suspended or revoked if the licensee (or his employee, agent, associate or controller), has:

(a) committed any offence involving fraud or other dishonesty or

1. For example, the encyclopedia racket is still active in Ontario in spite of years of licensing (personal experiences of the writer, 1977).
2. Interviews with trade association representatives in Ontario, 1972.

violence;

(b) contravened any provision made by or under this Act, or by or under any other enactment regulating the provision of credit to individuals or other transactions with individuals;

(c) practised discrimination on grounds of sex, colour, race or ethnic or national origins in, or in connection with, the carrying on of any business; or

(d) engaged in business practices appearing to the Director to be deceitful or oppressive, or otherwise unfair or improper (whether unlawful or not).[1]

Vague and subjective criteria, such as those in (d), can be criticised on the ground that they make flexibility a euphemism for arbitrariness. The refusal, suspension or revocation of a licence can be a severe sanction, more severe than a criminal conviction, and it would seem unjust if this sanction can be imposed for conduct that is not proscribed in advance, but only condemned in retrospect. These objections are surely compelling reasons why clause (d) should not normally be used. Perhaps the probabilities are either that it will not be used at all, or that it will be used only sparingly to catch any predatory behaviour that is plainly outrageous, but which may not be squarely covered by a specific offence. In so far as licensing adds any valuable flexibility in law enforcement processes, it is probably not because of any flexible features of the licensing system itself, but rather that licensing creates additional sanctions and so permits law enforcement agencies more choice in the selection of sanctions.

Under the *Consumer Credit Act*, 1974, the licensing system applies to credit extended by retailers, as well as cash lending and other forms of credit. But retailers who always sell for cash do not require a licence.

Thus the government had to decide whether, in the exercise of his licensing powers, the Director should consider only prior misconduct relating to credit, or whether he should also consider any prior misconduct relating to other aspects of trade. Consider, for example, a retailer who persistently sells shabby goods that do not meet the expectations created by his advertising. He may have several convictions under the *Trade Descriptions Act*. If there are no complaints about the credit aspects of his transactions, it could be argued that he should be treated in the same way as any merchant who sells only for cash, and who committed the same offences. On that view, licensing sanctions should not be invoked.

It is clear, however, that in his licensing decisions, the Director may and should consider any offences relating to the trade of the applicant, though

1. S.25(2).

they may not relate specifically to the credit aspects of transactions. Thus Section 25(2) provides that the Director 'shall have regard to', *inter alia,* any contravention of 'this Act, or by or under any other enactment regulating the provision of credit to individuals or *other transactions* with individuals'. Moreover, this is surely sound policy. To treat false advertising or other contraventions of the *Trade Descriptions Act* as nothing to do with the credit arrangements may be unrealistic. False representations relating to goods may be less effective when credit is not available. If the effectiveness of licensing is not to be stifled by technical jurisdictional arguments, the Director must, in the exercise of his licensing powers, be entitled to consider all offences relating to the trade of a licensee, not simply offences that may have a demonstrable connection with credit.

Requiring a licensee to display the licence at business premises is a technique sometimes used to aid the enforcement of a licensing system. But this is not required in the *Consumer Credit Act,* 1974.

While the modest display of licences can be beneficial, the advertising of licences is another matter. If care is not taken, licensing can be counter-productive by adding credibility to dubious operations. Thus in North America, advertisements stating that 'We are licensed by the government' have been used by many a shady operator to assuage public suspicion. A similar phenomenon appeared in Britain with regard to the Ministry of Transport Test Certificate for used motor vehicles. Instead of being treated cautiously by the public as indicating that the vehicle has probably been checked for compliance with minimum safety requirements, the certificate has sometimes been understood as a government assurance that the vehicle is mechanically sound. Moreover, dealers may not always resist the temptation to use language fostering that impression. In some jurisdictions in North America, licensing legislation includes a prohibition of any statement in advertising that the business is licensed by the government, or words to that effect.[1] It may be well to add such a provision to the *Consumer Credit Act,* perhaps by regulations under Section 26.

A technique sometimes used in association with licensing is bonding. Licensing and bonding commonly go together in Canada. To qualify for a licence, the applicant must either deposit securities of a specified value or file a surety bond. This requirement is imposed for categories of business thought to involve a high level of consumer grievances or a high level of insolvency among sellers, such as door-to-door selling and the motor trade. One purpose is to provide a fund from which the claims of aggrieved consumers can be met. Another purpose is to permit forfeiture of the bond

1. For example, The *Consumer Protection Act,* Rev. Stat. of Ontario, 1970, Ch. 82, S.4(3).

for a violation of the regulatory legislation, and in this way to provide an additional sanction.

One objection to bonding is that in some jurisdictions, anyone who can obtain a bond automatically obtains a licence. Thus the applicant for a licence becomes subject in effect to the scrutiny of the insurance industry rather than the licensing authority, and this shifts into the private domain regulatory responsibilities which people may feel should properly be a function of government.

The *Consumer Credit Act* requires licensing throughout the consumer credit industry, and given a system of this width, it seems unlikely that any additional achievement of bonding would be sufficient to justify the expense. It could be useful, however, to require bonding in respect of any category of the credit industry in which it may be found by experience that there is a high risk of insolvency and unpaid claims.

A theoretical possibility is to empower a licensing authority to require a bond on an *ad hoc* basis in marginal situations where a licence applicant has a dubious record, but not one that is clearly objectionable. It is doubtful, however, whether this would be practicable. The insurance industry can hardly be expected to offer bonds at reasonable rates if the only applications they receive are from bad risks.

Any need there may be for bonding is probably greatest not among traders who are credit grantors, but among those who are credit grantees; for example, any mail order companies that require payment before dispatch of the goods.

6. Undertakings (Assurances) and Prohibitory Orders

The use of undertakings and prohibitory orders (or injunctions) has long been a feature of consumer protection in many jurisdictions of North America. A tribunal or agency seeks and receives undertakings from traders for future compliance with legislative or other requirements. Failing an undertaking, the tribunal or agency may be empowered to issue prohibitory orders, or to take court proceedings for orders or injunctions.

For the United Kingdom, this type of structure is now provided in the *Fair Trading Act,* 1973. Under Part III of the Act, the Director General may seek undertakings, or apply to the court for prohibitory orders. This procedure would seem useful in two situations.

(1) Where the conduct is not seriously fraudulent and the trader has not previously been condemned for predatory practices, an undertaking or order may serve as a warning; an intermediate stage between an informal caution and a prosecution.

(2) In borderline cases where the legality of a trading practice is unclear,

undertakings or orders can add refinement to general prescriptions by specifying what is prohibited in the context of the particular trade.

Unfortunately, however, those are not the purposes for which Part III of the Act is being used. Some of the undertakings serve a definitional purpose, being more specific than the Act in identifying the prohibited conduct.[1] But many of the undertakings are in general terms that do not specify the prohibited conduct with any greater particularity than existing legislation.[2]

Moreover, a significant proportion of the undertakings are being sought not in novel or marginal cases, but in hardcore situations of serious and repeated crime. Thus one of the persons from whom an undertaking under Part III was being sought was described as: '. . .a secondhand motor car dealer who had been successfully prosecuted on a number of occasions for offences under the *Trade Descriptions Act* and the *Road Traffic Act*.'[3]

These undertakings are not being sought ahead of prosecutions as a first step in the response to deviational behaviour in the course of trade. They are being sought in desperation from traders against whom criminal sanctions have already proved an inadequate deterrent.

With regard to other types of crime, when moderate punishments fail to deter, the normal response is to impose more severe punishments. It seems incredible that, with regard to offences committed in the course of trade, when moderate punishments fail to deter, the response should be to seek undertakings of good behaviour.

A danger with undertakings and prohibitory orders is that they can enable an enforcement agency to appear productive without significant sanctions being imposed.

If an undertaking obtained by the Director General is violated, the result is not the imposition of sanctions even at that stage. Following the violation of an undertaking, the Director General may seek a prohibitory order from the court. If there is then a further violation of the court order, he may make a further application to the court for the committal of the

1. For example, 'In the conduct of its business, it will not demand final payment for work done without ensuring by inspection or otherwise that the said work has been done in accordance with the terms of the contract'. (Undertaking reported in the *Annual Report of the Director General of Fair Trading for 1975*, p.61, Clause 2.)

2. For example, 'Committing offences under section 1 of the Trade Descriptions Act 1968 by applying false trade descriptions to goods or by supplying or offering to supply goods to which a false trade description is applied'. (Undertaking reported in the *Annual Report of the Director General of Fair Trading for 1973-74*, p.47, Clause (a).)

3. *Annual Report of the Consumer Services Department of Greater Manchester Council for the year ending 31st March 1976*, p.15.

defendant to prison for contempt of court. It is difficult to see why the violation of an undertaking should not be made punishable immediately.

Even when an undertaking ends the misconduct by the particular trader, its overall effect may still be counter-productive. An undertaking may be no deterrent against perpetration of the same abuses by others, or against the imaginative introduction of other abuses by the same trader. Except for any type of business that requires a high investment of capital that cannot readily be withdrawn or transferred, it is no deterrent against a predatory course of trade to show that what happens to the trader concerned at the end of the line is that he is told to stop. By demonstrating that a predatory course of trade has not resulted in any significant punishment, undertakings and prohibitory orders could do more to promote than to prevent fraud and other abuses in marketing.

7. Terms Control

During the period of the survey, the Control Orders[1] required a minimum downpayment (deposit) for most consumer durables purchased by instalment credit, and a maximum period during which the instalments must be paid.

First introduced at the beginning of the war to divert resources to military purposes, the Control Orders were subsequently continued as an instrument of monetary policy. The minimum downpayment and maximum payment periods have varied with different categories of goods as well as being varied from time to time according to judgments about the extent to which consumer credit should be expanded or contracted.

For short periods, the Control Orders have been repealed, but they have subsequently been reinstituted. They were last repealed in 1972, and reinstituted in 1973.

The Control Orders are of interest in the study of consumer protection for two reasons. First, the system illustrates some broader problems in attempting government regulation of the terms of trade. Secondly, it has sometimes been suggested that terms controls should be used for consumer protection even when not required for reasons of military or monetary policy. Seductive offers of easy terms and no downpayment are the hallmark of high-pressure salesmanship and impulsive buying. Moreover people who cannot raise a significant downpayment or pay for an item within a reasonable time (say two and a half years for a motor vehicle) may be in such financial circumstances that the prudence of the transaction is at least doubtful. Thus terms controls may be advocated to prevent traders from talking consumers into the purchase of major items that they cannot

1. *The Hire-Purchase and Credit Sale Agreements (Control) Order 1964.*

afford.

> It is often said that a scale of mandatory down payments in various transactions would diminish impulsive or ill-considered purchases and no doubt in many cases this would be so.[1]

Studies in the United States have shown that repossessions increase with a reduction in downpayments, and an increase in the length of payment periods.[2]

> . . .repossession and loss rates are higher, on the average, when the down payment is small than when it is large.[3]
>
> . . .for both new and used cars the repossession ratio declines sharply and consistently as the down payment increases.[4]
>
> . . .for new cars the shorter the duration of contract, the smaller the repossession ratio. . .[5]

With regard to used cars, however, it was found in that study that repossession rates actually increased with shorter payment periods. The explanation suggested was that customers receiving longer contracts were selected with special care.

Describing the situation in England, other writers have said that

> During the period starting in 1958, without the Government's restraints of minimum deposits and maximum repayment periods, competition between lenders led to a large rise in bad debt experience, with consequential widespread and heavy losses by finance houses. As a result of this unhappy experience of unregulated competition, when the Government reimposed controls in the spring of 1960 they did not meet with the opposition from finance houses which they had suffered during the 1950's, but rather with scarcely concealed relief.[6]

Similarly, interviews by the writer revealed that the attitude of credit grantors to the Control Orders has not been one of universal resentment.

1. *Report of the Royal Commission on the Cost of Borrowing Money, Cost of Credit, and Related Matters*, 1965, Nova Scotia, p.387.
2. *The Quality of Consumer Instalment Credit*, G.H. Moore and P.L. Klein, 1967, National Bureau of Economic Research, Ch.3.
3. Ibid., p.61.
4. *Sales, Finance Companies and Their Credit Practices*, W.C. Plummer and R.A. Young, 1940, National Bureau of Economic Research, p.162.
5. Ibid., p.163.
6. 'The Economic Regulation of Instalment Credit in the United Kingdom', F.R. Oliver and N. Runcie, *Instalment Credit*, 1970, ed. A.L. Diamond, Stevens, London, p.141, 147-8.

Taking a significant deposit and requiring a relatively short period for paying off the instalments reduces the incidence of default, and thereby tends to confine credit transactions to the most profitable. To the extent that they are effective, the Control Orders can be a relief to some credit grantors in reducing any competitive pressure to engage in more risky transactions. It is the failure of enforcement, however, that has caused significant problems.

By the late 1960s, several techniques had evolved for avoiding the Control Orders. Check trading was among the most significant. The traditional type of check trading involved agents selling checks and collecting instalments often by calling at homes. These checks were usable at a range of retail outlets. The instalments were payable over a relatively short time, and the checks were commonly used for the purchase of clothing and household items rather than major durables. But a second type of check trading evolved as a device for avoiding the Control Orders. Many large retailers, including some department stores, established corporate affiliates that would issue trading checks for the purchase of a particular item from a particular shop.

Cash lending was not directly covered by the Control Orders. But the Bank of England issued directives from time to time to the clearing banks and to finance companies soliciting co-operation in the implementation of government policy relating to consumer credit. It does not appear, however, that this solicitation was effective in preventing the banks and finance companies from advancing loans for the purchase of consumer durables on terms that would have been a violation of the Control Orders if the same terms had been offered by a retailer on a hire-purchase contract. Thus with regard to the loan cases in the sample, enough data were available in 42 of them to determine whether the Control Orders would have been violated if those transactions had been financed on similar terms by a retailer using hire-purchase documentation. It was found that the deposit requirements would have been violated in 19 out of the 42.

Avoidance of the Control Orders through the arrangement of credit transactions in ways to which the Orders did not apply was well recognised in the credit industry. For example, '. . .the effect of the controls today is not so much to reduce the business done, but to channel it to those companies able and willing to use avoidance techniques.'[1]

What may have been less well recognised, however, is that violations were widespread even in situations to which the Control Orders clearly applied. These violations included not merely a failure to comply but also the adoption of techniques to conceal the non-compliance. For example, in

1. 'HPTA and the Controls', E. Etherington, (1971) 25 *Hire-Trading* 13.

one case on the survey the buyer stated: 'In the garage, the car was showing a price of £595, but in order to show a correct deposit in the agreement, the figure of £695 was written in the agreement.' In another case, the buyer of a motor cycle showed the interviewer a hire-purchase contract containing figures that complied with the Control Orders, but also showed her an invoice containing the figures that had been agreed between the seller and himself. In another case, the buyer of a television stated: 'there was no agreement written because I think what he does is against the law – you just get a book with payments written in.'

Of the 404 transaction credit cases in the survey, there were 350 in which enough data were available to determine whether, according to the figures contained in the agreement or reported by the buyer, there had been a violation of the Control Orders. In 78 of these, the Control Orders were most likely not applicable (either because they did not apply to the category of goods or because the transaction appeared to be a credit sale with the total price payable within 9 months). Of the remaining 272 cases, violations of the Control Orders appeared in no less than 63 (23 per cent). The ways in which the Control Orders appeared to be violated were as follows:

Never was a contract in writing	10
Contract signed without figures inserted	11
Fictitious cash price	12
Insufficient or no deposit	50
Excessive payment period	15
Instalments not approximately equal	7
TOTAL VIOLATIONS	105
Total number of transactions involved	63

Classified by types of Goods, the violations were as listed on page 401. (The list shows all transaction credit cases subject to the Control Orders in which enough data were available to indicate whether there was a violation.)

A substantial proportion of the transactions involved a higher deposit than the Control Orders required, or a payment period that was shorter. In these cases, the Control Orders would not in any event have had a limiting effect. Even for transactions completed exactly at the limits permitted by the Control Orders, it would sometimes be because those limits coincided with conventional terms rather than because the buyer had wanted easier terms but the seller had felt restrained from agreeing. Further, interviews with finance companies indicated that in so far as they sought adherence to the Control Orders, they were motivated at least as

Violation of Control Orders Classified by Type of Goods

Type of item	Total number of cases	Number appearing to involve a violation	%
Vacuum cleaner	20	4	20
Heating equipment	24	7	29
Sewing machine	10	0	0
New motor vehicle	13	6	46
Secondhand motor vehicle	62	10	16
Radio, TV, etc.	22	10	45
Furniture	43	13	30
Rug or carpet	17	6	35
Refrigerator or deep freeze	14	4	29
Gas or electric stove	32	2	6
Washing machine or dryer	15	1	7
Totals	272	63	

much by a desire to avoid risky transactions as by any fear of sanctions.

Thus of the 272 cases, a large proportion were transactions in which the buyer, the seller, or both wanted to consummate the transaction in any event upon terms that would comply with the Control Orders. Where both buyer and seller wanted to consummate the transaction upon terms that would violate the Control Orders, they probably did so. Considering that these figures relate only to cases in which the Control Orders were clearly applicable, and not to cases in which their application had been avoided (for example, by the use of a trading check or loan), it is clear that the Control Orders had become essentially a system of voluntary compliance.

Despite the widespread violations, prosecutions were running at the rate of only about 7 a year for the whole country.[1] The Board of Trade tried to secure compliance by informal contacts with finance companies and others concerned with consumer credit, but there was no serious machinery for detection and enforcement.

This research has not attempted to assess the dimensions of avoidance and evasion since the Control Orders were reinstituted in 1973. It is clear, however, that problems of non-compliance continued. As one knowledgeable observer has written:

> We are becoming seriously concerned. . .at the extent to which it is alleged that the Controls are now being avoided. Some of these allegations are probably untrue but some of them certainly are not

1. *Board of Trade Journal*, 2 July 1969, p.18.

> and as we have said the effect is cumulative and unless effective steps can be taken now to prevent avoidance, we fear that the situation will snowball within a few months to the position reached in 1971 when it was almost true to say that compliance with the controls was purely voluntary.[1]

Regulatory legislation of this type involves a cost, the more so if it is not well designed or seriously enforced. One of the problems with ineffective controls is that the techniques of avoidance or evasion are themselves likely to involve a cost. Consumers and credit grantors alike may feel impelled to consummate transactions in ways that may be more cumbersome, more expensive, or otherwise less desirable than the ways in which those transactions would otherwise have been undertaken.

Moreover it may be reasonable to assume a correlation between the level of fidelity with which a business enterprise observes the requirements of regulatory laws and the level of integrity in dealing with consumers, particularly when the requirements of the regulatory law are not seriously enforced by sanctions. Thus an effect of retaining the Control Orders without enforcement may be a tendency to drive those who are poor credit risks away from more reputable retailers (who are still complying with the Orders) to those with less concern for the fulfilment of obligations. If it is a goal of consumer protection to promote business dealings between conscientious and law-abiding merchants and low-income consumers, the Control Order system militates against that objective.

It may be that the Control Orders worked fairly well during the war. Patriotism was running high, and one of its demands was fidelity to government decree. Moreover the objectives of the system were understandable, and restrictions on consumption could be viewed as a temporary sacrifice to achieve urgent goals. This changed as the war years became more distant. Public support was more difficult to sustain for indefinite restrictions, the objectives and accomplishments of which were not obvious to large sections of the population. Perhaps most important, as terms controls appeared to the business community as a long-term rather than a short-term phenomenon, the incentive became greater to devise methods of avoidance or evasion.

For students of regulatory techniques, two lessons are clear. First, legislation to regulate business behaviour in ways that are contrary to the pressures of the market is difficult to enforce. Staff must be allocated specifically for the purpose, and there must be a vigorous programme of surveillance, detection and prosecution. Thus when considering the

1. (1974) 28 *Hire Trading* 2, 4.

enactment of this type of legislation, the value of the goals must be weighed not only against the cost in terms of market distortion, but also against the direct and ancillary costs of the enforcement process. Secondly, the proscriptions and definitions contained in such legislation must refer to the economic phenomena to be controlled, and not to concepts, institutions, or formalities that can be changed at the will of those subject to the regulation.

Finally if, as appears to be the case, the perceived need to restrain consumer credit is permanent, a reduction in creditors' remedies could well be more efficient and effective for that purpose than the Control Orders.[1]

8. Alternative to Sanctions

A. Market Pressures

For the reasons explained in this chapter, it is difficult to maintain effective sanctions in the regulation of business behaviour. For the promotion of honesty in business, the most viable alternative to sanctions may well be the pressures of a free market. But, for the reasons explained in Chapters 9 and 10, the legal system frustrates the operation of a free market by intervening predominantly on the side of credit grantors. By enforcing debt claims against consumers regardless of their legitimacy while failing to provide any effective machinery by which aggrieved consumers can obtain redress against sellers or lenders, the legal system operates to insulate business to a substantial degree from the losses that might otherwise result from the supply of defective goods, deceit and other predatory practices. Thus it is suggested, for the reasons given in Chapter 10(4), page 284, that the most effective way of promoting honesty in marketing would be to abolish debt claims arising out of retail transactions. Market pressures would then be allowed more influence.

B. Rewards

Another possibility, though perhaps not one with much potential, would be to supplement sanctions with a system of rewards. In the business community, rewards tend to be made by reference to success rather than integrity. For example, a manufacturer who has a phenomenal success in exports and thereby assists the balance of payments may receive a knighthood. But there is not much by way of public honour for a retailer who simply runs an honest business.

Grading or rating procedures might be regarded as one type of reward

1. This is explained in Chapter 10.

system. For example, the Consumers Association, through its magazine *Which?*, provides consumers with comparative information by which to assess different products and different manufacturers. There is, however, no comparable system covering all categories of local retailers.

For hotels, restaurants and garages, guide books and rating systems exist. With regard to hotels and garages, a common complaint has been that the rating systems tend to focus more on physical plant than on the honesty or quality of service. This problem has, however, received some attention in recent years. For example, the Automobile Association (AA) announced that it would supplement the evaluation of premises by a system of spot-checks to assess the reliability and quality of garage services.[1] Similarly with regard to hotels, AA inspectors are reported to make unannounced visits to the premises, and to make use of the services, including an overnight stay, before identifying themselves to the hotel management.[2] The investigation of members' complaints is another way in which organisations of this kind can monitor the performance of the hotels and garages being rated. There is, however, nothing comparable with regard to most retail trades.

C. Voluntary Compliance

One programme used with regard to the Control Orders was for the Board of Trade to seek voluntary compliance. This was also attempted with regard to some types of door-to-door selling. In both instances it was a failure. If a programme of voluntary compliance is operated as an alternative to enforcement, the deterrent value of sanctions has been abandoned.

In some circumstances, persuasion may be more effective than threats. For example, in a study of the compliance of ordinary citizens with income tax legislation in the United States, it was found in an experiment that appeals to conscience seemed to be more effective than the threat of sanctions.[3] When used with regard to major business institutions, however, an objection to reliance upon persuasion is that the Department concerned places itself under an obligation to the industries whose assistance has been sought. There is at least a risk that this obligation may add further to the lobbying power of those industries.

Voluntary compliance, particularly in situations of trade competition, may also promote suspicions of inequity. Each business may be unsure

1. See e.g. 'Garages Will Lose A.A. Link if Anonymous Spot Checks Disclose Shoddy Servicing', *The Times*, 14 January 1971, p.3.
2. *A.A. Hotels and the Automobile Association*, a pamphlet issued by the AA in 1977, p.14.
3. 'On Legal Sanctions', R.D. Schwartz and S. Orleans, (1967) 34 *University of Chicago Law Review*, 274, 295.

whether the same demands are being made on others, or whether they will be met to the same degree. Another limitation is that only some industries are sufficiently closely knit to be amenable to informal persuasion, particularly if it is essential for the persuasion to extend to the retail level. Hence those willing to co-operate with a government department may find themselves at a competitive disadvantage. This was happening with the Control Orders.

Thus in trade regulation, voluntary compliance has no widespread value as an *alternative* to sanctions. But a programme of persuasion and publicity can be helpful as a *supplement* to sanctions, particularly when a new system of regulation is being introduced, such as interest rate disclosure. Businessmen at the local level may well resent the regulation unless they are given a clear explanation of the objectives and the methods. Publicity pamphlets, and perhaps radio and TV programmes, can be used to explain to retailers the problems that the legislation is designed to remedy. If this results in willing compliance among a proportion of the trade, enforcement against the obdurate remainder should be easier.

13 CREDIT REPORTING

The successful operation of credit marketing partly depends on how far credit grantors can predict the probability of being paid. When dealing with a stranger, it is a great help if a credit grantor can obtain information about the paying habits of the customer. Various business organisations obtain, store and supply this type of information. These credit reporting agencies can be divided roughly into two types. First, there are those that report on trade buyers, i.e., business concerns that buy goods on credit, usually for manufacture or resale. Secondly, there are the agencies that report on consumers. In the *Consumer Credit Act*, 1974, these are now called 'Credit Reference Agencies'.

A credit reference agency obtains and stores information about consumers and their previous transactions, and supplies that information on request to credit grantors who are members of the agency. On receiving a credit report, the credit grantor determines the significance of the information for his purposes. This is generally more useful to credit grantors than would be a system of rating consumers, because the significance of the information may vary according to the type of business, the amount involved in the pending transaction and the proposed terms of the transaction, particularly the interest rate and the nature of any security.

The majority of credit reference agencies in Britain are local organisations. There are, however, two major ones operating nationally. One is the United Association for the Protection of Trade (UAPT). The UAPT caters to the general run of retail credit grantors dealing with consumers. It has regional offices with central co-ordination and administration in Croydon and London. The UAPT operates in conjunction with the Hire Purchase Trade Association, an organisation for credit grantors. At the UAPT offices, the credit information is filed by individual names. Approximately 7 million enquiries a year are received.[1]

The other national organisation is Credit Data Limited.[2] This too has regional offices. The information files are at Chesterfield, and the administrative head office is in Manchester. A large proportion of their enquiries are from mail order companies. The information is filed by address,

1. Credit enquiries of all types amounted to 6,870,161 in 1975. *Annual Report of the United Association for the Protection of Trade Limited for 1975*, p.2.

2. This company took over the business formerly known as British Debt Services. It is not a corporate affiliate of the US company Credit Data Corporation.

although names appear on the reports. Thus if it wishes, a mail order company can deny credit where someone at the same address, possibly a previous resident, has failed to pay. Some mail order companies may regard this as a necessary protection against a fraudulent individual writing from the same address under different names.

For the content of credit reports, both the UAPT and Credit Data rely largely on County Court judgments. By arrangement with the Lord Chancellor's Department, they record judgments for over £10 which remain unpaid for 28 days. Both agencies also record information from public registers, such as bankruptcies and bills of sale. Both also operate collection departments. At UAPT, information from the collection process is transmitted to the credit records, but apparently not at Credit Data.[1]

In two important respects, the UAPT system is more extensive. First, subscribers are required to report all accounts over 90 days in arrear. This is an important source of information. Credit Data may record any information of this type that it receives, but it does not require accounts in arrear to be reported. Secondly, the UAPT records enquiries received as well as adverse experience. An enquiry is an indicator that a credit transaction is imminent, and enquiries received are therefore a guide to accounts opened. Thus if an enquiry is followed by the absence of any adverse report, it indicates the probability of a satisfactory credit experience. A credit grantor receiving a report can compare these positive indicators with any adverse information. For example, a report that shows simply two accounts in arrear would look bleak. But a report that shows two accounts in arrear together with 17 enquiries (suggesting accounts opened) might not look too bad.

Members of the UAPT are asked to advise the agency of any accounts opened without a credit enquiry being made, but the response to this request is uneven.

The content of credit reports is determined more by the availability of data than by what credit grantors would ideally like to receive. No doubt it would be valuable to a credit grantor to know the current financial position of the customer, including his current income, and the amounts and terms of his obligations outstanding. Credit reference agencies are, however, not able to provide an up-to-date account of a consumer's financial position. The administrative cost of obtaining this type of information and keeping it up to date would be prohibitive, and there would be a high incidence of errors and omissions. Also many credit grantors are reluctant to feed positive information into a reporting system.

1. Interviews at UAPT and at Credit Data Limited, 1977.

Though it may be in the best interests of credit grantors to receive positive information out of the system, it may not be in their best interests individually to feed it in. For a credit grantor to provide such information could help competitors to lure away good paying customers.

Both the UAPT and Credit Data have routines for the removal of stale information:

> . . .BIDS [now Credit Data Limited] removes and destroys information in all categories after seven years, a time-span which was arrived at after consultation with their members who agreed that they would not find it useful to have older information. UAPT removes most entries over six years old, but holds details of bankruptcies for 15 years. Where there is a long history of defaulting payment and repossessions under judgments or other derogatory information still appearing, the file will not be pruned.[1]

A common misconception about credit reporting arises from the phrase 'credit rating'. In the context in which that phrase is generally used, it refers to something that does not exist. 'Credit rating' seems to imply that credit reference agencies apply a grade or code to individuals to designate credit worthiness. As explained above, however, this is not the nature of credit reporting at all.

Some credit bureaux in North America will classify individual files according to the specifications of a particular credit grantor, and some will provide lists of names with an overall rating. These general ratings, are, however, normally used not in response to enquiries for pending transactions, but to compile lists of names and addresses to whom advertising literature can be sent, or upon whom salesmen will call. There is a strong feeling that general ratings are contrary to the public interest. Thus the Federal Trade Commission reported:

> Credit guides are generally published by credit bureaus and leased on an annual basis to credit grantors. These 'guides' are alphabetical listings of certain information, usually in code, rating each consumer as to how he pays his bills. For example, a business dealing with a consumer rates the individual on a scale from 0 to 9 depending on the type of account, 9 being the most unfavourable rating a person may receive. This information is then forwarded to the credit bureau and is used in compiling the annual credit guide. All information is assembled into a book called a 'credit guide' which is

1. *Report of the Committee on Privacy*, 1972, Cmnd 5012, p.80.

> distributed, for a fee, to all bureau members wishing to make use of the information.[1]

The Commission concluded that the publication and distribution of these credit guides was a violation of the *Fair Credit Reporting Act* (US).

Credit reports are most commonly used by credit grantors to decide whether to consummate a credit transaction. But this is not their only use. There are two other principal uses, both extensive in North America but apparently not widespread in Britain. The first is for business solicitation. A company may make a list of names (perhaps from the voters' list or some other record), and obtain credit reports on everyone on the list to decide who to approach as potential credit customers. Secondly, credit reports can be used by employers in connection with the hiring or promotion of staff.

Apart from supplying the information on file, some credit reference agencies, including UAPT, will upon request have enquiries made by a local agent. Reports by local agents are known as 'status reports'. The enquiries may include telephone or personal contacts with the employer of the subject, his neighbours and local tradesmen. This aspect of credit reporting has probably been the most controversial, the criticisms of it including the invasion of privacy and the unreliable nature of the reports. The calibre of the agents making these enquiries has been questioned. Indeed, it may be impossible to maintain any effective quality control over the work of local agents and at the same time provide the service at a fee that would make it acceptable. This may be why the use of status reports for credit purposes seems to be decreasing, and is not a normal routine.

Credit reporting is an aid to credit grantors. It is probably also an aid to consumers. Without credit reference agencies, credit grantors would tend to rely on more general data, such as the income of the subject, the neighbourhood in which he lives, etc. People of modest means might then be denied credit, or charged a high rate of interest. With credit reporting, the paying habits of an individual become part of the data available to credit grantors. Thus one effect of credit reporting may be that people of modest means who budget well and pay their bills promptly are able to obtain credit on more favourable terms than would be possible if their paying habits were unknown.

Credit reporting may also serve a broader public interest by helping to promote competition. Without credit reference agencies, the same type of information could be gathered to some extent by larger credit grantors,

1. 'Fair Credit Reporting Act: Notice of Proposed Interpretations', Federal Trade Commission, 37 *Federal Register*, No. 46, 8 March 1972.

but much less readily by smaller ones. Thus the existence of credit reference agencies may help smaller credit grantors to remain competitive.

Another important aspect of credit reporting is the possible impact on the perimeters of consumer credit. It is arguable that by providing credit grantors with data to identify risky transactions, the system may restrain the over-extension of credit where a buyer would have difficulty in making the payments. A problem with that argument, however, is that the ordinary credit report does not show when someone's income is being over-burdened. Primarily it shows whether he has defaulted on credit transactions in the past. Credit reports distinguish those who pay their bills from those who do not. But they do not show whether a subject pays easily, or only with great difficulty and by inflicting privation on his family. Thus credit reporting may promote the extension of credit beyond healthy bounds. In other words, it is arguable that because the system shows only default, and does not show when someone is coming close to default, it promotes the extension of credit right up to the verge of default and in situations in which, if there were no credit reporting services, credit grantors might be more cautious.

It is the impression of the writer, however, that credit reporting is not an aggravating factor here. A credit grantor who wants to avoid over-commitment on the part of a consumer can usually obtain the necessary data by questioning the consumer. If credit is supplied to consumers who can only pay with great difficulty, this generally comes about not because credit grantors are inadvertently ignorant of the circumstances, but because they elect to extend credit in spite of them, or because they elect not to enquire. Indeed, some credit grantors have a reputation for encouraging a consumer to extend his commitments beyond his means. When credit grantors allow credit to the point where consumers are over-committed, it is not because they lack the information to do otherwise but because they lack the incentive.

> Bureaux quote instances of debtors whose only income is retirement pension or who are unemployed or on National Assistance who have been encouraged or urged to incur hire purchase commitments. One bureau quotes examples of cases of debtors unable to keep up payments on one purchase who, whilst owing money, were allowed to make another credit purchase. Another bureau quotes cases where credit has been allowed to individuals in the town against whom other traders have outstanding court orders.[1]

1. *Memorandum to the Committee on Enforcement of Judgments*, 1966 National Citizens' Advice Bureaux Council, p.5.

If the extension of credit is to be avoided where it is likely to cause hardship, this can be accomplished not by changes in the information available, but by reducing the pressure on consumers to make the payments; in other words, by reducing the strength of creditors' remedies as suggested in Chapter 10.

The only respect in which credit reporting seems relevant here is that the threat of an adverse credit report, when used in collection processes, can be a strong pressure to pay. It has been suggested in Chapter 10, page 296 and 314, that threatening an adverse credit report should be prohibited.

A related argument is that credit marketing could not prosper without an efficient system of credit reporting or strong collection methods. Credit grantors could operate profitably without one or the other, but not without either. Thus if credit grantors are not to be allowed strong sanctions for collections, they must be allowed an information system to distinguish people who are likely to pay from those who are not. Any harm that flows from credit reporting is slight compared with the social harm that flows from coercive methods of collection; and credit reporting is surely preferable.

Having a good credit record is commonly assumed to be desirable. It has the advantage of enabling an individual to obtain credit, and may occasionally assist in obtaining employment. But there can be some disadvantages. Some selling organisations focus a campaign on people whose credit records have been checked. When that happens, a good credit record can signal the advance of a doorstep salesman, nuisance telephone calls, or junk mail.

There has been a great deal of public apprehension about credit reporting. Much of it may be a reaction to the image created by the phrase 'credit rating', which has been widely used in the media. That phrase has even appeared in government documents, and in the publications of credit reference agencies themselves. Indeed, so firm is the popular view that everyone has a 'credit rating' that it seems almost useless to explain that no such thing exists.

Part of the public concern is about the invasion of privacy. A related fear is the manipulation of people's lives by those having control of comprehensive data banks. In a survey on attitudes to privacy conducted for the Younger Committee, the question was asked:

> Suppose you had wanted to buy a new washing machine recently and you had asked for hire purchase terms, and the dealer had told you that before giving you credit he would have to check with a credit rating agency. Would you regard the credit rating agency

knowing anything about you as an invasion of your privacy?[1]

The responses to that question were reported as follows:

> 46 per cent said they would regard this as an invasion of privacy and 53 per cent that they would not. 55 per cent said they would not be annoyed or upset; 19 per cent that they would be 'a bit' annoyed and 25 per cent said they would be 'very' annoyed. Asked whether they thought that it should be prohibited by law, 37 per cent said 'Yes' and 62 per cent 'No'. Since some forms of credit-worthiness checking involve knowledge of a credit seeker's income, it is perhaps worth noting that 78 per cent would object to such information being available to 'anyone who wanted to know'.[2]

It may be, however, that the percentage replying that they felt this activity an invasion of privacy would have been lower if the question had been asked in a different context; in particular, if it had not been preceded by questions that focused attention on the invasion of privacy.

Of complaints relating to the invasion of privacy, many refer to the actions of local enquiry agents making status reports. This activity must be distinguished from the ordinary in-file credit reporting described above.

The prospect of computers being used by credit reference agencies is viewed by some people with alarm. For example, the report of the Crowther Committee refers to '. . .these dangers to civil liberty that may arise from the growth of computerised credit registers. . .'.[3] Yet when the dangers are listed, it is difficult to find one that would arise from the use of a computer, i.e. a danger that would not be there in a manually operated system. The dangers perceived by the Crowther Committee were:

> . . .the capacity of the computer to assemble information, store a large quantity of data in a small space and transmit answers to enquiries at lightening speed, will generate a considerable increase in credit information. This will be due partly to the ability of a computer to marshal and record facts which hitherto would have been difficult to do and partly because the natural desire of any computer user is to see that he gets the maximum use from it. Hence quite irrespective of the value of the information which is being recorded, computers are likely, under Parkinson's Law, to lead to a steadily

1. *Report of the Committee on Privacy*, 1972, Cmnd 5012, p.73.
2. Ibid, p.74.
3. *Report of the Committee on Consumer Credit*, 1971, Cmnd 4596, para. 9.1.26.

> increasing output of data covering the individual consumer. The volume of information stored coupled with the complexity of computers themselves may make it difficult to discover the source of the error, even assuming the error is discovered at all. Moreover, information stored in a computer can be tampered with and altered without trace of interference. Computer tapes are also vulnerable to copying or even theft, a potentially serious problem where they combine sensitive information which may be improperly published or used as an instrument of blackmail. Hence the strong pressure building up in the United States for legislation requiring credit bureaux to maintain an effective system to safeguard records against theft, interference and unauthorized access and use.[1]

With respect, these fears are surely unfounded. The capacity of computers to transmit answers at lightning speed would be an advantage in credit transactions. If the answers are slow in coming, there is a risk of credit reporting being used less frequently than is desirable. Fear that the introduction of computers would increase the range of information stored may not be supported by American experience. When the Credit Data Corporation introduced a computer system in competition with the manual systems operated by the local bureaux, one of the objections to the new computer system was that the range of data stored and supplied was *less* extensive than that provided by the manual systems. The perceived need to reduce the data to standard codes that could be reproduced cheaply on standard forms limited the range of information recorded.[2]

The comment that it may be difficult to discover the source of error is true, but so it is with manually operated systems. The point that '. . .information stored in a computer can be tampered with and altered without trace of interference' is also true. But it can only be done by someone with technical knowledge and access to the computer equipment whereas in a manual system it can be done by almost anyone with access to the files.

It is the impression of the writer that public concern about putting records on a computer arises primarily out of fear of the unknown rather than fear of specific harm. In so far as a computer-operated credit reporting system would involve risks of harm to the public interest, those risks are already present, and probably in a greater degree, in manually operated systems.

The view that the Younger Committee took of 'computerisation' was

1. Ibid, para. 9.1.9.
2. Interviews at local credit bureaux in the US, and at Credit Data Corporation, 1967.

more sanguine, and, it is suggested, more realistic. 'None of the principles which we enunciate is in any way affected by what is, in our view, only a potentially more efficient method of record-keeping.'[1]

A possible result of switching to computer recording is that it might become feasible for large credit grantors to have their own computer terminals. If this happened, large companies might obtain credit reports faster than smaller merchants who would still communicate by telephone. This would tend to give larger credit grantors a competitive advantage: but this might still be regarded as a legitimate advantage of scale.

Another problem with credit reporting is the risk of inaccuracy. Probably the most significant cause is clerical errors in communication and recording. It is an old adage that a story changes in the retelling, and it would not be surprising if this is sometimes true in credit reporting. At the time of recording, clerical errors can result in data being entered against the wrong name, or wrong data being entered. On retrieval of the data, clerical mistakes can result in the wrong card being used to give the report, or information being omitted or inaccurately transmitted. An error or omission with regard to one item in a report may not be too significant if the report also contains a range of other information. But an error with regard to the identity of an individual can be more important.

A problem here is that there may be no coincidence between the level of accuracy that would be optimum in the interests of consumers and the level that would be optimum in the interests of credit grantors. For example, a system may aim at quick cheap reports because that is what the members want. The members may assess the risk of error by reference to probabilities, and they may not be willing to pay the cost of controls for more accuracy.

To illustrate the point with hypothetical figures, it might be optimum for credit grantors if 95 per cent of the data obtained on credit reports is correct. But it might be optimum for consumers if 98 per cent is correct. In other words, beyond the 95 per cent level, the cost of improving accuracy may not be matched by the increased profit from greater precision in business decisions. Consumers, on the other hand, might be willing to pay for a higher level of accuracy. Whether this is so cannot be discovered through the system because the choice is that of credit grantors. If the reality accords with economic theory, they can be expected to make the choice at the level of accuracy that will maximise their profit.

Other inaccuracies or false impressions can result from conflicts between the interests of each credit grantor and the interests of credit grantors as a whole. For example, a credit reference agency may record

1. *Report of the Committee on Privacy*, 1972, Cmnd 5012, p.82.

enquiries received, and sometimes the terms of an enquiry, such as '£500 over 10 months'. This may be taken by subsequent recipients of a report to indicate that credit was granted on those terms. But unless the agency is able to maintain a rigorous system for checking the results of enquiries, this may not be so. For example, the enquirer could have obtained a clear report from the credit reference agency, but then have obtained derogatory information from another source, and the credit may have been denied. Where a system operates in this way, it is another example of the content of credit reports being determined by what credit grantors are willing to allow into the system rather than by what they would like to receive out. In particular, there is no incentive for credit grantors to report up to date positive information.

When inaccuracies occur, it may usually be the result of inadvertence. But that is not always the case. Indeed, there is sometimes an incentive for a credit grantor to distort the information supplied. For example, suppose an appliance dealer is approached by Joe Bloggs about a colour television. Joe is an old customer with a previous account at a shop. He enquires about a television set and is quoted a price. He replies that he will think about it. The dealer understands this to mean that Joe will compare prices elsewhere. Suppose that a few hours later, the dealer receives an enquiry about Joe from a local credit reference agency. The dealer knows that information is being sought for a trade rival. The more favourable the reply, the more likely he is to lose a customer. How often situations of this type result in a distortion cannot be measured. But situations arise in which the opportunity and the incentive are both present.

Another example of false information is that the accounts reported to be in arrear include claims for money that is not lawfully due. There is nothing in the system to assure that a merchant, when reporting overdue accounts, will distinguish between debts and disputed claims.

Where a consumer communicates with a credit reference agency because of a suspicion that it may have inaccurate information about him on file, the matter is usually resolved by discussion:

> Experience gained in dealing with many hundreds of requests of this sort (before any statutory duty existed) strongly suggests that in the overwhelming majority of cases (in one of the largest agencies the figure was in fact 100%) the consumer and the agency quite easily and quickly agree on the truth and the record is amended, or not, as

the case may be.[1]

Often a credit report will include adverse information relating to a matter that the consumer had forgotten. In other cases, an error may appear that the agency is willing to correct.

The *Consumer Credit Act,* 1974, now provides a statutory procedure for consumers to question the records of credit reference agencies. Section 158 (1) provides that:

> A credit reference agency, within [7 working days][2] after receiving, –
> (a) a request in writing to that effect from any individual (the 'consumer'), and
> (b) such particulars as the agency may reasonably require to enable them to identify the file, and
> (c) a fee of 25 new pence,
> shall give the consumer a copy of the file relating to him kept by the agency.

Where the file is not in a readable form, for example because abbreviations or symbols are used, the copy supplied must be 'a transcript reduced into plain English'.[3]

There is no requirement that a consumer must have been denied credit, or that any other event must have occurred, before he is eligible to apply for a copy of the file. Nor need he give any reason for wanting to see it. But it would be natural to expect that the suspicion of error and the desire to see the file would usually arise following some denial or hesitation by a credit grantor. Probably in anticipation of this, the Act provides that within 28 days after the termination of antecedent negotiations, a debtor or hirer may request in writing that the creditor, owner or negotiator shall give him notice of the name and address of any credit reference agency from which information was sought about his financial standing.[4]

Where a consumer has received the file information from a credit reference agency, and considers an entry in the file to be incorrect, and that if it is not corrected he is likely to be prejudiced, he may give notice to the

1. *A Short Guide to the Consumer Credit Act 1974,* C. McNeil Greig, undated, Hire-Purchase Trade Association, p.69 Enquiries by the writer at the advisory agencies in 1977 indicated either a similar impression, or at least no substantial evidence to the contrary.

2. This is the period prescribed in the *Consumer Credit (Credit Reference Agency) Regulations 1977,* SI No. 329, Reg. 3.

3. S.158(5).

4. S.157(1).

agency requiring it either to remove the entry from the file or amend it.[1] Within 28 days after receiving such a notice, the agency must inform the consumer that it has: (a) removed the entry from the file, or (b) amended the entry (enclosing a copy of the amended entry), or (c) taken no action.

Unless the consumer has been informed by the agency that it has removed the entry from his file, he may serve a further notice on the agency requiring it to add to the file an accompanying notice of correction (not exceeding 200 words) drawn up by the consumer, and to include a copy of it when furnishing information included in or based on that entry.[2] If (a) the consumer has not received a notice from the agency that it intends to comply with the notice of correction requirement, or (b) the agency thinks that it would be improper to publish the notice of correction; the consumer or the agency, as the case may be, may apply to the Director General of Fair Trading 'who may make such order on the application as he thinks fit'.[3]

The jurisdiction of the Director is limited, however, to the two situations mentioned. He would appear to have no jurisdiction where the agency is willing to file the notice of correction, but the remedy that the consumer wants is the removal of the entry from the file. This could happen, for example, if the entry relates to a disputed claim. It is suggested that where a credit reference agency elects not to remove a disputed claim, there should be a procedure whereby a consumer can apply to a court for determination of the dispute and an order to correct the record. It may well be that few consumers would go to the trouble. But it would seem fair that the remedy should be there for any who may wish to use it.

As a vehicle for the detection and correction of error, the statutory procedure is limited, and the frequency of false information is still difficult to measure. First, the statutory procedure provides a check only when a consumer takes the initiative. It does not even require a consumer to be informed when a credit report about him is being obtained. It does not provide any system of monitoring or spot checks for system efficiency. Credit reference agencies say that mistakes are rare, and that if an error is discovered it is promptly corrected. This is hardly reassuring, however, if the design of the system does not provide automatic mechanisms for bringing mistakes to light.

Secondly, credit reference agencies usually prohibit their members from disclosing to a consumer the information received in a credit report. The

1. S.159(1).
2. S.159(3).
3. S.159(5). For a detailed critique of these provisions, see 'Credit Reference Agencies and the Consumer Credit Act', R.G. Lawson, (1977) 127 *New Law Journal* 57.

statutory procedure entitles a consumer to obtain a copy of the in-file information from a credit reference agency. But it does not entitle a consumer to obtain from a trader a copy of the credit report as received by the trader. In any event, this report is often by telephone and may not be recorded by the trader. Thus the statutory procedure offers a check only on the accuracy of the input, and on the in-file recording of a credit reference agency. It does not offer any check on the accuracy of transmission in the output. For example, if the agency makes a mistake by entering adverse information on the card of the wrong person, that might be discovered by the statutory procedure. But if the agency makes a mistake by extracting adverse information from the wrong card when composing a report for a member, that mistake may not be discovered even if the statutory procedure is invoked by the affected consumer.

Another difficult question is whether a credit reference agency, or those supplying information to an agency, should be liable to a consumer for losses resulting from inaccurate information. Where a credit report is used for routine credit transactions, and it is the refusal of credit that the consumer has suffered, it is surely not worthwhile for people to incur the cost of litigation. It is suggested that if the only loss is the denial of credit, there should be no liability. Apart from avoiding litigation costs, this would also avoid any fear of liability that might impede the willing compliance of credit reference agencies with the statutory disclosure procedure.

For credit marketing, it is in the public interest that a quick and cheap system of credit reporting should be maintained, including some risk of error. It is a different matter, however, if reports are used for personnel purposes, so that someone's career or livelihood may be at stake. It would seem more reasonable here to suggest that if an erroneous credit report results in the loss of a job opportunity, compensation in the form of damages should be paid out of the system. It would be cumbersome and perhaps too discouraging to the victims of such errors to make the result depend upon an inquiry into fault. It is suggested, therefore, that credit reference agencies should be strictly liable for inaccuracies in reports used for the hiring or promotion of personnel.

At the moment, credit reference agencies are not always aware of the purpose for which a credit report will be used. But they could protect themselves by:

(a) requiring members to state the purpose, and by charging a higher fee for personnel reports, or
(b) specifying that their reports are for credit purposes only, and requiring a contractual indemnity from members in respect

of any claims arising out of the use of a report for personnel purposes.[1]

Perhaps the most serious accuracy problem is the reporting of disputed claims. It may well be that few businesses would deliberately decide to report a disputed claim to a credit reference agency. But disputed claims generally appear in the accounts of credit grantors as debts. Hence if it is the general practice to report, say, all accounts 90 days in arrear, and if disputed claims are not screened out, they will be reported automatically along with undisputed debts.

The problem is mitigated to some extent when a credit report contains a variety of information. For example, if a credit report indicates 15 accounts opened over 5 years, and only 1 account in arrear, a reader of the report is likely to assume that the consumer generally pays his bills, but something went wrong on one transaction. The problem can be critical, however, in other situations. Suppose, for example, someone bought a major appliance on credit, but usually pays cash for everything. If he has refused to pay the instalments because the appliance does not work, and if this is reported to a credit reference agency as an account in arrear, the record of the consumer may look bleak.

Where a credit reference agency also operates a collection service, the problem is aggravated. The fear of an adverse credit report can then be more cogent in coercing the payment of claims. Even though the agency scrupulously refrains from threatening an adverse credit report, such a threat can still be seen by the consumer as implicit in the situation. This problem would be solved if, as suggested in Chapter 10, p.313, collection agencies are abolished.

A false impression can also be created when a consumer has fallen into arrear with the payment of bills, but has subsequently paid them. Judgments are usually recorded at credit reference agencies, and overdue accounts are recorded at some. But the subsequent payment of those judgments and accounts may never appear. A satisfaction of a judgment might be registered through a County Court office, and if so, it will usually find its way to the records of credit reference agencies. But unless the consumer initiates the process, which is unusual, there is nothing automatic in the system that will result in the payment of judgments and overdue accounts being noted on credit records.

For the reasons explained above, credit reporting, particularly if coupled with a reduction of creditors' remedies, can be a valuable public service. If

1. See e.g. *Gillett v. Nissen Volkswagen* (1975) 58 DLR 3d 104.

this is accepted, the problems of credit reporting must be tackled in some way that would still permit the operation of the system.

One possibility sometimes suggested is that credit reporting should be a state monopoly. A single reporting system could be more efficient in some respects. But the state already has a great deal of information about individuals accumulated in other departments for other purposes, and there is public apprehension about the power that would be derived from common control over all data banks about individuals. To this there is added the concern about record linkage which could result in information being procured for one purpose and subsequently used for another. As the Crowther Committee put it:

> This disquiet is likely to be the greater if one government file were allowed to 'talk' to another – if the information on a credit file, for example, were collated with the income tax file, the car registration file, the criminal justice file and the like.[1]

The most feasible alternative is that credit reporting should remain in private hands, but subject to government licensing. This is now provided for in the *Consumer Credit Act*, 1974.

It is suggested that the licensing system should include some control over the membership of credit reference agencies and access to credit records. One importance of this is that people who engage in business practices that reputable traders might see as dubious may also be strong competitors. A trader could be denied admission to an agency, or expelled from an agency, when competing vigorously with established members, but when allegations about the integrity of his business methods are also being made. It is surely not in the public interest that in such a situation, judgment on the integrity of his operation should be in the hands of an executive committee that may include his trade rivals or their associates.

Again, the files of credit reference agencies constitute a data bank with potential value for research, including research relating to credit marketing. It is surely not in the public interest that the availability of that research tool should be entirely at the discretion of those concerned with the protection of trade interests.

Having regard to these two examples, and there may be others, it is suggested that the Director General of Fair Trading should have some supervisory jurisdiction over access to credit records.

To sum up, it is suggested that credit reporting is on the whole more

1. *Report of the Committee on Consumer Credit*, 1971, Cmnd 4596, para.9.1.16.

beneficial than harmful. In so far as the systems have undesirable features, these can be remedied or at least mitigated by regulation without altering the basic structure.

14 CONSUMER INSOLVENCY

1. Introduction

There is no easy way to measure the full extent of consumer insolvency. No doubt it varies with swings in the economic cycle. It is clear, however, that consumer insolvency is a continuing and nowadays a substantial problem.

Often a consumer has commitments to the limit of his income. This may then be reduced unexpectedly, perhaps through sickness or unemployment. Or an unexpected event may demand an unplanned expenditure, perhaps for home repairs.

Consumer insolvency cannot, however, be attributed solely to unplanned events. In particular, the enticements of credit grantors are not directed only to those who can afford to pay. A correlation is also observable between consumer insolvency and marital disharmony; though it is unknown to what extent one is causative of the other, or to what extent they may be coincidental results of a common cause.

For reducing the incidence of consumer insolvency, there are several possibilities. Rigorous enforcement of the *Trade Descriptions Act* together with the introduction of interest rate disclosure could help. At least those measures could reduce the undertaking of obligations at a cost greater than people recognise.

Where consumer insolvency occurs, it becomes a feature in the interaction of the family and its creditors. There are, however, some limited opportunities for a more institutional response, and these are mentioned below.

2. Bankruptcy

The essence of bankruptcy is that the assets of an insolvent person are sold for the benefit of his creditors, and he subsequently becomes clear of his debts. The expense of the procedure, however, makes it unrealistic for the majority of consumers, and most bankruptcies are of business enterprises. From a creditor's point of view, putting a debtor into bankruptcy is not worthwhile unless the assets are of sufficient value to cover the costs of the bankruptcy proceedings and sale of the assets. Often that is not the case with insolvent consumers.

Nor is bankruptcy a procedure that insolvent consumers generally want to initiate. Assets are usually more valuable to a consumer than the amount they would yield on a bankruptcy sale. Moreover, bankruptcy can be embarrassing, possibly involving some loss of self-respect, and possibly having an adverse affect on future employment opportunities. Nevertheless, bankruptcy may be a wise course in some situations, and it is one of the options that an insolvent consumer might sometimes be well advised to consider.

3. Commercial Debt-pooling (Pro-rating)

The essence of debt-pooling is that a debtor pays his income, less his living expenses, to a debt-pooler who distributes (usually by a pro-rating formula) the amounts received among the creditors. In effect, the debt-pooler acts as a budget manager for the debtor.

Commercial debt-pooling has been fairly widespread in the United States, and is occasionally found in Britain.

There are many problems with this type of business. First, the debt-pooler charges a substantial commission, thus adding another debt on a family that is already over-burdened.

Secondly, the business has been rife with false advertising. Without actually saying so, advertisements often create the impression that the arrangement being made is a consolidation loan rather than debt-pooling. Many debt-poolers lure clients with attractive advertisements of no more garnishments, no more dunning letters, and no more phone calls from creditors. A debtor is given the impression that creditors will be 'off your back', and he is understandably disappointed when this does not happen. Some debt-poolers advertise themselves as 'credit counsellors', thereby creating the impression that they are qualified people dispensing impartial advise. Moreover, it has been a common complaint that people are not told about the commission and discover that it has been exacted only when they find that the total amount delivered to the debt-pooler has not been distributed among creditors.

Thirdly, awareness that the debt-pooler is a competitor for the available funds of a consumer may make traders suspicious of his services. There is no assurance that creditors will co-operate with the debt-pooler, and commonly they do not.

An aggravating factor is that abuses by debt-poolers do not readily come to the attention of government agencies or the public. The clients tend to be helpless people, quiescent in what happens to them and hesitant to complain. They may also feel reluctant to expand on the number of people becoming aware of their financial difficulties. Moreover, that they have gone to a debt-pooler at all indicates that they do not know where to go for the best sources of help.

In the United States, commercial debt-pooling has been banned in some states and regulated in others. In Britain, the Crowther Committee reported a preference for regulation:

> . . .we should not wish it to be thought that we are seeking to ban the activities of those who carry on the business of debt counselling and debt adjustment for reward. Such concerns, if suitably licensed and charging moderate fees, have a useful function to perform in that they are able not merely to advise but to take charge of a debtor's affairs and devote time to an individual consumer which could not be spared by other agencies covering a wider field. Nevertheless the disreputable conduct of some debt adjustment agencies has given cause for concern, and this form of business requires rigorous control.[1]

The recommendation of the Committee was adopted, and commercial debt-poolers now require a licence as 'debt-adjusters'.[2]

The Crowther Committee did not, however, really come to grips with the question of whether disreputable conduct by debt-poolers is a behavioural aberration or an inherent feature of this type of business. It is at least doubtful whether it is possible for a business of this type to operate profitably, with a fee structure that will attract clients, and honesty. It is the impression of the writer that debt-pooling cannot be operated honestly in the long run unless it is conducted by some social agency or other branch of government, or by some organisation of creditors, so that it can inspire the confidence of the business community and obtain co-operation from creditors in developing smooth routines. If this is right, attempts at regulation are futile and commercial debt-pooling should be banned.

4. Credit Counselling Services

As an alternative to commercial debt-pooling, the Crowther Committee recommended credit counselling services organised on a local basis with government support. The Committee wrote with approval of the service operating in Toronto.[3] Credit counselling services are found in most cities of North America. They have been set up in the United States by various organisations. Many resulted, directly or indirectly, from an initiative of the small loan industry during the 1960s in response to the rising incidence of consumer bankruptcy.

Since the cash loans of small loan companies were usually unsecured, they were often the creditors with the most to lose on a consumer

1. *Report of the Committee on Consumer Credit,* 1971, Cmnd 4596, para.9.3.8.
2. *Consumer Credit Act,* 1974, Part X.
3. *Report of the Committee on Consumer Credit,* 1971, Cmnd 4596, para.9.3.8.

bankruptcy. For reasons explained below, it is at least arguable that the initiators of these services have also been their principal beneficiaries.

In some areas, the small loan industry was so jealous of its control over credit counselling that it insisted on the counselling being done only by loan company personnel, even to the exclusion of bankers and other credit grantors. More recently, however, it seems to be more common for the counselling to be done by full-time staff.

Many credit counselling services are operated by social service agencies. But loan company personnel or former loan company officials can be found even on the governing bodies of social service agencies that administer credit counselling, and sometimes even on government bodies ostensibly responsible for monitoring the social service agencies.

The two main services performed by credit counselling agencies are budgeting advice (i.e. assisting a debtor to work out a budget so that he can organise the discharge of his debts), or debt-pooling (i.e. taking his income, and, after allowing for his living expenses, distributing it among his creditors according to a pro-rating formula).

Credit counselling with debt-pooling included is not organised on a national scale in England, but it has been done occasionally by some family service units and a few Citizens' Advice Bureaux. Also a regular credit counselling service is now operated in Birmingham by the Money Advice Centre of the Birmingham Settlement.

Credit counselling can obviously be useful to someone who needs help to organise a domestic budget. Also where a consumer is over-burdened, a credit counselling service may be more successful than an individual in obtaining the agreement of creditors to accept lower instalments over a longer period:

> The debtor is often afraid to reveal the full extent of his difficulties to his creditors, with the result that the creditors are bemused as to why they are receiving irregular payments. The intervention of a third party in possession of the full facts, is of benefit not only to the debtor but also to the creditor. Were this not so the work of the Centre would be practically impossible since one frequently has to rely on the co-operation of firms who need to see some practical business advantage to themselves in co-operating with such a service.[1]

There are, however, several objections to credit counselling services on the typical North American model. First, much of the literature on the subject,

1. *Debt Counselling*, J. Blamire and A. Izzard, 1975, Birmingham Settlement, p.43.

particularly in the United States, portrays saving people from the stigma of bankruptcy as the primary goal. Yet one thing that an insolvent person needs is an itemisation of the advantages and disadvantages of bankruptcy so that he can make a preference. Impartial advice of that kind can hardly be expected from an organisation that proclaims a dedication to the avoidance of personal bankruptcies, and which is organised and administered by people who, on the question of bankruptcy, are in a class adverse in interest to the consumer. No doubt paying debts is viewed by credit grantors as more honourable than bankruptcy. But that is an ethical question that an insolvent consumer should be free to decide after being appraised of the alternatives. An ethical judgment should not be thrust upon him under the guise of professional advice.

Secondly, what a consumer needs, and what he might think he is receiving, is impartial advice that will include a consideration of whether the claims being made on him are valid. Yet few, if any, credit counselling services are designed to provide this screening. There are several factors militating against the provision of this kind of advice. One is that where credit grantors organise the service, or participate in its management, they may have a natural preference for claims against consumers being paid rather than defended. Even when the service is operated by a social agency, the success of debt-pooling depends on the co-operation of credit grantors, and this may be jeopardised if many claims are defended on advice from the agency. Another factor is that the categories of staff engaged for debt-pooling and budgeting advice are not generally trained in consumer law to a sufficient degree to recognise when defences or counterclaims are available. Moreover, the staff do not have available any comprehensive manual of consumer law, or other documents, such as check lists of possible defences, that would enable them to advise on the validity of claims.[1]

Thirdly, the preference of credit grantors for debt-pooling rather than other kinds of advice or service may be reflected in the financing of an agency, even when financing is by government. For example, in some parts of Canada, the government determines the financial support that it will provide by counting the people on debt-pooling plans. No support is allowed for counselling on the defence of claims, or on the avoidance of debt. Even when the advising agency is part of a government department, its prescribed functions still do not include screening claims for their validity, or advising consumers on the defence of claims.[2]

Fourthly, the participation of credit grantors in counselling may

1. See Ch. 9, page 254.
2. See e.g. *Debtor Assistance Act*, Statutes of British Columbia, 1974, Ch. 25, S.5.

introduce other types of bias and conflicts of interest. For example, it is common in some areas of North America for a debt-pooling plan to end with a consolidation loan. That may sometimes be advantageous to a consumer. But in deciding on the wisdom of a consolidation loan, it is surely improper that a consumer should be dependent for advice on an organisation that is established or influenced by those in the business of making consolidation loans.

Fifthly, one of the ostensible objectives of credit counselling is to promote domestic budgeting so that people will not in future become insolvent. But here again, it is surely undesirable that people should be dependent for advice on budgeting, which includes advice on the wisdom of borrowing, from an organisation that is controlled or influenced by people in the business of lending.

Sixthly, debt-pooling, no matter how administered or by whom, may do more to aggravate than to mitigate the problems of consumer insolvency. By organising a system for the payment of claims which may not otherwise be paid, the aggregate effect is to reduce the risks for credit grantors, thereby tending to expand the perimeters of consumer credit. Moreover, since the situations affected are those in which people have difficulty in making payment, those are also the situations in which the incentive is increased for the expansion to occur. Thus to the extent that credit counselling services are successful in organising the payment of claims, they aggravate the very problem that they are there to solve.

Although debt-pooling may be useful in protecting credit grantors and in helping some consumers, it is suggested that its influence on the well-being of the consuming public as a whole is perverse. If debt-pooling is avoided, however, a credit counselling service could still be useful, and perhaps more useful, for advice on budgeting, the screening of claims for their validity, and advice and assistance on the defence of claims and on debtor strategy for achieving a balanced budget.

5. Administration Orders

An administration order is a form of debt-pooling operated by the court.[1] County Courts have been empowered for many years to make administration orders at the request of a debtor. These orders have been used extensively in some courts, but rarely in others. No doubt this partly reflects differences in attitudes towards administration orders by different registrars and court staffs.

During 1976, 2,568 applications were filed, and 1,971 orders were

1. For a more detailed discussion of administration orders, see e.g. *Report of the Committee on the Enforcement of Judgment Debts*, 1969, Cmnd 3909, pp.194-214.

granted on debtors' applications. (Another 60 orders were made under section 4(2) of the *Attachment of Earnings Act*.) Roughly half the applications (1,454) involved 6 or more creditors. Almost all the orders (2,001) provided for payment in full. However the number of orders discharged (715) was only about half the number rescinded (1,414). The average duration of discharged orders was 50 months.[1]

An administration order avoids most of the evils of commercial debt-pooling; and it has the advantage that the creditors covered by the order are precluded from issuing separate executions out of the court while the order remains in effect. But administration orders are open to the same basic objection as debt-pooling by credit counselling services. To the extent that they result in creditors being paid who would not otherwise be paid, they tend to expand the perimeters of consumer credit. Thus while the orders may help some insolvent consumers, they may in aggregate do more to aggravate than to mitigate the dimensions of consumer insolvency.

Another danger with administration orders is that if they ever became a normal routine, the pressure may develop to make them compulsory. Indeed, that pressure has been part of the political scene with regard to similar legislation in the United States and Canada. To have people bound for periods of years to pay all their discretionary income to creditors would be dangerously close to medieval concepts of bondage. It could undermine working morale and have a depressing effect on family life. Worse still, such a move would tend to expand even further the perimeters of consumer credit, and further aggravate, rather than mitigate, the dimensions of consumer insolvency.

6. Conclusions

Consumer insolvency will not be alleviated through debt-pooling: indeed, its dimensions are more likely to be enlarged than diminished. If it is right to assume that credit grantors are usually better equipped than consumers to make cautious judgments about financing and future commitments, the solution must come in creating a disincentive for credit grantors to advance credit when consumer insolvency is the likely result. Adoption of the proposal in Chapter 10, page 285, i.e., the abolition of debt claims in retail transactions, would be an important step in this direction.

If bankruptcy ever became cheap enough to be readily available to consumers, another possibility might be to consider whether, on a bankruptcy,

1. All figures from the *Judicial Statistics, England and Wales for the year 1976*, Cmnd 6875, p.80.

cash lenders should rank in order of their contractual interest rate, with those charging the highest ranking last. This could tend to discourage the extension of credit in marginal situations where the debtor is reaching the limits of his capacity to repay. Those are the transactions likely to be consummated at the highest rates. Moreover it is at least arguable that this formula for priority would be more equitable among credit grantors. Those who are charging an interest rate commensurate with a greater risk ought surely to be taking a greater risk.

15 CONCLUSIONS

Conclusions on particular matters have been included in the above chapters. It may be helpful, however, to summarise here some conclusions of broader application.

First, there is no correlation between consumer grievances suffered and complaints made. The latter are likely to be tiny in relation to the former.[1] Any government study for developing legislative policy in relation to consumer protection would, therefore, be inadequate if it were a response to the grievances of the minority of consumers who have sought government attention. Legislative changes will never be soundly based if they simply reflect the recommendations of a committee or commission proceeding by the 'sit back and listen' principle, or if the task is perceived as one of adjudication between bipolar adversaries, or an exercise in brokerage politics.

Fortunately, the Crowther Committee was sensitive to these points. Its procedures recognised a responsibility for initiative as well as judgment; a responsibility for ascertaining the problems and evolving solutions (rather than simply listening to submissions).

Fortunately too, there has been a shift of emphasis in the last decade from formalities to the substance of the matter. In adjudication, there has been some shift of emphasis from the exclusivity of form documents to the importance of parol evidence.[2] With regard to substantive law, the *Consumer Credit Act,* following the recommendations of the Crowther Committee, now applies protective clauses more according to the substance of a transaction, attaching less significance to the documentary choices of the parties.

Another strength of the Crowther Committee was its mandate to study consumer credit, not to study a particular statute. Unfortunately, however, the same approach was not taken subsequently with regard to trade practices. Instead of a committee or commission being established to study integrity in marketing, a committee was established simply to review the *Trade Descriptions Act.* Requiring the Committee to review an Act, rather than to review problems of integrity in marketing, created a risk that imagination and initiative might be curtailed by preconceptions based on

1. See Chapter 6(1).
2. See e.g. *Law of Contract : The Parol Evidence Rule,* 1976, Law Commission, Working Paper No. 70, pp.20-1.

the terms, context and institutional background of the existing statute. For example, in the dismissal of some proposals for reform,[1] it was considered relevant that the proposal would be inconsistent with the orientation of the Act as part of criminal law.

While the *Consumer Credit Act* brought significant reforms, it still reflects the common tendency in the legislative process to legitimate existing structures and practices, rather than to scan the range of available options. The tendency has been to attempt the prevention of abuses by regulating the status quo rather than by raising more fundamental questions about optimum structure. For example, collection agencies and commercial debt-poolers have been subjected to licensing without the question being fully explored of whether those organisations should exist at all. Similarly, debt claims by retailers against consumers and the pre-computation of interest in consumer credit transactions have both been allowed to develop and survive, though their abolition would surely be in the public interest. Private decisions made by those on one side of the marketplace still seem to govern the structure and practice of credit marketing more than the decisions made through the parliamentary process.

Another difficulty with consumer protection is that legislation, like case law, tends to focus on transactions involving substantial amounts while the bulk of consumer transactions involve small sums. For example, the *Consumer Credit Act* authorises the courts to grant relief from 'extortionate credit bargains'. Court proceedings of that type are not likely to become common in consumer cases. A statutory rate ceiling would surely have broader potential for transactions of modest amounts.

Much of this work has focused on the unsuitability of the adversary system in relation to small claims. Indeed, the adversary system may well do more to promote than to suppress fraud, other predatory practices in marketing and the supply of defective goods. Proposals relating to this are set out in Chapters 9 and 10.

As explained in Chapter 12, regulations requiring behaviour contrary to the pressures of the market can be difficult to enforce, the more so if enforcement is not actively and constantly supported by organised groups. Relevant to this, there is a natural tendency in the political process to seek compromise. This may be satisfactory if there is some ground between contending positions on which a compromise can rest. But in consumer protection, that is often not so. Interest rate disclosure illustrates the point. The tenable positions are the extremes. Interest rate disclosure should be required with thorough enforcement machinery to prevent

1. E.g. the proposal that corrective advertising might sometimes be required. (*Review of the Trade Descriptions Act 1968*, 1976, Cmnd 6628, paras.194-7.)

evasion or non-compliance, or alternatively, interest rate disclosure should not be required at all. To legislate compulsory rate disclosure without thorough enforcement machinery is the worst of all worlds. Yet it would not be too surprising if that result emerges from conflicting political pressures.

Often the accommodation or rejection of political pressures is avoided in legislation and deferred into the regulatory process. In this connection, the *Consumer Credit Act*, 1974, leaves many important provisions to be added by regulations or administrative arrangements. This permits flexibility to meet changing conditions and quick revision in the light of experience. But it also adds to the potential for untenable compromise. If it is right that the lobbying power of consumer organisations is generally stronger in the legislative process than in public administration, and conversely, that the lobbying power of corporate organisations is generally stronger and more continuously applied in administrative processes, regulation-making powers may not be as effective for consumer protection as substantive provisions contained in an act.

It has also been emphasised that credit transactions and collections are not just sequential processes, with the former sometimes leading to the latter but the latter having no effect on the former. Collection processes have a feedback influence on the integrity of selling and financing, and on the judgments of credit grantors about the provision of credit. It has been argued that the strengthening of credit reporting and the weakening of creditors' remedies offer the best hope of promoting a healthy credit industry while avoiding the social harms that can flow from harsh methods of collection.

In the discussion of consumer protection over the last two decades, the focus has been fairly constant, though there have been shifts of emphasis. The accelerating proliferation of gadgets may not seem as inevitable now as it may have appeared two decades ago. Pollution, uncertainty about the economy, and other problems affecting the quality of life may have come more to the forefront. But problems of integrity in marketing always remain. Moreover, they have an importance that goes beyond their immediate impact on consumers.

Businessmen set an example to others in their capacity of employers, and they often play leadership roles in other aspects of community life. Thus the standards of integrity observed in marketing can have spillover effects in society at large and in public affairs, both directly through the participation of businessmen and indirectly through the imitation of their standards. The enforcement, or non-enforcement, of legislation relating to integrity in marketing has, therefore, a potential impact on the public interest going well beyond its immediate role in consumer protection.

APPENDICES

APPENDIX A: THE SAMPLE

Introduction

The aim was to produce a random preselected sample of at least 1,500 households in England and Wales. To enable the selected households to be questioned by personal interview, the sample was clustered at 60 sampling points. This required a two-stage probability sample.

The First Stage: Selection of the Sampling Points (Polling Districts)

First, the 60 sampling points were allocated among the Registrar General's 10 standard regions in proportion to the adult population of each region.[1]

Within each standard region, a sampling frame was used that listed all the Local Authority Areas in England and Wales stratified in the following ways:

(1) By area type:
  (a) conurbations;
  (b) non-conurbation urban areas;
  (c) non-conurbation rural areas.
(2) Within each area type:
  (a) *conurbations*: by high employment areas/low employment areas;
  (b) *non-conurbations*: by high population density/low population density.
(3) Within each of the resultant cells, Local Authority Areas were arranged in descending order of a socio-economic index derived from the 1966 Census of Population.

The name of each Local Authority Area in the sampling frame was followed by the adult population[2] of that area, based on the 1966 Census. This was followed by a cumulative running total of the adult population for the standard region. Commencing at a random start and proceeding through this cumulative running total by a fixed interval, the sampling points were selected for each region, with each Local Authority Area

1. Because the demographic data was readily available in this form, the adult population was taken as those aged 15 years and over at the 1966 Census.
2. See footnote 1 *supra*.

having a probability of selection proportionate to its adult population.[1] Within each Local Authority Area, the polling districts were also listed with their total electorate, followed by a cumulative running total of the electorate for that Local Authority Area. Thus by applying a conversion factor to allow for the difference between the adult population and the electorate, the selection of a population point within the sampling frame identified not only the Local Authority Area within which the sampling point should be located, but also the particular polling district to be used as the sampling point.

In this way, 60 sampling points were identified. It was felt, however, that on this survey the risk of distortion through sampling imperfections was less than the risk of mistakes or incomplete results through interviewer error. To secure a high quality of interviewers, therefore, it was decided that some marginal sampling imperfections could be tolerated. Thus the list of sampling points that had been drawn was checked to ensure that good interviewers would be available for each point. Following this check, four of the points were changed. In each case, this was done by substituting

Table A.1: Distribution of Sampling Points

Standard region	Number of Sampling points			
	Conurbation	Urban	Rural	Total
North	1	2	1	4
North West	5	3	1	9
Yorkshire and Northumberland	2	3	1	6
West Midlands	3	2	1	6
East Midlands	–	3	1	4
East Anglia	–	1	1	2
South West	–	3	2	5
South East	–	8	3	11
Greater London	10	–	–	10
Wales	–	3	–	3
Totals	21	28	11	60

1. The sampling interval was determined by dividing the total adult population in each standard region by the number of sampling points allotted to that region. This figure, plus the remainder, was used to determine the range at the beginning of the sampling frame within which the random start should be selected. Within this range, the random start was picked by using a book of random numbers.

another Local Authority Area in the same standard region having demographic and socio-economic characteristics as close as possible to the one that had first been selected. A polling district within that Local Authority Area was then chosen by random selection. The 60 sampling points were distributed as shown in Table A.1.

The Second Stage: Selection of the Households (Addresses)

Within each selected polling district, a sample of 25 addresses was drawn from the current electoral register. This was done by going through the register applying a fixed sampling interval to a random start.[1] If the elector at whose name the sampling interval terminated was the first elector at his address, that address was included in the sample, but otherwise it was not. In either case, the name of that elector was used as the starting point for applying the sampling interval again. This procedure was used to ensure that each household would have approximately an equal chance of selection rather than a probability of selection in proportion to the number of registered electors at each address.

On arriving at the end of the register of electors for a polling district, a return was made to the beginning, thus passing through the register in a circular motion until 25 addresses had been drawn.[2]

Non-elector Households

Following each selected address, a note was made on the sample issue sheet of the next address in the electoral register. The interviewers were instructed that if any dwelling unit exists *between* the selected address and the next known address, contact should be made with that dwelling unit in addition to the selected address, and it should be added to the sample. In this way, it was hoped to include in the sample a random selection of non-elector households (for example aliens) in a proportion roughly equivalent to their occurrence in the population.

At six sampling points, all in rural areas, it was not possible to follow this procedure because of the difficulty of ensuring that the electoral register followed a geographic progression along one side of a street.

1. The sampling interval was determined by dividing the total electorate by 25. The resultant figure, plus the remainder, determined the range at the beginning of the register within which the random start was selected. Within that range, the starting point was selected by using a book of random numbers.

2. It would have been slightly more precise to have selected the random start anywhere within the polling district. But the register for each polling district was covered two or three times by the circular process described in the text. Moreover there is no reason to suppose that households at the beginning of the register would differ from those towards the end. It is not thought, therefore, that any significant bias will have resulted from selecting the random start close to the beginning.

However it was followed for 54 sampling points.

This procedure resulted in 23 households being added to the sample.

New Building Areas

While the procedure described in the preceding paragraphs might embrace some isolated instances of new building, it would not cover any substantial new building areas. A separate procedure was therefore used to include new building areas in the sample.

Using the *Monthly Digest of Statistics* for the basic data, an estimate was made of the proportion of new dwelling units completed since the electoral registers were last revised to dwelling units existing at that date. In this way, it was estimated that 40 addresses in the sample should be drawn from new building areas.

To permit clustering, it was decided that the new building area households should be drawn at not more than 10 of the sampling points. Using once more a book of random numbers, 10 sampling points were selected out of the 60, each having equal probability of selection.

For these 10 sampling points, the Local Authorities were asked if they could supply lists of all new residential accommodation completed within their Local Authority Areas since the electoral register was last revised. Two replied that no new residential building had been completed in their areas and the remaining 8 supplied lists. Some of these lists contained complete addresses. Others showed only the streets, and in these cases, the house numbers were ascertained by inspection and enquiry at the location. Once the complete street addresses were ascertained, random sampling procedures similar to those described above were applied so that 40 new building area addresses were selected, being 5 at each of the 8 sampling points. These selected addresses were then entered on the sample issue sheets for those 8 sampling points in substitution for addresses that had been drawn from the electoral register.

Multi-household Addresses

Although the sample required was a sample of households, the most suitable data base, i.e., the electoral register, only records names and addresses. Thus special provision was needed for multi-household addresses, for example, where a house has been divided into several flats but they are all still using the same postal address.

For each selected address, the interviewer was told to establish how many households were resident at that address. The instructions were that where more than one household was resident:

Either in the case of 2 or 3 households, treat each household

> separately by completing a Contact Report and interviewing at each.
>
> *Or* in the case of *4* or more households (e.g., large blocks of flats) the names of 3 persons have been entered on the SLS. Establish the households to which these belong and contact each one. (They may, by coincidence, be in the same household, in which case *do not* substitute.) If one of them has moved, contact the household now living at the flat where he used to live.

This instruction applied only where several households were living at one address. For most blocks of flats, however, this would not apply because each flat would be shown as a separate address in the electoral register. Where this was so, flats were selected in the same way as houses.

In the event, 17 households were added pursuant to this instruction. Thus the total for the final sample was 1,540 households.

Institutions

By using the electoral register for drawing the sample, institutions having no-one resident would automatically be excluded. For the purpose of this survey, it was also desired to exclude institutions having people who are resident, but not living in a household way, for example nursing homes and military barracks.

The instructions to the interviewers were as follows:

> Hotels, public houses, boarding houses and hostels, factories, business premises, hospitals, old people's homes, nursing homes, prisons, schools, colleges and other such establishments are defined as Institutions and are EXCLUDED from this survey. We have tried to exclude them at the sampling stage, but if one does occur, take no further action except entering it as unproductive both on your sample issue sheet and on a contact report. But if the selected address is a dwelling unit, it should not be excluded simply because it is attached to an institution.

APPENDIX B: HOUSEHOLD CONTACT REPORT

(Parts dealing with the identification of the household, introduction of the interviewer, and contact details omitted.)

J.6419

PART A – PRODUCTIVE CONTACT. ITEM SELECTION

ASK HEAD OF HOUSEHOLD OR OTHER ADULT MEMBER.

SHOW CARD A

Q1(a) I will read over this list of items and would like you to tell me whether you, or anyone in your household, have bought any during the *last two years*? Please include any item that was ordered though not received and also include items received on approval. Also please include anything that was bought, ordered or received, even if you don't have it now.

READ ALOUD SLOWLY AND RING CODE OF EACH 'YES'

KEY CODE

FOR EACH ITEM WHERE THE REPLY IS 'YES' (CODE RINGED) ASK:

(b) How long was ago was that?

IF UP TO 2 WEEKS, RING CODE X

IF OVER 2 WEEKS, ENTER IN MONTHS TO THE NEAREST MONTH (TWO FIGURE ENTRY)

PROCEED WITH REFERENCE TO ITEMS BOUGHT OVER TWO WEEKS AGO.

IF NO ITEMS – CLOSE INTERVIEW
IF 1 ITEM – INTERVIEW FOR THAT ITEM
IF 2 ITEMS – INTERVIEW FOR THOSE 2 ITEMS
IF MORE THAN 2 ITEMS – INTERVIEW FOR THE FIRST TWO ITEMS IN THE SEQUENCE
(KEY CODES 01, 02 etc.)

ENTER INITIALS OF THE BUYER(S) OF THE SELECTED ITEMS IN COLUMN 1, AND IN COLUMN 2 TICK (√) WHEN INTERVIEW FOR THE ITEM COMPLETED. (OTHERWISE GIVE REASONS WHY NOT COMPLETED.)

			1.	2.
Vacuum Cleaner	01	X		
Encyclopedia Set or reference books (over £20)	02	X		
Heating Equipment (total over £20 bought at one time)	03	X		
Cooking Utensils (total over £20 bought at one time)	04	X		
Sewing Machine	05	X		
Knitting Machine	06	X		
Typewriter	07	X		
New Motor Vehicle	08	X		
Secondhand Motor Vehicle	09	X		
TV, radio, tape recorder record player or combination	10	X		
Dishwasher	11	X		
Furniture (total over £20 bought at one time)	12	X		
Rug or Carpet (over £20)	13	X		
Refrigerator	14	X		
Deep Freeze	15	X		
Gas or Electric Stove	16	X		
Washing Machine, Dryer or combination	17	X		

Except for secondhand motor vehicles, check 'yes' responses to ensure that the item was NEW or intended to be NEW.

PART A SUMMARY: NO ITEMS BOUGHT OVER 2 WEEKS AGO – 0
INTERVIEW FOR 1 ITEM .... – 1
INTERVIEW FOR 2 ITEMS .... – 2

APPENDIX C: QUESTIONNAIRE

(Note: To facilitate printing, directional lines, colour coding, and office coding boxes have been omitted.)

		Code
Description of Item.	O.U.O.	
	Months Ago Bought	

SECTION 1 – ASK ALL

			Code
1.	What make is/was the ....? WRITE IN	O.U.O.	
		Don't know/remember	9
2.	When you bought the ...., how long had you been living at the address where you then lived?	Less than 1 month	Y
		1 month – less than 6 months	X
		6 months – less than 3 years	0
		3 years or over	1
		Don't remember	2
		O.U.O.	3
3.	a) Did you contact the seller in response to an advertisement for a *particular* ....?	Yes	Y
		No (Go to Q.4)	X
		Don't remember (Go to Q.4)	0
		O.U.O.	1

IF YES (Code Y)

b) Where did you see or hear the advertisement?	Newspaper or Magazine	Y	Y	Y
	Television	X	X	X
	Brochure delivered to home	0	0	0
	Brochure I picked up	1	1	1
	By telephone	2	2	2
MORE THAN ONE CODE MAY BE RINGED	On radio	3	3	3
	At a cinema	4	4	4
	Poster	5	5	5
	Catalogue	6	6	6
Other (STATE)		7	7	7
	Don't remember	8		
	O.U.O.	9		
c) Was the.............. that you bought exactly the same model as the one advertised?	Yes (Go to Q.5)		Y	
	No		A	
	Don't know (Go to Q.5)		0	
	O.U.O.		1	

IF NO (CODE A)

d) Why did you buy the one that you did rather than the one advertised?	One advertised was sold out	2		2
	One advertised not available for immediate delivery	3		3
	The salesman said the one I bought would be more satisfactory	4		4
MORE THAN ONE CODE MAY BE RINGED	Did not like the one advertised when I saw it	5		5
	Just preferred the one bought	6		6
Other (STATE)		7		7
	Don't know	8		
	O.U.O.	9		

		Code
e) What was the cash price of the one advertised?	WRITE IN £........ (Go to Q.5)	
	I never knew (Go to Q.5)	Y
	Don't remember	X
	O.U.O.	

IF DON'T REMEMBER (Code X)

		Code
f) Was the price of the one advertised more or less than the price of the one you bought?	One advertised was more	Y
	One advertised was less	X
	Both the same	0
	Don't remember	1
	O.U.O.	2
	→ NOW GO TO Q.5	

IF Q.3a) CODE X or O

		Code
4. a) Before you bought the .... do you remember seeing, or hearing, any particular advertising for ....s? (Doubtful answers code 0)	Yes	Y
	No (Go to Q.6)	X
	Don't remember (Go to Q.6)	0
	O.U.O.	1

IF YES (Code Y)

b) Where did you see or hear the advertising?	Newspaper or magazine	Y	Y	Y
	Television	X	X	X
	Brochure delivered to home	0	0	0
	Brochure I picked up	1	1	1
MORE THAN ONE CODE MAY BE RINGED	By telephone	2	2	2
	On radio	3	3	3
	At a cinema	4	4	4
	Poster	5	5	5
	Catalogue	6	6	6
Other (STATE)		7	7	7
	Don't remember	8		
	O.U.O.	9		

c) Did the advertising mention the make and model you bought?	Yes	Y
	No	X
	Don't remember	0
	O.U.O.	1
d) Did it (also) mention other makes or models?	Yes	Y
	No	X
	Don't remember	0
	O.U.O.	1
e) Did it mention the seller you bought the ....from?	Yes	Y
	No	X
	Don't remember	0
	O.U.O.	1
f) Did it (also) mention other sellers?	Yes	Y
	No	X
	Don't remember	0
	O.U.O.	1

5. ASK WHERE SOME ADVERTISING SEEN OR HEARD
Q.3a) CODED Y OR Q.4a) CODED Y

a) What did the advertising say?
LISTEN AND PROBE FULLY, BUT
DO NOT RECORD ANSWERS

b) Did any of this turn out to be wrong or untrue?
Yes A
No X
Don't know 0
O.U.O. 1

IF YES (CODE A)
c) What was wrong or untrue?
MORE THAN ONE CODE MAY BE RINGED

Goods not the quality advertised	2	2	2
Did not wear as well as advertising said	3	3	3
Did not perform as well as advertising said	4	4	4
Other (STATE)	8	8	8
O.U.O.	9		

ASK ALL
6. Before buying the ...., did you or anyone in the household discuss the matter outside the household; for example, with friends, relatives or neighbours?
Yes Y
No X
Don't remember 0
O.U.O. 1

7. a) Have you ever seen a magazine called "Which?"?
Yes A
No X
Don't know 0
O.U.O. 1

IF "YES" (Code A)
b) Did you check to see if there was any information about .... in "Which?" prior to buying this one?
Yes B
No 2
Don't know 3
O.U.O. 4

IF "YES" (Code B)
c) Was the one you bought recommended in "Which?"?
Yes 5
No 6
Don't remember 7
O.U.O. 8

8. Did you buy the .... at a shop/garage/etc. or from someone who called, or how?
At a shop/garage/etc. Y
At a wholesale warehouse X
From a heating engineer or builder 0
At the factory 1
Salesman called at home (Go to Q.13) 2
Salesman called at work (Go to Q.13) 3
By mail order (Go to Q.12) 4
Private seller (Item 09 only) (Go to Q.18) 5
O.U.O. 6

ASK WHERE ITEM BOUGHT FROM A SHOP/GARAGE ETC., WHOLESALE WAREHOUSE, HEATING ENGINEER, OR FACTORY Q.8 CODED Y, X, 0 or 1
9. Before going to the shop/garage/etc. where you bought the .... did you look at ....for sale at other places?
Yes Y
No X
Don't remember 0
O.U.O. 1

			Code	
10.	a) Before you went to the shop/garage/etc., where you bought the ...., did anyone from the shop/etc./get in touch with you?	Yes	A	
		No	X	
		Don't remember	0	
		O.U.O.	1	
	IF YES (Code A) b) How did they get in touch with you? MORE THAN ONE CODE MAY BE RINGED	Came to the home	2	2
		Came to where I work	3	3
		By telephone	4	4
		By mail	5	5
		Other (STATE)	6	6
		O.U.O.	7	
11.	SHOP SALES ONLY What type of shop was it where you bought the...........? MORE THAN ONE CODE MAY BE RINGED	Department Store	Y	Y
		Chain Store	X	X
		Discount Store	0	0
		Co-op	1	1
		Gas or electricity board	2	2
		Specialist shop	3	3
		Temporary or makeshift trade premises	4	4
	Other (STATE)		5	5
		Don't know	8	
		O.U.O.	9	
12.	MAIL ORDER CASES ONLY. ASK WHERE Q.8 CODED 4 How did you place the order?	With a salesman who came to the home (Go to Q.13)	Y	
		With an agent of mail order company who I know (Go to Q.18)	X	
		Sent it by mail (Go to Q.19)	0	
		At a mail order office (Go to Q.19)	1	
		By telephone (Go to Q.19)	2	
		O.U.O.	3	

SECTION 2

WHERE A SALESMAN CAME TO THE HOME OR PLACE OF WORK

ASK ALL WHERE Q.8 CODED 2 or 3
or Q.10 CODED 2 or 3
or Q.12 CODED Y

13.	Did you look around for a .... in the shops before you bought this one?	Yes	Y
		No	X
		Don't remember	0
		O.U.O.	1
14.	a) Before the salesman came was an appointment made for him to come and see you?	Yes	Y
		No	X
		Don't remember	0
		O.U.O.	1

b) Had you sent in your name in response to an advertisement?	Yes	Y	
	No	X	
	Don't remember	0	
	O.U.O.	1	

15. How did the salesman first introduce himself? Why did he say he wanted to talk to you? PROBE	Said he was selling..........	Y	Y
	Said he was taking a survey or opinion poll	X	X
	Said his firm was launching an advertising drive and wanted to place a .... with us for advertising purposes	0	0
MORE THAN ONE CODE MAY BE RINGED	Said I had won a contest or been selected for a prize	1	1
	Said he was from the education authority	2	2
	Said he was from some other public authority or department (STATE)	3	3
	Other (state)	4	4
	....		
	Don't remember (PROBE)	8	
	O.U.O.	9	

16. Did he say that your name had been suggested to him by someone you knew?	Yes	Y	
	No	X	
	Don't remember	0	
	O.U.O.	1	

17. a) About what time of day did the salesman arrive?	WRITE IN.		
	Don't remember		0
	A.M.		X
OFFICE USE ONLY	P.M.		Y
b) About what time did he leave?	WRITE IN.		
	Don't remember		0
	A.M.		X
OFFICE USE ONLY	P.M.		Y

SECTION 3 – ASK ALL

18. a) Were you thinking of buying a .... before you went to the shop/before the salesman called/etc.?	Yes	A
	No	X
	Don't remember	0
	O.U.O.	1
IF YES (Code A)		
b) Did you decide to the buy the model of .... that you actually bought before you went to the shop/before the salesman called/etc.?	Yes	2
	No	3
	Don't remember	4
	O.U.O.	5

19. a) In order to get the ...., did you agree to take some other thing, or some service, in addition to the ....?	Yes	A
	No	X
	Don't remember	0

		Code	
	O.U.O.	1	
PROBE IF NECESSARY, SEE EXAMPLES IN MANUAL, P.15			
IF YES (Code A)			
b) What was the other thing(s)?			
c) Were you satisfied with the (other thing)?	Yes	Y	
	No	B	
	Almost/not quite	C	
	O.U.O.	X	
IF NO OR ALMOST (Code B or C)			
d) What was unsatisfactory about it?	Poor quality or performance	1	1
	High price	2	2
Other (STATE)		3	3
MORE THAN ONE CODE MAY BE RINGED			
. . . .	O.U.O.9		

20. a) When you were buying the .... what did the salesman/seller/ agent/etc. tell you about it?	Nothing at all	Y		
	Never spoke to a salesman/etc.	X		
	All other answers	A		
	O.U.O.	0		
LISTEN AND PROBE FULLY, BUT DO NOT RECORD ANSWERS VERBATIM				
IF a) CODED A				
b) Did any of this turn out to be wrong on untrue?	Yes	1		
	No	2		
	Don't know	3		
	O.U.O.	4		
IF YES (Code 1)				
c) What was wrong or untrue?	Goods not the quality that salesman said	Y	Y	Y
	Goods did not wear as well as salesman said	X	X	X
MORE THAN ONE CODE MAY BE RINGED	Did not perform as well as salesman said	0	0	0
	Item was not new	1	1	1
	Operating cost more than salesman said	2	2	2
Other (STATE)		8	8	8
. . . .	O.U.O.	9		

21. a) Were you mislead or misinformed in any way about how much you would have to pay for the ....?	Yes	A	
	No	X	
	Don't remember	0	
	O.U.O.	1	
IF YES (Code A)			
b) What were you told that was wrong?			
c) How were you misinformed?	By the salesman I/we bought the .... from	Y	Y
	In the advertising	X	X

		Code	
MORE THAN ONE CODE MAY BE RINGED	By notices in the shop where .... was purchased	0	0
	Labels on the	1	1
Otherwise (STATE)		2	2
....	O.U.O.	9	

22\. a) Is there anything you feel you should have been told by the seller that you were not told?

Yes	A
No	X
Don't know	0
O.U.O.	1

IF YES (Code A)

b) What was it? ....

....

23\. a) Apart from any points just mentioned, was there anything about the sale transaction that you feel was unsatisfactory?

Yes	A
No	X
Don't know	0
O.U.O.	Y

IF YES (Code A)

b) What was it?

MORE THAN ONE CODE MAY BE RINGED

Excessive price	1	1	1
Excessive cost of credit/interest rate	2	2	2
Low part-exchange allowance	3	3	3
Have no use for the	4	4	4
High pressure sales tactics (Salesman talked me into it, etc.)	5	5	5
Salesman was not well informed about the product	6	6	6
Seller knew I couldn't afford it	7	7	7
I signed agreement in blank and seller inserted wrong figures	8	8	8
Other (STATE)	9	9	9
O.U.O.			Y

24\. a) At the time of the purchase, or before that, were you given to understand that the price you were paying for the .... was less than the usual price?

Yes	A
No	X
Don't remember	O
O.U.O.	Y

IF YES (Code A)

b) How were you informed of this?

MORE THAN ONE CODE MAY BE RINGED

By the salesman	1	1	1
In the advertising	2	2	2
By notices in the shop, or labels on the	3	3	3
Had a staff discount	4	4	4
Otherwise (STATE)........................	5	5	5
Don't remember	8		
O.U.O.	9		

25\. a) Were you informed that you could return the ...., or cancel the deal, within a limited time?

Yes	A
No	X
Don't remember	O
O.U.O.	Y

IF YES (Code A)

b) How were you informed of this?

In the advertising	1	1	1
The salesman told me	2	2	2

		Code		
	In the written contract	3	3	3
MORE THAN ONE CODE MAY BE RINGED	By a notice handed to me by the salesman	4	4	4
	By a notice received through the post	5	5	5
	In catalogue	6	6	6
	General knowledge/I know the law etc.	7	7	7
	Otherwise (STATE).	8	8	8
	Don't remember	9		
	O.U.O.		9	

26\. a) Did you attempt to return the ...., or to cancel the deal?

Yes	A
No	X
O.U.O.	O

IF YES (Code A)

b) Did you do this in writing?

Yes	1
No	2
Don't remember	3
O.U.O.	4

c) How long was this after you received the second copy of the agreement?

WRITE IN NUMBER OF DAYS	
There was no written agreement	Y
Only received one copy	X
Never received any copy	0
Don't remember	1
O.U.O.	2

d) Did the seller agree to take the .... back, or to cancel the deal?

Yes	A
No (Go to f)	B

IF YES (Code A)

e) Did you get back any money that you had paid?

Yes – all	Y
Part of it	X
No	0
Hadn't paid any money	1
Don't remember	2
O.U.O.	3

IF NO AT d) (Code B)

f) Please explain what happened . . . .

. . . .

. . . .

27\. At the time of the purchase, how was the particular .... you were going to buy identified for you?

SHOW CARD B AND READ ALOUD

RING ONE CODE ONLY

	See the actual one to be delivered	Y
	See another one of the same make and model	X
	See one similar to the one bought	0
	See a sample piece	1
Did you	Order by description because you were already familiar with this type of goods	2
	Order by catalogue description	3
	Order by description in advertisement	4
	Order by description of salesman	5
	O.U.O.	6

				Code
		IF Q.27 CODED Y		
28.	a)	Did you get the one you ordered	Yes	Y
		IF Q.27 NOT CODED Y	No	A
		Was the one you received exactly what you ordered in terms of make, model, colour, etc.?	Never received one at all	X
			Don't know	0
			O.U.O.	1
		IF NO (Code A)		
	b)	Was the one you received just as acceptable as the one ordered?	Yes	2
			No	3
			Almost/not quite	4
			O.U.O.	5
		ASK FOR MOTOR VEHICLES ONLY (ITEM CODES 08, 09)		
29.	a)	How long had you been driving before you bought this vehicle?	Over 1 year	Y
			3 months to 1 year	X
			Less than 3 months	0
			Never driven	1
			O.U.O.	2
		ASK IF SECOND-HAND VEHICLE (ITEM 09)		
	b)	Does the seller that you bought the vehicle from also sell new vehicles?	Yes	Y
			No	X
			Don't know	0
			O.U.O.	1
	c)	How old was the vehicle at the time when you bought it?	Les than 1 year	0
			1 up to –2 years	1
			2 up to –3 years	2
			3 up to –4 years	3
			4 up to –5 years	4
			5 up to –6 years	5
			6 up to –7 years	6
			7 years and over	7
			Don't know	8
			O.U.O.	9
	d)	Did you receive a Ministry of Transport Test Certificate with the vehicle?	Yes	Y
			No	X
			Don't know if received	0
			Don't know what that is	1
			O.U.O.	2
	e)	Did you have any mechanical check made yourself before you bought it?	Yes	A
			No	X
			O.U.O.	0
		IF YES (Code A)		
	f)	Who checked it for you?	Myself	1
			A garage	2
			A friend	3
			The A.A. or R.A.C.	4
		Other (STATE)		5
			Don't remember	6
			O.U.O.	9

Code

SECTION 4 – ASK ALL WHERE SOME ITEM WAS RECEIVED
(ASK ALL WHERE Q.28 CODED Y, A or 0)

30. a) Did you receive the .... at the time you ordered it or later?

At the time	Y
Later	A
Don't remember	X
O.U.O.	0

IF LATER (Code A)
b) Was it ready/delivered when promised, or was there a delay?

Ready/delivered on time	1
No particular time was promised	2
Delayed 1-7 days	3
Delayed 8-28 days	4
Delayed over 28 days	5
Delayed, but don't remember how long	6
Don't remember	7
O.U.O.	8

31. Where did you receive it

At home	Y
At the shop/garage/etc.	X
Elsewhere (STATE)	0
Don't remember	1
O.U.O.	2

32. a) Were any accessories missing that you were informed would come with the ....?

Yes	A
No	X
Don't know	O
O.U.O.	Y

IF YES (Code A)
b) What was missing? . . . .

. . . .

33. a) When you received it, was it in as good a condition as you expected it to be?

Yes	Y
No	A
Don't know	O
O.U.O.	X

IF NO (Code A)
b) What was wrong with it?

MORE THAN ONE CODE MAY BE RINGED

Chipped, scratched, or dented	1	1	1
Stained or rusty	2	2	2
Dirty or marked	3	3	3
Didn't work at all	4	4	4
Didn't work properly	5	5	5
Other (STATE)	8	8	8
O.U.O.	9		

34. a) Since you received the ...., have any (other) defects appeared?

Yes	A
No	X
O.U.O.	0

IF YES (Code A)
b) What are they?

Parts became loose	1	1	1
Parts broke too easily or went wrong	2	2	2
Colour faded	3	3	3

		Code		
MORE THAN ONE CODE	Creaks or other noises	4	4	4
MAY BE RINGED	Showing excessive wear	5	5	5
Other (STATE)		8	8	8
	O.U.O.	9		

35. ASK ONLY FOR HEATING EQUIPMENT, TELEVISION, RECORD PLAYER, CARPET, STOVE, WASHING MACHINE OR DRYER

a) Did the .... need any sort of installation or fitting?	Yes	A
	No	X
	O.U.O.	0
IF YES (Code A)		
b) Was the installation or fitting done properly?	Yes	1
	Almost/not quite	2
	No	3
	Never done at all (Go to Q.36)	4
	Don't know	5
	O.U.O.	6
c) Who did the installation or fitting?	Seller of the	Y
	Ourselves	X
	A friend	0
	Installation or fitting contractor (other than seller)	1
Other (STATE)		2
	O.U.O.	3

ALL ITEMS WHERE RECEIVED

36. a) Have you been using it during the last month?	Yes	Y	
	No	X	
	O.U.O.	0	
IF NO (Code X)			
b) Why not?	Never did have any use for it	Y	Y
	Don't use it very often	X	X
	Not the season for using it	0	0
MORE THAN ONE CODE MAY BE RINGED	It doesn't work/broke down	1	1
	It wore out	2	2
	Damaged or destroyed by accident	3	3
	Gave it away	4	4
	Sold it	5	5
	Repossessed by the seller or finance company	6	6
	It's dangerous to use	7	7
Other reason (STATE)		8	8
	O.U.O.	9	

37. In using the ...., have you found it to be as satisfactory as you expected?	Yes — completely	Y
	Almost/note quite	X
	No	0
	Only sometimes	1
	Only after it was repaired	2
	Doesn't work/no use at all	3
Other (STATE)		4
	O.U.O.	5

38. a) Since you bought the ...., have — Yes Y

		Code
you spent any money on repairs, apart from any routine maintenance?	No	X
	Don't remember	0
	O.U.O.	1

IF YES (Code Y)

b) About how much? WRITE IN £ ....

	Don't know	X
OFFICE USE ONLY	O.U.O.	Y

39\. a) Did you ever at any time complain to the shop/dealer/seller about this purchase, or ask for something to be put right, or ask for any repairs to be done?

Yes (Go to c)	Y
No	X
O.U.O.	0

IF NO (Code X)

b) Why not?

Nothing to complain about (Go to Q.43)	1
Too trivial to complain (Go to Q.43)	2
Defects were not more than expected (Go to Q.43)	3
Plan to complain soon (Go to Q.41)	4
Would not expect him/them to do anything (Go to Q.41)	5
Would take too much time and trouble (Go to Q.41)	6
Never knew where to find him/them (Go to Q.41)	7
No particular reason (Go to Q.41)	8
Other (STATE) . . . . (Go to Q.41)	9
O.U.O.	X

IF YES AT a) (Code Y)

c) What did you complain of? . . . .

. . . .

. . . .

d) What did you want them/him to do about it?

Repair item or replace parts	Y
Replace whole item	X
Re-install or re-fit	0
Supply additional parts or accessories	1
Cancel the deal and refund the price	2
Repay part of the price	3
Cancel the deal, refund the price and pay compensation in addition	4
Nothing	5
Other (STATE)	6
O.U.O.	7

e) What did they/he do?

Nothing (Go to Q.41)	Y
Repaired item or replaced parts	X
Replaced whole item	0
Re-Installed or Re-fitted	1
Supplied additional parts or accessories	2
Cancelled the deal and refunded the price	3
Refunded part of the price	4
Cancelled the deal, refunded the price and paid compensation in addition	5
Other (STATE)	6
O.U.O.	9

		Code
f) Were you satisfied with what they/he did?	Yes	Y
	Partly	X
	No	0
	Don't know	1
	O.U.O.	2
g) Were you charged anything for what they/he did?	Yes	Y
	No	X
	Don't remember	0
	O.U.O.	1

40. ASK ONLY IF BUYER ASKED SELLER FOR REPAIRS Q.39 d) CODED Y

a) Do you think you were entitled to have any of the repairs done under a guarantee?	Yes	A
	No	X
	Don't know	0
	O.U.O.	Y
IF YES (Code A)		
b) Did you ask for these repairs to be done under the guarantee?	Yes	1
	No	2
	Don't remember	3
	O.U.O.	4
c) Were these repairs actually done?	Yes	Y
	No	X
	Only some of them	0
	Don't know	1
	Still waiting	2
	O.U.O.	3
IF YES OR SOME OF THEM (Codes Y or 0)		
d) Were these repairs done willingly or did you have to insist?	Done willingly	Y
	Had to insist a little	X
	Had to insist a great deal	0
Other (STATE)		8
	O.U.O.	9
e) Were you charged anything for these repairs?	Yes	B
	No	X
	Don't remember	0
	O.U.O.	Y
IF YES (Code B)		
f) Do you think you should have been charged the amount that you were charged?	Yes	1
	No, should have been charged less	2
	No, should not have been charged at all	3
	Don't know	4
	O.U.O.	5

SECTION 5 — COMPLAINTS

ASK IF Q.39(a) CODED Y, OR
Q.39(b) CODED 4 TO 9 INCLUSIVE
OTHER CASES, GO TO Q.43

41. a) Did you ever complain to anyone about this purchase, or discuss any complaints with anyone apart from the seller?	Yes	A
	No	X
	O.U.O.	0

IF YES (Code A)

b) Who did you complain to, or discuss your complaints with

MORE THAN ONE CODE MAY BE RINGED

	Code		
The finance company	Y	Y	Y
The manufacturer	X	X	X
A solicitor	0	0	0
Citizens Advice Bureau	1	1	1
The police	2	2	2
A Social Worker	3	3	3
Wrote to newspaper	4	4	4
The A.A. or R.A.C.	5	5	5
Friend/s	6	6	6
Other (STATE)	8	8	8
O.U.O.	9		

c) What happened/what was the result of contacting (the finance co. etc.,)

(1st code at b) . . . .
. . . .

(2nd code at b) . . . .
. . . .

(3rd code at b) . . . .

42 a) Do you feel that the seller is/was/*entitled* to be *paid* in full for the.........?

Yes (Go to Q.43)	Y
No	X
Should be entitled to only part of price	0
Don't know	1
O.U.O.	2

IF a) CODED X, 0 or 1

b) Did you refuse to pay, or have you stopped making payments?

Yes	2
No	3
Refused to pay part	4
O.U.O.	5

IF NO (Code 3)

c. Why did you/do you still pay?

MORE THAN ONE CODE MAY BE RINGED

Can't afford legal advice	Y	Y	Y
Felt responsible for paying	X	X	X
My complaints are against the seller not the finance co.	0	0	0
To keep a good credit rating	1	1	1
Afraid they would take court proceedings	2	2	2
Afraid they would take the.........back	3	3	3
Paid before I discovered (the cause for not paying)	4	4	4
Afraid of trouble (no particular trouble specified)	5	5	5
Other reason (STATE)...	8	8	8
Don't know	9		
O.U.O.		9	

SECTION 6
ASK ALL

43. a) How did you finance or plan to finance the transaction?

Paid or planned to pay cash (including ordinary cheque)	A
Arranged a loan and paid cash (Go to Q.45)	X
Credit (H.P. or any other type of credit) (Go to c)	B

			Code	
	IF CASH (Code A)			
	b) Did you arrange a loan to pay for the............or to pay part of the price?	Yes (Go to Q.45)	1	
		No (Go to Q.45)	2	
		O.U.O.	Y	
	IF CREDIT (Code B at a)			
	c) What type of credit arrangement was it?	Hire-purchase or other credit arrangement made with seller specifically for this purchase (Go to Q.48)	3	
		Charge account or credit card of seller	4	
		Credit card of credit card company other than seller	5	
		Check obtained from Check Trader	6	
		O.U.O.	0	
	IF ACCOUNT OR CREDIT CARD (Codes 4 or 5)			
	d) Was this account payable at the end of month or by instalments?	At end of month	7	
		By instalments	8	
		Either at my option	9	
		O.U.O	Y	
44.	ACCOUNT, CREDIT CARD, or CHECK TRADER ASK IF Q.43 CODED 4, 5 or 6			
	a) Do you have any complaints about the way this account was opened, or about the way it is operated?	Yes	A	
		No	X	
		Don't know	0	
		O.U.O.	1	
	IF YES (Code A)			
	b) What complaints do you have?	High interest rate	2	2
		Payments are not recorded in an orderly way	3	3
	MORE THAN ONE CODE MAY BE RINGED	Other (STATE)	4	4
		O.U.O.	9	
	CASH, LOAN, ACCOUNT, CREDIT CARD OR CHECK TRADER. ASK WHERE Q.43 CODED A, X, 4, 5 or 6			
45	a) Did you trade-in anything in part exchange?	Yes	Y	
		No	X	
		Don't remember	0	
		O.U.O.	1	
	IF YES (Code Y)			
	b) How much was the part exchange allowance?	WRITE IN £......................		
		Don't remember		X
		OFFICE USE –		
46.	What was the total price of the........ (without deducting any part exchange allowance)?	WRITE IN £........................		
		Don't remember		X
		OFFICE USE –		

WHERE Q.43 CODED X or 1, GO TO Q.62
WHERE Q.43 CODED 2 or 7, GO TO Q.86

Code

47. ASK WHERE Q.43 CODED 6, 8 or 9

a) What rate of interest do you pay on this account?

WRITE IN ANNUAL OR MONTHLY RATE

........% a year	
.....% a month	
Don't understand	Y
Don't know	X
OFFICE USE –	

b) Was the whole price charged to your account, or did you pay a cash deposit?

Whole price charged to account	Y
Paid a deposit	X
Don't remember	O
O.U.O.	1

IF DEPOSIT (Code X)

c) How much was the deposit?

WRITE IN £..

Don't remember	X
OFFICE USE –	

WHERE Q.43 CODED 6, 8 or 9, GO TO Q.86

SECTION 7
INSTALMENT CREDIT CASES
HIRE-PURCHASE OR OTHER CREDIT ARRANGEMENT MADE WITH SELLER SPECIFICALLY FOR THIS PURCHASE

ASK WHERE Q.43 CODED 3

48. What rate of interest was payable on this agreement?

WRITE IN ANNUAL OR MONTHLY RATE

.......% a year	
.......% amonth	
Don't understand	Y
Don't know	X
OFFICE USE –	

49. a) Did you receive a copy of the agreement *at the time you signed it*?

Yes	Y
No	X
Don't remember	0
There never was any written agreement (Go to Q.52)	1
Never signed the agreement (Go to Q.51)	2
O.U.O.	3

b) Did you receive a copy of the agreement through the post?

Yes	Y
No	X
Don't remember	0
O.U.O.	1

IF YES (Code Y)

c) Was this before or after you received delivery of the............?

Before delivery of the..........	Y
After delivery of the..........	X
Same day	0
Don't remember	1
O.U.O.	2

		Code
50. Were all the figures and other terms of the agreement completely filled in before you signed it?	Yes	Y
	No	X
	Don't remember	0
	O.U.O.	1

51 a) Do you have a copy/the copies/of the agreement now?	Yes	A
	No	X
	Don't know	0
	O.U.O.	Y
IF YES (Code A) b) Could I please take a look at it/them?	Yes	1
	No	2
	Can't find it/them	3
	O.U.O.	4

IF YES (Code 1)
REMAINDER OF THIS QUESTION TO BE ANSWERED BY INTERVIEWER

		First Copy	Second Copy
c) Examine the copy(ies) and see if it (they) include the following statement in red print.	Yes – in red	Y	Y
	Yes – not in red	X	X
	No (If *both* 'No' go to Q.52)	0	0
	One copy only	–	1
	O.U.O.	2	2

NOTICE TO CUSTOMER –
RIGHT OF CANCELLATION
You have for a short time a legal right to cancel this agreement....................
....
....
send the goods to the person named above.

IF YES, Code Y or X) d) State if the above notice is concealed or camoflaged in any way	Yes	B	B
	No	0	0
	O.U.O.	1	1

IF YES (Code B)
e) How?

MORE THAN ONE CODE MAY BE RINGED

Surrounded by other print of larger size	2	2	2	2
Camouflaged by surrounding colours	3	3	3	3
Document folded and stapled so that the notice is out of sight	4	4	4	4
Other (STATE)	8	8	8	8
O.U.O.	9		9	

IN ASKING Qs. 52-61 CHECK WHAT THE INFORMANT SAYS WITH WHAT THE AGREEMENT STATES (WHERE AVAILABLE) AND PROBE ANY DIFFERENCES. IF THE INFORMANT INSISTS THAT THE AGREEMENT IS WRONG, CODE ACCORDING TO WHAT THE INFORMANT SAYS, AND THEN ADD IN WRITING "AGREEMENT STATES.........."

WRITE IN ANSWERS BELOW

OFFICE USE ONLY

52. How much was:
    a) The cash price (including any accessories)? £.........................
    LESS:
    b) Part exchange allowance £.........................
    c) Cash deposit £.........................
    DEDUCT b) AND c) £..........
    Balance of cash price £...........
    PLUS
    d) Interest/Hire purchase charges/ finance charges £.............
    e) Any other additions £.............
    f) Total deferred balance/ Balance of H.P. price £.............
    NIL FIGURES WRITE IN "NIL"
    DON'T KNOW WRITE "D.K."

52A IF A DEPOSIT (Figure entered at c.)
Did you arrange a loan to pay the deposit?

	Yes (See Manual p.17)	Y
	No	X
	Don't know	0
	O.U.O	1

53 Were the instalments payable weekly, monthly or quarterly?

	Weekly	Y
	Monthly	X
	Quarterly	0
	Other (STATE)	1
	Don't know	2
	O.U.O	3

54. How many instalments were to be paid? WRITE IN AS 3 FIGURE ENTRY

	Don't remember	X

55 a) Apart from the cash deposit (if any) were all the instalments for the same amount?

	Yes	Y
	Yes—but last one smaller	X
	Yes—but last one slightly larger	0
	Yes—but last one was more than double the other	1
	No	A
	Don't remember (Go to Q.57)	2
	O.U.O.	3

IF NO (Code A)
b) How did they vary?........................
.... (Go to Q.57)

56. How much was each instalment, except the last one?

WRITE IN POUNDS, SHILLINGS AND PENCE

£ : s. d.

	Don't know	X

OFFICE USE –

			Code
57.	How much would the cash price have been if you had paid cash?	WRITE IN £.................	
		Never knew	Y
		Don't remember	X
		OFFICE USE –	
58.	Was the agreement one of hire-purchase, conditional sale, or credit sale?	Hire purchase	Y
		Conditional sale	X
		Credit Sale	0
		Loan (See Manual)	1
		Don't know	2
		O.U.O.	3
59.	Did someone else as well as you (the buyer/s) have to sign something promising that the payments would be made?	Yes	Y
		No	X
		Don't remember	0
		O.U.O.	1
60	a) Who have you been paying the instalments to, or who were you expected to pay them to?	The seller	Y
		A finance company	X
		Other (STATE).	0
		Don't know	1
		O.U.O.	2
	IF A FINANCE CO. (Code X) b) What was the name of the finance company? WRITE IN		
		Don't know	8
		O.U.O.	9
61.	ASK FOR HEATING EQUIPMENT ONLY. ITEM 03 Did they require a mortgage on your house to secure the payments?	Yes	Y
		No	X
		Don't know	0
		Don't understand	1
		O.U.O.	2

SECTION 8
INSTALMENT CREDIT AND LOAN CASES
ASK WHERE Q.43 CODED X, 1 or 3

62	a) Did the salesman say that you could earn commissions on sales to people whose names you would give him, and in that way meet the payments?	Yes	A
		No	X
		Don't remember	0
		O.U.O.	1
	IF YES (Code A) b) Did you rely on these commissions to meet the instalments?	Yes	2
		No	3
		O.U.O.	4
	c) Did you earn any commissions?	Yes	B
		No	4
		Not yet	5
		O.U.O.	X

IF YES (Code B)

d) Have you been earning as much commission as you expected?

	Code
Yes	6
No	7
Never expected any particular amount	8
O.U.O.	0

63. IF ITEM IS A SEWING MACHINE, KNITTING MACHINE, or TYPEWRITER – ASK FOR ITEMS 05, 06 and 07

a) Did the seller say that you could earn money from things produced on the machine and in that way meet the payments?

	Code
Yes	A
No	X
Don't remember	0
O.U.O.	1

IF YES (Code A)

b) Did you rely on these earnings to meet the instalments?

	Code
Yes	2
No	3
O.U.O.	Y

c) Did you in fact earn anything from things produced on the machine?

	Code
Yes	B
No	4
Not yet	5
O.U.O.	X

IF YES (Code B)

d) Have you been earning as much as you expected?

	Code
Yes	6
No	7
Never expected any particular amount	8
O.U.O.	0

SECTION 9
LOAN CASES ONLY

ASK WHERE Q.43 CODED X or 1 OR
Q.52a CODED Y

64. What type of lender did you borrow the money from?

IF TWO LENDERS, SEE MANUAL P.22

	Code
Bank	Y
Loan or finance company	X
Mortgage company	0
Insurance company	1
Betting shop	2
Other bookmaker	3
Man/woman I haappened to meet	4
Personal friend/relative (Go to Q.86)	5
Other (STATE)	6
O.U.O.	7

65. Had you dealt with this (bank, mortgage company, etc.) before?

	Code
Yes	Y
No	X
Don't remember	0
O.U.O.	1

66. a) Before you borrowed the money, do you recall seeing or hearing any advertising of the lender?

	Code
Yes	Y
No	X
Don't know	0
O.U.O.	1

		Code		
IF YES (Code Y) b) Where did you see or hear the advertising?	Newspaper/magazines	Y	Y	Y
	Television	X	X	X
	Brochure delivered to home	0	0	0
	Brochure I picked up	1	1	1
MORE THAN ONE CODE MAY BE RINGED	By telephone	2	2	2
	On radio	3	3	3
	At cinema	4	4	4
	Poster	5	5	5
	Other (STATE)	6	6	6
	Don't remember	8		
	O.U.O.	9		

c) What did the advertising say?
LISTEN AND PROBE FULLY, BUT DO NOT RECORD ANSWERS

d) Did any of this turn out to be wrong or untrue?	Yes	A
	No	X
	Don't know	0
	O.U.O.	1

IF YES (Code A)
e) What was wrong or untrue? . . . .
. . . .
. . . .

67. a) Was the loan arranged by the seller of the.........?	Yes	Y
	No	X
	Don't know	0
	O.U.O.	1
IF NO, OR DON'T KNOW (Code X or 0) b) Was the lender suggested to you by the seller of the.........?	Yes	1
	No	2
	Don't remember	3
	O.U.O.	4

68. Where or how was the loan arranged?	At the office of the lender (the bank, etc.)	Y
	At the home of the lender	X
	At a pub, club, or other social institution	0
	At the shop/etc./where I bought the........	1 ┐
	At my home	2 │
	Where I work	3 ├ (Go to Q.70)
	By mail	4 │
	By telephone	5 │
	Other (STATE)	6 ┘
	O.U.O.	7

69. IF Q.68 CODED Y, X or O a) How far was the place where you arranged the loan from the place where you bought the........?	In same building	Y
	Less than 100 yards	X
	100 yards — less than 1 mile	0
	1 mile or more	1
	Don't know	2
	O.U.O.	3

		Code
b) Were you taken to (the place where the loan was arranged) by the seller of the........?	Yes	Y
	No	X
	Don't remember	0
	O.U.O.	1

70. ALL LOAN CASES
Was the seller of the........ recommended to you by the person/people you borrowed the money from?

Yes	Y
No	X
Don't remember	0
O.U.O.	1

71. When you decided to ask for the loan how much did you then plan to borrow? WRITE IN – £..................

No particular amount	Y
Don't remember	X
OFFICE USE –	

72. a) When you were arranging the loan, what did the lender tell you about it?

Nothing at all	Y
Never spoke to lender	X
All other answers	A
O.U.O.	0

LISTEN AND PROBE, BUT DO NOT RECORD ANSWERS

IF CODE A

b) Did any of this turn out to be wrong or untrue?

Yes	B
No	2
Don't know	3
O.U.O.	4

IF YES (Code B)

c) What was wrong or untrue . . . .

. . . .

. . . .

73. a) Was there anything you feel you should have been told by the lender that you were not told?

Yes	A
No	X
Don't know	0
O.U.O.	1

IF YES (Code A)

b) What was it? . . . .

. . . .

. . . .

74. a) Apart from any points just mentioned, was there anything about the *loan transaction* that you feel was unsatisfactory?

Yes	A
No	X
Don't know	0
O.U.O.	1

IF YES (Code A)

b) What was it

MORE THAN ONE CODE MAY BE RINGED

Excessive cost of loan (interest rate)	0	0
High pressure salesmanship of lender	1	1
Signed agreement in blank and lender inserted the wrong figures	2	2
Lender knew I couldn't afford to make repayment	3	3
Delay in supplying the money	4	4
Lender did not record payments in an orderly way	5	5
Other (STATE)	6	6
O.U.O.	9	

			Code
75.	a) Did you sign some document for the loan?	Yes	A
		No	X
		Don't remember	0
		O.U.O	1
	IF YES (Code A)		
	b) Were the figures and other terms of the loan completely filled in when you signed it?	Yes	2
		No	3
		Don't remember	4
		O.U.O.	5
	c) When did you receive a copy of it?	When the loan was made	6
		Later	7
		Don't remember	8
		Not at all	9
		O.U.O	0
	IF CODE 6, 7 or 8		
	d) Could I please take a look at it?	Yes	Y
		No	X
		Can't find it	0
		O.U.O.	1

IN ASKING Qs. 76-85, CHECK WHAT THE INFORMANT SAYS WITH WHAT THE DOCUMENT STATES (WHERE AVAILABLE) AND PROBE ANY DIFFERENCES. IF THE INFORMANT INSISTS THAT THE DOCUMENT IS WRONG, CODE ACCORDING TO WHAT THE INFORMANT SAYS, AND THEN ADD IN WRITING "AGREEMENT STATES........'

76\. How much did you actually borrow?

WRITE IN – £.....................
Don't remember X
OFFICE USE –

77\. a) What rate of interest was payable on the loan?

WRITE IN ANNUAL OR MONTHLY RATE ....% a year
......% a month
It was to vary with the bank rate Y
Don't understand X
Don't know X
OFFICE USE

b) Were you informed of this when the loan was arranged?

Yes Y
No, was not informed at all X
No, was informed the rate would be
WRITE IN ANNUAL OR MONTHLY RATE ......% a year
......% a month
Don't remember X
OFFICE USE

78\. a) What was the total amount to be paid back?

WRITE IN £.................
Don't know X
OFFICE USE –

b) Does this include interest?

Yes, interest included Y
No, Interest additional X
Don't understand 0
Don't know 1

		Code
79. Did someone else, as well as you (the buyer/s) have to sign something promising that the loan would be repaid?	Yes	Y
	No	X
	Don't remember	0
	O.U.O.	1

		Code
80. a) Did the lender take any sort of security?	Yes	A
	No	X
	Don't understand (PROBE)	0
	Don't remember	1
	O.U.O.	Y
IF YES (Code A) b) What was the security?	Mortgage of house	2
	Deposit of stocks or bonds	3
	Life assurance policy	4
	Chattel mortgage on the..........	5
	Other (STATE)	6
	O.U.O.	9

		Code
81. Was the loan to be repaid by instalments?	Yes	Y
	No (Go to Q.86)	X
	Don't know (Go to Q.86)	0
	It was not specified (Go to Q.86)	1
	O.U.O.	2

		Code
82. Were the instalments payable weekly, monthly or quarterly?	Weekly	Y
	Monthly	X
	Quarterly	0
	Other (STATE)	1
	O.U.O.	9

83. How many instalments were to be paid? ENTER AS 3 FIGURES

Don't remember X

		Code
84. a) Were all the instalments to be for the same amount?	Yes	Y
	Yes, but last was smaller	X
	Yes – but last was slightly larger	0
	Yes – but last was more than double the others	1
	No	A
	Don't remember (Go to Q.86)	3
	O.U.O.	4

IF NO (Code A)
b) How did they vary?. . . . . (Go to Q.86)

85. How much was each instalment, except the last one? WRITE IN POUNDS, SHILLINGS AND PENCE £ : s. d

Don't know X

OFFICE USE

Code

SECTION 10
ASK ALL

86. VARY ACCORDING TO CODING OF Q.43

WHERE Q.43 CODED 2 ASK:–	Were you ever notified that payment for the......was overdue?		
WHERE Q.43 CODED X or 1 ASK:–	Have you ever been advised that any repayment of the loan was overdue?		
WHERE Q.43 CODED 3 ASK:–	Have you ever been notified that any instalment was overdue?	Yes No (Go to Q.100) O.U.O.	Y X 0
WHERE Q.43 CODED 7 ASK:–	Now I want to ask you about the bill that covered this purchase. Were you ever notified that payment of this bill was overdue?		
WHERE Q.43 CODED 6, 8 or 9 ASK:–	Since you bought.............. have you ever been notified that any payment on the account was overdue?		

87. a) Why was payment overdue?

MORE THAN ONE CODE MAY BE RINGED

Didn't pay/stopped paying/because of dissatisfaction with the...........	Y	Y	Y
Didn't pay/stopped paying/because of seller's conduct as indicated above	X	X	X
Didn't pay/stopped paying/because of conduct of finance co./loan co./etc. STATE WHAT CONDUCT................	0	0	0
Interruption of earnings through sickness or injury	1	1	1
Out of work for other reasons	2	2	2
Money all spent on repairs to the.........	3	3	3
Money all spent paying other bills	4	4	4
For other reasons, did not have money to pay	5	5	5
Other reason (STATE)	6	6	6
Just forgot/too busy	7	7	7
Payment never was overdue. Notice I received was a mistake	8	8	8
O.U.O.	9		

IF NOTICE A MISTAKE (Code 8)

b) What happened? How was the matter cleared up? ....

(Go to Q.99)

Code

88. How did the people claiming payment get in touch with you?

MORE THAN ONE CODE MAY BE RINGED

By letter	Y	Y
By telephone	X	X
Called at the home	0	0
Called where I work	1	1
Other (STATE).	2	2
O.U.O.	9	

89. What did they say they would do about it?

ASK TO SEE LETTER IF AVAILABLE (Q.88 Coded Y)

MORE THAN ONE CODE MAY BE RINGED

Repossess the.........	Y	Y	Y
Take court proceedings	X	X	X
Send the van	0	0	0
Tell the neighbours	2	2	2
Adverse credit report (Blacklist me)	3	3	3
Make personal calls	4	4	4
Take action (no particular action specified)	5	5	5
Nothing	6		
Other (STATE)	7	7	7
O.U.O.	9		

90. a) Did anyone try to make you pay by harrassing you, or annoying you in any way?

Yes	A
No	X

IF YES (Code A)

b) What did they do?

MORE THAN ONE CODE MAY BE RINGED

Persistent phone calls	1	1
Phone calls in the night	2	2
Shouting on the doorstep	3	3
Other (STATE)	4	4
O.U.O.	9	

91. a) Did you consult a solicitor?

Yes	A
No (Go to d)	B

IF YES (Code A)

b) Did he agree to act for you?

Yes	1
No	2
Don't know	3
O.U.O	X

c) Were you granted LegalAid?

Yes	4
No	5
Don't know what Legal Aid is	6
Don't know whether it was granted	7
O.U.O.	8

IF NO AT a) (Code B)

d) Why not?

Couldn't afford the fees	Y	Y	Y
They charge too much	X	X	X
Don't know a solicitor	0	0	0
Don't know what a solicitor is	1	1	1

		Code		
MORE THAN ONE CODE MAY BE RINGED	Don't like solicitors	2	2	2
	Solicitors don't help people like me	3	3	3
	Solicitors don't help on problems like this	4	4	4
	Didn't need one	5	5	5
	Never thought of it	6		
	Don't know why not	7		
	Other (STATE)............	8	8	8
	O.U.O.	9		

92. Was a court summons issued against you?	Yes	Y
	No (Go to Q.96)	X
	Don't know (Go to Q.96)	0
	O.U.O.	1
93. a) Was there a trial?	Yes	A
	No	X
	Still pending	0
	Don't know	1
	O.U.O.	Y
IF YES (Code A)		
b) Were you (either buyer) present at the trial?	Yes	2
	No	3
	O.U.O.	4
c) Did a solicitor (or barrister) act for you at the trial?	Yes	Y
	No	X
	Don't know	0
	O.U.O.	1
94. a) What was the result of the court action?	Order that the..........be returned unless payments made	Y
	Order to pay money	X
	Order to give back the............	0
	Claim dismissed (I won the case)	1
	Case still pending	2
	Don't know	3
	O.U.O.	4
IF ORDERED TO PAY MONEY (Code Y or X)		
b) Did you pay/are you paying as the court ordered?	Yes	Y
	No	A
	Don't know	0
	O.U.O.	1

IF NO (Code A)

c) What steps were/are being/taken or threatened against you to enforce payment?

....

....

None that I know of	9

		Code	
95. a) Do you feel that you had/will have/a fair chance to defend yourself in court proceedings?	Yes	Y	
	No	X	
	Don't know	0	
	O.U.O.	1	
IF NO (Code X) b) Why not?	Don't understand all these forms	Y	Y
	Can't afford a solicitor	X	X
	Don't like going to a solicitor	0	0
	Don't like going to court	1	1
MORE THAN ONE CODE MAY BE RINGED	Can't afford time off work to go to court	2	2
	Don't understand court proceedings	3	3
	Judge was/will be/biased	4	4
	Could not get necessary evidence	5	5
	People like me never have a fair chance	6	6
	Other reason (STATE)	8	8
	O.U.O.	9	
96. a) Did the seller or finance company take the .... back?	Yes	A	
	No	X	
	O.U.O.	0	
IF YES (Code A) b) Did they take it back by court order, or by agreement with you?	Court order	1	
	I/We agreed to let them take it	2	
	I/We never agreed, but they took it anyway	3	
	Other (STATE).	4	
	O.U.O.	9	
c) Did the people who took the .... back tell you what effect this would have on your liability for payments?	No. Said nothing about it	Y	
	Said I/we would *not* have to pay any more	X	
	Said I/we might have to pay some more	0	
	Said repossession would reduce the amount owing	1	
	Other (STATE)	2	
	O.U.O.	9	
d) After the .... was taken back, did they still claim money from you?	Yes	Y	
	No	X	
	Not yet	0	
	O.U.O.	1	
97. a) Did they do anything else to try to enforce payment?	Yes	A	
	No	X	
	Don't know	0	
	O.U.O.	1	

IF YES (Code A)

b) What did they do? . . . .

. . . .

. . . .

		Code
98. What happened eventually with regard to the overdue payment(s)?	Paid off out of own resources	Y
	Refinancing was arranged with company/person to whom payment was due	X
	Refinancing was arranged by new loan with another company or person	0
	Nothing/nothing more/was paid	1
	Settled for a part of the sum claimed	2
	Matter still pending	3
	Other (STATE)	8
	O.U.O.	9

99. a) Did you incur any sort of hardship or difficulty or embarrassment because of this account, or because of any action taken to collect the money?	Yes	A
	No	X
	Don't know	0
	O.U.O.	Y

IF YES (Code A)

b) Please explain . . . .
. . . .
. . . .

SECTION 11
ASK ALL

100. Would you please look at this card and tell me which category the total weekly income of your household comes in, after deductions? SHOW CARD C	A. Up to £10 p. week	Y
	B. £11-£20 p. week	X
	C. £21-£30 p. week	0
	D. £31-£40 a week	1
	E. £41 or over	2
	Refused/not known	3
	O.U.O.	4

101. COMPOSITION OF HOUSEHOLD

WRITE IN NUMBERS

No. of males 16 and over
No. of females 16 and over
No. of children under 16

102. PARTICULARS OF BUYERS

a) Sex		First Buyer	Second Buyer
	Male	Y	Y
	Female	X	X
	Not applicable (one buyer)		0
	O.U.O.	1	1

b) What was your age on the date when you ordered the ....?

IF CLOSE TO 21, PROBE TO ENSURE ACCURACY

	First Buyer	Second Buyer
Under 21	Y	Y
21-24	X	X
25-29	0	0
30-39	1	1
40-64	2	2
65-79	3	3
80 or over	4	4
Not applicable (one buyer)		5
O.U.O.	6	6

c) Personal Occupation/Social Grade

GIVE DETAILS OF OCCUPATION AND CODE FOR EACH BUYER AND FOR HEAD OF HOUSEHOLD

WRITE IN OCCUPATION
1st Buyer (Personal)............................
2nd Buyer (Personal)...........................
Head of Household.............................

	First Buyer	Second Buyer	Head of Household
A	Y	Y	Y
B	X	X	X
C1	0	0	0
C2	1	1	1
D	2	2	2
E	3	3	3
Housewife (not working)	4	4	4
Not applicable (one buyer)		5	
O.U.O.	6	6	6

Code

103. What was the name of the shop or company that you bought the ....from?

It was. . . . .

Don't remember X

104. Other comments? (ASK FOR ANY OTHER COMMENTS, BUT ALSO NOTE HERE ANYTHING SAID DURING THE INTERVIEW NOT ADEQUATELY COVERED BY THE QUESTIONS).

. . . .
. . . .
. . . .
. . . .
. . . .

105. REASONS FOR REFUSAL. NOTE HERE ANY COMMENTS MADE DURING THE INTERVIEW BY WAY OF EXPLANATION FOR ANY REFUSAL TO ANSWER A QUESTION, OR TO SHOW DOCUMENTS'

Question No. . . . .
O.U.O.

Question No. . . . .
O.U.O.

(Interviewer's observations and identification particulars omitted.)

APPENDIX D: INTERVIEWERS' INSTRUCTIONS

(For brevity, less important instructions, or those that relate only to limited or exceptional situations, are omitted.)

Purpose of the Survey

. . . . . .

2. The survey is a random sample of households. Thus it is intended to seek information about satisfactory buying experiences, as well as about those that have involved problems.

3. The survey requires careful and detailed questioning about certain items of durable consumer goods. These are often bought on credit, but cash purchases are also within the scope of this study.

Preparations

4. To undertake this survey, it is essential to understand the questions and possible answers. To understand the different ways in which a credit transaction can be financed, please study the pamphlet *About Credit*, published by the Consumer Council. A copy is supplied. Then study carefully these instructions and the other survey documents before the briefing session.

Queries

5. For all queries about these instructions or the survey documents that occur to you prior to the briefing, make a note of them as they occur to you and then raise them at the briefing session. For particular queries that occur to you after the briefing, phone the client directly. He is Professor T.G. Ison, and his office number is............ Otherwise queries should be made to Research Services. . .in the usual way: about supplies, quotas and timetables to the Fieldwork Controller. . ., about sampling procedure to the Sampling Assistant. . ..

Supplies

6.

. . . . . .

The Sample

7. This is a national sample of households (addresses). Contact the households resident at the addresses listed on your [Sample Issue Sheets].

8. The addresses selected have been extracted from the National Register of Electors. The addresses refer mainly to private households, and a private household consists of –

   'either one person living alone or a group of persons, usually but not always, members of one family, who live together and whose food and other household expenses are managed as one unit. Resident domestic servants and "boarders", "lodgers" etc. (however described), are included in the household *provided* they have at least one main meal a day from the common source'.

9. For each address on the SIS [Sample Issue Sheet] establish how many households are at the address. Where more than one household is resident:

   either in the case of *2 or 3* households, treat each household separately by completing a Contact Report and interviewing at each. *or* in the case of *4* or more households (e.g. large blocks of flats) the names of 3 persons have been entered on the SIS. Establish the households to which these belong and contact each one. (They may, by coincidence, be in the same household and in which case *do NOT* substitute.) If one of them has moved, contact the household now living in the flat where he used to live.

Institutions

10. Hotels, public houses, boarding houses and hostels, factories, business premises, hospitals, old people's homes, nursing homes, prisons, schools, colleges and other such establishments are defined as Institutions and are EXCLUDED from this survey. We have tried to exclude them at the sampling stage, but if one does occur, take no further action except entering it as unproductive, both on your Sample Issue Sheet and on a Contact Report.

11. But if a selected address is a dwelling unit, it should not be excluded simply because it is attached to an Institution.

Additions to the Sample

12. After your first call at a selected address, look at the number of the next known address on the SIS in the column headed 'House number of next address in the register'. Where a dwelling unit exists *between* the selected address and the next known address, make contact also

with that dwelling and add it to your sample.

Example

Serial No.	Address	House number of next address in Register
02	1, Bradley Walk	3

If 1a, (or 2), for example, exists on the same side of the street between 1 and 3, contact 1a in addition to 1. Similarly if, for example, 1a is a flat attached to No.1, contact both 1 and 1a.

13. The procedure ensures coverage of new households and non-elector households. On this survey, it is important that such households should not be omitted. In addition in certain areas we will require interviews in newly built streets which have come into occupation since the Registers were compiled. A special instruction will be issued to those interviewers concerned.

Serial Numbers

. . . . . .

Making Contact (General Notes)

16. A Contact Report (explained in detail below) must be completed for every selected household, i.e., each address on the SIS and each household that you add following the instructions in paragraph 9 and paragraph 12 above. Begin this report at your first call.

17. First of all, seek the head of the household if he is immediately available. Otherwise, speak to whoever appears to be the most responsible member of the household present and who is over 16. If the first visit to a selected dwelling fails to make contact, make a second visit later, and if necessary a third. Make enquiries in the neighbourhood about when the family is at home, and use your initiative and judgment about the timing of subsequent visits. If they are on holiday, propose the recall until their return. If a third visit fails to make contact, consider, having regard to information obtained (from neighbours and tradesmen, etc.) whether a fourth visit is likely to succeed. If the household is on the phone, use the telephone at this stage to try to arrange an interview. Try your utmost to contact every selected household. But if, after the third or a subsequent visit, there is nothing to indicate that a further

visit is likely to succeed, abandon the attempt and complete the Contact Report, Part B.

. . . . . .

19. If you meet with a refusal, use your judgment in deciding whether a re-call is appropriate. For example a refusal by the head of the household must be accepted. But if the refusal is by an elderly relative, try tactfully to arrange a re-call when the head of household is at home.

The Introduction

20. Upon making contact, introduce yourself and the survey as indicated in the 'Introduction' on the Contact Report. The exact wording can be varied or abbreviated according to the circumstances. Then go to the screening questions on the Contact Report, Part A.

. . . . . .

23. As long as the screening questions show that one or more of the items on the list have been bought within the household, as indicated in the Contact Report, proceed with one or two item interviews as the case may be.

24. The interview should proceed *whether or not the goods were retained.* As long as the item was bought, or ordered, or received on approval for use in the household, it doesn't matter if it was subsequently returned to the seller, given away, thrown away or traded-in. *This instruction is vital*, because we are particularly interested in cases where something was bought on credit, and then later repossessed by the seller or a finance company. Also it doesn't matter if the item was never received. If it was bought or ordered, proceed with the interview.

25. The survey relates to the purchase or ordering of new items only, except for the addition of secondhand motor-vehicles.

. . . . . .

The Interview (General Notes)

27. To proceed with each interview, ascertain the buyer or buyers of the item, i.e. the person or persons who were present at the time of buying and participating in the decision to buy. Note their initials on Part A – Column 1. If two members of the household over 16 were present when the item was bought, *interview both together.* Arrange another visit for the purpose if necessary.

28. Where the household is being interviewed about two items, use a

separate questionnaire for each, and complete one before proceeding to the other.

29. You may find a case in which the buyer knows little about the subsequent use of the item. e.g. where the husband bought a vacuum cleaner that is used mainly by the wife. In a case of this sort, the user must be interviewed as well as the buyer.

. . . . . .

31. On many surveys, the objective is to record the spontaneous response of a particular informant. This is usually the case where attitudes are being sought. On this survey, however, *the objective is to obtain factual information about the experience of the household.* Hence this survey differs in two respects.

    (1) You should *probe* more freely than usual to ensure that the questions are correctly understood and that the responses are correctly classified, using neutral probes of course, and taking care not to influence the informant. Ask each question exactly as it stands in the first instance, but if it is not obviously understood after repeating it, use your judgment in explaining the question. (Refer to the manual notes). Again, if the answer is ambiguous, or it is doubtful how it should be classified, use your judgment in asking supplementary questions. In particular probe 'don't know' responses to ensure that the question was properly understood.

    (2) The response should *not* be limited to the personal knowledge of the buyer. Allow him to refresh his memory in any way he wishes, e.g. by referring to documents or by speaking to other members of the household. If the answer to a question is within the knowledge of another member of the household, seek the information from the other member wherever possible.

31a The pre-coded responses should not be read out to informants except at Q1a) on the Contact Report and Q.27 on the questionnaire.

32. Where there are two buyers, they may sometimes give different but consistent answers. Remember that it is *the collective experience of the household* that is being recorded. For example, in reply to Question 6, the husband may say that he spoke to friends about it, but the wife may say that she did not. Record the response as 'Yes'.

In some cases, however, they may give inconsistent answers. For example, they may disagree about what the salesman said or about whether the item is satisfactory. In a case of this sort, use your judgment and record whichever answer seems more likely to be right. For example, the husband may generally be more reliable if it is a car you are talking about, the wife if it is kitchen equipment.

33. Keep these instructions with you so that you can refer to them as necessary during the interview.

34. Please *use a blue or black ball pen*. You may find that after you have ringed a code, the informant changes his mind and corrects his answer. In this case, strike through the incorrect code with a diagonal line and ring the correct one.

35. If the informant interrupts with chatter between questions, this must obviously be kept in check, but it should not be prevented entirely. A moderate amount of chatter can be helpful in three ways:

    (1) To maintain a cordial atmosphere.
    (2) To show whether any of the questions have been misunderstood, or any answers wrongly classified.
    (3) To provide other comments, to be noted at question 104. In particular, if there is something bothering the informant, we want to know what it is.

36. The questionnaire calls for you to look at any documents the informant has relating to the transaction. Return them when you have finished looking at them. If the informant seems to have the documents but refuses to show you, note any explanation he gives at question 105.

...

Sending in Work

...

The Contact Report

...

46. Ask Part A, Screening Questions, of any member of the household over 16. But where you have a choice, prefer the head of the household, or whoever appears to be the most responsible of those immediately available. Show the list of items and read out slowly. Ring the

code applicable to each item that was bought, ordered, or had on approval within the past 2 years. It is very important that the informant understands Q.1(a) on the Contact Report. Note that the question relates to three situations:

(1) Goods that were bought (for cash or on credit terms) and received.
(2) Goods that were ordered but not received (either because the seller failed to deliver or because the buyer cancelled the order).
(3) Goods that were received on approval but not bought.

. . .

48. Regarding furniture, cooking utensils, and heating equipment, it is not necessary that any single piece should cost over £20. Several pieces *bought together* can be treated as one item. Apart from furniture, cooking utensils, and heating equipment, if two or more items were bought on the same agreement, or at the same time, treat as separate items.

49. If two items of the same key code have been bought, but on separate occasions, enter the one bought nearest to four months ago and ignore the other.

Gifts

50. Deal with gifts as follows:

(1) If the item was bought as a gift from one member of the household to another, *include*. Interview the giver and the receiver of the gift.
(2) If the item was bought for use in the household, but later given away, *include*. Interview the buyer/s/.
(3) If cash was given to a member of the household and the item bought with the money, *include*. Interview the buyer/s/.
(4) If the item was given to a member of the household by someone outside, *exclude*.
(5) If the item was bought and then (without use) given to someone outside the household, *exclude*.

51. The guiding principle here is that we want interviews only where the household had both the buying and using experience.

52. Sometimes people are induced to buy something by the salesman

telling them initially that it is a gift. Then it transpires that they are expected to pay for it. Treat these cases as an ordinary purchase and proceed with interview.

53. This survey does not include goods hired under a straight rental agreement where there is no provision for purchase. (This is often the case with television.)

54. The responses to Q.1(b) are your guide in selecting the items for interview. Follow the instructions on the Contact Report.

Example

1(a)	01	02	03	04	05	06	etc.
(b)	X 15	X –	X –	X 12	X –	X 07	
1.	DAW NW			AJW			
2.	✓			✓			

. . .

The Questionnaire

General Instructions

Cash figures. Where the question asks for a cash figure, record the answer to the nearest pound, except where shillings and pence are indicated. If the informant does not remember the exact amount, approximate figures are acceptable.

Unlisted responses. If the answer does not fit one of the listed responses, write it out verbatim.

Other. To many of the questions, one of the listed responses is 'Other (STATE)'. Where this is applicable, write in the response and ring the code.

Multiple responses. Where more than one answer is possible, probe for any additional responses after one response has been received. Where more than one answer is possible, two or more code columns have been provided.

If only one response is received, use the first column. If several responses are received, code one in each column. If there are more responses than columns, code the additional responses in the last column.

Example

. . . . . .

'Seller'. Where goods are bought on hire-purchase or other credit terms, then as a matter of technical law, a finance company often has the legal status of owner or seller. But throughout the questionnaire, 'seller' has the ordinary colloquial meaning. It means the dealer, or the company or person selling the goods, whether or not he was in strict law the seller.

Also 'the seller' includes any manager, salesman, agent, collector or other person representing the seller.

'Salesman'. Similarly 'salesman' includes anyone participating in the selling of the item whether or not he is actually called a salesman.

'Bought'. Several questions refer to when the item was 'bought'. This refers to the occasion of ordering or agreeing to buy the item, not to the delivery of the item.

'OUO'. Boxes marked OUO (office use only) should be ignored.

'...........'. Where '...........' appears in a question, read the type of item, E.g. 'the car', 'the refrigerator', etc.

Horizontal lines. Where there is no horizontal line between questions, this indicates that the next question should be asked in the same situation as the preceding one. Conversely a horizontal line indicates that the next question applies to a different situation from the preceding one. Follow the instruction under the line.

Indentation. Where a sub-question is indented, this indicates that whether or not to ask the question depends on the answer to the preceding sub-question. Conversely where there is no indentation, the asking of the sub-question does not depend on the preceding sub-question.

Section 1

. . . . . .

For 'Description of Item' write the particular item rather than the group.

E.g. put

'car' rather than 'motor vehicle';
'radio' rather than 'TV, radio, tape recorder, record-player or combination';
'bedroom suite' rather than 'furniture';
'electric fire' or 'immersion heater' rather than 'heating equipment'.

Question 1. Write in the name of the maufacturer, not the brand name. E.g. for a Ford Zephyr car, put 'Ford' not 'Zephyr'.

If the buyer doesn't know, ask to look at the item if it is convenient to do so.

If the item consists of several units, enter the make of whichever appears to be the most costly unit.

. . . . . .

Question 2. If there were two buyers, take the one who has lived there the longest.

Question 3(a). We want to know whether the buyer, or one of them, responded to an advertisement for a particular item or a particular model.

. . . . . .

Question 8. 'Shop' means any retail premises at which goods are normally sold. But if it was simply a mail order office, ring code 4.

If the buyer says something like 'My friend is an agent', probe. It probably means that the friend takes orders for a mail order company, in which case ring code 4.

Question 9. It does not matter whether the buyer looked at the same make. If he looked at the same category of goods at other places, record as 'Yes'. Also it does not matter if he was looking to buy in the other shops, etc., or just browsing.

Question 10(a). We want to know if the shop first took the initiative to make personal contact with the buyer. If the buyer first took the initiative to get in touch with the shop, record as 'No'.

Question 11. To classify the shop, you may use your own knowledge as well as answers obtained from the buyer/s.

'Department Store' means a shop appearing to have at least 25 sales staff and at least 3 departments.

'Chain Store' means a seller having shops at 3 or more locations.

'Discount Shop' means a shop that continually advertises cut prices on its whole range of goods, not just on a few items.

'Specialist Shop' means any shop selling one category of goods. E.g. a furniture shop, a household appliances shop, etc.

Ring as many codes as applicable.

Question 14(a). If an appointment was made, it will usually have been done by telephone. But it does not matter how it was done. If there was any sort of appointment record as 'Yes'.

Question 15. The object here is to find out what the salesman's opening line was, i.e., what he first said to capture the attention of the household. Probe fully and ask any necessary supplementary questions.

Question 17. For example, if the salesman came at about five past four in the afternoon, record as 4.05 p.m.

If the informant does not remember, ask for about how long the salesman was there. Then see if the arrival and departure times can be estimated.

Question 18(b). If the item is an *encyclopedia*, change the question to 'Did you decide to buy the particular encyclopedia you actually bought before you went to the shop/before the salesman came/etc.?'

Question 19. Some common examples of such agreements are:

1. To get a deep freezer, they may have agreed to buy a frozen food plan.
2. To get an encyclopedia set, they may have agreed to subscribe to an information service.
3. To get a TV, they may have signed a maintenance contract.

Question 20. Try to induce the buyers to remember everything they can about what the salesman said. Listen, but do not record. Then ask (b) if any of this turned out to be wrong or untrue.

People tend to remember their experiences with the goods more readily than what the salesman said. So it is important to probe here and give them a chance to think.

Question 23. Only deal here with complaints about the sales transaction, or the way the goods were sold. Subsequent experience with the goods is covered later.

Question 24. For example, the price ticket may have said 'Regular £85, sale price £60'. Or the salesman may have said 'this is a special offer', or simply 'sale price'.

Question 25(a). If the buyer was informed of this at or before the time of ordering the goods, record 'Yes' even if he was told something else later.

The wording of the information does not matter. E.g. '10 days free trial', 'on approval', or 'if you don't like it you can send it back'.

Question 26(a). For goods received on approval that were sent back, record as 'Yes'.
(c) Write number of days as a two digit entry. E.g. if it was 5 days, record as 0 5. If the buyer does not remember exactly, an approximate figure is acceptable. But if he is vague about it, leave the boxes blank and ring code 1.
(d) If the seller agreed, record as "Yes" even if he protested.

Question 27. Show Card B and read aloud slowly. Probe if necessary to ensure correct answer.

Question 28. Question must be asked in all cases under Section 3, but the form of the question varies according to the coding of Q.27.

Question 29(a). If there were two buyers, code the one who had been driving the longest.

Section 4

This section applies to all cases where an item was received. But it may not necessarily be the one ordered.

Question 30. The response 'at the time' refers to where the buyer received the item on the same occasion as he agreed to buy it. If he took delivery on any occasion after that, record as 'later', even though it may be the same day.

Questions 30-39. You may find a situation where an item was supplied but later the seller replaced it by another one. In such a case, read these questions as applying to the first item supplied. Buyer satisfaction with the second item will appear in response to Q.39(f).

Questions 32-34. Record all defects, whether or not they are subsequently remedied. Seller action to remedy defects is covered at Q.39.

Question 39(a). It does not matter whether the household regarded the communication as a complaint. Record 'Yes' if there was any expression of dissatisfaction, any request for something to be put right, or any request for repairs.

Record 'Yes' at (a) if there were any complaints or requests to the seller, whether or not the complaint was remedied.

(f) If there were several complaints and the buyer was satisfied about some but not others, ring code X. Code X also applies where there was one complaint and the buyer was partly satisfied about it.

Question 40(a). Sometimes the word 'warranty' is used. 'Warranty' and 'guarantee' mean the same thing.

Question 41(a). Again, it does not matter whether the household used the word 'complain'. Code 'yes' if any dissatisfaction was expressed, or any advice was sought about the purchase.

(c) Include any advice received, as well as any action taken, and the result. After '(1st code at b)' write the result of contacting the person or institution coded in the first column at b. Similarly after '(2nd code at b)' etc.

Question 42(a). We want to know whether the buyer feels that, despite his complaints, the seller had a right to be paid.

If there are two buyers and they disagree, code the response of the one who handled the finances.

(c) If the informant says he was afraid of trouble, ask 'What sort of trouble?' If he does not specify, ring code 5. If he does specify, use the other codes applicable.

Question 43(a). This is a key question. Great care must be taken with it, because a mistake in classification here would result in the wrong questions being asked later.

Avoid 'Don't know'.

If the informant does not understand the question, probe by asking what sort of credit arrangement was made. If he still does not understand, say, 'For example, did you arrange hire-purchase terms with the seller, or did you go somewhere else and arrange a loan?' Do *not* probe by asking if he paid cash. Some people feel that there is something wrong with buying on credit. Thus if asked whether they bought for cash or on credit, they might feel impelled to reply cash. But if people are asked how they financed the transaction, or what the credit arrangement was, those who paid cash can be expected to say so.

'Planned to pay cash' (included in code A) refers to the situation where the buyer intended to pay cash, but never actually paid.

In many cases, the buyer will have paid part of the price in cash and arranged credit or a loan for the balance. Classify these cases according to how the balance was financed. In other words, only ring A if the whole price was paid (or planned to be paid) in cash.

If the price was paid by someone else as a gift to the informant, ring code A.

'Credit', code B, includes situations:

(1) Where the buyer used a continuing account, (a charge account or credit card). This may be an account with the seller or a credit card company.
(2) Hire-purchase or other credit terms arranged with the seller specifically to purchase this item.

You could find a case where the buyer bought on hire-purchase and also raised a loan to pay the deposit. If so, treat initially as a hire-purchase case, i.e. ring codes B and 3. The loan will then be mentioned at Q.52A and dealt with more fully in Section 9. This is the only situation in which Sections 7 and 9 will both be applicable.

If a loan was arranged, it makes no difference whether the cash was actually handed to the buyer and paid to the seller, or whether it was paid directly by the lender to the seller. Either case should be coded as X. If there is any doubt as to whether the financing was by loan or credit terms, try to look at the documents. The words 'hire-purchase', 'credit sale', 'seller', 'buyer' or 'hirer' indicate code B. The words 'lender' and 'borrower' in the documents indicate code X.

You could find a case where the salesman is acting as agent for a loan company. Thus instead of selling on hire-purchase or other credit terms, he arranges a loan for the buyer. This will usually be clear from the documents, and such a case should be coded X. It is fairly common for central heating, but otherwise is not usual.

(b) For cases where the buyer replied 'cash' at (a), this question is an additional check to discover whether a loan was arranged.

(c) Code 3 applies where hire-purchase or other credit terms were arranged with the seller specifically to purchase this item. This is common for more expensive items.

Code 4 applies where the item was charged to a continuing account with the seller. It may be called a charge account or something else. To use the account, the buyer often produces a credit card of the seller. This is common for goods bought from department stores and from oil companies.

Code 5 applies where a credit card was used other than the card of the seller. For example, code 5 applies to a Barclaycard or Diners' Club card. These companies are not selling the goods; they are just operating a credit card system.

A Check Trader is a company issuing checks that enable people to buy goods at specified outlets. The retailers are then paid by the Check Trader (less a discount) and the buyer pays the Check Trader for the checks by instalments. Any arrangement that fits this description should be classified under 6, whether or not the company calls itself a 'Check Trader'. In other situations, however, credit checks are issued by the seller. This is equivalent to a budget account and should be coded as 4.

The same classifications apply whether the item was bought at a shop, by mail order, or from an itinerant salesman.

Most credit transactions with a salesman who calls at the home are in one of two categories:

(1) The salesman comes regularly and a continuing account is main-

tained with the customer. New purchases are debited to the account and periodic payments are credited. Companies operating this way are sometimes known as credit pedlers, credit draperies, or credit traders. Code these cases as 4.

(2) There is no continuing business between the customer and the salesman. He is going round selling a particular item, and he arranges hire-purchase or other credit terms for that item. Code these cases as 3. (But if he arranges a loan to cover the purchase, then of course the case should be coded as X.)

To ensure correct classification, it will often be necessary to ask supplementary questions. For example, suppose in reply to (a), the buyer says 'I used my credit card'. This should be code B at (a) but could be 4 or 5 at (c). So you would ring code B and then ask 'Which credit card did you use?' This would enable you to distinguish between codes 4 and 5.

(d) Some charge accounts (credit card accounts) are payable monthly for the full amount owing. For these, ring code 7. But on some charge accounts (credit card accounts) the buyer pays the balance by instalments. These are often called revolving credit or budget accounts. For these ring code 8.

If the buyer has the choice of paying the full amount owing monthly, or paying by instalments, ring code 9. This is common for accounts at department stores.

. . . . . .

Questions 47 and 48. Record the percentage as either per year or per month.

Sometimes interest is called a service charge.

If no interest is payable, record as NIL per cent a year.

. . . . . .

Question 51(b). If they ask why you want to see it, say that you would like to see exactly what sort of document was used.

If they appear unwilling to show you, ring code 2 and dispense with seeing it.

When you see the document, look for the cancellation notice. Read the beginning and end to ensure that it corresponds with the notice in the questionnaire. Otherwise it is easy to confuse a cancellation notice with the signature box. Repeat for the second copy where available.

Note that (c) to (e) are to be answered by your own observation without questioning the informant.

Question 52. Where a copy of the agreement is available these figures will usually be clear. Specimen hire-purchase and credit sale contracts are included in your supplies so that you can see how the figures are commonly arranged. If the agreement is not available, rely on the memory of the buyer as far as possible. If he cannot remember any figure, write D.K. in the space for that figure. If appropriate, help the informant with the arithmetic.

(a) Cash price means whatever price was agreed as the cash price, including the price of any accessories.
(b) If there was no trade-in, write £NIL.
(c) If there was no deposit, write £NIL.
(d) Usually the interest is pre-computed. It is calculated in advance, usually called a finance charge or hire-purchase charge and quoted as a lump sum. It is the difference between the hire-purchase (or credit) price and the cash price. However, you could come across an exceptional case where the interest has not been pre-computed. For example, an agreement might say: 'Price £100, payable at £10 a month with interest at 3 per cent a month on the outstanding balance.' In such a case write in, for example, '3 per cent a month on the outstanding balance'.

Question 52A. If the answer is 'yes', it means that the buyer financed in two ways:

(1) By hire-purchase or other credit terms arranged with the seller. Qs. 48-63 deal with this.
(2) By loan. Qs. 64-85 deal with this and should also be asked.

If Q.52A is answered 'yes', make a mark by Q.86 to remind yourself to check the manual again at that question.

Question 54. This refers to the number of instalments payable according to the agreement. The number actually paid could be different.

Question 57. This is not necessarily the same as the figure shown at Q.52(a). For example, the buyer might reply 'The price was £100, but the salesman said if I paid cash I could have a 10 per cent discount'. This reply should be recorded as £90.

Question 58. Usually this will be clear in the agreement. A hire-purchase agreement is one under which the buyer agrees to hire the goods, and then has an option to purchase for a nominal sum after he has paid a specified number of instalments. Usually the words 'hire' and 'option to purchase' are used. . .

. . . . . .

The easiest way to distinguish is to look in the signature box. Usually it will say: 'This document contains the terms of a hire purchase agreement. . . .' (or conditional sale agreement, or credit sale agreement, as the case may be).

If it was a casual arrangement with the seller with no formal documents, this will be a credit sale, code 0.

If it is a *loan* document, treat as follows:

(i) If the loan was *in addition* to hire-purchase or other credit terms, ensure that Q.52A is coded Y. Then continue through sections 7, 8 and 9.

(ii) If the loan is the *only source* of financing, a mistake has been made in coding Q.43. Go back to Q.43, strike out the codes ringed at that question and ring code X. Then follow the skip instructions applicable where Q.43 coded X.

Question 59. The other person (the non-buyer) may have been asked to sign the agreement itself, or more likely he will have been asked to sign another document entitled 'indemnity', 'guarantee', or 'promissory note'.

. . . . . .

Question 62(a). If this was the gist of what the salesman said, ring code A. It does not matter if he used different language to express the idea.

Question 63(a). This may have been said by the salesman or in the advertising.

. . . . . .

Question 71. The figure required is the amount the buyer thought he wanted to borrow prior to any discussion with the lender.

Question 72(a). Try to induce the buyer to remember everything he can about what the lender said. Listen but do not record. Then ask (b) if any of this turned out to be wrong or untrue.

Question 77(a). Write in either annual or monthly rate if known. A rate of less than 4 per cent will usually be a monthly rate.

. . . . . .

Question 86. It does not matter whether the notification was formal or casual. If there was any type of communication indicating that payment was overdue, ring code Y.

The first form of the question (where Q.43 coded 2) applies where it was intended to be a cash transaction, but for some reason the buyer did not pay.

. . . . . .

Question 89. We want to know here what action was *threatened.* In the following questions, we ask what action was *taken.*

If the informant still has letters claiming payment, try to look and see what the letters threaten.

. . . . . .

Question 102. '1st buyer' and '2nd buyer' refer to the buyer(s) of this item. If another selected item was bought within the household, the buyer(s) of that item will be dealt with in the questionnaire for that item.

. . . . . .

(c) Note that under 'personal occupation/social grade' we are asking you to record details separately for each buyer *and also* for the head of household. In many cases of course the head of the household will also be a buyer and then the first (or second) and third columns will have the same code.

Where a buyer is not the head of household, we are using the standard social grade classification as a personal occupation grading. Unlike the normal practice therefore you may have a different grading within the same household.

As well as ringing codes for both buyer(s) and head of household, full supporting details of occupation should be given in the usual way. 'Housewife (Not working)' means with neither full time or part time occupation. A housewife who has any occupation, whole or part time, will have a personal occupation grading.

. . . . . .

Question 104. Note anything which the informant regards as significant, *or* anything which you think might be significant.

In particular, if there is anything bothering the informant we would like to know what it is.

Question 105. No question to be asked here. Just note any reasons for refusal given during the interview.

. . . . . .

APPENDIX E: FORMULAE BY WHICH THE TRANSACTIONS IN THE SAMPLE WERE CLASSIFIED

Classification by Selling Methods

1. Major Objections

Cases where any of the following conditions was present.

(1) Buyer signed contract in blank, and seller inserted figures higher than those agreed to by the buyer.
(2) Lies told by a door-to-door salesman for the purpose of obtaining admission to the home.*
(3) Four or more things said by the salesman when the item was bought about the item turned out to be wrong or untrue.*
(4) High-pressure sales tactics.*
(5) Delay in delivery over 28 days beyond date by which delivery was promised.*
(6) Advertised as a private sale whereas seller was in the trade.*
(7) Item not new, although sold as new.*
(8) Apart from the responses to particular questions, other comments by the buyer indicated major objections to the selling methods.

2. Substantial Objections

Cases not classified above and where any of the following conditions was present.

(1) Item delivered not the one ordered, and not just as acceptable.
(2) The probability of a bait and switch technique.
(3) Lies told by a door-to-door salesman for the purpose of obtaining admission to the home.†
(4) Something in the advertising turned out to be wrong or untrue.†
(5) Something said by the salesman when the item was bought about the item turned out to be wrong or untrue.†
(6) Buyer misled or misinformed about how much he would have to pay for the item.†
(7) Buyer misled about the terms of payment.†
(8) High-pressure sales tactics.†

**Unless* it appeared from other parts of the questionnaire that this was less serious.
†Unless it appeared from other parts of the questionnaire that this was not serious.

(9) Figures and other terms of the contract were not completely filled in before the buyer signed it.†
(10) Item sold by a man allowed into the home to repair a similar item that the household already had.†
(11) Sale tied in with the supply of some other item or service which the buyer found unsatisfactory.†
(12) Delay in delivery 8-28 days from the date by which delivery promised.†
(13) Item delivered not the one ordered and not quite as acceptable as the one ordered.†
(14) Buyer charged for delivery, installation or accessory that he had been told was included in the price.†
(15) Charged more than quoted for delivery, installation, or accessory.†
(16) Unreasonably high price of accessories or installation.†
(17) Item unsafe or unfit to function at all.†
(18) Seller subsequently attempted inertia selling[1] of other goods.
(19) Apart from the responses to particular questions, other comments by the buyer indicated substantial objections to the selling methods.

3. Minor Objections

Cases not classified above and where any of the following conditions was present.

(1) Something in the advertising turned out to be wrong or untrue.
(2) Something said by the salesman when the item was bought about the item turned out to be wrong or untrue.
(3) Item was sold by a man allowed into the home to repair a similar item that the household already had.
(4) Item was sold by someone allowed into the home after purporting to be interested in buying old models rather than selling new ones.
(5) Salesman said that buyer could earn commissions on sales to people whose names buyer would give him and in that way meet the payments.
(6) Figures and other terms of the contract were not completely filled in before the buyer signed it.
(7) Sale was tied in with the supply of some other item or service which the buyer found unsatisfactory.

† *Unless* it appeared from other parts of the questionnaire that this was not serious.
1. The practice of sending goods that have never been ordered and expecting the recipient to pay for them.

(8) Salesman was not well informed about the product.
(9) Miscellaneous grievances about, for example, the seller refusing to put the guarantee in writing or demanding payment before delivery of the goods.
(10) Buyer felt that he should have been told something by the salesman that he was not told.
(11) Buyer contacted the seller in response to an advertisement for a particular item but bought a different one of the same type.
(12) Salesman disinterested or inattentive.
(13) Buyer charged for delivery, installation or accessory that he had been told was included in the price.
(14) Unreasonably high price of accessories or installation.
(15) Delay in delivery 1-7 days beyond date by which delivery promised.
(16) Item delivered was not the one ordered, and was not quite as acceptable.
(17) Seller subsequently attempted inertia selling of other goods.
(18) Apart from the responses to particular questions, other comments by the buyer indicated minor objections to the selling methods.

(Note. Cases that would otherwise have been classified in this category might be classified above under 1(8) or 2(19) if other comments on the questionnaire indicated that this was appropriate.)

4. Entirely Satisfactory

Cases where none of the conditions listed above was present.

Classification by Condition of Goods

1. Major Objections

Cases where any of the following conditions was present.

(1) Buyer spent £50 or more on repairs (apart from routine maintenance) and the item was not a secondhand motor vehicle.
(2) Buyer spent £5 or more on repairs (apart from routine maintenance) and the item was not a motor vehicle or central heating.
(3) Part or accessory was missing that the buyer had been informed would come with the item, and the absence of which prevented the item from functioning at all.*
(4) When received, the item did not function at all.*
(5) Multiple defects appeared after delivery.*

**Unless* the seller remedied the defects without charge, or other parts of the questionnaire or other comments indicated that the matter was less serious.

(6) Item no use at all.*
(7) Substantial part or accessory missing that the buyer had been informed would come with the item.†
(8) Significant defects in the item when received.†
(9) Installation by the seller was not properly done.†
(10) Significant defects subsequently appeared in the item.†
(11) Item not in use because broken down.†
(12) Item not in use because too dangerous to use.†
(13) Performance unsatisfactory or only sometimes satisfactory.†
(14) Seller failed to effect repairs which the buyer requested under the guarantee.†
(15) Buyer was charged for repairs done under the guarantee when he thought he should not have been.†
(16) Apart from the responses to particular questions, other comments by the buyer indicated major objections to the condition of the goods.

2. Substantial Objections

Cases not classified above and where any of the following conditions was present.

(1) Buyer spent £10 or more on repairs (apart from routine maintenance) and the item was not a secondhand motor vehicle.
(2) Buyer spent £3 or more on repairs (apart from routine maintenance) and the item was not a motor vehicle or central heating.
(3) Seller failed to effect repairs which the buyer requested under the guarantee.
(4) Seller failed to effect repairs under the guarantee until the buyer insisted a great deal.
(5) Buyer was charged for repairs done under the guarantee when he thought he should not have been.
(6) Substantial part or accessory missing that the buyer had been informed would come with the item.**
(7) Significant defect in the item when received.**
(8) Significant defect appeared in the item subsequently.**
(9) Installation by the seller was not properly done.**
(10) Item not in use because broken down.**

**Unless* the seller remedied the defects without charge, or other parts of the questionnaire or other comments indicated that the matter was less serious.
†*And* seller failed to remedy the complaint. *Unless* other parts of the questionnaire or other comments indicated that the matter was less serious.
***Unless* the seller remedied the defects, or other parts of the questionnaire or other comments indicated that the matter was not serious.

(11) Item not in use because too dangerous to use.*
(12) Performance unsatisfactory or only sometimes satisfactory.*
(13) Buyer requested repairs under the guarantee and only some of them were done.*
(14) Seller failed to effect repairs under the guarantee until the buyer insisted a little.*
(15) Buyer was charged for repairs done under the guarantee when he thought he should have been charged less.*
(16) Apart from the responses to particular questions, other comments by the buyer indicated substantial objections to the condition of the goods.

3. Minor Objections

Cases not already classified above, and where any of the following conditions was present.

(1) An accessory was missing that the buyer had been informed would come with the item.
(2) The item was defective when received.
(3) Defects subsequently appeared in the item.
(4) Installation by the seller was not properly done.
(5) Item was not in use because broken down or too dangerous to use.
(6) Performance unsatisfactory or only sometimes satisfactory.
(7) Buyer complained to the seller about the purchase, or asked for something to be put right, or asked for repairs to be done.
(8) Buyer did not complain, but for reasons indicating that he had cause for complaint.
(9) Money spent on repairs (apart from routine maintenance) and the item was not a secondhand motor vehicle.
(10) Buyer requested repairs under the guarantee and only some of them were done.
(11) Seller failed to effect repairs under the guarantee until the buyer insisted a little.
(12) Buyer was charged for repairs done under the guarantee and felt that he should have been charged less.
(13) Buyer stopped payment because of dissatisfaction with the item.
(14) Buyer disappointed with the item.
(15) Poor service by the seller after sale.
(16) Apart from the responses to particular questions, other comments

* *Unless* the seller remedied the defects, or other parts of the questionnaire or other comments indicated that the matter was not serious.

by the buyer indicated minor objections to the condition of the goods.

(Note. Cases that would otherwise have been classified in this category might be classified above under 1(16) or 2(16) if other comments on the questionnaire indicated that this was appropriate.)

4. Entirely Satisfactory

Cases where none of the above conditions was present.

APPENDIX F: SOCIAL GRADES

On this survey, each buyer of an item was allocated a social grade according to his own occupational category, and in addition, a social grade was allocated to the head of the household.

A housewife who also had an outside occupation, whether full time or part time, was classified according to her outside occupation. If she had none at all, she was classified in a separate grade of 'housewife'. The social grades used were:

A A business or professional person who has reached a high rank in his field, or a person having substantial private means. Examples: bishop, surgeon, senior civil servant, commercial airline pilot, senior business executive, chief constable.

B People holding intermediate positions in the professions, business, or the civil service. Examples: vicar, nursing sister, industrial scientist, advertising manager in a medium sized company, army captain or major.

C1 Generally people in administrative, supervisory, or clerical positions. Examples: nurse, telephonist, driving instructor, librarian, police sergeant, or a retired person who before retirement would have been C1 grade, and who has a pension other than the state pension, or private means.

C2 Skilled manual workers. Examples: bricklayer, coal cutter, welder, shoemaker, ambulance driver, radio mechanic.

D Generally semi-skilled or unskilled workers. Examples: apprentice, fisherman, textile printer, dough mixer, bus conductor, cleaner.

E Old age pensioners, widows, casual workers and those who, through sickness or unemployment, are dependent on social security schemes, and have small or no private means.

Housewife: a woman engaged in looking after a home for herself and at least one other, and who does not have any outside occupation.

The above is a very abbreviated version of the grading manual used on the survey. Except for the addition of the housewife grade, it was the manual that the interviewers of Research Services Ltd were accustomed to using. The manual had much longer lists of examples.

Where there were two buyers, the higher social grade of the two was used in analysis.

APPENDIX G: CLASS ACTIONS

The following discussion of class actions was written by Professor M.J. Trebilcock of the Faculty of Law, University of Toronto. It first appeared as part of an article entitled 'Private Law Remedies for Misleading Advertising' (1972) 22 *University of Toronto Law Journal*, p.1, 20-29. It is now reproduced by kind permission of the University of Toronto Press and of the author.

"......

2. Collective Rights of Action

(a) The Consumer Class Action

Probably the most controversial development in the whole consumer protection area in the recent past has been the rise of the class action.

This procedure enables representatives of a class of persons, named or unnamed, to sue on behalf of the class in respect of some claim in which the class has a common interest. Typically in a consumer context, a class action will involve a suit for an injunction and/or damages against a named defendant who perhaps through a misleading advertising campaign or the sale of a defective line of products or the use of an irregular form of contract, has prejudiced a whole class of consumers, conceivably running into millions in number, and perhaps involving millions of dollars in damages. If each consumer were compelled to sue individually for redress, the cost of proceedings would often render an action pointless. However, when the individual claims are 'consolidated' into a class action, the damages then in issue may in aggregate become very substantial and render worthwhile the legal overheads involved in bringing an action, both from the point of view of the consumer, and from the point of view of legal counsel.

To highlight the impact that class actions can have in the consumer protection area, it is worth citing some recent recoveries in the USA under this procedure.

In *State of West Virginia v Pfizer & Co.,*[1] various states and municipalities recovered $120m from five pharmaceutical companies in settlement of complaints alleging price-fixing of certain antibiotics in

1. U.S.D.G., S.D.N.Y., 68 Civ. 240.

violation of anti-trust laws. $37m of this was made available to individual consumers who had been prejudiced. The balance was to be used by the states, etc., on public health facilities. In *Illinois Bell Telephone Co. v Slattery,*[1] the defendant telephone company was required to refund over $18m to customers whom it had overcharged, by deducting overcharges from future accounts. In *Daar v Yellow Cab Co.,*[2] the Supreme Court of California held well-founded a class action brought on behalf of all persons who had used the defendant company's taxis claiming in excess of $100,000 in damages being illegal overcharges for its fares over a four year period. In *Bebchick v Public Utilities Commission,*[3] illegal overcharges on fares exacted by a bus company from over a million passengers who regularly used the defendant's buses were ordered to be 'refunded' by reducing fares in future until the amount of the overcharge had been exhausted. In *Eisen v Carlisle and Jacquelin,*[4] a class action was brought on behalf of nearly 4 million odd-lot buyers in which it was claimed that defendants had been guilty of a breach of anti-trust laws in fixing their fees for odd-lot transactions. It is estimated that the action, if it proceeds, could involve damages running into over $100m. The average individual claim, on the other hand, amounts to only about $9 and, as such, is clearly not worth litigating. The Court of Appeals for the Second Circuit has held that the action in this form is in principle maintainable. Presently, a class action (importantly, in our present context) claiming an injunction and damages is filed in Washington in respect of misleading advertising claims alleged to have been made by Bristol-Meyers Ltd., manufacturers of Excedrin head-ache cure. Also, a class action is in progress for $427.5m in respect of the 200,000 GM commercial vehicles alleged to be fitted with dangerously defective wheels.

The potential impact of the class action procedure in any jurisdiction, if admitted, can readily be appreciated from the foregoing examples. However, the question of the legitimacy of the procedure has generated enormous controversy.

What are the arguments for and against the class action procedure?

FOR

Professor Benjamin Kaplan, one of the drafters of the current US Federal Rules of Procedure on Class Actions, has said that 'the historic mission of the class action is taking care of the smaller guy.'[5] Abraham

1. (1939), 102 F. 2d. 58.
2. (1967), 433 P. 2d. 732 (Cal.).
3. (1963), 318F. 2d. 187 (U.S. Court of Appeals. D.C.).
4. (1968), 391 F. 2d. 555 (U.S. Court of Appeals, 2nd Circ.).
5. Quoted by Ford, (1969), 10 *Bost. College Ind. and Comm.L.Rev.,* 505, n22.

L. Pomerantz writes: 'The class action is born of economics – the economics of the client as well as that of the lawyer. . .The class action is mushrooming throughout the courts of our land. It has become one of the most socially useful remedies in history. . .Heretofore, sanctions against consumer frauds consisted of a fine, injunction, or administrative wrist slapping. Now, the class action is striking at the malefactors' nerve endings: their pocketbooks. There is no more persuasive sanction.'[1]

Professor Starrs writes: 'The class action is clearly the kind of organised pressure which is often needed to force into public and judicial view the widespread evils of a system, a place or a person. It is the judicial analogue to the mass demonstrations of the streets. Its success often hinges less on the ultimate outcome of the particular case than on the publicity, visibility and aroused popular reaction it evokes. The class action, therefore, serves multiple purposes, some of which are tactical rather than legal. . .In short, the class action compensates for a lack of cohesiveness, accessibility and willingness to participate among poor persons which makes joint action by them often ineffectual. There is now a common fight against a common foe. The whip is no longer in the hands of the merchant or the collection agent who can divide and conquer. Now the talisman is combine and defeat through a class action, and the cause of having the oppressors on the receiving end for a change is sweet indeed.'[2]

Mrs Bess Myerson Grant, Commissioner of Consumer Affairs of the City of New York, in hearings before the US Senate Committee on Commerce said:

The class action bill. . .is one of the most powerful instruments of economic justice which the Senate has ever considered. . .The idea of consumer class actions is one of the most important proposals for economic reform which has appeared on the Nation's legislative agenda since the New Deal. . .

A Federal class action law will have more impact on the marketplaces of the Nation than all the myriads of laws and ordinances against fraud and deception which are hidden away in the statute books of the 50 States and their various subdivisions, put together. All these laws make fraud illegal. But they have not made fraud unprofitable. Many of these laws can only be invoked by administrative agencies, which long ago lost their concern for the consumer and their appetite for action.

A Federal class action law – at least one which is not hamstrung by needless procedural roadblocks to consumer justice – will put the power

1. (1970), 25, *Bus. Lawyer* 1259, 1260.
2. (1969), 49 *Bost. Univ. L. Rev.* 408, 410.

to seek justice in court where it belongs – beyond the reach of campaign contributors, industry lobbyists, or Washington lawyers – it will put power in the hands of the consumers themselves and in the hands of their own lawyers, retained by them to represent their interest alone.[1]

AGAINST

Thomas J. Weithers, a Chicago defence counsel, in a recent paper,[2] argues: '[The class action] provides a new device for bringing before the court great numbers of passive litigants who would otherwise have remained silent. Unless restricted to those cases where, in the discretion of the trial judge, such actions can achieve economies of time, effort and expense [ie, in respect of individual actions that would otherwise still have been brought], class actions will become "Frankenstein monsters," disrupting the administration of the judicial system.'[3]

Business interests have been outspoken critics of the development of the class action. The US Chamber of Commerce has described the procedure as 'ineffective, excessive and unnecessary.'[4] The Wall Street Journal reports a spokesman for the American Retail Federation as saying: 'The potential impact of indiscriminate consumer class actions on business is devastating.'[5] Other critics have contended that legitimate business would be the target of frivolous lawsuits that would cost thousands of dollars to defend: It is claimed that the greatest beneficiaries would be lawyers who would prod consumers into filing massive claims in the hopes of collecting large settlements and fat fees (ie, the analogy of the 'strike action' in the corporate context). President Nixon has himself warned that too liberal a development of the class action 'might flood the courts with a whole mass of actions which lawyers are perfectly capable of thinking up in the interests of a fee.'[6] Both Chief Justice Burger[7] and Justice Black[8] of the US Supreme Court have warned of the crippling burden that could be placed on the courts if often enormously complex class actions were to be too easily maintainable. Professor Chafee has written: 'The situation is so tangled and bewildering that I sometimes wonder whether the world would be any the worse off if the class-suit device had been

1. Hearings before the Consumer Subcommittee of the U.S. Senate Committee on Commerce, No. 91-48, 1970, at 172.
2. (1969), 10 *Bost. College Ind. and Comm. L. Rev.* 515.
3. At 525.
4. *Wall Street Journal* 30 April 1970.
5. Ibid.
6. Ibid.
7. Speech to the American Bar Association, 10 August 1970.
8. In *Snyder v Harris* (1969), 394 U.S. 332, at 341.

left buried in the learned obscurity of Calvert on *Parties to Suits in Equity*.'[1]

Readers may find it easier to make an evaluation of these arguments for and against the class action if some of the procedural issues that fall to be resolved in the course of such an action are briefly canvassed. Rule 23 of the US Federal Rules of Procedure, which has been used most frequently in recent cases as the basis for a class action, will be used as the point of reference for the discussion.[2]

1 Adequacy of Representation The Court must ensure that those claiming to represent the class are capable of doing so adequately. This question involves examining whether the representatives have the resources necessary to prosecute the case fully, whether counsel retained by the representatives are adequate.

One point worth mentioning here in passing is that the diversity of citizenship jurisdiction of the US federal courts can apparently only be used as a means of bestowing on consumers the benefits of rule 23 if one of the plaintiff representatives by himself has a claim exceeding the $10,000 needed to found this jurisdiction. The US Supreme Court in *Snyder v Harris*[3] has ruled that it is not possible for the representatives to aggregate their claims in order to satisfy this requirement. This decision creates an unfortunate limitation on the scope of rule 23.

2 A Common Class Interest Rule 23 requires that there be questions of law or fact common to the class. This is probably one of the most crucial requirements in rule 23, as in most other class action statutes. Examples cited above of recent recoveries in class actions indicate that some courts have been prepared to interpret the requirement of 'common interest' imaginatively.

However, a recent decision of the New York Courts of Appeals, *Hall v Coburn Corporation*,[4] has held that class actions brought by

1. *Some Problems of Equity* (1950), at 200.
2. Detailed studies of the consumer class action procedure in the U.S.A. are to be found in (1969), 10 *Bost. College Ind. and Comm. L. Rev.* (symposium issue on the class action); James E. Starrs, 'The Consumer Class Action' (1969), 49 *Bost. Univ. L. Rev.*, at 210 and 406; Kalven and Rosenfield, 'The Contemporary Function of the Class Suit' (1941), 8 *U. Chicago L. Rev.* 684; Dole, 'Consumer Class Actions under the Uniform Deceptive Practices Act' (1968), *Duke, L.J.* 1101; Dole, 'Consumer Class Actions under Recent Consumer Credit Legislation' (1969), 44 *N.Y.U.L. Rev.* 80; Smit, 'Are Class Actions for Consumer Fraud a Fraud on the Consumer?' (1971), 26 *Bus. Lawyer*, 1053.
3. (1969), 394 U.S. 332.
4. (1969), 31 App. Div. 2d. 892, 298 N.Y.S. 2d. 894 aff'd No. 16 (N.Y. Ct. of App. 13 May 1970).

persons whose causes of action arise out of distinct transactions are not maintainable in New York state, even though the transactions are similar and are with a single defendant. In this case, the defendant finance company had used contracts the type of which did not comply with size requirements in the New York Retail Instalment Sales Act. The statute provided that, in these circumstances, a consumer was entitled to recover all the finance charges on his transaction. The class action had been brought on behalf of all consumers who had been induced to sign these irregular contracts.

Hall v Coburn Corporation should be contrasted with cases such as *Daar v Yellow Cab Co.*[1]

3 Notice to Class Members Rule 23 requires that once a court has held that a class action is maintainable, 'the best notice practicable under the circumstances' must be given to members of the class.

The purpose of this notice is to advise the class member: (A) that the court will exclude him from the class if he so requests by a specific date; (B) that the judgment, whether favourable or not, will bind all members who do not request exclusion; and (C) that any member who does not request exclusion, may if he so desires enter an appearance through his counsel.

Because all members of a class are bound by a judgment in a class action under rule 23, it is only reasonable that they should be given the opportunity of opting out and bringing an individual action on their own account, if they so wish.

From the point of view of defendants to a class suit, it has been suggested that this procedure is objectionable because it is a form of barratry or champerty. It is a way of dredging up litigants who would otherwise not have bothered to make a claim.[2] The only way of meeting this charge is to confess and avoid. The point of the criticism is precisely the rationale for class actions. Without the availability of the class action, in many cases it is simply not worth a consumer's while to sue. Thus, a class action, almost by definition, dredges up claims that would otherwise not have been made. The criticism of this seems a very dubious one: it seems to contemplate that it is in order for the law to confer generous substantive rights on consumers, provided that the law at the same time ensures that they are never enforceable. This proposition is not, at first sight, a compelling one.

Any dangers involved in the notice procedure of inflammatory exhortations to members of the class to sue and be damned can readily

1. *Supra*, note 1, p.498.
2. See Weithers, *supra*, note 1, p.500.

be safeguarded against by the court either drafting the notice or at least approving a notice drafted by the plaintiffs.

From a consumer's point of view, there are also, however, dangers in the notice procedure. How *much* notice has to be given? In a large class of ill-defined consumers, individual notice may be impracticable, or even if it is practicable, may be prohibitively expensive. Rule 23 seems only to require reasonable notice in the circumstances, but in *Eisen v Carlisle and Jacquelin,*[1] the decision of the US Courts [sic] of Appeals (2nd circ.), while acknowledging in principle the right of the plaintiffs to bring an action on behalf of the 4 million odd-lot buyers, seemed sympathetic to the defendants' argument that because they could (and with alacrity) supply the names of one million of the customers affected, individual notice ought to be given to these customers, and, in respect of the remainder, the plaintiffs should publish notices in newspapers throughout the country. The cost of mailing 1 million letters was estimated to be $200,000, the cost of advertising in newspapers a further substantial sum. These requirements, if insisted on, would spell the end of many class actions. However, in other cases[2] because of the fact that the defendants were entitled to the benefit of res judicata in the class action, and provided the plaintiffs could make out a prima facie case, courts have been prepared to require the defendants to pay for the notice. Moreover, advertising in newspapers which a substantial proportion of the class were likely to read has been held to be adequate notice.

In order to meet the criticism that the class action procedure might be used as a form of 'strike suit' simply to generate fees for attorneys and intimidate defendants into unjustified settlements, rule 23 requires the approval of the court to dismissals or compromises of class actions. It is hard to conceive of any other expedient that might be adopted to meet the risk of strike suits.[3]

Finally, the argument that class actions will generate so much new and complicated litigation that the courts will collapse under its weight seems at best an argument for reforming the court system rather than for denying justice to large sections of the community.

4 Judgment; Allocation and Distribution of Damages A judgment on the questions of law or fact common to the class may still leave a mul-

1. *Supra*, note 3, p.498.
2. Eg, *Dolglow v Anderson* (1968), 43 F.R.D. 472.
3. Cf, Lawrence Committee on Company Law Reform (Ont.) (1967). The Committee in recommending a wide scope for the shareholder's derivative action also recommended similar restrictions on settlements etc. (p.64).

titude of individual claims to be dealt with. For example, while in the class action there may be a general finding of liability, individual members of the class may still have to prove the damage that each has suffered.

Kalvin and Rosenfield[1] outline the following steps as being typical following an order in favour of the class:

1 The case will be referred to the Master of the Court to administer the details of participation by absentees. The defendant may be compelled to produce the names and addresses of members of the class that he is holding.
2 The plaintiff's attorney or the Master will prepare and submit to the court for approval forms for proof of claims and accompanying explanatory material which the Master should then mail to all absentees, or where this is impracticable, advertise in appropriate newspapers.
3 Members of the class should file claims within a prescribed time, and defendant should be permitted to file objections to the claims, but only as to issues not common to the original class judgment.
4 The Master should hold a hearing as to the objections and, if appropriate, as to the damages of each claimant, and then should file a report with the court.
5 The court, after disposing of all objections to the Master's report, should enter a final decree ordering the defendant to pay all who have proved their claims and make provision for costs and legal fees in the latter case, on a *quantum meruit* basis. The Master himself may distribute the damages, or, the representatives may be appointed trustees for collecting judgment and distributing on the claims.

One final problem must be mentioned. In some cases, because of the smallness of individual claims, the difficulty of notifying unidentified members of a class of their rights, and the difficulty of proving an individual's claim to damages, only a very small percentage of the members of the class may come forward and seek a recovery. Is this prospect a bar to a class action?

Recent American cases deny this, and instead apply what Pomerantz has described as a 'cy-pres' doctrine.[2] Under this doctrine, the court will direct the distribution of the unclaimed damages in a way which as nearly as possible compensates the class of persons aggrieved. The cases

1. See original article, note 1.
2. (1970), 25 *Bus. Lawyer* 1259, 1260 ff

of *State of West Virginia v Pfizer and Bebchick v Public Utilities Commission* have already been cited. In the first, unclaimed damages for which the pharmaceutical companies were liable were distributed to the states concerned for expenditure on public health projects. In the second, future bus fares were required to be reduced until the amount of the illegal overcharge had been consumed. In *Market St. Ry. Co. v Railroad Commission*,[1] in a similar situation, only two per cent of the affected class presented claims. The balance of the illegal overcharge was directed to be applied to the improvement of the defendant's railroad facilities for the benefit of all its riders.

These are the procedures typically involved in the bringing and conduct of a class action. Admittedly, the action does violence to some of our more cherished notions of due process, res judicata, non-champerty, compensatory damages, etc. However approximate as may be the justice done by the class action in some cases, it is still immeasurably better than a system that provides no justice at all. In a situation where the claims of individual members of a class are very small, the class action holds out the only prospect so far conceived for dispensing justice. In the absence of the class action procedure, these claims lie entirely outside our legal process. The tragedy of this is that for the ordinary citizen, this kind of claim is often the only kind of claim for which he has occasion to have resort to the legal system. Until this claim can be enforced, the legal process is worth nothing to him.

The importance of the class action as a response to this problem is now, as the above developments suggest, widely recognised in the US. Moreover, presently, there are a number of bills before the US Congress designed to extend the scope of the class action further.[2] It may be useful to mention bills at either end of the spectrum. The Administration's bill, S.3201, provides for consumer class actions in federal courts in eleven categories of wrongs, all involving some form of fraud or deception. However, before a consumer class action can be brought, there is a 'triggering' device under which either the Justice Department or the FTC must have first proceeded to a final cease and desist order against the defendant in question.

The Administration's bill has attracted strong criticism from consumerists. For example, Mrs Bess Myerson Grant, the head of the New York City Consumer Affairs Division described the bill as 'a fraud': 'Deceptive packaging and mislabeling are as insidious on the con-

1. (1946), 171 P. 2d. 875 (Calif.).
2. See articles by U.S. Rep Eckhardt (1970), 45 *Notre Dame Lawyer* 663; former senator Tydings, (1970), 45 *Notre Dame Lawyer* 478.

gressional calendar as they are in the supermarket shelf. The administration's so-called class action bill is like balloon tread. Substantial at first glance but short on weight.[1]

Former Senator Tydings states: 'It appears that the American public is the victim of a consumer fraud. The consumer was promised protection, and he has received from the Administration only artifice.'[2]

The specific points of criticism of the bill are that the categories of situations in which a class action can be brought are far too narrow and exclude, for example, breach of warranty, non-fraudulent misrepresentation, and breach of statutory duty. Secondly, to make the consumer class action subject to the suggested triggering device is to make the consumer totally dependent on the whims of the administrative agencies involved. If they decided, or were persuaded, not to prosecute, or proceeded as slowly as they often do, the consumer stands to be severely prejudiced, if not prevented entirely from receiving justice.

At the other end of the spectrum is bill S.3092 introduced into the Senate by Senator Tydings. This confers jurisdiction upon federal courts to hear, without preconditions, class actions based on acts in defraud of consumers. An 'act in defraud of consumers' is defined as '(1) an unfair or deceptive act or practice which is unlawful within the meaning of sections 5(a)(1) of the *Federal Trade Commission Act* or (2) an act that gives rise to a civil action by a consumer or consumers under State, statutory or decisional law for the benefit of consumers.'

Under this bill, obviously enough, almost any cause of action could be the subject of a consumer class action.

. . . . . .

. . .The provinces [of Canada] have adopted a rule governing representative actions which follows the terms of order 16, rule 19 of the UK Rules of the Supreme Court 1883. For example, rule 75 of the Ontario Rules of Practice of the Supreme Court provides: 'Where there are numerous persons having the same interest, one or more may sue or be sued or may be authorised by the court to defend on behalf, or for the benefit of all.'

This rule, and its English counterpart, sought to crystallize a body of case law in equity dating back to the early years of the eighteenth century.[3] Some of the early cases show an encouraging readiness on

1. Senate Committee Hearings, *supra* note 2, p.499, at 172.
2. *Supra* note 1, p.505, Tydings, at 480.
3. For detailed accounts of the history of the representative action, see Chafee, *Some Problems of Equity*, chaps. 6 and 7; Stoljar, (1956), 3 *Univ. of Western Australia L. Rev.* 479, and (1957), 4 *Univ. of Western Australia L. Rev.* 58.

the part of the courts to adapt the rules of procedure to the demands of justice in the particular case. For example, Lord Eldon in 1809 in *Cockburn v Thompson*[1] felt able to say 'The strict rule was that all persons interested in the subject of a suit, however numerous, ought to be parties. . .but that being a general rule established for the convenient administration of justice must not be adhered to in cases which consistently with practical convenience it is incapable of application... It was better to go as far as possible towards justice than to deny it altogether.'

However, the tenor of these views was unfortunately not maintained in later cases. Because the representative suit was primarily a creature of equity, relief sought in such a suit prior to the Judicature Acts tended to be either declaratory or injunctive. Following the Judicature Acts, the question fell to be determined whether this equitable procedure could be employed in damages claims. The question was answered in the negative in the leading case of *Markt & Co. v Knight Steamship Co.*[2] The plaintiffs sued on behalf of themselves and forty-four other persons for damages for cargoes lost on the defendant's boat. The Court of Appeal held that a representative suit would not lie, because the plaintiffs and their representees were together not 'persons having the same interest in one cause or matter'. Fletcher Moulton LJ went on to declare: 'To my mind, no representative action can lie where the sole relief sought is damages, because they have to be proved separately in the case of each plaintiff, and therefore the possibility of representation ceases.'[3] Buckley LJ's vigorous dissenting judgment was unfortunately to no avail. . .

. . . . . ."

1. (1809), 33 E.R. 1005.
2. [1910], 2 K.B. 1021.
3. At 1040-1.

TABLE OF CASES

TABLE OF STATUTES

TABLE OF STATUTORY INSTRUMENTS

INDEX

For Product Safety Concerns and Information please contact our EU representative GPSR@taylorandfrancis.com Taylor & Francis Verlag GmbH, Kaufingerstraße 24, 80331 München, Germany

Printed and bound by CPI Group (UK) Ltd, Croydon, CR0 4YY
14/09/2026
02216243-0001